ESSAYS ON ICTY PROCEDURE AND EVIDENCE IN HONOUR OF GABRIELLE KIRK McDONALD

International Humanitarian Law Series

VOLUME 3

The *International Humanitarian Law Series* is a series of monographs and edited volumes which aims to promote scholarly analysis and discussion of both the theory and practice of the international legal regulation of armed conflict.
The series explores substantive issues of International Humanitarian Law including,

- protection for victims of armed conflict and regulation of the means and methods of warfare

- questions of application of the various legal regimes for the conduct of armed conflict

- issues relating to the implementation of International Humanitarian Law obligations

- national and international approaches to the enforcement of the law and

- the interactions between International Humanitarian Law and other related areas of International law such as Human Rights, Refugee Law, Armed Control and Disarmament Law and International Criminal Law.

Essays on ICTY Procedure and Evidence in Honour of Gabrielle Kirk McDonald

Editors

Richard May, Judge, ICTY

David Tolbert, Senior Legal Adviser, Registry, ICTY

John Hocking, Senior Legal Officer, Appeals Chamber, ICTY

Ken Roberts, Legal Officer, Chambers, ICTY

Bing Bing Jia, Legal Officer, Chambers, ICTY

Daryl Mundis, Associate Legal Officer, Office of the Prosecutor, ICTY

Gabriël Oosthuizen, Associate Legal Officer, Chambers, ICTY

KLUWER LAW INTERNATIONAL

THE HAGUE - LONDON - BOSTON

A C.I.P. Catalogue record for this book is available from the Library of Congress.

ISBN 90-411-1482-3

Published by Kluwer Law International,
P.O. Box 85889, 2058 CN The Hague, The Netherlands

Sold and distributed in North, Central and South America
by Kluwer Law International,
675 Massachusetts Avenue, Cambridge, MA 02139, U.S.A.

In all other countries, sold and distributed
by Kluwer Law International, Distribution Centre
P.O. Box 322, 3300 AH Dordrecht, The Netherlands

Printed on acid-free paper

Printed and bound in Great Britain by MPG Books, Bodmin, Cornwall.

Judge Gabrielle Kirk McDonald
Former President of the ICTY

Table of Contents

PART III: THE PRESIDENCY AND JUDGES

PART IV: INDICTMENTS

PART V: DEFENCE COUNSEL

PART VI: FAIR TRIALS

PART VII: EVIDENCE

PART VIII: VICTIMS AND WITNESSES

PART IX: POWER OF CHAMBERS TO CONTROL PROCEEDINGS

PART X: STATE CO-OPERATION AND COMPLIANCE ISSUES

PART XI: APPEALS

PART XII: REVIEW AND ENFORCEMENT OF SENTENCES

PART XIII: THE ICTY AND ITS RELATIONSHIP WITH THE FORMER YUGOSLAVIA AND THE ICC

Foreword

The twentieth century was one of unparalleled progress in the history of humanity. It was also one of unspeakable horrors, committed on an unprecedented scale. This was not for want of laws. Through a series of initiatives, beginning with the second Hague Peace Conference in 1907, diplomats and lawyers gradually put in place, over the course of the century, a comprehensive set of international legal instruments designed to prevent the commission of atrocities and to curb the inhumanities of war. Too often lacking, though, was the will to enforce the laws that those instruments laid down. Serious violations of international humanitarian law went unpunished. The message sent to those who might be tempted to violate the law was clear: they had nothing to fear. The trials at Nürnberg and Tokyo stood out as isolated and increasingly historic exceptions.

The decision of the Security Council in 1993 to establish an international tribunal for the prosecution of persons responsible for serious violations of international humanitarian law committed in the territory of the former Yugoslavia since 1991 marked a decisive break with this record of inaction. Faced with deeds of unimaginable savagery drawn, in Judge Riad's words, from the darkest pages of human history, States proclaimed their determination at last to take concrete steps to enforce the rules of international humanitarian law. These rules were reaffirmed a year later when the Security Council established an international criminal tribunal for the prosecution of persons responsible for genocide and other serious violations of international humanitarian law committed in the territory of Rwanda, and further endorsed at the 1998 Rome Conference which successfully adopted a Statute for a permanent international criminal court.

As one of the eleven Judges who were appointed to the International Tribunal for the former Yugoslavia in the first elections to its bench in 1993, Judge Gabrielle Kirk McDonald made a key contribution to putting in place the procedures, mechanisms and structures which were needed to put the Tribunal in a position to undertake its substantive work of conducting criminal trials. Subsequently, as its President from 1997 to 1999, she led the Tribunal through a pivotal stage in its history as it made the transition to a fully functioning international criminal court, trying cases, hearing appeals and administering and enforcing a system of international criminal justice.

R. May et al., Essays on ICTY Procedure and Evidence in Honour of Gabrielle Kirk McDonald, xi–xii.

Perhaps equally important was the role that Judge McDonald played as an advocate of the cause of international criminal justice. As President of the International Tribunal for the former Yugoslavia, she worked tirelessly to secure the good will of Governments and enlist their cooperation in investigating crimes and in apprehending suspects and transferring them to the custody of the Tribunal. More generally, she used her position to bring international humanitarian law and its enforcement to the attention of the peoples of the world. If the public has come to demand respect for the basic values of humanity and the rule of law in the resolution of armed conflicts and the restoration of peace, that is due in no small part to Judge McDonald's efforts.

This collection of essays is a fitting tribute to Judge McDonald and her work. In a very short time, a comprehensive, functioning and effective system of international criminal law and procedure has been brought into being. In that process, Judge McDonald played a historic role. Indeed, perhaps more than any other single person, Judge McDonald helped bring us closer to a world which once seemed beyond attainment – a world in which those whose deeds offend the conscience of humankind will no longer go unpunished, in which human rights will be truly universal and in which the rule of law will finally prevail.

Kofi A. Annan
UN Secretary-General

Preface

It is a privilege for us to edit these essays in honour of Gabrielle Kirk McDonald, the former President of the International Criminal Tribunal for the former Yugoslavia. It is however a privilege tinged with sadness, marking, as it does, the departure of an esteemed friend and colleague. President McDonald provided instrumental leadership to the Tribunal at a critical time during its development. Moreover, she was an innovative Judge and a tireless advocate for the Tribunal. This book is but a small token of gratitude for her great efforts.

This is an unusual composition in that the contributions address a relatively narrow theme, which is reflected in the title. Moreover, the essays have been written by those closely involved in the practice of the ICTY. The essays, therefore, are more than mere descriptions of the rules and the decisions of the Judges: they analyse the topics about which they are written.

Apart from honouring Gabrielle Kirk McDonald for her contribution to the work and development of the ICTY, the aim of this volume is to give an overview of some of the important procedural and evidentiary aspects of the Tribunal's jurisprudence and practice. It is also to be hoped that the Tribunal itself will benefit from a new light being shone on certain practices and rules, which may well lead to their amendment.

The volume covers a range of topics, starting with a biographical note on Gabrielle Kirk McDonald and two introductory essays on the ICTY, its origins, structure, Statute and Rules. Part II deals with jurisdictional matters, including illegal arrests, defects in the composition of Chambers and the inherent powers of the Chambers. The Office of the President, the President's role in detention matters and the judicial independence of the Judges are considered in Part III. Part IV covers some issues relating to indictments and plea-bargaining before the ICTY. Included under Part V are essays on the right to counsel for indigent suspects and the assignment of defence counsel, whilst Part VI deals with the right to an expeditious trial, provisional release and the status of the accused before the ICTY. Part VII covers various evidentiary matters, including essays on the admissibility of evidence, hearsay evidence, discovery, judicial notice and precedent in the practice of the ICTY. The two essays in Part VIII deal with the protection of the interests of victims and witnesses in the context of fair trials and

R. May et al., Essays on ICTY Procedure and Evidence in Honour of Gabrielle Kirk McDonald, xiii–xiv.

restitution of property and compensation to victims. Part IX covers matters such as contempt and non-compliance with the Rules, and Part X covers non-compliance by states with Tribunal orders and the immunities of ICTY staff members, assets and archives. The essays in Part XI deal with various matters relating to appeals, including interlocutory appeals and the question whether administrative decisions from the Registry are appealable. Part XII is comprised of essays on state requests for review and the enforcement of sentences. Finally, Part XIII covers the Outreach Programme and aspects of the ICTY contribution to the procedure of the ICC.

Generally, the essays cover the various stages of proceedings before the Tribunal. Reference to the procedural and evidentiary law of the ICTY's sister Tribunal, the International Criminal Tribunal for Rwanda, is also made in these pages. This is to be expected, because the rules of procedure and evidence of the two Tribunals are largely similar and the Appeals Chambers of the two Tribunals are comprised of the same judges. There are, of course, other interesting topics on the procedural and evidentiary law of the ICTY that have not been covered, but it is hoped that these essays will be of assistance to all those interested in the work and practice of the Tribunal. With a few exceptions, this collection of essays states the law as of the end of May 2000.

The editorial board would like to express our gratitude to everyone who has assisted in making this volume possible. In particular, we would like to thank Janice Looman-Kearns and Sharon Bloomfield for their administrative assistance, and Lindy Melman of Kluwer.

The Editors
The Hague

Abbreviations

ABA-CEELI	American Bar Association – Central and East European Law Institute
A.B.A.J.	*American Bar Association Journal*
A. Ch.	Appeals Chamber
ACHR	American Convention on Human Rights 1969
ACHRPR	African Charter on Human Rights and People's Rights 1981
AJIL	*American Journal of International Law*
BYIB	*British Year Book of International Law*
CEDH	*Cour européenne des droits de l'homme*
CIJ	Coalition for International Justice
CONF.	Conference
DCU	Defence Counsel Unit
Doc.	Document
ECHR	European Convention on Human Rights 1950
ECtHR/Eur. Ct. H. R.	European Court of Human Rights
FRY	Federal Republic of Yugoslavia
GAOR	Official Records of the UN General Assembly
GDR	German Democratic Republic
Geo. J. I. C. L.	*Georgia Journal of International and Comparative Law*
Hague Recueil	*Recueil des cours de l'Académie de droit international*
ICC	International Criminal Court
ICCPR	International Covenant on Civil and Political Rights 1966
ICJ	International Court of Justice
ICJ Rep.	Reports of Judgments, Advisory Opinions and Orders of the ICJ
ICRC	International Committee of the Red Cross
ICTR	International Criminal Tribunal for Rwanda
ICTY	International Criminal Tribunal for the former Yugoslavia
IFOR	International Implementation Force
ILC	International Law Commission
ILM	International Legal Materials
ILR	International Law Reports

IMT	International Military Tribunal, Nuremberg
NGO	Non-governmental organisation
No.	Number
OLAD	Office for Legal Aid and Detention Matters
PCA	Permanent Court of Arbitration
PCIJ	Permanent Court of International Justice
Res.	Resolution
RPE	Rules of Procedure and Evidence (of the ICTY)
RPP	*Règlement de procédure et de preuve*
SCOR	Official Records of the UN Security Council
Sess.	Session
SFOR	Stabilisation Force
SFRY	Socialist Federal Republic of Yugoslavia
S.M.U. L. Rev.	*Southern Methodist University Law Review*
UDHR	Universal Declaration of Human Rights
UK	United Kingdom
UN	United Nations
UNCC	United Nations Compensation Commission
UNGA	United Nations General Assembly
UNHCR	United Nations High Commissioner for Refugees
UNRIAA	United Nations Reports of International Arbitral Awards
UNSC	United Nations Security Council
UNTAES	United Nations Transitional Administration for Eastern Slavonia
UNTS	United Nations Treaty Series
US	United States
USA	United States of America
Yale J. Int. L.	*Yale Journal of International Law*

Table of Cases

A. ICTY cases

1. Prosecutor v. Aleksovski (Case No. IT-95-14/1-PT, T, AR73, AR77, A)

*2. Prosecutor v. Blaškić (Case No. IT-95-14-PT, T, AR72, AR108*bis*)*

*12. Prosecutor v. Kordić and Cerkez (Case No. IT-95-14-I, PT, T, Case No IT-95-14/2-AR108*bis, *Case No. IT-95-14/2-T, AR73.5, AR73.6)*

13. Prosecutor v. Kovačević (Case No. IT-97-24-T, AR73, AR73(B).2, AR73(B).3)

23. Prosecutor v. Simić and Others (Case No. IT-95-9-PT, AR65, AR72, AR73, AR73.2, R77)

24. Prosecutor v. Tadić (Case No. IT-94-1-T, AR72, A, A-R77, Tbis-*R117, A*bis*)* – p. 6

11. Prosecutor v. Musema (Case No. ICTR-96-13-T)

Judgement, 27 Jan. 2000 – pp. 277, 278, 286

12. Prosecutor v. Ngirumpatse (Case No. ICTR-98-44-A)

Decision, 28 Apr. 2000 – p. 46

13. Prosecutor v. Nsengiyumva (Case No. ICTR-96-12-A)

Decision on Appeal against Oral Decision of Trial Chamber II of 28 September 1998, 3 June 1999 – p. 46

14. Prosecutor v. Nyiramasuhuko and Ntahobali (Case No. ICTR-97-21-T)

Decision on a Preliminary Motion by the Defence for the assignment of a Co-counsel to Pauline Nyiramasuhuko, 13 March 1998 – p. 184

15. Prosecutor v. Rutaganda (Case No. ICTR-96-3-T)

Decision on the Defence Motion to Direct the Prosecutor to Investigate the matter of False Testimony by Witness "CC", 26 March 1998 – p. 88
Judgement and Sentence, 6 Dec. 1999 – p. 281

16. Prosecutor v. Semanza (Case No. ICTR-97-20-A)

Decision, 31 May 2000 – p. 344, 350, 373
Separate Opinion of Judge Shahabuddeen, 31 May 2000 (appended to *Decision*) – pp. 350, 351, 495

17. Prosecutor v. Serushago (Case No. ICTR-98-39-S)

Sentence, 5 Feb. 1999 – pp. 152, 568

18. Prosecutor v. Ruggiu (Case No. ICTR-97-32-I)

Judgement and Sentence, 1 June 2000 – p. 152

C. World War II cases

D. European Court of Human Rights cases

E. International Court of Justice cases

Temple of Preah Vihear, 1962 ICJ Rep. 6 (Separate Opinion of Vice-President Alfaro). – p. 475
US Diplomatic and Consular Staff in Tehran, 1980 ICJ Rep. 3 ("Iran case"). – p. 373

F. Permanent Court of International Justice cases

Chorzow Factory (Interpretation of Judgements Nos. 7 and 8), 1927 PCIJ Series A, No. 13 (Dissenting Opinion by Judge Anzilotti). – p. 373
Chorzow Factory (Merits), 1928 PCIJ Series A, No 17. – p. 475
Diversion of the Water from the River Meuse, 1937 PCIJ Series A/B, No. 70 (Dissenting Opinion of Judge Anzilotti). – p. 475
Lighthouses in Crete and Samos, 1937 PCIJ Series A/B, No. 71 (Separate Opinion of Judge Séfériadès). – p. 475

G. Arbitration cases

Trial Smelter Arbitration (Award II) (1941), UNRIAA iii. 1905.

H. National cases

Abrahams v. Minister of Justice – p. 40
Anisminic, Ltd. v. the Foreign Compensation Commission and Another – p. 50
Attorney General v. Eichmann – p. 40
Betts v. Brady – p. 168
Connelly v. DPP – p. 478
Doney v. The Queen – p. 147
Exall – p. 256
Fédération Nationale des Déportés et Internes Résistants et Patriotes and Others v. Barbie – p. 40
Filartiga v. Pena-Irala – p. 285
Gideon v. Wainwright – p. 168
Green v. US – p. 478
Haw Tua Tau v. Public Prosecutor – p. 147
Jayasena v. The Queen – p. 147
Karadzic v. Kadic *et al.* – p. 382
Kepner v. US – pp. 478, 480
Klopfer v. North Caroline – p. 198
Levinge v. Director of Custodial Services – p. 40
Liangsiriprasert v. US – p. 40
Oscroft v. Benabo – p. 47

Table of Treaties

PART I

Introductory

RICHARD MAY*

1. Gabrielle Kirk McDonald: A Biographical Note

In her final message to the staff of the International Criminal Tribunal for the former Yugoslavia on United Nations Day in October 1999, President McDonald said this:

> [The] Tribunal is now an effective international criminal court, conducting fair trials and appellate proceedings. By dispensing justice, the value of the rule of law is vindicated [...] By holding fair trials which both allow the victims of atrocities to tell their stories and bring perpetrators to justice, the Tribunal is laying the groundwork for building a civil society in the war torn areas of the former Yugoslavia [...] Thus, our mission is an historic one that is not only vital to the peoples of the former Yugoslavia but to humanity generally. The ideals of the United Nations, most notably reflected in the Universal Declaration of Human Rights are ever present in our work. These fundamentally important principles are the foundation of the work of the Tribunal and guide us as we work for justice in difficult and trying circumstances.

In these words President McDonald encapsulated themes which have run through her career: belief in the rule of law and its part in bringing peace and reconciliation; belief in judging individuals rather than groups in order to avoid stereo-typing and prejudice; belief in using the law creatively to fight injustice. That career has involved many different aspects of the law and enabled Gabrielle Kirk McDonald to make an innovative contribution to international criminal law during her time as a Judge and President of the International Tribunal.

Gabrielle Kirk McDonald was born in 1942 in St. Paul, Minnesota, USA where her father worked for the railroad. After her parents' divorce her

---

*The author is grateful for the assistance of Judge Patricia Wald, David Tolbert, Daryl Mundis and Jenny Martinez.

R. May et al., Essays on ICTY Procedure and Evidence in Honour of Gabrielle Kirk McDonald, 3–8.

mother took her and her brother to New York. There her mother worked as a journalist and editor with Prentice Hall, publishers. Her mother, whom Gabrielle McDonald describes as a free spirit and very determined, was a formative influence on her. For instance, it was her mother who resisted the racial discrimination which the family encountered in New York. This experience of discrimination and her education led Gabrielle Kirk McDonald, during her high school years, to decide that she wanted to become a civil rights lawyer. She studied first at Boston University, then moved to Hunter College in New York, before transferring to Howard University Law School in Washington, D.C. This law school has been called the think-tank of the American civil rights movement and has produced many famous alumni including Thurgood Marshall, the first African-American to be appointed a Justice of the United States Supreme Court. At Howard University Gabrielle Kirk McDonald was taught by, among others, Patricia Roberts Harris, who was to be an Ambassador and Secretary of Housing and Urban Development in the Carter Administration and from whom she learnt a determination to do well. As a result she graduated *cum laude* from Howard and first in her class. After graduation she became a staff attorney with the NAACP Legal Defense and Educational Fund in New York, working to make the 1964 Civil Rights Act a reality by combating segregation in housing, education and employment. In 1967 she was the NAACP Legal Defense Fund's Chief Attorney in an important employment discrimination case against Philip Morris Companies Inc., under Title VII of the Civil Rights Act, a case which she won, marking the first such victory for the NAACP. While she was working for the Fund she experienced much prejudice and remembers the courageous stance taken by lawyers who co-operated with the civil rights movement in the face of outright discrimination.

In 1969 Gabrielle McDonald set up in practice with Mark T. McDonald, her then husband, in Houston, Texas. Their practice, built up over 10 years, was in employment discrimination cases against such companies as Monsanto Company and Union Carbide Corporation. Their biggest success came in negotiating a settlement of $1.2 million from the Lone Star Steel Company in back pay for four hundred African-American workers. Meanwhile, she had also become the mother of two children, Michael and Stacy, and had taught labour law as a lecturer at the University of Texas School of Law. In recognition of her achievements Gabrielle Kirk McDonald was to receive the first Annual Equal Justice Award from the National Bar Association which stated, "as one of the leading Title VII Attorneys … today your contribution to the fundamental area of equal opportunity has enabled many to achieve more than their full potential as citizens of the United States."

In 1979, at the age of 37, Gabrielle Kirk McDonald was appointed a Federal District Judge for the Southern District of Texas by President Carter: she was the first African-American to be appointed to the Federal

Bench in Texas and only the third African-American woman to be appointed in the country. While on the bench she won the accolade from a former US Attorney in Houston that "she was always even-handed and did not permit her civil rights background to cloud her judgment as a Federal judge". She remained on the bench until 1988 during which time she took part in a number of high profile cases. These included her decision in *SDJ Inc. v. City of Houston* that a Houston ordinance regulating the location of strip bars did not infringe the Freedom of Expression clause of the Constitution; her dismissal of a plea bargain for a sentence of three years imprisonment made between the Federal Prosecutor and a sheriff who had pleaded guilty to violating the Civil Rights of prisoners in his care (he was later sentenced to ten years imprisonment by another court); and her refusal to recuse herself *Le Roy v. City of Houston*, in a dispute involving the Houston City Council, the latter alleging that as an African-American she was a member of a class which stood to benefit from the suit (the U.S. Court of Appeals for the Fifth Circuit upheld her decision). She was also asked to recuse herself on racial grounds in a famous case in which a group of Vietnamese fishermen sued the Ku Klux Klan for harassing and intimidating them over access to shrimp stocks in the Gulf of Mexico: *Vietnamese Fishermens Association v. The Knights of the Ku Klux Klan*. Judge McDonald refused to recuse herself, subsequently saying: "if my race is enough to disqualify me hearing this case then I must disqualify myself as well from a substantial portion of cases on my docket [...] an action which would cripple my efforts to fulfil my oath as a Federal Judge". She proceeded to hear the case in the face of death threats to her and her family. She found in favour of the fishermen and ruled that the Klan was interfering with their right to free competition. She ordered the Klan to cease its harassment and to close its paramilitary training camps.

On retiring from the bench Gabrielle Kirk McDonald resumed private practice in Austin, Texas, dealing with employment discrimination defense work. She also resumed teaching, now at St. Mary's University School of Law in San Antonio. In 1993 she was about to start a full-time teaching career, having accepted a post as Distinguished Visiting Professor at Texas Southern University Thurgood Marshall School of Law in Houston, when she was approached and asked if she would be interested in returning to the bench, this time for a new court, the International Tribunal created by the United Nations to deal with the atrocities of the war in the former Yugoslavia. Despite some initial hesitation, due to her self-confessed lack of knowledge of international humanitarian law, she accepted and was elected as a judge of the Tribunal in 1993 by the General Assembly of the United Nations, receiving the most votes of all candidates.

Judge McDonald, together with the ten other judges of the Tribunal, took office in November 1993. At the time the Tribunal, with its judges and a handful of secretaries, was housed in a room in the Peace Palace, the home of the International Court of Justice, having no premises of its own, no defendants and (in Judge McDonald's own words) "no jurisprudence we could rely upon". The judges then began on the task of drafting the Rules of Procedure and Evidence.

In time, however, rules were drafted, premises were found, indicted persons were arrested and brought to The Hague and the first trial, that of Dusan Tadić, was begun. As Presiding Judge of Trial Chamber II, Judge McDonald presided over this trial. She told the Los Angeles Times that her background as a civil rights lawyer proved useful for her work at the Tribunal and founded her belief that facing the aftermath of Yugoslavia's ethnic warfare was possible and that she could take on Tribunal tasks for which there was little precedent. "I learned from the Civil Rights Movement", she said. "There we were dealing with a minority and with confrontation. And, at the same time, we got new laws and we had to use them to enable people to live and work together."

Since *Tadić* was the Tribunal's first trial, the Trial Chamber was, in a very real sense, breaking new ground. As Judge McDonald was to say in an interview later, it gave her and her colleagues (Judge Stephen and Judge Vohrah) the "chance to use the law creatively". During the course of the trial a number of important procedural and other issues had to be resolved: whether the Tribunal was bound by the decisions of other international bodies; how to maintain the balance between the need to protect victims and witnesses and sustaining the accused's right to a public hearing; laying down special rules for evidence from victims and witnesses in cases of sexual assault; general principles for a grant of anonymity to witnesses; providing guidelines relating to the safe-conduct of witnesses and to the provision of testimony by video link; and whether hearsay evidence was to be admitted. The Trial Chamber's rulings on all these issues have played an important part in establishing precedents for the Tribunal's practice and procedure.

Judge McDonald also presided over Trial Chamber II in the evidence hearings (Rule 61) in the *Rajić* case (April–September 1996), the deferral hearings in the *Lasva Valley* case (May 1995) and in the *Erdemović* case (May 1996). She was also in charge of proceedings in the *Dokmanović* case, presided over the hearing of preliminary motions in the *Čelebići* case, and initiated a series of hearings on the Subpoena issue. Judge McDonald also sat as a member of the Appeals Chamber in the *Erdemović* case.

By presiding over the *Tadić* trial Judge McDonald secured her place in history. However, within a few months of the Judgement being given in that case, she was elected President of the Tribunal in November 1997. She was to serve in this capacity for a term of two years before her retirement from the Tribunal in 1999. Her predecessor as President, Judge Antonio Cassese, said this in nominating her for the post:

> She has shown great competence, integrity and impartiality. She has demonstrated admirable equanimity and a deep sense of humanity, in particular in dealing with witnesses. She has always maintained and required a high standard of professionalism in the courtroom. May I add, on a personal

> basis, that Judge McDonald represents to me the best that America can offer: she is straightforward, she is direct, she is intelligent and unstintingly hard-working [...] In short, I am sure that she would be an outstanding President and would offer the Tribunal strong moral leadership for the next two years.

This is precisely what she proceeded to do. Thus, a month after taking up her post in November 1997 she said in an address to a plenary meeting of the Peace Implementation Council in Bonn:

> The Tribunal is the golden thread that runs through the cloth of the peace process. It is to attempt to ensure respect for the principles of equality of all human life, the universality of justice and consistency in application of the law.

On her election President McDonald set herself three goals for the International Tribunal. The first concerned the number of Trial Chambers. One courtroom only had manifestly been inadequate for the Tribunal's functioning and the Tribunal premises were adapted to include two more; but there were now insufficient numbers of judges to try the growing number of persons held in the detention centre at The Hague. President McDonald went to the United Nations Security Council in New York and argued persuasively for three more judges; three were duly elected.

Another goal was to obtain changes in the rules relating to pre-trial procedures because of the increasing number of detainees. (Ten indictees had surrendered voluntarily in October 1997 and over thirty were in detention when President McDonald retired in 1999.) These detainees were spending longer times in custody because of the increasing number of detainees and the unforeseen complexity and, therefore, length of the trials. In 1998 the Rules of Procedure and Evidence were amended to provide for stronger case management by the judges during the pre-trial phase of the proceedings. In 1999 the President established a Working Group on Trial Practices with a mandate to make practical recommendations that would reduce the length of trials.

A third goal was to spread the word of what the Tribunal was doing and address misunderstandings. In particular, President McDonald was at all times deeply aware of the situation in the former Yugoslavia, not only as it had been during the various conflicts but also afterwards. To this end she promoted the Outreach Programme (discussed elsewhere in this work). The purpose was to explain the work of the Tribunal to the peoples of the former Yugoslavia. As she explained in an interview with the Los Angeles Times:

> Our decisions are to help bring about reconciliation (of the various factions within the former Yugoslavia) but our decisions cannot do that [...] if there is not a belief that the Tribunal is fair, that the decision-makers are fair. And that is why I am interested in Outreach, or what I call 'awareness projects'.

Thanks to President McDonald's efforts, the Outreach Programme is now functioning. She was able to inspire a number of organisations and States to provide voluntary funding so that the peoples of the former Yugoslavia now have the chance to learn about the real work of the International Tribunal.

The Appeals Chamber for the International Tribunal also functions as the Appeals Chamber for the International Criminal Tribunal for Rwanda. As President, Gabrielle Kirk McDonald thus presided over the Appeals Chambers of both Tribunals and made a number of visits to Arusha, the seat of the Rwanda Tribunal. She has spoken of her deep distress at being taken to the Genocide Museum in Rwanda: she described to CNN her feelings when she saw rooms full of skeletons and asked what should she, as a mother, say to her children about these terrible events? However, President McDonald's concern for the victims in Rwanda did not prejudice her even-handedness. One of her last acts as President was to preside over the Appeals Chamber's first decision in *Barayagwiza* which concerned the rights of the accused in the context of numerous pre-trial delays. In its conclusions to that Judgement the Appeals Chamber used language which reflected President McDonald's concerns, not only for the victims but also for those accused of serious violations of international humanitarian law:

> The crimes for which the Appellant is charged are very serious. However, in this case the fundamental rights of the appellant were repeatedly violated [...] The Tribunal – an institution whose primary purpose is to ensure that justice is done – must not place its imprimatur on such violations. To allow the Appellant to be tried on the charges for which he was belatedly indicted would be a travesty of justice. Nothing less than the integrity of the Tribunal is at stake in this case. Loss of public confidence in the Tribunal, as a court valuing human rights of all individuals – including those charged with unthinkable crimes – would be among the most serious consequences of allowing the Appellant to stand trial in the face of such violations of his rights. *Barayagwiza v. Prosecutor*, Decision, Case No. ICTR-97-19-AR72, 3 November 1999 at paragraphs 106, 109.

Although the Decision was later overturned for procedural reasons on review by the Appeals Chamber, these statements stand as an accurate reflection of Gabrielle Kirk McDonald's deep concern for justice for all, no matter whom. Thus ended what she described as the most fulfilling part of her long, varied and distinguished career.

GABRIËL OOSTHUIZEN*

2. Sketching the Framework: The ICTY, its Structure, Statute and Rules

The aim of this piece is to briefly introduce the reader to the historical origins of the International Criminal Tribunal for the former Yugoslavia ("ICTY", "the Tribunal"), its organisation and its workings.[1]

1. Establishment of the ICTY

The establishment of the ICTY took place against the backdrop of the armed conflict that engulfed the former Socialist Federal Republic of Yugoslavia ("former Yugoslavia") in the 1990s. The international community, through the United Nations ("UN") Security Council, responded to the war by establishing an international tribunal "for the prosecution of persons responsible for serious violations of international humanitarian law committed in the territory of the former Yugoslavia since 1991".[2] The Security Council hoped to achieve three principal objectives with the establishment of the ICTY, namely, put an end to the crimes being committed in the former Yugoslavia, bring to justice those responsible for the crimes and contribute to the restoration and maintenance of peace.[3]

Following a request from the Security Council[4], the UN Secretary-General presented a report on all aspects of the establishment of such an International Tribunal to the Security Council on 3 May 1993.[5] Acting

*Associate Legal Officer in Chambers, ICTY; BLC LLB (University of Pretoria, South Africa) LLM Public International Law *cum laude* (Leiden University). The views expressed herein are those of the author and not of the Tribunal or the United Nations.

[1]For more information, visit the ICTY's website at http://www.un.org/icty.

[2]SC Res 808, UN Doc S/Res/808 (22 Feb 1993), para. 1.

[3]Id.

[4]Id., para. 2.

[5]Report of the Secretary-General Pursuant to Paragraph 2 of Security Council Resolution 808 (1993), S/25704, 3 May 1993.

R. May et al., Essays on ICTY Procedure and Evidence in Honour of Gabrielle Kirk McDonald, 9–12.

under Chapter VII of the Charter of the UN, the Security Council approved the report of the Secretary-General and established an *ad hoc* international criminal tribunal for the former Yugoslavia by its Resolution 827 on 25 May 1993.[6] The Security Council adopted without change the Statute of the International Tribunal proposed by the Secretary-General.[7]

2. THE STATUTE OF THE ICTY

The opening passage of the Statute provides that the ICTY shall function in accordance with the provisions of the Statute. Some of the more pertinent provisions of the Statute are highlighted below.

The ICTY has jurisdiction over natural persons[8] who allegedly committed grave breaches of the Geneva Conventions of 1949[9], violations of the laws or customs of war[10], genocide[11] and crimes against humanity[12] on the territory of the former Socialist Federal Republic of Yugoslavia since 1 January 1991[13].

The basic organisational structure of the ICTY comprises three organs: the Chambers comprising three Trial Chambers and an Appeals Chamber; the Prosecutor; and a Registry, servicing both the Chambers and the Prosecutor.[14] Each of the Trial Chambers is composed of three Judges, and the Appeals Chamber is composed of five.[15] The members of the Appeals Chamber of the ICTY also serve as members of the Appeals Chamber of the International Criminal Tribunal for Rwanda ("ICTR").[16] The President of the ICTY is elected from among their own ranks by the Judges.[17] The Judges

[6]SC Res 827, UN Doc S/Res/827 (25 May 1993), paras. 1 and 2. The opening passage of the Statute refers to the full title of the International Tribunal, namely the "International Tribunal for the Prosecution of Persons Responsible for Serious Violations of International Humanitarian Law Committed in the Territory of the Former Yugoslavia since 1991".

[7]SC Res 827. UN Doc S/Res/827 (25 May 1993), para. 2.

[8]Art. 6.

[9]Art. 2.

[10]Art. 3.

[11]Art. 4.

[12]Art. 5.

[13]Art. 8. The temporal jurisdiction of the ICTY is open-ended.

[14]Art. 11. The Security Council amended ICTY Statute Art. 11 by its Resolution 1166 to establish a third Trial Chamber: SC Res 1166, UN Doc S/Res/1166 (13 May 1998), para. 1.

[15]Art. 12.

[16]Art. 12 of the Statute of the International Tribunal for the prosecution of persons responsible for genocide and other serious violations of international humanitarian law committed in the territory of Rwanda and Rwandan citizens responsible for genocide and other such violations committed in the territory of neighbouring States, between 1 January and 31 December 1994, annexed to SC Res 955, UN Doc S/Res/955 (8 Nov. 1994), by which the ICTR was created.

[17]Art. 14.

are also responsible for the adoption and amendment of the Rules of Procedure and Evidence of the ICTY ("Rules").[18] The Prosecutor is responsible for the investigation and prosecution of persons falling within the ICTY's jurisdiction and acts independently as a separate organ of the ICTY.[19] The Prosecutor fulfils the same role for the ICTR.[20] The Registry is responsible for the administration and servicing of the ICTY, including the Chambers and the Prosecutor.[21]

The Statute further provides for the investigation and the preparation of indictments by the Prosecutor,[22] the review of indictments by a judge of a Trial Chamber,[23] the commencement and conduct of trial proceedings,[24] the rights of the accused[25] and the protection of victims and witnesses.[26] Decisions and judgements of the Trial Chambers can be appealed[27] or reviewed.[28] The enforcement of sentences,[29] the pardon or commutation of sentences[30] and the co-operation and judicial assistance of states with the ICTY[31] are also provided for.

3. The Rules of Procedure and Evidence of the ICTY

Of great importance to the work of the ICTY, are its rules of procedure and evidence. Article 15 of the Statute provides as follows:

> The judges of the International Tribunal shall adopt rules of procedure and evidence for the conduct of the pre-trial phase of the proceedings, trials and appeals, the admission of evidence, the protection of victims and witnesses and other appropriate matters.

The first version of the Rules was adopted on 11 February 1994; at the time of writing, it has been amended 17 times and comprises more than 120 rules. Rule 6 of the Rules deals with the amendment of rules. It provides that proposals for amendment of the Rules may be made by a Judge, the Prosecutor or the Registrar and shall be adopted if agreed to by not less than

[18] Art. 15 and Rule 6.
[19] Art. 16.
[20] ICTR Statute Art. 15(3).
[21] Arts. 11(c) and 17.
[22] Art. 18.
[23] Art. 19.
[24] Art. 20.
[25] Art. 21.
[26] Art. 22.
[27] Art. 25.
[28] Art. 26.
[29] Art. 27.
[30] Art. 28.
[31] Art. 29.

nine Judges at a plenary meeting, consisting of all the Judges, of the ICTY.[32] An amendment to the Rules may be otherwise adopted, provided the Judges unanimously approve it.[33]

4. Other rules and regulations

Apart from the Rules, the judges have also adopted the Rules Governing the Detention of Persons awaiting Trial or Appeal Before the Tribunal or Otherwise Detained on the Authority of the Tribunal.[34] These Rules were adopted to govern the administration of the UN detention unit and to ensure the continued application and protection of the individual rights of those detained.[35]

The Registrar has also issued various directives and regulations, including the Regulations for the Establishment of a Complaints Procedure for Detainees,[36] the Regulations for the Establishment of a Disciplinary Procedure for Detainees,[37] the Regulations to Govern the Supervision of Visits to and Communications with Detainees[38] and the Directive on Assignment of Defence Counsel.[39]

The Prosecutor is empowered by Rule 37(A) of the Rules to adopt provisions for the purpose of directing the functions of the Office of the Prosecutor.[40]

---

[32]Rule 6(A). Rule 24 provides that the Rules are to be adopted and amended at the plenary meetings of the ICTY.

[33]Rule 6(B).

[34]IT/38/Rev.7, 5 May 1994.

[35]Id., Preamble.

[36]IT/96, April 1995.

[37]IT/97, April 1995.

[38]IT/98/Rev. 2.

[39]IT/73/Rev. 6.

[40]Rule 37(A). At the time of writing, only two Regulations have been issued by the Prosecutor, namely, the Regulation No. 1 of 1994 (17 May 1995), "Prosecutor's Policy on *Nolle Prosequi* of Accomplices"; and Regulation No. 2 of 14 September 1999, "Standards of Professional Conduct for Prosecution Counsel".

KELLY DAWN ASKIN*

3. The ICTY: An Introduction to its Origins, Rules and Jurisprudence

The expansion and evolution of international humanitarian law, international criminal law, and international human rights law, which often intersect and overlap, exploded in the 1990s, largely as a result of the establishment of the International Criminal Tribunals for the former Yugoslavia ("ICTY") and for Rwanda ("ICTR") in 1993 and 1994 respectively. The Statute, Rules, practices, and jurisprudence of these Tribunals have had and will continue to have an enormous impact upon the development of international law. Indeed, it is highly unlikely that recent efforts to increase respect for and enforcement of international law – such as the adoption of a Statute for a permanent International Criminal Court, the arrest and detention of General Augusto Pinochet, the concerted efforts to establish a tribunal to prosecute the Khmer Rouge leadership of the Cambodian regime, the NATO intervention in Kosovo, the investigative commissions in Sierra Leone and East Timor, the Historical Clarification Commission in Guatemala, investigations into massacres by U.S. troops in Korea, and domestic trials for war crimes in Chechnya – would have occurred had the ICTY not been established.

While the ICTY and ICTR are the first international criminal tribunals established by the United Nations, their predecessors, the International Military Tribunals for Nuremberg ("Nuremberg Tribunal")[1] and for the Far

*Kelly Dawn Askin, B.S., J.D., Ph.D. (law), ICTY Consultant; author of various publications in international human rights, humanitarian law, and criminal law, including War Crimes Against Women: Prosecution in International War Crimes Tribunals (1997), and chief editor of Women and International Human Rights Law (3 vols, 1999–2000). The views expressed herein are those of the author and do not represent the views of the ICTY or the UN.

[1]See Agreement for the Prosecution and Punishment of Major War Criminals of the European Axis, signed at London, August 1945, 83 UNTS 279, 59 Stat. 1544; annex, Charter of the International Military Tribunal.

R. May et al., Essays on ICTY Procedure and Evidence in Honour of Gabrielle Kirk McDonald, 13–23.

East ("Tokyo Tribunal"),[2] were established in 1945 and 1946 respectively by the Allied victors of World War II to prosecute alleged Axis war criminals in Europe and Asia. The Nuremberg and Tokyo Tribunals adjudicated primarily charges of aggression, crimes against humanity, and war crimes, each holding joint trials against political, military, and civilian leaders of the war. These trials, while sometimes accused of rendering "victor's justice," nonetheless established important principles and provided crucial foundations upon which the Yugoslavia and Rwandan Tribunals have built and improved. The attribution of individual criminal responsibility for gross violations of international law, and its application at Nuremberg and Tokyo, helped establish norms of individual accountability and develop the notion of individual rights and responsibilities in international law. Indeed, a progressive aspect of the Nuremberg Trial was its efforts in holding state leaders responsible for crimes committed against particular persons residing within state borders, particularly Jews, Roma, mentally ill, and others deemed "undesirable" in achieving an Aryan state of Germanic purity. These prosecutions confirmed that in certain circumstances state actors could be held accountable by the international community for crimes committed within a state's own borders, including against its own citizens.

In 1945, the establishment of the United Nations immediately following World War II was a driving force in consolidating, codifying, and promoting international standards and agreements as to minimum duties of states vis-à-vis other states and, increasingly, toward individuals. During the 50 years between the Nuremberg and Tokyo Tribunals and the Yugoslavia and Rwandan Tribunals, international treaties designed to protect, promote, and enforce international humanitarian law,[3] international human rights law,[4] and international criminal law[5] impacted greatly the developing standards and norms toward accountability of states and individuals. Also during this period, regional human rights courts or commissions were established in Africa, Europe, and the Americas to monitor and enforce human rights, and these bodies have made significant contributions to furthering respect for and commitment to the rule of law and their establishment has also facilitated erosion of the once inviolability of state sovereignty.

[2]See Charter of the International Military Tribunal for the Far East, Special Proclamation by the Supreme Commander for the Allied Powers at Tokyo, 1946, TIAS 1589, 4 Bevans 20.

[3]E.g., the 1949 Geneva Conventions and the 1977 Additional Protocols to the 1949 Geneva Conventions.

[4]E.g., the Universal Declaration of Human Rights, the International Covenant on Civil and Political Rights, the International Covenant on Economic, Social and Cultural Rights, and the Convention on the Elimination of All Forms of Discrimination Against Women.

[5]E.g., the Genocide Convention and the Torture Convention. Other pertinent treaties recognising international crimes, such as the 1926 Slavery Convention, were promulgated prior to this period.

Despite these achievements, as has often been noted, the twentieth century was the bloodiest in history, with armed conflict and internal strife occurring in every region of the globe. The two World Wars, which were waged in the first half of the twentieth century, and the prosecution of the leaders and others deemed most culpable for the Holocaust and its systematic slaughter of millions of civilians, did seemingly little to effectively deter international and internal wars during the second half of the twentieth century. In countries as vast and varied as Vietnam, Angola, Korea, Pakistan, Iran, Spain, Ethiopia, Azerbaijan, Nicaragua, Somalia, Afghanistan, Chile, Northern Ireland, Colombia, Algeria, China, Libya, and dozens of others, bloody battles raged, with enormous losses to unarmed men, women, and children, members of the armed forces, cultural and religious objects, property, and the environment. It appears that the increase in military technology,[6] combined with the decrease of notions of chivalry and honour for combatants,[7] particularly when integrated with prejudice, hatred, fear, and revenge, resulted in civilians suffering the greatest casualties in and of war (e.g., as direct losses to the civilian population and as indirect losses as a result of long term effects of the war or through destruction of civilian objects). In addition, the twentieth century has increasingly seen civilian populations intentionally targeted for attack as part of an official or tolerated military strategy to terrorise, demoralise, dispel, and destroy the enemy group.

In 1992, pictures of emaciated detainees starving behind barbed wire fences and reports that women were enslaved for systematic rape in detention camps in the former Yugoslavia stunned the world community, evoking images of World War II's Nazi concentration camps in Europe and the sexual slavery of the former "comfort women" by the Japanese Imperial Army in Asia.[8] In response, the United Nations established a Commission of Experts to investigate abuses,[9] and after confirmation of gross violations of humanitarian law committed during the conflict, including reports of ethnic cleansing, unlawful killing of civilians, forced expulsion, and widespread and

---

[6]For most of the twentieth century, technological advancements allowing aerial bombardments and creating weapons of mass destruction resulted in indiscriminate attacks against the civilian population. In recent years, however technology has continued to advance such that precision targeting is available, thus hopefully decreasing the danger of incidental damage to civilian populations.

[7]See Michael Ignatieff, The Warrior's Honour (1998).

[8]Many of the first reports are reproduced in a book by Roy Gutman, the New York Times reporter who first broke the story of Omarska camp in an August 2, 1992 article in New York Newsday, and this report, and its haunting photographs, galvanised support for an international response to the crisis. See Roy Gutman, A Witness to Genocide (1993).

[9]SC Res. 780, UN SCOR, 47th Sess., at 36, UN Doc. S/INF/48 (1992).

systematic detention and rape of women,[10] the UN Security Council decided to establish an international tribunal to prosecute persons responsible for serious violations of international humanitarian law in the territory of the former Yugoslavia, and requested the Secretary-General to proceed accordingly.[11] Thus on 25 May 1993, the Statute of the International Criminal Tribunal for the former Yugoslavia was adopted by the UN Security Council, acting under Chapter VII of the UN Charter.[12]

The Statute of the ICTY grants the Tribunal subject matter jurisdiction over genocide, crimes against humanity, and war crimes.[13] Personal jurisdiction may be exercised over natural persons charged with individual criminal responsibility for having planned, instigated, ordered, committed or otherwise aided and abetted in a crime, or with superior criminal responsibility for persons who had authority and control over subordinates and who knew or had reason to know subordinates were committing or about to commit a crime and failed to take necessary and reasonable measures to prevent, halt, or punish the crimes.[14] Territorial jurisdiction is limited to the former Yugoslavia, although the temporal jurisdiction is open-ended as to events occurring in the territory after 1 January 1991.[15] Thus the recent Kosovo conflict also comes within the jurisdiction of the Tribunal, which has concurrent jurisdiction with and primacy over national courts.[16]

The first session of the Tribunal was held in 1993.[17] In the first years of its existence, no accused were in the Tribunal's custody,[18] so the Judges, as required by Article 15 of the Statute, used this period to draft and adopt the Rules of Procedure and Evidence ("Rules") to be interpreted and applied by the Tribunal. In designing these Rules, the Judges took note of the patterns of crimes and the forms these crimes took in the Yugoslavia conflict, and thus endeavoured to devise a "purpose-made" set of Rules that would

---

[10]See e.g. SC Res. 798 (1993). See also the Report of the European Community investigative mission into the treatment of Muslim women in the former Yugoslavia, S/25240, Annex 1 (1993).

[11]SC Res. 808 (1993).

[12]SC Res. 827 (1993). See also the Secretary-General's Report.

[13]Arts. 4 (genocide), 5 (crimes against humanity), and 2–3 (grave breaches of the 1949 Geneva Conventions and violations of the laws or customs of war, respectively).

[14]Arts. 6, 7(1), 7(3).

[15]Art. 8. More precisely, according to SC Res. 827, at para. 2, temporal jurisdiction extends from 1 January 1991 "and a date to be determined by the Secretary Council upon the restoration of peace".

[16]Art. 9.

[17]Antonio Cassese (Italy) was elected President of the Tribunal in 1993. He was re-elected for a final term of office in 1995, pursuant to Rule 18(A) of the Rules of Procedure and Evidence, after which he was succeeded first by Gabrielle Kirk McDonald (U.S.) in 1997, and later by Claude Jorda (France) in 1999.

[18]Duško Tadić was first transferred to Tribunal detention facilities on 24 April 1995, and it would be nearly a year before other accused came within the Tribunal's custody.

facilitate their work in adjudicating justiciable crimes within the context of the crimes actually committed.[19]

This once nascent institution has grown into a sizeable, thriving organisation, employing in excess of 1000 staff members from over 70 countries, and expending an annual budget of more than 100 million U.S. dollars. Over 94 individuals have been publicly indicted since the Tribunal's inception, and an unknown number have been charged in secret indictments, pursuant to Rule 53(C). As of May 2000, thirty-nine accused were in the custody of the Tribunal at its detention facilities in The Hague; Trial Chamber Judgements have been rendered against 13 accused after trials on the merits, and against another two accused who entered guilty pleas; trials against another 11 defendants are ongoing in the Tribunal's three Trial Chambers; additional accused are in various stages of pre-trial proceedings; and post-trial proceedings, including Appeals on the merits, are pending in several cases.

The Statute and Rules are interpreted and applied on a regular and ongoing basis during the course of pre-trial, trial, and post-trial proceedings. Indeed, thousands of decisions have been rendered on interlocutory motions[20] covering a vast array of both standard challenges and novel issues, such as jurisdictional scope, defects in the form of the indictment, protective measures, provisional release, evidentiary standards, ineffective assistance of counsel, judicial recusal, and production of documents, with the Tribunal attempting to balance the rights of the accused against the rights of victims and witnesses in an effort to ensure fair, impartial, and expeditious trials. Indeed, one of the greatest obstacles currently facing the Tribunal involves constraints concerning getting a case to trial within a reasonable time after the accused is in detention.[21]

As noted in the following pages, the Tribunal is making significant progress in prosecuting some of the crimes committed on the territory of the former Yugoslavia, although clearly the scope of crimes and large number of perpetrators preclude the Tribunal's ability to provide prosecutorial redress for all crimes committed during the conflict. Perhaps one of the Tribunal's greatest accomplishments – although simultaneously the impetus for some of the harshest criticisms of the Tribunal – is the range of persons indicted at all levels of the hierarchical structure, thus confirming that low level

---

[19]Report of the International Tribunal for the Prosecution of Persons Responsible for Serious Violations of International Humanitarian Law Committed in the Territory of the former Yugoslavia since 1991, A/49/342, S/1994/1007, 29 Aug. 1994, at paras. 75 and 76.

[20]For example, in the *Blaškić* case alone, 160 interlocutory decisions were rendered during the pre-trial and trial phases. See *Prosecutor v. Blaškić,* Judgement, Case No. IT-95-14-T, 3 March 2000, at para. 19 (stating that 82 interlocutory decisions were rendered during the pre-trial proceedings and 78 were rendered during trial).

[21]See e.g. Patricia M. Wald, "Judging War Crimes", 1(1) Chicago Journal of International Law (Spring, 2000), pp. 189–196, at p. 190. See also *Barayagwiza v. Prosecutor, Decision (Prosecutor's Request for Review or Reconsideration)*, ICTR-97-AR72, ICTR A. Ch., 31 March 2000.

individual civilian actors or common soldiers, prison camp guards, businesspersons, members of the media, and top military or political leaders may each be held accountable. While the intended strategy is to try the leaders most culpable for the crimes once custody is gained over them, the precedent set in adjudicating crimes committed by lower level perpetrators is constructive, as it is typically those at the bottom of the hierarchical ladder who physically commit the crimes sanctioned or ordered by their superiors. It is also significant that individuals of all sides are being prosecuted, with charges brought against the three major ethnic groups participating in the conflict.

The Tribunal's mandate has a much broader impact than exclusively being limited to the conflict region, and its work is rapidly filling much lacuna in this previously underdeveloped and under-utilised body of law. Through the establishment of judicial norms, procedures, and jurisprudence, developed principally through its Rules and case law, precedent emerging from the Tribunal will undoubtedly be of great practical use to international, regional, and domestic prosecutions of international crimes committed in wartime or peacetime.[22] Since 1996, trials covering such atrocities as genocide, sexual slavery, persecution, mass expulsion or deportation, systematic rape, unlawful detention under horrific conditions, and intentional destruction of religious and cultural property have commenced in The Hague. While these international prosecutions serve as merely one form of redress to the countless victims and but one means of response to the conflict, it is hoped that the Tribunal's work will also facilitate peace, reconciliation, and healing in the Balkans, and provide at least some deterrence to the commission of future crimes. In its successful prosecution of several forms of gender based crimes, the two Tribunals have already made significant contributions to an area of law that has historically been ignored.[23] In addition, the daunting task of adjudicating the aforementioned crimes has resulted in judgements that are facilitating the creation of an historical record of the conflict.

---

[22]Unless specifically required under the authorising Statute or law, only war crimes require a nexus to an armed conflict, as crimes against humanity and genocide are justiciable whether committed in wartime or peacetime. The precedent established will not, of course, be legally binding on other judicial systems, but can serve as useful guidance and persuasive authority.

[23]See e.g., Patricia Viseur Sellers, "The Context of Sexual Violence: Sexual Violence as Violations of International Humanitarian Law", in Gabrielle Kirk McDonald and Olivia Swaak-Goldman (Eds.), Substantive and Procedural Aspects of International Criminal Law: The Experience of International and National Courts (vol. I, 2000); Patricia Viseur Sellers, "Emerging Jurisprudence on Crimes of Sexual Violence", 13(6) American University International Law Review (1998), p. 1523; Kelly Dawn Askin, "The International Criminal Tribunal for Rwanda and Its Treatment of Gender-Based Crimes", in John Carey and John Pritchard (Eds.), International Humanitarian Law: Origins, Challenges, and Prospects (2000); Kelly D. Ashkin [sic], "The International War Crimes Trial of Anto Furundžija: Major Progress Toward Ending the Cycle of Impunity for Rape Crimes," 12 Leiden Journal of International Law (1999), pp. 935–955.

Judge Gabrielle Kirk McDonald made a considerable contribution to international law in general and the Tribunal in particular. Her participation – including in drafting, interpreting, and applying the Rules of Procedure and Evidence, sitting on the first international war crimes trial held under UN auspices, as Presiding Judge over Trial Chamber II, member of the Bureau, then as President of the Tribunal, and Presiding Judge over the Appeals Chamber of both Tribunals – greatly influenced the practice of and impacted the jurisprudence of the Tribunal. In reviewing the evolution of case law of the Tribunal as highlighted in the following pages, it should be remembered that President McDonald had a major influence on various facets of the Tribunal's work.

In 1996, after jurisdictional challenges were exhausted,[24] the first international war crimes trial since World War II began against Duško Tadić, the first (and for a while, the sole) indictee over whom the Tribunal had gained custody. In the *Tadić* case, the accused, a low level Serbian civilian and part time traffic cop, was tried for some 31 counts alleging grave breaches of the Geneva Conventions, violations of the laws or customs of war, and crimes against humanity for a broad range of crimes including murder, torture, persecution, cruel treatment, wilfully causing great suffering, and inhumane acts. He was found guilty by the Trial Chamber of 9 counts plus part of 2 counts: 4 counts and in part on 1 count for violations of the laws or customs of war for cruel treatment; 4 counts and in part on one count for crimes against humanity for inhumane acts; and one count of persecution as a crime against humanity.[25] During the course of this trial, many Rules were added or amended to reflect evolving needs and unforeseen circumstances affecting the defendant and the victims and witnesses. Particularly notable aspects of the *Tadić* case concerned jurisdictional challenges,[26] the scope and application of Articles 2, 3, and 5 of the Statute, measures and standards for the protection of victims and witnesses and how to balance these needs against the rights of the accused,[27] classification of the armed conflict, clarifications on protected person status under the

[24]See *Prosecutor v. Tadić, Decision on the Defence Motion for Interlocutory Appeal on Jurisdiction*, Case No. IT-94-1-AR72, A. Ch., 2 Oct. 1995.

[25]*Prosecutor v. Tadić, Opinion and Judgment*, Case No. IT-94-1-T, 7 May 1997.

[26]Judge McDonald lodged a Dissenting Opinion in regards to the application of Article 2, grave breaches, of the Statute: see *Prosecutor v. Tadić, Separate and Dissenting Opinion of Judge McDonald Regarding the Applicability of Article 2 of the Statute*, Case No. IT-94-1-T, 7 May 1997. This dissent helped create much needed dialogue and research on the correct means to characterise armed conflicts, the interpretation of protected person status under the 1949 Geneva Conventions, and the application of grave breaches to internal armed conflict. See e.g., Theodor Meron, "Classification of Armed Conflict in the former Yugoslavia: Nicaragua's Fallout", 92 *AJIL* (1998), p. 236.

[27]*Prosecutor v. Tadić, Decision on the Prosecutor's Motion Requesting Protective Measures for Victims and Witnesses*, Case No. IT-94-1-T, 10 Aug. 1995.

Geneva Conventions, definitions of vague enunciations of crimes, and effective assistance of counsel. The proceedings also raised human rights issues concerning rights of appeal, as the Appeals Chamber found Tadić guilty of additional 9 charges for which he had been found not guilty by the Trial Chamber and as yet, no provisions have been made for challenging these new convictions.[28]

In the *Erdemović* case, the accused, a Bosnian Serb soldier, originally pleaded guilty to murder as a crime against humanity for his participation in the killing of numerous unarmed Bosnian Muslim men at Pilica farm in July 1995, shortly after the Bosnian Serb Army take-over of the UN "safe haven" of Srebrenica. After the Trial Chamber sentenced Erdemović to 10 years' imprisonment, he appealed, asserting that he had not intended to plead guilty to murder as a crime against humanity, and that his initial appearance had been uninformed as to the precise nature of the crime. Accepting this assertion, the Appeals Chamber remitted the case to a new Trial Chamber and allowed Erdemović to be given an opportunity to re-plead. At the second sentencing hearing, Erdemović pleaded guilty to murder as violation of the laws or customs of war, and he was sentenced to 5 years' imprisonment. Neither party appealed; with the proceedings thus concluded, Erdemović was transferred to Norway to serve his sentence,[29] less the time already spent in detention. Particularly notable aspects of this case concerned entering guilty pleas, sentencing differences between crimes against humanity and war crimes, and whether genuine duress serves as a mitigating factor or as a defence when war crimes are committed under orders to do so by a superior, and the subordinate fears for his life or safety if he fails to comply.[30]

In the *Čelebići* case,[31] the 4 accused, Bosnian Muslims and Croatians who held positions of authority in or over Čelebići prison camp, were charged with various forms of severe mistreatment of male and female Bosnian Serb detainees in the camp. More specifically, the accused were charged with grave breaches of the 1949 Geneva Conventions and violations of the laws or customs of war for abuses at the prison camp in which detainees were unlawfully killed, tortured, detained, beaten, sexually assaulted, and

---

[28] Instinctively it would seem that convictions by the Appeals Chamber should warrant an appeal to a differently constituted Appeals Chamber.

[29] As of May 2000, agreements to enforce the sentences of the Tribunal have been secured with 7 states. See discussion in David Tolbert, "The International Tribunal for the former Yugoslavia and the Enforcement of Sentences", 11 Leiden Journal of International Law (1998), pp. 655–669.

[30] *Prosecutor v. Erdemović, Judgement*, Case No. IT-96-22-T, A. Ch., 7 October 1997. The majority opinion, in which Judge McDonald participated, held that duress was not a complete defence to crimes against humanity or war crimes for unlawful killings, although it could be considered in mitigation.

[31] *Prosecutor v. Delalić and Others, Judgement*, Case No. IT-96-21-T, 16 Nov. 1998 ("*Čelebići* ").

otherwise subjected to cruel and inhuman treatment by the accused and/or persons under their authority and control. One of the accused was found not guilty of all charges, whereas the other three were found guilty on various counts, with 7–20 year sentences imposed. Appeals are pending. Particularly notable aspects of this case concerned concurrent sentencing practices (as opposed to consecutive sentencing or a mixture thereof), command responsibility, holdings regarding various forms of sexual violence committed against both female and male detainees, and guilty verdicts for grave breaches committed in international armed conflicts.

In the *Furundžija* case,[32] the accused, a local commander of a special unit of the Bosnian Croat military police, was charged with violations of the laws or customs of war for torture and outrages upon personal dignity including rape, for the sexual violence inflicted on a women during the course of interrogation, and a Croatian soldier forced to watch the attack as part of his interrogation as to whether he had betrayed them to the enemy. Lasting a total of 10 trial days, this was the shortest trial thus far held in the Tribunal. Particularly notable aspects of this case concerned the application of Common Article 3 provisions, definitions and other determinations concerning rape and other forms of sexual violence, including the legal acknowledgement of torture by means of rape, allegations of judicial bias and prosecutorial misconduct, the impact of trauma on testimony reliability, and war crimes committed against a member of the same side as the perpetrator.

In the *Aleksovski* case,[33] the accused, a Bosnian Croat commander of the Kaonik prison facility, was charged with two counts of grave breaches of the Geneva Conventions for inhuman treatment and wilfully causing great suffering or serious injury to body or health and one count of violations of the laws or customs of war for outrages upon personal dignity. Essentially, Aleksovski was accused of individual and superior responsibility for various forms of physical and mental harm allegedly caused to detainees under his authority within and outside the prison camp, committed as a result of violence and both intentional and incidental inhumane living conditions at the camp. Found guilty solely for one count of violations of the laws or customs of war, under both theories of responsibility, Aleksovski was initially sentenced to two and a half years' imprisonment. Because he had already spent two years and nearly 11 months in detention, Aleksovski was ordered immediately released. On appeal, the sentence was increased to seven years imprisonment. Aleksovski, who showed up for the appeal, was re-arrested.[34] Of particular importance here are the sentencing practices of the Tribunal and issues concerning responsibility for conditions of detention during armed conflict situations.

---

[32] *Prosecutor v. Furundžija, Judgement,* Case No. IT-95-17/1-T, 10 Dec. 1998.
[33] *Prosecutor v. Aleksovski, Judgement,* Case No. IT-95-14/1-T, 25 June 1999.
[34] *Prosecutor v. Aleksovski, Judgement,* Case No. IT-95-14/1-A, A. Ch., 24 March 2000.

In the *Jelisić* case,[35] the accused, a Bosnian Serb who called himself the "Serb Adolf" and who held a *de facto* position of authority at Luka prison camp, was tried for one count of genocide after pleading guilty to 31 counts of crimes against humanity and violations of the laws or customs of war. The genocide count was charged exclusively under Article 4(2)(a), which concerns a genocidal act committed with an intent to destroy a protected group by killing members of the group. After the Prosecution completed its case-in-chief and before the Defence had presented its defence, the Trial Chamber essentially directed a verdict for the Defence, rendering a Judgement acquitting the accused on the genocide charge. The Trial Chamber determined that the Prosecutor had failed to establish beyond a reasonable doubt that Jelisić acted with the requisite intent to destroy in whole or in part a national, ethnic, racial, or religious group as such. However, finding that there was a sufficient basis to establish the culpability of Jelisić as to the guilty plea entered, the Trial Chamber sentenced Jelisić to 40 years' imprisonment. Both sides have appealed. While the Rwandan Tribunal has held several genocide trials, this was the first genocide trial held before the Yugoslavia Tribunal. Of particular importance here is the proof requirement vis-à-vis genocidal intent, issues concerning finding fairly low level perpetrators guilty of genocide, adequacy of pleading and evidence regarding genocide charges, and perhaps the utility of holding a trial for one charge when a guilty plea has been entered for dozens of other counts.

In the *Kupreškić* case,[36] 6 soldiers of the Croatian Defence Council were charged with violations of the laws or customs of war and crimes against humanity for murder, persecution, cruel treatment, and inhumane acts allegedly committed against Bosnian Muslims in the village of Amici-Santici and its environs, such that after attacking the village by shelling, the HVO soldiers entered the village to harm or expel the occupants and to destroy houses, cultural and religious objects, property, and livestock. One accused was acquitted, and the other five convicted of a crime against humanity for persecution on political, racial or religious grounds. However, due to judicial determinations concerning cumulative charging, each was found not guilty of crimes against humanity for murder and inhumane acts and not guilty of violations of the laws or customs of war. Sentences ranged between 8–25 years' imprisonment. Particularly notable aspects of this case involve persecution as a crime against humanity, issues concerning joint trials, and the appropriateness of cumulative charging.

In the *Blaškić* case,[37] the accused, a high level Croatian military officer, was charged with grave breaches of the Geneva Conventions, violations of the laws or customs of war, and crimes against humanity for a variety of alleged acts committed against Bosnian Muslims, including persecution,

[35]*Prosecutor v. Jelisić, Judgement,* Case No. IT-95-10-T, 14 Dec. 1999.
[36]*Prosecutor v. Kupreškić and Others, Judgement*, Case No. ICTY-95-16-T, 14 Jan. 2000.
[37]*Prosecutor v. Blaškić, Judgement*, Case No. IT-95-14-T, 3 March 2000.

murder, inhumane acts, inhuman treatment, excessive destruction of property, wilful destruction to religious or educational institutions, taking civilians as hostages, and other forms of physical or mental violence against persons or property. The trial, lasting over 2 years, was the longest trial held by the Tribunal thus far. In the Judgement, Blaškić was found guilty of 18 counts and not guilty of 2 counts (in relation to shelling of a town), and sentenced to one lump term of 45 years' imprisonment (thus, a proportioned amount was not attributed to each specific count on which the accused was found guilty). Of particular importance in this case were issues concerning command responsibility and the chain of command, targeting of military objectives, and issues relating to the Tribunal's inability to force states to comply with its orders or requests, including compelling a sovereign state to turn over documents.[38]

Indisputably, the Yugoslavia Tribunal has made an indelible mark on international law and global events. And perhaps none have left a greater imprint on the Tribunal than former Judge and President, Gabrielle Kirk McDonald.[39] Her dynamic voice and thoughtful vision helped direct the course of the Tribunal, and the impact that she – as a woman, an experienced trial court judge, an African-American, a domestic court common law practitioner, a civil and human rights litigator, a legal scholar and law professor, and a tireless advocate for criminal justice and judicial reform – had on the progressive development of international law has been phenomenal. As the following chapters indicate, the Tribunal is well on its way toward revolutionising international criminal law and its application to states and individuals violating its prescriptions, and the drafting and development of the Rules have been an essential component of the Tribunal's progress.

---

[38]See *Prosecutor v. Blaškić, Judgement on the Request of the Republic of Croatia for Review of the Decision of Trial Chamber II of 18 July 1997,* Case No. IT-95-14-AR108*bis*, A. Ch., 29 Oct. 1997; *Prosecutor v. Blaškić, Decision on the Objection of the Republic of Croatia to the Issuance of Subpoenae Duces Tecum*, Case No. IT-95-14-PT, 18 July 1997.

[39]It is of course impossible to rank objectively the impact that individuals make on such an institution, but it is indisputable that such notable figures as Judges McDonald, Cassese and Jorda, Prosecutors Goldstone, Arbour and Del Ponte, and Registrar de Sampayo have left their signatures, and indeed the course of the Tribunal has been in large part guided by their individual personalities, goals, decisions and influence.

PART II

Jurisdiction

SUSAN LAMB[1]

4. Illegal Arrest and the Jurisdiction of the ICTY

1. Introduction

The power of international forces in Bosnia and Herzegovina to arrest indictees of the International Criminal Tribunal for the former Yugoslavia ("ICTY") was originally disputed by the forces themselves and, until recently, no explicit powers of arrest were set forth in the ICTY's Statute or Rules of Procedure and Evidence ("Rules").[2] Although the legal basis for the arrest of ICTY indictees was put on a firmer footing by the enactment of additional Rules, the scope and extent of these powers remain controversial.[3] The ICTY has itself since passed judgment upon the validity of the first of the recent forcible arrests in-field by UN forces[4] and issues

[1]Legal Advisor, Office of the Prosecutor, UN ICTY, The Hague, Netherlands. The views expressed herein are those of the author alone and do not represent the views of the ICTY or the UN.

[2]International Forces in Bosnia and Herzegovina originally took the view that the arrest of indicted war criminals was beyond their force mandates. (See Amnesty International Report, EUR 63/11/96, April 1996.) The view of the American contingent of the Stabilisation Force ("SFOR") was, until recently, that SFOR "had the authority to arrest any indicted war criminals it encounters or who interfere with its mission, but it will not try to track them down" (Amnesty International, Bosnia: The International Community's Responsibility to Ensure Human Rights, EUR 63/14/85, June 1996).

[3]Security Council Resolution 827, issued pursuant to Chapter VII of the UN Charter and establishing the ICTY, makes no specific reference to arrests (SC Res 827, UN Doc S/RES/827 (25 May 1993)). Rule 59*bis* refers to many different modalities of the arrest of war crimes suspects indicted by the ICTY: those which have occurred to date have been carried out either by a UN body specifically named in an ICTY arrest warrant or by SFOR or its component forces. The ICTY's Rules also countenance the issuing of arrest warrants directly to the Prosecutor of the ICTY, although the Rules do not specify exactly how such arrests are to be effected.

[4]*Prosecutor v. Dokmanović, Decision on the Motion for Release by the Accused Slavko Dokmanović*, (*"Dokmanović"*), Case No. IT-95-13a-PT, 22 Oct. 1997; leave to appeal denied in *Prosecutor v. Dokmanović, Decision on Application for Leave to Appeal by the Accused Slavko Dokmanović*, Case No. IT-95-13a-AR 72, A. Ch., 11 Nov. 1997.

R. May et al., Essays on ICTY Procedure and Evidence in Honour of Gabrielle Kirk McDonald, 27–43.

concerning the legitimacy of the ICTY's arrest powers remain pending in other cases.[5] Given the uncertain legal basis for arrests, a related question is the consequences of a wrongful arrest – i.e. one effected in the absence of an adequate legal basis – for the subsequent exercise by the ICTY of jurisdiction over an accused.[6]

2. Pertinent Provisions of the ICTY Statute and Rules

Powers designed to facilitate the arrest of persons indicted by the ICTY are outlined in Articles 19, 20 and 29 of the Statute and Rules 54–59*bis*. Article 19(2) of the Statute provides that

> [u]pon confirmation of an indictment, the judge may, at the request of the Prosecutor, issue such orders and warrants for the arrest, detention, surrender or transfer of persons, and any other orders as may be required for the conduct of the trial.

This provision appears to be an extremely open-textured authorisation for a judge to issue any such orders requested by the Prosecutor and which a judge deems necessary. Article 20(2) of the Statute provides, in turn, that

> [a] person against whom an indictment has been confirmed shall, pursuant to an order or an arrest warrant of the International Tribunal, be taken into custody, immediately informed of the charges against him and transferred to the International Tribunal.

Article 29, addressed to States, mandates their co-operation with the Tribunal in the investigation and prosecution of persons accused of committing serious violations of international humanitarian law. In particular, it obliges States to comply with any request for assistance or an order issued by a Trial Chamber, including, but not limited to, orders for the arrest or detention of persons.

---

[5]In proceedings initiated by its *ex parte* "Notice of Motion for Judicial Assistance in connection with the Stabilisation Force ("SFOR") or other military and security forces operating on the territory of Bosnia and Herzegovina," filed 24 Nov. 1999, the Defence sought the assistance of the Trial Chamber in obtaining information and documents in relation to the evidentiary hearing to be held on the Defence's "Motion for an order directing the Prosecutor to forthwith return the Accused Stevan Todorovic to the country of refuge" and "Petition for a Writ of Habeus Corpus", filed on 21 Oct. and 15 Nov. 1999 respectively (together "Motions for release"). These evidentiary proceedings and both Motions for release remain pending. See infra regarding the subsequent cases in which the lawfulness of the accuseds' arrest may in future be challenged.

[6]See Susan Lamb, "The Powers of Arrest of the International Criminal Tribunal for the Former Yugoslavia," British Yearbook of International Law (1999), pp. 167–244 and infra.

The ICTY Statute's provisions are somewhat general, and matters of detail pertaining to arrests are set forth in the Rules.[7]

Detailed arrest procedures are set forth in Rules 54–59*bis*. The primary rule, contained in Rule 54, provides that "at the request of either party or *proprio motu*, a Judge or a Trial Chamber may issue such orders, summonses, subpoenas, warrants and transfer orders as may be necessary for the purposes of an investigation or for the preparation or conduct of the trial." No limitations upon this general power to issue orders are expressed.[8]

Rule 55 creates an obligation upon State authorities to give effect to arrest warrants. On the basis of this rule, arrest warrants were usually sent to the authorities in appropriate States with respect to every indictment confirmed by a Judge of the Tribunal.[9] This constitutes the primary, though not exclusive, method for the arrest and transfer of persons to the Tribunal.[10] Additionally, after the signing of the Dayton Accord, all arrest warrants previously issued by the Tribunal were transmitted to the International Implementation Force ("IFOR") deployed on the territory of Bosnia and Herzegovina under the Dayton Accord.[11]

The rule which has, in practice, provided the most dramatic impetus to ICTY arrests is Rule 59*bis*, adopted in January 1996 principally to provide for the transmission of arrest warrants to international bodies such as SFOR. Rule 59*bis* reads as follows:

[7]The Tribunal's rule-making powers are outlined in the Statute, Art. 15 which states that "[t]he judges of the International Tribunal shall adopt rules of procedure and evidence for the conduct of the pre-trial phase of the proceedings, trials and appeals, the admission of evidence, the protection of victims and witnesses and other appropriate matters." The Tribunal thus appears, on the face of it, to have plenary competence under the Statute to adopt any rules of procedure and evidence it deems appropriate.

[8]See, however, the new Rule 54*bis*, enacted 30 Nov. 1999, which grants to States requested under Rule 54 to produce documents or information the opportunity to be heard and to apply to a Judge or Trial Chamber to have any resultant order set aside on the grounds that disclosure would prejudice that State's national security interests.

[9]This did not occur, exceptionally, with respect to the arrest of Dokmanović, who was arrested pursuant to a sealed arrest warrant which was transmitted only to the United Nations Transitional Administration for Eastern Slavonia ("UNTAES") and not the Government of Croatia or the Federal Republic of Yugoslavia ("FRY"). The secret character of the indictment and its non-transmission to States was justified on the grounds both that this would have been futile (due to the history of non-co-operation with the ICTY by these states) and so as to preserve the reasonable prospect that was believed to exist for effecting Dokmanović's arrest within the UNTAES area of administration. Judge McDonald in *Dokmanović* declared sealed indictments to be "envisioned and acceptable" according to Rule 53 (supra note 4, at p. 12).

[10]Id., at p. 20.

[11]Note also Rule 61(D), which confers a power to issue international arrest warrants, following the failure of a State to arrest and transfer an indicted person. These have also been transmitted to IFOR (and latterly its successor body, the Stabilisation Force (SFOR)).

(a) Notwithstanding Rules 55 to 59, on the order of a Judge, the Registrar shall transmit to an appropriate authority or international body or the Prosecutor a copy of a warrant for the arrest of an accused, on such terms as the Judge may determine, together with an order for his prompt transfer to the Tribunal in the event that he be taken into custody by that authority or international body or the Prosecutor.

(b) At the time of being taken into custody an accused shall be informed immediately, in a language he understands, of the charges against him and of the fact that he is being transferred to the Tribunal and, upon his transfer, the indictment and a statement of the rights of the accused shall be read to him and he shall be cautioned in such a language.

All arrests so far carried out by SFOR have been effected on the basis of this provision. The exact procedures envisaged are nevertheless left somewhat opaque and a degree of uncertainty surrounds the modalities of any arrest effected on the basis of Rule 59*bis*.[12] In particular, it is unclear from the language of the Rules what constitutes an arrest, and little clarification is provided by the nascent arrest practice of the ICTY.[13]

The Trial Chamber in *Dokmanović* viewed a restraint upon a person's free movement imposed by law enforcement personnel as "a necessary component of arrest."[14] Applying this test, it found that Dokmanović was arrested and detained only after he had arrived at the UNTAES base in the

[12]Rule 59*bis* is in many respects not clearly drafted. It appears to suggest that once an arrest warrant has been issued to a State, a judge may then order the Tribunal Registrar to transmit "copies" of that original warrant to "an appropriate authority or international body." In practice, warrants are issued to a body such as SFOR and include instructions to "detain" the indictee and to transfer them to The Hague. Despite this wording, however, at no stage in the course of effecting Dokmanović's arrest was an order made by a judge directing the Registrar to transmit to UNTAES a copy of the arrest warrant. Instead, Judge Riad addressed the warrant directly to UNTAES, and the role of the Registrar remained unclear. As UNTAES was the direct addressee of the arrest warrant (rather than the recipient of, for example, a photocopy of a warrant addressed to another body), the term "copy" does not appear to have been understood in its ordinary meaning. Rather, it referred to a warrant substantively identical to the warrant issued to the State except for its addressee; it was, in effect, an original. On the considerable procedural confusion that surrounded the original issuance of the Dokmanović arrest warrant, see *Dokmanović*, at p. 3, n. 1.

[13]"Arrest" is defined in Rule 2(A) as "the act of taking a suspect or an Accused into custody by a national authority." Note, however, the broadened definition of "State" under this Rule, which is designed to allow judicial documents to be transmitted to the non-State entities found in the former Yugoslavia.

[14]*Dokmanović*, at p. 14, para. 28, citing, *inter alia*, Article 5(1) of the European Convention for the Protection of Human Rights and Fundamental Freedoms ("ECHR") ("liberty" meaning the physical liberty of the person) and Article 9(1) of the International Covenant on Civil and Political Rights ("ICCPR") ("arrest and detention" referring to the act of depriving a person of his liberty, and the state of deprivation of liberty).

eastern Slavonian region of Croatia.[15] Dokmanović's arrest was held by the Trial Chamber to have been effected only once the UNTAES vehicle had crossed into the military compound in Croatian territory, when the arrest had been formally declared, the charges against Dokmanović announced and his rights read out. The Trial Chamber placed emphasis upon the fact Dokmanović had not expressed any desire for the vehicle to stop or to be let out, nor was he handcuffed or forcibly restrained in any way until he arrived at the military compound in the UNTAES area of administration.[16] The arrest of Dokmanović constituted the first arrest by international forces and the OTP in the field and clearly practices were still evolving.[17]

In addition, the Trial Chamber in *Dokmanović* sought to ascertain the compatibility of arrests with the mandate of UNTAES. UN Security Council Resolution 1037, establishing UNTAES, makes no express reference to the arrest of ICTY indictees. Instead, UNTAES' mandate re-states the primary obligation of States to co-operate with the ICTY and then creates a parallel obligation upon UNTAES to co-operate with and support the Tribunal.[18]

In the course of the Security Council debate which led to the adoption of Resolution 1037 however, at least two Security Council members appeared to envisage that UNTAES's obligations of co-operation might include the power to effect arrests.[19] Moreover, the importance of UNTAES' obligation

---

[15]In fact Dokmanović's arrest had been effected by an elaborate ruse on the part of the Office of the Prosecutor ("OTP") and UNTAES whereby he had been enticed to enter a UN vehicle on the Serbian side of the border with Eastern Slavonia, driven to a military base in the UNTAES area of administration and there detained (id., at pp. 15–16).

[16]The Trial Chamber rejected the contention that a *de facto* arrest had occurred before this point explicitly on the basis that Dokmanović had entered the UNTAES vehicle which carried him to the compound of his own free will. This was despite the fact that Dokmanović had probably lost his liberty the moment he entered the UNTAES vehicle, for if he had attempted to leave the UNTAES vehicle before it had reached the military compound, he would have almost certainly been restrained (id.).

[17]As to the respective roles of the parties effecting the arrest, the Trial Chamber seemed content to view the arrest as a "joint operation" on the part of the ICTY and UNTAES (id., at p. 25). The decision highlights the reality that there is a considerable fudging of the distinction between words such as "arrest" and "detention" both in the ICTY Statute and in the nascent arrest practice in the field.

[18]The operative parts of Security Council Resolution 1037 read as follows: "The Security Council [...] (21) *Reaffirms* that all States shall cooperate fully with the International Tribunal for the Former Yugoslavia and its organs in accordance with the provisions of Resolution 827 (1993) of 25 May 1993 and the Statute of the International Tribunal and shall comply with requests for assistance or orders issued by a Trial Chamber under Article 29 of the Statute; (21) *Stresses* that UNTAES shall cooperate with the International Tribunal in the performance of its mandate [...]" (SC Res. 1037, S/RES/1037 (15 January 1996)).

[19]See for instance the statement of Mr. Elaraby, Representative of Egypt, Provisional Verbatim Records of the 3619th Meeting of the Security Council, Monday 15 Jan. 1996, S/PV.3619, at p. 8 and that of Mr. Martinez Blanco, Representative of Honduras, Provisional Verbatim Records, id., at p. 14.

to co-operate with the ICTY was certainly stressed in the Security Council debates leading up to the adoption of Resolution 1037.[20]

Certain aspects of UNTAES' mandate also contain an explicit human rights dimension, although this stops short of authorising UNTAES to effect the arrest of persons accused of having committed serious breaches of international humanitarian law.[21] Certainly, the arrest of an ICTY indictee known to be at large in Eastern Slavonia could contribute to such an "atmosphere of confidence" and thereby promote respect for those human rights standards which were explicitly embodied in UNTAES's mandate. A power to arrest may thus be compatible with the overall scheme and object of the UNTAES mandate and its duty to co-operate with the ICTY, provided assistance in this regard is requested by the Tribunal. Indeed, the co-operation of UNTAES in effecting Dokmanović's arrest had in fact been requested by the ICTY; a point emphasised by the Trial Chamber in declaring that the arrest of Dokmanović was consistent with the powers expressly and impliedly conferred by Resolution 1037.[22]

However, this analysis is rather thin. An obligation to "co-operate" with the Tribunal is not necessarily synonymous with a power of arrest. Nor could a request from the ICTY for assistance in carrying out an arrest have the effect of granting additional powers to UNTAES or of legitimising any act by UNTAES which would otherwise be beyond the powers conferred upon it by Resolution 1037.[23] Although Resolution 1037 did not refer explicitly to powers of arrest, it is nevertheless possible that, for the reasons just outlined, it could be interpreted as supporting such a power by implication. Regrettably, no analysis of this type was undertaken by the Trial Chamber.

3. The Scope of the ICTY's Rule-Making Powers

The ICTY Rules pertaining to arrests also raise difficult and complex questions concerning the overall scope of the ICTY's rule-making powers.[24] The

[20]See for example the comments of the Representatives of Italy and Poland (id., at pp. 7, 17).

[21]For example, para. 12 of Resolution 1037 provided that UNTAES should promote "an atmosphere of confidence" among local residents and "respect for the highest standards of human rights and fundamental freedoms."

[22]The Trial Chamber held that "Resolution 1037 places responsibility on UNTAES for cooperating with the Tribunal. [...] UNTAES [...] was executing its mandate to cooperate with the Tribunal by effecting the arrest of the Accused." (*Dokmanović*, at pp. 21–24). See also Article 20(2) of the Statute, which is a mandatory provision, thus binding those named in an arrest warrant to take the indictee into custody (id., at p. 23).

[23]While UNTAES' co-operation in the arrest of an indicted suspect for crimes against humanity is probably not *incompatible* with its mandate, this mandate was less than explicit on the issue of arrests. (See further Lamb, supra note 6, at p. 185.)

[24]An evaluation of the legitimacy of the ICTY's formulation of Rule 59*bis* requires an analysis of its conformity with the ICTY's delegated grant from the Security Council resolutions establishing the Tribunal and the express terms of the Tribunal's Statute (id., at pp. 195–202).

Statute confers extensive powers upon the judges of the Trial Chamber to issue any order or arrest warrant it sees fit and the Tribunal's rule-making competence is therefore broad and open-textured.[25]

Moreover, the Security Council established the ICTY as a measure deemed necessary for the restoration of international peace and security in the former Yugoslavia, pursuant to Chapter VII of the UN Charter. As the Statute derives its authority from Security Council Resolution 827, the decisions of the Tribunal are thus also to be considered binding enforcement measures under Chapter VII of the UN Charter.[26]

Although arrest warrants constitute binding enforcement measures, it nevertheless does not follow that such measures are non-derogable in all circumstances.[27] Recent arrest practice provides few, if any, unambiguous examples of where the exercise by the Tribunal of its enforcement powers could be said to be patently unlawful.[28] Nevertheless, certain recent arrests give grounds for caution as to the possible dangers of the unchecked use of coercive powers by international forces.

Controversial in this regard is perhaps the case of Simo Drljača, who was shot and killed by SFOR during an attempt to arrest him. Security Council

---

[25]See ICTY Statute, Arts. 19(2) and 15, supra. Consequently, it is unlikely that Rule 59*bis* is *per se ultra vires* (at least not on its face). The nub of the issue is instead likely to be the limits to particular *applications* of the Tribunal's enforcement powers (id., at p. 180).

[26]This conclusion follows from a plain reading of SC Res. 827, supra. The UN Secretary-General has also affirmed that the binding nature of the Security Council decision to create the Tribunal entails the obligation for all States to co-operate with the Tribunal at any stage of the proceedings. (See Secretary-General's Report, paras. 23 and 125.) Pursuant to UN Charter Arts. 25 and 103, decisions of the Security Council taken under Chapter VII of the UN Charter create binding obligations upon UN Member States which prevail over any other inconsistent international obligations. *(Application and Interpretation of the Montreal Convention (Libya v. US, France and UK) Provisional Measures*, ICJ Reports 1992). See further Lamb, supra note 6, at pp. 197–199.

[27]For instance, the exercise of such powers may not be unlimited in circumstances where their exercise clashes with jus cogens or peremptory norms of international law. *Jus cogens* norms have a special character and the hierarchy of norms under Art. 103 of the UN Charter thus does not envisage a conflict between action under Chapter VII and a breach of a peremptory norm. For a definition of *jus cogens*, see Art. 53 of the Vienna Convention on the Law of Treaties; for a list of some of the least controversial examples of this class, see Ian Brownlie, Principles of Public International Law (1998), at pp. 514–517. See also *Application of the Convention on the Prevention and Punishment of the Crime of Genocide, (Bosnia and Herzegovina v. Yugoslavia (Serbia and Montenegro)), Provisional Measures*, ICJ Reports 1993, 3, Diss. Op., Judge Lauterpacht, at p. 15, para. 39.

[28]In *Dokmanović*, individual rights such as liberty and due process were clearly implicated, although there had been no breach by the ICTY of such rights. In any event, it is doubtful whether any purported violation of these rights in effecting the arrest would support an allegation that the ICTY acted beyond the scope of its competence in effecting an arrest (see further Lamb, supra note 6, at pp. 202–3).

Resolution 1088 does mandate the use of force by SFOR in self-defence.[29] In the absence of explicit, enumerated criteria in Resolution 1088 for its evaluation, it is difficult to identify with any precision what constitutes legitimate self-defence on the part of SFOR troops.[30] In order for the effecting of an arrest to exceed the bounds of the Tribunal's designated Chapter VII competence, the relevant international case law nevertheless suggests that the conduct of the arresting agents would have to be of a character shocking to the conscience of the international community; such as, for instance, where the arrest was effected in violation of a peremptory norm of international law.[31]

A recent example of an alleged clash between ICTY arrest powers and fundamental human rights norms is provided by the arrest of Stevan Todorović.[32] Todorović was arrested in the FRY on 27 September 1998, transported into Bosnia and Herzegovina and handed over to the custody of

---

[29]Paragraph 20 of Resolution 1088 "recognizes the right of the force to take all necessary measures to defend itself from attack or threat of attack" (SC Res. 1088, UN Doc. S/Res/1088 (10 December 1996)). Drljača was alleged to have opened fire on the SFOR troops who had ambushed him, wounding one of them.

[30]It is thus likely that the legitimacy of SFOR's actions will be evaluated on a case by case basis, in terms of what was thought by SFOR to have been required by the circumstances. The necessity or otherwise of this response is likely to be evaluated contemporaneously with the threat confronting the forces in the field rather than on an *ex post facto* basis and with the wisdom of hindsight. (See in this regard *Prosecutor v. Tadić, Decision on the Defence Motion for Interlocutory Appeal on Jurisdiction*, Case No. IT-94-1-AR72, A. Ch., 2 Oct. 1995, at para. 45 where the Appeals Chamber, in addressing the discretionary power of the Security Council to take measures under Chapter VII of the UN Charter, held that "[i]t would be a total misconception of what are the criteria of legality and validity in law to test the legality of such measures *ex post facto* by their success or failure to achieve their ends [...]").

[31]See supra notes 26, 27 and accompanying text. An example of this sort might be if Drljača, rather than being killed, was instead apprehended by SFOR and subjected to torture, as it is extremely difficult to conceive of permissible derogations from the prohibition against torture in general international law. (Indeed, Art. 2(2) of the 1984 UN Convention Against Torture and other Cruel, Inhuman or Degrading Treatment or Punishment provides that "[n]o exceptional circumstances whatsoever, whether a state of war or a threat of war, internal political instability or any other public emergency may be invoked as a justification of torture.") Beyond the case where resort to force is demonstrably and unambiguously necessary (such as, for instance, where it is required in self-defence), the killing of a suspect by international forces in the course of effecting an arrest is not justifiable: at least, the ICTY could not kill a suspect *in lieu* of arresting him. However, where SFOR is validly attempting to arrest a suspect who is using all means to resist arrest, including the resort to force, they can persist in their attempt to arrest him even to the point where it is necessary to shoot the indictee in self-defence.

[32]The modalities in which the accuseds Dragan Nikolić and Momčilo Krajišnik were apprehended raise similar issues to Todorović and the lawfulness of these arrests may thus also in future be challenged; see infra.

SFOR and officials of the ICTY.[33] During the pre-trial proceedings, it was alleged that the accused had been abducted by ICTY agents from the FRY and thus should be returned to that territory.[34] In a separate memorandum filed in support of the accused's motion, the Defence stated that the ICTY "does not have the right to subject the Accused to prosecution following such illegal abduction" and requested the Trial Chamber "to refrain from exercising its jurisdiction in this case over the Accused who was seized and abducted by means in violation of international law."[35]

The Prosecution opposed the accused's motion on the basis that it was supported by no evidence disclosing a *prima facie* basis for judicial enquiry. It alleged, further, that even if the motion was considered on its merits, the facts alleged by the accused, even if they could be proved, would not as a matter of law entitle the accused to the remedy sought.[36]

At the conclusion of an oral hearing on 4 March 1999, the Trial Chamber ruled that the accused's motion would be rejected. The Trial Chamber justified its initial refusal to grant an evidentiary hearing on the grounds that

---

[33]During his first appearance before the Trial Chamber on 30 Sept. 1998, Todorović stated that he did not feel well because he had received a heavy blow over his head "during the kidnapping" and that he had been transported from Serbia by boat. (Transcript of Trial Chamber hearing of 30 Sept. 1998, at 102, *Prosecutor v. Todorović*, Case No. IT-95-9-PT ("*Todorović*"). A motion was filed on his behalf alleging that "according to published reports, [...] the Defendant Stevan Todorović was illegally abducted from the territory of the Federal Republic of Yugoslavia. Such abduction, if it be the case, may not and must not be countenanced by this court." ("Notice of Motion for Evidentiary Hearing on Arrest, Detention and Removal of Defendant Stevan Todorović and for Extension of Time to Move to Dismiss Indictment," D2989–D2984, 10 Feb. 1999). Although the accused's motion referred to "published reports," the attachment to the accused's motion appeared to be a copy of a message, posted by a private individual to an e-mail bulletin board, containing what purported to be the text of an article from *The Times*. This report referred to claims attributed to unspecified "Western diplomatic sources," to "angry relatives of Mr Todorović" and other unnamed persons. The report suggested that his removal from the FRY had been effected by the British SAS or the American Delta Unit.

[34]The motion filed by Todorović requested various orders including (i) an order directing that a preliminary evidentiary hearing be had as to the facts and circumstances of the arrest; (ii) an order directing the Prosecutor to make available to the Defence all documents in the Prosecutor's files as to the manner, method and individuals who detained and delivered the accused to the jurisdiction of the Court and (iii) an order directing the Prosecutor to show cause why an order of dismissal of the indictment against the accused should not be made and the defendant be freed from custody "absent proof that the arrest of the Accused was in accordance with customary international law, practice and usage." ("Notice of Motion for Evidentiary Hearing," id.).

[35]Id. See also "Memorandum of Law in Further Support for an Evidentiary Hearing as to abduction and Detention of Accused Todorović," D3163–D3155, filed 1 March 1999, at pp. 3156–8.

[36]See "Prosecutor's Response to the 'Notice of Motion for Evidentiary Hearing on Arrest, Detention and Removal of Defendant Stevan Todorović and for Extension of Time to Move to Dismiss Indictment' filed by Stevan Todorović on 10 February 1999," D3128–D3105, 22 Feb. 1999.

the motion did not contain sufficient factual and legal material as to the circumstances of the arrest to warrant such a hearing.[37] Leave to appeal was nevertheless granted on the question of "whether the Trial Chamber erred in denying the Defence request for an evidentiary hearing and an order directing the Prosecutor to afford discovery."[38]

On 13 October 1999, the Appeals Chamber dismissed this appeal, ruling that the Trial Chamber had not abused its discretion in denying the original motion, on the basis that the accused's Motion had not contained sufficient factual and legal material regarding the circumstances of his arrest and that the onus of proof with regard to establishing the unlawfulness of the arrest lay with the accused.[39] The accused subsequently filed two further motions, arguing that his arrest, detention and delivery was in violation of State sovereignty and contrary to customary international law.[40] At a hearing on 24 November 1999, the Trial Chamber, having ascertained that the Defence accepted that it was they who bore the onus of proof with regard to the alleged irregularities in the accused's arrest, decided to deal with the merits of both Defence motions simultaneously and granted the accused an evidentiary hearing.[41]

Todorović's allegations concerning the legality of his arrest raise difficult questions regarding the correct balance to be struck between the exercise of the Tribunal's powers of arrest and the individual rights of the accused. The

---

[37]Written reasons for the decision were subsequently issued by the Trial Chamber on 25 March 1999. (*Prosecutor v. Todorović, Decision Stating Reasons for Trial Chamber's Order of 4 March 1999 on Defence Motion for Evidentiary Hearing on the Arrest of the Accused Todorović*, Case No. IT-95-9-PT, 25 March 1999).

[38]*Prosecutor v. Todorović, Decision on Application by Stevan Todorović for leave to Appeal against the Oral Decision of Trial Chamber III of 4 March 1999*, A. Ch., Case No. IT-95-9-PT, 1 July 1999.

[39]*Prosecutor v. Todorović, Decision on Appeal by Stevan Todorović against the Oral Decision of 4 March 1999 and the Written Decision of 25 March 1999 of Trial Chamber III*, A. Ch., Case No. IT-95-9-PT, 13 Oct. 1999.

[40]"Notice of Motion for an Order Directing the Prosecutor to Forthwith Return the Accused Stevan Todorović to the Country of Refuge," filed 20 Oct. 1999 and "Petition for a Writ of Habeas Corpus," filed 15 Nov. 1999. The latter motion was based on the Appeals Chamber decision in *Barayagwiza v. Prosecutor*, A. Ch., Case No. ICTR-97-19-AR72, 3 Nov. 1999, which the accused interpreted as authority for the proposition that ICTY procedural law recognises the remedy of *habeas corpus*. The better view is that the Appeals Chamber in Barayagwiza upheld the fundamental right of detainees to challenge the legality of their detention. However, this right is provided for in particular Tribunal Rules rather than through the Tribunals' adoption of ancient national remedies such as the common law prerogative writs. ("Prosecutor's Response to Stevan Todorović's Document Entitled "Petition for a Writ of Habeas Corpus,"" D4752-D4738, 19 Nov. 1999). This view has subsequently been endorsed by Hunt J in *Prosecutor v. Brđanin, Decision on Petition for a Writ of Habeus Corpus on Behalf of Radislav Brđanin*, Case No. IT-99-36-PT, 8 Dec. 1999.

[41]The accused provided testimony on that same day. (Transcript of hearing of 24 Nov. 1999, *Prosecutor v. Todorović*, at pp. 542–86). This matter is still pending.

first concerns the nature of the accused's rights allegedly violated.[42] Secondly, even if a violation of the accused's rights such as liberty and due process could be established, or if it were proven that the accused was taken from the FRY against his will in violation of the sovereignty of the FRY, the appropriate remedies in such a case would still fall to be determined.[43] As it appeared that SFOR and Tribunal procedures pertaining to the detention and transfer of suspects to The Hague came into play only following the delivery of Todorović to SFOR in Bosnia and Herzegovina, Todorović's arrest also raises the issue of the effect of any potentially illegal acts committed prior to the handing over of Todorović by entities other than international forces, for instance by the authorities of another State or by

---

[42]The manner in which Todorović was taken from the former Yugoslavia was said by the Defence to involve a violation of his right to liberty and security of person as recognised in the International Covenant on Civil and Political Rights and the European Convention on Human Rights. Although Tribunal indictees do have the right to liberty and security of the person under international law, it is nevertheless far from clear that such rights are violated by the forcible effecting of Tribunal arrests. In such cases, defendants are deprived of their liberty only on grounds and in accordance with procedures that are established by law; namely, pursuant to lawful arrest and detention by a competent legal authority on the basis of an arrest warrant. (See further Lamb, supra note 6, at pp. 202–3).

[43]In particular, it is by no means certain that the accused would necessarily be entitled to the remedy sought, namely the dismissal of the indictment against the accused or his release. While certain cases decided by national courts have affirmed that a court should decline to exercise criminal jurisdiction over an accused who has been brought within the jurisdiction of a court by unlawful means, these cases generally do not afford a valid analogy to Tribunal arrests, on the grounds that such decisions were premised on the fact that the removal of the accused from the other State involved a circumvention of applicable extradition procedures. However, the regime of extradition is patently inapplicable to the case of the Tribunal, as the Tribunal is not a foreign jurisdiction or a State but a unique international organisation created pursuant to Chapter VII of the UN Charter. Furthermore, a violation of State sovereignty is a violation of the rights of the relevant State; to be entitled to a remedy, the accused may need to establish that this violation of a State's sovereignty also constituted some violation of his own fundamental rights. (See *Attorney-General v. Eichmann*, 36 ILR 5, 62 (Israeli Sup. Ct., 1968) at p. 305 ("*Eichmann*"); cf. *Dokmanović*, at para. 55). Furthermore, even if it could be shown that breaches of international law had occurred in the course of effecting an arrest, it would be necessary to show collusion between the Prosecution in this unlawful activity in order to establish the responsibility of the ICTY. The need to show official involvement was conceded by the Defence ("Memorandum of Law," supra note 35, at p. 3157). The Prosecution denied that it had had any involvement in any alleged activity relating to the accused's removal from the FRY, claiming that it had no prior information concerning any proposed operation to secure the arrest of the accused and that the first knowledge that the Prosecutor had of the matter was on the 27 Sept. 1998, when it was informed by SFOR that it had the accused in custody in northern Bosnia. (Transcript of Trial Chamber hearing of 4 March 1999, *Prosecutor v. Todorović*, at pp. 344, 348). The Defence indicated that while it was not prepared to argue that the Prosecution was in collusion with whoever was alleged to have kidnapped the accused, they contended that SFOR forces were acting as agents of the Prosecution (Transcript of Trial Chamber hearing of 24 Nov. 1999, id., at 547–8). See further infra.

private individuals.[44] To the extent that Todorović's apprehension by unspecified authorities or individuals was effected in violation of FRY sovereignty and hence international law, can the OTP be said to have adopted and ratified any such violations?[45]

Despite the expressed preference of the Prosecutor that close judicial scrutiny of the facts surrounding arrests effected by multinational forces be avoided, it would nevertheless be highly undesirable for an ICTY Trial Chamber to abdicate its judicial function in this manner.[46] There is, however, a real conflict between the need for the Trial Chamber to have as full and accurate representation as possible of the methods used by SFOR to effect arrests and the practical consequences that such disclosure may have for safety and security in the field.[47] Lacking any police or other enforcement agency of its own, the Tribunal must rely upon the military forces of certain State and super-State entities such as SFOR to arrest its indictees, giving rise to concern on the part of the Prosecution that any requirement by the Tribunal that these states and entities disclose details of

---

[44]In *Dokmanović*, at para. 78, the Trial Chamber expressly left open the question "whether the International Tribunal has the authority to exercise jurisdiction over a defendant illegally obtained from abroad." The Prosecution contended with regard to Todorović that any irregularities in an arrest conducted by the authorities of another State and prior to the delivery of the accused to the jurisdiction of the Tribunal should not constitute a bar to the ICTY's exercise of jurisdiction, adverting to the danger that "to hold otherwise would provide an inducement to certain States, such as the FRY, to ensure that serious irregularities are committed in the arrest process before handing the Accused to the Tribunal, being confident that after review, the indictment would be dismissed and the defendant released because the defendant's rights had been violated by the authorities in the FRY. Under that scenario, the States concerned could claim that they are fulfilling their obligation of co-operation while, at the same time, sabotaging the Prosecution because the Defendant's fundamental rights were violated by the irregularities in the process" (Transcript of Trial Chamber hearing of 4 March 1999, id., at pp. 351–2).

[45]This question is likely to re-emerge in relation to the *Nikolić* case, where the accused similarly alleges that he was abducted by unknown agents from the FRY. See further supra note 32.

[46]The need for judicial scrutiny is necessary so as to ensure that unlawful measures are not resorted to by law enforcement personnel, to maintain the integrity of the international judicial process and to safeguard the fairness of the trial process. As the Defence emphasised, "[t]he Prosecutor is [in this regard] not only charged with prosecuting the Accused. The Prosecutor's role before this International Tribunal is of far greater import. The Prosecutor speaks for [the] rule of law and [ought not pay] mere lip service to it." ("The Accused/Appellant Stevan Todorović's Reply Brief," A153-A137, 16 Aug. 1999). This idea found some support before the Trial Chamber (Transcript of Trial Chamber hearing of 4 March 1999, id., at pp. 363–4).

[47]In this regard, the Prosecution cited the concern of SFOR and the police forces of the States involved in arresting Tribunal indictees that disclosing details of their operational orders, methods of operating in the field and means of undertaking their arrest operations would undermine security and confidentiality, endanger the lives of their personnel and would seriously jeopardise both their ability and willingness to conduct these arrests (id., at p. 356).

this nature to the Trial Chamber may lead to a withdrawal of their willingness to provide such voluntary assistance.[48] A fundamental dilemma therefore exists where the Tribunal wishes simultaneously both to encourage the continued apprehension of Tribunal suspects still at large and to fulfil its duty, as a judicial organ, to check against any alleged abuses of power committed by international forces in the field. The ICTY's dependence upon such forces to carry out arrests and other enforcement functions thus creates a basic structural constraint upon the capacity of the ICTY to uphold the rule of law within the United Nations system.

4. The Consequences of Irregularities in Arrests of Indictees

Where a violation of international law does occur in the method used to arrest an accused, the question of whether this debars the Tribunal from proceeding to try the accused has been the subject of keen controversy.[49] It is often argued that a kidnapping is an international wrong and the application of the principle *ex injuria juris non oritur* means that an otherwise existing basis of jurisdiction should therefore not be exercised.[50] At least in cases where Tribunal employees or their agents have been complicit in such wrongdoing, it has been reasoned, by analogy, that the ICTY, just as any State, may therefore exercise jurisdiction and prosecute an individual charged only by means that do not violate international law, but may not do so by means that infringe upon the territorial sovereignty of another State, absent protest by that State.[51]

However, a review of State practice suggests that the illegality of an arrest at international law has frequently constituted no bar to a domestic court's subsequent attempt to exercise jurisdiction over an accused, where the jurisdiction of that Court is otherwise well founded.[52] It nevertheless cannot be denied that there are important policy factors that support the view that international illegality is to be discouraged, and that to permit jurisdiction is to encourage such illegality: a rationale which would arguably apply all the

---

[48]Id., at pp. 356, 357–8.

[49]Historically, the normal and generally accepted remedy in the event of a wrongful abduction was the return of the victim (i.e. restitution in kind). (See *inter alia* Mann, "Reflections on the Prosecution of Persons Abducted in Breach of International Law," in Dinstein (Ed.), International Law at a Time of Perplexity (1989), at p. 411). The fact that an arrest may violate the law of the State where the arrest took place is of no consequence, due to the explicit subordination of national law to the provisions of the Statute (ICTY Rule 58).

[50]Mann, id., at p. 407. For a different formulation of the policy underpinnings of the *ex injuria* rule, however, see Higgins, Problems and Process: International Law and How we Use It (1994), at p. 72.

[51]Shen, "Responsibilities and Jurisdiction Subsequent to Extraterritorial Apprehension," 23 Denver Journal of International Law and Policy (1994), at 74–9.

[52]See Ian Brownlie, Principles of Public International Law (1998), at p. 320.

more strongly to the ICTY, as a custodian of international legality and fundamental human rights standards.[53] On the other hand, there are also important policy considerations that support the bringing to trial of those who engage in serious crime, especially universally condemned offences such as war crimes or crimes against humanity.[54]

State practice in this area is also far from uniform. Some national courts have been willing to exercise criminal jurisdiction over a defendant who has been forcibly abducted from the territory of another State, in violation of the sovereignty of that State. In so doing, they have generally insisted that how a person is brought before them is not a matter for them and are concerned only with the fact of his presence and the need to establish a separate basis of jurisdiction. This approach has historically been adopted in the United Kingdom[55] as well as in Australia,[56] France,[57] Israel,[58] South Africa[59] and the United States.[60] By contrast, other cases decided by national courts have held that a court should decline to exercise jurisdiction over an accused who has been brought within the jurisdiction of the court by means of an irregular rendition.[61]

---

[53]As the South African Supreme Court noted in setting aside jurisdiction over a defendant kidnapped from Swaziland by the security services, "[s]ociety is the ultimate loser when, in order to convict the guilty, it uses methods that lead to decreased respect for the law." (*State v. Ebrahim*, South Africa Supreme Court, Appellate Division (1991), 2 S.A. Rep. 553(q)), 16 Feb. 1991, 31 ILM (1992) 888 at p. 898).

[54]Higgins, supra note 50, at p. 72. See further infra.

[55]See, *inter alia, R. v. O/C Depot Battalion R.A.S.C. Colchester, Ex parte Eliot*, (1949) 1 All. E.R. 373; *R. v. Plymouth Justices, Ex parte Driver* (1986) Q.B. 95; *Liangsiriprasert v. United States* [1991] 1 App. Cas. 225; *In re Schmidt*, [1995] 1 App. Cas. 339 (Eng. H.L. 1994).

[56]See, *inter alia, Levinge v. Director of Custodial Services* (1987) 9 NSWLR 546.

[57]See, *inter alia, Re: Argoud*, 45 ILR 90 (Court of Cassation (Criminal Chamber), 4 June 1964; *Fédération Nationale des Déportés et Internes Résistants et Patriotes and Others v. Barbie*, 78 ILR 124 (Court of Cassation (Criminal Chamber), 20 Dec. 1985).

[58]See *inter alia, Attorney General v. Eichmann*, 36 ILR 5, 62 (Israeli Supreme Court, 1968).

[59]See *inter alia Abrahams v Minister of Justice*, (1963) 4. S.A.L.R. 542.

[60]See for instance *US. v. Alvarez Machain*, 504 U.S. 655, 112 S.Ct. 2188 (June 15, 1992). Several cases have subsequently reaffirmed this position *(inter alia Gerstein v. Pugh*, 420 U.S. 103, 119 (1975); *I.N.S. v. Lopez-Mendoza*, 468 U.S. 1032 (1984); *US v. Verdugo-Urquidez*, 110 S. Ct. 1056 (1990) and *US v. Matta-Ballesteros*, 71 F. 3d 754, at 762 (1995)), even though the *Alvarez-Machain* case has been subjected to widespread criticism. (See *inter alia* the UN Working Group on Arbitrary Detention which concluded that "[the] detention of Humberto Alvarez-Machain is declared to be arbitrary, being in contravention of [...] Article 9 of the International Covenant on Civil and Political Rights." (Report of the Working Group on Arbitrary Detention, UN Commission on Human Rights, 50th Session, UN Doc. E/CN.4/1994/27 (1993), at pp. 139–40) and Reisman, "Covert Action", 20 Yale Journal of International Law (1995) 419, at pp. 422–424.

[61]*R. v. Horseferry Road Magistrates Court, Ex parte Bennett*, [1994] 1 AC 42 (H.L.). See also, *inter alia,* the judgment of the Swiss Federal Supreme Court (EUGRZ (1983) 435) of 15 July 1982 (involving the circumvention of a bilateral extradition treaty between Germany and Belgium) and *R. v. Bow Street Magistrates, Ex Parte Mackeson*, 75 Crim. App. R. 24 (1981).

The dual tensions observable in the national case law – namely, to ensure that the perpetrators of serious crimes are brought to justice as against the need to prevent abuses of power by law enforcement personnel – may also arise within the practice of the ICTY, particularly in view of the willingness of international forces to actively arrest Tribunal indictees, if necessary by force. National cases in which an otherwise competent national court has declined to exercise jurisdiction over an accused stress the unacceptable and egregious nature of the violations of the accused's rights which have occurred and the fact that all judicial bodies have an inherent jurisdiction to guard against abuses of their own process.[62] Many of these considerations will be applicable, *mutatis mutandis*, should the ICTY be called upon to decide whether or not to exercise jurisdiction over any accused who may have been brought before the Tribunal in violation of international law, at least in circumstances where there is evidence that the Prosecution or other Tribunal personnel or their agents have committed or colluded in the commission of internationally unlawful conduct.

Against this, however, it appears that where an accused is charged with the most serious offences known to international humanitarian law, the presumption in favour of trying him is strengthened.[63] Special consequences are also entailed by the unique character of the Tribunal as a Chapter VII enforcement measure designed to effectively prosecute and punish serious violations of international humanitarian law committed in the former Yugoslavia and the hierarchical relationship which is thereby established between the ICTY Statute and national legal systems.[64]

The question of the effects upon the ICTY's jurisdiction of any arrest by Tribunal staff or multinational forces which circumvents the Tribunal's *own*

---

[62]Most of the national and international decisions in which courts have refused to exercise jurisdiction on the basis of the manner in which the accused was brought before the court cite either official collusion in illegal conduct, or the use of unjustified violence against the accused or similar unconscionable behaviour. (See further supra note 43 and Lamb, supra note 6, at pp. 228–44).

[63]Id., at pp. 237–40.

[64]Consequently, the law of the State in which an arrest is effected and bilateral extradition regimes do not bind the Tribunal when acting to take an accused into custody (see further Lamb, supra note 6, at pp. 197–199).

arrest procedures has nevertheless still to be determined.[65] In the light of the careful balance required by the applicable national and international case law, the legal consequences of such arrest scenarios would have to be carefully evaluated by the ICTY in any given case. It is, however, clear that withdrawal of the indictment altogether and the release of the accused would be required only in extreme cases, where any continuation of the trial proceedings would in all the circumstances be fundamentally incompatible with the right to a fair trial and the integrity of the judicial process.[66]

5. Conclusion

The arrest of persons indicted by the Tribunal is clearly vital to the achievement of the object and purpose of the ICTY: to prosecute and punish serious violations of international humanitarian law and thereby to contribute to the maintenance or restoration of international peace and security in the territory of the former Yugoslavia. Hence, extensive powers of arrest have been provided *expressis verbis* in the ICTY's Rules and few challenges to the legitimacy of the Tribunal's powers of arrest vis-à-vis the overall scope of the ICTY's general framework of delegated competence from Security Council Resolution 827 and Chapter VII of the UN Charter appear convincing.

---

[65]Thus far, the Trial Chamber has left open the broader question of whether it has the authority to exercise jurisdiction over a defendant illegally obtained from abroad (*Dokmanović*, at para. 78). It should be borne in mind, however, that multi-State entities such as NATO and SFOR, who in practice conduct the majority of ICTY arrests, are not agencies of the Tribunal. Their conduct, as such, cannot be imputed automatically to that of the Prosecutor. This is so at least where it is unproven that the Prosecutor was involved in or ordered that conduct. Where violations of international law are committed by such forces however, there may be cases in which the Tribunal, by accepting custody of the accused, is alleged to have adopted and ratified such conduct, thus assimilating these violations to itself. (See *United States Diplomatic and Consular Staff in Tehran*, ICJ Reports 1980, 3, at pp. 29–30, 33–6, where responsibility for breaches of the law of diplomatic relations was based upon the failure of the Iranian authorities to control the militants (in the early phase) and also upon the adoption and approval of the acts of the militants (at the later stage)). In *Eichmann*, Israel contended that Eichmann had not been abducted by Israeli government agents, while Argentina contended that Israel's decision to detain and try him rendered Israel responsible for the abduction even if it had originally been a private act. See further infra.

[66]While the release of the accused may not be an appropriate remedy, where irregularities in the method used to effect an arrest are established, civil remedies may exist against his captors and the accused may be able, in the course of the trial process, to avail himself of certain exclusionary rules of evidence. This was conceded by the Prosecution in *Todorović* (see transcript of Trial Chamber hearing of 4 March 1999, *Prosecutor v. Dokmanović*, at p. 353) and appears to have been accepted by the ICTR. (See *Prosecutor v. Kabiligi, Decision on the Defence Motion to Lodge Complaint and Open Investigations into Alleged Acts of Torture under Rules 40(C) and 73(A) of the Rules of Procedure and Evidence*, Case No. ICTR-97-34-I, 5 Oct. 1998). See also Higgins, supra note 50, at p. 72 and infra.

Recent arrest practice sheds some light upon the tension which may arise, on the one hand, between the exercise by the Tribunal of its enforcement functions and its duty, on the other, to ensure respect for the fundamental procedural rights of the accused. Even where irregularities on the part of Tribunal officials in a suspect's mode of capture are proven, however, the remedy of dismissal is certainly not automatic[67]; indeed, in most cases, the extreme remedy of release of a person indicted for the commission of serious violations of international humanitarian law will not be seen to comport with justice. Nevertheless, the release of the accused must, *in extremis*, remain as the ultimate remedy on the grounds that it constitutes the strongest deterrent and sanction against the abuse of power by law enforcement personnel and serves as a remedy of last resort in those truly exceptional circumstances where the divestiture of its jurisdiction is thought by the Tribunal to be necessary to safeguard the integrity of the conduct of international criminal justice.

---

[67]See ICTY Rule 5(C) which states that "[t]he relief granted by a Trial Chamber under this Rule shall be such remedy as the Trial Chamber considers appropriate to ensure consistency with the fundamental principles of fairness." See also *Prosecutor v. Barayagwiza, Prosecutor's Request for Review or Reconsideration*, Case No. ICTR-97-19-AR72, A. Ch., 31 March 2000 where the Appeals Chamber revised its earlier decision to release the accused (on the grounds of serious irregularities which were found to have vitiated his detention) and instead allowed the case against him to continue. This case did not pertain to illegal arrests and it justified this revision principally upon the discovery of new facts which the Appeals Chamber deemed could have been decisive in reaching the initial decision had they been known at the time. It nevertheless underscores the radical nature of the remedy of the release of the accused and the fact that such remedies are rarely (and reluctantly) resorted to even in cases where irregularities have been proven and are clearly attributable to the Prosecution.

WANG TIEYA* AND BING BING JIA**

5. Is Defective Composition a Matter of Lack of Jurisdiction within the Meaning of Rule 72?

This paper is proposed to deal with a question which has engaged the attention of the Appeals Chamber of the ICTR on numerous occasions.[1] The question itself, embodied in the topic, is practical in origin, as it does not correspond to any of the articles of the Statute or of the Rules of Procedure and Evidence of the ICTR.[2] It therefore calls for some consideration as to why and how it arises in the ICTR practice. Interpretation of the Rules in connection with an unprecedented question of practice is an exercise that always fascinates the authors in their practice that involves ICTR appeals.

The question is not unique to the practice of the ICTR.[3] However, for one reason or another, it arises surprisingly frequently in that practice. It begins with the terms of Rule 72, paragraph (A) of which provides that preliminary motions may be filed by either party "within sixty days following disclosure by the Prosecution to the Defence of all the material envisaged by Rule 66(A)(i), and in any case before the hearing on the merits".[4] Rule 72(B)(i) provides that preliminary motions may contain objections based on lack of jurisdiction. Rule 72(D) provides that "[D]ecisions on preliminary motions are without interlocutory appeal, save in the case of dismissal of an objection

*Formerly Judge of the Appeals Chamber, ICTY and ICTR (Nov. 1997–March 2000); formerly professor of public international law, Law School, Beijing University; Member of the Institute of International Law.

**Legal Officer, Chambers Legal Support, ICTY (1998-); D.Phil.(Oxon.).

[1]The views expressed in this paper do not in any way reflect the position of the ICTY or ICTR or the United Nations. They are personal thoughts of the authors.

[2]In the following pages, the designations "Statute" and "Rules" will be used.

[3]See para. 10, below. However, it has not arisen in the ICTY practice.

[4]Rule 66(A)(i) provides that "The Prosecution shall disclose to the Defence: i) Within 30 days of the initial appearance of the accused copies of the supporting material which accompanied the indictment when confirmation was sought as well as all prior statements obtained by the Prosecution from the accused...".

R. May et al., Essays on ICTY Procedure and Evidence in Honour of Gabrielle Kirk McDonald, 45–53.

based on lack of jurisdiction, where an appeal will lie as of right". The generality of the terms of Rule 72(B) incites certain not unfounded inquiries into the meaning and scope of the word "jurisdiction". Does it encompass a variety of situations where powers of the organs of the ICTR are called into question? Does it refer only to the powers of the Chambers in respect of cases before them? Can it mean that, since challenges to jurisdiction are brought before Trial Chambers and the Appeals Chamber, the Chambers have final say in this question even in relation to the powers of the Prosecution or the Registry? Be that as it may, Rule 72(B)(i) is the only general ground on which an interlocutory decision by a Trial Chamber can be appealed to the Appeals Chamber.[5] This restriction in the Rules may well be the reason behind the multiple attempts by, notably, the Defence to refer various decisions of the Trial Chambers to the Appeals Chamber on the ground of Rule 72(B)(i).[6] The composition of a Trial Chamber has been used in support of such attempts.[7]

As an example, the interlocutory appeal, *Kanyabashi v. Prosecutor*,[8] is recalled to place the topic in context; yet, this is not intended to be an insider's guide to something which we once worked on in our official capacity. The appeal arose from a decision of Trial Chamber I, dated 24 September 1998, allowing two motions of the Prosecution to amend the indictment and to join the trial of Mr. Kanyabashi with that of some other accused. The appeal was lodged by the Appellant on the ground that Trial Chamber I lacked jurisdiction to hear the two motions, because his initial appearance was made before Trial Chamber II which had the exclusive jurisdiction over his case, the re-composition of Trial Chamber I violated Article 13 of the Statute and rendered the Chamber incompetent,[9] the re-composition violated his right to be tried by independent and impartial judges, and the change in the composition of the Chamber was not justified by exceptional circumstances and was dictated by factors that affected the

[5]Relief may be sought under Rule 73, which, however, does not include a right of interlocutory appeal. Rule 65 allows appeals from a decision relating to provisional release to be filed subject to leave granted by a bench of three appellate judges of the Appeals Chamber.

[6]Cf. Rule 72(C) of the ICTY Rules, which provides for the parties to apply for leave to appeal Trial Chambers' decisions over preliminary motions unrelated to objection on the basis of lack of jurisdiction. There have consequently been far fewer applications based on lack of jurisdiction in interlocutory appeals before the ICTY.

[7]Cf. *Nsengiyumva v. Prosecutor, Decision on Appeal against Oral Decision of Trial Chamber II of 28 September 1998*, Case No. ICTR-96-12-A, 3 June 1999; *Ngirumpatse v. Prosecutor, Decision*, Case No. ICTR-98-44-A, 28 April 2000; *Kajelijeli v. Prosecutor, Decision*, Case No. ICTR-98-44-A, 28 April 2000; and *Karemera v. Prosecutor, Decision*, Case No. ICTR-98-44-A, 22 May 2000.

[8]*Joseph Kanyabashi v. The Prosecutor, Decision*, Case No. ICTR-96-15-A, 3 June 1999.

[9]The reference to Article 13 is limited to Article 13(2), which provides that "After consultation with the Judges of the International Tribunal for Rwanda, the President shall assign the Judges to the Trial Chambers. A Judge shall serve only in the Chamber to which he or she was assigned".

impartiality of the judges. The second ground raised the issue that is subject to discussion in this paper.[10]

The Joint and Separate Opinion of Judge Gabrielle McDonald and Judge Lal Chand Vohrah held that the re-composition of a Trial Chamber by the President was an administrative decision that did not offend the Statute of the ICTR or the Rules.[11] The Joint Separate and Concurring Opinion of Judge Wang Tieya and Judge Rafael Nieto-Navia held that the matter of composition was in no way concerned with the jurisdiction of a Trial Chamber, and that the relevant rules regarding composition were concerned with judicial administration.[12] However, Judge Mohamed Shahabuddeen dissented, stating that "[W]hen there is an error in the composition of the bench, the court is not properly constituted. And where the court is not properly constituted, it cannot exercise its jurisdiction ... I think it is also possible to extract some support from the jurisprudence of the International Court of Justice for the proposition that an error in the composition of a judicial, or quasi-judicial, body goes to jurisdiction."[13] The learned Judge refers to a passage from an English case wherein it was stated that a "court may lack '*jurisdiction*' to hear and determine a particular action or application because (i) of the *composition* of the court (for example, the bias of the judge)."[14]

The starting point for this paper would be the meaning given to the word "jurisdiction". *Black's Law Dictionary* defines the word as signifying "a court's power to decide a case or issue a decree".[15] It goes without saying that, in national legal systems, such power normally comes from statutes, and no court may take on a case clearly outside its statutory jurisdiction. The ICTR is in an essentially similar position. Its jurisdiction is set forth in the Statute, and it cannot extend its jurisdiction beyond the reach of the Statute. Following numerous challenges to jurisdiction allegedly made pursuant to Rule 72(B)(i), the latest revision of the rule at the 7th plenary session of the ICTR in February 2000, defines the range of challenges to jurisdiction with reference to the personal, territorial, temporal, and subject-matter jurisdiction laid down in Articles 1 through 8 of the Statute of the ICTR, thus narrowing the scope of Rule 72(B)(i) jurisdictional motions to the substantive jurisdiction of the ICTR. However, the question this paper is exploring does not disappear.

It is necessary to state that the *constitution* of the Chambers is decided by Article 10 of the ICTR Statute, which provides for three Trial Chambers and

[10]This second ground does not correspond to the second ground of appeal in the case.

[11]See supra, footnote 8, *Joint and Separate Opinion of Judge McDonald and Judge Vohrah*, para. 46.

[12]See supra, footnote 8, *Joint Separate and Concurring Opinion of Judge Wang and Judge Nieto-Navia*, para. 19.

[13]See supra, footnote 8, *Dissenting Opinion of Judge Shahabuddeen*, p.7.

[14]Judge Shahabuddeen cites *Oscroft v. Benabo* [1967] 2 All ER 548 at 557, C.A. per Lord Diplock.

[15]1999.

an Appeals Chamber; whereas Article 11 regulates the *composition* of the Chambers, stipulating for three judges to sit in each of the Trial Chambers and five in the Appeals Chamber. These articles deal with matters which are distinct from those under Articles 1 to 8 of the Statute.

Another point, which is more important due to its general nature, is the distinction between the possession of jurisdiction and the exercise of that jurisdiction. It may be that jurisdiction cannot be exercised by a court even though it is formally in its possession. The relevance of this point is that, it is arguable that a jurisdictional challenge in terms of Rule 72 does not have to be confined to the issue of whether a Chamber or the Tribunal possesses jurisdiction, as it may also be based on the fact that the Chamber has lost competence to exercise that jurisdiction. We submit, however, that the terms of Rule 72(B) are probably more restrictive than they appear to be, as "lack of jurisdiction" is hardly equivalent to "lack of competence to exercise jurisdiction". If a court is for certain reasons unable to exercise jurisdiction over a case, this presupposes that it had that jurisdiction. It may even be argued that such jurisdiction, once lawfully conferred on an ICTR Chamber, cannot be lost under the Statute. A lawful conferment would be by way of presidential assignment of a case to a Trial Chamber, this being shown when an accused is brought before a Trial Chamber for initial appearance under Rule 62. This view seems to be specifically apt to describe the practice of the ad hoc ICTR and ICTY, but not what is current in public international law.

Public international law appears to consider in different terms the difference between jurisdiction and competence.[16] A leading authority states generally that:

> There is the question of the general class of case in respect of which a given tribunal has jurisdiction – the tribunal's jurisdictional field, whether *ratione materiae, personae* or *temporis*; and there is the question of its competence to hear and determine a particular individual case – e.g. the case may not fall, *ratione materiae*, within the tribunal's general field; or even if it does, may be excluded on grounds arising *ratione personae* or *ratione temporis*. A tribunal may have jurisdiction in the "field" sense, yet lack competence as regards the particular case: basic jurisdiction does not necessarily entail competence in the particular case.[17]

[16]This is said with the caution that there is in this body of law the independent subject of jurisdiction which is concerned with the *right* of a State to exercise certain of its powers: see F. A. Mann, "The Doctrine of Jurisdiction in International Law", 111 *Recueil des cours* (1964), at p. 9.

[17]G. Fitzmaurice, "The Law and Procedure of the International Court of Justice, 1951–4: Questions of Jurisdiction, Competence and Procedure", 34 *British Yearbook of International Law* (1958), at pp. 8–9.

He remarks later:

> In short, the jurisdiction of any tribunal can be faulted under any of these heads [i.e. *ratione materiae, personae, or temporis* – added by the authors] by showing either that the tribunal does not possess jurisdiction in the particular material, personal or temporal field to which the case relates, or that, the tribunal being possessed of a certain field of jurisdiction, material, personal and temporal, the particular case falls in some essential respect outside that field.[18]

He refers also to the question of the propriety of exercising jurisdiction, but does not seem to construe the meaning of propriety as covering the cases where the composition of a certain tribunal is questioned by parties before it.[19] It is felt that the question a criminal tribunal may encounter does not necessarily arise before a tribunal is set up and operated on the basis of consensual jurisdiction, such as the International Court of Justice. Composition would be a matter resolved first of all to the satisfaction of the States that initially set up the tribunal, and then of the States that bring their cases before it: this is, in fact, the case in respect not only of arbitral tribunals, but of permanent institutions like the International Court.[20]

In international criminal law, jurisdiction, in the sense of one over a "field" – to use the term of the quoted authority referred to in the preceding paragraph, is, and should be, as pre-determined as in a national system. It is determined by way of agreement reached among entities that are not subject to the jurisdiction – States. That jurisdiction encompasses only natural persons who cannot influence the existence and conferment of that jurisdiction. The administering of international criminal law may therefore be more closely reflective of the practice in domestic law than in public international law, opening the way for international criminal tribunals to borrow from general principles of law recognised in national practice. Similar questions may arise in international criminal law and municipal law. Disqualification of judges, or composition of a bench, is one such example.

In terms of municipal law, the English case quoted by Judge Shahabuddeen in *Kanyabashi* is obviously supportive of the position that disqualification affects jurisdiction. In other English cases where jurisdiction is a matter for contention, if in the course of deliberation and drafting of the judgement a court took into account a factor that was not within its power to consider, its decision would be a nullity, as it had no jurisdiction to do so,

---

[18]Id., p. 9.

[19]Id., pp. 21–22 and pp. 143–47. See also, H. Thirlway, "The Law and Practice of the International Court of Justice 1960–1989, Part Nine", 69 *British Yearbook of International Law* (1998), p. 1 at 34–57.

[20]Art. 26 (2) of the Statute for the International Court provides that the Court may "at any time" form a chamber for dealing with a particular case, with the number of judges to sit in the chamber determined by the Court "with the approval of the parties". Under Art. 26(3), cases shall be heard and determined by the chambers formed pursuant to Art. 26 "if the parties so request".

or, in terms of the ICTR Statute, it lacked jurisdiction to do so.[21] Lord Reid stated thus:

> It has sometimes been said that it is only where a tribunal acts without jurisdiction that its decision is a nullity. But in such cases the word "jurisdiction" has been used in a very wide sense, and I have come to the conclusion that it is better not to use the term except in the narrow and original sense of the tribunal being entitled to enter on the enquiry in question. But there are many cases where, although the tribunal had jurisdiction to enter on the enquiry, it has done or failed to do something in the course of the enquiry which is of such a nature that its decision is a nullity. It may have made a decision which it had no power to make.[22]

In the same breath, he also included the cases where a tribunal misconstrued the provisions giving it its powers so that it failed to deal with the matter remitted to it but dealt with matters not remitted to it and where the tribunal failed to consider matters which it was required to consider. Concurring, his colleague Lord Pearce pointed out that lack of jurisdiction might arise in various forms, such as where a court made decisions which it had no power to make, departure by the court from the rules of natural justice, wrong questions asked of itself, or consideration of matters which it was not asked to consider. Any of such will lead to a legal error that a supervisory court should intervene to correct.[23]

The preceding paragraph merely shows that, in certain English cases, the consequence of *a court* stepping outside its jurisdiction is the nullity of its decision made in such circumstances which leads to the intervention by a supervisory court to correct the error that led the lower court to make that decision. It is plain that the action of a court taken outside its jurisdiction will be an act done in lack of jurisdiction. The point is that a party in the case can raise this matter to a superior court for remedy, but that this happens only *after* the error of the lower court was committed.

However, Rule 72 provides for preliminary motions, which are by nature confined to the pre-trial stage. There is no question of acting outside jurisdiction, if the trial is yet to commence, unless concerns are raised in respect of the possession of jurisdiction by the Tribunal including the Trial Chambers to deal with the case (it is noteworthy that none of the ICTR interlocutory appeals seem to have raised such concerns as regard the possession of jurisdiction of the Tribunal). On this account, the ICTR is like

---

[21]E.g., *Anisminic, Ltd. v. the Foreign Compensation Commission and Another*, [1969] 1 All ER 208, HL (Lord Morris and Lord Pearson dissenting); *Pearlman v. Keepers and Governors of Harrow School*, [1979] 1 All ER 365, C.A. (Civil Division, Lane LJ dissenting).

[22]*Anisminic, Ltd. v. the Foreign Compensation Commission and Another*, [1969] 1 All ER 208 at p. 213.

[23]Id., para. 233.

the International Court, its jurisdiction over a whole case having to be determined prior to the opening of the trial or the commencement of the merits stage. Once a decision is made by a Trial Chamber, without knowing that a legal error has been committed that compromises the fairness of the trial, there is the remedy of lodging an appeal. Errors of this type do not undermine the possession of jurisdiction by the Trial Chamber. They concern the way of exercise of that jurisdiction. They do not fall under Rule 72.

It is of course arguable that the composition of a Chamber, as distinct from the constitution of the Chamber, may have impact upon the competence of the Chamber to *exercise* jurisdiction over a certain case. If the composition of the Chamber, in terms of which judges are assigned to it by the President of the ICTR,[24] is somehow defective, but the Chamber nevertheless proceeds with motions in a pending case, there is a realistic chance of bias and violations of the rights of the accused to a fair trial. However, this consequence does not make the issue of disqualification of judges or, conversely, of composition of the Chambers, jurisdictional, in the sense that jurisdiction would be lost over a pending case. It can only be said that, defective composition will affect the impartiality of the composing judges to try the case, and their continuation with the trial in spite of the partiality concern will give rise to appeal. In terms of the whole case, therefore, the interests of the accused would not be undermined irreparably. It may be, however, arguable that, as defective composition will entail that some judges cannot sit on a case, it affects the exercise of jurisdiction by the relevant Chamber, and that therefore, this matter can be deemed jurisdictional. The problem with this latter view is that it may be useful only if the Rules are silent over the issue of the impartiality of judges.[25] However, the Rules are not silent in this regard.

Rule 15(A) provides, inter alia, that "[A] Judge may not sit at a trial or appeal in any case in which he has a personal interest or concerning which he has or has had any association which might affect his impartiality. He shall in any such circumstance withdraw from that case." Rule 15(B) states that "[A]ny party may apply to the Presiding Judge of a Chamber for the disqualification of a Judge of that Chamber from a trial or appeal upon the above grounds. After the Presiding Judge has conferred with the Judge in question, the Bureau, if necessary, shall determine the matter. If the Bureau upholds the application, the President shall assign another Judge to sit in place of the disqualified Judge."

On the basis of Rule 15(A), it would be difficult to maintain that the composition of a Chamber is lawful if one of the members of the Chamber were found to be associated with the case in a way that is anticipated by Rule

---

[24]The power of the ICTR President to assign judges applies only to Trial Chambers, as the Appeals Chamber is filled with the appellate judges from the ICTY Appeals Chamber: see Article 12(2) of the ICTR Statute.

[25]The issue of disqualification of judges is not discussed in this paper. But see the contribution by Morrison in this collection of essays.

15(A). There is the sense that the act of composition of the Chamber may well be flawless, but that the result of the act, reflected in the membership of the Chamber, is not beyond reproach. The Defence could feel unsettled by the knowledge that a judge who had been vocally advocating a particular cause before taking up the office with the Chamber will sit on the bench assigned to deal with its case that focuses on that very cause. It could be forgiven for questioning the impartiality of the Chamber in this composition, with suitable submissions.

There is, however, a distinction between the competence to exercise jurisdiction and the possession of jurisdiction. If the ICTR has jurisdiction over the case, the Trial Chambers will have delegated jurisdiction to handle the case. Can that jurisdiction be lost due to factors that will disqualify one of the judges? The answer is negative. The relevant Trial Chamber is an institution of itself, insomuch as it can exist, in theory, without judges. Of course it always comes to life only with judges. But whatever judges are assigned, they are assigned under the presumption that the Trial Chamber is duly seized of the case and has jurisdiction over the whole case. The change in the membership of the Chamber cannot therefore affect its jurisdiction. Where impartiality of one or several members of the Chamber is called into question, resort should first be had to Rule 15, rather than Rule 72. A judge may decline to exercise the jurisdiction of the Trial Chamber for reasons of propriety, but he cannot divest the Chamber of its jurisdiction by continually sitting in it.

In connection with what is said in the previous paragraph, it is conceded that a particular Trial Chamber may sometimes lack jurisdiction. This is a situation which has also occurred in *Kanyabashi*. In the case, Trial Chamber I was requested by the Prosecution to consider two motions from it, one of which was concerned with the amendment of the indictment. Under Rule 50, such a motion shall be considered by the Chamber before which the accused made his initial appearance. The appropriate Chamber in this case would be Trial Chamber II. The majority of the Appeals Chamber held that Trial Chamber I lacked jurisdiction over the amendment motion.[26] It ordered the motion to be returned to Trial Chamber II for decision. This shows that jurisdiction goes along with a Chamber, rather than the constituent judges of that Chamber.

The presumption is not helpful that any challenge to jurisdiction could be submitted on the premise that the exercise of jurisdiction would be affected if a Trial Chamber carried on its proceedings in a given case. This seems a confusion of the two issues of possession and exercise of jurisdiction. The competence of a Trial Chamber to correctly exercise jurisdiction may be affected by procedural errors in composing the bench of the Chamber, but

[26]*Joseph Kanyabashi v. The Prosecutor, Joint and Separate Opinion of Judge McDonald and Judge Vohrah*, Case No. ICTR-96-15-A, 3 June 1999 at para. 28; and *Joint Separate and Concurrent Opinion of Judge Wang and Judge Nieto-Navia*, 3 June 1999 at para. 9.

not the ab initio power of the Chamber to adjudicate this case. Rule 72 (B) (i) concerns "lack of jurisdiction" only.

It is recognised that the paper has so far relied on an interpretation of Rule 72(B)(i) that appears to be strict. After all, the provision refers only to "objections based on lack of jurisdiction". It seems that, as long as an objection is claimed to be based on the ground of lack of jurisdiction, an interlocutory appeal will lie as of right pursuant to Rule 72(D). We consider, however, that whether an objection can be regarded as a challenge to jurisdiction depends on whether the cause of the objection is genuinely linked with jurisdiction. There has to be an objection, but there must also be a case regarding jurisdiction, which the objection manifests. It is stretching reason to argue that matters like assignment of counsel by the Registrar or failure to provide translation of court documents in time can also give rise to a contention over jurisdiction, if only a party claims this to be the case. A right of appeal cannot be lightly given under the Rules, because the interests that right protect cannot be trivial.

In short, the matter of the composition of Chambers is not a matter that falls under Rule 72(B)(i), but only under Rule 15. It may affect the competence of a Chamber to exercise its jurisdiction over a case, but has no bearing on the possession or lack of jurisdiction of the Chamber that is regulated by the Statute and the Rules. It cannot therefore lead to a claim of lack of jurisdiction. Not completely paralleling the existing pattern in public international law, the matter also assumes less urgency for criminal tribunals than for tribunals settling disputes among States, because there is always the remedy of post-trial appeal available to parties before a criminal tribunal to correct legal errors even regarding jurisdiction or composition. To this extent, the ICTR procedure likens to municipal law procedure; whereas the former differs significantly from the latter in allowing jurisdiction to be challenged prior to trial.

MOHAMED BENNOUNA*

6. The Characterisation of the Armed Conflict in the Practice of the ICTY

Several legal consequences derive from characterising an armed conflict as either internal or international, including whether, for example, maintenance of international peace and security, State succession or humanitarian law are at issue.[1] We shall focus our attention on this last aspect, especially since Judge Gabrielle McDonald rendered an important Separate and Dissenting Opinion on this subject.[2]

Initially, one may not have envisioned that the ICTY would commit so much time and energy to determining the nature of the conflict, or conflicts, in the former Yugoslavia. In fact, when this Tribunal was established in 1993 the armed conflict was raging, and a commission of experts set up by the United Nations Secretary General at the request of the Security Council had established that serious violations of humanitarian law had occurred in the territory of the former Yugoslavia. According to Article 1 of the Statute, the ICTY was indeed to be competent to "prosecute persons responsible for serious violations of international humanitarian law committed in the territory of the former Yugoslavia since 1991". Probably in order to accomplish this objective as soon as possible, a Trial Chamber ruled from the outset that its jurisdiction was not dependent on the character of the armed conflict, and that it was consequently not obliged to rule on its international or internal character.

---

*Judge, ICTY. Former Professor of International Law and Dean of the Faculty of Law of Rabat (Morocco). Former member of the UN International Law Commission.

[1]Christine Gray, "Bosnia and Herzegovina: civil war or interstate conflict? Characterisation and consequences", 67 British Yearbook of International Law (1996), pp. 157–197.

[2]*Prosecutor v. Tadić, Separate and Dissenting Opinion of Judge McDonald regarding the Applicability of Article 2 of the Statute*, appended to *Judgement*, Case No. IT-94-1-T, 7 May 1997 ("*Dissenting Opinion*").

R. May et al., Essays on ICTY Procedure and Evidence in Honour of Gabrielle Kirk McDonald, 55–64.

The Trial Chamber indeed considered that Article 2 which gives it the power to prosecute grave breaches of the Geneva Conventions was drafted "autonomously"[3]; in other words, that it needed not refer to the legal system established by these conventions, except as regards the identification of the victims to be considered as "persons protected" by the Conventions (persons in the hands of one of the parties to the conflict or of an occupying power of which they are not nationals).[4] It is accepted that the two conditions set out in the Geneva Conventions for the implementation of "grave breaches" concur to a large extent, namely the international nature of the conflict and "protected persons". However, for the Trial Chamber, proof that the conflict is international is admittedly justified when the grave breaches are prosecuted before a national tribunal (under the universal jurisdiction provision of the Geneva Conventions), but this is no longer so before an international tribunal established by the Security Council on the basis of Chapter VII of the Charter.

The "autonomy" principle in Article 2 of the Statute, which would have immediately made it possible to settle the controversy on the nature of the conflict, did not survive in ICTY practice as it was quickly rejected by the Appeals Chamber.[5]

It must however be pointed out that in the *Tadić Interlocutory Appeal Decision* on jurisdiction Judges Li and Abi-Saab avoided the question of the characterisation of the conflict in their respective opinions by taking different approaches. On the basis of the *travaux préparatoires*, Judge Li considered that the conflict in the former Yugoslavia was characterised as international from the time the Statute was adopted.[6] Judge Abi-Saab went further still, as he considered that the development of international customary law in this area permitted the punishment of the "grave breaches" provided for in the Geneva Conventions, within the context of both an international and internal conflict. This was another way of going beyond the controversy on the nature of the conflict "instead of reaching, as the Decision does, for the acts expressly mentioned in Article 2 via Article 3 when they are committed in the course of an internal armed conflict".[7]

[3]*Prosecutor v. Tadić, Decision on the Defence Motion on Jurisdiction*, Case No. IT-94-1-T, 10 Aug. 1995 at para. 49.

[4]See Article 4 of 1949 Geneva Convention IV relative to the protection of civilian person in time of war.

[5]*Prosecutor v. Tadić, Decision on the Defence Motion for Interlocutory Appeal on Jurisdiction*, Case No. IT-94-1-AR72, A. Ch., 2 Oct. 1995 ("*Tadić Interlocutory Appeal Decision*").

[6]*Prosecutor v. Tadić, Separate Opinion of Judge Li on the Defence Motion for Interlocutory Appeal on Jurisdiction*, Case No. IT-94-1-AR72, A. Ch., 2 Oct. 1995. For a similar opinion see Theodor Meron, "International Criminalisation of Internal Atrocities", 89 *AJIL* (1995), pp. 554–577 at p. 556; and Hervé Ascensio et Alain Pellet, "L'activité du Tribunal pénal international pour l'ex-Yougoslavie (1993–1995)", Annuaire français de droit international, pp. 101–136, at p. 130.

[7]*Prosecutor v. Tadić, Separate Opinion of Judge Abi-Saab on the Defence Motion for Interlocutory Appeal on Jurisdiction*, Case No. IT-94-1-AR72, A. Ch., 2 Oct. 1995.

The *Čelebići* Trial Chamber held in 1998 that "the possibility that customary law has developed the provisions of the Geneva Conventions since 1949 to constitute an extension of the system of "grave breaches" to internal armed conflicts should be recognised."[8] It should also be recalled that Judge Rodrigues took up the issue once again in the *Aleksovski* case in 1999 in order to defend the "autonomy" principle in a dissenting opinion.[9]

The purpose of these attempts was to simplify the subsequent treatment of the different cases based on Article 2 by the Tribunal. The *Tadić Interlocutory Appeal Decision* of the Appeals Chamber in 1995, however, decided otherwise and reached the conclusion on "the changing nature of the conflicts" in Yugoslavia where "the conflicts have both an international and internal character".[10] Following this Decision, the Trial Chambers were required to settle the question of the characterisation of the conflict on a case by case basis, which obliged the Prosecutor to provide evidence and arguments for characterising the armed conflict where the crimes alleged were said to have been perpetrated in each case.[11] Moreover, any decision of the Appeals Chamber on this issue would have binding force (*res judicata*) only insofar as the place and the persons concerned are the same.[12] The result is that, although the case law will admittedly limit the scope of the debate, it will not entirely dispose of it. The question of the characterisation of the conflict could recur in every trial before the ICTY.

It is worth noting that on one occasion the Prosecutor attempted to address the issue of the nature of the conflict at the pre-trial stage by requesting a Trial Chamber to take judicial notice of the international character of the conflict. The Trial Chamber denied the motion, considering *inter alia* that it could only take judicial notice of factual findings but not of a legal characterisation based on such facts.[13]

---

[8] *Prosecutor v. Delalić and Others, Judgement,* Case No. IT-96-21-T, 16 Nov. 1998 at para. 202.

[9] *Prosecutor v. Aleksovski, Dissenting Opinion of Judge Rodrigues*, appended to *Judgement*, Case No. IT-95-14/1-T, 25 June 1999.

[10] *Tadić Interlocutory Appeal Decision* supra note 6. According to Judge Shahabuddeen in his Declaration attached to the *Blaškić Judgement* of 3 March 2000 (infra note 23), the *Tadić Interlocutory Appeal Decision* opens up the possibility of a "dual characterisation" since it adds that there can be a combination of internal and international aspects of the conflict.

[11] George Aldrich, "Jurisdiction of the International Criminal Tribunal for the Former Yugoslavia", 90 *AJIL* (January 1996), pp. 64–69 at p. 69.

[12] The *Čelebići* Trial Chamber held: "There can be no question that the issue of the nature of the armed conflict relevant to the present case is not *res judicata*." Supra note 8 at para. 228.

[13] *Prosecutor v. Simić and Others, Decision on the pre-trial motion by the Prosecution requesting the Trial Chamber to take judicial notice of the international character of the conflict in Bosnia-Herzegovina*, Case No. IT-95-9-PT, 25 March 1999.

Apart from the assessment of the facts at issue, the essential legal question that needed to be resolved was that of the criteria the Tribunal should apply in characterising a conflict as either international or internal. From a legal standpoint, some harmonisation is necessary to ensure that each Trial Chamber employs the same criteria when characterising conflicts in the former Yugoslavia. Taking a conflict which was initially internal as the starting point, the criteria of whether, in the light of each situation, it was internal or international, must in fact be established. In practice, this will mean characterising the conflicts in Bosnia and Herzegovina covered in the indictments. Starting with the *Tadić Interlocutory Appeal Decision* in 1995, the Appeals Chamber referred to the first criterion on the "direct participation" of the Federal Republic of Yugoslavia (Serbia and Montenegro) (FRY).[14] In other words, so long as the conflict is between the government and rebels forces within the country, it is presumably internal and becomes international only when a foreign State intervenes directly on behalf of one of the parties in question. In applying this first criterion, the Appeals Chamber considered that there was an international armed conflict in at least part of Bosnia and Herzegovina up until 19 May 1992, the date on which the JNA – the army of the FRY – withdrew from the country. The existence of an international armed conflict arose out of the participation of the armies of two countries, even though one of them (the FRY) was allied with the Bosnian Serb forces and operated from within its midst; this finding allowed the application of Article 2 of the Statute of the ICTY.[15] Should one, therefore, conclude that one is faced with an internal conflict in the absence of "direct participation" or where the foreign army withdraws? This would not appear to be the case since it has been known for many years that a State can intervene through an intermediary (a party to the conflict) and thus act indirectly to pursue its own strategy. The primary issue in such a case is to determine the degree of dependence that would allow the conclusion that one party is acting for the benefit of a foreign State. Taking its inspiration from the *Nicaragua Judgement* of the International Court of Justice,[16] the ICTY first established the criterion of "effective control" to evaluate the international character of the conflict, before abandoning it in favour of "overall control". The question of the connection between the international character of the conflict and the law on State responsibility runs through this case law.

We shall review the two criteria envisaged in the practice of the ICTY in turn – effective control and overall control.

[14]Supra note 5.

[15]See also *Prosecutor v. Karadžić* and Mladić, *Review of the indictments pursuant to Rule 61 of the Rules of Procedure and Evidence*, Case No. IT-95-5-R61/ IT-95-18-R61, 11 July 1996. In its decision the Trial Chamber considered that the rules governing the armed conflict of an international character should be applied until peace was re-established (based on the 4th Geneva Convention).

[16]*Case Concerning Military and Paramilitary Activities in and Against Nicaragua (Nicaragua v. United States of America), Judgement of 27 June 1986* (hereinafter "*Nicaragua Judgement*"), ICJ.

1. The Criterion of Effective Control

In order to characterise the armed conflict in Bosnia and Herzegovina, the Trial Chamber in the *Tadić Judgement* issued on 7 May 1997 commenced its analysis in the field of state responsibility. After the withdrawal of the Yugoslav Army (the JNA and subsequently the VJ) on 19 May 1992, it was necessary to demonstrate that the acts of the Bosnian Serb forces (VRS) could be attributed to the FRY to reach the conclusion that the conflict remained international. For that reason, the Trial Chamber concentrated on examining the *Nicaragua* case, which shares certain similarities with the *Tadić* case, and accepted the assertion of the ICJ that "for this conduct to give rise to legal responsibility of the United States it would in principle have to be proved that the State had effective control of the military or paramilitary operations in the course of which the alleged violations were committed."[17]

Evidently inspired by the International Law Commission's draft on State responsibility and, in particular, Article 8 thereof on attributing to the State the behaviour of persons purportedly acting on behalf of the State,[18] the *Nicaragua Judgment* led the Trial Chamber to consider that only proof of Belgrade's exercise of "direction and command" of Republika Srpska – including the issuance of specific instructions – satisfied the requirements of the effective control criterion. However, if the Trial Chamber had relied only on *jus ad bellum*, the law of the use of force, it could have found an entire set of elements in its analysis of this case such as the "shared strategic objectives", the "plan to create a Greater Serbia" or the "co-ordination of activities at the highest levels" between the RS and the FRY. On that basis, it would have seemed difficult to characterise the conflict in Bosnia and Herzegovina as internal.

Nonetheless, the reasoning based on the responsibility of States prevailed to such an extent that the Trial Chamber concluded that "the armed forces of RS could not be considered as organs or *de facto* agents of the FRY (Serbia and Montenegro)" and, implicitly, that from 19 May 1992, the conflict was no longer international.

In her *Dissenting Opinion*, Judge McDonald adopted a different interpretation of the *Nicaragua Judgment*. In her view, imputability depended on

[17] *Nicaragua Judgement* at para. 115.

[18] Draft adopted by the International Law Commission ("ILC") in 1996, see Report of the ILC, UN Doc. A/51/10. The commentary of this article states: "it must be genuinely proved that the person or group of persons were actually appointed by organs of the State to discharge particular function or to carry out a particular duty, that they performed a given task at the instigation of those organs." Yearbook of the ILC, 1974, vol. II (Part One), at p. 285.

the nature of an agent, which is based on "dependence and authority", and it was only where this nature was absent that the ICJ would advocate use of the criterion of effective control. However, she considered that effective control was inappropriate in the case in point because the circumstances of the *Tadić* case lead to the inference that the VRS was an agent of the FRY by reference to the more general criterion of "dependence and control". In so doing, Judge McDonald opened the way to calling the "effective control" criterion into question and finally to its rejection on appeal – albeit by way of another reasoning.

The literature, however, went even further by denying that the *Nicaragua* case and its criteria were of any relevance in characterising the armed conflict. For Theodor Méron: "in practice, applying the *Nicaragua* test to the question in *Tadić* produces artificial and incongruous conclusions".[19] He counted on the Appeals Chamber to seize the only opportunity offered to make adjustments by relying simply on the identification of the foreign intervening actor. For public international law indeed, the presence or absence of foreign intervention allows a conflict to be characterised as internal or international.[20] It is true, in any case, that in the face of uncertainty on the part of the Trial Chambers, some harmonisation was necessary.

In the *Aleksovski* case in 1999, the majority applied the strict criterion of control based on "the direction and command" of military forces by the State and held that, the HVO could not be considered as a *de facto* agent of Croatia.[21] However, in the *Rajić* case in 1996 the Trial Chamber's ruling pursuant to Rule 61 concluded that the HVO had the character of an agent, and taking the *Nicaragua* case as its basis, considered it sufficient for the HVO to be under Croatia's overall military and political control.[22]

However, in the *Tadić* case, the Appeals Chamber would not go as far as Professor Meron suggested, since it maintained that it is necessary to resort to legal criteria "provided by general rules on the responsibility of States" in

---

[19]Theodor Meron, "Classification of Armed Conflict in the former Yugoslavia: Nicaragua's Fall Out", 92 *AJIL* (1998), pp. 236–242, at p. 237.

[20]See my book: *Le consentement à l'ingérence militaire dans les conflits internes*, L.G.D.J., Paris, 1974.

[21]*Prosecutor v. Aleksovski, Judgement*, Case No. IT-95-14/1-T, 25 June 1999 ("*Aleksovski Judgement*"). See *Joint Opinion of the majority, Judge Vohrah and Judge Nieto-Navia, on the applicability of Article 2 of the Statute pursuant to paragraph 46 of the Judgement*. The majority however used the notion of "overall control", linking it to the issuing of instructions. The Appeals Chamber, in its Judgement of 24 March 2000, found that "notwithstanding the express reference to "overall control", the *Aleksovski Judgement* did not in fact apply the text of overall control". *Prosecutor v. Aleksovski*, Judgement, Case No. IT-95-14/1-A, A. Ch., 24 March 2000 ("*Aleksovski Appeal Judgement*") at para. 142.

[22]*Prosecutor v. Rajić, Review of the indictment pursuant to Rule 61*, Case No. IT-95-12-R61, I, 13 Sept. 1996.

order to characterise the conflict.[23] Still, it would seize the opportunity to refute the criterion of "effective control" because, in its opinion, this does not fit in with the reasoning of the law on State responsibility since that law is so flexible that "the degree of control required may vary depending on the factual circumstances of each case." Furthermore, the Appeals Chamber criticised the criterion derived from the *Nicaragua* case for not according with the legal and State practice it analysed in depth. In particular, this criterion would be used in practice only "with regard to individuals or unorganised groups of individuals acting on behalf of States. By contrast, it has applied a different test with regard to military or paramilitary groups"[24] which the Appeals Chamber termed "overall control".[25]

2. The Criterion of Overall Control

Although it is sufficient for armed forces, militia or paramilitary units to be under "the overall control" of a foreign State for one to consider them as *de facto* organs of that State, the degree of control on which characterisation of the conflict as international depends should still be defined. The Appeals Chamber initially proceeded by elimination and attempted to determine what does not constitute overall control rather than to formulate its positive constituent elements. Thus it would go beyond mere financial aid, the provision of equipment or military training and be less than the issuance of specific orders or the conducting of each of the State operations. When dealing with the positive aspect of the definition, "the overall criterion" appears to be particularly flexible since for the Chamber it is sufficient for the State to have "a role in the organising, co-ordinating, or planning the military actions of the military group in addition to financing, training and equipping or providing operational support [to that group]".[26]

Yet it is the very flexibility of the criterion that allows it to be adapted to the tremendous diversity of situations in the field. Thus, in the *Tadić* case in which one of the parties to the conflict in Bosnia and Herzegovina was in the service of a foreign State or acted to satisfy the clearly declared "expansionist goals" of that State, it is easier to prove overall control and there can be no doubt as to the ensuing internationalisation. This is the case even if the Bosnian Serb party's choice of means and tactics was autonomous (that is, it did not receive precise instructions) although

[23] *Prosecutor v. Tadić, Judgement*, Case No. IT-94-1-A, A. Ch., 15 July 1999 ("*Tadić Appeal Judgement*") at paras. 104 and 105.
[24] *Tadić Appeal Judgement* at para. 124.
[25] The Appeals Chamber in the *Aleksovski Appeal Judgement*, supra note 21, held: "The "overall control" test, set out in the *Tadić* Judgement is the applicable law." (At para. 134). In fact, the "overall control" test should be referred to as a criterion for the interpretation of the applicable law, rather than the applicable law itself.
[26] *Tadić Appeal Judgement* at para. 137.

participating in a common strategy (the construction of a Greater Serbia) along with the FRY.

Having examined the actual relationship between the Bosnian Serb Army and the FRY Army, the Appeals Chamber concluded that there were shared objectives and strategies before and after 19 May. This was the date when direct participation gave way to overall control. As Judge McDonald pointed out, the VRS was no more than a "legal fiction"[27] or, according to the Appeals Chamber, the formal framework intended to allow Belgrade's intervention to continue.

One can wonder, like Judge Shahabuddeen,[28] whether it was necessary for the Appeals Chamber to make such a formal challenge to the *Nicaragua Judgment* in order to come to this conclusion. After all, in that case, the ICJ accepted the external illegal intervention of the United States, through the interposition of *contras*, without however concluding that the United States was responsible for the violations of humanitarian law that they committed. One would thus move away from *jus in bello* to rely on *jus ad bellum*, when characterising the conflict, to render the participation in acts of civil war in the territory of another State, through threat or the use of force, the operative criteria. As Judge Shahabuddeen stated: "On the basis of *Nicaragua*, I have no difficulty in concluding that the findings of the Trial Chamber (in the *Tadić* case) suffice to show that the FRY was using force through the VRS against BH even if it is supposed that the facts were not sufficient to fix the FRY with responsibility for any delictual acts committed by the VRS."[29] However, one may wonder whether Judge Shahabuddeen does not, in the end, come to the same conclusions as in the *Tadić Appeal Judgement* via a different route, since he considers that, in the *Nicaragua* case, the proof of indirect recourse to force stems from the application of the criterion of effective control "applied with the desired flexibility." Thus, one can say that even if he does not adopt the "criterion of overall control" in his Separate Opinion, he is not very far from it. For this reason, when he did finally adopt it in the *Blaškić Judgement* of 3 March 2000, since from an institutional point of view he agrees that the Trial Chamber should conform to the Judgement rendered on appeal, he nevertheless pointed out, citing Judge Gros, that "a change in terminology does not suffice to avoid a problem."[30] In a way, Judge Shahabuddeen continues to show a preference for effective control in judging the degree of control necessary to come to the conclusion that a State resorted to force through a foreign military entity. But, in the end, he agrees that applying the criterion with the

[27]The *Čelebići* Trial Chamber shared this opinion in its *Judgement*. Supra note 8 at para. 223.

[28]*Prosecutor v. Tadić, Separate Opinion of Judge Shahabuddeen*, appended to *Judgement*, Case No. IT-94-1-A, A. Ch., 15 July 1999.

[29]Id. at para. 14.

[30]*Prosecutor v. Blaškić, Declaration of Judge Shahabuddeen* appended to *Judgement*, Case No. IT-95-14-T, 3 March 2000 ("*Blaškić Judgement*").

requisite flexibility makes it possible to arrive at the same conclusion with regard to the characterisation of the conflict in both cases, *Tadić* and *Blaškić*.

In fact, in the *Blaškić* case the Trial Chamber clearly declared its intention to take up the conclusions of the *Tadić Appeal Judgement* since "the legal criteria which allow the international nature of an armed conflict to be demonstrated have been set out exhaustively by the Appeals Chamber."[31]

In the *Blaškić Judgement*, the Trial Chamber first evoked the evidence attesting to Croatia's direct intervention in Bosnia and Herzegovina before noting that Croatia had indirect control over the HVO and the Croatian community of Herceg-Bosna. From this point of view, in line with the reasoning of the Appeals Chamber in the *Tadić Appeal Judgement*, it considered that "overall control" arises in particular from the existence of objectives common to the intervening State and the entity considered to be a party to a civil war. "The HVO and paramilitary or similar forces fought for Croatia, defended the 'Croatian' people and territory, and wanted this territory which they considered as Croatian to be integrated into the Republic of Croatia".[32] According to the Trial Chamber, it is therefore established that Croatia had "territorial ambitions" in Bosnia and Herzegovina and that it sought to accomplish its objectives through an entity, the HVO, and paramilitary groups which were closely linked to it, to such an extent that it had "overall control" over them. The *Blaškić Judgement* further holds that the same type of relations would exist in reality at the level of the political party (the HDZ, the Croatian Democratic Union) and the Croatian community of Herceg-Bosna.

However, although in the *Blaškić* case the Chamber considered that the "overall criterion" serves to determine the "imputation" of acts of a given entity to a foreign State, it no longer evokes the debate that this notion gave rise to the law on the State responsibility. In this context the appeal to "imputation" serves to demonstrate outside intervention through recourse to force and, consequently, the international character of the conflict.

3. Conclusion

In characterising the armed conflict, it seems that ICTY case-law has gradually moved away from the law of international responsibility in favour of proof of outside intervention of a State through the intermediary of one of the parties to the conflict within another State. This was achieved in two

[31]*Blaškić Judgement*, supra note 30 at paragraph 75. It is worth noting that the Appeals Chamber concluded in the *Aleksovski Appeal Judgement*: " In the interests of certainty and predictability the Appeals Chamber should follow its previous decisions, but should be free to depart from them for concrete reasons in the interests of justice." Supra note 21 at para. 107.

[32]*Blaškić Judgement*, supra note 30 at para. 108.

stages – initially by distinguishing the military or paramilitary groups so as to no longer apply to them the criterion of "effective control" but rather the criterion of "overall control" and, then, by defining the latter with the necessary flexibility so as to include cases in which an entity is in the service of a foreign State with which it shares the same objectives and strategy. This is what international law characterises as "proxy war", the indirect resort to force by one State against another State, which undoubtedly constitutes an international conflict.

MICHÈLE BUTEAU* and GABRIËL OOSTHUIZEN**

7. When the Statute and Rules are Silent: The Inherent Powers of the Tribunal

When, in the course of proceedings, a Trial or Appeals Chamber of the International Criminal Tribunal for the former Yugoslavia ("Tribunal") is faced with a problem for which provision is not made either in its Statute or its Rules of Procedure and Evidence ("Rules"), how does it proceed? This contribution intends to show that in such instances the Chambers have resort to what is commonly referred to as the "inherent powers" or the "inherent jurisdiction" of the Tribunal.

The main cause of the need to resort to such powers lies in the relatively rudimentary nature of the Tribunal's constituent instrument, the Statute, and its Rules and other formal documents.[1] The Statute, for example, sets out the Tribunal's jurisdiction, structure and basic procedural framework in merely 34 Articles. The equally crucial Rules – the crafting of which is provided for in Article 15 of the Statute[2] and which is continuously being

*Associate Legal Officer, Appeals Chamber, ICTY; LL.M International Human Rights Law (University of Essex, England); Juris Doctor (City University of New York Law School, USA). The views expressed herein are those of the author and not of the Tribunal or the United Nations.

**Associate Legal Officer in Chambers, ICTY; BLC LLB (University of Pretoria, South Africa) LLM Public International Law *cum laude* (Leiden University). He has previously worked for the Deputy Agent for Bosnia and Herzegovina in the genocide case of *Bosnia and Herzegovina v Yugoslavia (Serbia and Montenegro)* before the International Court of Justice. The views expressed herein are those of the author and not of the Tribunal or the United Nations.

[1]E.g., the Directive on the Assignment of Counsel (IT/73/Rev. 6). Courts in many national jurisdictions are of course familiar with the need to resort to such powers, albeit probably less frequently.

[2]Art. 15 ("Rules of procedure and evidence") provides: "The judges of the International Tribunal shall adopt rules of procedure and evidence for the conduct of the pre-trial phase of the proceedings, trials and appeals, the admission of evidence, the protection of victims and witnesses and other appropriate matters."

R. May et al., Essays on ICTY Procedure and Evidence in Honour of Gabrielle Kirk McDonald, 65–81.

supplemented[3] – numbers just over 150 and certainly adds some flesh to the Statute, but is still fairly basic. What follows is a largely descriptive exposition of the various principal instances, in chronological order, where the Chambers referred to and applied the Tribunal's inherent powers.[4]

1. The Tadić Jurisdiction Decisions

In the *Tadić* case, the first case to have come before the Tribunal, the Trial Chamber considered in August 1995, a defence preliminary motion challenging, *inter alia*, the legality of the establishment of the Tribunal, the implication being that the Tribunal lacks jurisdiction to try the accused.[5] In the Chamber's view, essential to the defence submissions was the concept that the Chamber has the capacity to review and rule upon the legality of the acts of the Security Council ("SC") in establishing the Tribunal.[6] Distinguishing between jurisdictional matters, which it can consider,[7] and the matter of the lawfulness of the Tribunal's creation, which is not truly a jurisdictional matter,[8] the Chamber held that the Tribunal is not a constitutional court set up to scrutinise the actions of organs of the United Nations ("UN").[9] On the contrary, it is a criminal tribunal "with clearly defined powers, involving a quite specific and limited criminal jurisdiction" and if it were to "confine its adjudications to those specific limits, it will have no authority to investigate the legality of its creation by the [SC]."[10] The "competence of the [Tribunal] is precise and narrowly defined" in Article 1 of the Statute, which states the "full extent" of the Tribunal's competence and does not empower it to question the legality of the law which established it.[11]

---

[3]Rule 6(A) provides: "Proposals for amendment of the Rules may be made by a Judge, the Prosecutor or the Registrar and shall be adopted if agreed to by not less than nine Judges at a plenary meeting of the Tribunal [...]."

[4]Given the space provided, justice cannot really be done to this very important subject; the risk of oversimplifying the issues faced by the Chambers should also be obvious.

[5]*Prosecutor v. Tadić, Decision on the Defence Motion on Jurisdiction*, Case No. IT-94-1-T, 10 Aug. 1995 ("*Tadić* Jurisdiction Decision").

[6]Id. at para. 3.

[7]Like "questions of time, place and nature of an offence charged": *Tadić* Jurisdiction Decision at para. 4.

[8]*Tadić* Jurisdiction Decision at para. 4.

[9]Id. at para. 5.

[10]Id. at para. 5.

[11]Id. at para. 8. Art. 1 provides: "The International Tribunal shall have the power to prosecute persons responsible for serious violations of international humanitarian law committed in the territory of the former Yugoslavia since 1991 in accordance with the provisions of the present Statute."

As regards the defence argument that Rule 91 ("False Testimony under Solemn Declaration")[12] is an example of the exercise by the Tribunal of powers that are not explicitly provided for in its Statute, the Chamber observed that there is "no analogy to be drawn between the inherent authority of a Chamber to control its own proceedings and any suggested power to review the authority of the Security Council."[13]

On appeal, the *Tadić* Appeals Chamber in October 1995 took a different view of the same issue.[14] The Chamber, *inter alia*, rejected the Trial Chamber's narrow definition of the concept of jurisdiction.[15] It distinguished between what it stated is termed in international law as "original" or "primary" and sometimes "substantive" jurisdiction on the one hand (what the Trial Chamber described as the full extent of the Tribunal's competence)[16] and "'incidental' or 'inherent' jurisdiction which derives automatically from the exercise of the judicial function."[17] The Appeals Chamber also referred to the latter as "residual powers which may derive from the requirements of the 'judicial function' itself."[18]

Emphasising that the SC created a special kind of subsidiary organ, namely, a judicial body,[19] the Chamber stated as follows:

> [18.] This power, known as the principle of "*Kompetenz-Kompetenz*" in German or "*la compétence de la compétence*" in French, is part, and indeed a major part, of the incidental or inherent jurisdiction of any judicial or arbitral tribunal, consisting of its "jurisdiction to determine its own jurisdiction." It is a necessary component in the exercise of the judicial function and does not need to be expressly provided for in the constitutive documents of those tribunals,

---

[12]Rule 91 provides: "(A) A Chamber, *proprio motu* or at the request of a party, may warn a witness of the duty to tell the truth and the consequences that may result from a failure to do so. (B) If a Chamber has strong grounds for believing that a witness has knowingly and wilfully given false testimony, it may direct the Prosecutor to investigate the matter with a view to the preparation and submission of an indictment for false testimony. [...] (E) The maximum penalty for false testimony under solemn declaration shall be a fine of Dfl. 200,000 or a term of imprisonment of seven years, or both. [...] (F) Sub-rules (B) to (E) apply *mutatis mutandis* to a person who knowingly and willingly makes a false statement in an affidavit or formal statement which the person knows or has reason to know may be used as evidence in proceedings before the Tribunal."

[13]*Tadić* Jurisdiction Decision at para. 9.

[14]*Prosecutor v. Tadić, Decision on the Defence Motion for Interlocutory Appeal on Jurisdiction*, A. Ch., Case No. IT-94-1-AR72, 2 Oct. 1995 ("*Tadić* Appeal Jurisdiction Decision").

[15]Id. at paras. 9–12.

[16]Id. at para. 14, essentially encapsulated in Art. 1 of the Statute.

[17]Id. at para. 14.

[18]Id. at para. 14.

[19]Id. at paras. 15–17, with reference to *Effect of Awards of Compensation Made by the United Nations Administrative Tribunal, Advisory Opinion of 13 July 1954*, 1954 ICJ Reports 47 ("*Effect of Awards case*") at pp. 51–52 and 60–1.

> although this is often done (*see*, e.g., Statute of the International Court of Justice, Art. 36, para. 6). But in the words of the International Court of Justice: "[T]his principle, which is accepted by the general international law in the matter of arbitration, assumes particular force when the international tribunal is no longer an arbitral tribunal [...] but is an institution which has been pre-established by an international instrument defining its jurisdiction and regulating its operation." (Nottebohm Case (*Liech. v. Guat.*), 1953 I.C.J. Reports 7, 119 (21 March).) This is not merely a power in the hands of the tribunal. In international law, where there is no integrated judicial system and where every judicial or arbitral organ needs a specific constitutive instrument defining its jurisdiction, "the first obligation of the Court – as of any other judicial body – is to ascertain its own competence." (Judge Cordova, dissenting opinion, advisory opinion on Judgements of the Administrative Tribunal of the I.L.O. upon complaints made against the U.N.E.S.C.O., 1956 I.C.J. Reports, 77, 163 (Advisory Opinion of 23 October) (Cordova, J., dissenting).) [19.] It is true that this power can be limited by an express provision in the arbitration agreement or in the constitutive instruments of standing tribunals, though the latter possibility is controversial, particularly where the limitation risks undermining the judicial character or the independence of the Tribunal. But it is absolutely clear that such a limitation, to the extent to which it is admissible, cannot be inferred without an express provision allowing the waiver or the shrinking of such a well-entrenched principle of general international law. As no such limitative text appears in the [Tribunal's Statute], the [Tribunal] can and indeed has to exercise its "*compétence de la compétence*" and examine the jurisdictional plea of the Defence, in order to ascertain its jurisdiction to hear the case on the merits.

The Chamber concluded that whilst the Tribunal's primary or substantive jurisdiction does not permit it to review the acts of other UN organs it could, in exercising its incidental jurisdiction, examine the legality of its establishment by the SC "solely for the purpose of ascertaining its own 'primary' jurisdiction over the case before it."[20]

---

[20] *Tadić* Appeal Jurisdiction Decision at para. 20. Judge Li, in a separate opinion, opined that, properly understood, the doctrine of competence-competence only allows the Tribunal to examine and determine its own jurisdiction, not to review the legality of the SC resolution establishing the Tribunal. In his opinion, the review is *ultra vires* and unlawful and the appeal on this question should have been dismissed without examining the legality of the Tribunal's establishment to the *Tadić* Appeal Jurisdiction Decision: *Separate Opinion of Judge Li on the Defence Motion for Interlocutory Appeal on Jurisdiction* at paras. 2 and 4. On another unrelated question, Judge Sidhwa, also in a separate opinion, remarked that courts have no inherent powers, under any concept of inherent jurisdiction, to create appellate provisions or acquire jurisdiction where none is granted in their statutes: *Separate Opinion of Judge Sidhwa on the Defence Motion for Interlocutory Appeal on Jurisdiction* at para. 6.

2. The Blaškić Subpoena Decisions

In July 1997, the *Blaškić* Trial Chamber considered a challenge by Croatia to the legal authority of the Tribunal to issue compulsory orders to states and high government officials.[21] The Chamber distinguished between the Tribunal's inherent and express power to issue such orders. On the former, it stated that the "absence of an express grant of power, however, does not negate the existence of such a power if it can be considered to be inherent and implied."[22] Having considered three cases of the International Court of Justice ("ICJ")[23] and the *Tadić* Appeal Jurisdiction Decision in this respect,[24] the Chamber observed that

> [30.] [...] the power of the [Tribunal] to issue a *subpoena duces tecum* to a State may similarly be implied if it is necessary in order to fulfil its fundamental purposes and to achieve its effective functioning. [31.] The [Tribunal] is, primarily, a criminal judicial institution, with jurisdiction over individuals charged with the most serious offences. It is imperative that a Trial Chamber, which must ultimately make a finding of the guilt or innocence of such individuals and impose the appropriate sentence as penalty, has all the relevant evidence before it when making its decisions [...].

Following an analysis of the Statute, the Rules and the position adopted by courts in some national jurisdictions, the Chamber, held with respect to its inherent power that

> [...] Thus, taking into consideration its nature and purposes, the Trial Chamber finds that the (Tribunal) has the inherent power to compel the production of documents necessary for a proper execution of its judicial function. To hold to the contrary would prevent the [Tribunal] from effectively redressing serious violations of international humanitarian law, its very *raison d'être*.[25]

---

[21] *Prosecutor v. Blaškić, Decision on the Objection of the Republic of Croatia to the Issuance of Subpoenae Duces Tecum*, Case No. IT-95-14-PT, 18 July 1997 ("*Blaškić Subpoena Decision*") at para. 14.

[22] Id. at para. 26.

[23] *Reparations for Injuries Suffered in the Service of the United Nations*, 1949 ICJ Reports ("*Reparations* case") at p. 171; *Effect of Awards* case at p. 47; *Certain Expenses of the United Nations*, 1962 ICJ Reports ("*Certain Expenses* case") at p. 151.

[24] *Blaškić Subpoena* Decision at paras. 26–29.

[25] Id. at paras. 32–40. The Chamber examined Arts. 20 ("Commencement and conduct of trial proceedings", providing for, *inter alia*, fair and expeditious trials), 21 ("Rights of the accused", providing for, *inter alia*, the right of an accused to examine, or have examined, the witnesses against him and to obtain the attendance and examination of witnesses on his behalf under the same conditions as witnesses against him) and 9 ("Concurrent jurisdiction") of the Statute and Rule 54.

The Chamber then stated that the Statute and Rules demonstrate that express authority is given to the Tribunal to direct mandatory orders to States.[26] Before reaching that conclusion, the Chamber made reference to Rule 77 ("Contempt of the Tribunal"). The Chamber observed that although the Tribunal's function is the prosecution of international humanitarian law violations, this does not mean that it cannot address itself incidentally to other functions in the fulfilment of this task, referring to Rule 77 as an example.[27]

By addressing an order to a state the Tribunal is merely exercising its "necessary incidental judicial functions in fulfilment of its purpose", not attempting to extend its competence beyond that established in the Statute.[28] Concluding its examination of the question as to whether it can issue specifically a *subpoena* to a state, the Chamber held that

> the issuance of a *subpoena duces tecum* to a State for the production of government documents is nothing more than an order compelling the production of those documents. The [Tribunal] has the inherent power and express authority to issue such orders. Resort to the mechanism of subpoenas is provided for in Rule 54. The Trial Chamber declines to invalidate that Rule, which effectuates the duty of States and individuals to comply with orders of the [Tribunal].[29]

Concerning the Tribunal's power to issue a *subpoena* to an individual, including government officials, the Chamber held that there is no doubt that a Judge or Trial Chamber may issue such an order to acquire information required for an investigation or trial as a necessary exercise of the Tribunal's incidental powers.[30] As regards the duty of states and individuals to comply with the Tribunal's binding orders, in relation to the former the Chamber stated that a "refusal must be evaluated by the [Tribunal] for merit, and it retains the power – to the extent it is expressly authorized or inherent because of the nature of the institution – to penalize the non-complying party if appropriate."[31] In relation to the latter, the Chamber stated that

---

[26]Id. at paras. 42ff. It examined Arts. 1 ("Competence of the International Tribunal"), 15 ("Rules of procedure and evidence"), 18 ("Investigation and preparation of indictment"), 19 ("Review of the indictment") and 29 ("Cooperation and judicial assistance") of the Statute and Rule 54.

[27]Id. at para. 49.

[28]Id. at para. 49, with reference to para. 14, *Tadić* Appeal Jurisdiction Decision.

[29]*Blaškić Subpoena* Decision at para. 64. Rule 54 provides: "At the request of either party or *proprio motu*, a Judge or a Trial Chamber may issue such orders, summonses, subpoenas, warrants and transfer orders as may be necessary for the purposes of an investigation or for the preparation of the trial."

[30]Id. at paras. 65, 66 and 69.

[31]Id. at para. 77.

Rule 77 confirmed that individuals generally have a duty to comply with such orders.[32]

An appeal followed the Trial Chamber's decision and the Appeals Chamber rendered its *Blaškić Subpoena Judgment* in October 1997.[33] The Chamber held that a "*subpoena*" (in the sense of injunction accompanied by threat of penalty) couldn't be applied or addressed to states; only binding orders or requests can be addressed to them.[34] The Appeals Chamber considered that one of the reasons justifying this finding is that in the case of an international judicial body the power to take enforcement measures against states cannot be regarded as inherent in its functions; the drafters of the Statute would have expressly provided for such a power had they so intended.[35] The Appeals Chamber considered preferable the use of the term "inherent powers" with regard to those functions of the Tribunal which are judicial in nature and which are not expressly provided for in the Statute. With respect to "implied powers", the Appeals Chamber stated that it has normally been applied by the ICJ with a view to expanding the competencies of political organs of political organisations.[36]

Moreover, with respect to the question whether the Tribunal can issue binding orders to states, the Chamber referred to its primary jurisdiction as being encapsulated in Article 1 of the Statute.[37] Article 29 of the Statute ("Cooperation and judicial assistance")[38] accounts for the novel and unique

---

[32]Id. at para. 87.

[33]*Prosecutor v. Blaškić, Judgement on the Request of the Republic of Croatia for Review of the Decision of Trial Chamber II of 18 July 1997*, A. Ch., Case No. IT-95-14-AR108*bis*, 29 Oct. 1997 ("*Blaškić* Supoena Judgement").

[34]Id. at para. 25.

[35]Id. at para. 25 ("Under current international law States can only be the subject of countermeasures taken by other States or of sanctions visited upon them by the organized international community, i.e., the [UN] or other intergovernmental organizations.").

[36]Id. at fn 27. In the same footnote, the Appeals Chamber further stated that "As is well known, reference to the Court's "inherent powers" was made by the [ICJ] in the *Northern Cameroons* case (I.C.J. Reports 1963, p. 29) and in the *Nuclear Tests* case. In the latter case the Court observed that it "possesses an inherent jurisdiction enabling it to take such action as may be required, on the one hand to ensure that the exercise of its jurisdiction over the merits, if and when established, shall not be frustrated, and on the other, to provide for the orderly settlement of all matters in dispute... Such inherent jurisdiction, on the basis of which the Court is fully empowered to make whatever findings may be necessary for the purposes just indicated, derives from the mere existence of the Court as a judicial organ established by the consent of States, and is conferred upon it in order that its basic judicial functions may be safeguarded" (*Nuclear Tests* case, I.C.J. Reports 1974, pp. 259–60, para. 23)."

[37]Id. at para. 26.

[38]Art. 29, in part, provides: "(1) States shall cooperate with the [Tribunal] in the investigation and prosecution of persons accused of committing serious violations of international humanitarian law. (2) States shall comply without undue delay with any request for assistance or an order issued by a Trial Chamber [...]."

power granted to the Tribunal to issue orders to sovereign states.[39] The Tribunal does not have ancillary jurisdiction over states; instead, Article 29 embodies the Tribunal's "ancillary (or incidental) mandatory powers" *vis-à-vis* states.[40]

Furthermore, on the question concerning the legal remedies available to the Tribunal in case of non-compliance by a state with a binding order, the Chamber restated that the Tribunal is not vested with any enforcement power *vis-à-vis* states.[41] However, it is endowed with the inherent power to make a judicial finding concerning a state's failure to observe the provisions of the Statute or the Rules and to report that finding to the Security Council:

> [...] [T]he [Tribunal] must possess the power to make all those judicial determinations that are necessary for the exercise of its primary jurisdiction. This inherent power inures to the benefit of the [Tribunal] in order that its basic judicial function may be fully discharged and its judicial role safeguarded. The [Tribunal's] power to report to the Security Council is derived from the relationship between the two institutions. The Security Council established the [Tribunal] pursuant to Chapter VII of the [UN] Charter for the purpose of the prosecution of persons responsible for serious violations of international humanitarian law [...]. A logical corollary of this is that any time a State fails to fulfil its obligation under Article 29, thereby preventing the [Tribunal] from discharging the mission entrusted to it by the Security Council, the [Tribunal] is entitled to report this non-observance to the Security Council.[42]

Considering the question of whether the Tribunal may issue binding orders in the form of *subpoenas* (that is, under threat of penalty) to individuals acting in their private capacity, the Appeals Chamber observed that the "spirit and purpose of the Statute" as well as Articles 18(2)[43] and 19(2)[44] of the Statute confer on the Tribunal "an incidental or ancillary jurisdiction" over individuals other than those whom the Tribunal may prosecute and try but may be of assistance in the task of dispensing criminal justice entrusted to the Tribunal.[45] The Chamber also assumed that an inherent power to

---

[39]Id. at para. 26.

[40]Id. at para. 28.

[41]Id. at para. 33.

[42]Id. at para. 33. The Chamber also stated that "The adoption of Rule 7*bis* ("Non-compliance with Obligations") is therefore to be regarded as clearly falling within the authority of the Tribunal." (at para. 33).

[43]Art. 18(2) provides: "The Prosecutor shall have the power to question suspects, victims and witnesses, to collect evidence and to conduct on-site investigations. In carrying out these tasks, the Prosecutor may, as appropriate, seek the assistance of the State authorities concerned."

[44]Art. 19(2) provides: "Upon confirmation of an indictment, the judge may, at the request of the Prosecutor, issue such orders and warrants for the arrest, detention, surrender or transfer of persons, and any other orders as may be required for the conduct of the trial."

[45]*Blaškić Subpoena* Judgment at para. 48.

address itself directly to individuals and thereby to bypass national authorities inures to the advantage of the Tribunal where the attitude of a state or entity jeopardises the discharge by the Tribunal of its functions: "Were it not vested with such a power, the International Tribunal would be unable to guarantee a fair trial to persons accused of atrocities in the former Yugoslavia."[46] As regards the legal remedies for non-compliance by an individual with a *subpoena* or order issued by the Tribunal, they are available to it once resort to national remedies or sanctions are unworkable. In this connection the Chamber held as follows:

> The remedies available to the [Tribunal] range from a general power to hold individuals in contempt of the [Tribunal] (utilising the inherent contempt power rightly mentioned by the Trial Chamber) to the specific contempt power provided for in Rule 77.[47]

3. Various other Orders, Decisions and Judgments

In June 1999, the *Delalić* Appeals Chamber considered a motion by a co-counsel of an accused to be immediately relieved of his duties.[48] Under the express provisions of the Directive on Assignment of Counsel ("Directive"), the Chamber did not have the power to consider the motion at that particular stage, since neither the Registrar nor the President had previously considered it. However, the Chamber referred to

> the inherent power which the Tribunal has, deriving from its judicial function and from the provisions of Articles 20 and 21 of its Statute, to control its proceedings in such a way as to ensure that justice is done and, particularly in relation to matters of practice, that the trial proceeds fairly and expeditiously [...]

The Chamber considered it appropriate to exercise that power in the particular circumstances and denied the motion.[49]

---

[46]Id. at para. 55.

[47]Id. at para. 59.

[48]*Prosecutor v. Delalić and Others, Order on the Motion to Withdraw as Counsel Due to Conflict of Interest,* Case No. IT-96-21-A, A. Ch., 24 June 1999 ("*Delalić* Counsel Order").

[49]The Chamber held that, even if proved, the assertion by the co-counsel that he will be unable to provide effective assistance to his client without risking his employment, would not constitute a proper basis upon which to withdraw the assignment just days before the appellant brief of his client is due, as to do so on the grounds of co-counsel's personal interests is contrary to counsel's obligations under the Code of Professional Conduct for Defence Counsel Appearing before the International Tribunal, and to the interests of his client and of justice (*Delalić* Counsel Order).

In July 1999, the *Simić* Trial Chamber examined the issue as to whether a former employee of the International Committee of the Red Cross ("ICRC") may be called to give evidence of facts that came to his knowledge by virtue of his employment.[50] The majority of the Trial Chamber answered the question in the negative on the basis of an international customary right to non-disclosure accruing in favour of the ICRC.[51] In his appended separate opinion, Judge Hunt explained that he was not persuaded that the answer to the problem at hand is supplied by customary international law.[52] He opined that

> It is the fundamental obligation of this Tribunal, imposed by Articles 20 and 21 of its Statute, to ensure the fair and expeditious trial of those indicted before it. A fair trial is one which is fair to both the accused who is on trial and to the prosecution which, as I have already said, acts on behalf of the international community, including the victims of the offences charged. The Tribunal also has an inherent power, deriving from its judicial function, to control its proceedings in such a way as to ensure that justice is done. Whether or not evidence which is relevant should nevertheless not be permitted to be given is a matter of procedural rather than substantive law, and it is in relation to such procedural matters that the Tribunal's obligation and inherent power become particularly important, for it is these matters which primarily ensure that the trial proceeds fairly and expeditiously. It is against this background that the present application must be determined.[53]

In July 1999, the Tadic Appeals Chamber resolved an evidentiary problem for which there is no express provision under the Statute or the Rules. It concerned whether a Trial Chamber has the power to order the disclosure of a prior defence witness statement once a witness has testified.[55] Rather than deriving the power to order such disclosure – in order to ascertain the credibility of that witness' testimony – from the broad powers conferred to it under Rule 89(B),[56] the Chamber held that

---

[50]*Prosecutor v. Simić and Others, Decision on Prosecution Motion Motion Under Rule 73 for a Ruling Concerning the Testimony of a Witness*, Case No. IT-95-9-PT, 27 July 1999 ("*Simić* Decision").

[51]*Simić* Decision at paras. 45–80.

[52]*Separate Opinion of Judge David Hunt on Prosecutor's Motion for a Ruling Concerning the Testimony of a Witness* at paras. 19–23 ("*Simić* Separate Opinion of Judge Hunt").

[53]*Simić* Separate Opinion of Judge Hunt at para. 25. *Inter alia*, the *Blaškić Subpoena* Judgment and the *Tadić* Appeal Judgment were referenced.

[54]*Prosecutor v. Tadić, Judgement*, A. Ch., Case No. IT-94-1-A, 19 July 1999 ("*Tadić* Appeal Judgement").

[55]Id. at para. 320.

[56]Rule 89(B) provides: "In cases not otherwise provided for in this Section, a Chamber shall apply Rules of evidence which will best favour a fair determination of the matter before it and are consonant with the spirit of the Statute and the general principles of law."

> this power is inherent in the jurisdiction of the [Tribunal], as it is within the jurisdiction of any criminal court, national or international. In other words, this is one of those powers mentioned by the Appeals Chamber in the *Blaškić* [*Subpoena* Judgment] which accrue to a judicial body even if not explicitly or implicitly provided for in the statute or rules of procedure of such a body, because they are essential for the carrying out of judicial functions and ensuring the fair administration of justice.[57]

The Appeals Chamber, in the *Tadić* Sentencing Appeal Judgment of January 2000,[58] recommended a minimum sentence to be served by Mr. *Tadić*. The Chamber noted that neither the Statute nor the Rules provide guidance for judicial discretion with respect to the recommendation of a minimum sentence.[59] It held, however, that

> The discretion of a Trial Chamber to recommend a minimum sentence flows from the powers inherent in its judicial function and does not amount to a departure from the Statute and the Rules. However, the judicial discretion of Trial Chambers to attach conditions to sentences is subject to the limitations imposed by fundamental fairness.[60]

4. The Tadić Contempt Judgment

In January 2000, the *Tadić* Appeals Chamber issued the *Tadić* Contempt Judgment.[61] Mr. Vujin, former defence counsel for the accused Duško Tadić, stood accused of having committed contempt of the Tribunal by knowingly and wilfully interfering with the administration of justice.[62] The allegations against Mr. Vujin were made in accordance with the contempt rule, Rule 77.[63] Rule 77 identifies several situations which are stated to

---

[57] *Tadić* Appeal Judgment at para. 322.

[58] *Prosecutor v. Tadić, Judgement in Sentencing Appeals*, A. Ch., Case No. IT-94-1-A & IT-94-1-A*bis*, 26 Jan. 2000.

[59] Id. at para. 28.

[60] Id. at para. 28.

[61] *Prosecutor v. Tadić, Judgment on Allegations of Contempt Against Prior Counsel, Milan Vujin*, A. Ch., Case No. IT-94-1-A-R77, 31 Jan. 2000 ("*Tadić* Contempt Judgement").

[62] By, *inter alia*, putting forward a case which was known to him to be false and by manipulating witnesses to provide incomplete statements.

[63] *Tadić* Contempt Judgment at paras. 1–2 and 160.

constitute contempt of the Tribunal, but Rule 77(E) provides that "Nothing in this Rule affects the inherent power of the Tribunal to hold in contempt those who knowingly and wilfully interfere with its administration of justice."[64]

Considering the Tribunal's jurisdiction to deal with contempt, the Chamber noted that the Statute makes no mention of the Tribunal's power to deal with contempt. The Chamber stated that the

> [13.] Tribunal does, however, possess an inherent jurisdiction, deriving from its judicial function, to ensure that its exercise of the jurisdiction which is expressly given to it by that Statute is not frustrated and that its basic judicial functions are safeguarded. As an international criminal court, the Tribunal must therefore possess the inherent power to deal with conduct which interferes with its administration of justice. The content of that inherent power may be discerned by reference to the usual sources of international law. [...] [18.] A power in the Tribunal to punish conduct which tends to obstruct, prejudice or abuse its administration of justice is a necessity in order to ensure that its exercise of the jurisdiction which is expressly given to it by its Statute is not frustrated and that its basic judicial functions are safeguarded. Thus the power to deal with contempt is clearly within its inherent jurisdiction. That is not to say that the Tribunal's powers to deal with contempt or conduct interfering with the administration of justice are in every situation the same as those possessed by domestic courts, because its jurisdiction as an international court must take into account its different setting within the basic structure of the international community.

---

[64]The remainder of the Rule provides, in pertinent part: "(A) Any person who (i) being a witness before a Chamber, contumaciously refuses or fails to answer a question, (ii) discloses information relating to those proceedings in knowing violation of an order of a Chamber, or (iii) without just excuse fails to comply with an order to attend before or produce documents before a Chamber, commits a contempt of the Tribunal. (B) Any person who threatens, intimidates, causes any injury or offers a bribe to, or otherwise interferes with, a witness who is giving, has given, or is about to give evidence in proceedings before a Chamber, or a potential witness, commits a contempt of the Tribunal. (C) Any person who threatens, intimidates, offers a bribe to, or otherwise seeks to coerce any other person, with the intention of preventing that other person from complying with an obligation under an order of a Judge or Chamber, commits a contempt of the Tribunal. (D) Incitement to commit, and attempts to commit, any of the acts punishable under this Rule are punishable as contempts of the Tribunal with the same penalties. (E) Nothing in this Rule affects the inherent power of the Tribunal to hold in contempt those who knowingly and wilfully interfere with its administration of justice. [...]. (H) The maximum penalty that may be imposed on a person found to be in contempt of the Tribunal: (i) under Sub-rules (A) and (E) above is a term of imprisonment not exceeding twelve months, or a fine not exceeding Dfl. 40,000, or both; (ii) under Sub-rules (B), (C) or (D) above is a term of imprisonment not exceeding seven years, or a fine not exceeding Dfl. 200,000, or both. [...] (J) Any decision rendered by a Trial Chamber under this Rule shall be subject to appeal in cases where leave is granted by a bench of three Judges of the Appeals Chamber, upon good grounds being shown. [...]."

The Chamber also considered the defence arguments pertaining to whether the various changes made to Rule 77 over the period relevant to the case qualified such an inherent power and increased the extent of the conduct which amounts to contempt, to the prejudice of the respondent's rights. Having considered the elaboration of Rule 77 since the Tribunal's creation,[65] the Chamber noted that the considerable amount of elaboration which has occurred in relation to Rule 77 over the years is not to be treated as if it had produced a statutory form of offence enacted by the judges of the Tribunal.[66] However, Article 15 of the Statute does not provide judges with the power to create new offences, only that to adopt rules of procedure and evidence for the conduct of matters falling within both the Tribunal's inherent and statutory jurisdiction.[67] The content of these inherent powers may be discerned by reference to the usual sources of international law, but not by reference to the wording of the rule.[68] Rules 77(A)–(D) are

> [25.] [...] statements of what was seen by the judges at Plenary meetings of the Tribunal to reflect the jurisprudence upon those aspects of the law of contempt as are applicable to the Tribunal. Those statements do not displace the underlying law; both the Tribunal and the parties remain bound by that underlying law.
> [26.] In the opinion of the Appeals Chamber: (a) the inherent power of the Tribunal as an international criminal court to deal with contempt is for present purposes adequately encompassed by the wording of the reservation inserted in Rule 77 in November 1997 – that the Tribunal has the power "to hold in contempt those who knowingly and wilfully interfere with its administration of justice" – as such conduct would necessarily fall within the general concept of contempt, being "conduct which tends to obstruct, prejudice or abuse the administration of justice"; and (b) each of thc formulations in the current Rules 77(A) to (D), when interpreted in the light of that statement of the Tribunal's inherent power, falls within – but does not limit – that inherent power, as each clearly amounts to knowingly and wilfully interfering with the Tribunal's administration of justice.[69]

The Chamber rejected the respondent's arguments that the nature of the conduct which amounts to contempt had been greatly increased to the prejudice of his rights by the amendments made to Rule 77 both after the commencement of the relevant period in this case and after its conclusion.[70] The Chamber held that

---

[65]*Tadić* Contempt Judgment at paras. 19–23.
[66]Id. at para. 24.
[67]Id. at para. 24. Rule 91, which deals with false testimony, was referred to as another provision concerning the conduct of a matter falling within the inherent jurisdiction of the Tribunal (Id., fn. 25).
[68]Id. at para. 24.
[69]Footnote 26, added to para. 25, states: "Rule 96, which deals with evidence in cases of sexual assault, is a similar statement insofar as it deals with the admissibility of evidence of consent by the victim."

> The inherent power of the Tribunal to deal with contempt has necessarily existed ever since its creation, and the existence of that power does not depend upon a reference being made to it in the Rules [...]. As the Appeals Chamber is satisfied that the current formulation of Rules 77(A) to (D) falls within that inherent power, the amendments made in December 1998 did not increase the nature of the conduct which amounts to contempt to the prejudice of the Respondent's rights.[71]

5. The *Kunarac* Decision

In March 2000, the *Kunarac* Trial Chamber had to consider a request from the defence that Mr. Milan Vujin, who was found to be in contempt of the Tribunal in the *Tadić* Contempt Judgment as referred to above, be granted audience as co-counsel for one of the accused on a *pro bono* basis, not as assigned counsel under the Directive on the Assignment of Defence Counsel.[72] The Chamber noted that although there was no expressed provision under the Rules or any other provision of the Tribunal's jurisprudence from which guidance can be obtained as to whether a person found to be in contempt of the Tribunal could appear without payment by the Tribunal,[73]

---

[70]*Tadić* Contempt Judgement at paras. 27–28. Those were the amendments made (i) in November 1997, which refer for the first time to the inherent power of the Tribunal to hold in contempt those who knowingly and wilfully interfere with its administration of justice, and (ii) in December 1998, which are said to have widened the conduct amounting to contempt to include for the first time any coercion of witnesses by threats, intimidation or bribes. [71]*Tadić* Contempt Judgment at para. 28. The *Simić* Trial Chamber recently considered allegations of contempt against an accused and an assigned counsel, arising in connection with alleged harassment and bribery of a potential defence witness (*Prosecutor v. Simić and Others, Judgement in the Matter of Contempt Allegations Against an Accused and his Counsel*, Case No. IT-95-9-R77, 30 June 2000 (*Simić* Contempt Judgment)). The Chamber, apparently incorporating the relevant findings on contempt made in the *Tadić* Contempt Judgment, stated: "The Tribunal's jurisdiction to deal with contempt was recently considered in detail [in the *Tadić* Contempt Judgment]. The Chamber held that the power to deal with contempt was within the inherent jurisdiction of the Tribunal, deriving from its judicial function, in order to ensure that its exercise of the jurisdiction which is expressly given to it by its Statute is not frustrated and that its basic judicial functions are safeguarded. The inherent power is to hold in contempt those who knowingly and wilfully interfere with the Tribunal's administration of justice. The Chamber included that intimidation of, interference with, or an offer of a bribe to, a potential witness before the Tribunal, or any attempt to intimidate or to interfere with such a witness. That inherent power exists independently of the terms of Rule 77, and the amendments made to that Rule from time to time do not limit that inherent power" (at para. 91). In the event, neither the accused nor the counsel were in contempt of the Tribunal (at para. 101).

[72]*Prosecutor v. Kunarac and Others, Decision on the Request of the Accused Radomir Kovač to Allow Mr. Milan Vujin to Appear as Co-Counsel Acting Pro Bono*, Case No. IT-96-23-PT & IT-96-23/1-PT, 14 March 2000 ("*Kunarac* Decision").

[73]Id. at para. 7.

> the jurisprudence of the Tribunal has long accepted that the Chambers possess an inherent power to control the proceedings in such a way as to ensure that justice is done and to deal with conduct which interferes with the Tribunal's administration of justice.[74]

The Chamber considered "the inherent power by necessity to include the power to refuse audience to counsel, notwithstanding that he may be otherwise qualified under Rule 44(A) [...], but who is for other reasons not a fit and proper person to appear before the Tribunal."[75] After having recounted the conduct for which Mr. Vujin was found to be in contempt, the Chamber concluded that he is no longer fit to appear before the Tribunal and refused to grant him audience, notwithstanding his pending appeal against the Vujin Judgment.[76]

6. Final Observations

The Chambers' rulings assert that the limits to the Tribunal's jurisdiction are more apparent than real. The general argument on existence and scope of the Tribunal's inherent powers goes as follows: where the Statute is silent, the Tribunal's inherent power may be invoked nonetheless as a legal basis for resolving an issue. This power automatically flows from the Tribunal's judicial nature and has been an inherent feature since its creation. A particular general attribute of this is that it is necessary for the full discharge and safeguarding of the Tribunal's judicial function, its primary jurisdiction as expressed in its constituent instrument. This power does not float around

[74]Id. at para. 9. The Chamber referred at some length to the treatment of the Tribunal's inherent powers in the Vujin Judgment, the *Blaskić Subpoena* Judgment, the *Tadić* Appeal Judgment and the *Simić* Separate Opinion of Judge Hunt (at paras. 9–12).

[75]*Kunarac* Decision at para. 13.

[76]Id. at paras. 14–20. Judge Hunt appended a separate opinion to the decision: *Prosecutor v. Kunarac and Others, Separate Opinion of Judge David Hunt on Request by Radomir Kovač to Allow Milan Vujin to Appear as Counsel Acting Without Payment by the Tribunal*, Case No. IT-96-23-PT & IT-96-23/1-PT, 24 March 2000. Notwithstanding that the Statute, Rules and other formal documents of the Tribunal do not expressly state the jurisdiction of a Trial Chamber to determine such a matter, Judge Hunt opined that "The Tribunal does, however, possess an inherent jurisdiction, deriving from its judicial function, to ensure that its exercise of the jurisdiction which is expressly given to it by the Tribunal's Statute is not frustrated and that its basic judicial functions are safeguarded. As an international criminal court, the Tribunal therefore possesses the inherent power to deal with conduct which interferes with its administration of justice. I am satisfied that such an inherent power includes the power to refuse audience to counsel – notwithstanding that he may be otherwise qualified to appear in accordance with Rule 44, and notwithstanding that he is the counsel chosen by the accused – who is not a fit and proper person to appear before the Tribunal." (at para. 8).

at large.[77] Such a power may be expressed in the Rules, without sacrificing its continued independent existence outside the content of those Rules.

As formulated, this general argument can be considered to be misleading. For example, the Chambers have in various instances referred to the power at issue as an "inherent" or an "implied power", and as an "incidental" or "ancillary jurisdiction", often apparently interchangeably, in similar contexts. However, should one simply presume that these powers and jurisdictions are substantially and consequentially the same, and if not, would any distinction matter in the context of the Tribunal?[78] In this respect, could it be argued that the Tribunal and the ICJ are of the same flock, but not necessarily of the same feathers?

The aforementioned general argument also suggests that by invoking the power at issue the Chambers fill both substantive and procedural *lacunae* in the Statute, notwithstanding some assertions and suggestions that only the latter can be so filled. However, does not even a cursory glance at, for example, the inherent power to impose a considerable fine and/or a term of imprisonment for contempt of the Tribunal or for giving false testimony under oath raise some doubt as to those very assertions and suggestions?

---

[77] Judge Shahabuddeen, in his dissenting opinion in the *Case concerning the Land, Island and Maritime Frontier Dispute (El Salvador v. Honduras), Order of 28 February 1990*, 1990 ICJ Reports at 41, stated that: "This implied prohibition [against giving parties any say in the selection of judges to hear a case] is not neutralized by approaching the matter from the point of view of the doctrine of implied powers. True, the fact that specific powers are conferred on a body does not necessarily imply the non-existence of others. But the latter do not float around at large. In the last analysis, all the powers of a body must be conferred by its constituent instrument, whether expressly or impliedly. [...] Putting greater emphasis on the extent to which such additional powers must be so required, Judge Hackworth, dissenting, stated: 'Powers not expressed cannot freely be implied. Implied powers flow from the grant of expressed powers, and are limited to those that are "necessary" to the exercise of the powers expressly granted.' ([*Reparations* case], p. 198.) [...]."

[78] Apart from the suggested differences between "inherent" and "implied powers" in the *Blaskić Subpoena* Judgment, also see Ian Brownlie, Principles of Public International Law (1998) at pp. 687–689 for a pointed discussion of inherent and implied powers; and Henry G. Schermers and Niels M. Blokker, International Institutional Law: Unity Within Diversity (1997) at 158–163 on implied powers. Schermers and Blokker note that a distinction is occasionally made between powers implied from explicit powers as opposed to powers implied from purposes and functions of organisations; the latter basis is broader than the former. They further note, however, that purposes, functions and explicit powers are mostly used interchangeably as a basis for implied powers (at 159). Also see Black's Law Dictionary (1999), for example, defines "implied power" as a "political power that is not enumerated but that nonetheless exists because it is needed to carry out an express power." (at 1189); "incidental power" as a "power that, although not expressly granted, must exist because it is necessary to the accomplishment of an express purpose." (at 1189); "inherent power" as a "power that necessarily derives from an office, position, or status." (at 1189); and "ancillary jurisdiction" as a "court's jurisdiction to adjudicate claims and proceedings that arise out of a claim that is properly before the court." (at 855).

Does Article 15 of the Statute, for example, necessarily preclude the judges from adopting Rules, based on the Tribunal's inherent powers, which extend beyond procedural and evidentiary matters, but which are crucial for its effective functioning?

The argument that the SC could not, and should not have exhaustively spelt out all of the Tribunal's powers, is an agreeable proposition. That the Tribunal in practice therefore needs inherent powers or something akin to it to determine matters where the Statute is silent, is clear, bearing in mind of course that needs, real or perceived, usually inform invocations of power. Less clear, however, is whether the judges should not provide for Rules related to all inherent powers foreseen or shown by practice to exist. In any event, it is also clear that the judges cannot reasonably be expected to foresee and provide for all instances where the Tribunal's inherent powers might have to come into play.

Questions also may be raised with respect to the scope of such powers, which should be determined by various considerations, including the Tribunal's independent and effective functioning in a decentralised international legal environment, the rights of the accused, the concerns of the international community and the SC's grant of powers to the Tribunal. Further clarity is necessary with regard to the relationship between such inherent powers and the Statute and between such powers and the Rules, especially where a Rule relates to an inherent power. Should interested parties consider such a related Rule as but a mirage of that power or as its only justiciable contours? Virtual reality should not encroach upon the domain of the law.

A flexible, fair and reasonable means of solving problems not provided for in either the Statute or the Rules suggests itself, should the following general considerations, amongst others, be taken into account. Reliance by courts on inherent powers, involves the potential for arbitrariness. Therefore, serious consideration should be given to the power expressly granted in Article 15 of the Statute to adopt only rules of procedure and evidence. The question whether the invocation of such powers is *necessary* for the full discharge and safeguarding of the Tribunal's judicial function requires as much examination as the question whether inherent powers constitute a sufficient basis for the Chambers to depart in any direction they wish. What should be opted for, are Rules that are more than mere manifestations of the Tribunal's inherent powers.

PART III

The Presidency and Judges

JON CINA* AND DAVID TOLBERT**

8. The Office of the President: A Third Voice

1. Introduction

The Presidency of the ICTY is a unique office with a wide array of responsibilities. The President is not only the *de jure* head of an organisation with some 1000 staff and a budget of over $100 million, but he or she also has critical substantive duties and key leadership responsibilities, including substantial judicial, administrative, diplomatic and political roles. The judicial functions include presiding over the five-judge appeals courts of both the ICTY and the ICTR, which in a sense, at least for the time being, is a "supreme court" of international humanitarian law. The President's diplomatic and political roles include representing the ICTY within the framework of the international community's attempts to foster and secure peace in the Balkans. The President has additional significant administrative responsibilities in relation to the Chambers specifically and the Tribunal generally.

The role of the President has changed considerably since the establishment of the Tribunal in 1993. The comprehensive normative development of the Tribunal has caused a steady increase in the nature and responsibilities vested in the President. Moreover, the vicissitudes of the political context in which the Tribunal has operated have produced an institution – the Office of the President – that has surpassed the expectations, and perhaps intentions, of the court's founders and early supporters.

*PhD Candidate, University of Melbourne. Formerly: Special Assistant to President McDonald; Legal Assistant, Registry, ICTY. LL.B (Hons) University of Strathclyde.

**Senior Legal Adviser, Registry and Chef de Cabinet, to President McDonald, ICTY. B.A. *magna cum laude*, Furman University; J.D. University of North Carolina; LL.M. *with distinction*, University of Nottingham. Formerly: Chief, General Legal Division, UNRWA; Lecturer, University of Hull School of Law; Partner, Gerdes, Mason, Wilson, Tolbert & Simpson. Member of North Carolina Federal and State Bars.

The views expressed herein are those of the authors and do not necessarily represent those of the United Nations, ICTY or ICTR.

R. May et al., Essays on ICTY Procedure and Evidence in Honour of Gabrielle Kirk McDonald, 85–97.

The President or the Office of the President,[1] the latter term being of recent vintage, has matured into an identifiable entity within the Tribunal, and in the process, as will be argued below, has developed into its "third voice". The Presidency's status as a political actor provides an additional means with which to facilitate the work of the ICTY, complementing its primary mechanisms: the court's judicial determinations and the activities of the Prosecutor. It is suggested, however, that the resulting structural tensions within the Tribunal and the competing priorities pertaining to the functions of the President now support reform of the office.

2. Early Developments

This has not always been the case. The Statute of the Tribunal appears to envision the President's role as a relatively narrow, and to some extent incoherent, one. Although one Article is devoted to the Presidency, the Statute provides only that "[t]he judges of the International Tribunal shall elect a President", that he or she "shall be a member of the Appeals Chamber and shall preside over its proceedings" and that after consulting the other Judges, he or she "shall assign the judges to the Appeals Chamber and to the Trial Chambers".[2] The other three references to the President in the Statute concern such diverse issues as consultation over the appointment of a Registrar,[3] the determination of questions of pardon or commutation of sentence where convicted persons are so eligible[4] and the submission of the annual reports to the General Assembly.[5] It was with only this guidance that Judge Antonio Cassese was elected as the first president in November 1993 by his fellow Judges.

Cassese then headed an institution in law and name only: the United Nations had yet to secure a Prosecutor, a building, a meaningful staff or budget. Acknowledging their situation and the need to create *ab initio* instruments to give meaning to the Statute, the Judges began drafting Rules of Procedure and Evidence to govern the operation of the Tribunal. The initial version of the Rules was necessarily limited in scope.[6] However, as one of the very few aspects of the Tribunal in which practical experience already existed, albeit the most limited sort – a President had been elected – the Presidency was a subject of this first period of judicial legislation.

At this early stage, the election of the President had provided impetus and structure to the Judges' activities, with the new President acting naturally as manager and facilitator of their Plenary work. As noted, however, the

[1]For convenience, the terms are used interchangeably in this paper.

[2]Art. 14 (1), (2), (3).

[3]Art. 17 (3).

[4]Art. 28.

[5]Art. 34.

[6]Practice and the availability of research resources would subsequently inform their comprehensive expansion into a detailed code of international criminal procedure.

Statute made no mention of this co-ordinating aspect of the role. Moreover, it implicitly contemplated the President performing additional duties, flowing from its substantive provisions. These related to the judicial and rule-making responsibilities of the Judges and their cohabitation in an institution that included its own criminal justice administration and prosecutor. In addition, no other appropriate leadership mechanism existed and the powers the Statute vested in the President pertained to judicial management and miscellaneous other matters. The election of the first President thus led logically to the explicit delineation of a coherent set of functions for the office.

3. The Functions and Responsibilities of the President[7]

The Rules include a section establishing, and concerning, the Presidency as a separate entity within the Tribunal.[8] Various other Rules create powers relating to other elements of the court. Rules 18 and 20 expand the procedural foundations of the Statute, describing the mechanism for selecting the President and Vice-President[9] and stipulating a two-year maximum term of office with re-election permitted once.

The President is vested with important administrative responsibilities under Rule 19, which provides that he or she "shall coordinate the work of the Chambers and supervise the activities of the Registry". This provision logically establishes the role of the President as the chief administrator of the Chambers. On the other hand, the extension of the President's power to supervise the Registry cannot be so clearly derived from the Statute and has been the subject of not inconsiderable controversy at both *ad hoc* Tribunals.[10] While the Statute provides that the Registrar will provide administrative support to the Chambers, the Registrar is also to provide similar support to the Prosecutor.[11] Thus, Rule 19 can be interpreted as placing the Registrar in the anomalous position of providing administrative support to the Prosecutor, who is independent under the Statute, but yet supervised by the President, who is a judge. Although conflicts have largely been avoided in practice,[12] Rule 19 sits uneasily with the principle that the Prosecutor and the Chambers are separate, independent organs.

---

[7]These responsibilities touch upon a great variety of other aspects of the Tribunals' work, outside the scope of the present discussion. The remainder of this paper is therefore limited to an analysis of those aspects which are directly relevant to the Office of the President. Other chapters in this collection of essays provide more detailed information.

[8]ICTY Rules, Part Three, Section Two: "The Presidency". Judge Elizabeth Odio Benito was elected Vice President on the same date as Cassese was voted President.

[9]See ICTY Annual Report 1994, at paras. 68–70.

[10]See Report of the Expert Group to Conduct a Review of the Effective Operation and Functioning of the International Criminal Tribunal for the Former Yugoslavia and the International Criminal Tribunal for Rwanda, A/54/634, 22 November 1999 ("*Experts Report*"), at paras. 237–245.

[11]Art. 17.

[12]*Experts Report*, supra note 10, at para. 238.

Substantively, the development of ICTY law and practice and a variety of additional instruments and agreements have attached further layers of responsibility to the Office of the President. The broad range of duties now incumbent on the President comprises four categories.

3.1 Judicial[13]

As noted, the President presides over the ICTY Appeals Chamber, and by virtue of Article 12 of the ITCR Statute and the practice of the two Tribunals, over the ICTR Appeals Chamber.[14]

The early years of the Tribunals' life created little work for either Appeals Chamber, the result both of the low number of accused in custody, particularly at the ICTY, and the grounds of appeal being limited by narrow statutory provisions.[15] No appeals were brought from ICTY Trial Chambers until mid-1995,[16] while the first time the ICTR Appeals Chamber considered a matter was in mid-1998.[17] As of March 2000, however, the Chamber is seized of over forty matters on appeal from ICTY and ICTR Trial Chambers. The majority of these appeals are interlocutory, but the number of appeals against judgements has been on the increase.

While this figure represents a normal, or even light, workload for a national court, it is a onerous number for the Tribunals. The small number both of Appeals Judges and their research and support staff considering extremely complex questions of law for which there is little if any precedent; in so doing, it is they who are creating the body of case law in this field. It was, moreover, almost certainly not envisaged by the drafters of the Statute. The increase in appeals has flowed from both the addition of a third trial chamber to each Tribunal and the Judges' expansion of appellate grounds through the promulgation of Rules permitting interlocutory appeals, either

[13] See also id., at paras. 102–108, "The Appeals Chamber".

[14] Article 12 (2) of the ICTR statute provides that "[t]he members of the Appeals Chamber of the [ICTY] shall also serve as the members of the [ICTR] Appeals Chamber." Although strictly speaking the text is silent on the question over who should preside over the latter, by default the role has been performed by the presiding Judge of the ICTY Chamber.

[15] The Statutes permit appeals from either party on an error of law invalidating the impugned decision, on an error of fact that has occasioned a miscarriage of justice, or an application for review of a decision if new facts emerge which could have been a decisive factor in reaching the impugned decision. ICTY Statute, Arts. 25 and 26; ICTR Statute, Arts. 24 and 25.

[16] *Prosecutor v Tadić, Defence Motion for Interlocutory Appeal on Jurisdiction* Case No. IT-94-1-AR72, 2 Oct. 1995 (appealing against *Decision on the Defence Motion on Jurisdiction in the Trial Chamber of the International Tribunal*, Case No. IT-95-1-T, 10 Aug. 1995).

[17] *Prosecutor v Rutaganda, Notice of Appeal Against the Decision of Trial Chamber I Dismissing the Defence Motion for an Order to the Prosecutor to Investigate A Case of False Testimony (Witness "CC")*, Case No. ICTR 96-3-A, 19 March 1998 (appealing against *Decision on the Defence Motion to Direct the Prosecutor to Investigate the matter of False Testimony by Witness "CC"*, Case No. ICTR-96-3, 26 March 1998).

as an inherent function of the court,[18] in the interests of justice or international law, or on the showing of good cause.[19]

Clearly, the President must accord priority to his or her judicial appellate work: the incumbent is a Judge first, President second. The interests of justice demand expeditious adjudication, while the characteristics of the interlocutory process – every application for leave to appeal is assessed by a three-Judge panel, constituted afresh in each situation – have the potential to suspend Trial Chamber proceedings for long periods of time,[20] are such that judicial obligations require and absorb the greatest part of the President's attention and efforts. Whereas Cassese's tenure saw intermittent appeals that were dealt with promptly, the Chamber his successor Gabrielle Kirk McDonald inherited was in effect permanently running to stand still. While this has eased somewhat under President Claude Jorda with the increased involvement of other members of the Appeals Chamber in active case management, it remains true that at this juncture in the Tribunals' development, the volume of cases together with the number and complexity of issues raised is such that presiding over the Appeals Chamber is itself sufficient to occupy the President to the exclusion of all other tasks. It is, moreover, doubtful that this would be offset by the acquisition of additional Appeals Chamber Judges, as is currently being proposed by the ICTY.[21] They are likely to be necessary simply to maintain the present rate of adjudication, as the number of cases is likely to continue rising: both Tribunals continue to gain custody of accused with increasing frequency; the Appeals Chamber also has acted as a necessary and vocal check against prosecutorial carelessness.[22]

In fact, as head of the ICTR Appeals Chamber, the ICTY President is subject to other demands. The Judges travel to the ICTR's seat in Tanzania, both to participate in ICTR Plenaries and to hold hearings. In the early years, this required only short-term annual relocation from The Hague (and the President's other ICTY responsibilities). However, recognising the amount of ICTR work and the imbalance and perceived lack of priority accorded to it that results from the Chamber sitting in northern Europe to

---

[18]ICTY Rule 72 permitted the Court to review its own jurisdiction, the first ground of interlocutory appeal.

[19]Note, however, that the scope for interlocutory action before the ICTR Chamber is significantly more restrictive than before the ICTY, excluding appeals from decisions on motions filed under ICTR Rule 73.

[20]"Indeed trials before ICTR were suspended for almost nine months pending an interlocutory appeal relating to the authority of the (ICTR) President to make changes in the composition of Trial Chambers and the effect of such changes on the jurisdiction of the Trial Chambers ..." *Experts Report*, supra note 10, at para. 104.

[21]Id., at para. 107.

[22]See *Prosecutor v Bagosora, Decision On The Admissibility Of The Prosecutor's Appeal From The Decision Of A Confirming Judge Dismissing An Indictment Against Théoneste Bagosora And 28 Others*, Case No. ICTR-98-37-A, 8 June 1998; and *Prosecutor v Bayaragwiza, Decision and Decision on Prosecutor's Request For Review Or Reconsideration*, Case No. ICTR-97-19-AR-72, 3 Nov. 1999 and 31 March 2000.

deliberate on crimes committed in central Africa, the ICTR Appeals Chamber is now hearing appeals in Arusha on a regular basis. Clearly, this trend should continue; however, this obviously removes the President from the ICTY for a number of weeks at any given time.

3.2 Quasi-Judicial

Rule 19 establishes in broad terms the non-statutory "functions of the President".[23] The power to supervise the Registry, together with the stipulation in Rule 33 that the Registrar acts under the authority of the President to administer and service the Tribunal and acts as its channel of communication, is the basis for a series of what are essentially administrative law powers and functions exercised by the President. The Registry, *inter alia*, maintains the Detention Unit, protects the welfare of its inhabitants and ensures that their rights, including the right to representation, are upheld. A number of subsidiary directives, rules and regulations have been adopted and amended by the Judges to govern these activities. Each vests in the President a form of appellate power in relation to the Registrar's decisions. The President thus functions both as a restraint against any erroneous actions by the Registry and as an additional means of refining procedures relating to suspects and accused.[24]

Thus, persons detained by the Tribunal who have complained to the Commanding Officer of the Detention Unit and received an unsatisfactory response may appeal via the Registrar to the President.[25] Textually, there is no limit to what may constitute the subject of a complaint: Rule 84 permits that "[e]ach detainee may make a complaint to the Commanding Officer". Although successive Presidents have interpreted this provision contextually, a broad reading of it would arguably allow appeals on a wide range of non-detention issues: once confined to the Detention Unit, anything ostensibly troubling an individual becomes, at least potentially, an issue relating to detention. The possibility exists, therefore, of a flood of appeals, particularly as the population of the Detention Unit grows. In practice, appeals have

[23]"(A) The President shall preside at all plenary meetings of the Tribunal. The President shall coordinate the work of the Chambers and supervise the activities of the Registry as well as exercise all the other functions conferred on the President by the Statute and the Rules. (B) The President may from time to time, and in consultation with the Bureau, the Registrar and the Prosecutor, issue Practice Directions, consistent with the Statute and the Rules, addressing detailed aspects of the conduct of proceedings before the Tribunal." Under ICTY Rule 21, "the Vice-President shall exercise the functions of the President in case of the latter's absence or inability to act."

[24]Notably, following the deaths of Slavko Dokmanović and Milan Kovaćević inside the Detention Unit in June and July 1998, President McDonald spent several days with the remaining detainees, commissioned separate inquiries into the deaths and proposed a series of reforms to the detention regime framework.

[25]Rules Governing the Detention of Persons awaiting Trial or Appeal before the Tribunal or Otherwise Detained on the Authority of the Tribunal, IT/38/Rev.8, 22 November 1999, Rule 85.

been relatively few and have been resolved co-operatively by the President and Registrar: with respect to questions of welfare, an agreed compromise that respects the rights of the detainee is an inherently more desirable outcome than the imposition of Presidential authority on the Registrar. Similar situations pertain with respect to the Regulations to Govern the Supervision of Visits to and Communications with Detainees,[26] and the Directive on the Assignment of Defence Counsel.[27]

The Practice Directions contemplated in Rule 19 are best viewed as being analogous to national secondary legislation.[28] To date, four have been issued, progressively as the need has arisen to establish procedures for designating States for the enforcement of ICTY Sentences; considering applications for pardon, commutation and parole; the amendment of the Rules; and submissions to the Appeals Chamber.[29]

The President also has several responsibilities regarding the enforcement of sentences. The determination as to which State an accused shall serve his or her sentence is "primarily an administrative decision but with certain political and quasi-judicial elements as well".[30] Moreover, under Article 28, the President is responsible for making decisions relating to the pardon or early release of convicted persons; this power has in effect also been extended to questions of early release under the agreements the Tribunal has negotiated with various States.[31] In cases where there is a request by the enforcing State for pardon, commutation of sentence or early release, the

---

[26]IT/98/Rev.3, 22 July 1999, under whose provisions detainees may appeal to the President any decision of the Registrar made under the Regulations (Regulation 10). This includes the right to request the President to reverse the Registrar's decisions to monitor the detainee's telephone calls (Regulations 21 (A), 22) or visits (Regulations 44 (A), 45) or to deny a visitor permission to see a detainee (Regulations 33 (B), 35). The Registrar is further required to inform the President of any renewal of a decision under the Regulations to record detainee phone calls and visits (Regulations 21 (C), 44 (B)).

[27]IT/73/Rev.7, 22 July 1999, permitting the President to review Registry decisions denying assignment or withdrawal of counsel from a suspect or accused (Art. 13 (A)), allowing reversal of a decision not to assign; Art. 20 (E)), obliging the Registrar to consult the President in resolving financial disputes with counsel and requiring the President to consult the Advisory Panel on defence counsel issues as appropriate (Art. 32 (C)).

[28]For example, United Kingdom Ministers frequently promulgate regulations establishing uniform criteria relating to the implementation of specific legislation.

[29]Practice Direction on the Procedure for the International Tribunal's Designation of a State in which a Convicted Person is to Serve his/her Sentence for Imprisonment, IT/137, 10 July 1998; Practice Direction on the Procedure for Determination of Applications for Pardon, Commutation of Sentence and Early Release of Persons convicted by the International Tribunal, IT/146, 7 April 1999; Practice Direction on Procedure for the Proposal, Consideration of and Publication of Amendments to the Rules of Procedure and Evidence of the International Tribunal, IT/143, 18 December 1998; Practice Direction on Procedure for the Filing of Written Submissions in Appeals before the International Tribunal, IT/155, 1 October 1999.

[30]David Tolbert, "The International Tribunals for the former Yugoslavia and the Enforcement of Sentences", 11 *Leiden Journal of International Law* (1998), pp. 655–669, at p. 668.

[31]Id., at 665–66.

relevant Practice Direction provides that the President will review various documents and information about the conduct and mental status of the convicted person. Then after hearing the convicted person and consulting with the sentencing Chamber and the Bureau, the President will make a decision regarding the request.[32]

Finally, under Rule 7*bis* the President has the duty to report to the Security Council non-compliance by a State under Article 29. Rule 7*bis* raises a number of difficult issues, as it places the President in the unenviable position of making a judicial decision in a non-judicial context; however, this Rule is discussed extensively elsewhere in this book and is thus outside the scope of the present discussion.[33]

3.3 Administrative

The President is in effect the head of the Chambers judicially and administratively,[34] charged with a number of management tasks. The Bureau, a quasi-cabinet, was established by the Judges to assist the officeholder, thereby emphasising "the collegiate direction of the Tribunal's work."[35] These entities together formulate the working policies of the Chambers. The Bureau's other members, the Vice-President and the Presiding Judges of the Trial Chambers, provide advice and assistance to the President on carrying out functions including assigning Judges to Chambers and budgetary matters, offering views on the appointment of the Registrar and Deputy Registrar, and setting Plenary dates and agendas. More importantly, it provides a forum for Judges to raise issues of concern, such as the need for clarity concerning the disqualification of Judges from proceedings. Except on specific matters,[36] its role is merely consultative, although past Presidents have generally adhered to the principle of *de facto* majority rule during its deliberations. It is *prima facie* undesirable for one Judge – albeit the President – to override the wishes of thirteen equal colleagues where the issue is common to all.

In contrast is the President's most significant non-judicial responsibility: the Budget. The office-holder participates in detail in the annual assessment of the Chambers' financial requirements and the submission of a comprehensive budget covering the whole Tribunal.[37] This has been a source of tension between the Chambers and Registry: while the Registry consults the Judges concerning the resources of the judicial support branch of the

[32] See Tolbert and Rydberg, "Enforcement of Sentences", infra, in this collection of essays.

[33] See Mundis, "Reporting non-compliance: Rule 7*bis*", infra, in this collection of essays.

[34] See ICTY Rules 17 (B), and Rule 19(A), establishing the President's judicial precedence.

[35] Supra note 9.

[36] For example, ICTY Rule 15: Disqualification of Judges.

[37] Members of Chambers do not comment on the submissions of the Office of the Prosecutor.

Registry, there has been some disagreement about the respective roles of the Chambers and Registry in the process.[38] The Judges have expressed concern over their ability to control their own work, thus illustrating some of the difficulties inherent in creating and operating a UN court.[39] In this connection, the Expert Group found: "[t]he judges are in the best position to determine their own needs and should be entitled to submit proposals which they feel satisfy [them]".[40] Prior to the report of the Experts Group, McDonald proposed and the judges approved, the Registry's judicial support section being refocused towards Chambers. Although this is less than recommended by the Experts Group,[41] Jorda appears to have greater control over Chambers administrative questions than his predecessors.

3.4 Political

The President represents the Tribunal, in public and in private. At its most basic, this involves projecting the Tribunal's image, work and principles, through countless media interviews and speeches to fora around the world. Given the nature of the court and the conflicts it is charged with adjudicating, the President is a powerful symbol.[42] The most notable aspect of the Presidency, however, is the political activism that has characterised its history thus far.

In 1994, President Cassese and Prosecutor Goldstone headed a Tribunal buried in apathy. If rhetoric had a practical use, the ICTY would have overcome many, if not all, of the initial obstacles it faced. However, as the conflict in the former Yugoslavia continued and increased in savagery, the Tribunal's chief resource was its principal officers. Alarmed at the failure to translate the Security Council's commitment into a working court, a failure symptomatic of the incoherence that characterised the response of the international community to the wars, Cassese and Goldstone separately engaged in a progressively more proactive political effort to protect the moral investment that the Tribunal represented. As one of the group of initial Judges, Cassese had few other ICTY responsibilities and, thus, in addition to working on the Rules, focused with Goldstone on obtaining

---

[38]*Expert Report,* supra note 10, at paras. 237–247.

[39]Id.

[40]Id., at para. 245.

[41]It proposed that authority over Chambers administration and budgetary matters should be realigned from the Registry to the Bureau; id., at para. 246.

[42]Although the ICTR has endured a more problematic history, the Rwandan Government hosted McDonald as Presiding Judge of its Appeals Chamber in 1998. Following meetings with the President and Government, she visited Murambi in Nyamagabe Commune, where she spoke with survivors of the genocide and saw the remains of some of the reported thirty-five to fifty thousand individuals killed there, left intact in memoriam.

resources and co-operation.[43] As the lack of support, particularly for the Office of the Prosecutor, became more acute, Cassese's private and public lobbying stressed the court's conceptual significance and the consequent importance of its success. This theme and his accompanying assertive tone continued through the end of his second Presidency, by which time his entreaties to States, the Security Council, the General Assembly, the Council of Europe and the Peace Implementation Council centred on the obligation to arrest indictees.[44] Non-compliance by the States and entities of the former Yugoslavia following the conclusion of the General Framework Agreement for Peace in Bosnia and Herzegovina[45] and the failure of NATO to carry out arrests raised the spectre of impunity to a serious impediment to the Tribunal's work, practically and theoretically given the ultimate aims of the ICTY's creation.

As McDonald succeeded him, two years of deficient "peace implementation" had been marked by near total default on the parties' obligations to co-operate with the Tribunal.[46] She articulated four aims, including the addition of a third Trial Chamber, increasing formal State co-operation,[47] increasing awareness of the court and contributing the ICTY's experience to the campaign for a permanent International Criminal Court. This represented a clear continuation of Cassese's use of the Presidency as the Tribunal's third voice: disseminating the ICTY's judicial findings and, where appropriate, complementing the Prosecutor's efforts to build State co-operation to secure custody of accused and adequate resources.

McDonald consolidated and expanded the base she inherited. She lobbied strongly for additional funding for the court, throughout early 1998 assertively and successfully campaigning with the major powers individually and the Security Council collectively for the third Trial Chamber. While momentum was finally gathering behind the Tribunal as she assumed office,

---

[43]Cassese wrote to all Member States of the UN detailing their obligations to ensure domestic legal compliance with the ICTY and requesting assistance in the form of material resources and agreements to host convicted persons. The Prosecutor's struggle to acquire adequate resources continues six years later, events in Kosovo acting first as a further drain on over stretched staff and then as a catalyst for increased international support.

[44]This is a necessarily brief outline, which fails to do justice to Cassese's efforts. See ICTY Annual Reports 1994, 1995, 1996, 1997, 1998 and 1999, and ICTY Yearbooks 1996 and 1997 for a detailed and progressive history of the problems the Tribunal has faced in securing State co-operation, including with the General Framework Agreement for Peace in Bosnia and Herzegovina (hereinafter: *GFAP*), and the roles of Cassese and McDonald in response.

[45]The GFAP was initialled in November 1995 in Dayton, Ohio and signed December 1995 in Paris by Bosnia and Herzegovina, Croatia and the Federal Republic of Yugoslavia (on behalf of itself and the Republika Srpska).

[46]Only in July 1997 did NATO forces begin arresting indicted persons. Until then, only eight were in custody. US pressure on Croatia led to the voluntary surrender of ten further individuals in October 1997.

[47]Implementing legislation, agreements on the enforcement of sentences and protection of witnesses.

shortfalls in funding and co-operation remained the norm. She focused on the emerging complacency surrounding the Tribunal, pointing out that efforts to date had merely ensured that the ICTY was finally able to begin discharging its mandate[48] and urged more States to join the small group of "collective activist" nations that shoulder the burden of supporting the Tribunal.[49] Internally, McDonald encouraged a more activist publicity policy:[50] an Outreach Programme was established and press and information efforts were reorganised and directed towards the former Yugoslavia.

Other features of McDonald's tenure, however, reveal the extent to which the President's political function has developed. The central premise of her Presidency was that, in addition to the office's judicial duties, the President should be concerned with matters that affected the institution *qua* institution and should act in its name.[51] Thus, she made extensive use of the Presidential power to report non-co-operation to the Security Council.[52] Following the Security Council's repeated failure to address effectively the Government of the Federal Republic of Yugoslavia's (hereinafter: FRY) rejection of the Tribunal's legitimacy, she *proprio motu* extended the principle to report the FRY to the Contact Group, the Peace Implementation Council and the North Atlantic Council.[53] More significantly, McDonald (with Prosecutor Arbour) objected to a proposed Truth and Reconciliation Commission for Bosnia and Herzegovina, citing likely conflict with ICTY investigations and rulings, and potential manipulation of the Commission. While supporting the principle behind the proposal, they asked the Office of the High Representative to address the matter, the Presidency thereby explicitly involving the Tribunal in the domestic affairs of a State.[54] Further, as the conflict in Kosovo intensified throughout 1998 and the FRY refused the Prosecutor investigative access there, McDonald adopted a stance of public activism within the context of the international community's overall

---

[48]Six trials of twelve individuals commenced and four Judgements against seven were rendered during McDonald's Presidency.

[49]She was referring to Canada, The Netherlands, the UK, and the US, the principal donors of equipment, personnel and political will, all of which are finite.

[50]See Vohrah and Cina, "The Outreach Programme", infra, in this collection of essays, for an analysis of this aspect of McDonald's Presidency.

[51]This was partly a response to the media habit of characterising the Prosecutor as speaking on behalf of the Tribunal as a whole.

[52]See Mundis, "Reporting non-compliance: Rule 7*bis*", infra, in this collection of essays.

[53]Organisations overseeing the peace agreements in Kosovo and Bosnia and Herzegovina.

[54]While the ICTY is intimately involved with the State in question – Bosnia and Herzegovina – it is only through Prosecutorial activity or judicial order that it has addressed it with such specificity. Although McDonald and Arbour met with OHR and the chief advocates of the proposal, the conflict in Kosovo led to its suspension. It is understood that efforts to establish a commission have been resumed.

initiative to secure peace as being more likely to lead to specific co-operation with the ICTY.[55] While the Prosecutor necessarily sought to meet specific operational requirements, McDonald stressed the need for genuine acceptance and endorsement of the Tribunal conceptually, both in the conflict itself and in any peace settlement. Thus, following the commencement of NATO action against the FRY, she urged support for the Prosecutor and attempted to counter the multitude of reports presenting an erroneous view of the Tribunal's mandate and capabilities with respect to Kosovo.[56]

Jorda succeeded McDonald in November 1999. It is far too early to reach any conclusions on the way in which the Presidency will evolve during his tenure, although his public statements indicate a focus on managing the Tribunal's judicial affairs: maximising use of resources by overhauling pre-trial and trial management procedures.[57] It will be interesting to see if the Tribunal is sufficiently developed and stable to support such a relatively narrow focus.

4. Reform?

It is not entirely clear that the Office of the President as currently constituted should have a public or political profile. There is no question that the Tribunal needs to continue an assertive public relations policy or that the symbolism inherent in the role of ICTY President lends itself to a prominent role in such a policy. Equally, the capacity for impartial public activism independent of the Prosecutor is necessary to ensure that a neutral voice is also heard highlighting the imperatives on which support for the Tribunal is founded. However, one must ask whether that person should be a sitting judge, as this role runs counter, at least to some extent, to the duties of the Tribunal's Judges to provide for fair trials.

Moreover, the current number and demands of the President's responsibilities are without question too onerous to remain the sole province of one incumbent. As noted, judicial appellate work alone is a full time occupation. Jorda's emphasis on internal affairs may anyway necessarily reduce the extent of Presidential public activities.

---

[55]McDonald held a press conference and wrote to the Security Council following the signing of the Holbrooke-Milosevic agreement in October 1998 to express her alarm at the omission of the ICTY. She believed any final settlement should avoid repeating the vague co-operation commitments contained in the GFAP, whose language provided the rationale for both the parties' and NATO's subsequent inaction. During the Rambouillet peace negotiations in early 1999, McDonald and Arbour, based on independent advice and assurances, differed on the acceptability or otherwise of the proposed terms relating to the ICTY.

[56]See address to the Council on Foreign Relations, 12 May 1999 "The International Criminal Tribunal for the former Yugoslavia: Making A Difference or Making Excuses".

[57]See, e.g., Press Release, "The Judges Mandate The President to Present a Long-term Judicial Strategy for the Tribunal", The Hague, 18 April 2000.

Serious consideration should therefore be given to reforming the Office of the President. One proposal would involve removing the President's judicial role, allowing him or her to focus on administrative, political and or diplomatic responsibilities. This approach has a precedent of sorts in the Statute for the International Criminal Court.[58] It has much to commend it: the President would still be a judicial colleague, but with the time to focus on the critical policy and political issues that face the ICTY and without the constraints that would otherwise affect him or her as a sitting judge. An alternative, more radical, proposal would transform the Presidency into the fourth branch of the Tribunal without any formal connection to the Chambers. This would allow even more scope for Presidential public and political engagement, liasing with the Judges, Prosecutor and Registrar over issues of common concern,[59] and an increased involvement in ICTY public relations, without reducing the court's judicial capacity.[60]

In any event, it is clear that some reform of the Office of the President is necessary so that the President can focus his or her energies in specific directions rather than dissipating the moral authority of the office in sundry directions. The past Presidents have used the office to great effect, as is demonstrated by the evolution of the office and the development of the Tribunal; however, as the Tribunal's judicial work increases, it is time for further change to meet the Tribunal's current needs.

---

[58]The Presidency of the International Criminal Court forms the fourth organ of the court, although its responsibilities would appear to include many of the quasi-judicial and administrative functions currently the responsibility of the ICTY President. Rome Statute of the International Criminal Court, PCNICC/1999/INF/3, Arts. 34 and 38.

[59]This would obviously have no effect on the Prosecutor's ability to pursue his or her agenda.

[60]Both of these proposals would appear to necessitate amendment of the ICTY Statute.

JEAN-JACQUES HEINTZ* et MÓNICA MARTÍNEZ**

9. La Compétence du Président quant aux Questions Relatives au Quartier Pénitentiaire et son Rôle en Matière de Contrôle et de Détention

Les fonctions du Président du Tribunal comprennent le contrôle du Greffier s'agissant de l'administration et de la gestion matérielle du quartier pénitentiaire des Nations Unies, ainsi que des conditions de détention applicables à tous les détenus. Les juges des Chambres de première instance et de la Chambre d'appel sont habilités, aux termes du Règlement de procédure et de preuve ("le Règlement"), à statuer sur certaines questions relatives à la détention, en particulier les demandes de mise en liberté provisoire. Ils ont aussi parfois été amenés à statuer au cas par cas sur d'autres questions indirectement liées au régime de détention de l'accusé. De fait, tous les juges du Tribunal ont ainsi une part de responsabilité dans la détermination et le contrôle des conditions de détention au Quartier pénitentiaire des Nations Unies.

La première partie du présent article s'intéressera au sens à donner aux dispositions du Statut, du Règlement et du Règlement portant régime de détention des personnes en attente de jugement ou d'appel devant le Tribunal

*Jean-Jacques Heintz, Maîtrise en droit privé à Strasbourg en 1969; Ecole Nationale de la Magistrature de 1971 à 1973; Juge au TGI de Mulhouse de 1973 à 1983, Chargé de cours à l'Université de Haute Alsace; Maître de conférences à l'Ecole Nationale de la Magistrature à Bordeaux de 1983 à 1986; Président du TGI de Montbéliard de 1986 à 1990; Directeur de l'Ecole Nationale des Greffes (Dijon) de 1990 à 1997; Expert-consultant auprès de la Commission Européene et de la Banque Mondiale dans le domaine de l'organisation judiciaire et du fonctionnement des jurisdictions; Depuis 1997, détaché au TPIY en qualité de Greffier Adjoint.

**Mónica Martínez, Maîtrise en droit à Oviedo, Espagne en 1992; Maîtrise en droit européen et international à Bruxelles en 1993; Membre du barreau de Gijón, Espagne; Membre de l' «I.B.A.»; *Juriste* associée au TPIY aux services d'appui juridique et judiciaire du Greffe (de mars 1995 à mars 1996; de avril 1997 à décembre 1997 et depuis juin 1998 jusqu'à present).

Les opinions exprimées dans cet article sont celles des auteurs et n'engagent nullement le TPIY ou l'Organisation des Nations Unies.

R. May et al., Essays on ICTY Procedure and Evidence in Honour of Gabrielle Kirk McDonald, 99–110.

ou détenues sur l'ordre du Tribunal ("le Règlement sur la détention préventive").

Dans une deuxième partie nous exposerons la pratique du Tribunal s'agissant du rôle du Président en matière de contrôle des conditions de détention. Nous énoncerons les différents scénarios qui ont conduit à des mesures s'écartant du principe de compétence du Président, au profit des Chambres de première instance, lesquelles traitent occasionnellement de questions relatives à la détention à différents stades de la procédure judiciaire.

La troisième partie présentera brièvement les principales caractéristiques des diverses modalités de contrôle des centres de détention provisoire, tant en droit international que dans les systèmes de *common law* et de tradition romano-germanique.

Nous analyserons ensuite l'évolution de la pratique du Tribunal à la lumière du Statut et du Règlement du Tribunal ainsi que des normes internationales et nationales existantes, et nous évaluerons en conclusion s'il est plus approprié de réserver au Président le contrôle de toutes les questions relatives à la détention ou de déléguer cette fonction au corps judiciaire.

1. L'ESPRIT DU STATUT ET DU RÈGLEMENT

La responsabilité de contrôle du Président sur les conditions de détention des accusés avant leur possible condamnation n'est pas explicitement régie par le Statut.[1] Toutefois, le principe d'un tel contrôle peut être déduit du fait que les accusés, une fois arrêtés, sont transférés au Tribunal et placés sous la garde de celui-ci.[2] Le Statut ne fournit pas d'avantage de précisions quant à la répartition des fonctions de contrôle et des responsabilités entre le pays hôte et le Tribunal en matière de détention des accusés.

Les articles 19 et 33 du Règlement définissent les fonctions du Président et du Greffier respectivement. Le Règlement a été adopté pour la première fois à l'issue de la deuxième session plénière, qui s'est tenue du 17 janvier au 11 février 1994. Les juges se sont réunis et ont débattu de chaque article à partir d'un projet, préparé sur la base de propositions formulées par des Etats et des organisations non gouvernementales et complété par d'autres articles élaborés par les juges eux-mêmes. Trois groupes de travail se sont réunis, d'abord séparément puis ensemble, afin d'apporter les modifications nécessaires au projet initial et de proposer un libellé pour chaque article en vue de débats ultérieurs en session plénière; l'un des groupes de travail s'est consacré exclusivement au Règlement sur la détention préventive.

---

[1]L'article 27 du Statut ne parle que d'emprisonnement faisant suite à la sentence. "*La réclusion est soumise aux règles nationales de l'État concerné, sous le contrôle du Tribunal international*".

[2]Cf. article 20, par. 2 du Statut.

La formulation de la version originelle de l'article 19 du Règlement (portant alors le numéro 3.8), qui régit les fonctions du Président, a été débattue en session plénière. Un grand nombre de tâches exigeaient que le Président soit en contact avec le Greffe. On aurait pu retenir l'emploi du terme "*diriger* les activités du Greffe". Néanmoins, la formule selon laquelle le Président *coordonne* les travaux des Chambres et *contrôle* les activités du Greffe a été estimé plus opportune.

Il avait également été suggéré que la disposition relative aux questions à débattre en session plénière[3] porte également sur la question de la détermination et du contrôle par le Tribunal des conditions de détention au Quartier pénitentiaire des Nations Unies.[4] Les juges ont donc assumé la responsabilité de l'institution et du contrôle du régime de détention. Il a été décidé à l'unanimité que les normes des Nations Unies devaient s'appliquer au quartier pénitentiaire.[5]

En ce qui concerne le contrôle quotidien des conditions au quartier pénitentiaire, les Juges s'en chargeraient eux-mêmes, en désignant à cet effet un ou deux d'entre eux, ou un organe international comme le Comité du Conseil de l'Europe pour la prévention de la torture et des traitements inhumains ou dégradants. Toutefois, puisque les normes des Nations Unies étaient censées s'appliquer, on n'a pas considéré nécessaire d'inscrire cette condition dans un article du Règlement. Par conséquent, la question des autorités d'inspection a été renvoyée au Règlement sur la détention préventive.[6]

---

[3]Cf. article 24 v) du Règlement (alors article 3.13).

[4]Le quartier pénitentiaire des Nations Unies est établi au sein d'une maison d'arrêt du pays hôte ("Complexe pénitentiaire de Scheveningen").

[5]Le Règlement sur la détention préventive est conforme à l'Ensemble de règles minima (pour le traitement des détenus) des Nations Unies de 1997 et aux Règles pénitentiaires européennes tel qu'adoptées par le Conseil de l'Europe sur la base des règles des Nations Unies. Par principe, il a été décidé que les règles des Nations Unies devaient s'appliquer conjointement aux dispositions applicables du pays hôte.

[6]En application de l'article 6 A) du Règlement sur la détention préventive, "Le Bureau peut à tout moment charger un juge ou le Greffier du Tribunal d'inspecter le quartier pénitentiaire et de faire rapport au Tribunal sur les conditions générales ou tout aspect particulier d'application du présent Règlement".

Il convient de mentionner l'accord existant entre le TPIR et le TPIY permettant aux autorités officielles d'un Tribunal d'inspecter à l'improviste le quartier pénitentiaire de l'autre, en vue de soumettre au Président du Tribunal concerné des rapports confidentiels sur les conditions de détention.

En application de ce Règlement,[7] le Greffier a délégué au Commandant du quartier pénitentiaire ses fonctions de responsable de l'administration et de la gestion matérielle; ce dernier l'informe de tout problème naissant de l'administration quotidienne du centre de détention. Le Président peut agir soit en tant qu'autorité d'inspection soit comme instance appelée à trancher les recours contre les décisions du Greffier. Le Président est également informé et consulté à propos de toute question susceptible de porter préjudice aux droits individuels des détenus.

Un mécanisme de recours hiérarchique a dès lors été établi dans le Règlement sur la détention préventive: les détenus s'entretiennent d'abord de toute question avec le Commandant du quartier pénitentiaire, qui est responsable devant le Greffier. En application du Règlement et du Règlement sur la détention préventive, le Greffier intervient à son tour, sous le contrôle du Président qui, comme mentionné ci-dessus, supervise les conditions de détention tant d'un point de vue administratif que judiciaire.

En effet, le Règlement sur la détention préventive permet aux détenus de solliciter l'examen par le Président de toute décision prise par le Greffier lorsque cellc-ci est susceptible de porter préjudice à leurs droits individuels.[8] Les détenus peuvent également soumettre des questions directement au Greffier ou au Président. De fait, le Président soumet toute question au Greffier dans le cas où ce dernier n'a pas encore pris de décision en premier ressort.[9]

Par conséquent, le Président est compétent en matière de détention pour: 1) évaluer les conditions de détention et s'assurer, lorsque les droits individuels des détenus sont en jeu, que le personnel du quartier pénitentiaire n'abuse pas de ses pouvoirs ni des procédures en vertu desquels il exerce un contrôle sur les prisonniers; 2) remédier s'il y a lieu à de tels abus dans le but d'améliorer les conditions de détention.

---

[7]Le Règlement sur la détention préventive a été adopté lors de la troisième Session plénière qui s'est tenue en mai 1994. Tandis qu'ils débattaient de la hiérarchie, les Juges ont envisagé la possibilité que ce soit le Président ou le Bureau, saisi par le Greffier, qui, après avoir consulté le Commandant, sollicite la collaboration des autorités du pays hôte s'agissant de toute question liée à la mise en œuvre de l'Accord de siège conclu entre le Tribunal et le pays hôte, par exemple en cas d'évasion.

[8]Cf. notamment articles 36*ter*, 66 et 76.

[9]Tandis qu'ils débattaient du Règlement sur la détention préventive, les Juges ont traité la question du contrôle des conditions de détention. Il fut décidé que les détenus devaient d'abord soumettre une plainte au Commandant. Dans le cadre de la procédure de plaintes, le fait que le Greffier ne dispose pas de toute l'indépendance nécessaire a également été soulignée; il est avant tout le chef de l'administration du Tribunal et a donc une fonction plus exécutive que judiciaire. Le rôle du Président a de même été considéré comme très problématique, parce que le fait même d'assumer cette fonction de contrôle pourrait l'empêcher de siéger par la suite au sein de la Chambre d'appel lorsque celle-ci examinerait l'appel au fond du même détenu. Le Président est également garant, devant le Conseil de Sécurité, de l'exécution des missions du Tribunal dans son ensemble et, en outre, assume, en cette qualité, un certain nombre de tâches administratives et de responsabilités liées au contrôle de la mise en œuvre des peines prononcées par le Tribunal.

2. La Pratique du Tribunal

La pratique du Tribunal confirme que les Juges ont pleinement exercé leur responsabilité s'agissant non seulement de la mise en détention mais également du contrôle des conditions de celle-ci. Au demeurant, la possibilité de traiter des questions relatives aux conditions de détention des accusés aux conférences de mise en état a été intégrée aux missions des Juges de la mise en état.[10] Nous allons donner ci-après quelques exemples du rôle joué par les Juges du Tribunal dans des questions relatives à la détention.

2.1 Restrictions aux contacts entre détenus

Dans l'affaire *le Procureur c./Delalić et autres* (Affaire no. IT-96-21-T), en se fondant sur l'article 33 du Règlement, sur l'article 85 du Règlement sur la détention préventive et sur certaines règles de détention, la Chambre de première instance a estimé que la décision du Greffier de refuser de communiquer au Procureur tout ou partie de certains documents confisqués aux détenus relevait de la compétence du Président. Cependant, pour le Procureur, il appartenait à la Chambre de première instance de se prononcer sur la question, en application des articles 72 A), 99 iv) et 54 du Règlement.

La question préliminaire était donc de savoir si le point soulevé relevait de la compétence du Président. Celui-ci a estimé que le litige découlait de l'exercice par le Greffier de ses responsabilités sur le quartier pénitentiaire. Aux termes du Règlement sur la détention préventive, les détenus peuvent se plaindre par écrit au Président. Le Président a donc conclu qu'il avait compétence pour trancher la question que lui avait renvoyée la Chambre de première instance et qu'il pouvait légitimement passer à l'examen de la question au fond.[11]

2.2 Requête du Défendeur relative à la mise sur écoute des appels téléphoniques

Un des accusés dans l'affaire *le Procureur c./Delalić et autres* (Affaire no. IT-96-21-T), a adressé au Président une requête aux fins de contester la décision de mise sur écoute de ses appels téléphoniques,[12] rendue par le Greffier en application de l'article 21 du Règlement interne définissant les modalités des visites et des communications avec les détenus.[13] L'accusé voulait connaître les détails des motifs sur lesquels se fondait la décision du

---

[10] Cf. article 65*bis* du Règlement.

[11] *Le Procureur c./Delalić et autres, Décision du Président sur la requête du Procureur afin de la production des notes échangées entre Zeijnil Delalić et Zdravko Mucić*, Affaire no. IT-96-21-T, TPIY Chambre de première instance II, 11 novembre 1996, Section III, p. A.

[12] *Le Procureur c./Delalić et autres, Demande concernant la surveillance des appels téléphoniques de M. Zdravko Mucić*, Affaire no. IT-96-21-T, TPIY Chambre de première instance II, 28 mai 1997.

[13] Document IT/98.

Greffier, afin de la contester devant le Président. C'est en définitive le Greffier qui a tranché la question, celle-ci ne mettant pas en cause la violation d'un droit fondamental de l'accusé.[14]

2.3 Modification des conditions de détention/mise en liberté provisoire/aptitude de l'accusé à être jugé

Dans l'affaire *le Procureur c/ Blaskić* (Affaire no. IT-95-14-PT), le Président a rendu une décision relative à la requête introduite par la Défense aux fins de modification des conditions de détention et, éventuellement, de sa mise en liberté provisoire, en application de l'article 64 du Règlement.[15] Le Président a ordonné que l'accusé soit transféré du quartier pénitentiaire vers un lieu où il serait assigné à résidence et où sa détention préventive serait assortie de conditions particulières et ce, jusqu'à ce que le Président en décide autrement ou jusqu'à la fin du procès en première instance et, le cas échéant, en appel. Le Greffe a été chargé d'assurer le suivi permanent de la détention et d'informer le Président dans les plus brefs délais. Le Président a ultérieurement modifié les conditions de détention en résidence surveillée suite aux requêtes introduites par l'accusé en vertu du même article 64 du Règlement.[16]

Dans l'affaire *le Procureur c./Delalić et autres* (Affaire no. IT-96-21-T), une requête a été introduite auprès de la Chambre de première instance aux fins d'obtenir la mise en liberté provisoire de l'un des accusés en application de l'article 65 du Règlement.[17] Une autre demande a été adressée à titre subsidiaire au Président sur la base de l'article 64, afin d'obtenir la modification des conditions de détention de l'un des accusés.[18] Dans le cadre de cette seconde requête, le Procureur a demandé au Président de donner au Greffier les consignes qui s'imposent pour modifier les conditions de détention de l'accusé de manière à ce qu'il bénéficie du soutien nécessaire pour demeurer apte à être jugé.[19] La Chambre de première

[14]*Le Procureur c./Delalić et autres, Décision* du Greffier en date du 19 juin 1997, Affaire no. IT-96-21-T, Chambre de première instance II.

[15]*Le Procureur c/ Blaškić, Décision sur la requête de la défense filée en vue de l'article 64 du Règlement,* Affaire No. IT-95-14-T, TPIY Chambre de première instance I, 3 avril 1996.

[16]*Le Procureur c./Delalić et autres, Décisions relatives aux requêtes de la défense demandant modification des conditions de détention du General Blaškić*, Affaire no. IT-95-14-T, TPIY Chambre de première instance I, 17 avril 1996, 9 mai 1996, 9 janvier 1997 et 26 mai 1997.

[17]Requête du conseil de la défense filée le 1er avril 1996 et réponse du Procureur filée le 2 avril 1996.

[18]*Le Procureur c./Delalić et autres, Demande aux fins de modifier les conditions de détention de l'accusé Esad Landzo adressée au Président conformément à l'article 64 du Règlement*, Affaire no. IT-96-21-T, TPIY Chambre de première instance II, 26 décembre 1996.

[19]*Le Procureur c./Delalić et autres, Réponse du Procureur à l'application devant le Président en vue de modifier les conditions de détention de l'accusé Esad Landzo conformément à l'article 64 du Règlement*, Affaire no. IT-96-21-T, TPIY Chambre de première instance II, 7 janvier 1997.

instance a, en application des articles 64 et 65 du Règlement, rejeté tant la demande de mise en liberté provisoire de l'accusé, que la demande de transfert vers un hôpital neuro-psychiatrique.[20]

Le Greffier, conformément à la demande du Président, a fait connaître son avis sur la question. Elle a affirmé qu'aux termes du Règlement et du Règlement sur la détention préventive, elle est responsable du quartier pénitentiaire sous le contrôle du Président. Elle a précisé que c'est le Président, et non les Chambres, qui est habilité à donner des instructions au Greffier à propos de toute question liée à la détention. Elle a fait valoir enfin, qu'en tout état de cause, il appartient au Greffier de veiller à ce que le Règlement sur la détention préventive soit correctement appliqué et à ce que les droits des accusés soient pleinement respectés.

Le Président a, en vertu de l'article 64 du Règlement, rejeté la demande de transfert de l'accusé en résidence surveillée ou vers un établissement médical et a enjoint au Greffier de prendre les mesures qui s'imposent pour préserver la santé mentale de l'accusé.

2.4 Correspondance entre le Président et le Greffe à propos des visites collectives

Le 28 octobre 1998, le Président a sollicité l'avis du Greffe à propos du refus – prétendument discriminatoire – de permettre à un groupe de détenus de recevoir des visites collectives. Le Greffier adjoint, après avoir consulté le Commandant du quartier pénitentiaire, a répondu au Président le 6 novembre 1998 en communiquant un aperçu des modalités des visites prévues par la réglementation en vigueur et applicables à tous les visiteurs du quartier pénitentiaire des Nations Unies.

2.5 Correspondance entre la Chambre de première instance et le Greffe à propos des restrictions imposées à un accusé en ce qui concerne les communications avec sa famille

En exécution d'une ordonnance en date du 17 septembre 1999, rendue par la Chambre de première instance III aux fins de modifier les restrictions imposées à un accusé en ce qui concerne les communications avec sa famille, le Greffier adjoint a été amené à examiner les difficultés pratiques de la mise en œuvre de ces restrictions dans un mémorandum intérieur daté du 24 septembre 1999. En accord avec les juges, l'exécution de l'ordonnance s'est faite sur la base des propositions faites par le greffe.

---

[20] *Le Procureur c./Delalić et autres, Décision sur la requête en vue de la libération provisoire filée par l'accusé Esad Landzo*, Affaire no. IT-96-21-T, TPIY Chambre de première instance II, 16 janvier 1997.

2.6 Correspondance entre le Président/le Greffier et les détenus à propos des conditions de détention en général

A l'initiative des détenus, une délégation de ceux-ci a rencontré le porte-parole du Tribunal au quartier pénitentiaire des Nations Unies les 10 et 12 août 1998. Ils ont exprimé leur souhait d'évoquer publiquement leurs conditions de détention en publiant une lettre ouverte au Président du Tribunal signée par tous les détenus. Le Greffier a consenti à cette demande et le Président a approuvé la publication de ladite lettre le 3 août 1998.

Le Tribunal s'est entretenu avec les autorités néerlandaises compétentes et, les 16 et 30 septembre 1998, le Président a répondu à la lettre ouverte des détenus en se penchant sur leurs préoccupations essentielles en matière de conditions de détention. Il a également précisé que, dans le cadre de l'enquête menée par l'un des juges du Tribunal sur le décès récent de deux détenus, les conditions de détention en vigueur à l'époque étaient examinées en vue de possibles améliorations. Une réponse plus détaillée aux griefs des détenus a donc été reportée jusqu'à ce que le Président prenne connaissance des recommandations du juge concerné.

2.7 Procédure de dépôt d'une plainte

Le Président, après avoir examiné la plainte officiellement adressée au Greffier le 21 avril 1997 par le détenu Duško Tadić et après avoir entendu toutes les parties intéressées, y compris le Commandant du quartier pénitentiaire, a considéré qu'il s'agissait d'une question d'intérêt général ou d'ordre administratif, et a invité le Greffier à prendre des mesures supplémentaires pour veiller au maintien de l'ordre dans le quartier pénitentiaire.

3. Les Normes Internationales et Nationales

3.1 Normes internationales

En vertu des normes internationales pertinentes relatives aux droits de l'homme, notamment la Convention européenne des Droits de l'Homme ainsi que la jurisprudence qui s'en est dégagée,[21] une autorité judiciaire

---

[21]P.ex. *Letellier c France, arrêt du 26 juin 1991, CEDH série A, vol. 207.* Selon la requérante, qui contestait la légalité de sa détention devant le juge d'instruction d'abord, puis devant la chambre d'accusation en tant qu'instance de recours, l'insuffisance du contrôle judiciaire n'a pas permis d'atteindre les objectifs poursuivis. La Cour, compte tenu des circonstances de l'espèce, n'était pas convaincue que la détention préventive prolongée de la requérante se justifiait: [...] «les considérations stéréotypées de la chambre d'accusation n'étaient guère compatibles avec la vigilance constante dont les juridictions nationales doivent faire preuve pour assurer la protection appropriée des intérêts de l'individu détenu dans l'attente de son procès».

dotée de l'indépendance et de l'objectivité requises pour permettre un recours judiciaire effectif doit être investie du pouvoir de contrôler les conditions de détention imposées par les autorités administratives.

Le droit à un recours effectif est consacré par l'article 13 de la Convention européenne des Droits de l'Homme,[22] l'article 8 de la Déclaration universelle des droits de l'homme,[23] et par l'article 2.3) du Pacte international relatif aux droits civils et politiques.[24]

En effet, pour protéger les droits des détenus, il est primordial que ceux-ci puissent se plaindre auprès d'organes indépendants concernant toute question liée à leurs conditions de détention.

3.2 Normes nationales

3.2.1 Systèmes de tradition romano-germanique

Dans certains pays de tradition romano-germanique, il a été affirmé que les juges ne disposaient pas tous des compétences requises en matière pénitentiaire et n'étaient pas tous suffisamment au fait des exigences administratives. À la lumière de cet argument, un compromis s'est dégagé, qui a abouti à la création d'une fonction de magistrat spécifiquement chargé de l'exécution des peines, dont les responsabilités juridictionnelles s'accompagnent d'une fonction de contrôle administratif des conditions de détention. Il en va notamment ainsi du juge de l'application des peines en France et du *Juez de Vigilancia Penitenciaria* en Espagne.[25]

En droit français, «le juge de l'application des peines, le juge d'instruction, le président de la chambre d'accusation ainsi qu'il est dit à l'article 222, le procureur de la République et le procureur général visitent les établissements pénitentiaires. Auprès de tout établissement pénitentiaire est instituée une commission de surveillance dont la composition et les attributions sont déterminées par décret» [...].[26] Dans la pratique, en matière de détention provisoire, c'est le juge d'instruction compétent qui supervise les conditions de celle-ci en première ressort et la chambre d'accusation en appel.

3.2.2 Systèmes de Common Law

(i) Royaume-Uni

En vertu de la loi de 1952 sur les prisons, le ministre de l'Intérieur peut prendre des dispositions aux fins de réglementer et d'administrer les établissements de détention préventive, ainsi que des dispositions

[22] 213 RTNU 221; 4 novembre 1950.

[23] R.A.G. 217A (III); 10 décembre 1948.

[24] R.A.G. 2200A (XXI); 16 décembre 1966.

[25] Le rôle de ces magistrats spécialisés est toutefois *essentiellement* (en droit espagnol) ou *exclusivement* (en droit français) lié aux détenus qui ont été condamnés.

[26] Voir article 727 du Code de procédure pénale.

concernant la classification, le traitement, l'emploi, la discipline et le contrôle des personnes qui y sont détenues.

C'est le ministre de l'Intérieur qui est officiellement responsable du système pénitentiaire devant le Parlement. Des fonctionnaires dûment autorisés par le ministre de l'Intérieur visitent les prisons pour inspecter leur état général, contrôler le traitement dont les prisonniers font l'objet et pour se renseigner sur toute autre question indiquée par le ministre. Le *Chief inspector* procède à l'inspection régulière des divers établissements et enquête sur des incidents ou des situations spécifiques sur instruction du ministre de l'Intérieur. Par contre, il n'a aucune compétence en ce qui concerne les griefs individuels.

Il existe également un *conseil des visiteurs*, chargé d'enquêter et de faire rapport sur toute question à la demande du ministre de l'Intérieur. En cas d'extrême nécessité, cet organe peut également suspendre tout fonctionnaire dans l'attente d'une décision du ministre. Toutefois, le conseil doit demander l'avis du directeur de la prison avant de prendre une décision d'éventuelle portée disciplinaire.

Les *magistrates* peuvent à tout moment visiter une prison située sur le territoire dans le ressort duquel ils exercent les fonctions de juge de paix ou dans laquelle est incarcéré un détenu ayant commis une infraction dans leur ressort territorial. Ils peuvent examiner l'état des prisons et contrôler les conditions de détention des prisonniers. Ils peuvent aussi inscrire dans le registre des visiteurs, tenu par le directeur de la prison, des remarques relatives à l'état de la prison ou à d'éventuels abus. Ces observations doivent être notifiées au conseil des visiteurs lors de sa visite suivante. Les magistrats ne peuvent toutefois pas s'entretenir avec les détenus de questions étrangères au traitement qui leur est réservé dans la prison.

(ii) États-Unis

La législation américaine permet aux prisonniers d'introduire une action en justice lorsqu'ils estiment que leurs droits ont été violés dans le cadre de leur détention préventive. Ce recours trouve généralement son fondement dans la Constitution américaine. La portée des garanties constitutionnelles est limitée et le système judiciaire ne permet pas aux détenus d'obtenir réparation pour toutes les violations de droits de l'homme qu'ils subissent pendant leur détention. Les moyens dont disposent les tribunaux pour garantir l'exécution de leurs décisions sont limités, surtout lorsque des mesures correctives s'imposent.

Les détenus ayant introduit une action, tout comme les autorités administratives, sont appelés à témoigner. De surcroît, certaines juridictions recourent aux services d'experts qui donnent leur avis sur les conditions de détention. Il arrive parfois que les juges aillent se rendre compte personnellement de la situation.

4. Conclusion

Les conditions de détention se sont améliorées sous l'effet de la pratique du Tribunal en matière de contrôle par le Président ou par les juges (*stricto sensu*) des actes de l'administration du quartier pénitentiaire. Les systèmes romano-germanistes prévoient en général un contrôle juridictionnel des conditions de détention imposées par les directeurs de prison. Les systèmes de *Common Law* autorisent même les détenus à s'adresser directement aux juges pour contester leurs conditions de détention bien que la portée des garanties est limitée.

Le Tribunal a mis en œuvre un système mixte : le contrôle des décisions prises par le Greffier ou, au nom de celui-ci, par l'administration du quartier pénitentiaire, appartient exclusivement au Président. Les détenus peuvent soumettre toute question directement au Greffier qui, le cas échéant, peut la transmettre au Président pour examen. Ils peuvent également s'adresser directement au Président qui consulte le Greffier dans le cas où ce dernier n'a encore rendu aucune décision en premier ressort.

En outre, les juges ont également un rôle à jouer quant aux conditions de détention en général, qu'ils peuvent modifier,[27] ainsi qu'en tant qu'autorité chargée d'inspecter le quartier pénitentiaire.[28] On peut donc affirmer que, dans le régime instauré par le Tribunal, le Président combine certains pouvoirs juridictionnels avec une fonction de contrôle administratif des conditions de détention. Seules les questions spécifiquement prévues par le Règlement, à savoir la mise en liberté provisoire, font l'objet d'un véritable examen juridictionnel *stricto sensu*.[29]

On pourrait aussi envisager de réserver le contentieux de la détention au Président et, partant, de lui conférer la compétence exclusive d'établir et de modifier les conditions de détention. Néanmoins, les juges semblent être l'organe le mieux à même de trancher ces questions en toute impartialité et sans idée préconçue. En tant qu'organe indépendant, ils devraient au moins être habilités à donner des instructions et faire des suggestions concernant les conditions et le régime de détention. Les autorités administratives, sous la supervision du Greffier et du Président, devraient être chargées d'exécuter ces instructions et d'informer le Tribunal, dans un délai donné, de leur mise en œuvre.

Examinons enfin l'importance que pourrait revêtir le développement parallèle de voies de recours extrajudiciaires permettant d'améliorer les conditions de détention et, notamment, l'introduction de mécanismes destinés à répondre efficacement aux griefs des détenus. De tels mécanismes

---

[27]Aux termes de l'article 24 du Règlement, les juges se réunissent en plénière pour la détermination ou le contrôle des conditions de détention. En conséquence, les propositions visant à modifier les diverses dispositions réglementaires pertinentes ne peuvent être examinées, voire adoptées, qu'en session plénière.

[28]Voir note 6 plus haut.

[29]Article 65 du Règlement.

ont déjà été mis en œuvre au quartier pénitentiaire et permettent notamment aux détenus de s'adresser à des inspecteurs indépendants[30] ou au Greffier adjoint qui assure un suivi régulier des conditions de détention. Aucun de ces mécanismes ne doit toutefois empêcher les détenus de s'adresser officiellement au Président.

[30]Le Comité International de la Croix Rouge a des contacts réguliers avec les détenus et fait un rapport au Tribunal à la suite de ses visites.

HOWARD MORRISON*

10. Judicial Independence – Impartiality and Disqualification

The growth in the number of International Courts and Tribunals since the end of the Second World War has generated a rapid demand for International Judges. Jurisdictions range from the ad hoc mandates over the former Yugoslavia and Rwanda, the broader international jurisdictions of such as the International Court of Justice and the European Court of Human Rights to the more specific and, perhaps, esoteric determinations of more regionally based Courts and Tribunals concerned, *inter alia*, with trade, commercial, maritime and investment disputes and human rights.

Holding sway over all of the various Judges of this distinguished array of judicial entities, however, are the same vital principles of judicial independence that set apart truly fair and objective systems of national courts from those few remaining totalitarian and corrupt regimes that, at best, serve to remind us all of what Sir Ninian Stephen, a former judge of the ICTY, described as "the fragile bastion" which is judicial independence.[1]

Those principles have been reflected recently in a number of important cases, perhaps none so well-reported, nor illustrative of the foundations of judicial independence and impartiality, than the United Kingdom House of Lords decision concerning the role of Lord Hoffman in the *Pinochet* case.[2] The involvement of Lord Hoffman with Amnesty International was never claimed to have actually influenced any of his decision making. In dealing with the fundamental principle as to faith in the transparency of any judicial process, Lord Nolan said "in any case where the impartiality of a judge is in question the appearance of the matter is just as important as the reality."[3]

---

*Howard Morrison is an English barrister who has experience as both co-counsel and Lead Counsel before the ICTY and ICTR, in the latter case defending the former Rwanda cabinet minister Justin Mugenzi on charges of genocide. He also sits judicially as a Recorder of the Crown Court in the UK.

[1]Report of the World Jurists Association 1991, p. 529.

[2]*Regina v. Bow Street Metropolitan Stipendiary Magistrate and others, Ex Parte Pinochet Ugarte* (no.2) [H.L.(E.)] 2 W.L.R. 1999.

[3]Id., p. 288.

R. May et al., Essays on ICTY Procedure and Evidence in Honour of Gabrielle Kirk McDonald, 111–120.

For his part, Lord Hutton stated:

> In his judgement in *Regina v. Gough* [1993] AC 646, my noble and learned friend Lord Goff of Chievely, made reference to the great importance of confidence in the integrity of the administration of justice, and he said: "In any event, there is an overriding public interest that there should be confidence in the administration of justice, which is always associated with the statement of Lord Hewart C.J. in *Rex v. Sussex Justices, Ex Parte McCarthy* [1924] 1 K.B. 256, that it is of fundamental importance that justice should not only be done, but should manifestly and undoubtedly be seen to be done."[4]

With respect, it seems self-evident that "undoubtedly" is the key consideration; the removal of doubt as to true independence and impartiality is the touchstone of faith in the system in respect of both those who are affected and those who merely observe.

Such is the fundamental importance of the correlation between independence, impartiality and disqualification, that it is to be found in every governing Article or Statute of any International Covenant, Declaration or Convention concerning the judiciary.

The historical roots are impressive. As long ago as 1328 The Statute of Northampton recognised the importance in England of an independent judiciary, declaring that a royal command should not disturb the course of the common law and stating that, should such a command be issued, the judges were to ignore it.[5] By the early seventeenth century, Sir Edward Coke, Chief Justice of England, maintained that, "the King cannot change any part of the common law, nor create any offence by his proclamation, without Parliament, which was not an offence before."[6] In the Act of Settlement of 1701, it was enshrined that judges should be appointed for life, allowing only for their removal on the grounds of serious offences. With the publication of *De l'espirit des lois* in 1748, Montesquieu gave form to judicial independence as part of the doctrine of the separation of powers. He wrote:

> When the legislative and executive powers are united in the same person, or in the same body of magistrates, there can be no liberty. Again, there is no liberty if the judicial power be not separated from the legislative and the executive. Were it joined with the legislative, the life and liberty of the subject would be exposed to arbitrary control for the judge would be the legislator. Were it joined to the executive power, the judge might behave with violence and oppression. There would be an end to everything, were the same man, or the same body, whether of the nobles or of the people, to exercise those three

[4] Id., p. 292.
[5] Statute of Northampton 1328. Stat. Realm [1328].
[6] Coke's Reports 1572–1616.

> powers, that of enacting laws, that of executing the public resolutions, and that of trying the cases of individuals.[7]

Apart from the obvious innate value in any subjective case, the essential importance of an independent judiciary is the role that such independence plays in safeguarding fundamental liberties and human rights. As much is expressed in, or implied from, various international and regional instruments, beginning with the Universal Declaration of Human Rights. Article 10 of the Declaration provides:

> Everyone is entitled in full equality to a fair public hearing by an independent and impartial tribunal in the determination of his rights and obligations of any criminal charge against him.[8]

Further, Article 14 of the International Covenant on Civil and Political Rights provides, *inter alia*,

> All persons shall be equal before the courts and tribunals in the determination of any criminal charge against him, or of his rights and obligations in a suit at law, everyone shall be entitled to fair and public hearing by a competent, independent and impartial tribunal established by law.[9]

The importance of such an institution in a democracy was again reiterated with greater emphasis in the Vienna Declaration and Programme for Action in 1993. In paragraph 27, the Member States present declared, *inter alia*,

> Every state should provide an effective framework of remedies to address human rights grievances of violations. The administration of justice including law enforcement and prosecutorial agencies and, especially, an independent judiciary and legal profession in full conformity with applicable standards contained in international human rights instruments, are essential to the full and non-discriminatory realization of human rights and indispensable to the processes of democracy and sustainable development.

On the regional levels, Article 8(1) of the American Convention on Human Rights[10] ("Pact of San Jose, Costa Rica") provides:

> Every person has the right to a hearing with due guarantees and within a reasonable time, by a competent, independent, and impartial tribunal previously established by law, in the substantiation of any accusation of a criminal

---

[7]As quoted by M.J.C.Vile, Constitution and the Separation of Powers (1967).
[8]UN Doc. A/811 (10 Dec. 1948) ("Declaration").
[9]999 UNTS 171 (16 Dec. 1966) ("Covenant").
[10]1144 UNTS 123 (22 Nov. 1969).

> nature made against him or for the determination of his rights and obligations of a civil, labour, fiscal or any other nature.

Article 6(1) of the European Convention for the Protection of Human Rights[11] provides:

> In the determination of his civil rights and obligations or any criminal charge against him, everyone is entitled to a fair and public hearing within a reasonable time by independent and impartial tribunal established by law.

Article 7 of the African Charter on Human and People's Rights[12] provides:

> Every individual shall have the right to have his cause heard. This comprises:
>
> (a) the right to an appeal to competent national organs against acts of violating his fundamental rights as recognized and guaranteed by conventions, laws, regulations and customs in force;
>
> (b) the right to be presumed innocent until proved guilty by a competent court or tribunal;
>
> (c) the right to defence, including the right to be defended by counsel of his choice;
>
> (d) the right to be tried within a reasonable time by impartial court or tribunal.

It will be noted that, while the Declaration and the Covenant together with the American and European Conventions refer to an "independent and impartial tribunal", the Vienna Declaration refers to an "independent judiciary" and the African Charter to an "impartial court or tribunal".

In a landmark judgment on judicial independence delivered by the Supreme Court of Canada recently, Antonio Lamer, C.J., said:

> Judicial independence is valued because it serves important social goals, it is a means to secure those goals. One of those goals is the maintenance of public confidence in the impartiality of the judiciary, which is essential to the effectiveness of the court system. Independence contributes to the perception that justice will be done in individual cases. Another social goal served by judicial independence is the maintenance of the rule of law, one aspect of which is the constitutional principle that the exercise of all public power must find its ultimate source in a legal rule.[13]

---

[11] 213 UNTS 221 (4 Nov. 1950).

[12] 21 ILM 58 (27 June 1981).

[13] *Re. Remuneration of Judges of the Provincial Court of Prince Edward Island and the Jurisdiction of the Legislature in Respect thereof* [1998] 2 S.C.R. 443.

It seems clear that the concept of judicial independence, and the separation of executive and judicial office, is not simply a right, requirement or obligation which is personal to an individual judge or judicial body. It is not analogous to a legal privilege which a holder may waive when it best suits him. Rather, it is a fundamental and constituent part of both natural law and natural justice going to the root and foundation of the rule of law.

The essence of judicial independence and impartiality was formulated succinctly by Dr. L. M. Singhvi in his final report to the UN Sub-Commission on Prevention of Discrimination and Protection of Minorities:

> Judges must be impartial and independent and free from any restrictions, inducements, pressures, threats or interference, direct or indirect, and should have the qualities of conscientiousness, equipoise, courage, objectivity, understanding, humanity and learning because those are the prerequisites of a fair trial and credible and reliable adjudication.[14]

In a similar vein, the Supreme Court of Canada in the case of *Valente v. The Queen*[15] observed that "[judicial] independence focused on the status of the court or tribunal in its relationship with others particularly the executive branch of the Government". The Court went on to add that the traditional objective guarantees for judicial independence must be supplemented with the requirement that the court or tribunal be reasonably perceived as independent. The reason for this additional requirement was that the guarantee of judicial independence has the goal not only of ensuring that justice is done in individual cases, but also of ensuring public confidence in the justice system. The Court further added:

> Without that confidence the system cannot command the respect and acceptance that are essential to its effective operation. It is, therefore, important that a tribunal should be perceived as independent, as well as impartial, and that the test for independence should include that perception.[16]

It can be concluded that the greater part of judicial independence is the perception of the independence of the Tribunal as an entity.

If that is true for the national public perception of a national court, then how much greater, in the overall amalgam of jurisprudence and lay confidence, is the need for a positive international perception of an international tribunal. The only two universal treaties establishing international adjudicative organs include in their statutes express provisions forbidding judges from exercising "any political or administrative function". Article 16(1) of the Statute of the International Court of Justice provides

---

[14]Commission on Human Rights, E/CN.4Sub.2/1985/18/Add.l, 38th session, 22 July 1985 at para. 76.

[15][1985] 2 S.C.R. 673.

[16]Id.

that "no member of the Court may exercise any political or administrative function, or engage in any other occupation of a professional nature". The second judicial organ to which all States of the international community may be party, the International Tribunal for the Law of the Sea, incorporates verbatim the provisions of Article 16(1) of the International Courts Statute and defines the subject matter further:

> [N]o member of the Tribunal may exercise any political or administrative function, or associate actively or be financially interested in any of the operations of any enterprise concerned with the exploration for, or exploitation of, the resources of the sea or the sea-bed or other commercial use of the sea or the sea-bed.[17].

Beyond the provisions found in these universal treaties, States have also shown, through the establishment of regional courts, that the requirement of judicial independence is a part of State practice. The fact that the 1950 Convention for the Protection of Human Rights and Fundamental Freedoms, establishing the European Court of Human Rights, did not have provisions requiring the independence of its judges was not lost on the Council of Europe. Thus, in drawing up Protocol No. 11, which came into force on 1 November 1998, the Council determined that a criterion for office would be that "judges shall not engage in any activity that is incompatible with their independence, impartiality or with the demands of full time office".[18]

More precise in their nature are the provisions of the Inter-American system as found in both the American Convention on Human Rights and in the statute of the Inter-American court. The Inter-American court would seem to have the most explicit and restrictive annunciation of occupations that are incompatible with being a judge at the international level. While the American Convention provides that the position of Judge of the court is incompatible with any other activity that might affect the independence or impartiality of such a judge, the Statute of the court goes further by determining that the position of a judge of the Inter-American Court of Human Rights is incompatible with the following oppositions and activities:

> Members or high-ranking officials of the executive branch of government, except for those who hold positions that do not place them under the direct control of the executive branch and those of diplomatic agents who are not chiefs of missions to the OAS or to any of its member states.[19]

---

[17]Art. 7, United Nations Convention on the Law of the Sea (Annex VI-Statute of the International Tribunal for the Law of the Sea).

[18]Art. 21, Protocol No. 11 to the Convention for the Protection of Human Rights. [11 May 1994] ETS n. 155.

[19]Art. 18, Statute of the I-ACHR, OAS Res. 448 (IX-0/79), OAS Off. Rec. OEA/Ser.P/IX.o.2/80, Vol. 1, p. 98.

Opinio juris on the issue of judicial independence was expressed recently as a by-product of the movement towards establishing an International Criminal Court. The 1998 Rome Statute provides that a judge may not participate in a case where his or her impartiality may be questioned. The Prosecutor or an accused may request disqualification of a judge for lack of impartiality.[20] The court may also determine whether the activities or additional occupations of a judge are compatible with the office he or she holds, pursuant to Articles 40(2)-(4). In that regard the ICC broadly follows the contemplation of Rule 15(A) of the ICTY and ICTR Rules of Evidence and Procedure, notably that "a judge may not sit at a trial or appeal in any case in which he has a personal interest or concerning which he has or has had any association which might affect his impartiality". As always, it is the interpretation in practice that is of moment rather than a mere recitation of noble ideals in the formality of the text.

The United Nations International Law Commission completed a draft statute for the International Criminal Court that included a provision, which reads, *inter alia*, that:

> Judges shall not engage in any activity which is likely to interfere with their judicial functions or to affect confidence in their independence. In particular they shall not while holding the office of judge be a member of the legislative or executive branches of the Government of State, or of a body responsible for the investigation or prosecution of crimes.[21]

In its commentary to this Article, the International Law Commission amplifies its understanding that a judge is not to be "a member of the legislative or executive branches."[22] The Preparatory Committee on the Establishment of an International Criminal Court requested proposals from States to supplement the International Law Commission's draft. With respect to Article 10, no State took issue with the notion that judges would violate their independence if they were a member of the legislative or executive branches.

It is evident that beyond customary norms there is a general principle of law precluding an international judge from being a member of any municipal government's executive organ. A "general principle of law" is a rule common to the internal laws of the majority of States. According to a former Judge of the International Court of Justice, Kotaro Tanaka, the

---

[20] Id., Art. 41(2).

[21] Arts. 10(1) and (2) of the International Law Commission Draft Statute for an International Criminal Court in Yearbook of the International Law Commission, Volume 11, (Part 2), 1994, p. 32. Since no State raised any negative observations – even at the discussion stage – when signing the Treaty of Rome, this may be taken as a settled legal view.

[22] Id.

> Principle of independence of judges and other provisions concerning the judicial administrations are more or less the same in almost all civilized nations. It is not an exaggeration to mention that there exist general principles of law recognized by civilized nations [Article 38, paragraph 2 of the Statute of the Court] or a world law, namely a unified law on this matter.[23]

Judge Tanaka goes on to say that the criteria required of International Judges are the same as those for municipal judges: "The principle of the independence of judges in general can be conceived as one of the general principles of law recognized by civilized nations."[24]

In addition, the UN Special Rapporteur also considers that judicial independence is a general principle. In relation to the underlying concepts of judicial independence and impartiality, which the Special Rapporteur asserts are "general principles of law recognised by civilised nations" in the sense of Article 38(1)(c) of the Statute of the International Court of Justice, the Special Rapporteur quoted the following passages of Mr Singhvi's lucid final report to the Sub-Commission in 1985:

> Historical analysis and contemporary profiles of the judicial functions and the machinery of justice shows the worldwide recognition of the distinctive role of the judiciary. The principles of impartiality and independence are the hallmarks of the rationale and the legitimacy of the judicial function in every State. The concepts or the impartiality and independence of the judiciary postulate individual attributes as well as institutional conditions. These are not mere vague nebulous ideas but fairly precise concepts in municipal and international law. Their absence leads to a denial of justice and makes the credibility of the judicial process dubious. It needs to be stressed that impartiality and independence of the judiciary is more a human right of the consumers of justice than a privilege of the judiciary for its own sake.[25]

In the context of this book it is interesting to see how this important facet of jurisprudence is reflected in the framework and concluded decisions at the ICTY. ICTY Rule 15(A) sets out the fundamental principle:

> A Judge may not sit on a trial or appeal in any case in which he has a personal interest or concerning which the Judge has or has had any association which might affect his or her impartiality. The Judge shall in any such circumstances withdraw, and the President shall assign another Judge to the case.

It would only follow the golden rule of "justice being seen to be done" if that subsection were to be read as if the first sentence included the phrase "or

[23]Kotaro Tanaka, "Independence of International Judges", Comunicazioni e Studi, Vol. 14, 1997.

[24]Id., pp. 859–860.

[25]Id., paras. 34–35.

might appear to any observer to..." after the word "might" in the text. The words "shall in any such circumstances withdraw..." are plainly, and, with respect, essentially, imperative.

The principle has given rise to legal debate and determination in several cases before the ICTY. In subpoena proceedings in the *Blaškić* case in April 1997,[26] Judge McDonald, who had issued the original order at issue in those proceedings, was requested by the Government of Croatia to recuse herself from participating in the hearing by virtue of her having issued the disputed order. Croatia specifically stated in the request, "Although we do not doubt your integrity, we believe that both the appearance and substance of fairness and due process require you not to take part in this hearing, or in determining the validity of the subpoena at issue".[27]

Judge McDonald requested that the matter be referred to the Bureau of the Tribunal, the latter considering the issues pursuant to Rule 15 and rejecting the recusal request, fundamentally upon the basis that as a professional Judge, Judge McDonald would be able to determine the matter at issue with all proper independence, the fact that Judge McDonald had issued the subpoena being removed from jurisprudential tests as to its validity.

It is noteworthy that it was Judge McDonald herself who invited *amicus curiae* Briefs to be prepared to assist in the determination of the powers of a Judge or Trial Chamber of the ICTY to issue a *subpoena duces tecum* to a sovereign State or to a high government official of a State and the appropriate remedies for ensuing non-compliance with respect to such a *subpoena*.

In May 1998, following the application by the accused for the disqualification of Judge Jorda and Judge Riad in the *Kordić* and *Čerkez* case,[28] it was determined by the Bureau that it was not a ground for disqualification for Judges to be allocated to sit in separate trials arising out of the same series of events; in these instances the allegations of 'ethnic cleansing' by Bosnian Croat forces in central Bosnia in 1992–93.

In the 4 May 1998 decision the Bureau held:

> [...] It does not follow that a judge is disqualified from hearing two or more criminal trials arising out of the same series of events, where he is exposed to evidence relating to these events in both cases. This applies also to the situation where an accused in the later case was previously named as a co-accused in the first indictment. A judge is presumed to be impartial. In this case there is nothing to rebut that presumption.

The decision is, perhaps, unremarkable in that the application was misconstrued from a Rule 15 viewpoint. The determination of guilt in these, as in any cases, is dependent upon the subjective assessment of evidence rather

---

[26] *Prosecutor v. Blaškić*, Indictment, Case No. IT-95-14-T.
[27] *Prosecutor v. Blaškić*, Order, Case No. IT-95-14-PT, 14 March 1997.
[28] IT- 95-14/2-T

than any judicial disposition influenced, or potentially influenced, by extra-evidential associations.

What is perhaps worthy of a cautious approach, is the possible interpretation that the presumption of impartiality is an equivalent presumption to that of innocence in an accused. The real distinction is that the *appearance* of impartiality is the key.

In March 1999, following a post-trial application in the *Furundžija* case, the Bureau held, perhaps unsurprisingly on the facts, that an application for the disqualification of a Judge had to be made during the trial before any judgement was issued. Plainly, if a matter only came to light following a determination, as in the *Pinochet* case, then wholly different considerations must apply. It is noteworthy that the application by *Furundžija*[29] relied extensively upon the *Pinochet* judgement.

The most important determination of the principle of justice not only being done, but manifestly being seen to be done, is likely to be determined in the forthcoming appeal in the *Čelebići*[30] case concerning the appointment to the Vice Presidency of Costa Rica by the then sitting Judge, Judge Odio-Benito, and her involvement as a trustee in a UN fund committed to the relief of victims of torture whilst trying a case where torture featured on the indictment.

Concerns as to raising contentious matters that are subject to *sub judice* considerations rightly preclude any detailed comment.

The factual determinations to date, however, revolve around the decision of the Bureau of 4 September 1998 when it was held that the assumption of the office of Vice-President of Costa Rica did not disqualify Judge Odio-Benito on the basis that she was not exercising any political or administrative function and had undertaken not to until she had completed her judicial duties.

The determination of the appeal as to that decision will plainly go to the practical interpretation of the safeguards contained in Rule 15 as well as the broader determinations of the standard of "independence" set out in Article 12 and "impartiality" set out in Article 13 of the Statute.

The upholding of the integrity and impartiality of International Courts and Tribunals is a task inseparable from the maintenance of the amalgam of judicial independence and impartiality. The basics are not difficult to achieve. When a person accepts a judicial post he or she declares and forsakes all political and executive positions for at least the tenure of the judicial appointment; if the choice is later made to take up or resume any such position it is preceded by resignation. Self-disqualification sends out a clear signal of truly independent integrity.

The signal to all will be clear; international Judges are as independent and honourable as any. A signal which is simple, effective and essential.

---

[29]Dated 3rd February 1999, Case No. IT-95-17/1-A.

[30]IT-96-21-A. Oral arguments were heard in the case from 5–8 June 2000.

PART IV

Indictments

MICHAEL J. KEEGAN* and DARYL A. MUNDIS**

11. Legal Requirements for Indictments

1. Introductory Issues

The drafting of an indictment or charging document in many national jurisdictions is considered to be an almost mechanical step in the pre-trial process. National requirements for a legally sufficient indictment are well defined in the applicable codes and jurisprudence. In most instances, the facts and circumstances of the subject crime involve a single act or event and one accused. Even when dealing with "multiple crimes" or "multiple defendants," the number of acts or perpetrators is generally small. Thus, the drafting of the indictment or charging document for the average national case is a comparatively simple exercise and all parties to a criminal proceeding are well aware of what is required for a valid indictment. Nevertheless, despite hundreds of years of jurisprudence or statutory

*Michael J. Keegan is a Legal Officer in the ICTY Office of the Prosecutor and a graduate of Case Western Reserve University School of Law and Northeastern University. He has prosecuted several cases, including *Tadić, Kovačević, Omarska, Keraterm, Brđjanin & Talić*. He is a former Judge Advocate in the U.S. Marine Corps and was recently appointed as the first Prosecutor General for East Timor by UNTAET.

**Daryl A. Mundis is an Associate Legal Officer in the OTP and is assigned to the *Foča, Keraterm* and *Nikolić* cases. He was formerly an Associate Legal Officer in the Office of President McDonald and a U.S. Navy Judge Advocate and is a graduate of the London School of Economics (LLM *with Merit*), Columbia (MIA and JD *with Honours in Foreign and Comparative Law*), and Manhattanville College (BA *magna cum laude*).

The views expressed herein are solely those of the authors and are not to be imputed to the UN or the ICTY.

R. May et al., Essays on ICTY Procedure and Evidence in Honour of Gabrielle Kirk McDonald, 123–136.

requirements, there are still objections to the form or substance of indictments raised on a daily basis in national courts in regard to these "simple" cases.

For the International Criminal Tribunal for the former Yugoslavia ("ICTY"), the unique nature of its mandate and operations has made the development of indictments anything but simple. Since the Trial Chambers must evaluate the evidence to determine the guilt or innocence of the accused in light of the charges set forth in the indictment, it is important that the indictment conform to the technical legal requirements set forth in the Statute, Rules of Procedure and Evidence ("Rules") and jurisprudence of the ICTY. Several factors may necessitate amending the indictment, however, raising other issues. For example, despite intensive investigations, additional information concerning uncharged criminal conduct may come to light during the time between indictment and arrest, or even during the trial itself. Moreover, since many of the ICTY indictments charge more than one individual with offences, other potential issues arise when only one of the multiple indictees is arrested.

To give the proper perspective to the issue of drafting indictments, one has to consider both the mandate and character of the ICTY. For those of us at the ICTY charged with drafting the first indictments there was an absolute lack of any well-defined statutory standards, judicial precedents, or prior indictments to look to. We were guided only by the general requirements of the ICTY Statute and Rules. Additionally, the nature of the crimes within the mandate of the ICTY is drastically different from the national prosecution experience of any individual. There is no legal system in the world that deals on a routine basis with the types of cases that fall within the mandate of the ICTY or with the limitations that the ICTY faces in the exercise of its jurisdiction. The ICTY is the first international criminal tribunal since the Nuremberg and Tokyo War Crimes Trials with the mandate to prosecute serious violations of international humanitarian law. It is also significant that the conflict from which its mandate arose was still ongoing at the time the ICTY began its operations. Thus, the Office of the Prosecutor ("OTP") began drafting indictments during the conduct of ongoing hostilities and investigations.

Any review of the development of indictments at the ICTY must also take account of the fact that the Tribunal is international in character as well as name. It is made up of professionals from many different cultures and legal systems, all of whom view the requirements of the Tribunal's Statute and Rules from the perspective of their professional experience, training and national legal system. These various viewpoints reflect the differences, both in terms of concepts and procedures, of the various legal systems of the world. Therefore, even a simple issue such as what an indictment should look like generates many different opinions.

The task gets even more difficult when considering the issue of what degree of detail is necessary to meet the statutory requirement that a *prima facie* case exists or what amounts to a concise statement of facts.[1] In national legal systems, procedural issues such as the form of the indictments and the statutory or legal requirements for sufficient pleadings is well developed and understood. Although in national legal systems there is usually jurisprudence governing the type of information required for a sufficient indictment and the particular form that it should take, no such jurisprudence existed in the early years at the ICTY. It was left to the Prosecutor to determine what the indictment should look like and what level of information was sufficient to meet the requirements of the Statute and the Rules.

The development of the form of ICTY indictments has been a long and difficult process; one that is still undergoing a course of development and refinement. This process has primarily occurred through the ongoing internal review process of the OTP and decisions rendered by the Appeals and Trial Chambers of the ICTY as a result of motions brought both by the Prosecution and the Defence.[2] The issues raised by the parties in their motions have generally fallen into two broad categories, the form of the indictment and amendments of the indictment.

---

[1]See ICTY Statute Articles 18(4) and 21(4)(a) and Rule 47(C) of the ICTY Rules. Article 18(4) of the Statute states that "[u]pon determination that a *prima facie* case exists, the Prosecutor shall prepare an indictment containing a concise statement of the facts and the crime or crimes with which the accused is charged under the Statute." Article 21(4)(a) provides that the accused shall be entitled "to be informed promptly and in detail in a language he understands of the nature and cause of the charge against him". The definition of "nature" and "cause" appear to be self-evident. The "nature" of the charge is a full description of the legal characterisation of the charge, that is, the specific provision of the ICTY Statute that has allegedly been violated. The "cause" of the charge is the factual basis or description of the charge, the "concise statement of the facts of the case." It is Rule 47 that fleshes out the requirements of Articles 18 and 21. Rule 47(C) requires that the Indictment "set forth the name and particulars of the suspect and a concise statement of the facts of the case and of the crime with which the suspect is charged." Rule 47(B) requires that the Prosecutor prepare supporting material with the Indictment to forward to the Confirming Judge. Rule 47(E) states the purpose of the supporting material. It directs that the "reviewing Judge shall examine each of the counts of the indictment, and any supporting materials the Prosecutor may provide, to determine [...] whether a case exists against the suspect." Thus, Rule 47(E) of the Tribunal Rules recognises that the purpose of the supporting material is to assist the reviewing Judge to determine if there is a *prima facie* case. It directs that the reviewing Judge "shall" review any supporting material provided. In other words, the indictment provides the "nature and cause" of the charges, that is the concise statement of the facts underlying the charges, and the supporting material provides the evidence to support those charges. It is knowledge of the details in that evidence, more so than the information in the indictment, which the accused needs to be able to prepare for trial.

[2]It is worth noting in this respect that although the Prosecutor drafts the indictment, it is then submitted to a Confirming Judge to determine whether a *prima facie* case exists. Pursuant to Rule 72(A), the Defence may file a preliminary motion challenging the form of the indictment or for either severance of counts joined in one indictment or, in the case of joint accused, for separate trials. Thus, both parties, the Confirming Judge, the Trial Chamber, and even the Appeals Chamber may affect the indictment that the accused is eventually tried on.

2. Form of the Indictment

The issues confronting the drafters of the first indictments ranged from the basic question of what the indictment should physically look like to complex legal issues, including how to plead the elements of the offences, whether multiple offences could be charged, whether certain crimes could be considered to be lesser included offences of other crimes, when it was appropriate to join accused in an indictment, and the role or purpose of the supporting material. In light of the significance of these issues, the Prosecutor eventually developed a particular form that was designed to state the technical charges, while also fulfilling the important role of informing the public. The unique nature of the crimes under the jurisdiction of the ICTY dictated that the indictments be drafted in such a manner to ensure that the allegations are placed in the proper context so that the charges can be fully understood. In the view of the OTP, this was particularly critical in the early stages of the Tribunal to ensure that that both the accused and the international community would be able to understand the basis for the charges from the indictment itself.

The basic format of the indictment consists of several sections. Those sections are labelled: Background, the Accused, Superior Authority or Individual Criminal Responsibility, General Allegations, and the Charges. The Background section is designed to describe the relevant historical facts necessary to place the alleged crimes in the proper context. The next section contains the biographical information of the accused. The section on Superior Authority or Individual Criminal Responsibility describes the basis of the accused's criminal responsibility under Articles 7(1)[3] and/or 7(3)[4] of the Statute. The General Allegations section sets forth both the common elements for any offence under Articles 2 to 5,[5] as well as certain common elements for particular offences, such as torture or murder. The Superior Authority or Individual Criminal Responsibility section and the General Allegations section were designed to allege the required elements of the crimes without having to unnecessarily repeat them for each count. To achieve this, both of these sections are incorporated by reference into each

[3]Article 7(1) provides: "A person who planned instigated, ordered, committed or otherwise aided and abetted in the planning, preparation or execution of a crime referred to in Article 2 to 5 of the present Statute, shall be individually responsible for the crime."

[4]Article 7(3) enshrines the theory of command responsibility, and states: "The fact that any of the acts referred to in Articles 2 to 5 of the present Statute was committed by a subordinate does not relieve his superior of criminal responsibility if he knew or had reason to know that the subordinate was about to commit such acts or had done so and the superior failed to take the necessary and reasonable measures to prevent such acts or to punish the perpetrators thereof."

[5]These articles of the Statute set forth the subject matter jurisdiction of the ICTY. Article 2 governs graves breaches of the four Geneva Conventions of 1949. Article 3 covers violations of the laws or customs of war. Article 4 and Article 5 provide jurisdiction for genocide and crimes against humanity respectively.

of the specific counts alleged. The final section of the indictment contains the particular charges and is broken down into two sections. The first section contains a precise statement of the facts necessary to establish the substantive elements of the charges alleged, based on the relevant violations of Articles 2–5 of the Statute. The relevant counts are then set forth in descending order of "importance": genocide, crimes against humanity, grave breaches of the Geneva Conventions and violations of the laws or customs of war.

The intent of this format was to include all possible legal and factual aspects that might be necessary to meet the standard required by the Statute and Rules in as brief a form as possible. However, it was impossible to anticipate all of the possible issues or viewpoints that would affect how the indictment would be perceived or operate and the only thing that could have been anticipated with certainty is that the indictments would be challenged. Through the ongoing process of trials, however, the Appeals and Trial Chambers have addressed a number of issues regarding the indictments,[6] and as a consequence, the legal standards governing the sufficiency of indictments are becoming better established.

3. Basic Requirements of an Indictment

Several decisions of the Trial Chambers have clarified some of the basic legal requirements of indictments. Many of these decisions have also recognised the differences between the unique jurisdiction of the ICTY and national jurisdictions and have shed light on what are appropriate subjects for defence objections to the form of the indictment.

All of the Chambers that have considered the question thus far have decided that the basic requirement for a sufficient indictment, as set forth in the ICTY Statute and Rules, is a concise statement of the facts and of the

[6]More than 30 decisions have been rendered by the Trial Chambers or Appeals Chamber relating to the form and/or substance of the indictment.

crime or crimes with which the accused is charged.[7] The different Trial Chambers have also generally agreed on the nature of the information that should be contained in the concise statement of the facts: time and place of the offences, identity of the victims, and the acts or conduct of the accused. They have not, however, had a consistent approach on how to frame that requirement.

In the *Prosecutor v. Krnojelac*, the Trial Chamber noted that:

> The extent of the Prosecution's obligation to give particulars in an indictment is to ensure that the accused has "a concise statement of the facts" upon which reliance is placed to establish the offences charged, but only to the extent that such statement enables the accused to be informed of the "nature and cause of the charge against him" and in "adequate time […] for the preparation of his defence."[8]

The Trial Chamber went on to state that an indictment "must contain information as to the identity of the victim, the place and the approximate date of the alleged offence and the means by which the offence was committed."[9] In determining if this standard had been met the Trial Chamber noted that an indictment is not defective "provided that, when taken as a whole, the indictment makes clear to each accused (a) the nature of the

---

[7]See, for example, *Prosecutor v. Tadić, Decision on Defence Motion on the Form of the Indictment*, Case No. IT-94-1-T, 14 Nov. 1995 ("*Tadić* Indictment Decision"); *Prosecutor v. Delalić and Others, Decision on Motion by the Accused Zejnil Delalić Based on Defects in the Form of the Indictment*, Case No. IT-96-21-T, 2 Oct. 1996 ("*Čelebići* Indictment Decision"); *Prosecutor v. Kovačević, Decision on Defence Motion for Provisional Release*, Case No. IT-97-24-PT, 20 Jan. 1998 ("*Kovačević* Provisional Release Decision"); *Prosecutor v. Kupreškić and Others, Decision on Defence Challenges to Form of the Indictment*, Case No. IT-95-16-PT, 15 May 1998 ("*Kupreškić* Indictment Decision"); *Prosecutor v. Krnojelac, Decision on Defence Preliminary Motion on the Form of the Indictment*, Case No. IT-97-25-PT, 24 Feb. 1999 ("*Krnojelac* Indictment Decision I"); *Prosecutor v. Krnojelac, Decision on Preliminary Motion on Form of the Indictment*, Case No. IT-97-25-PT, 11 Feb. 2000 ("*Krnojelac* Indictment Decision II"); *Prosecutor v. Krnojelac, Decision on Form of Second Amended Indictment*, Case No. IT-97-25-PT, 11 May 2000 ("*Krnojelac* Indictment Decision III"); *Prosecutor v. Kunarac, Decision on Defence Preliminary Motion on the Form of the Indictment*, Case No. IT-95-23-PT, 23 Oct. 1998 ("*Kunarac* Indictment Decision"). *Prosecutor v. Kordić* and *Čerkez, Decision on Defence Application for Bill of Particulars*, Case No. IT-95-14/2-PT, 2 Mar. 1999 ("*Kordić* Bill of Particulars Decision"); *Prosecutor v. Kvočka and Others, Decision on Defence Preliminary Motions on the Form of the Indictment*, Case No. IT-98-30-PT, 12 Apr. 1999 ("*Kvočka* Indictment Decision").

[8]*Krnojelac* Indictment Decision I, para. 12 (footnotes omitted).

[9]*Krnojelac* Indictment Decision I, para. 12 citing to *Prosecutor v. Blaškič, Decision on the Defence Motion to Dismiss the Indictment Based upon Defects in the Form Thereof*, Case No. IT-95-14-PT, 4 Apr. 1997, para. 20. ("*Blaškič* Indictment Decision") ("A valid indictment must specify the essential factual ingredients of the offence charged; it must specify the approximate time, place and manner of the acts or omissions of the accused upon which the prosecution relies, and it must provide fair information and reasonable particularity as to the nature of the offence charged.")

responsibility (or responsibilities) alleged against him and (b) the material facts – but not the evidence – by which his particular responsibility (or responsibilities) will be established."[10]

In addressing the question of the sufficiency of the indictment in the *Kvočka* case, the Trial Chamber recognised the impact of the unique nature of the jurisdiction of the ICTY on the form of indictments. Noting the use of national authorities by the Trial Chamber in the first *Krnojelac* Indictment Decision in fashioning its holding, the *Kvočka* Trial Chamber found that while references to national practice are helpful, the "sole determinant of the law applied by the International Tribunal is its Statute and Rules; moreover, the influence of domestic criminal law must take due account of the very real differences between a domestic criminal jurisdiction and the system administered by the International Tribunal."[11] While stating clearly that there was a "minimum level of information that must be provided by the indictment" in order for the indictment to be "valid as to its form", the Trial Chamber held that "as a general rule, the degree of particularity required in indictments before the International Tribunal is different from, and perhaps not as high as, the particularity required in domestic criminal law jurisdictions."[12]

The Trial Chamber noted that this rationale was due, in part, to "the massive scale of the crimes with which the International Tribunal has to deal."[13] The Trial Chamber held that the degree of specificity required in an indictment will depend on the particular circumstances of that case. Where specific information is available as to location and time of the offence, the identity of the victims, and the means by which the accused committed the offences, the Prosecution should be required to allege that information in the indictment. The Trial Chamber also recognised, however, that there may be cases where the massive scale of the crimes made it impracticable or impossible to identify all the victims, the specific identity of co-actors, or the

---

[10]*Krnojelac* Indictment Decision I, para. 7.

[11]*Kvočka* Indictment Decision, paras. 14–18.

[12]Id.

[13]Id., para. 17. In addition to the massive scale of the crimes with which the ICTY has to deal, it is also important to note that many of these crimes involve multiple perpetrators and common plans or schemes of criminal activity, such as the running of prison camps or widespread attacks on the civilian population. In *Krnojelac* Indictment Decision III, the Trial Chamber specifically addressed what must be alleged in an indictment charging some form of "joint criminal enterprise:" "In order to know the nature of the case he must meet, the accused must be informed by the indictment of: (a) the nature or purpose of the joint criminal enterprise (or its "essence"…), (b) the time at which or the period over which the enterprise is said to have existed, (c) the identity of those engaged in the enterprise – so far as their identity is known, but at least by reference to their category as a group, and (d) the nature of the participation by the accused in that enterprise. Where any of these matters is to be established by inference, the prosecution must identify in the indictment the facts and circumstances from which the inference is sought to be drawn." *Krnojelac* Indictment Decision III, para. 16.

specific means by which all the criminal acts were committed. What the Trial Chamber did find was required in the pleadings was "the specific acts alleged to have been committed by the accused." The Trial Chamber indicated that this information was a part of the required "concise statement of facts." The *Kvočka* Indictment Decision reinforces the consistent thread found in the other Trial Chamber decisions regarding the basic requirement for a sufficient indictment: a concise statement of the material facts of the case.[14]

The second *Krnojelac* Indictment Decision elaborated on what constitutes material facts and held that:

> Whether a particular fact is material depends in turn upon the nature of the case which the prosecution seeks to make. The materiality of such things as the identity of the victim, the place and date of the events for which the accused is alleged to be responsible, and the description of the events themselves, necessarily depends upon the alleged proximity of the accused to those events.[15]

The Trial Chamber then set forth three different situations and discussed the legal requirements of materiality in each of the situations, with the least precision required in the first category and the highest degree of precision in the last category.

In the first situation, an indictment charging superior responsibility under Article7(3), what is most material is the relationship between the accused and those who did the acts for which the accused is allegedly responsible, and

> [T]he conduct of the accused by which he may be found (a) to have known or had reason to know that the acts were about to be done, or had been done, by those others, and (b) to have failed to take the necessary and reasonable measures to prevent such acts or to punish the persons who did them.[16]

The second situation entails a case based upon what the Trial Chamber characterises as "aiding and abetting" responsibility.[17] In this situation what is most material is the "conduct of the accused by which he may be found to have planned, instigated, ordered, committed or otherwise aided and abetted in the planning, preparation or execution of those acts."[18]

---

[14]The significance of its holding, however, is the clear articulation of the necessity to consider those requirements in terms of the unique nature of the mandate of the ICTY.

[15]*Krnojelac* Indictment Decision II, para 18. However, in the same decision (at para. 57) the Trial Chamber emphasised that "the prosecution cannot be obliged to perform the impossible. Where appropriate, the prosecution must, of course, make it clear that it has provided the best particulars it can. An inability to provide better particulars will inevitably reduce the value of the witnesses who are unable to be more specific, but it does not affect the *form* of the indictment." (Emphasis added.)

[16]*Krnojelac* Indictment Decision II, para. 18.

[17]Id.

[18]Id.

In the third situation, the accused is alleged to have personally committed the acts charged in the indictment. In this case, the material facts must be stated with the greatest precision:

> [T]he information pleaded as material facts must, so far as it is possible to do so, include the identity of the victim, the place and approximate date of those acts and the means by which the offence was committed.[19]

In the course of rendering their decisions with regard to the form of indictments, the Trial Chambers have also determined what are not appropriate defence objections to the form of the indictment. Principal among those are objections to the indictment based upon a disagreement with the facts as alleged in the indictment.[20] Other inappropriate objections have included assertions that *mens rea* must be proven in order to establish the existence of a reasonable suspicion,[21] and other issues, such as cumulative charging, that require decisions on the merits of the evidence to be lead at trial.[22]

4. Elements of the Offence

The Prosecution has from the very first indictment included factual assertions as to the elements of offences charged in the indictment. It would appear from the decisions of the Trial Chambers that have considered this issue, however, that it may not be necessary to do so. For example, in the *Kvočka* case,[23] the Defence asserted that the indictment was defective due to a failure to allege the legal elements of Articles 5 and 7(3). The Trial Chamber ruled that there is no requirement under the jurisprudence of the Tribunal for the indictment to allege the legal elements of the particular crimes and that a failure to do so did not render the indictment defective. The Trial Chamber noted that reference in the indictment to the specific Article of the Statute that was allegedly violated incorporated all the elements set out therein. The Trial Chamber also noted that the "Prosecutor is not conducting a tutorial when she drafts an indictment."

In *Kordić*,[24] the Trial Chamber denied a Defence motion requesting, *inter alia*, that the Prosecution identify with specificity the facts supporting each element of the offences charged and to specify the *mens rea* element for

---

[19]Id.

[20]*Kvočka* Indictment Decision, para. 40; *Krnojelac* Indictment Decision I, para. 20, *Čelebići* Indictment Decision, para. 10.

[21]*Kovačević* Provisional Release Decision, para. 19.

[22]See, for example, *Kunarac* Indictment Decision.

[23]*Kvočka* Indictment Decision, para. 36.

[24]*Kordić* Bill of Particulars Decision, paras. 6–8. See also *Prosecutor v. Kordić and Čerkez, Decision on Joint Defence Motion to Strike All Counts Arising Under Article 2 or Article 3 for Failure to Allege a Nexus Between the Conduct and an International Armed Conflict*, Case No. IT-95-14/2-PT, 1 Mar. 1999, p. 1.

each offence. The Trial Chamber held that the indictment need not identify the precise legal elements of each crime since all that is required under Article 18(4), and Rule 47(C)[25] is a concise statement of the facts and the crime or crimes which the accused allegedly committed.

5. Cumulative Charging

A significant issue for the Prosecution has been the question of the most appropriate method to charge an accused that does not appear to be unduly burdensome, but that also reflects the gravity of his conduct, supports the international norms or values recognised by Articles 2–5 of the Statute and also accounts for the inevitable variations of proof at trial. In some jurisdictions this difficulty is addressed by the concept of "lesser included offences." A lesser-included offence exists where all of the elements of a particular crime are included within the elements of another crime. The application of this concept recognises that many crimes are related, separated only by degrees of intent or by outcome, and that the facts as established at trial may be somewhat different from those alleged by the Prosecution in the indictment. Thus, the Prosecution may prove at trial that the accused committed a crime, but it may not be the specific crime alleged. In those States that recognise this doctrine the court could automatically find the accused guilty of the lesser included offence on the theory that when an accused is charged with the greater offence he is also put on notice as to the other possible offences that may derive from or be an inherent part of the offence charged.

In those States that accept the doctrine of lesser-included offences, the laws prohibiting the separate crimes are designed to protect the same societal values or norms, such as the protection of human life or the protection of property.[26] In the *Tadić* case, in response to motions from the Defence on the form of the indictment and other issues, the OTP specifically asked the Trial Chamber in pre-trial motions to rule on the issue of lesser-included offences and the elements of the offences. The Trial Chamber refused to do so. The Trial Chamber stated that it would only consider charges that were specifically alleged in the indictment. This rationale was followed in the *Čelebići* case as well.[27]

---

[25]See footnote 1, supra.

[26]The doctrine of lesser-included offences must be distinguished from the situation where two distinct offences are committed during a single transaction. For example, if the accused commits a murder in the course of a burglary, he can be convicted for both crimes in order to protect those different societal values. By contrast, the doctrine of lesser-included offences, for example, covers the situation where the indictment alleges that the accused committed murder and the evidence at trial supports a finding of manslaughter. Notwithstanding the fact that the lesser-included offence was not specifically charged, the accused is not prejudiced, in theory, since he was on notice as to the greater offence.

[27]*Prosecutor v. Delalić* and Others, *Judgement*, Case No. IT-96-21-T, 16 Nov. 1998, paras. 1020, 1041–1045 ("*Čelebići* Judgement").

Although the doctrine of lesser-included offences has not been recognised by the ICTY, the Chambers have consistently accepted the position of the Prosecution regarding multiple charges and held that accused may be charged and convicted under different Articles of the Statute for the same conduct in order to protect the different international societal values or norms reflected Articles in 2 to 5 of the Statute.[28] This has generally been referred to as "cumulative" charging. The Chambers have held that the effect of cumulative charging on an accused is an issue for sentencing,[29] and thus far the Trial Chambers have found that the penalty for each of the cumulative charges should be served concurrently.

There still remains the issue of whether an accused, in the appropriate case, could be sentenced to serve consecutive terms of imprisonment for the cumulative charges. If it is recognised that the crimes under each Article exist to protect separate international values, then it should be recognised that there also may be violations that are so egregious as to warrant the imposition of consecutive sentences.

6. Other Issues Related to Form of the Indictment

Part of the analysis undertaken in reaching the decision of which offence under the Statute is the most appropriate to charge in a particular case is the determination of how to characterise the acts that occurred. An interesting development that was originally connected to the form of the indictments has also resulted in a significant development in law as well. In the *Tadić* case, the Prosecution faced for the first time the challenge of how to effectively capture and charge the criminal conduct that was commonly described as "ethnic cleansing." The Prosecution team responsible for drafting the amended indictment determined that the crime of persecution, as a crime against humanity under Article 5, was the most appropriate charge to incorporate all of the various acts of the accused. Until that time, persecution as a crime against humanity had been considered by many as the

[28] *Prosecutor v. Tadić, Opinion and Judgment*, 7 May 1997, para. 609; *Kupreškić* Indictment Decision, p. 3; *Krnojelac* Indictment Decision I, para. 8.

[29] *Tadić* Indictment Decision, paras. 15–18; *Čelebići* Indictment Decision, para. 24; *Blaškić* Indictment Decision, para. 32; *Kupreškić* Indictment Decision, p. 3; *Kvočka* Indictment Decision, para. 25. But see *Prosecutor v. Kupreškić and Others, Judgement*, Case No. IT-95-16-T, 14 Jan. 2000, at pp. 253–294, where Trial Chamber II undertook an extensive analysis of cumulative charging and stated, at para. 727: "The Prosecution: (a) may make *cumulative* charges whenever it contends that the facts charged violate simultaneously two or more provisions of the Statute […] (b) should charge *in the alternative* rather than cumulatively whenever an offence appears to be in breach of more than one provision, depending on the elements of the crime the Prosecution is able to prove. […] (c) should *refrain* as much as possible from making charges based on the same facts but under *excessive multiple heads*, whenever it would not seem warranted to contend […] that the same facts are simultaneously in breach of various provisions of the Statute." (Emphasis in original.)

least important – if there can be such a thing – of the crimes enumerated in Article 5. Partially as a result of the decision to charge persecution for the acts encompassing ethnic cleansing, however, this offence has become a crime of great significance.

The issue of the joinder of several accused can be problematic for the Prosecution in a situation where the commission of criminal acts was so pervasive and involved the participation of numerous people in various ways. The question arises as to what is the most effective and just way to group various perpetrators in any indictment. The determination of which perpetrator to indict is clearly within the authority of the Prosecutor in the exercise of her discretion,[30] and in determining how to structure the indictment and which co-accused should be joined, the Prosecution has been guided by the plain language definition of "transaction" in ICTY Rule 2. The Trial Chambers have generally accepted the Prosecution's position in this regard.[31] The issue of joinder of accused after the initial appearance of the accused, however, is a matter of discretion for the Trial Chamber. As with other issues related to the trial process, the standard to be applied is whether the joinder is in the interests of justice. The main consideration involved is the impact of the joinder on the right of the accused to a fair and expeditious trial.[32]

The other issue related to the form of the indictment has been the question of the purpose of the indictment vis-à-vis the supporting and disclosure material. It is unclear from the decisions of the Trial Chambers what role the disclosure material plays (in contrast to the indictment) in providing the factual information required to satisfy the accused's right to prepare his defence. In *Tadić*, the Trial Chamber indicated that prior to requesting a bill of particulars, the accused should examine the disclosure material to determine if that satisfied his questions. This holding was also followed in the *Čelebići* case. Those decisions indicate that the supporting and other disclosure material play a significant role in providing an accused with the relevant factual material necessary to allow him to prepare his defence. This analysis appears to be consistent with Article 18 and Rule 47.

In his decision of 24 May 1999 regarding the confirmation of the indictment against *Slobodan Milošević and Others*, however, Judge Hunt stated that Rule 47(E) did not allow him to consider whether the supporting material might cure any gaps in the indictment that he might find as the Confirming Judge. As Judge Hunt recognised, the Confirming Judge cannot look to the supporting material to find material facts that must be alleged in

[30] *Čelebići* Judgement, para. 179.

[31] See, for example, *Kvočka* Indictment Decision, para. 55.

[32] *Prosecutor v. Kolundžija and Došen, Decision on Prosecutor's Motion for Joinder*, Case No. IT-98-30-PT and IT-95-8-PT, 19 Oct. 1999.

the indictment in order to have a legally sufficient charge. In the event that the necessary material facts were missing, the Confirming Judge must deny confirmation of the indictment.[33]

7. Amendment of Indictments

Perhaps the most contentious issue regarding indictments thus far has been the amendment of indictments, which is governed by Rule 50. Most national systems allow for amendment of the indictment during the proceedings. The issue with respect to amendments of the indictment, as with most other trial issues, is whether the amendment may cause any prejudice to the accused's right to a fair trial. This can be both a question of the timing of the amendment as well as the substance of the amendment. If there is no prejudice to the accused or there is a mechanism to cure any potential prejudice, then there should be no reason to deny an amendment. The aspects of the amendment process that have presented the most difficulty have been the issue of when the Trial Chamber becomes the arbiter of that question and whether the accused has a right to make submissions on a proposed amendment to the indictment.

The original Rule 50 was simple in its construction. It directed that the authority to grant leave to amend switched from the Confirming Judge to the Trial Chamber when the case was "at trial". The difficulty with that Rule was the interpretation of the phrase "at trial." As the work of the Tribunal has grown more complex there have been several amendments to Rule 50, directed at clarifying when the authority to grant leave to amend vests with the Trial Chamber, rather than the Confirming Judge.

The later changes to Rule 50 also defined what types of amendments did not require confirmation. These changes recognised that there were some amendments that would not result in prejudice to an accused and therefore there was no need for a Confirming Judge or Trial Chamber to be involved. There is no question that a Trial Chamber needs to have the authority over the issue of amendments at the point in time that any amendments may affect the fair and efficient conduct of the trial, the question is when is that point in time. With the number of cases now pending before the Tribunal, the reality is still that the Trial Chamber may not need to be involved from the time of initial appearance. However, in light of the efforts by Chambers to streamline the pre-trial and trial processes to complete the trials as

[33]However, in the *Krnojelac* Indictment Decision I at paragraph 15, the Trial Chamber stated: "[I]n a limited class of case, less emphasis may be placed upon the need for precision in the indictment where complete pre-trial discovery has been given. For example, if all of the witness statements identify uniformly and with precision the circumstances in which the offence charged is alleged to have occurred, it would be a pointless technicality to insist upon the indictment being amended to reflect that information. That is, however, a rare situation."

quickly as possible, the Trial Chambers need the authority to control amendments at an early stage. The issue is the how to define that stage clearly for the benefit of all parties, but also in a fashion that will survive the changes in practice as the Tribunal continues to develop.

Finally, the impact of amending indictments may be felt in cases other than the one in which leave to amend is sought. Rule 50(C) provides that "where necessary the date for the trial shall be postponed to ensure adequate time for the preparation of the defence." Of course, amendments made shortly before the scheduled start of a trial may delay the proceedings, affecting not only the accused but also the Trial Chamber involved, potentially affecting the commencement of other trials, since each Trial Chamber has several cases assigned to it.

8. Future Developments

As the jurisprudence of the Tribunal continues to develop, so too will the form of the indictments. There are a number of areas where clear decisions by the Chambers could have a significant effect on the form of the indictments and result in more streamlined and focused indictments. Those areas relate to the elements of the offences, judicial notice of adjudicated facts, and lesser-included offences.

If a definitive position is taken with respect to the elements of the various offences within the mandate of the Tribunal such that they become a settled aspect of the ICTY jurisprudence, the Chambers could make a specific determination that elements of offences do not need to be pleaded in the indictment. It is possible that Rule 47 could be amended to provide further details as to the form and substance of the indictments. With regard to reducing the size of the indictments, if the Chambers judicially note the historical facts of the conflict in the former Yugoslavia as adjudicated facts, such that they become universally accepted by the Chambers, it might alleviate the need to continue to allege the background facts and many of the facts related to common elements of offences that are currently found in the prefatory paragraphs of the counts. Finally, if the Chambers accept the doctrine of lesser-included offences and a schedule of lesser-included offences was established, that would obviate the need to charge all possible violations of the Statute.

DAVID HUNT*

12. The Meaning of a "*prima facie* Case" for the Purposes of Confirmation

This essay is concerned with the meaning of a "*prima facie* case" for the purposes of confirming an indictment,[1] and with the approach which a judge should take when assessing the evidence in order to determine whether such a case has been established for that purpose.

Article 18.4 of the ICTY Statute permits the Prosecutor to present to a judge of a Trial Chamber an indictment following the Prosecutor's "determination that a *prima facie* case exists". Article 19.1 permits a judge to confirm the indictment if "satisfied that a *prima facie* case has been established by the Prosecutor". Article 19.2 permits the judge who has confirmed the indictment to issue a warrant for the arrest of the accused person. A *prima facie* case is not defined in the Statute. However, ICTY Rule 47(B) (which deals with precisely the same issue as Article 18.4 of the Statute) appears to provide such a definition – at least for that Article. It permits the Prosecutor to present an indictment –

> [...] if satisfied [...] that there is sufficient evidence to provide reasonable grounds for believing that a suspect has committed a crime within the jurisdiction of the Tribunal [...].

My contentions are:

(1) that Rule 47(B) is *ultra vires* the Statute;
(2) that a *prima facie* case is established for the purposes of confirmation only where the indictment pleads facts which, if accepted, are such that

*By the Hon David Hunt, Presiding Judge of Trial Chamber II in the ICTY. Formerly a judge (1979–1991), and Chief Judge of the Common Law and Criminal Divisions (1991–1998), of the Supreme Court of New South Wales, Australia.

[1]Every indictment must be confirmed by a judge of a Trial Chamber before a warrant may be issued for the arrest of the accused.

R. May et al., Essays on ICTY Procedure and Evidence in Honour of Gabrielle Kirk McDonald, 137–149.

a reasonable Trial Chamber *could* be satisfied beyond reasonable doubt of the guilt of the accused; and

(3) that it is for the Trial Chamber to say later whether the evidence should be accepted; but

(4) that, in the assessment of whether such a case has been established, where the sole evidence upon an essential ingredient of the offence has been conceded by the witness to be false or is unreliable upon its face, that evidence may be disregarded.

It is a basic step in my argument in support of these contentions that, where relevant, a *prima facie* case necessarily, as a matter of common sense, has the same meaning at every stage of the proceedings – in particular at the first three of the four vital stages of the criminal justice process when the rights of a suspect or an accused person are most affected. Those four are the decisions (i) to arrest him, (ii) to put him on trial, (iii) that he has a case to answer and (iv) to convict him.

Most (if not all) national criminal justice systems recognise certain rights of the suspect or the accused person which must be respected by the relevant authorities at each of these stages. The fourth stage never involves the concept of a *prima facie* case, and it need not be considered further in this essay.

As to the first stage (the decision to arrest a person), there are various formulations in the different legal systems as to the circumstances which will justify the arrest in situations other than being caught in *flagrante delicto*. In the common law systems (at least in those with which I am more familiar), an arrest is justified only if the authority effecting the arrest (usually a police officer) has a suspicion (or belief) based upon reasonable grounds that the suspect has committed a particular crime. That is not a very onerous requirement; it is also not substantially different from the requirements of Rule 47(B).

In some respects, the position in the civil law systems does not appear to be substantially different from the common law position. For example, in France, the police may detain a person for an identity check (*contrôle d'identité*) where an officer suspects on reasonable grounds that that person is either planning, or has recently attempted or committed, a serious or grave offence,[2] although they may also detain a suspect for interrogation and investigation (*garde à vue*) upon the basis only that they have formed the view that the suspect is able to supply material evidence.[3] In Germany, an arrest (*vorläufige Festnahme*) is justified, *inter alia*, upon compelling suspicion that the person detained has committed an offence.[4]

The requirements are more onerous at the next two stages in both the common law and the civil law systems – when it must be decided, first, whether to commit or to put the accused on trial and, secondly, whether he has a case to answer. The requirement in the ICTY Statute that every

---

[2]Hatchald, Huber & Vogler, Comparative Criminal Procedure (1996), p. 35.
[3]Id., p. 36.
[4]Id., pp. 121–123.

indictment must be confirmed is equivalent to the process in national systems by which the decision is made to commit the accused, or to put him on trial.[5]

In the common law systems, the accused is committed for trial after a preliminary hearing by a magistrate who must determine whether, on the material put forward at that hearing, there is a case for the accused to answer. The universal test as to whether such a case exists is whether there is evidence which, if accepted, could establish beyond reasonable doubt that the accused is guilty of the offence charged – in other words, that there is a *prima facie* case. At the trial, the trial judge may be called upon by the accused at the end of the prosecution case to determine whether the accused has a case to answer. At this stage, the test is the same but the decision must be made upon the basis of the evidence which has been given at the trial – when it is not necessarily the same as that which had been put forward in the preliminary hearing.

Although the various civil law codes do not, in general, refer to the concept of a *prima facie* case, there are nevertheless generally similar tests stated in relation to the decision to send a case for trial. In France, for example, a case will be sent for trial where the facts stated in the *dossier* would support a conviction.[6] In Spain, the case will be sent for trial if there is rational evidence of the crime charged.[7] In Germany, the code requirement for sending a case for trial has been interpreted by the Federal Supreme Court (*Bundesgerichtshof*) as a "preliminary evaluation" of the contents of the case file as making "the conviction of the accused probable".[8] It has been said that, except in Spain, the civil law systems do not have a procedure whereby it may be held that there is no case to answer.[9] In Spain, the trial judge may dismiss the jury at the conclusion of the prosecution case if there is no evidence to support the conviction of the accused.[10]

When in 1993 the framers of the ICTY Statute undertook their task of setting up a new international criminal court, they were sailing in truly uncharted international waters in relation to procedures for the arrest of the accused and for committing him for trial. The only previous such court to

---

[5]*Prosecutor v Kordić and Others, Decision on the Review of the Indictment,* Case No. IT-95-14-I, 10 Nov. 1995, (1995) II ICTY JR 1119 at 1125; *Prosecutor v Milošević and Others, Decision on Review of Indictment and Application for Consequential Orders*, Case IT-99-37-I, 24 May 1999 at para. 2.

[6]*Code de Procédure Pénal*, Arts. 212, 214.

[7]*Ley de Enjuiciamiento Criminal*, Art. 384.

[8]*Amtliche Sammlung der Entscheidungen des Bundesgerichtshofes in Strafsachen*, Vol. 23, p. 306. (This imposes a greater burden on the prosecution than do most other legal systems.)

[9]*Prosecutor v Kordić and Čerkez, Decision on Defence Motions for Judgment of Acquittal*, Case IT-95-14/2-T, 6 Apr. 2000 at para. 24.

[10]Id., para. 24.

have existed, the International Military Tribunal at Nürnberg,[11] already had all but one of the accused persons in custody before any charges were laid, and the Charter of that Tribunal therefore had no need to make any provisions in relation to arrest. Nor was there any provision made by the Charter for a preliminary hearing to determine whether there was a case against the accused warranting them being put on trial; the indictment and the documents submitted by the Chief Prosecutors (to which the prosecution could add during the trial) had only to be approved by the four Chief Prosecutors acting as a committee for that purpose.[12]

The solution reached by the framers of the ICTY Statute was to equate the requirements for the issue of an arrest warrant to those for confirmation (or putting the accused on trial) by having the indictment confirmed before it is served on him. At both stages, a *prima facie* case has to be shown. However, as already noted, the original Rules of Procedure and Evidence provided, by what is now ICTY Rule 47(B),[13] that the Prosecutor could forward the indictment to the judge of a Trial Chamber –

> [...] if satisfied in the course of an investigation that there is sufficient evidence to provide reasonable grounds for believing that a suspect has committed a crime [...].

It is unlikely to have been accidental that the wording of Rule 47(B) is different from that of Article 18 of the Statute. It must be assumed that the judges intended to express in Rule 47(B) their interpretation of what a *prima facie* case was within the meaning of Article 18 for the purposes of justifying the presentation of an indictment for confirmation. As Article 19 of the Statute imposes the same requirement for the Prosecutor to satisfy for both the confirmation of the indictment and the issue of an arrest warrant, the judges may appear to have intended to interpret what a *prima facie* case is within the meaning of Article 19 as well.[14] Such an interpretation is not substantially different from the requirements generally accepted in national systems as justifying an arrest.

If, however, a case to answer is the same as a *prima facie* case (as logically it must be), a significant question arises as to whether the interpretation expressed in Rule 47(B) is correct. What may be appropriate as a

---

[11]The "Special Tribunal" for which provision was made by Article 227 of the 1919 Treaty of Versailles to try the Kaiser of Imperial Germany never came into operation, and those who were to be tried before an "International High Tribunal" in accordance with that treaty were ultimately tried before German national courts in Leipzig.

[12]Charter annexed to the London Agreement, 1945, Art 14(C).

[13]What is now Rule 47(B) was originally Rule 47(A), but I have for convenience given it its current description.

[14]Such a possibility is supported by the terms of Rule 61(C), which permits a Trial Chamber to issue an international arrest warrant where it is satisfied "that there are reasonable grounds for believing that the accused has committed all or any of the crimes charged in the indictment".

justification for the issue of an arrest warrant constitutes a very substantial reduction in the generally accepted rights of the accused both for putting him on trial and for calling upon him to answer a case, if all that has to be demonstrated at each of these stages are reasonable grounds for believing that he has committed the crime charged.

Yet this was the initial interpretation of Articles 18.4 and 19.1 made judicially within the Tribunal. In August 1995, when confirming the indictment in *Prosecutor v Rajić*,[15] Judge Sidhwa examined the Treaty of Versailles, the Charter of the Nuremberg International Military Tribunal and various proposals for other international criminal courts which were never put into effect.[16] He concluded that the expression "*prima facie* case" was not grounded in "any uniform principle or set parameters" so far as international criminal law was concerned.[17] He thought that the object of the ICTY Statute, the offences which it covered, the need for expediency, the necessity of effective disposal "and a host of other complex matters" all invited "new and adventurous ideas", and he concluded:

> He who wants to serve international law, must ride the crest of high flood to reach the evolutionary source i.e. the new mutations that human knowledge and wisdom throws [sic] up.[18]

The requirement that there be reasonable grounds for believing that the suspect has committed a crime, Judge Sidhwa said, means that it is sufficient for the Prosecutor to point to "such facts and circumstances as would justify a reasonable or ordinary prudent man to believe that a suspect has committed a crime".[19]

Judge Sidhwa then determined that Rule 47(B) was "explanatory or declaratory of Article 18.4". He thought it strange that there was not a similar rule which explained Article 19.1, but he said that this was "an inadvertent case of *casus omissus*", and that he would adopt the interpretation given by Rule 47(B) for Article 19.1 as well.[20] Judge Sidhwa did not consider the effect which that interpretation would have upon any subsequent submission by the accused that there was no case to answer.

---

[15]*Prosecutor v Rajić, Review of the Indictment*, Case No. IT-95-12-I, 29 Aug. 1995, (1995) II ICTY JR 1051.

[16]The Convention for the Creation of an International Criminal Court for the Prevention and Punishment of Terrorism (1937), the Report of the UN Committee on International Criminal Jurisdiction (1951), the Interim Report of the Ad-Hoc Group of Experts to the Commission on Human Rights (1981), and the Draft Statute for an International Criminal Court adopted by the International Law Commission (1994). Id., pp. 1057–1061.

[17]Id., p. 1063.

[18]Id., p. 1063.

[19]Id., p. 1065.

[20]Id., pps. 1065, 1067.

In November 1995, in *Prosecutor v Mrkšić*,[21] Judge Riad confirmed an indictment after assessing whether the facts stated in "the record" could establish the ingredients of the crimes charged,[22] and he concluded that:

> […] there is sufficient evidence to provide reasonable grounds for believing that [the accused], by virtue of their position of authority, committed crimes which […] fall under the jurisdiction of the Tribunal.[23]

Although Articles 18 and 19 of the Statute were mentioned in passing,[24] there is no reference to the apparent difference between Rule 47(B) and those Articles, and there is no express reference in the decision to the requirement of those Articles that a *prima facie* case be established. Nevertheless, Judge Riad's assessment that the facts pleaded "could" establish the crimes charged would appear to have been intended to demonstrate that a *prima facie* case had been pleaded.

A few days later, when confirming the indictment in *Prosecutor v Kordić*,[25] Judge McDonald considered the earlier decision of Judge Sidhwa, but she was not convinced that the wording of Article 18.4 requiring the existence of a *prima facie* case was satisfied by the standard of "reasonable grounds" provided by Rule 47(B).[26] However, as Article 19.1 requires the judge to be satisfied that a *prima facie* case exists before confirming the indictment and issuing an arrest warrant, Judge McDonald said that she did not need to decide whether Rule 47(B) sufficiently reflected the requirements of Article 18.4.[27] Such an approach necessarily rejected the view of Judge Sidhwa that the interpretation given by Rule 47(B) to Article 18.4 applied also to Article 19.

For a suitable interpretation of what a *prima facie* case is, Judge McDonald turned to the commentary accompanying the draft Statute for an International Criminal Court adopted by the International Law Commission in 1994. Article 27.1 of that draft Statute permitted the Prosecutor to file an indictment upon concluding that there is a *prima facie* case. The commentary added that:

> […] a *prima facie* case for this purpose is understood to be a credible case which would (if not contradicted by the Defence) be a sufficient basis to convict the accused on the charge.[28]

---

[21] *Prosecutor v Mrkšić and Others, Confirmation of the Indictment,* Case No. IT-95-13-I, 7 Nov. 1995, (1995) II ICTY JR 1089.

[22] Id., p. 1093.

[23] Id., p. 1093.

[24] Id., p. 1089.

[25] *Prosecutor v Kordić and Others, Decision on the Review of the Indictment,* Case No. IT-95-14-I, 10 Nov. 1995, (1995) II ICTY JR 1119.

[26] Id., p. 1121.

[27] Id., pp. 1121, 1123.

[28] Report of the International Law Commission on the Work of its 46th Session, UN Doc A/49/10 (1994), at p. 95.

Judge McDonald then applied that interpretation to the requirement in Article 19.1 that she be satisfied that a *prima facie* case exists before confirming the indictment and issuing an arrest warrant. This interpretation of a *prima facie* case places a much more onerous requirement upon the Prosecutor than that adopted by Judge Sidhwa. It is also an appropriate requirement for the prosecution to satisfy at the stage of demonstrating that the accused has a case to answer.

A week later, when confirming the indictment in *Prosecutor v Karadžić & Mladić*,[29] Judge Riad expressed his satisfaction that a *prima facie* case had been disclosed by the indictment, but he concluded again that there was "sufficient evidence to provide reasonable grounds for believing that 'the accused' committed the crimes charged in the indictment".

In May 1996, in *Prosecutor v Erdemović*,[30] Judge Sidhwa listed the supporting material provided by the Prosecutor with the indictment to be confirmed in accordance with Rule 47, he stated that it showed reasonable grounds to believe that the accused had committed the crimes charged, and he made a finding in the terms of Article 19.1 that the Prosecutor had established a *prima facie* case. He did not discuss the nature of the *prima facie* case required by that Article, but it may be assumed that he was still riding "the crest of high flood" which he had ridden the previous year.

In July 1997, Rule 47 was amended by the addition of a requirement that the reviewing judge is to examine each of the counts in the indictment and any supporting materials the Prosecutor may provide, in order:

> [...] to determine, applying the standard set forth in Article 19, paragraph 1, of the Statute, whether a case exists against the suspect.[31]

The amendment would appear to have been made in response to the comment made by Judge McDonald in *Kordić*, that the judge is bound by the terms of Article 19.1 whereas Rule 47(B) is directed to Article 18.4. It is unfortunate, however, that the judges did not take advantage of the amendments being made to Rule 47 at that time either to alter the interpretation in Rule 47(B) of the *prima facie* case required by Article 18.4 or to make that interpretation expressly applicable to the *prima facie* case required by Article 19.1 as well. Or perhaps on this occasion the judges recognised that the Rules of Procedure and Evidence are not really a suitable vehicle for the expression of their interpretation of the Statute.[32]

---

[29] *Prosecutor v Karadžić and Mladić, Review of the Indictment*, Case No. IT-95-18-I, 16 Nov. 1995, (1995) II ICTY JR 1153 at 1161.

[30] *Prosecutor v Erdemović, Review of Indictment*, Case IT-96-22-I, p. 3.

[31] This is now ICTY Rule 47(E).

[32] Cf *Prosecutor v Tadić, Judgment on Allegations of Contempt Against Prior Counsel*, Milan Vujin, Case IT-94-1-A-R77, 31 Jan. 2000 at paras. 24–25.

In May 1999, when confirming the indictment in *Prosecutor v Milošević*,[33] and faced with this conflict of authority as to the proper interpretation of Article 19.1, I followed that of Judge McDonald in *Kordić*. With all due respect to Judge Sidhwa, I have no doubt that his enthusiastic adventure on the high seas of international law led him into fundamental error, in that he did not take into account that the necessary consequence of the low level of satisfaction which his interpretation of Articles 18 and 19 permitted was that the generally accepted rights of the accused as to what is required for him to be put on trial and for the establishment of a case to answer were also reduced.

In the meantime, and apparently without reference to the effect which Rule 47(B) was having on the interpretation of the expression *prima facie* in Articles 18 and 19, the Trial Chambers were interpreting the prosecution's obligation to establish a case to answer in the way traditionally understood in national systems. In considering the Tribunal's jurisprudence upon this issue, it should be pointed out that, until ICTY Rule 98*bis* was added in March 1998, there was no rule of procedure and evidence specifically directed to applications made at the conclusion of the prosecution case for a judgment of acquittal based upon there being no case to answer. Applications prior to the addition of that rule were made pursuant to ICTY Rule 54 ("General Rule"), which permitted a Trial Chamber to make such orders as may be necessary for the conduct of the trial.

In the first case to be tried by the Tribunal, *Prosecutor v Tadić*, the Trial Chamber (Judge McDonald presiding) held that, in an application for a ruling that there was no case to answer, the test to be applied was:

> [...] whether as a matter of law there is evidence, were it to be accepted by the Trial Chamber, as to each count charged in the indictment which could lawfully support a conviction of the accused.[34]

In the second case to be tried, *Prosecutor v Delalić*, the Trial Chamber held that the test was whether:

> [...] as a matter of law, there is evidence relating to each element of the offences in question which, were it to be accepted, is such that a reasonable Tribunal might convict.[35]

The next case in which consideration was given to this issue was *Prosecutor v Blaskić*, by which time ICTY Rule 98*bis* had been added. Rule 98*bis*(B) provides:

---

[33] *Prosecutor v Milošević and Others, Decision on Review of Indictment and Application for Consequential Orders*, Case IT-99-37-I, 24 May 1999 at para. 4.

[34] *Prosecutor v Tadić, Decision on Defence Motion to Dismiss Charges*, Case IT-94-1-T, 13 September 1996 at p. 2.

[35] *Prosecutor v Delalić and Others, Order on the Motions to Dismiss the Indictment at the Close of the Prosecutor's Case*, Case IT-96-21-T, 18 March 1998 at p. 4.

> The Trial Chamber shall order the entry of judgment of acquittal on motion of an accused or *proprio motu* if it finds that the evidence is insufficient to sustain a conviction on that or those charges.[36]

In *Blaskić*, the Trial Chamber said that this rule:

> [...] means that the Trial Chamber must grant the Motion if it is convinced that, at this stage of the proceedings, the prosecution has not provided sufficient evidence to justify immediately a judgment of conviction based on the various counts invoked by counsel for the accused.[37]

and that:

> [...] the required standard is that the evidence presented by the prosecution be insufficient to justify from this time forth a conviction for all or part of the counts concerned.[38]

Notwithstanding these relatively traditional statements in relation to finding that there is or is not a case to answer, the same Trial Chamber said of Rule98*bis* later, in *Prosecutor v Jelisić*:

> [...] one must not confuse the notion of acquittal [under Rule 98*bis*] with that of lack of evidence, that is, no prosecution case.[39]

As the judgment in *Jelisić* has been appealed by the Prosecutor, it would be inappropriate to comment upon this statement beyond saying that its logic is difficult to discern. In its written judgment, the Trial Chamber said that it had:

> [...] concluded that, without even needing to hear the arguments of the Defence, the accused could not be found guilty of the crime of genocide.[40]

In *Prosecutor v Kupreškić*,[41] the Trial Chamber adopted the test laid down in *Tadić*, which I have already quoted. In *Prosecutor v Kordić*,[42] after a review of many of the decisions, the Trial Chamber stated the test as being "whether there is evidence on which a reasonable Trial Chamber could

[36] *Prosecutor v Blaskić, Decision of Trial Chamber I on the Defence Motion to Dismiss*, Case IT-95-14-T, 3 Sept. 1998.

[37] Id., p. 4.

[38] Id., p. 5.

[39] *Prosecutor v Jelisić*, Case IT-95-10-T, 19 Oct. 1999, Transcript p. 2333.

[40] *Prosecutor v Jelisić, Judgment*, Case IT-95-10-T, 14 Dec. 1999 at para. 15.

[41] *Prosecutor v Kupreškić, Decision on Motion for Withdrawal of the Indictment Against the Accused Vlatko Kupreškić*, Case IT-95-16-T, 18 Dec. 1998 at p. 3.

[42] *Prosecutor v Kordić and Čerkez, Decision on Defence Motions for Judgment of Acquittal*, Case IT-95-14/2-T, 6 Apr. 2000, para. 26.

convict". It considered that the decision in *Jelisić* was one on its own particular facts and stated that, if it purported to establish a different test, it declined to follow it.[43]

Thus, with the possible exception of *Jelisić*, every decision in relation to whether the accused has a case to answer at the conclusion of the prosecution case has expressed the test in terms equivalent to whether a *prima facie* case has been established.

It is fundamental that the same phrase should be interpreted in the same way wherever it appears in a statute such as the ICTY Statute unless the context otherwise dictates. There is no suggestion in either Article 18 or Article 19 of the ICTY Statute that the phrase "*prima facie* case" should be interpreted differently for each. As a matter of logic and common sense, that phrase should also convey the same meaning where it has been adopted throughout the Tribunal's jurisprudence, unless the context otherwise dictates. There is no suggestion that a *prima facie* case should mean anything different when used as the test under Rule 98*bis* in determining whether there is a case for the accused to answer.

It necessarily follows that – if a *prima facie* case for the purposes of determining whether the accused has a case to answer means that the evidence, if accepted, is such that a reasonable Trial Chamber *could* be satisfied beyond reasonable doubt of the guilt of the accused – it must mean the same thing for the purposes of presenting an indictment to a judge of a Trial Chamber in accordance with Article 18.4, of confirming the indictment in accordance with Article 19, and of issuing an arrest warrant also in accordance with Article 19. If this be so, it inevitably follows that ICTY Rule 47(B) is *ultra vires* the Statute. This is so because, as it provides a less onerous task for the Prosecutor than does Article 18.4, it is inconsistent with the Statute to the detriment of fundamental rights of the accused.

It is noticeable that in only one of the decisions to which I have referred is there any discussion of the approach which the judge or the Trial Chamber should take when assessing the indictment or the evidence in order to determine whether a *prima facie* case has been established.[44] To this issue I now turn.

As a matter of ordinary English, the Latin phrase *prima facie* accords with its translation. As an adjective, *prima facie* means arising at first sight, or based on the first impression obtained. That is the approach taken in the common law systems. In other words, neither the committing magistrate nor the trial judge investigates the weight to be afforded to the evidence in the prosecution case. Whether there is a *prima facie* case depends solely upon the quantity, not the quality, of the evidence. This is because the issues of fact in criminal trials in the common law systems must generally be determined by a jury and not by a judge. The assessment proceeds upon the

[43] Id., para. 17.

[44] That was in the most recent decision in *Prosecutor v Kordić and Čerkez, Decision on Defence Motions for Judgment of Acquittal*, Case IT-95-14/2-T, 6 Apr. 2000.

bases (1) that the jury will accept all of the evidence in support of the prosecution case, and the inferences from that evidence, without reference to any contradiction, qualification or explanation also present in that evidence,[45] and even if the evidence is tenuous or inherently weak or vague,[46] and (2) that all of the evidence which supports the accused's case will be rejected by the jury,[47] even if the evidence comes from a witness upon whose other evidence the prosecution relies.[48] This is because it is for the jury to determine what part of the evidence they accept and what part they reject.[49]

The literature available does not disclose any judicial exegesis as to the approach taken in the civil law systems in determining whether a *prima facie* or equivalent case exists but, from my own discussions with civil lawyers, it appears that, despite the greater participation by the suspect in the investigative stage, the approach of the *juge d'instruction* (or similar judicial officer) does not substantially differ from that in the common law systems. In other words, the judicial officer leaves it to the Trial Chamber to determine whether the evidence should be accepted.

In the Tribunal, of course, there is no jury, and the zealous concern of the common law courts that it is for the jury to determine whether to accept even a tenuous or inherently weak or vague case is not appropriate. However, both in principle and logically, there should be no difference in general terms in the approach to be taken by the Tribunal to that taken in both the common law and civil law systems – that it should be left to the Trial Chamber to say whether the evidence should be accepted.

That is because it is a fundamental rule in relation to determining issues of fact that no conclusion should ever be reached in relation to the credit of a witness until *all* the evidence has been given. A tribunal of fact must never look at the evidence of each witness separately, as if it existed in a hermetically sealed compartment; it is the accumulation of *all* the evidence in the case which must be considered. The evidence of one witness, when considered by itself, may appear at first to be of poor quality, but it may gain strength from other evidence in the case. Conversely, apparently credible evidence of another witness may lose that appearance in the light of other, subsequently given, evidence.[50]

If the Trial Chamber *were* entitled to weigh questions of credit when determining whether a *prima facie* case existed, and if it found that such a

---

[45]*Jayasena v The Queen* (1970) AC 618 at 624.

[46]*Doney v The Queen* (1990) 171 CLR 207 at 214–215.

[47]*Rex v Rothery* (1925) 25 SR(NSW) 451 at 461.

[48]Cf *Regina v Brent* (1973) Crim LR 295; *Haw Tua Tau v Public Prosecutor* (1982) AC 136 at 150–151; *Regina v Towers* (1984) 14 A Crim R 12 at 15.

[49]See, generally, *Regina v Galbraith* (1981) 1 WLR 1039; *United States v Mariani*, 725 F 2d 862, 865 (1984); *Wentworth v Rogers* (1984) 2 NSWLR 422 at 429, 431; *Regina v Towers* (at 15); *Regina v Haas* (1986) 22 A Crim R 299 at 304; *Regina v R* (1989) 18 NSWLR 74 at 81.

[50]*Prosecutor v Tadić, Judgment on Allegations of Contempt Against Prior Counsel, Milan Vujin*, Case IT-94-1-A-R77, 31 Jan. 2000 at para. 92.

case had been established, the perception would necessarily be created (whether or not it is accurate) that the Trial Chamber had accepted the evidence of the prosecution's witnesses as credible. Such a consequence would then lead to two further perceptions: (1) that the accused will bear at least an evidentiary onus to persuade the Trial Chamber to alter its acceptance of the credibility of the prosecution's witnesses, and (2) that the accused will be convicted if he does not give evidence himself. He would virtually be required to waive the right given to him by the ICTY Statute to remain silent.[51]

In *Prosecutor v Kordić*,[52] and after the close of the prosecution case, the defence moved for a judgment of acquittal pursuant to ICTY Rule 98*bis*, and it argued that, in order to find that there was a case to answer, the Trial Chamber had to be satisfied beyond reasonable doubt at *that stage* that each element of the offences charged *had* been established – to the extent that, if two reasonable inferences were available from the evidence found to be credible (one of guilt and the other of innocence), the prosecution case had to be dismissed.[53] Such an approach would be the same as that taken at the end of *all* the evidence, when determining whether to convict the accused. In response, the prosecution relied upon the test applied in the previous decisions to which reference has already been made.[54] The Trial Chamber held that the true test to be applied was not whether there was evidence which satisfied the Trial Chamber beyond reasonable doubt of the guilt of the accused (as the defence had argued), but rather it was whether there was evidence on which a reasonable Trial Chamber could convict.[55]

The Trial Chamber said that the approach to be taken in determining whether this test was satisfied is that questions of credibility or reliability should not generally be considered, leaving those matters to be considered at the end of the case.[56] The Trial Chamber said that a case to answer would not be constituted by *any* evidence; there must be evidence which could *properly* lead to conviction,[57] and the Trial Chamber went on to identify as one situation in which it *would* be obliged to consider questions of credibility or reliability:

> [...] where the Prosecution's case has completely broken down, either on its own presentation, or as a result of such fundamental questions being raised through cross-examination as to the reliability and credibility of witnesses that the Prosecution is left without a case.[58]

---

[51]Article 21.4(g).

[52]*Prosecutor v Kordić and Čerkez, Decision on Defence Motions for Judgment of Acquittal*, Case IT-95-14/2-T, 6 Apr. 2000.

[53]Id., para. 1.

[54]Id., para. 5.

[55]Id., para. 26.

[56]Id., para. 28.

[57]Id., para. 26. (Emphasis added.)

[58]Id., para. 28.

A question arises as to whether this exception to the "true test" which the Trial Chamber introduced is either necessary or wise. The true test was stated to be whether there is evidence on which a reasonable Trial Chamber could convict. If the prosecution is "left without a case" – either on its face or through concessions made in cross-examination – then surely there would not be evidence upon which a reasonable Trial Chamber could convict. This would perhaps be more readily the case where questions of reliability rather than credibility are concerned. If the only witness to give evidence of a fundamental ingredient of the offence charged concedes either in his evidence in chief or in cross-examination that his evidence is based on second- or third-hand hearsay, it is difficult to see how a reasonable Trial Chamber could convict.

But necessarily more difficult cases would arise where questions of credit are concerned. If the only witness to give evidence of a fundamental ingredient of the offence charged concedes in cross-examination that his initial evidence is false, again a reasonable Trial Chamber could not convict. However, for the reasons already given, it may be thought to be highly dangerous for the Trial Chamber to resolve disputed questions of credit when rejecting an application for a judgment of acquittal. The Trial Chamber in *Kordić* imposed a requirement that "fundamental questions" of credit be raised before questions of credit would be considered, but it is not made clear just what was intended by this phrase beyond, for example, a concession by a vital witness that his initial evidence is false.

I agree that the basic test of whether a *prima facie* case exists should be whether, if accepted, the evidence is such that a reasonable Trial Chamber *could* convict, and that it is for the Trial Chamber to say later whether the evidence should be accepted. However, in making that assessment, I suggest that, where the sole evidence upon an essential ingredient of the offence has been conceded by the witness to be false or is unreliable upon its face, that evidence may be disregarded. There are many reasons why a witness may seek to deny the truth of a version of the facts which he has previously given and which is inconsistent with the evidence which he has given of those facts. Questions of his credit necessarily arise in such a case. The mere fact that he has given different versions and asserts that one of them is false would not mean that that version may be disregarded for the purposes of this assessment. On the other hand, it could be manifestly unfair to an accused person to hold that he has a case to answer where the sole evidence upon an essential ingredient of the offence with which he has been charged is on its face unreliable. It is for these reasons that the approach which I have formulated gives a greater flexibility to the basic test of whether the evidence, if accepted, is such that a reasonable Trial Chamber could convict.

MICHAEL BOHLANDER*

13. Plea-Bargaining before the ICTY

1. Introduction

Plea-bargaining is a well-known institution in most common law systems. They have a formalised procedure of pleading guilty to the charges of the indictment, and very often the prosecution and the defence get together before a case goes to trial in order to find a solution which is acceptable to both sides. Most civil law countries do not have such a formal plea but regulate the same issue under the provisions for confessions in the material sense made at the trial stage. Often the mere fact that the accused has made a confession does not relieve the court of the task of finding out whether this confession is credible and supported by corroborating material.[1] In adversarial systems, plea-bargaining takes two basic forms, charge bargaining and sentence bargaining. The former means that the accused agrees to plead guilty to a less severe offence in return for the prosecution's dropping heavier charges, like pleading guilty to voluntary manslaughter instead of murder. This is very often done in order to avoid mandatory sentence provisions and here charge bargaining blends to some extent into the second form, where the accused pleads guilty to the charges as brought forward by the prosecution, thus saving them and the court a lengthy trial and expecting a reduced sentence in return. This paper deals with plea-bargaining before the ICTY and the ICTR, with the plea-bargaining procedure under the

*Dr. iur. (Saarbrücken University); Richter am Landgericht (Meiningen); Honorary University Fellow, Exeter University School of Law; Legal Officer, Trial Chamber II, International Criminal Tribunal for the Former Yugoslavia. – The views expressed in this article are solely those of the author and do not represent the opinions of the UN or the ICTY. – The manuscript was finished in June 2000.

[1]This was even the case under the law of the former German Democratic Republic (GDR), which was widely regarded as a system of injustice ("Unrechtssystem"). See e.g. the materials of the 3. Wissenschaftliche Konferenz des Straf- und Militärkollegiums des Obersten Gerichts of 25 June 1987, Gerichtliche Beweisführung und Wahrheitsfindung im sozialistischen Strafprozeß, 1987.

R. May et al., Essays on ICTY Procedure and Evidence in Honour of Gabrielle Kirk McDonald, 151–163.

Statute of the permanent International Criminal Court ("ICC"), and lastly with some comments as to the appropriateness of such bargains in the context of serious violations of international humanitarian law.

2. The Law of the ICTY and ICTR

The Statute of the ICTY does not contain any provision about the admissibility and the procedure to be followed in the case of guilty pleas, let alone plea bargains. However, the Judges of the Tribunal based on their rule-making power under Article 15 of the Statute have incorporated Rule 62*bis* in the Rules of Procedure and Evidence.[2] The ICTR has a similar rule in its own Rules of Procedure and Evidence under Rule 62(v) which is in effect identical with that of the ICTY.[3]

Valid guilty pleas have been received and decided upon at the time this paper was written at the ICTY in the cases of *Erdemović* and *Jelisić*,[4] and at the ICTR in the cases of *Kambanda*,[5] *Serushago*[6] and *Ruggiu*.[7] *Kambanda* does not really fall under the category of plea-bargaining, as the accused there pleaded guilty to all the charges as presented by the Prosecutor. No sentence agreements had been made, the main purpose of the agreement appears to be that the accused's family received protective measures from the Prosecutor's Office for fear of reprisals.[8] Serushago pleaded guilty to four out of five counts, including genocide, as well as murder, extermination and torture as crimes against humanity, but pleaded not guilty to one count of rape as a crime against humanity, which was then withdrawn by the Prosecutor according to a plea agreement between the parties and with the leave of the Trial Chamber. Serushago received a sentence of 15 years' imprisonment on the basis of a number of mitigating circumstances, among others the full and effective co-operation with the Prosecutor which led to several other indictments. Ruggiu, a Belgian journalist, pleaded guilty to incitement to genocide and to persecution, for which he received 12 years imprisonment. Again, the plea agreement was not a real agreement on a *quid pro quo* basis. Jelisić pleaded guilty to crimes against humanity and war crimes, but not

[2]The Rule was adopted at the fourteenth plenary session on 12 Nov. 1997. The amendment was adopted after the first sentencing judgement in the *Erdemović* case (IT-96-22-A), discussed below. The word "guilt" in the last line of this Rule had read "guilty" before the current wording was introduced at the eighteenth plenary session on 9–10 July 1998. The new sub-rule (b) was added at the nineteenth plenary session, on 17 Dec. 1998, namely the condition that "the guilty plea is informed".

[3]The ICTY Rules of Procedure and Evidence contain Rule 92, a provision dealing with confessions made by the accused during questioning. It is identical with Rule 92 of the ICTR. So far the ICTY has not yet ruled on this matter.

[4]*Prosecutor v. Jelesić, Judgement*, Case No. IT-95-10-T, 14 Dec. 1999.

[5]*Prosecutor v. Kambanda, Judgement and Sentence*, Case No. ICTR-97-23-S, 4 Feb. 1999.

[6]*Prosecutor v. Serushago, Sentence*, Case No. ICTR-98-39-S, 5 Feb. 1999.

[7]*Prosecutor v. Ruggiu, Judgement and Sentence*, Case No. ICTR-97-32-I, 1 June 2000.

[8]At paras. 48–49.

guilty to genocide. He received a 40-year sentence for the former, but was acquitted of genocide.

3. The *Erdemović* Case

The first and so far only case of a real plea bargain before the ICTY was the prosecution of Drazen Erdemović.[9] Erdemović had originally been indicted for taking part in a massacre in a so-called 'safe area' near Srebrenica. The indictment charged him with two alternative counts: A violation of the laws or customs of war under Article 3 of the Statute together with Common Article 3 of the 1949 Geneva Conventions, and a crime against humanity under Article 5 of the Statute. At his initial appearance, Erdemović pleaded guilty to the charge under Article 5 and was subsequently sentenced to 10 years' imprisonment. Erdemović appealed this judgement on the grounds that his guilty plea was uninformed and that the Trial Chamber had failed to take sufficiently into account the defence of duress raised by him. The Appeals Chamber in its decision of 7 October 1997 quashed the sentencing judgement on the basis that the plea was indeed uninformed.[10] The issues of informed pleas and duress are not of importance here. Rule 62*bis* was not yet in force at that time.[11] The Appeals Chamber had to deal with the question of whether guilty pleas are a part of international criminal proceedings at all. The majority relied to a large part on the legal reasoning of the joint separate opinion of Judges McDonald and Vohrah. The question was, however, not addressed explicitly. The majority obviously had no problem whatsoever with the notion of guilty pleas. The separate opinion state:[12]

> 1. The guilty plea in the procedure of the Tribunal
>
> The institution of the guilty plea, though securing "administrative efficiency", must not in any way prejudice the Appellant's rights [...]
>
> [...] the immediate consequences which befall an accused who pleads guilty are that he forfeits his entitlement to be tried, to be considered innocent until proven guilty, to test the Prosecution case by cross-examination of the Prosecution's witnesses and to present his own case. It follows, therefore, that certain pre-conditions must be satisfied before a plea of guilty can be entered.

[9] *Prosecutor v. Erdemović*, Case No. IT-96-22-T at the trial level, *Prosecutor v. Erdemović*, IT-96-22-T*bis* in the second sentencing hearing and *Prosecutor v. Erdemović*, Case No. IT-96-22-A in the Appeals Chamber.

[10] For a fervent criticism of the Trial Chamber before the appellate court handed down its decision see Sienho Yee, "The Erdemović, sentencing judgment: a questionable milestone for the international criminal tribunal for the former Yugoslavia", *26 Geo. J.I.C.L.* 1997, p. 263.

[11] See footnote 2 supra.

[12] Joint Separate Opinion of Judge McDonald and Judge Vohrah, at p. 6 – Footnotes omitted.

> In our view, the minimum pre-conditions are as follows:
>
> (a) The guilty plea must be voluntary. It must be made by an accused who is mentally fit to understand the consequences of pleading guilty and who is not affected by any threats, inducements or promises.
>
> (b) The guilty plea must be informed, that is, the accused must understand the nature of the charges against him and the consequences of pleading guilty to them. The accused must know to what he is pleading guilty;
>
> (c) The guilty plea must not be equivocal. It must not be accompanied by words amounting to a defence contradicting an admission of criminal responsibility;
>
> We find ample support for our view that the above three pre-conditions must be satisfied in a consistent and long-established line of authorities obtaining throughout the common law jurisdictions of the world. We would like to reiterate, however, that we do not in any way consider the common law authorities as binding upon us; we merely consider them as relevant material, throwing light upon the proper construction to be given to the guilty plea as employed in the procedure of the International Tribunal [...].

Judge Cassese in his separate opinion addressed the question on a more fundamental level and tried to avoid mere reference to national jurisdictions.[13] He then went on to apply these principles to the question of the admissibility of guilty pleas under international criminal law, and more specifically, under the law of the ICTY:

> The system, laid down in Article 20, paragraph 3, of the Statute and enunciated in Rule 62 of the Rules, of pleading guilty or not guilty to the charges set out in the indictment against an accused, is clearly drawn from the criminal procedure of common-law countries. This practice does not have a direct counterpart in the civil-law tradition, where an admission of guilt is simply part of the evidence to be considered and evaluated by the court. However, notwithstanding its origin in a particular national setting, the true import and scope of this notion may be grasped without necessarily referring to the legislation and case-law of common-law countries.
>
> It is apparent from the whole spirit of the Statute and the Rules that, by providing for a guilty plea, the draftsmen intended to enable the accused (as well as the Prosecutor) to avoid a possible lengthy trial with all the attendant difficulties. These difficulties – it bears stressing – are all the more notable in international proceedings. Here, it often proves extremely arduous and time-consuming to collect evidence. In addition, it is imperative for the relative officials of an international court to fulfil the essential but laborious task of protecting victims and witnesses. Furthermore, international criminal proceedings are expensive, on account of the need to provide a host of facilities to the various parties concerned (simultaneous interpretation into various languages;

[13]Separate and Dissenting Opinion of Judge Cassese at p. 3 – Footnotes omitted.

provision of transcripts for the proceedings, again in various languages; transportation of victims and witnesses from far-away countries; provision of various forms of assistance to them during trial, etc.). Thus, by pleading guilty, the accused undoubtedly contributes to public advantage. At the same time, the accused may find his pleading guilty beneficial to his own condition. Firstly, it may help him to salve his conscience and atone for his wrongdoing. Secondly, he will avoid the indignity and the possible demoralisation of undergoing a trial, as well as the psychological ordeal he would have to go through during examination and cross-examination of witnesses (and possibly also of himself as a witness); he will also eschew the public exposure that may ensue from trial, and the adverse consequences for his social position and the life of his family and relatives. Thirdly, the accused may expect that the court will recognise his co-operative attitude by reducing the sentence it would have imposed had there not been a plea of guilty: in other words, the accused may hope that the court will be more lenient in recognition of his admission of guilt.[14]

The accused Erdemović entered a second plea on 14 January 1998. He pleaded guilty to the count of violations of the laws or customs of war and the charges under Article 5 of the Statute were then withdrawn by the Prosecutor. The plea was made on the basis of a plea bargain agreement the contents of which were set out in the second sentencing judgement of 5 March 1998:[15]

The essential elements of the plea agreement were that:

(a) The accused would plead guilty to count 2, a violation of the laws or customs of war, in full understanding of the distinction between that charge and the alternative charge of a crime against humanity, and the consequences of his plea.

(b) The accused's plea was based on his guilt and his acknowledgement of full responsibility for the actions with which he is charged.

(c) The parties agreed on the factual basis of the allegations against the accused, and in particular the fact that there was duress.

(d) The parties, in full appreciation of the sole competence of the Trial Chamber to determine the sentence, recommended that seven years' imprisonment would be an appropriate sentence in this case, considering the mitigating circumstances.

(e) In view of the accused's agreement to enter a plea of guilty to count 2, the Prosecutor agreed not to proceed with the alternative count of a crime against humanity.

[14]It is interesting to note that Cassese talks of an "admission of guilt", which is the language of the ICC Statute under Rules 64 and 65. In addition, this section of his opinion seems to imply that he did not necessarily want to view the "guilty plea" in the dispositive character it usually has under the common law, especially when occurring in the form of charge bargaining.

[15]Case No. IT-96-22-T*bis* at p. 20.

> [...] There is no provision for such agreements in the Statute and Rules of Procedure and Evidence [...]. This is the first time that such a document has been presented to the International Tribunal. The plea agreement [...] is simply an agreement between the parties, reached on their own initiative without the contribution or encouragement of the Trial Chamber. [...] the accused confirmed his agreement to and understanding of the matters contained therein. The parties themselves acknowledge that the plea agreement has no binding effect on this Chamber. [...] Whilst in no way bound by this agreement, the Trial Chamber has taken it into careful consideration in determining the sentence to be imposed upon the accused.

The Trial Chamber subsequently sentenced Erdemović to 5 years' imprisonment on the charges he had pleaded guilty to; Erdemović served his sentence and was subsequently released. The obvious question is whether the Trial Chamber could – or even *should* – have found Erdemović guilty under Article 5 as he had also admitted all the relevant *facts*. On the face of it the Trial Chamber did not consider itself to be bound by the plea agreement. In fact, it appears to have been the other way round. As the last sentence of the excerpt appears to indicate, the Trial Chamber took the agreement into account for purposes of sentencing, but, it would seem, not for the determination of guilt, i.e. the charges on which the accused was convicted. Apparently the decision of the prosecution not to proceed with the count of crimes against humanity was sufficient for the Trial Chamber not to address the issue any further. This decision of the Trial Chamber reveals another unsolved fundamental problem in international criminal law, which cannot be addressed here for lack of space, namely whether there is a duty to prosecute and try international crimes under all permissible legal characterisations, once the facts underlying the offence have themselves been admitted by the accused (the so-called "legality principle"). This is especially important in cases like this, where the plea-bargaining leads to the prosecution dropping a more serious charge in favour of obtaining a guilty plea, albeit to a lesser charge.

4. The Statute of the ICC

The Rome Conference of July 1998 resulted in the signing of the Statute of the new permanent International Criminal Court.[16] The Statute makes express provision for a procedure resembling a guilty plea. However, the term "guilty plea" is not used; rather the Statute chose the words "admission of guilt" as the opposite to a formal plea of not guilty. The ICC Statute does not use the word "confession" either. The only two references to "confessing" are in Articles 55 and 64 on the right of the accused not to be compelled to

[16] UN Document A/Conf. 183/9 (1998), 17 July 1998.

testify against himself. In the preparatory stages of the Statute the general problem of plea-bargaining had been discussed and the rift between common law and civil law on this issue had become apparent. In the Report of the Preparatory Committee on the Establishment of an International Criminal Court after August 1996, Australia and the Netherlands proposed the possibility of a plea of guilty with the immediate consequence of setting a date for a pre-sentencing hearing; a trial was not necessary by definition.[17] A note to the proposal contains the words:

> The proposal that a guilty plea would lead directly to a pre-sentencing hearing would also raise concerns from the perspective of a civil law system.[18]

These concerns were voiced also in the summaries in Volume I of the report,[19] and additionally the interests of the international community in achieving high publicity for these trials were stressed. The relevant provision in the draft

> [...] was described as relating to the question of plea bargaining, which should be excluded given the fact that it is in contradiction with the structure of the court and also given the serious nature of the crimes which affected the interests of the international community as a whole. However, it was also stated that guilty pleas were not inseparable from plea bargaining.[20]

Following this report the subsequent debates contained the phrase "admission of guilt"[21] as the opposite to a plea of not guilty. The relevant provisions of the Statute are set out in Articles 64 and 65, and the latter are mostly self-explanatory. From the structure of the ICC Statute it appears to be clear that its framers did have a concept in mind which would give the Court the discretion to accept an admission of guilt whilst not relieving it of its duty to ascertain a sufficient factual basis for the admission. As sub-section 5 of Article 65 makes clear, plea bargains have no binding force whatsoever on the Court. This sub-section, however, also signals that charge bargaining is still going to be an admissible feature under the ICC's law. Yet it is clear that if a charge bargain is not binding on the ICC, then the accused may be found guilty of any offence under which the Court deems the admitted facts to be subsumable. Just what purpose charge bargaining is supposed to achieve under the ICC Statute if all the relevant facts are admitted is open to question.

---

[17]See M. Cherif Bassiouni, The Statute of the International Criminal Court, A Documentary History (1998), at p. 533.

[18]Id., p. 533.

[19]Id., pp. 423–44.

[20]Id., p. 424.

[21]Id., pp. 172, 278 and 364.

Arguably one field of application might be that of the Prosecutor dropping certain factual charges in return for an admission of guilt on others. For example, if there are two separate charges of rape against two women and one charge of destruction of property, the Prosecution may decide to drop the latter charge in return for an admission of guilt on the first two charges. The Statute does address the situation under Article 61 with different results, depending on whether the deal between the prosecution and the accused is made before or after the confirmation hearing before the Pre-Trial Chamber or after the start of the trial before the Trial Chamber. The Statute does not require the Prosecutor to seek the permission of the Pre-Trial Chamber for withdrawing charges prior to the confirmation of the charges, as is clear from Article 61(4) which only requires the Prosecutor to notify the Pre-Trial Chamber of the withdrawal and the reasons for it. At this stage, therefore, charge bargains may have binding effect on the Court after all if the bargain relates to a distinct set of facts. After the charges have been confirmed but before the start of the trial, the Prosecutor may ask the Pre-Trial Chamber's permission to amend the charges, e.g. to introduce more serious ones, under Article 61(9). Although the Statute does not mention it explicitly for the period after the confirmation and uses the words "amend" and "withdraw" in a way as to signify different meanings, one might still be inclined to argue *a maiore ad minus* that amending also encompasses withdrawing if even more serious charges may be brought. After the commencement of the trial the Prosecution must seek the permission of the Court under Article 61 (9) for the withdrawal of charges. There can thus be no fact bargaining after the confirmation of the charges without the consent of the Court.

It should be noted on the other hand that the Statute does not expressly create a duty on the Trial Chamber to try all the facts of the case, which are before it. The withdrawal under Article 61(9) may even be made after the Trial Chamber has heard all the relevant evidence from both sides as to the charges that are to be withdrawn. The wording of the Statute implies a discretion of the Trial Chamber, without saying anything about the guiding principles that the Trial Chamber should adhere to when making its decision as to whether to grant its permission or not. It does not say whether the decision is final or whether the Trial Chamber may renege on it, as is the case, for example, under German law (see below under section V). Can any assistance be found by looking at the national systems?

5. National Law as a Basis for Plea-Bargaining in International Criminal Tribunals

International criminal courts do not apply domestic law merely on a grander scale. Given the fact that there is no genuine criminal law in the international forum so far – especially as far as a "general part" and procedural law are concerned – but only a few basic and rather vaguely defined offences, and the procedural rules made by the judges of the ICTY and ICTR, these tribunals will for some time to come have to go back to general principles of law embedded in all sorts of jurisdictions, not just the ones governed by common law. Cassese rightly stated in his separate opinion in *Erdemović* that it would be a futile exercise to try and adapt national systems to the international level without first reflecting which are the really basic principles and concepts that are quintessential to those system and how one may glean rules of international law from them. Especially with regard to plea-bargaining, a field which is a grey-zone, it may be very difficult to find such common ground.

Much has been written about plea-bargaining in the United States of America, one of the major representatives of the common law systems. There the process is used most widely. I do not wish to dwell on the American debate, but it is easy to see from looking at the literature and the jurisprudence that even the American law is far from representing a uniform picture.[22] Yet it is an undeniable fact that in everyday practice and in the preparation of international documents and rules the influence of the common law system of thought and doctrine is overwhelming. A look at the so-called civil law countries is therefore more than necessary. However, such an endeavour requires thorough comparative research, which is outside the scope of this paper. Yet for the purposes of showing the vast potential for differences in approach, a brief look at the example of German law shall be sufficient here.

German law finds the idea of bargaining for lesser charges unacceptable and allows sentencing bargain only in very limited circumstances. This follows from the fact that German criminal procedure seeks to find out the material truth, not just the "truth" put forward through the arguments and evidence of the parties. Although there had been some debate about a proliferation[23] of plea-bargaining in German criminal procedure,[24] the Federal Court of Justice (Bundesgerichtshof) in its judgement of 28 August 1997[25] has set strict guidelines as to how far plea bargains should be allowed.

- Plea negotiations with regard to a confession by the defendant and the sentence to be imposed are not as a matter of principle admissible. They must, however, take place in open session in the presence of all the

[22]See e.g. Abraham S. Goldstein, "Converging Criminal Justice Systems: Guilty Pleas and the Public Interest", 49 *S.M.U.L. Rev*. (1996), p. 567.

[23]Whether that is still the case is open to question. See Klaus Malek, Verteidigung in der Hauptverhandlung (1994), p. 21 and accompanying footnotes.

[24]See Bernd Schünemann, Absprachen im Strafverfahren? Grundlagen, Gegenstände und Grenzen, Gutachten B zum 58. Deutschen Juristentag (1990), and Karl F. Schumann, Der Handel mit Gereichtigkeit, Funtkionsprobleme der Strafjustiz und ihre Lösungen – am Beispiel des amerikanischen plea bargaining (1977).

[25]Amtliche Sammlung der Entscheidungen des Bundesgerichtshofes in Strafsachen (BGHSt) vol. 43, p. 199.

judges, lay assessors and the parties to the case. Prior preparatory talks are hereby not ruled out.

- The court is not allowed to indicate to the accused a certain sentence, it may only indicate an upper limit for the case of a confession. The court is not bound by this if during the hearing, new and aggravating circumstances arise. The intention to renege on the indication must be notified to the defendant in open session.
- The court when indicating a possible sentence and imposing it later on in the trial must adhere to the general sentencing principles. The punishment must be commensurate with the guilt of the accused.
- The fact that a confession was made as part of a sentencing negotiation does not invalidate its use as a mitigating factor for the proper sentencing decision.
- It is not lawful to negotiate a waiver of appeal before the sentence has been handed down.

In fact, negotiations violating these guidelines may bring the parties to the agreement and the judges in danger of incurring criminal liability.[26] Breaches of the agreement by the court or the prosecution do not render the whole trial unfair, but will usually result in the inadmissibility of a bargained confession. The fact of the confession must, however, always be taken into account as a mitigating factor for the purposes of sentencing, even if the court reneges on the agreement.[27] The position of the German law is dictated by a strict adherence to the principles of *iura novit curia* and the search for the material truth.[28] Any agreement between the prosecution and the defence does not bind the court at all. It arguably does not even bind the prosecution or the defence. It thus is much like an imperfect or non-actionable obligation in contractual terms. The prosecution and the court do not even need the consent of the accused to drop the charges. In connection with the wider-ranging provision of section 154 under which whole offences

[26]See for an overview Christian Pfeiffer, "Einleitung", in Karlsruher Kommentar zur Strafprozessordnung und zum Gerichtsverfassungsgesetz (1999), para. 29 et seq.

[27]Judgement of the Bundesgerichtshof in (1996) *Strafverteidiger*, p. 521.

[28]The reference to section 154 a of the Code of Criminal Procedure, which might be raised by somebody intent on showing that German law does know charge bargaining, does not really hold. Section 154 a empowers the prosecution to drop certain charges provisionally if in comparison to the remaining ones they do not have any significant weight, and the court can do so as well with the consent of the prosecution, but it may at any stage re-introduce the dropped charges after giving the defendant sufficient notice and a discretionary adjournment under section 265 of the Code of Criminal Procedure.

may be excluded from the trial this power is often used to avoid an otherwise possible acquittal on these offences in cases of doubtful evidence.[29]

Looking only at the example of German law as one representative of the wide variety of civil law thinking, it becomes clear that no general principles of domestic law will emerge on which an international court may base its procedure with regard to plea-bargaining apart from the provisions mentioned above. This is even more so if one bears in mind that the conceptual differences between the individual civil law systems are often much more substantial than those between the different varieties of the common law jurisdictions. The ICC Statute is an attempt to bridge the gap between the two systems by allowing for more flexibility in the proceedings following an admission of guilt instead of obviating the need for any scrutiny of the evidence by implementing the full effects of the common law guilty plea based on an agreement between the parties. Yet the law under the Statute is far from being clear on all points and much will be left to the Rules of Procedure and Evidence to be established by the State Parties.

6. Plea-Bargaining as Serving the Public Advantage?

Cassese made express reference to the practical usefulness of plea-bargaining. The fact that the accused who pleads guilty saves the Tribunal from having to conduct a lengthy trial with all the ensuing financial and logistical problems is considered to be contributing to the public advantage. Not mentioned by Cassese, but also imaginable as being a part of the public advantage, is the idea that the witnesses would be spared the ordeal and the secondary traumatisation of having to testify before the Trial Chambers. However, that is where the public advantage argument stops. The rest of the opinion merely deals with the benefits the accused may draw from a guilty plea. It is important to note that this argument on the face of it only applies to guilty pleas as such, but does not have an immediate bearing on the question of whether the guilty plea may be bargained between the Prosecution and the accused. Here another factor, a moral issue, comes into play, which may provide a kind of "public policy" counterbalance to the "public advantage" considerations, namely the final argument put forward during the preparation of the ICC Statute relating to the serious nature of the crimes. Especially the victims of the crimes or their relatives, or whole

[29]The recent jurisprudence of the second Senate of the Bundesgerichtshof (Decision of 10 June 1998: *Neue Zeitschrift für Strafrecht* (1999), p. 92) has come under heavy criticism from one of the leading German criminal law commentators, Thomas Weigend, in his article "Eine Prozeßordnung für abgesprochene Urteile?" in *Neue Zeitschrift für Strafrecht* (1999), p. 57. There the court considered a confession made on the basis of a sentence bargain a sufficient basis for the judgement although no other evidence was heard by the court. Weigend rightly calls this a first step towards a change in the paradigm of ascertaining the material truth of a case underlying German criminal procedure.

segments of a country's population will not understand the fact that their tormentors escape public scrutiny and may hide behind an agreement with the very institution that is supposed to ensure that justice is being done to the victims. Criminological research of domestic systems tends to show that it is not only the severity of the sentence that matters to the victim, but also the public admission or confirmation that he or she was wronged by the accused. The victims very often also want their day in court in order to confront the accused with their grievances. If this applies to ordinary theft, how much more must it be relevant to crimes against humanity. The issues at stake are too important to argue away the need for a public trial with a cathartic function on the basis of financial, staffing and docket calendar constraints, and to justify plea and especially charge bargaining on the same grounds. What tribunals like the ICTY and ICTR, and hopefully soon the ICC, are dealing with is much more serious than any domestic murder prosecution. These crimes strike at the heart of peaceful human co-existence. The confession of the accused in open session will possibly fulfil the need for public justice, but any suspicion of covert dealings between Prosecution and Defence, in which the Trial Chambers might appear to be involved as well, will raise doubts as to whether the principle of just deserts has been respected, and undermine the public's trust in the work of the Tribunals.[30]

7. Concluding Remarks

> Ein Geständnis ist niemals ein Strafmilderungsgrund: das haben die Richter erfunden, um sich Arbeit zu sparen. Das Geständnis ist auch kein Zeichen von Reue, man kann von außen kaum beurteilen, wann ein Mensch reuig ist, und ihr sollt das auch gar nicht beurteilen.[31]

Criminal law in the international legal forum is a very recent phenomenon; it lacks the sharp features that domestic systems have acquired over centuries of refining their concepts in a continuous tug-of-war between the lower and appellate courts, the legal literature and the legislature. If one looks at the dissenting and sometimes even contradictory opinions of judges at the ICTY and ICTR on one and the same issue, combined with the dearth of authoritative statements of the Appeals Chamber on matters of substantive law due to the fact that the jurisprudence of the Appeals

[30]This general concern is shared by Suzannah Linton in her article "Reviewing the case of Drazen Erdemović: Unchartered waters at the International Criminal Tribunal for the Former Yugoslavia", 12 LJIL (1999), p. 251 at p. 270.

[31]A confession is never a reason to reduce the sentence: the judges have invented this in order to have less work to do. A confession is not a sign of remorse, one cannot judge from the outside when a man feels remorse, and it is not for you to do that (translation by the author): Kurt Tucholsky, "Merkblatt für Geschworene (Leaflet for Jurors)", in: Gesammelte Werke, Vol. 7 (1929), Rowolt Publishers, rororo-Series, at pp. 159–160.

Chamber is still in its formative stages,[32] an accused will very often not really know what he is pleading to.[33] The same risk applies for the Prosecutor who may inadvertently bargain away a more serious and adequate valid charge. There is no solid basis for bargaining yet. It is not surprising that the ICC Statute contains much narrower offence descriptions and will be supplemented by a catalogue of elements of the respective crimes. This reflects the uncertainty prevalent among the international community about the exact content of international criminal law proper. It is thus in my view a better approach to have the accused admit the facts alleged in the indictment and leave it to the court to apply the law to them. The mere admission of facts is a feature common to all legal systems; the reduction of sentence for a frank admission of responsibility, too.

If the international community is serious about international criminal prosecution of those responsible for atrocities like in Yugoslavia and Rwanda, then it must be prepared to fund this enterprise accordingly in order to be able to afford full public trials and at the same time to avoid overloaded dockets like those of the ICTY and ICTR. Understaffing and underfunding such highly visible institutions with equally high-minded goals and principles makes a mockery and a farce of the ideas behind international criminal justice. The commitment to the reign of the rule of law and international criminal prosecutions can no longer conveniently be used as a mere platform for displaying a nation's or international organisation's high moral stance. During all those years when the ICC seemed far away there was no real danger of any actual obligation arising out of professing one's deep belief in that cause. Those days are over. Now this commitment means not only moral, but constant financial and diplomatic commitment. With the advent of the two ad hoc tribunals the winds of change have become stronger and will hopefully continue to blow at full force until the implementation of the ICC and help strengthen its presently rather weak position. There is no way back.

---

[32]One should bear in mind that as yet there is no permanent Appeals Chamber, because under Rule 27 of the RPE of the ICTY, the judges of the Trial Chambers rotate on a regular basis between the latter and the Appeals Chamber, something which was criticised by the Expert Group that looked at the efficiency of the proceedings before the ICTY and ICTR. See the Report of the Expert Group to Conduct a Review of the Effective Operation and Functioning of the International Tribunal (sic!) for the Former Yugoslavia (ICTY) and the International Criminal Tribunal for Rwanda (ICTR), UN Document No. A/54/634 of 22 Nov. 1999, at paras. 105–106.

[33]I would like to thank my colleague Olivier Fourmy, Senior Legal Officer of Trial Chamber I (ICTY), for drawing my attention to this particular angle.

PART V

Defence Counsel

JOHN E. ACKERMAN*

14. Assignment of Defence Counsel at the ICTY

1. Introduction

It is a great honour to have been invited to submit an article for this book honouring Judge Gabrielle McDonald. I have had the pleasure of acquaintance with Judge McDonald for several years, having practiced in Houston, Texas where she worked and sat for many years as a Federal District Judge. I experienced her commitment to the rights of the accused first-hand in a trial in which she presided in the early 1980s in Houston, in which I served as counsel for an accused. On another occasion I assisted in a case in which the Ku Klux Klan was engaged in harassment of Vietnamese fishermen on the Gulf coast of Texas. Judge McDonald took severe actions against the Klan and effectively ended the difficulties.

Judge McDonald grew up in the 1950s in New York City. She witnessed her mother fight battles against racism and injustice. These experiences led her to law school and to a career in civil rights law. During her formative years and continuing into her years in university and law school the civil rights movement exploded onto the American scene. It is very appropriate that in a book honouring this distinguished jurist that there be an article on the rights of indigent accused to the assignment of effective defence counsel.

Throughout the 1950s and early 1960s, it was the practice in many States of the United States to deny appointed counsel to indigent defendants charged with offenses that did not carry the death penalty. This was especially true in the southern states and as a result carried racial undertones with it. Parallel to the civil rights movement came the Warren Court. The Supreme Court of

*Mr. Ackerman practices criminal defence law in Houston, Texas and before the ICTY. He previously served as Dean of the National College for Criminal Defense at the University of Houston and as President of the National Association of Criminal Defense Lawyers. He was appointed by Governor Ann Richards of Texas to the Criminal District Court of Harris County, Texas where he served as the Judge for a six-month period. The views expressed herein are those of the author and not of the Tribunal or the United Nations.

R. May et al., Essays on ICTY Procedure and Evidence in Honour of Gabrielle Kirk McDonald, 167–176.

the United States under Chief Justice Earl Warren began expanding the rights of the accused by applying the Federal Bill of Rights to State criminal justice systems through the due process provisions of the Fourteenth Amendment. On 18 March 1963, the Supreme Court issued its famous decision in the case of *Gideon v. Wainwright ("Gideon")*.[1] Gideon had been convicted in the State of Florida of the felony offense of breaking and entering with intent to commit a misdemeanour. Prior to his trial he had asked to be assigned a lawyer to defend him. The request was denied and he was tried, convicted and sentenced without benefit of counsel. He did not appeal his conviction through the Florida appellate system, but filed a petition for a writ of habeas corpus with the Florida Supreme Court which petition was summarily denied. He then filed a hand written *pro se* Petition for Certiorari with the United States Supreme Court. His petition was granted. A Washington D.C. lawyer, Abe Fortas, was appointed by the Supreme Court to represent Gideon. Fortas was later appointed Associate Justice on the Supreme Court; a shining example of the importance with which the Supreme Court viewed the necessity of competent and effective counsel.

The issue of assigned counsel had last been comprehensively addressed by the Supreme Court in 1942 in *Betts v. Brady ("Betts")*.[2] In that case, the Court had decided that the Sixth Amendment of the Federal Constitution did not require appointment of counsel in all State cases. The Court said, "appointment of counsel is not a fundamental right, essential to a fair trial."[3] The Court specifically directed the parties in *Gideon* to brief the question of whether *Betts* should be reconsidered.

In the *Gideon* decision, the Court held that the Sixth Amendment right to counsel was made obligatory on the States under and by virtue of the language of the Fourteenth Amendment. The Court said:

> From the very beginning, our state and national constitutions and laws have laid great emphasis on procedural and substantive safeguards designed to assure fair trials before impartial tribunals in which every defendant stands equal before the law. This noble ideal cannot be realized if the poor man charged with crime has to face his accusers without a lawyer to assist him.[4]

Meanwhile great strides were being taken internationally with regard to human rights. Soon after it was established the United Nations, through the General Assembly adopted and proclaimed the Universal Declaration of Human Rights of 1948. Although not mentioned specifically, it can be argued that the right to counsel for the indigent is implicit in the language of Articles 10 and 11 of the Declaration. The Council of Europe adopted the European Convention on Human Rights in 1950. The right to assigned counsel for indigent accused is specifically enshrined in Article 6, thereof.

---

[1]372 U.S. 335, 83 S.Ct. 792, 9 L.Ed.2d 799 (1963).
[2]316 U.S. 455 (1942).
[3]Id. at 471.
[4]*Gideon*, at 344.

The same right is established in the International Covenant on Civil and Political Rights at Article 14, adopted in 1966. Finally the right to assigned counsel was recognised in the 1969 American Convention on Human Rights. Thus, the necessity of providing counsel for indigent criminal accused has now received universal recognition by the community of nations.

Implicit in the entire concept of providing counsel for the indigent accused is the proposition that counsel is provided to ensure that the accused is in an equal position vis-à-vis his accuser before the tribunal before which he will be adjudged. This is an important component of the concept of Equality of Arms between the prosecutor and the accused in a criminal trial that goes to be very heart of the notion of a fair trial.[5] Prosecuting offices world-wide are usually staffed by lawyers with experience and training in both the criminal law and trial procedures and practices. It follows that assigned counsel should have similar experience and training. Unfortunately, this is not always the case. To implement fully the "noble ideals" of the International Conventions and proclamations discussed above, it must be the case. There really could be no tenable argument to the contrary. Chief Justice Burger, of the United States Supreme Court once likened the criminal justice system to a three-legged stool; the court, the prosecutor and the defence. If any leg is weak the stool will fall. A decision in a criminal court can have no legitimacy if there is even the suggestion that it came about due to weakness of the judiciary, the prosecutor or the defence. To be accepted, all three components must be competent and effective.

2. Right to Counsel at the ICTY

In this background the United Nations Security Council created the ICTY. The provision of counsel to indigent accused was specifically mandated in the Tribunal's Statute. Article 18 provides that a "[...] suspect shall be entitled to be assisted by counsel of his own choice, including the right to have legal assistance assigned to him without payment by him [...] if he does not have sufficient means to pay for it [...]." Similarly Article 21 extends this right to the trial stage. The accused has the right "[...] to have legal assistance assigned to him, in any case where the interests of justice so require, and without payment by him [...]."." Article 21 describes this stated right as a "minimum guarantee" to be provided in "*full equality*."[6]

This statutory right to counsel before the Tribunal was implemented by the adoption of Rules 42, 44 and 45 of the Rules of Procedure and Evidence. An accused may be represented by counsel of his own choice, paid by him or someone of his behalf or, if indigent, by counsel assigned to him by the

[5] See, *Prosecutor v. Tadić, Judgement,* Case No. IT-94-1-A, A. Ch., 15 July 1999 ("*Tadić* Judgment") at para. 44.

[6] Emphasis supplied.

Registrar. The mechanics of this process was placed in the hands of the Registrar of the Tribunal. Rule 44(A) defines the qualification of counsel engaged by a suspect or accused to be someone admitted to practice law in a State, or a University Professor.[7] These are, perhaps, the least stringent requirements that could conceivably be imposed. Rule 44 refers to and incorporates the Directive on Assignment of Defence Counsel. Such a Directive was adopted on 28 July 1994. Article 14 of this directive sets out the qualifications for counsel to be assigned by the Registrar to the indigent. He or she must meet the following qualifications: (i) he is admitted to the practice of law in a State, or is a University professor of law; (ii) he speaks one of the two working languages of the Tribunal; (iii) he agrees to be assigned as counsel by the Tribunal to represent any indigent suspect or accused; and (iv) his name has been included in the list envisaged in Rule 45(A) of the Rules. There is an exception as to the second requirement. Counsel who speaks the language of the suspect, but not one of the working languages can be assigned if authorised by a Judge or a Trial Chamber.[8]

The procedure for assignment of defence counsel and provision for their support is in need of substantial revisiting and restructuring. One of the major criticisms levelled at the Tribunal is the length of trials. To some extent, at least, trials are lengthened by the lack of experience and training of defence counsel appearing before the Trial Chambers. Many have no experience whatsoever with criminal law. Many have no experience whatsoever with the adversary nature of trial proceedings before the ICTY. Many are unfamiliar with the Statute and Rules of Procedure and the practice before the Tribunal that has developed through the case law that has interpreted and applied the provisions of the Statute and Rules.

Recently, the issue of assignment of counsel was examined by the Expert Group to Conduct a Review of the Effective Operation and Functioning of the International Tribunal for the Former Yugoslavia and the International

---

[7]This rule can be read to establish these minimum requirements only for lawyers engaged by the accused himself, not for those assigned by the Tribunal. There is precedent for the argument that an accused is in a poor position to complain about the competence of a lawyer he has himself engaged. However, when the court supplies a lawyer, or a list from which a lawyer may be chosen, then the accused is in a position to complain bitterly if that lawyer is not competent and does not render effective assistance of counsel.

[8]In this writer's opinion, this should only occur if there is, at the same time, a counsel assigned who speaks one of the official languages. A lawyer who does not speak either English or French cannot even read the transcript of proceedings. This is crucial to be able to afford effective assistance. There have been numerous instances in trial where the translation has not reflected the true meaning of what was intended and the counsel was unable to notice the error. Where Trial Chambers frequently announce their decisions orally only, such counsel is not in a position to later review the decision without access to a readable transcript. Thus, if the Registry determines, with leave of a Judge or Chamber to assign someone who does not speak one of the official languages, it should, at the same time, assign someone who does. Furthermore, if the second assigned counsel who speaks either English or French does not share a common language with his colleague, the Registry must provide an interpreter to ensure that they are able to communicate effectively.

Criminal Tribunal for Rwanda.[9] Unfortunately, the Expert Group's examination was sometimes cursory and as a result, on occasion, they missed the mark. It is, however, a useful document from which to gain an understanding of the problems facing the Tribunal in the area of assignment of counsel.

3. Assignment and Qualifications of Counsel

The first issue, one demanding rather immediate attention, deals with the quality of assigned counsel. Rule 44 and the Directive on Assignment of Counsel should be amended to enhance the quality of counsel appearing in Tribunal cases. Perhaps the most efficient way to effect the necessary changes would be to remove from Rule 44 all language dealing with the qualifications of defence counsel and simply refer to the Directive for that purpose.

The Directive could then be amended to heighten the requirements for defence counsel at the Tribunal. A proposed lead counsel should demonstrate at least 10 years experience in criminal trial practice and a proposed co-counsel should demonstrate at least 5 years of such experience.[10] This could all be accomplished with a comprehensive application form devised by the Registry.

In addition there should be a mandatory training requirement of a minimum of fifteen hours to be completed before someone could be added to the list, or at least to be completed within 90 days of inclusion on the list. This training could be provided by the Registry or by independent organisations with curricula approved by the Registry. All training should be at the expense of the trainee, excepting the cost for faculty and facilities. It would be appropriate to charge a fee for attendance at such training sessions. Fifteen hours of such training should be an annual requirement due to the continuing changes in the Tribunal's jurisprudence.

Once the Directive has been amended, as recommended above, the Registrar should remove from the Rule 45(A) list all persons who are not currently assigned to Tribunal cases or who have not had significant experience before the Tribunal either in the Trial or Appellate Chambers. Those removed should be advised of the new requirements and invited to resubmit an application on a form prepared by the Registry.[11] Two lists would

[9]Report of the Expert Group to Conduct a Review of the Effective Operation and Functioning of the International Tribunal for the Former Yugoslavia and the International Criminal Tribunal and Rwanda United Nations General Assembly, Doc. A/54/634 ("Expert Group").

[10]This recommendation is in accord with the recommendation of the Expert Group found at para. 210 of their report; modified by recommendations from the Association of Defence Counsel.

[11]There are as many as 350 lawyers currently on the list. Such a change would also have the effect of reducing the list to a more useful and workable number. It must be daunting indeed for a detainee to be handed a list of 350 lawyers and asked to choose one from the list. How is the detainee to know if he is making a wise and valid choice when the list has been so poorly screened in the first instance?

then be created. A list of enrolled lead counsel and a list of enrolled co-counsel.

Since the Tribunal functions on the adversary, common-law system, it should be considered whether it would be advisable to provide that where two counsel are assigned, at least one of those counsel be a person with experience in an adversary trial system.

The Tribunal should consider the formation of a Tribunal Bar Association, membership in which would be required for appearance before the Tribunal. All the requirements discussed above could then be incorporated and would apply to both Prosecutors and Defence. Such a bar association could then promulgate disciplinary rules with an appropriate enforcement mechanism, including suspension and disbarment.

The Expert Group, having observed some proceedings before Trial Chambers was highly critical of the interrogation of witnesses "characterized by the absence of crisp, focused questions and by long, rambling answers tending to be narratives, at times vague, repetitive and irrelevant. ... Such answers seem to be evoked by vague, multiple or compound questions and the relative infrequency of objections to them."[12] It is very likely that the situation described arose from a counsel unfamiliar with the adversary system. Lawyers in the adversary system are trained to ask crisp, focused questions and to object to answers that are not responsive, although some fail to do either.

The Expert Group was critical of what they saw as an unusual level of motion practice before the Tribunal. With respect, this writer suggests that they were wrong in their appraisal of this issue. The Tribunal is, in effect, a new criminal justice system. Its Statute and Rules raise as many questions as they answer. Motion practice is the chief way by which jurisprudence is developed in an adversary criminal justice system. It is too much to expect all issues to be settled with only three Appeals judgements[13] having been issued. In addition the Rules are constantly being amended which raise new questions. Lastly, the jurisprudence of the Tribunal is not readily available to counsel. Many motions are filed which raise settled issues simply because counsel, for whatever reason, do not know the issue has been settled. Training requirements would go a long way toward solving this problem. Although the Tribunal makes an effort through its web site to make decisions and orders available, the web site is wholly inadequate for this purpose. Many

[12]Expert Group, para. 75.

[13]*Tadić* Judgment, supra note 5; *Prosecutor v. Erdemović, Judgement,* Case No. IT-96-22-A, A. Ch., 7 Oct. 1997 ("*Erdemović* Judgment"); and *Prosecutor V. Aleksovski, Judgement,* Case No. IT-95-14/1-A, 24 March 2000. The *Erdemović* Judgment contributed little to the jurisprudence of the Tribunal since he pleaded guilty and the issue revolved primarily around the guilty plea.

decisions and orders never appear on the web site. Steps should be taken to improve access to these materials.[14]

4. Compensation and Support of Assigned Counsel

The Expert Group discussed at some length the issue of compensation of assigned defence counsel. The Group pointed out that the Defence Counsel Unit of the Registry consumes as much as 15% of the Tribunal's budget. The implication was that this is too much and steps should be taken to reduce this expenditure.[15]

On 7 April 2000, the Registry took such a step, although a seriously misguided one. The solution was to dramatically reduce the number of hours that a counsel could work for his client each month, thus having the effect of reducing the expenditure for assigned defence counsel. Such a scheme, of course, will likely dramatically affect other issues of importance to the Tribunal, such as the time between arrest and trial and the time taken to resolve appeals. It is clear that if counsel must work less hours on a case then the time necessary for preparation for trial or for preparing appellate briefs will need to be extended. If is difficult to imagine that any money will really be saved since the total hours expended on a case are likely to be roughly the same in any event.

On 28 April 2000, twenty-eight detainees, through their counsel filed a Motion with the Bureau of the Tribunal challenging the new Registry scheme as being violative of the Statute of the Tribunal and international law principle of Equality of Arms.[16] No decision has been reached as to this Motion.

In over thirty years experience with numerous criminal justice systems, this writer has observed that it is endemic in criminal justice systems that when budgets are reduced, the first place to cut is compensation for assigned counsel. The Prosecutor and Judges generally have significant power to control their budgetary allowances while the defence is largely powerless. Thus, the defence, as the weakest leg of the triumvirate, becomes the target for budget cutting and manipulation.

---

[14]At para. 183, the Expert Group speaks of a new software program designed to make all these materials easily available to all counsel and suggests that it is now operational. This writer has seen no indication of that at the ICTY. One would hope that such a plan is actually being implemented.

[15]See Expert Group Report, paras. 202–208.

[16]*Emergency Motion Filed on Behalf of Various Accused Directed to the Bureau of the International Criminal Tribunal for the Former Yugoslavia to Declare the Registry's "Modifications of Remuneration for Counsel, Assignment Practice for Support Staff" to be in Violation of Articles 20 and 21 of the Statute of the ICTY and in Violation of the Principle of Equality of Arms between the Prosecution and the Defence,* Case No. IT-00-38-Misc. 4, 28 Apr. 2000.

It must be kept in mind throughout that indigent accused are entitled, in full equality, to the effective assistance of counsel in their defence. While the Expert Group was concerned with a defence counsel unit budget that consumed 15% of the Tribunal's resources no concern was expressed about the Office of the Prosecutor that consumes nearly 30%.

When a case is indicted and the indictee is arrested, the Office of the Prosecutor assigns a trial team to the case. The team consists of a Senior Trial Attorney, two Co-Counsel, one Legal Officer, a Trial Support Assistant and a Case Manager. The accused gets one assigned counsel until trial begins and, if approved, a legal assistant and an investigator. He may also receive the assistance of a translator. If the Registrar considers that "exceptional circumstances" exist, co-counsel may be assigned to a case, sixty days prior to the commencement of the trial. However, the accused is never provided anything approaching the resources committed to a case by the Prosecutor. Just this issue alone can occasion significant pre-trial delay. By the time an indictment is confirmed and the detainee arrested the Prosecutor has spent many months in gathering evidence and preparing the case. Only when the detainee is arrested does defence counsel begin the task of gathering evidence, digesting and organising it, conducting an investigation, interviewing witnesses, getting documents translated and generally preparing to meet the Prosecutor's case and prepare a case for the defence. It is somehow expected that one lone counsel with limited support can do this, while working on the other side is the Prosecution trial team discussed above. This expectation is manifestly unrealistic.

Article 21 of the Statute promises the assignment of defence counsel as a "minimum guarantee" in "full equality". This is the promise, but the reality is quite different. The Tribunal should not proclaim to the World that it provides assigned counsel as a minimum guarantee in full equality and then fail to do so in reality. One lone defence counsel labouring against three Prosecution counsel hardly can be seen as providing "full equality."[17]

Clearly there is justification for the budget of the Office of the Prosecutor being somewhat larger than that for defence counsel because of the investigative aspects of the office and the fact that the office appears in all cases where assigned defence counsel only appears in indigent cases. Furthermore, the Office of the Prosecutor has the expense of maintaining offices, equipment and staff which costs are borne personally by defence counsel. Rather than showing an unacceptably large commitment to the defence, the above figures seem to show a rather paltry commitment to the defence as compared with the Prosecutor.

A huge, practical disparity exists in rates paid to defence counsel due to the differing economies of the nations of the world. This results in some lawyers being paid vastly more than the prevailing rates in their home

[17]This disparity is sometimes exacerbated by limits placed by the Registrar on the investigative and translation work that needs to be completed, such as limiting hours or in some cases refusing payment for the translation of documents.

countries and some being paid considerably less. The Expert Group was critical of the Registry's position that there could be no variation between national groups and the hourly rates paid based upon UN regulations. The Expert Group pointed out that these regulations do not apply since defence counsel are not UN employees but independent contractors.[18]

It is clearly in the best interests of the Tribunal to be able to attract the best-qualified lawyers to appear in cases before the Tribunal. As it stands today, the maximum hourly rate payable to counsel is $110 per hour for those with 20 years professional experience or more. Comparably experienced trial lawyers from developed countries such as the United States, the United Kingdom and Australia would earn an average of $250–$350 per hour for the same work.[19] Such lawyers are significantly under-compensated by the Tribunal and discouraged by these rates form even considering taking a case here.[20] Lawyers from less-developed countries, on the other hand, are experiencing a windfall. Such a system is decidedly unfair.

The Expert Group has indicated that the Registry is considering a lump-sum fee arrangement. This would be completely unworkable. It is impossible at the outset of a case to predict its length and complexity. No one would accept a case unless the lump sum is paid in advance. What happens, as occurs with some frequency, when that lawyer who has been paid his lump sum is dismissed by his client? How does the Registry get its money back? Although such a system could conceivably work in a confined and tightly controlled national system, it could never work in this Tribunal and should be rejected.

5. Conclusion

At some point the world will deliver its judgment of this Tribunal. It will not be praised for doing its work quickly, nor will it be praised for doing its work cheaply. The post-World War II Tribunals are not remembered for the swiftness of their trials, nor the expense of their operations. They are remembered for whether or not justice was done there; and many argue

---

[18]Expert Group Report, para. 206.

[19]The writer can say from his own personal experience that the remuneration problem is only a part of it. When one takes on a case at the Tribunal he must spend weeks or months at a time away from this family and loved ones and his private law practice. The private law practice effectively disappears because of the all-consuming nature of a major Tribunal case.

[20]This contention is not diminished by the fact that several lawyers from developed countries have applied to be included in the list. Many have an interest beyond the financial – either an interest in international criminal law or in accepting a new and different challenge. Few who apply for the list are fully aware of the all-consuming commitment involved with assignment to such a case. The new scheme of the Registry further exacerbates this problem.

effectively that it was not. If this Tribunal is to achieve a lasting and favourably legacy it will be for having provided fair trials to persons brought before it and setting a shining example for the world to follow. The controlling *raison d'être* for this Tribunal is to contribute to bringing peace and security to former Yugoslavia. It thus becomes crucial that those living in former Yugoslavia view the Tribunal as a fair institution. A fair trial is only possible when all three legs of the stool are strong. Unless care is taken to strengthen and maintain the defence leg of the stool the Tribunal will ultimately be seen as a failure.

MICHAEL GREAVES[1]

15. The Right to Counsel before the ICTY and the ICTR for Indigent Suspects: An Unfettered Right?

Each of the two *ad hoc* Tribunals set up by the United Nations in the 1990s with which Judge Gabriel McDonald has been associated, whether as President of the ICTY or as President of the Appeals Chamber of the ICTR, guarantees to the Defendant the right to counsel "of his or her own choosing" in more or less identical terms. The ICTY Statute Article 21(4)(d) reads as follows:

> (4) In the determination of any charge against the accused pursuant to the present Statute, the accused shall be entitled to the following minimum guarantees, in full equality: [...]
>
> (d) to be tried in his presence, and to defend himself in person or through legal assistance of his own choosing; to be informed, if he does not have legal assistance, of this right; and to have legal assistance assigned to him, in any case where the interests of justice so require, and without payment by him in any such case if he does not have sufficient means to pay for it;

ICTR Statute Article 20(4)(d) merely adds an alternative feminine to the same phraseology.

In practice, as will be seen, this right has not been an unfettered right but has been subject to some restrictions before both Tribunals. There has also been a markedly different approach by each Tribunal to the concept of "counsel of the Defendant's own choice".

[1]Michael Greaves was called to the Bar of England and Wales in 1976. Following 20 years in practice at common law Bar on the Midland and Oxford Circuit, he has since 1997 acted as Defence Counsel in two trials before the ICTY and has made various other appearances before both the ICTY and the ICTR.

R. May et al., Essays on ICTY Procedure and Evidence in Honour of Gabrielle Kirk McDonald, 177–185.

A. Who May Act as Counsel Before the ICTY and ICTR

Before considering these matters one may ask: who may act as counsel before the International Tribunals?

Though slightly different in language, Rule 44 of each Tribunal's Rules of Procedure and Evidence states that, subject to proper verification by the Registrar, counsel "shall be considered" qualified to represent a suspect or accused if counsel is either "admitted to the practice of law in a State" or "is a University professor of law".

Each Registry maintains a list of those who have submitted the appropriate information about themselves and who thereby indicate a willingness to be assigned as Counsel to a suspect or an accused. The criteria by which each Tribunal measures the eligibility of counsel are, however, slightly different. The ICTY Directive on the Assignment of Defence Counsel Revision 7 Article 14[2] states:

> Pre-requisites for the assignment of counsel
>
> (A) Any person may be assigned as counsel if the Registrar is satisfied that he fulfils the following pre-requisites;
> (i) he is admitted to the practice of law in a State, or is a University professor of law;
> (ii) he speaks one of the two working languages of the Tribunal;
> (iii) he agrees to be assigned as counsel by the Tribunal to represent any indigent suspect or accused;
> (iv) his name has been included in the list envisaged in Rule 45 (A) of the Rules.
>
> (B) In particular circumstances, upon the request of an indigent suspect or accused, the Registrar may assign counsel who speaks the language of the suspect or the accused but does not speak either of the two working languages of the Tribunal.

It is notable that no restriction exists which excludes from the list of assignable counsel those who have only been admitted to practise law for a short period and who therefore are relatively inexperienced. Indeed Annex VI of the Directive which sets out the fees payable to counsel clearly implies that anyone who has just been admitted to practise law in their country or who have only just achieved their professorship can act as Leading Counsel for a suspect or an accused.[3] Thus a suspect or accused could, in a case where he or she is facing a charge of genocide which, after a trial, is likely to attract a very long sentence, probably life imprisonment, be represented by counsel who has only a few weeks experience as a lawyer or, in the case of a

---

[2] As amended on 19th July 1999.

[3] A differential hourly rate is payable for varying levels of experience: those of 0–9 years' professional experience receive a gross hourly rate of US$ 80.

University Professor, no trial experience at all. The *onus* for taking such a decision is thus placed squarely upon the shoulders of the suspect or the accused to examine carefully the *curriculum vitae* of those counsel on the Registrar's list and to make his choice accordingly. In that sense a suspect or an accused is given a wide choice when it comes to a request for the assignment of counsel. In practice, though there have been examples of an accused selecting counsel who have little or no experience of conducting complex criminal trials, there has not, as yet, been an appeal mounted because of the incompetence of or negligence of counsel.

The comparable provision of the ICTR Directive on the Assignment of Defence Counsel, Article 13, is more restrictive as to who can be assigned:

> Pre-requisites for the assignment of counsel
>
> Any person may be assigned as counsel if the Registrar is satisfied that he fulfils the following pre-requisites:
>
> (i) he is admitted to practice law in a State, or is a professor of law at a university or similar academic institution *and has at least 10 years' relevant experience*,
> (ii) he speaks one of the working languages of the Tribunal, namely French and English,
> (iii) he agrees to be assigned as counsel by the Tribunal to represent a suspect or accused, and
> (iv) his name has been included in the list envisaged in Rule 45(A) of the Rules. [emphasis added]

It will be seen that a significant and crucial difference has been introduced which restricts those who have less than ten years relevant experience from being assigned as counsel. Thus, at a stroke, a vast swathe of legal practitioners and junior University Professors is rendered ineligible for practice before the ICTR.

In this regard it may be argued that the ICTY position on the issue of experience gives full effect to ICTY Statute Article 21, allowing a suspect or an accused, subject to the matter of working languages, an uninhibited choice, regardless of experience or suitability, as to who is going to represent him at trial. The ICTR, on the other hand, prevents the suspect or accused from choosing anyone as his counsel who has less than ten years' relevant experience. On the face of it the ICTY position adheres more faithfully to the clear words of its Statute than does the ICTR to its Statute.

Plainly it is reasonable to insist that those assigned are in one degree or another qualified as lawyers. But there is a proper argument to be made that the restrictions made by the ICTR's Rules are neither sensible nor lawful.

As to the first proposition there are often counsel of, for example, seven or eight years' experience in the criminal courts who are eminently suited to act as co-counsel to a more experienced leading counsel. Indeed, many might find such a relationship much easier to manage given that having two counsel of equal experience can sometimes lead to stresses that do not obtain where there is a clear difference in experience, though this will always be a matter of individual circumstance dependent entirely upon the character of counsel.

As an example there is at least one counsel who has been assigned in several cases before the ICTY who has demonstrated clearly the requisite skills and knowledge as an advocate who cannot, because of this arbitrary restriction, even get on the list of counsel at the ICTR. This particular lawyer would be a considerable asset for the ICTR which thus deprives itself and defendants of the widest possible selection of lawyers.

The second issue is as to whether such a restriction is lawful? The ICTY approach is, it may be submitted, one designed to give as full effect as possible to the phraseology of counsel "of his or her own choosing". It is properly arguable that the restriction which exists as to experience in the ICTR is one which is not justifiable on the clear wording of its Statute. Whilst it may be desirable to encourage suspects and defendants to select only those with experience, it must be very doubtful that there is a legal entitlement to impose such a restriction.

It might be lawful to have such a restriction if one could say that such a restriction existed in many of the world's jurisdictions and had thus acquired the status of a "general principle of law" but such restrictions do not appear to exist elsewhere. Indeed if such restrictions do exist in a national jurisdiction they may well fall foul of national laws on restraint of trade and thus be held unlawful in any event. This is in distinction to the other restriction which exists, that of language:[4] in most jurisdictions there is a clear requirement that lawyers are fluent in the official language of their country. It may be said that the requirement that an individual lawyer speaks one of the working languages of the Tribunal is one which may properly be justified on the basis that it reflects a general principle of law well established in the national jurisdictions of the world.

2. The Language Requirement

The language requirement imposed by the ICTY Directive on the Assignment of Defence Counsel Article 14 (A) (ii) and by the ICTR Directive on the Assignment of Defence Counsel Article 13 (ii) are, on the face of it, identical. The ICTR, however, admits of no exception to this and therefore counsel for an accused will speak either French or English. The ICTY's position is, however, different. As will have been seen from the ICTY Directive on the Assignment of Defence Counsel Article 14 (B), in particular circumstances, a Judge or the Trial Chamber seized of the case may, upon the request of an indigent suspect or accused, authorise the Registrar

[4] See below.

to assign counsel who speaks the language of the suspect or the accused but does not speak either of the two working languages of the Tribunal.

In practical terms the lack of an exceptional power has not had any or any significant effect at the ICTR. Although the native language of most Rwandans is Kinyarwanda, many people are fluent in French. In addition the accused detained by the ICTR are, almost without exception, highly educated and sophisticated individuals, many of whom speak both French *and* English.[5] Many Counsel are native French speakers or have a reasonable facility in French and the language issue has not presented direct problems of the kind which have arisen at ICTY, save that language produced, in effect, the thorny problem of the "moratorium" against French and Canadian Counsel of which more below.

Language is, however, an issue of some concern at the ICTY. Initially there was a clear requirement that counsel must be able to speak one of the two official languages of the Tribunal. This has gradually been eroded over time to a situation where it has become not unusual for an accused at the ICTY to be represented by someone who does not speak or read either of the two official languages of the Tribunal.

The history of the Rules and the Articles of the ICTY Directive on the Assignment of Defence Counsel demonstrate the erosion. In October 1995, ICTY Rule 44 was the only criterion for the assignment of counsel:

> Rule 44
>
> Appointment and Qualifications of Counsel
>
> Counsel engaged by a suspect or an accused shall file his power of attorney with the Registrar at the earliest opportunity. A counsel shall be considered qualified to represent a suspect or accused if he satisfies the Registrar that he is admitted to the practice of law in a State, or is a University professor of law.[6]

By December 1996, ICTY Rule 45 showed that a first crack in thc wall had appeared:

> Rule 45
>
> Assignment of Counsel
>
> (A)(i) A list of counsel who speak one or both of the working languages of the Tribunal, meet the requirements of Rule 44 and have indicated their willingness to be assigned by the Tribunal to indigent suspects or accused, shall be kept by the Registrar.

[5]The UN Detention Unit has the services of a first class English teacher who has converted the writer's client's English from non-existent to a passable command and understanding of the language in just ten months.

[6]ICTY Rules, as amended 6 Oct. 1995 (IT/32/REV.6).

> (ii) In particular circumstances, upon the request of an indigent suspect or accused, *the Registrar may be authorised, by a Judge or a Trial Chamber seized of the case*, to assign counsel who speaks the language of the suspect or the accused but does not speak either of the two working languages of the Tribunal.[7] [emphasis added]

It will be noted that the assignment of counsel who did not speak an official language of the Tribunal was a matter that was considered of sufficient importance to require the authorisation of a Judge or of a Trial Chamber.

By 1998 the importance of this matter being reserved to a Judge or a Trial Chamber had, however, been downgraded, in that the intervention of a Judge or a Trial Chamber was no longer required and such a decision could be taken by the Registrar alone:

> Rule 45
>
> Assignment of Counsel
>
> (A) A list of counsel who speak one or both of the working languages of the Tribunal, meet the requirements of Rule 44 and have indicated their willingness to be assigned by the Tribunal to indigent suspects or accused, shall be kept by the Registrar.
> (B) In particular circumstances, upon the request of an indigent suspect or accused, *the Registrar may assign* counsel who speaks the language of the suspect or the accused but does not speak either of the two working languages of the Tribunal.[8] [emphasis added]

There are aspects of grave concern in this.

Firstly, Leading Counsel who does not speak one of the official languages of the Tribunal cannot readily study the jurisprudence of international criminal law. A quick perusal of the shelves of the ICTY library will reveal just how little of the necessary jurisprudence is available in the Bosnian/Croatian/Serbian group of languages. Translations of the latest judgement or decision of the ICTY tend to appear after a lapse of some months. On any view this must seriously inhibit the ability of counsel properly to represent their client, especially in the early days of their case when so many crucial decisions must be taken. A clear understanding of the jurisprudence of the law and of the Rules of Procedure and Evidence is an essential prerequisite at this time so that no irreparable mistake is made which may fatally harm the client's interests.

Secondly, in such a situation Leading Counsel cannot communicate easily with the Prosecution. Speaking through an interpreter is no substitute for

[7] ICTY Rules, as amended 3 Dec. 1996 (IT/32/REV.10).
[8] ICTY Rules, as amended 9 and 10 July 1998 (IT/32/REV.13).

direct communication on matters which will be of considerable importance in the preparation of the case and dealing with all those issues which inevitably arise both pre-trial and during the trial.

Thirdly, Leading Counsel may be co-defending alongside other counsel who do not speak Bosnian/Croatian/Serbian. Thus he or she cannot, save through an interpreter, properly discuss matters which must be discussed between co-defending counsel. Not only may this damage the client's interests but it may also have the effect of damaging the interests of a co-accused. Although this situation might also occur with a French speaker who does not speak any English co-defending with English speaking counsel who has no French, this does not appear to have happened as yet whereas numerous lawyers from the former Yugoslavia have been assigned without being capable in either of the two official languages. In any event the monolingual French- or English speaker has the significant advantage of ready access to the relevant jurisprudence.

It is sometimes said that this problem can be offset by the assignment of co-counsel who does have the appropriate language skills. But, under present highly restrictive guidelines, it is difficult to have co-counsel assigned until the case is far advanced, indeed near to trial, and long after an adequate facility in an official language of the Tribunal is required.

It is very difficult to believe that, unless there are *genuinely* exceptional circumstances (as opposed to the demands of mere expediency), the assignment of counsel who cannot speak an official language is really in the interests of justice. This is no mere theoretical concept of the problem of language but is one which has been seen to operate in practice to the considerable detriment of Defendants' interests by many who have had the privilege of practising before the ICTY.

3. The ICTR Moratorium against French and Canadian Counsel

Turning back now to the ICTR, one must examine the issue which came to be known as "the moratorium". Because of the fact that most Defendants spoke and were fluent in French, many chose counsel from Canada (particularly from the Province of Quebec who were both francophone and, because criminal law is a matter reserved to Federal rather than Provincial jurisdiction, common lawyers for the purposes of criminal law and procedure) or from France.[9] In time there came to be a heavy preponderance of such counsel. As a result a decision was taken to impose a moratorium against further assignment of counsel from Canada and France.

---

[9]For reasons, one suspects, of history both recent and longer ago, few Belgian counsel have been chosen by Rwandan accused.

The matter first appears to have troubled the Tribunal judicially in the case of *Prosecutor v. Nyiramasuhuko and Ntahobali*[10] in which counsel for Nyiramasuhuko sought the assignment of co-counsel. The Learned Judges in that case, Kama P., Aspegren and Pillay JJ., held:

> That to ensure the most efficient defence possible in the context of a fair trial, and where appropriate, the accused and Counsel should be offered the possibility of designating the counsel of their choice from the list drawn by the Registrar for this purpose, the Registrar having to take into consideration the wishes of the accused and Counsel, *along with namely the resources of the Tribunal, competence and recognized experience of counsel, geographical distribution, a balance of the principal legal systems of the world, irrespective of the age, gender, race or nationality of the candidates*. [emphasis added][11]

This was taken by the Registry as sanction for a policy of exclusion from consideration for assignment of counsel from Canada and France, although the decision was careful to claim that there would be no discrimination on the grounds of race or nationality.

Thus a situation arose where members of the various Provincial Canadian and French Bars, overwhelmingly but not exclusively Canadian and French by nationality, were being excluded because of a desire to take into consideration the "geographical distribution" of the candidates and to achieve "a balance of the principal legal systems of the world". One might be forgiven for thinking that, whatever the semantic nuances, this amounted to discrimination of a kind that the Tribunal claimed to be avoiding. It is very difficult to see how this decision could have been thought to have allowed a genuinely free choice of counsel for an accused. The right under ICTR Statute Article 20 which guarantees a Defendant legal assistance "of his or her own choosing" is not qualified in any way that would appear to permit such a moratorium, however, desirable or laudable some might believe it to be.

Though the moratorium has recently been lifted, the jurisprudence of the Tribunal remains as has been set out above and has been lately reiterated in the case of *Prosecutor v. Bicamumpaka*.[12] This restatement came despite an earlier Appeals Chamber decision in the case of *Prosecutor v. Akayesu*[13] which said that the provision by the Registrar of the ICTR of a list of counsel

---

[10]Case No. ICTR-97-21-T.

[11]*Prosecutor v. Nyiramasuhuko and Ntahobali, Decision on a Preliminary Motion by the Defence for the Assignment of a Co-counsel to Pauline Nyiramasuhuko*, Case No. ICTR-97-21-T, 13 March 1998 at p. 6.

[12]*Prosecutor v. Bicamumpaka, Decision on the Motion Requesting the Assignment of Francine Veilleux as Defence Counsel for Jérôme Clément Bicamumpaka*, Case No. ICTR-99-50-I, 6 Oct. 1999 at para. 11.

[13]*Prosecutor v. Paul Akayesu, Decision Relating to the Assignment of Counsel*, Case No. ICTR-96-4-A, 27 July 1999.

to an accused effectively raised a legitimate expectation that counsel selected by the Appellant would be assigned to represent him. Lately new Counsel from both Canada and France have in fact been assigned. Whatever the state of the jurisprudence, the moratorium seems now to be dead in the water. In any event, one finds it difficult to believe that such a policy would survive an effective challenge in an appropriate case to the ICTR Appeals Chamber.

Furthermore, it is absolutely plain that the operation of this policy has caused enormous resentment amongst Defendants detained in Arusha. They perceive the policy as being one which not only denies them a genuine free choice but is also evidence of how the Tribunal views the guarantees apparently made in the ICTR Statute. This has seriously undermined any belief that those guarantees will be honoured and has gravely affected the legitimacy of the Tribunal in the eyes of the accused. Perhaps for that reason alone the policy ought to be definitively abandoned.

4. Conclusion

In conclusion one may properly say that the approach of the two Tribunals to the right to counsel has been very different. The ICTY has pursued a course of giving wide effect to the concept of "counsel of choice", some would argue with a degree of liberality which may not ultimately be to the benefit of either the accused or the interests of justice. Sometimes this has led to a bewildering series of changes of counsel representing an individual Defendant. In one instance a defendant is currently being represented by his fifth leading Counsel and his fourth co-counsel. Few believe he has been well served by this situation but at least he has been given full rein to make the choice guaranteed to him under the ICTY Statute and, if any harm has accrued to him, then he is very much the author of his own misfortunes. There is little sense of dissatisfaction amongst the accused at the present state of affairs concerning choice of counsel at the ICTY.

The ICTR, however, has initiated a policy of seeking to restrict choice on purported public policy grounds that *prima facie* undermine, at the very least, the concept of an individual having a free and unfettered choice of counsel. This policy, whether it is yet declared to be *ultra vires* the ICTR Statute or not, has the appearance, at its lowest, of subverting those same guarantees and has undoubtedly provoked intense dissatisfaction amongst the accused.

Whilst not wishing to encourage the tail to wag the dog, the contrasting reactions of the ICTY and ICTR detainees to the different regimes may well provide a useful bell-weather as to which approach is right and which is wrong.

TOMA FILA*

16. The ICTY from the Perspective of Defence Counsel from the Former Yugoslavia: My Point of View

1. Introduction

It is no easy matter for any attorney to act as counsel before the ICTY, irrespective of the country he comes from and the legal system he was trained in and within which he pursued his professional career, since the ICTY is in the process of creating a new law, neither Anglo-Saxon nor continental, that is to say, a new international criminal law.

To be a member of one of the nations which was a combatant and whose members are being tried at the ICTY represents an additional human and professional burden.

To be more precise, another element emerges in addition to the standard professional engagement before any court, when the attorney finds himself in an inevitable interactive relationship extending to the framework of the client–court–prosecutor–administration–the family of the accused, and so forth. I refer to the public opinion, be it professional or lay, well meaning or malevolent, politicised or petty political, but in any event insufficiently or entirely uninformed.

Namely, day-to-day politics have formed and continue to form "day-to-day" positions, depending on whether the party in power or opposition parties are involved. For the former, defence counsel are unreliable citizens, associates of a hostile court, and for the latter, the extended hand of the state or regime. Such a simplified, black and white, point of view is greatly in evidence in the Yugoslav media to this day.

In exchanging views with my colleagues from other states which have emerged on the territory of the former Socialist Federative Republic of

*Toma Fila is a Belgrade attorney. He was born in Bitolj in 1941. He has practiced law for 35 years. Before the ICTY, he has acted as counsel for Đorđe Đukić, Goran Lajić, Slavko Dokmanović and Mlađo Radić.

R. May et al., Essays on ICTY Procedure and Evidence in Honour of Gabrielle Kirk McDonald, 187–194.

Yugoslavia, I have concluded that they have been subjected to very similar or even identical experiences.

I think therefore that we should inevitably remind ourselves of the chronology of missed opportunities to inform the public in a timely manner about all the functions of this international court, in order, perhaps, to avoid future misunderstandings. It is especially important to inform intellectuals and legal experts, all those with an open mind, so that in the future they can contribute to the affirmation of the ICTY as the predecessor of a permanent international criminal court.

This brief survey comprises my personal selection of the most significant themes, such as the ICTY's establishment, legality, legitimacy, jurisdiction in Kosovo and a review of some practical aspects of its work.

2. The Establishment, Legality and Legitimacy of the ICTY

The ICTY, as an instrument of the United Nations, was conceived as a means to implement international legal mechanisms, with a view to achieving at least three objectives:

(a) to have those suspected of serious violations of international humanitarian law answer for their actions, whereby justice would be served from both a moral and a legal standpoint;
(b) to stabilise the peace process in the former Yugoslavia by affirming the principle of individual responsibility for crimes, rather than the collective responsibility some hoped would be ascribed to nations in their entirety;
(c) to speed up the process of reconciliation amongst nations at bitter odds because of war.

Once the International Tribunal was established, legal experts in Serbia and Montenegro expressed differing opinions, for the most part negative, about the legitimacy of the court. Most legal experts took the position that the Security Council could not establish the International Criminal Tribunal since the possibility of its establishment fell within the scope of authority of the UN General Assembly. Citing Chapter VII of the UN Charter was legally unacceptable because the Security Council is authorised to form, pursuant to the provisions of this Chapter, auxiliary organs, while the International Tribunal could not possibly constitute an auxiliary organ of the Security Council. The prevailing view among legal experts was that in establishing the Tribunal, the Security Council had overstepped its authority as envisaged in the United Nations Charter. Moreover, the application of Article 29 of the UN Charter which entitles the Security Council to establish auxiliary organs, on the basis of which the International Tribunal was formed, constitutes a poor precedent for equating the International Criminal Court with an auxiliary organ of the Security Council. The Government of the

Federal Republic of Yugoslavia expressed its disagreement over the establishment of the International Tribunal.

Professor Smilja Avramov pointed out the following:

> The Hague Tribunal is illegal, in my opinion as an attorney, and Yugoslavia should thoroughly consider whether it should accept it, because an illegal act may become legal once accepted. The Security Council does not have the jurisdiction to establish an international court such as the Hague Tribunal. This can only be done by an executive political organ, while Resolution 827 violates all the elementary principles of the UN and is not binding in character.[1]

The official political structures advocated the same views. The establishment of the International Tribunal represented an act of discrimination. Federal Justice Minister Uroš Klikovac was the mouthpiece of this official position, stating the following in the public media: "The Federal Government does not recognise, on its territory, the purview of the International Tribunal for crimes perpetrated on the territory of the former Yugoslavia. We support the establishment of a Tribunal whose jurisdiction would not extend to one state only, but would apply to all equally."[2]

A year later, the attitude towards the ICTY remains the same still. The Justice Minister, Uroš Klikovac, stated the following in large-circulating dailies:

> The ICTY is an auxiliary body of the Security Council, and ad hoc tribunal designed to conduct proceedings and adopt decisions only for the area of Yugoslavia. The Federal Republic of Yugoslavia could not extend its support to the establishment of the Tribunal, irrespective of the fact that it advocates, on a permanent basis, bringing to justice all violators of international humanitarian law and having them punished in the appropriate manner. Yugoslavia supports the establishment of a permanent international court which would treat equally all events and take steps against citizens from all countries in the international community.[3]

The opinion of professor Ranko Petković expressed in large circulation dailies is illustrative:

> When the International Tribunal in The Hague was formed, Yugoslavia's position was one of rejection. The first objection was that in conformity with traditional international law, the Security Council was not authorised to create

[1]Avramov, Smilja, International Law Professor at the Belgrade Faculty of Law, *Nedeljna borba,* 22–23 July 1995.

[2]Klikovac, Uroš, Justice Minister of the Federal Republic of Yugoslavia, radio broadcast "Pečat vremena", 10 Oct. 1994.

[3]Klikovac, Uroš, Justice Minister of the Federal Republic of Yugoslava, interview in the *Dnevnik* daily, Novi Sad, 17 Jan. 1995; the statement was carried by all dailies: *Politika, Večernje novosti* and *Borba.*

> an International Criminal Tribunal. The second objection was that the International Tribunal in The Hague was formed as part of the escalating pressures on the Federal Republic of Yugoslavia and the Serbs and that only they would be tried. The third objection was that there have been innumerable wars and crises since World War II, such as the Korean war or the war in Vietnam, and yet it occurred to no one to establish a court to try those who perpetrated war or other crimes … Because of the given reasons, the Federal Republic of Yugoslavia refused to recognise the jurisdiction of the Hague Tribunal.[4]

Professor Vladan Vasiljević points out that the "Paris Agreement makes it binding on all signatories to cooperate with the Hague Tribunal, but that Yugoslavia continues to obstruct the Tribunal's work."[5]

Dr. Konstantin Obradović, an expert in international law at the Belgrade Institute for International Politics and Economics, remarks that the Tribunal is entirely legitimate. As to the question of whether the Tribunal will be objective, he notes: "Crimes committed on the territory of the former Yugoslavia are involved. We shall see whether the Tribunal will be objective once it begins work, but the Statute is certainly impartial."[6]

In my opinion, all discussions in favour of and against the ICTY ceased the moment the Dayton Agreement was signed. The representatives of all the parties in conflict recognised both the legality and legitimacy of the ICTY and accepted future cooperation with this institution of the international community.

For example, Democratic Party Chairman Zoran Đinđić held the opinion that "cooperation was necessary so as to identify the perpetrators of war crimes and thereby avoid collective national guilt,"[7] while Vesna Pešić considered that "concealing crimes is not in any state's interest."[8] Likewise, Milan Miković, member of the SPO/Serbian Renewal Movement party/ Main Board, joined in with his statement that "Yugoslavia, its bar association and attorneys cannot ignore the War Crimes Tribunal in The Hague, and the defence of suspects needs to be organised."[9]

An opposing view was expressed by Aleksander Vučić: "The Hague Tribunal was established to conduct political trials for war crimes committed on the territory of the former Yugoslavia, and the question arises why there was no reaction to what the Americans did in Vietnam or Panama."[10]

---

[4]Petković, Ranko, the then editor-in-chief of the journal *Međunarodna politika, Večernje novosti*, 2 Feb. 1995.

[5]Vasiljević, Vladan, then a criminologist in Belgrade, *Naša Borba,* 26 Dec. 1995.

[6]Obradović, Konstantin, then a Professor of International Law at the time at Belgrade University, *Vreme,* 31 May 1993.

[7]Đinđic, Zoran, Democratic Party Chairman, *Politika,* 17 July 1995.

[8]Pešic, Vesna, the then President of the Serbian Civic Alliance, *Politika,* 17 July 1995.

[9]Miković, Milan, attorney and member of the SPO Main Board, *Politika,* 15 July 1995.

[10]Vučić, Aleksandar, General Secretary of the Serbian Radical Party, address in the National Assembly of the Republic of Serbia, July 1995.

I would particularly like to say that in late 1998, an exceptionally favourable opportunity was missed to acquaint, first hand, interest experts and professionals thoroughly with the functioning of the ICTY. A workshop was organised in Belgrade by the Humanitarian Law Fund which was attended by prominent individuals from the diplomatic corps and professional and intellectual circles in Belgrade and Serbia. However, the distinguished guests who at the time held the highest-ranking positions in the ICTY were absent. Nataša Kandić, Executive Director of the Humanitarian Law Fund of the Federal Republic of Yugoslavia, said the following in her introductory address to the participants:

> We all know that Prosecutor Louise Arbour and President McDonald refrained from coming to Belgrade because of the decision reached by the Government of the Federal Republic of Yugoslavia to ban Prosecutor Arbour's entry into Kosovo. I personally have deep understanding for their decision. On 4 November 1998, Prosecutor Arbour obtained a seven-day visa to visit Yugoslavia, along with a warning, in writing, that the Government of the Federal Republic of Yugoslavia does not permit the International War Crimes Tribunal for the former Yugoslavia to conduct investigations in Kosovo. Prosecutor Arbour was in effect being told that she was banned from going to Kosovo after the Conference in Belgrade to carry out the announced mission of determining the actual state of affairs.[11]

Since I was present and took part in the Conference, voicing my opinion that the ICTY also enjoyed jurisdiction over Kosovo, I regretted that President McDonald was not present to support with her arguments this rather isolated position at the time. Both the personal and professional authority of President McDonald would have, perhaps, changed certain ingrained positions held by official political circles which adapted themselves to the newly-emerged situation with great difficulty.

3. THE TRIBUNAL AND KOSOVO

The developments which ensued in Kosovo brought to the fore the question of the ICTY's jurisdiction in terms of conducting proceedings against persons who allegedly committed violations of international humanitarian law in that region. Official circles *a priori* rejected any possibility of accepting the ICTY's jurisdiction over Kosovo. Officials cited the Statute and the Security Council Resolution on the basis of which the ICTY was established.

Only a limited number of individuals voiced their opposing views and attempted to explain (I humbly count myself among them) that the ICTY

[11] Kandić, Nataša, Director of the Humanitarian Law Fund, "International Conference on War Crimes Trials," Belgrade, 7 and 8 Nov. 1998, published by the Humanitarian Law Fund, Belgrade.

was established for the territory of the former Socialist Federative Republic of Yugoslavia with a mandate beginning with 1 January 1991 and unlimited in time, and that from that standpoint, the Tribunal indeed had jurisdiction over Kosovo, while cooperation with Yugoslav authorities was inevitably implied.

The views expressed in professional and political circles in the Federal Republic of Yugoslavia were controversial. In an interview with *Večernje Novosti*, the Federal Justice Minister, Zoran Knežević, stated the following: "Not a single international document indicates the possibility of the Hague Tribunal's jurisdiction for Kosovo and Metohija."[12] He also pointed out that the Milošević-Holbrooke agreement did not refer to the possibility of foreign investigators being present in Kosovo.

The statement given by ICTY President Gabrielle Kirk McDonald in late 1999 to the popular Zagreb paper *Globus* was given wide publicity. "The pilots," she said, "who bombed the refugee column in Kosovo during NATO's intervention in Yugoslavia as well as all those who participated in similar actions and their superiors could, theoretically speaking, come under the jurisdiction of the International Tribunal for war crimes committed in Kosovo following the arrival of KFOR troops."[13]

4. Some Practical Aspects of the ICTY's Work

As counsel before the ICTY, I confronted a whole series of practical issues, some of fundamental and some of lesser importance.

The financing of the ICTY represents a highly important question. Bearing in mind that this Tribunal is an organ of the United Nations, it would be ideal if it were to cover its expenditures from the UN budget. Special funds should be allocated within the regular budget for the implementation of special-purpose projects, such as the investigation of mass graves and so forth. I am, however, aware of budgetary restrictions, and consider that donations by states are inevitable for the implementation of serious projects falling within the Tribunal's jurisdiction. I am hopeful that the UN will find a way to cover both the regular and the special expenditures of the Tribunal in order to ensure the continuity of financing all of the Tribunal's spheres of activity.

Another issue of importance for the independence and impartiality of the ICTY was the possibility of employing personnel without remuneration. I think that this was a great test in terms of defending the position of the Tribunal's autonomy. Fortunately, I can say, with satisfaction, that this problem was perceived and efficiently eliminated, and that the relevant UN decisions pertaining to this field were applied.

---

[12]Knežević, Zoran, Justice Minister in the Government of the Federal Republic of Yugoslavia, *Večernje novosti,* 1 Nov. 1998.

[13]*Globus,* 6 Nov. 1999 and 7 Nov. 1998.

A third question is that of the Tribunal's organisational structure. The fact that the Prosecutor's Office and Trial Chambers function in conjunction with a common administration, and that they are even in spatial proximity since they are located in the same building could be indicative in certain respects of the privileged position of the Prosecutor's Office in relation to the defence. According to fundamental principles, the two sides should enjoy completely equal status.

The fourth issue I think needs to be raised is the manner of arresting and taking into custody those indicted by the ICTY. I will cite the example of IFOR's arrest of the late General Đorđe Đukić on 30 January 1996. After their arrest, General Đukić and Colonel Krsmanović were illegally detained by the police in Sarajevo, and after all anticipated deadlines had elapsed, a decision was reached to launch investigative proceedings. At the ICTY Prosecutor's request of 12 February 1996, Đorđe Đukić was transferred, in the capacity of a witness, to The Hague where he was indicted, although no indictment had previously existed. The second example is the arrest of the late Slavko Dokmanović who was, without any doubt, arrested on the territory of the Federal Republic of Yugoslavia, although UNTAES did not have a mandate to act on the territory of the Federal Republic of Yugoslavia.

I consider this to be a highly sensitive legal question because it deals with the basic human right to freedom, and the violation of this right represents one of the most sensitive points for commencing proceedings before the Tribunal. The question of the lawfulness of arrests demands special attention and caution.

The ICTY, as the basis of the future permanent International Criminal Court, has the difficult task of pioneering legal practice which will represent an unavoidable guidepost in the process of creating international criminal law which is recognised, respected and applied by all countries world-wide.

The Tribunal should exclusively operate as a professional and impartial organ guided by the rules and moral norms of contemporary jurisprudence.

5. In Place of a Conclusion

As an attorney with a long-standing practice, especially in the defence of persons who have perpetrated the most heinous crimes, I confronted a great dilemma when I was engaged to work before the ICTY. The dilemmas derived from the different approaches to the work method and the application of law in cases where I acted as counsel. An additional dilemma that emerged resulted from the fact that as an attorney trained in the area of the former Yugoslavia, I found that my previous professional practice and experience before Yugoslav courts did not represent an adequate basis for adjusting to the new and different legal approach.

I am glad to acknowledge that my work before the Tribunal has been an abundant source of new knowledge and experience for me personally, that my professional positions were exposed to strong influence and probably evolved further as I acquired new insights.

I retain exceptionally pleasant memories of the first ICTY President with whom I had the honour to cooperate, Professor Antonio Cassese, who invested great efforts to explain the ICTY's mission patiently and persistently both to my colleagues and myself.

Furthermore, a series of questions which emerged in the course of pursuing justice before the Tribunal opened up an entire gamut of different legal systems being applied. Cooperating with and learning from the great attorney, Judge Gabrielle Kirk McDonald, long-standing ICTY President, I am convinced that a large segment of the Yugoslav public is not familiar with the top-notch quality of the experts working for the ICTY. I perceive the significant role played by President McDonald primarily in her specific contribution to and personal engagement in establishing high standards in the application of international humanitarian law.

I am convinced that the ICTY will remain consistent with respect to the elevated principles of humanism and justice to which top legal experts such as the esteemed Judge, Madame McDonald, and her colleagues will continue to devote all their energy. As both a human being and a professional, I believe, with optimism, that with the passage of time the ICTY will receive its historical recognition and contribute to generations of future attorneys as a true source of inspiration and a professional example.

PART VI

Fair Trials

HAFIDA LAHIOUEL[1]

17. The Right of the Accused to an Expeditious Trial

One of the last appeal decisions rendered by the former President of the ICTY, Gabrielle Kirk McDonald, was of particular interest in regard to the right of the accused to a fair trial. The finding of a grave violation of one of the accused's rights was sanctioned by discontinuance.[2] The question whether the violation of the accused's right to be tried without undue delay would lead to the same remedy is raised because "major concerns have been voiced not only by UN officials, Members States and others, but also by all organs of the Tribunals with regard to the slowness of the pace of proceedings, the associated length of detention of accused [...]".[3] Thirty-nine accused are currently held in ICTY custody, many of whom have been held for more than three years.[4] Considering the present pace of ICTY proceedings, it is likely that trials of the majority of the detained accused will not start and subsequent possible appeal judgements will not be rendered for several years.

It is therefore important to consider the question of the right of the accused to an expeditious trial. This right is enshrined in the Statute of the

[1]The author is currently employed at the International Criminal Tribunal for the former Yugoslavia as Associate Legal Officer. The views expressed herein are those of the author and do not represent the views of the ICTY or the United Nations.

[2]*Prosecutor v. Barayagwiza*, *Decision*, Case No. ICTR-97-19-AR72, A. Ch., 3 Nov. 1999. A grave violation of the right of the accused to be informed promptly of the nature and causes of the charges against him was found.

[3]By its Resolution 53/212 dated 18 Dec. 1998, the General Assembly requested the Secretary General to evaluate the efficiency of the Tribunals operations and functioning. The Experts appointed to carry out this evaluation were particularly requested to try to explain why after six years and budgets totaling $ 400 millions, only 15 ICTY and ICTR trials have been completed. Report of the General Assembly on the functioning and operations of the ICTY and ICTR, UN Doc. A/54/634, ("Report of the Expert Group") par. 35. See the Web site of the U.N.: <http://www.un.org/doc>.

[4]See the Web site of the Tribunal: <http://www.un.org/icty>.

R. May et al., Essays on ICTY Procedure and Evidence in Honour of Gabrielle Kirk McDonald, 197–213.

Tribunal.[5] When the length of detention is assessed as unacceptably long, it is then necessary to determine the cause of delay. Once reasons for delays are determined it is finally necessary to examine how the ICTY is expediting trials or preventing delays.

1. Right to an Expeditious Trial

The right to an expeditious trial, generally considered to be an essential aspect of a fair trial, is enshrined in the Statute of the Tribunal and takes effect upon the arrest of the accused. The Rules of the Tribunal provide for the implementation of this right.

1.1 The interests protected by this right

This right has its roots at the very foundation of criminal proceedings. Recognition of a right to a speedy trial may be traced back to the twelfth century.[6] Today, all major international and regional instruments provide that everyone is entitled to a fair and public hearing within a reasonable time.[7]

The right to a speedy trial has traditionally been perceived as protecting three basic interests of the accused. First, and most important, the accused should not for any unduly long period remain in a state of uncertainty about his fate or be subjected to a series of disabilities normally associated with criminal proceedings.[8] Secondly, speedy proceedings are designed to safeguard the right of the accused to mount an effective defence; the passage of time may result in loss of exculpatory evidence. Thirdly, if the verdict is reached a considerable time after the offence has become the subject of controversy, the public confidence in the system of criminal justice is undermined. This last interest is important. The Tribunal's mandate includes bringing peace in the territory of the former Yugoslavia.

---

[5]The length of detention coincides in the ICTY with the length of the proceedings as the accused is held on remand until a judicial decision is brought to the charges against him. By examining the framework of such a right in the ICTY (see infra), one may consider that a pre-trial phase must last no more than six months and in case of pre-trial detention time having lasted two years, the accused may claim an unreasonable delay.

[6]*Klopfer v. North Carolina*, 386 U.S. 213, 87, S.Ct.988, 18 L.Ed.2d 1 (1967).

[7]Article 6 (1) of the European Convention, Article 14 (3) (c) of the International Covenant for the Political Rights, Article 7 (1) of the African Charter, Article 8 (1) of the American Charter of Human Rights.

[8]The European Commission and the European Court of Justice (the "European Convention organs"), have attached the greatest significance to this reason, the existence of the violation being therefore independent of the existence of a prejudice. Indeed, the time spent in detention while awaiting trial often means loss of earnings, disruption of family life and enforced idleness.

1.2 A statutory right

Article 20 of the ICTY Statute requires the Trial Chambers to

> ensure that a Trial is fair and expeditious and that proceedings are conducted in accordance with the rules of procedure and evidence, with full respect for the rights of the accused and due regard for the protection of victims and witnesses.

Article 21(4)(c), which provides that the accused shall be tried without undue delay, is the replica of Article 14 of the International Covenant on Civil and Political Rights ("ICCPR").[9] Both Articles 20 and 21 of the Statute guarantee an expeditious trial; this dual guarantee of the Statute distinguishes between the duty of the Judges to expedite proceedings and the right of an accused to be tried without undue delay. In the first case, an assessment of the length of the proceedings is necessary while in the second case, an assessment of the cause of the delay is needed in order to show whether the delay is justified. One may stretch the interpretation of this provision and could consider that in this latter case a long delay, if not undue or justified, may still be consistent with the rights of the accused.[10] Arguably, it is first necessary to assess the length of the proceedings and only when this is excessive, it becomes necessary to assess whether delay was reasonable in the circumstances; therefore to identify delays and link each delay to its cause. The exercise of determining whether or not a delay is justified by a reasonable cause is not easy. Each delay must be assessed with regard to different circumstances, such as the complexity of the case, the conduct of the parties or the approach taken by the court.[11]

1.3 The duration of this right

The purpose of this right is to guarantee an end to the uncertainty into which a person is put because of criminal charges. One can consider that the

[9]This Article states that "everyone shall be entitled to a fair and public hearing" and "to be tried without undue delay".

[10]It is important in this matter to recall the opinion of Judge Yakov Ostrovsky who submitted in his Separate Opinion on the *Prosecutor's Motion for Adjournment* in *Prosecutor v. Bagosora*, Case No. ICTR-98-37-T, 17 March 1998 that the reason that "[…] Bagosora trial cannot be postponed is that he has been in custody for two years without trial. It is inadmissible when an international Tribunal such as ours, due to the position of the Prosecutor, fails to act in conformity to Article 20 of its Statute […]. It is commonly accepted that justice delayed is justice denied".

[11]"The Prosecutor noted with regards to the length of trials that the true measure of the duration of a trial is not the time period over which the trial extended, but rather the actual number of days of trial, excluding periods when courtrooms or Judges were unavailable for various reasons and excluding trial suspensions due to interlocutory appeals, the need to deal with motions, illness or unavailability of attorneys or other necessary parties, etc." Report of the Expert Group, par. 170.

right runs from the moment criminal charges are brought to the attention of the accused to his final sentence. Although an accused may be in a state of uncertainty even before he is arrested, the particular situation of the Tribunal makes it more appropriate that the beginning of the period be the moment of the arrest and not the moment when criminal charges are brought against a person. The ICTY relies on the assistance of States and international military forces in arresting suspects or indictees and turning them over to the Tribunal for detention. The ICTY does not control the timing or the number of cases that will be tried as it is dependent on State co-operation in obtaining custody of indictees. It has to be noted that uncertainty is not ended by the conviction but by the combination of the conviction and sentence.

1.4 The implementation of this right

The need of parties for adequate time to prepare the case must be balanced with the right to expeditious trial. The accused should also be aware of the reasonable time each stage of procedure should last and when he should expect a decision.

Upon arrest, the initial appearance of the accused must take place without delay,[12] and within thirty days following the initial appearance, the Prosecutor must provide the Defence with the supporting material of the indictment in the language of the accused.[13] Upon completion of the Prosecutor's obligation of disclosure,[14] the Defence has thirty days to challenge the jurisdiction of the Tribunal, to allege defects in the form of the indictment, to seek separate trial or severance of counts joined in one indictment and/or to raise objection based on the refusal of a request for assignment of Defence counsel.[15] The Prosecutor has fourteen days to answer to the motion and the Defence has fourteen days to answer in rebuttal. Another time limit of sixty days is set for the Trial Chamber to rule on those motions. Further, it has to be noted that either party may at any time move before the Chamber by way of motion for appropriate ruling or relief. All decisions on preliminary or other motions, with the exception of decisions on jurisdiction, are without interlocutory appeal save with leave of a bench of three Judges of the Appeals Chamber filed within seven days of the decision challenged.[16]

When time limits are respected, a case is ready to go to trial in six months. However, time-limits may be varied by the Chamber in accordance with

[12] ICTY Rule 62.
[13] ICTY Rule 66(A).
[14] This obligation of disclosure is reciprocal; the Defence must, for instance, inform the Prosecutor of its intention to offer special defence within a particular time: ICTY Rule 67(A)(ii)(b).
[15] ICTY Rule 72.
[16] ICTY Rule 73.

Rule 127, which provides that upon good cause being shown a time-limit may be enlarged or reduced. Prior to the commencement of the presentation of the Prosecution and Defence cases, a pre-trial conference and a pre-defence conference are held[17] and parties must file pre-trial briefs and lists of witnesses and exhibits. These conferences are intended to focus the attention of the parties on the important issues and in so doing to reduce the time required at trial. Finally, during the trial, rules concerning the presentation of the case ensure that the trial is expeditious. For instance, each party starts the presentation of its case by an opening statement that may allow the other party to envision its strategy. The Trial Chamber may also exercise control over the mode and order of the interrogation of witnesses and the presentation of evidence so as to avoid needless consumption of time.[18]

In seven years of existence, the ICTY has so far concluded four cases: *Erdemović*, *Tadić*, *Aleksovski* and *Furundžija*.[19] Four cases including twelve accused mostly detained on remand since 1997 are at the appellate stage.[20] Four cases including eleven accused mostly detained since 1998 are currently being tried,[21] and eight cases including eleven accused mostly detained since 1999 are at the pre-trial phase.[22] A general observation of the length of the proceedings shows that each stage of proceedings, namely the pre-trial, trial and appellate phases, lasts between one and two years. In total, an accused may remain in detention for up to four years. This record seems poor especially in comparison with the pace of trials in the International Military Tribunals at Nuremberg, which lasted ten months.[23] However, the European organs have found that a period of delay of five years was not unreasonable.[24] Comparison must be made with due regard to the difference of the legal systems.

---

[17]ICTY Rule 73*bis* and Rule 73*ter*. The pre-trial conference must be held but there is a discretion with regard to the pre-Defence conference.

[18]ICTY Rule 90(G)(ii). The purpose of the Rules is to promote a fair and expeditious trial as stated by the Appeals Chamber in *Prosecutor v. Aleksovski, Decision on Prosecutor's Appeal on Admissibility of Evidence*, Case No. IT-95-14/1-AR73, A. Ch., 16 Feb. 1999.

[19]Drazen Erdemović was arrested on 2 March 1996, his trial began on 16 Nov. 1996 and he was discharged from detention on 26 Aug. 1998. Dusko Tadić was arrested on 12 Feb. 1994 and the appeal judgement on his sentence was rendered on 12 Feb. 2000. Zlatko Aleksovski was arrested on 8 June 1996, transferred to the ICTY Detention Unit on 28 Apr. 1997 and the final judgement on his sentence was rendered on 9 March 2000. Anto Furundžija was arrested on 18 Dec. 1997, the appeal judgement on his sentence was rendered on 25 July 2000.

[20]*Blaskić*, *Čelebići*, *Kupreskić* and *Jelisić*. The accused Tihomir Blaskić surrendered on 1 April 1996 and his judgement, which is being appealed, was rendered on 3 March 2000.

[21]*Kordić, Kvočka, Krstić* and *Kunarac.*

[22]*Simić, Galić, Naletilić, Kovać, Kolundžija, Kronojelac, Brđanin* and *Krajišnik.*

[23]Robert H. Jackson, Nuremberg in Retrospect: Legal answer to International Lawlessness, 35 A.B.A.J. (1949), 83, at 881.

[24]*Ringeisen v. Austria*, 16 July 1971. All cases of the European Court of Human Rights referred to below, can be found on <http:/www.cedh.eu/cases>.

The ICTY does not explicitly provide for the sanction of violations of the right to a trial without undue delay. Article 5(3) of the European Convention, Article 7(5) of the American Convention or Article 9(4) of the ICCPR appear to make trial within a reasonable time an alternative to release pending trial. The ICCPR speaks of release if it is determined that detention is unlawful. The Tribunal considers pre-trial detention as a necessity in light of the gravity of the crimes.[25] The Rules, therefore, do not grant automatic release pending trial after spending a certain amount of time in detention. The Tribunal may consider an application for provisional release with guarantees that the accused will appear for trial or will not threaten witnesses and victims. However, the Secretary-General's Report submitted that "the tribunal must fully respect internationally recognised standards regarding the rights of the accused at all stages of its proceedings".[26] There is evidence that Judges would increasingly be favourable to grant a motion for provisional release in case of a prima facie excessive long length of detention and with no perspective of a coming trial.[27]

2. Causes of Delays in ICTY Proceedings

Once started, trial proceedings may be lengthened by different problems. The European organs considered that three kinds of difficulties could delay criminal proceedings:[28] the complexity of the case, the conduct of the accused and the conduct of the relevant authorities.[29] These may be applied in the ICTY as well.

---

[25]The European Court considers that detention is exceptional. Therefore, to determine whether a delay is reasonable, the European Court examines first the reason of the detention, e.g. the possibility to escape proceedings or the possibility to interfere with or intimidate victims. *Letellier v. France*, 26 June 1991. The ICTY's "Rules have incorporated the principle of preventive detention of accused persons because of the extreme gravity of the crimes for which they are being persecuted by the international Tribunal": *Prosecutor v. Blaškić, Order Denying a Request for Provisional Release*, Case No. IT-95-14-PT, 25 Apr. 1996 at par. 4.

[26]Report of the Secretary-General pursuant to Paragraph 2 of the Security Council Resolution 808, UN Doc. S/25704 (1993), reprinted in 32 I.L.M. 1159 (1993) par. 106.

[27]*Prosecutor v. Simić and Others, Decision on Milan Simić's Application for Provisional Release*, Case No. IT-95-9-PT, 19 May 2000.

[28]Those factors were determined in *Huber v. Austria*, Report 2D & R11, 8 Feb. 1973.

[29]The European Court ruled for instance, that in a criminal case involving two accused with one causing delay, the Prosecution should consider separating the case in two, if possible, so that the other accused is not victimised by his co-accused: *Kemmache v. France*, 29 June 1991.

2.1 The complexity factor

A case may be rendered complex by the seriousness of the offences involved or the number of acts underlying a pattern of criminal behaviour, by the distance in time and place between the criminal operation and the investigations or by the question of transfer of jurisdiction of the case to another court. Any of those consideration may create delays.[30]

2.1.1 Delays arising out of the legal complexity of cases

The most important problem lengthening proceedings before the ICTY is the legal complexity of cases.

The way in which offences are defined makes it difficult, since the four offences set out in the Statute of the Tribunal[31] can be committed in numerous ways. No less than eight individual types of conduct amount to grave breaches of the Geneva Conventions. The offence of violation of customs of war specific to ICTY is not fully defined, rather, five acts are indicated as non-exhaustive examples. The rest has to be found in customary international law. Therefore, the position of the Prosecution has been that it has no choice but to indict for as many crimes as appear to have been committed and to introduce as much evidence and as many witnesses as appear necessary to establish guilt beyond a reasonable doubt for all of them. With multi-count indictments, the norm before the ICTY,[32] this tendency of cumulative charging complicates and prolongs pre-trial and trial proceedings.

2.1.2 Delays arising out of the distance in place and time

The ICTY has jurisdiction to prosecute crimes committed in the territory of the former Yugoslavia since 1991. Motions to amend or to joint indictments are often filed by the Prosecutor, because new evidence has been obtained in the time between indictment and arrest. This can lengthen the proceedings, since amendments are usually followed by a response from the

[30]For example, the accused Naletilić was transferred to the ICTY custody by the Croatian authorities on March 2000 after a long procedure, while his co-accused Martinović was waiting in the ICTY custody since 1999.

[31]ICTY Statute, Arts. 2, 3, 4 and 5.

[32]For instance, the accused Tadić was tried on 34 counts, the accused Blaškić was tried on 20 counts but the accused Furundžija was tried on 2 counts. The accused Nikolić, arrested on 22 April 2000, is charged with 80 counts: 29 counts of crimes against humanity, 29 counts grave breaches of the Geneva Conventions and 22 counts of violations of the laws or customs of war. This represents the highest number of counts contained in a public indictment issued by the Tribunal so far.

Defence counsel, oral hearings or written briefs and finally a decision by the Chamber concerned. In some cases, the resulting delay can be serious.[33]

2.1.3 Delays due to the number of witnesses

A case before the Tribunal may be assessed either as complex[34] or simple,[35] as indicated by the number of witnesses called by parties, by the number of pages of the case transcript, the number of exhibits introduced and the number of pages of the judgement rendered. In 1997 and 1998, 699 witnesses testified before the Tribunal and their testimonies covered almost 90,000 pages of transcript.

Furthermore, proceedings may be lengthened by practical difficulties linked to the lack of certainty as to exactly when a witness will be testifying, how long the testimony will last, whether trials will be interrupted or rescheduled, and whether there will be a last minute change in the willingness of a witness to testify or in respect of the content of a witness' testimony. In addition, the Tribunal's witnesses are mainly victims or close relatives of victims. Therefore, they tell their stories in their own way and at their own pace. It is difficult to ensure that the examination is rapidly focused on a particular piece of evidence.[36] Few domestic trials have as many as fifty witnesses for both parties, even when the accused is tried for the commission of an international offence.[37] It is true that in common law

---

[33]*Prosecutor v. Nsengiyumva, Decision on Appeal Against Oral Decision of TCII of 28 September 1998*, Case No. ICTR-96-12-A, A. Ch., 6 June 1998. The interlocutory appeal on the procedural issue of the correct composition of a Trial Chamber to consider amended indictments resulted in a delay of almost nine months, not only in the case in respect of which the appeal was filed but also in 8 others in which amended indictments had been submitted by the OTP.

[34]The accused Tadić, whose pre-trial detention lasted one year and five months, was tried in six months, the transcript of the hearings consisted of 7,015 pages, 86 Prosecution witnesses were heard within 100 days and 40 Defence witnesses were heard within 50 days, 367 exhibits were admitted. The *Čelebići* trial which started in 1997 extended over a period of almost 18 months and the judgement rendered on Nov. 1999 comprised 452 pages plus annexes containing 1291 paragraphs. The *Blaškić* judgement was rendered on 3 March 2000, three years after the beginning of the trial, which began on 24 June 1997 and ended on 31 July 1999. The Prosecution called 104 witnesses, the Defence called 46 witnesses and the Trial Chamber called 9 witnesses. The Prosecution and the Defence presented 788 and 614 exhibits respectively and the trial brief of the Prosecutor was over 1000 pages.

[35]Some cases were less lengthy. The accused Erdemović pleaded guilty at this initial appearance on 31 May 1996, the trial proceedings were completed on 29 Nov. 1996 and the appeal process, during which a re-definition of a valid guilty plea was made, ended on 5 March 1998. Aleksovski's trial took only 41 trial days over a 13 weeks period with a total of 64 witnesses and 175 exhibits.

[36]For instance, counsel may informally indicate that he or she is unable to state whether the evidence is disputed.

[37]See *Prosecutor v. Touvier*, Ch. Appel de Paris, 1ère ch., Gaz. du Palais 1993, 13 April 1992 or Fédération nationale des déportés et internés et autres v. Barbie, Cass. Crim., Gaz. du Palais 1989, 3 June 1988.

adversarial proceedings, it is primarily the parties who determine the manner in which they will conduct their cases, the number of witnesses they will call, the number of exhibits they will submit, and the amount of testimony to be elicited. The extent of cross-examination and rebuttal is also largely in the hands of the parties. Furthermore, the corpus of human rights law stresses the rights of the accused, which may result on a time-consuming trial but fairer trial process. Cases presented before the ICTY are very complex; however, this should not be overrated as a primary factor causing delay.

2.2 *The behaviour of the accused*

An obstructionist attitude on the part of the accused may also cause delay. Such an attitude may take two principal forms: the accused may rely on his procedural rights to the extent of abusing them or may fail to adopt a co-operative attitude.

2.2.1 Delays arising out of the exercise of procedural rights

One of the most fundamental rights of the accused is the right to legal assistance. The accused may fail to appoint counsel or do so after considerable delay.[38] Furthermore, the Statute of the Tribunal provides that indigent suspects or accused are entitled to legal assistance assigned to them at no cost.[39] Almost all accused detained by the Tribunal are indigent and ten per cent of the annual budget of the Tribunal is allotted to free legal assistance. A phenomenon of "excessive lawyering" has been noticed and this results in delay in the administration of justice. Other delays are linked to changes of Defence counsel. Many accused in the Tribunal have requested successive changes of defence counsel. Such changes have been granted by the Registrar where exceptional circumstances have been demonstrated and upon the assurance that delays in trials will be kept to a minimum.[40]

Another right of the accused is to exercise available remedies. However, the exercise of remedies and other applications, which are retrospectively judged as unnecessary or which apparently offer no prospects of success

---

[38] *Prosecutor v. Kovač, Decision on the request of the accused Radomir Kovač to allow Mr. Milan Vujin to appear as co-counsel acting pro-bono*, Case No. IT-96-23-T, 14 March 2000. The accused Kovač persisted in requiring the appointment of and right of audience before the Trial Chamber for Mr. Vujin as Defence Counsel, whereas Mr. Vujin was charged before the ICTY in another case. The Trial Chamber denied the right of audience to Milan Vujin.

[39] ICTY Statute, Arts. 18 and 21.

[40] *Prosecutor v. Simić, Decision of the Registrar,* Case No. IT-95-9-PT, 8 Sept. 1998. The policy of the Registry is to prevent any delay by requesting the former counsel to brief the new counsel or to decide the change effective to be effective at an appropriate moment, such as after expiration of time-limit for filing of preliminary motions.

from the outset, may be considered to be deliberate obstruction on the part of the accused.[41] The accused may also exercise such remedies on a repetitive and tardy manner and this can be considered as obstructionist as it causes delays.[42] The lodging of successful applications may also create delays, but one may consider it as abusive when it does nothing to protect the rights of the accused. As a general remark, motions during a trial tend to slow the pace of ongoing trials, and some accused may believe it to be in their interests to engage in obstructive and dilatory tactics before and during trial.

2.2.2 Delays arising out of lack of co-operation

The failure to co-operate may take various forms. The accused is not under an obligation to either renounce his procedural rights or to co-operate in the criminal proceedings against him, but failure to do so may cause delay. For example, an accused may fail to volunteer information to investigators. This can prolong investigations, which often continue after the trial starts. It is also true that further delays appear when there is negative or hesitant co-operation by the State involved. Delay may also be caused by a change of tactics at trial.[43] One may consider that the accused should not use dilatory tactics or abuse his procedural rights. But an accused whose behaviour is obstructionist may not be considered as waiving his right to a speedy trial; however, such behaviour may be seen to weaken his claim of undue delay.

It should be added that responsibility to avoid delays must be shared by both parties to the proceedings and by the Tribunal. The Prosecution, like the defence, is under an obligation to avoid procedural delays and to avoid calling excessive or repetitive evidence. ICTY Judges have expressed the belief that the prolonged nature of the Tribunal proceedings is due in part to the manner in which the prosecution and defence present their cases, but also to a significant degree to not enough control being exercised by the Judges over the proceedings.[44]

2.3 The conduct of the Tribunal

2.3.1 Delays arising out of conduct of the proceedings

Delays can result from the time taken by the court for the completion of specific procedural steps or measures. In the early stages of the Tribunal's

---

[41] Many accused in the Tribunal file motions to request provisional release, some of which are not reasoned and/or do not provide the conditions required to meet such a request, e.g. bond bail. *Prosecutor v. Kunarac*, *Further Decision on Request for Provisional Release of Dragoljub Kunarac*, Case No. IT-95-23-PT, 17 Nov. 1999.

[42] *Prosecutor v. Talić, Decision on motions by Momir Talić for a separate trial and for leave to file a reply*, Case No. IT-99-36-PT, 9 March 2000.

[43] In accordance with ICTY Rule 67, the Defence must indicate whether it intends to offer a special defence or a defence of alibi.

[44] Report of the Expert Group, para. 77.

work, a large number of motions were to be expected since many questions of procedure and practice had to be settled. The Tribunal has gradually established its jurisprudence matters such as jurisdiction,[45] protective measures to be granted to witnesses[46] or video-link conferences.[47] Time will inevitably be taken in drafting judgements. Delays may also result from time taken for a sensitive matter under investigation, such as State security matters, or from belated execution of letters rogatory by foreign States.[48] Finally, some delays result from the legal system of the Tribunal. The work of the Tribunal is rendered complex and lengthy by the structure of the Statute and the Rules of Procedure and Evidence, which combine characteristics of the common-law adversarial system with, to a lesser extent, the civil law inquisitorial system and also involves a corpus of comparative and international humanitarian law.

2.3.2 Delays arising out of practical difficulties

Another reason for delay is the inadequacy of personnel and resources. Delays in translation of documents into the official languages of the Tribunal and the language of the accused[49] can be significant. A second problem concerns the courtrooms. The first trial of the ICTY started in 1996 and occupied the only courtroom for six months, four days a week, this in order to make the courtroom available to other proceedings. Currently, a problem faced by Judges is courtroom size, which can be a factor in setting a trial date as only two of the three courtrooms can accommodate more than two accused. The 1998–1999 courtroom utilisation records indicate unused courtrooms on numerous days. Since April 2000, however, three courtrooms are being used continuously by the three trial Chambers, Trial Chamber I sitting in two cases in parallel.[50] Trials are conducted for no more than some hours per day, in order to make the courtrooms available for other cases. As courtroom availability is a limiting factor, the same is true of the number of Judges. Up to November 1998, the Tribunal operated with two Trial Chambers and a rule that limited the flexibility of Judges and their availability especially in case of illness or otherwise. Rule 15 formerly provided that a Judge who confirmed an indictment was automatically disqualified from any further participation in the case at the trial level in order to avoid a perception of bias against the accused in the subsequent trial. This reduced the number of

[45] *Prosecutor v. Tadić, Decision on the Defense Motion for Interlocutory Appeal on Jurisdiction*, Case No. IT-94-1-AR72, A. Ch., 2 Oct. 1995.

[46] *Prosecutor v. Blaškić, Decision on the Application of the Prosecutor dated 17 October 1996 Requesting Protective Measures for Victims and Witnesses*, Case No. IT-95-14-T, 5 Nov. 1996.

[47] *Prosecutor v. Tadić, Decision on the Defense Motion to Summon and Protect Defense Witnesses, and on the Giving of Evidence by Video-Link*, Case No. IT-94-1-T, 25 June 1996.

[48] *Prosecutor v. Naletilić*, Case No. IT-99-34-PT.

[49] *Prosecutor v. Talić, Further Order for Filing of Motions*, 26 Oct. 1999 and *Decision on Motion to Translate Procedural Document into French*, Case No. IT-99-36-PT, 16 Dec. 1999.

[50] The *Kvočka* and *Krstić* cases.

Judges eligible to participate. Furthermore, the schedule of a trial may be delayed due to a Judge's obligations in other cases.[51] All delays lead to a temporary backlog of cases, which can become a structural challenge. The framework of the right to expeditious trials implies that it is necessary to assess whether the delay, if any, is justifiable by the circumstances of the case or undue because of a failure of the judicial system. The Tribunal has a duty to organise its legal system so as to comply with the requirements of the Statute. Procedures causing undue delays must therefore be corrected or alternative measures should be adopted, for instance by hiring additional personnel.[52]

3. Judges' Duty to Ensure an Expeditious Trial: Measures Taken

The Tribunal may take different kinds of measures to expedite trials or prevent delays. Cases can be simplified and Trial Chambers can urge the parties to avoid delays. Further, the legal system of the Tribunal can be modified.

3.1 Measures to simplify cases

As the Tribunal develops and matures, the most useful aspects of both common and civil legal systems have been incorporated in the Rules. The result of such combination, which prolonged proceedings at the beginning, now tends to expedite trials.

3.1.1 Measures to reduce the number of offences

The more judgements are issued, the easier it is for the Prosecutor to discern the amount of evidence needed to prove multiple counts. The Prosecution is therefore in a position to reduce the size of its case without fearing that it has failed to sustain its burden of proof.

3.1.2 Measures to reduce the number of witnesses

Considerable judicial time may also be saved by the reduction of the number of witnesses. In order to avoid trials lasting years, the Trial Chambers have urged parties to reduce the estimated number of witnesses. First, parties are urged to use judicial notice[53] as a means of reducing the time devoted to

[51] Trial Chambers I*bis* or Trial Chamber III*bis* or *ter* were formed and Appeals Chambers are composed differently in order to overcome the problem of disqualification of Judges in particular cases.

[52] The ICTY Budget amounted to almost 100 million US$ in 2000.

[53] Rule 94 dealing with judicial notice was amended on June 1998 to further facilitate its use.

establishing background facts that have been already established in another case.[54] It is worth noting that the arrest of an accused often results in the severance of cases, with the result that a co-accused arrested subsequently or one who surrenders later is tried separately on the same indictment. However, the accused retains the right to contest evidence derived from a different case, so, in practice, cautious use is made of this rule.

The use of exhibits in lieu of testimony has been examined in order to save judicial time, as the Tribunal's rules do not prohibit hearsay. Another possible means of reducing the length of trials is provided by Rule 94*ter*, which allows the use of affidavits. Affidavits are submitted to the Trial Chamber as documentary evidence and are subject to cross-examination if the Trial Chamber so rules.[55] Judges also encourage parties to use Rule 71, which allow depositions to be taken by a Presiding Officer.[56]

3.1.3 Measures to encourage co-operation

The Tribunal requires more co-operation from States or relevant authorities, the lack of which has complicated and prolonged pre-trial and trial proceedings. The Tribunal regularly issues requests for co-operation in the arrest of indictees and for assistance with investigations to obtain evidence and witnesses more easily.

3.2 Measures to monitor the parties

The Tribunal has a duty to expedite proceedings by monitoring the parties. In this regard, the Tribunal has exploited different ways of speeding up the proceedings by more efficient use of the available Rules or by adopting or modifying Rules.

3.2.1 Measures against dilatory tactics

ICTY Rule 73(A) provides that motions may be ruled orally[57] but since the legal questions raised by the parties are sometimes complex it is on occasion more efficient to request written pleadings. As the Tribunal matures, it is easier to curtail excessive motions and Judges request parties to present motions after discussion between themselves, in an effort to resolve the matter by agreement without the intervention of the court. The Chambers may then rule in an oral hearing.[58] ICTY Rule 73*bis* entitles Judges to hold

---

[54] *Prosecutor v. Blaškić*, Case No. IT-95-14 was separated in three indictments and identical repetitive testimony and exhibits were noted.

[55] *Prosecutor v. Dokmanović, Scheduling Order*, Case No. IT-95-13-PT, ICTY TC II, 28 Nov. 1998, the Trial Chamber requested that witness statements were to be presented to the Chamber not as evidence but to enable the Chamber to familiarize itself with the case.

[56] *Prosecutor v. Kvočka, Defense List of Deposition Witnesses*, Case No. IT-98-30-PT, 25 Feb. 2000.

[57] ICTY Rule 72(C) also mentions that preliminary motions can be ruled orally.

[58] Trial Chambers expressly require the parties to bring their motions orally, whenever it is possible.

pre-trial conferences and pre-defence conferences during which Judges may limit the amount of time each party has to present evidence in the interest of an expeditious trial and the efficient administration of justice.[59] By this, Judges may encourage the parties to agree more readily as to certain facts that are not in dispute. As the number of judgements rendered increases, the defence will become less reluctant to agree on facts that are not really in dispute, facilitating the presentation of the Prosecution's case.[60]

3.2.2 Measures against lack of co-operation
Judges recently modified Rule 67 regarding reciprocal disclosure, which requires the defence, following the Prosecutor's disclosure, to describe in general terms the nature of its defence and to indicate issues on which it is in agreement with the Prosecutor and issues which are contested, enabling the parties and the Chamber to focus on the real issues. However, the defence may fail to do so or may provide what appears later in trial to be an inconsistent defence. A sanction for the defence's failure in its obligation of timely disclosure is still to be considered by Judges. The loss of time can be considerable, as the Prosecution may have to recall a witness for rebuttal after the completion of the defence case. Another attempt to expedite trials is reflected in the newly adopted Rule 84*bis* providing that an accused may make a voluntary statement, not under oath, to the Trial Chamber at the outset of the trial. The concept is drawn from the civil law inquisitorial system in which it is common for the accused to make whatever statement he wishes about the case. This could have an effect of shortening the trial.[61]

3.3 Measures to organise the ICTY legal system

In October 1997, a surge in the number of detainees prompted the President to appoint a working group aimed at streamlining procedures for fair and expeditious trials. As a result, the July 1998 Plenary of Judges adopted 8 new rules and amended 26 others. Following the July 1999 Plenary, the President

[59]*Prosecutor v. Blaškić, Decision on the Length of the Proceedings and the Time Allocated to the Parties to Present their Evidence*, Case No. IT-94-14-T, 17 Dec. 1997. The Chamber allocated a limited number of days to parties to present their evidence and required convincing grounds in support of any possible motion for the extension of the time limits imposed.

[60]*Prosecutor v. Kvočka and Others, Decision on Judicial Notice*, Case No. IT-98-30/1-T, 8 June 2000. Trial Chamber I took judicial notice from facts from *Tadić* and *Čelebići* judgements upon which parties were in agreement and drew legal conclusions from these facts. As a consequence, in that trial the Prosecutor does not need to prove the common elements of Articles 3 and 5 of the Statute, for instance the existence of an armed conflict at the time and places of the indictment.

[61]In the *Blaškić* case, had the accused testified prior to the presentation of the defence case, time would have been saved in proving facts that were admitted later by the accused. The *Kvočka* trial started with the testimonies of two co-accused and it appears that many witnesses are not needed anymore.

appointed a "Group on Judicial Practices"[62] to recommend measures to expedite trials. Judges, sensitive to the issue of unduly long detention period, intend to expedite pre-trial and trial proceedings by improving judicial management, with full respect for the rights of the accused.

3.3.1 Measures enhancing judicial control

In accordance with the newly adopted Rule 65*ter*,[63] a Judge of a Trial Chamber may be designated as pre-trial Judge. The pre-trial Judge oversees through meetings with both parties, efforts to reach agreements on facts and law, witnesses, exhibits, scheduling, etc. The issues in dispute are determined through this increased degree of judicial control, utilising existing rules such as Rule 65*bis* for status conferences and Rule 90(G) enabling judicial control over the presentation of evidence. Judges adopted Rule 65*ter* to codify a previous practice by some Judges to request the parties to present in advance of the trial copies of witness statements and other documents identifying points of dispute and agreement. Judges had started taking a more active role in trials by questioning counsel and witnesses, cutting off irrelevant or repetitive testimony and excluding witnesses whose testimony is cumulative or of no material assistance with respect to disputed issues.[64] The result has been expedition of the proceedings.[65] However, the pre-trial Judge is not empowered to take any substantial decision on behalf of the Chamber.[66]

3.3.2 Measures against inadequacy of personnel and resources

The delays arising out of the inadequacy of resources and personnel, such as the number of Judges, number of courtrooms and number of qualified staff have resulted in a backlog of cases.

The Tribunal has alerted the UN Security Council to the problem of inadequate resources and the United States General Accounting Office has been requested to conduct a survey. This Office concluded that the ICTY's capacity in terms of the number of Judges and courtrooms was inadequate to handle its workload without significant delays. As a result, the Security Council created a third Trial Chamber. Extra courtroom space was added in 1998. This has significantly improved the situation in regard to the backlog

[62]The Group is composed of representatives of the three organs of the ICTY and of Defence counsels.

[63]Rule 65*ter* was adopted during the Plenary of Judges held in June 1998.

[64]*Prosecutor v. Naletilić and Martinović, Scheduling Order*, Case No. IT-98-34-PT, 16 June 2000. The pre-trial Judge requested the Prosecution to indicate whether or not a fact was going to be proven by more than two witnesses.

[65]Under the guidance of the pre-trial Judge, the practice is more and more to request parties to discuss each paragraph of the indictment as soon as possible in order to determine the points in agreement.

[66]One may therefore consider that the pre-trial Judge may delegate some tasks to the senior legal officer appointed to assist Judges of a Trial Chamber in order to manage the pre-trial phase of a case.

of cases. The year 1998 was also marked by an increase in the number of arrests. Another solution was then proposed: the amendment of Rule 15 of the ICTY Rules. After the modification of Rule 15 on 22 November 1999, a confirming Judge is no longer automatically disqualified from participating in later proceedings. The limited nature of the indictment confirmation process, coupled with the professionalism and integrity of Judges, is indeed a guarantee of fair treatment of the accused. This amendment has the advantage of conserving judicial resources to aid in expediting trials of accused without infringing their rights.

Another means used to expedite trials with the available resources is for each Trial Chamber to conduct two trials at the same time, allowing six trials to be conducted in parallel.[67] Another option to deal with undue delay in the lengthy pre-trial detention could be the use of temporary Judges in charge of handling the entire pre-trial process as well as collateral matters such as contempt committed outside the seat of the Tribunal. Such an approach would however require the amendment of the Statute. The Tribunal's Registry has also alerted the relevant authorities to delays caused by lack of translators.[68] The year 2000 budget allows for extra staff to be hired in this area.

3.3.3 The provisional release of accused

As examined above, the Tribunal is taking active measures in order to comply with its duty to expedite trials, especially in view of the fact that accused remain in detention. To be realistic, all those measures do not have a great effect of converting the proceedings of the Tribunal into short-term events between arrest and final outcome. Future cases are still likely to involve extended pre-trial and trial proceedings, and the Tribunal will continue dealing with complex legal points or facts to establish the responsibility of the accused beyond reasonable doubt. It is foreseeable that the Defence will continue using its procedural rights to a maximum, challenging the Prosecution's position wherever possible and conceding on factual matters only when there is no other viable alternative. Moreover, the Prosecution in turn has often insisted on presenting voluminous evidence.

The provisional release of an accused is an alternative to dramatically reduce the prejudice caused by long criminal proceedings. Judges have showed their ability to overcome the problem of delayed trials by adopting

---

[67]Trial Chamber is conducting two cases in parallel, hearing the *Kvočka* case the first two weeks of the month and the *Krstić* case during the other two weeks. The trials started on 28 Feb. and 13 March 2000 respectively.

[68]It has to be noted that the Registry of the Tribunal is in charge of assisting Judges and the Prosecution and that no delay was found to be due to the functions and operations of this organ. "The Expert Group deems it a remarkable tribute to the executive and administrative ability of the ICTY Registrar that the administration aspects of ICTY's functions and operations have been found in UN audits to have been conducted in an efficient manner with only relatively minor improvements or remedial measures recommended" Report of the Expert Group, par. 237.

and amending the Rules, and one of the major amendments adopted lately concerns Rule 65, which provides for the possibility of provisional release of an accused on bail and other conditions. Such a release is no longer restricted by the requirement of exceptional circumstances, but reluctance to use the provision may remain until it becomes possible for the Tribunal to rely on States to guarantee that indictees will be produced for trial and will comply fully with provisional release conditions imposed by the Tribunal. Consideration may be given to the fact that if an accused is provisionally released and absconds, the trial may go forward to a conclusion in his absence;[69] every system that generally prohibit trial in *abstentia*, allows it in these circumstances.

4. Conclusion

The Tribunal has maintained the highest possible standards of fairness for the right of the accused but the search for a balance between the rights of the accused and the rights of the victims is difficult. Furthermore, establishing a new and unique prosecutorial and judicial institution with the task of implementing a complex and not well defined set of legal norms was inevitably going to involve a lengthy development period. The ICTY has now existed for seven years and the overall length of detention of an individual accused has not yet, exceeded four years. Should a violation of the accused's right to an expeditious trial be found, a remedy will have to be determined. However, an order for discontinuation as a sanction would not appear satisfactory.[70] Rather, the accused could be entitled to a mitigating circumstance when time comes to determine a sentence, or possibly to compensation if acquitted.[71]

---

[69]However, in some national jurisdictions, like France, if the accused later appears in court, a guilty verdict being reached *in absentia* will be set aside and the case retried.

[70]For example, in *Prosecutor v. Barayagwiza*, (Case No. ICTR-97-19-A, A. Ch., 31 March 2000), the Appeals Chamber cancelled the discontinuation previously ordered and compensated the prejudice caused by deciding that the violation of the accused's right will be a mitigating circumstance or in case of acquittal, a financial compensation. However, the Appeals Chamber did not state that discontinuance would never be possible.

[71]The accused would be entitled to two types of compensation, one because he was wrongly charged and detained and one because he was detained for an unduly long time. No such procedures exist at the present time.

CLAUDE JORDA* et JÉRÔME DE HEMPTINNE**

18. Un Nouveau Statut pour l'Accusé dans la Procédure du Tribunal Pénal International pour l'ex-Yougoslavie

1. Introduction

Le Statut et le Règlement de procédure et de preuve du Tribunal pénal international pour l'ex-Yougoslavie (ci-après "Règlement" ou "RPP") confient à l'accusé un rôle fondamental lorsqu'il comparaît pour la première fois devant le juge : il doit déclarer solennellement s'il est coupable ou pas des crimes qui lui sont reprochés.[1]

Par la suite, au cours des débats à l'audience, l'accusé ne s'exprime plus en principe que par la voix de son avocat. En effet, il ne prend généralement pas la parole, car il doit alors prêter serment,[2] au risque d'être poursuivi s'il ne dit pas la vérité.[3] Il doit également subir le contre-interrogatoire du procureur.[4] L'accusé n'est de surcroît pas interrogé par le juge pendant le procès, celui-ci n'étant pas autorisé à lui poser des questions.

Il a donc un statut hybride: il possède à la fois une fonction de première importance en tout début de procédure et un rôle de second plan pendant le reste de l'instance répressive.

Ce système est-il adapté à la répression des violations graves du droit humanitaire qui relève de la compétence du Tribunal international? Assure-t-il au mieux l'équilibre entre le respect des droits fondamentaux de l'accusé et le devoir du Tribunal de rechercher la vérité des crimes? Telles sont les questions auxquelles nous tenterons de répondre dans cet article.

---

*Président du Tribunal pénal international pour l'ex-Yougoslavie.

**Juriste assistant au Tribunal pénal international pour l'ex-Yougoslavie.

Les opinions exprimées dans cet article sont celles des auteurs et n'engagent nullement le TPIY ou l'Organisation des Nations Unies.

[1]Article 20 § 3 du Statut, articles 62 §§ 4, 5 et 6 ainsi que 62*bis* du RPP.

[2]Article 90 B) du RPP.

[3]Article 77 du RPP.

[4]Article 85 du RPP.

R. May et al., Essays on ICTY Procedure and Evidence in Honour of Gabrielle Kirk McDonald, 215–229.

Nous tâcherons dans une première partie de définir précisément le statut de l'accusé dans la procédure et de présenter les principes sur lesquels il repose. Cette analyse nous permettra dans une seconde partie d'examiner quelle place l'accusé devrait occuper au procès pénal international afin que la vérité sur les crimes soit établie sans pour autant, bien entendu, nuire à la défense de ses droits légitimes. Notons dès à présent que cette recherche ne portera que sur le rôle de l'accusé dans les débats à l'audience. Elle ne traitera donc pas de la procédure initiale d'enquête.

1.1 Description et fondements

Excepté à l'occasion de la procédure de plaidoyer de culpabilité, l'accusé n'intervient généralement pas personnellement dans les débats entre son conseil et le procureur. Il n'est pas non plus soumis à l'interrogatoire du juge (1(a)). Ce système résulte d'abord de la procédure principalement accusatoire prévue au Règlement. Il se justifie également par la préoccupation majeure des rédacteurs du Statut et du Règlement de sauvegarder pleinement les droits de l'accusé à un procès équitable et impartial tels qu'ils sont garantis par les Conventions internationales de protection des droits de l'homme (1(b)).

1.1.1 Description

Rappelons brièvement la procédure de plaidoyer de culpabilité et ses conséquences avant d'examiner la place de l'accusé durant les débats à l'audience.

Lors de sa première comparution, l'accusé est tenu de plaider coupable ou non coupable séparément sur chacun des chefs d'accusation dont il est inculpé.[5] Sa parole revêt alors une importance toute particulière et a des implications fondamentales sur la procédure de jugement. En effet, s'il reconnaît sa culpabilité sur tout ou partie des crimes qui lui sont reprochés, les débats ne portent plus à leurs égards que sur la détermination d'une peine.[6] Les juges doivent bien évidemment s'être préalablement assurés de la sincérité et de la validité du plaidoyer.[7] Dans le cas où l'accusé plaide non coupable, le procès se déroule normalement: l'accusation et la défense mènent les débats tant sur la culpabilité que sur la peine.[8]

En principe, l'accusé est étranger au déroulement de la procédure de jugement et ne s'exprime que par l'entremise de son conseil qu'il a

---

[5]Article 20 § 3 du Statut et articles 62 et 62*bis* du RPP.

[6]Article 62*bis* du RPP.

[7]Selon les termes de l'article 62*bis* du RPP, la chambre de première instance doit s'assurer que "i) le plaidoyer de culpabilité a été fait délibérément, ii) [qu'] il est fait en connaissance de cause, (iii) [qu'] il n'est pas équivoque et iv) qu'il existe des faits suffisants pour établir le crime et la participation de l'accusé à celui-ci, compte tenu soit d'indices indépendants soit de l'absence de tout désaccord déterminant entre les parties sur les faits de l'affaire".

[8]Article 62 v) du RPP

personnellement choisi ou qui lui a été commis d'office par le Tribunal.[9] Son rôle se cantonne à celui de spectateur passif du débat judiciaire.

Deux exceptions atténuent toutefois cet état de fait.

1. Lors de la présentation par le conseil de la défense de ses moyens de preuve, et le plus souvent en fin de procès, l'accusé peut décider d'être entendu en qualité de témoin. Dans ce cas, il est soumis aux restrictions et obligations qui s'imposent à ce dernier: 1) il doit prêter serment avant de déposer[10] et, au cas où il ne dit pas la vérité, peut faire l'objet de poursuites;[11] 2) il ne peut s'exprimer que dans le cadre des interrogatoires des parties[12] et enfin 3) il est soumis au contre-interrogatoire du procureur.[13]
2. Depuis la récente réforme du Règlement du 2 juillet 1999, l'accusé peut aussi intervenir personnellement dans la procédure et non plus, dès lors, uniquement comme témoin. Il est en effet autorisé à faire une déclaration pour sa défense à l'ouverture du procès, "[a]près les déclarations liminaires des parties ou si [...] la Défense choisit de présenter sa déclaration liminaire après celle, le cas échéant, du Procureur."[14] Il peut dans ce cas s'exprimer plus librement puisqu'il ne doit pas prêter serment et qu'il n'est pas interrogé sur le contenu de sa déclaration.[15] Notons cependant, que l'accusé doit y avoir été préalablement autorisé par le juge.[16]

1.1.2 Fondements

Distinguons comme précédemment le plaidoyer de culpabilité du procès.

Le plaidoyer de culpabilité résulte principalement de l'adoption par les auteurs du Règlement d'une procédure fortement inspirée par le système accusatoire de type anglo-saxon. Ce système conçoit le procès pénal comme un litige entre deux adversaires, le procureur et l'accusé, auquel ce dernier peut mettre fin en reconnaissant sa responsabilité en début de procédure.[17] Selon les mots du professeur Fortin,

> [...] le système qui s'en remet aux parties pour établir les questions en litige doit nécessairement leur reconnaître la faculté de ne pas contester celles-ci. *Le tribunal n'a pas pour fonction d'assurer la manifestation de la vérité matérielle des*

[9]Article 45 du RPP. Cf. aussi la Directive relative à la commission d'office de conseil de la défense telle qu'amendée le 22 juillet 1999 (IT/73/Rev. 7).

[10]Article 90 B) du RPP.

[11]Article 77 du RPP.

[12]Article 85 du RPP.

[13]Id.

[14]Article 84*bis* du RPP.

[15]Id.

[16]Id.

[17]Cf. aussi S. Ginossart, "Eléments du système anglais de la preuve judiciaire", XLII *Revue de droit international et de droit comparé*, 1965, p. 9 à 19; J. Richert, "La procédure de "plea-bargaining" en droit américain", 1 *Revue de science criminelle et de droit pénal comparé*, 1975, p. 375 à 392.

> *faits de l'inculpation, mais plutôt celle de trancher le litige d'après la preuve que les parties lui soumettent*. Or, le plaidoyer de culpabilité, en mettant fin au litige, enlève au tribunal la raison d'être de sa fonction[18] (italiques ajoutés).

La procédure de plaidoyer de culpabilité se justifie par des considérations d'ordre matériel: elle raccourcit le procès et accélère ainsi la résolution des affaires particulièrement complexes dont les juges sont saisis.[19] Cette justification revêt aujourd'hui une importance spéciale à un moment où le Tribunal doit faire face à une charge de travail considérablement accrue par des arrestations de plus en plus régulières.

Elle se fonde également sur des raisons économiques:[20] chaque fois qu'une personne plaide coupable, le Tribunal fait l'économie d'un long procès.[21]

Aussi, la procédure de plaidoyer de culpabilité facilite-t-elle considérablement la tâche du procureur qui, grâce aux aveux de l'accusé, est assuré d'obtenir la condamnation de celui-ci sans avoir à rechercher toutes les preuves qui lui seraient nécessaires pour conduire un procès.[22] Cette dernière considération est d'autant plus importante que l'accusation est confrontée à des difficultés particulières pour rechercher les preuves dont elle a besoin.[23] Ne disposant pas de force de police, celle-ci est en effet entièrement tributaire de la coopération des autorités de la communauté internationale et de ses Etats membres.

Enfin, la procédure de plaidoyer de culpabilité permet d'éviter les dangers qui peuvent résulter de la venue à La Haye d'un grand nombre de victimes et de témoins dont la protection est particulièrement difficile à assurer en dehors de l'enceinte du Tribunal.[24]

---

[18]J. Fortin, "Preuve pénale", Thémis, 1984, p. 387.

[19]J. Cedras, supra note 17, p. 250; J. Richert, supra note 17, p. 384.

[20]J. Fortin, supra note 18, p. 387; J. Richert, supra note 17, p. 383.

[21]Comme l'ont souligné Mme le juge McDonald et M. le juge Vohrah dans leur opinion individuelle de l'arrêt "*Le Procureur c/ Drazen Erdemović*" du 7 octobre 1997, "[l]e concept du plaidoyer de culpabilité est en soi un produit spécifique au système contradictoire de la *common law* qui reconnaît l'avantage qu'il présente pour la communauté. Il *réduit en effet les frais, il fait gagner du temps à la cour et il permet d'éviter des désagréments à de nombreuses personnes, en particulier aux témoins*. Selon nous, cette institution de la *common law* qu'est le plaidoyer de culpabilité devrait trouver sa place dans une instance pénale internationale comme le Tribunal international qui connaît d'affaires par nature très complexes et qui exigent nécessairement, lorsqu'un procès a lieu, des audiences très longues dans des conditions financières difficiles. Ces contraintes financières tiennent à ce que les ressources du Tribunal lui sont allouées par l'Organisation des Nations Unies dont les moyens dépendent à leur tour des contributions des Etats" (italiques ajoutés) (Opinion individuelle présentée conjointement par Mme le juge McDonald et M. le juge Vohrah, "*Le Procureur c/ Drazen Erdemović*", 7 octobre 1997, affaire no IT-96-22-A, § 2).

[22]J. Richert, supra note 17, p. 383.

[23]Cf. aussi l'opinion individuelle et dissidente de M. le juge Cassese, "*Le Procureur c/ Drazen Erdemović*", arrêt du 7 octobre 1997, affaire no IT-96-22-A, § 8.

[24]Id., p. 10.

La quasi-absence de participation personnelle de l'accusé dans la procédure de jugement tient également à la procédure accusatoire prévue au Règlement, laquelle ne permet généralement pas que celui-ci soit entendu autrement qu'en qualité de témoin. Plus fondamentalement, elle se justifie par le fait que, lors de l'adoption du Règlement, les juges se sont principalement préoccupés d'assurer une parfaite protection des droits de l'accusé, notamment du droit de se taire et de ne pas contribuer à sa propre incrimination.[25] Dans son rapport à l'origine de la création du Tribunal, le Secrétaire général de l'Organisation des Nations Unies a d'ailleurs insisté sur cet impératif:

> "[i]l va sans dire que le Tribunal international doit respecter pleinement les normes internationalement reconnues touchant les droits de l'accusé à toutes les phases de l'instance", parmi lesquelles, l'article 14 du Pacte international relatif aux droits civils et politiques (1966) (ci-après "Pacte").[26]

Certes, permettre à l'accusé de participer aux débats soit en qualité de témoin, soit plus spontanément – sans avoir à prêter serment, ni à se livrer au contre-interrogatoire du procureur – ne semble pas formellement incompatible avec les dispositions du Pacte.[27] Il n'en demeure pas moins vrai que lui donner ce choix peut potentiellement porter atteinte à ses droits fondamentaux, notamment à son droit à la présomption d'innocence. En effet, dès lors que l'accusé choisit de faire une déclaration sans prononcer de serment, ni répondre aux questions du procureur, plutôt que d'intervenir comme témoin, le risque est que le juge déduise de ce seul fait qu'il cherche à mentir ou à dissimuler des éléments révélateurs de sa culpabilité.

Permettre au juge de poser des questions directement à l'accusé n'est pas non plus formellement interdit par les Conventions internationales de protection des droits de l'homme. La plupart des systèmes de droit civil prévoit d'ailleurs qu'il peut être interrogé à l'audience; la loi belge faisant même de cette interrogatoire une formalité substantielle de la procédure.[28] En contrepartie, ces systèmes reconnaissent à l'accusé un droit fondamental au silence: il peut, selon les mots du Professeur Hoeffler, "[...] refuser de répondre si sa réponse est susceptible de l'incriminer".[29] Nous reviendrons sur le droit au silence dans la seconde partie de notre recherche.

---

[25]Article 21 § 4, g) du Statut.

[26]Rapport du Secrétaire général, S/25704 (3 mai 1993), § 106.

[27]Il convient de rappeler que, depuis la réforme de juillet 1999, le Règlement autorise l'accusé à s'exprimer spontanément, toutefois, rappelons-le, dans des conditions strictes: en début de procès et avec l'accord du juge. Le Statut de la Cour pénale internationale lui reconnaît également ce droit: il peut "faire sans prêter serment, une déclaration écrite ou orale" (article 67 § 1, h) du Statut de la Cour pénale internationale, PCNICC/1999/INF/3 (17 août 1999)).

[28]Articles 190, 266 et 293 du Code belge d'instruction criminelle.

[29]J. Hoeffler, *Traité de l'instruction préparatoire en matière pénale*, Les Editions Administratives UGA, 1956, p. 216, no 222 cité dans O. Klees, "De l'obligation de témoigner au droit au silence", 17 *Revue trimestrielle des droits de l'homme* (1994) p. 250.

Il y a cependant un danger que le juge interprète ce silence comme un aveu de culpabilité. Les propos de l'ancien procureur général près la Cour de Cassation de Belgique sont significatifs à cet égard: "il est évident que l'inculpé innocent désirera toujours concourir à la manifestation de la vérité".[30] A l'inverse, le coupable cherchera toujours à se réfugier dans un silence révélateur de sa responsabilité criminelle.[31] Ainsi existe-t-il un risque que le droit au silence – même formellement garanti – devienne en pratique

> illusoire par le seul fait que, psychologiquement, le refus d'explication de l'inculpé acquiert [chez le juge] une valeur d'aveu, de non-contestation des charges externes ou à tout le moins la volonté de cacher une vérité que l'on n'ose révéler.[32]

1.2 Repenser le rôle de l'accusé dans le procès pénal international

La place de l'accusé dans le procès pénal international est critiquable et peut même être dommageable. Elle est critiquable car elle ne favorise pas la manifestation de la vérité des crimes. Elle peut être dommageable car elle s'est révélée avec l'expérience ne pas garantir au mieux la protection de ses droits légitimes (2(a)). La place de l'accusé devrait dès lors être repensée dans une perspective plus conforme aux exigences de la répression pénale internationale. Tout d'abord, la procédure de plaidoyer de culpabilité devrait être redéfinie. Ensuite, l'accusé devrait être autorisé à s'exprimer plus librement et spontanément à l'audience, sans avoir à prêter serment, ni à répondre aux questions du procureur. Le juge devrait enfin pouvoir lui poser toutes les questions précises qu'il estime nécessaires à la recherche de la vérité (2(b)).

1.2.1 Critiques

Reprenons notre distinction entre la procédure de plaidoyer de culpabilité et le procès.

Le plaidoyer de culpabilité ne favorise pas la découverte de la vérité. A l'occasion de cette procédure, l'accusé doit se prononcer sur sa culpabilité en quelques mots seulement. Il doit dire par oui ou non s'il est coupable ou pas des crimes qui lui sont reprochés, tels qu'ils sont décrits et qualifiés dans l'acte d'accusation dont il fait l'objet. Il n'est pas autorisé à préciser ses affirmations en les nuançant ou en donnant, par exemple, des explications sur les circonstances qui ont entouré la commission de ses actes. De surcroît, si l'accusé reconnaît sa responsabilité, et que ses aveux sont libres et éclairés,

---

[30] H. Bekaert, "La manifestation de la vérité dans le procès pénal", éd. 1972, p. 17 cité dans Ph. Quarré. "Le droit au silence", *Journal des Tribunaux*, 4 oct. 1974, p. 525. Il se dit par ailleurs favorable au "droit au silence".

[31] P. Legros, Communication in *Le droit au silence et la détention provisoire*, Bruylant, 1997, p. 14.

[32] Ph. Quarré, supra note 30, p. 526.

les débats sont écourtés pour des raisons, nous l'avons dit, d'ordre principalement matériel et économique. Il n'y a pas de véritable procès: aucun témoin, victime ou expert n'est appelé à la barre pour témoigner sur les crimes et la responsabilité. Seules quelques personnes sont invitées à se prononcer sur la personnalité de l'accusé en vue de permettre au juge de prononcer une peine juste et équitable.

A l'évidence, cette procédure simplifiée, qui confére à l'accusé une portée exceptionnelle, ne permet pas de faire complètement la lumière sur les infractions perpétrées et sur la culpabilité de leurs auteurs. En effet, les crimes qui relèvent de la compétence du Tribunal sont particulièrement complexes et semblent, par leur nature, souvent échapper à la raison. Ils sont complexes, car d'une part ils exigent, en plus de la commission répétée d'actes criminels individuels, le rattachement de ceux-ci à un conflit armé – interne ou international – ou à une entreprise de persécution ou d'extermination systématique. Ils sont d'autre part le plus souvent commis sur une longue durée et sur une vaste zone géographique, parfois même sur le territoire de plusieurs Etats. Enfin ils impliquent généralement, au-delà de la responsabilité personnelle de l'accusé, celle d'un système politique ou militaire. Ces crimes semblent échapper à la raison par le fait qu'ils sont particulièrement odieux et qu'il est très difficile, en l'absence de témoignage, de comprendre les motifs – à première vue souvent irrationnels – qui ont poussé leurs auteurs à agir.

Mais le Tribunal peut-il faire primer, par un procès écourté, des préoccupations principalement matérielles et économiques sur la recherche de la vérité? N'est-il pas impératif qu'il mette tout en oeuvre pour analyser les exactions dont il juge les auteurs et pour décortiquer les mécanismes qui ont entraîné leur commission, à la lumière notamment des témoignages de ceux ou celles qui les ont personnellement vécus?

Il y va tout d'abord du rôle préventif du Tribunal. Si la genèse, les causes et la spécificité de crimes aussi graves pour l'ordre public international que ceux dont il est saisi ne sont pas comprises, ni explicitées, ceux-ci se reproduiront inévitablement. Comme le dit M. Joinet dans le Rapport final sur "la question de l'impunité des auteurs des violations des droits de l'homme",

> Chaque peuple a le droit inaliénable de connaître la vérité sur les événements passés, ainsi que les circonstances et les raisons qui ont conduit, par la violation massive ou systématique des droits de l'homme, à la perpétration de crimes aberrants. *L'exercice plein et effectif du droit à la vérité est essentiel pour éviter qu'à l'avenir de tels actes ne se reproduisent*[33] (italiques ajoutés).

---

[33]Question de l'impunité des auteurs des violations des droits de l'homme (civils et politiques), Rapport final établi par L. Joinet, en application de la décision 1996/119 (E/CN.4/Sub.2/1997/20, 17).

Il y va également de sa fonction pédagogique: le Tribunal doit, en plus de châtier les coupables et rendre justice aux victimes, faire comprendre à l'opinion publique internationale comment, pourquoi et dans quelles circonstances les crimes qui relèvent de sa compétence ont été commis. Ses jugements constituent à cet égard des documents historiques fondamentaux qui permettront aux générations actuelles et futures de mieux appréhender les crimes de masse et leurs origines.

Il y va enfin de sa mission de paix:[34] en donnant la parole aux victimes, le Tribunal doit leur permettre de retrouver un certaine dignité et par là contribuer au rétablissement de relations sociales harmonieuses entre des communautés en guerre depuis parfois plusieurs mois, voire même plusieurs années.[35]

Le Tribunal ne peut bien entendu remplir pleinement ces trois missions sans entendre publiquement ceux et celles qui ont été victimes ou témoins des crimes, ni procéder à une analyse minutieuse de leurs dépositions afin de déterminer comment, et surtout pourquoi, des crimes de guerre et des crimes contre l'humanité ont été perpétrés.

La procédure de plaidoyer de culpabilité n'est pas aisée à mettre en pratique et ne garantit pas au mieux la protection des droits de l'accusé. Certes, elle peut favoriser sa réinsertion sociale, en l'incitant à prendre conscience de la cruauté de ses actes et en le ramenant au sens de ses responsabilités humaines et sociales. Elle lui épargne également un procès long et humiliant et lui assure une peine plus clémente.[36]

Il n'en demeure pas moins malaisé pour un accusé de devoir porter un jugement sur sa culpabilité lors de sa première comparution devant le juge.[37] Sa responsabilité porte, nous l'avons dit, sur des crimes particulièrement

---

[34]Le Tribunal a été institué par le Conseil de sécurité, en vertu du Chapitre VII de la Charte des Nations Unies, pour assurer le retour et la maintien de la paix en ex-Yougoslavie.

[35]Claude Jorda et Jérôme de Hemptinne "Status and Role of the Victims", à paraître dans *The Statute of the International Criminal Court and International Law*, Oxford University Press.

[36]Comme l'a souligné M. le juge Cassese, "[...] l'accusé en plaidant coupable sert son propre intérêt. En premier lieu, cela peut l'aider à *soulager sa conscience* et à racheter ses propres erreurs. En deuxième lieu, il *s'épargnera le sentiment d'indignité* qui accompagne la tenue d'un procès et n'aura pas à vivre cette expérience potentiellement démoralisante. Il *évitera aussi l'épreuve psychologique* que constitue le fait d'avoir à assister à l'interrogatoire et au contre-interrogatoire des témoins (il se peut aussi qu'il soit lui-même témoin). Il évitera également l'exposition au public que suppose tout un procès et les conséquences préjudiciables que cela entraînera pour son statut social ainsi que pour la vie de sa famille et de ses proches. En troisième lieu, l'accusé peut espérer que le tribunal tiendra compte de son attitude coopérante et *réduira la peine* qui lui aurait été infligée s'il n'avait pas plaidé coupable. En d'autres termes, l'accusé peut espérer que le tribunal fera preuve de plus de mansuétude en raison de son aveu de culpabilité" (italiques ajoutés) (opinion individuelle et dissidente de M. le juge Cassese, supra note 23, § 8).

[37]N'ignorons pas non plus que l'aveu peut être mensongé et destiné, par exemple, à dissimuler le véritable coupable (J. Magnol, "L'aveu dans le procès pénal", 1 *Revue de droit pénal et de criminologie*, 1950, p. 245).

compliqués. Ceux-ci doivent en effet s'inscrire dans un contexte général – qu'il s'agisse du conflit armé (élément constitutif des "Infractions graves aux Conventions de Genève de 1949"[38] et des "Violations des lois ou coutumes de la guerre")[39] ou de l'attaque massive ou systématique (élément constitutif des "Crimes contre l'humanité")[40] – dont l'existence ne dépend généralement pas de ses seules actions criminelles, ni de sa seule volonté, mais également de celle d'un système de terreur auquel il a adhéré ou à tout le moins participé.

De surcroît, à ce stade initial du procès, l'accusé n'a pas eu le temps ni l'opportunité de juger des qualités professionnelles de son avocat – qui, le plus souvent, lui a été assigné par le Tribunal –, alors même qu'il doit largement compter sur ses compétences pour faire le choix décisif d'avouer ou pas les crimes qui lui sont reprochés.

Il n'est pas non plus facile pour le juge qui, en principe, ne possède pas en début de procédure les éléments de preuve rassemblés par les parties au cours de leurs enquêtes respectives, d'apprécier, comme il est tenu de le faire,[41] la validité d'un plaidoyer de culpabilité.

Il convient cependant d'atténuer cette seconde critique par les deux considérations suivantes.

1. Lors de la session plénière du mois de juillet 1999, les juges, soucieux de garantir au mieux la protection des droits de l'accusé, ont modifié l'article 62 du Règlement: l'accusé peut désormais plaider coupable ou non coupable dans les 30 jours de sa comparution initiale et non plus, comme auparavant, obligatoirement lors de celle-ci. L'accusé dispose dès lors d'un laps de temps supplémentaire pour examiner, avec l'aide de son conseil, les accusations dont il fait l'objet et réfléchir à la stratégie qu'il souhaite adopter.
2. A l'occasion de la même réunion plénière, l'article 62*bis* du Règlement a également été modifié: les juges sont dorénavant tenus de vérifier non plus seulement que le plaidoyer est libre et éclairé[42] mais aussi qu' "[...] il existe des faits suffisants pour établir le crime et la participation de l'accusé à celui-ci, compte tenu soit d'indices indépendants, soit de l'absence de tout désaccord déterminant entre les parties sur les faits de l'affaire".[43] Ainsi, par exemple, les juges de la Chambre de première instance I ne se sont-ils pas contentés d'examiner si le plaidoyer de culpabilité de Goran Jelisić avait été fait délibérément et en connaissance de cause, ni seulement de prendre acte de l'existence d'un accord

[38]Article 2 du Statut.
[39]Article 3 du Statut.
[40]Article 5 du Statut.
[41]Article 62 du RPP.
[42]Article 62*bis*, i), ii) et iii) du RPP.
[43]Article 62*bis*, iv) du RPP.

entre l'accusation et la défense sur les faits et le droit de la cause.[44] Ils ont succinctement analysé dans leur jugement final si, d'après les dépositions de victimes et de témoins qui leur avaient été remises par le procureur, les crimes avoués avaient bien été commis par l'accusé.[45]

Le statut de l'accusé au procès ne favorise pas la découverte de la vérité. L'accusé ne participe généralement pas au débat judiciaire qui se déroule entre son conseil et le procureur. Il est le plus souvent réduit à n'être qu'un spectateur passif de son propre procès. En effet, comme il n'est pas autorisé à s'exprimer librement, – excepté, nous l'avons souligné, en tout début d'instance –,[46] il préfère garder le silence. Rappelons à cet égard, que pour prendre la parole, l'accusé doit prêter serment et peut, dès lors, faire l'objet de poursuites pénales s'il ne dit pas la vérité. Il doit également accepter de se soumettre au contre-interrogatoire, souvent virulent, de l'accusation.

Et lorsqu'il décide malgré tout d'intervenir aux débats – le plus souvent en fin de procédure –, l'accusé ne s'exprime pas spontanément: il se contente de répondre aux questions de son avocat qu'il a minutieusement préparées à l'avance avec lui.

Enfin, l'accusé n'est pas interrogé par le juge. En effet, le Règlement ne prévoit pas que ce dernier puisse lui poser directement les questions qu'il estime nécessaires et, le cas échéant, confronter sa parole aux dires des victimes et des témoins.

N'est-il cependant pas important d'entendre l'accusé pour établir la vérité des crimes?[47] A cette fin, ne faudrait-il pas trouver un système qui permette de mieux concilier la protection de l'intérêt public international – qui, comme nous l'avons mis en évidence, exige que toute la lumière soit faite sur les crimes – avec les droits fondamentaux de l'accusé, tels qu'ils sont garantis, dans les Conventions internationales de protection des droits de l'homme?

La protection de l'intérêt public international. Entendre l'accusé s'expliquer sur les événements qui lui sont reprochés et sur les raisons qui ont motivé ses actes – autrement que par le truchement des questions que lui pose son avocat – permettrait sans aucun doute au juge de faire plus complètement la lumière sur l'origine des crimes de guerre et des crimes

---

[44]Les juges ont affirmé dans le jugement "*Le Procureur c/ Goran Jelisić*" du 14 décembre 1999 que "[b]ien que la Chambre note que les parties aient pu s'accorder sur le crime reproché, encore faut-il que les juges trouvent des éléments de l'affaire de quoi asseoir leur conviction, tant en droit qu'en fait, que l'accusé est bien coupable de ce crime" (IT-95-10-T) § 25.

[45]Id., p. 7 à 18.

[46]Article 84*bis* du RPP.

[47]La déposition de A. Eichmann devant la Cour de District de Jérusalem n'a-t-elle pas été décisive pour comprendre la nature de ses activités criminelles et, de façon plus générale, l'industrie des crimes perpétrés par les nazis ? Cf. R. Brauman, E. Sivan, "*Eloge de la désobéissance, A propos d' "un spécialiste", Adolf Eichmann*", Le Pommier-Fayart, 1999.

contre l'humanité, ainsi que sur le passé et la personnalité de leurs auteurs.[48] Grâce à l'audition de l'accusé, le juge pourrait à l'évidence mieux comprendre – et faire comprendre à la société – les causes des crimes particulièrement graves dont il est saisi, en vue de protéger pleinement les intérêts légitimes de la communauté internationale.[49]

Les droits fondamentaux de l'accusé. Nul doute que cette recherche de la vérité ne peut se faire au mépris du respect de la dignité et de la liberté de l'homme "qui exige que tout suspect soit totalement libre de décider de l'attitude à adopter face aux accusations portées contre lui."[50] Nul doute également que l'accusé doit être protégé contre toute forme de coercition abusive dont il pourrait faire l'objet de la part des autorités du Tribunal.[51] Nul doute enfin que celui-ci doit être présumé innocent et qu'il ne peut être tiré de présomption de culpabilité de son silence.[52]

Rappelons à cet égard, que tant le Statut du Tribunal[53] que le Pacte[54] garantissent à l'accusé les droits à ne pas être forcé de témoigner contre lui-même et de s'avouer coupable. Bien qu'ils ne soient pas formellement envisagés dans la Convention européenne des droits de l'homme, ces droits ont été affirmés par la Cour européenne de droits de l'homme comme étant

---

[48]Est-il pensable que, lorsque les grands chefs militaires et hauts fonctionnaires comparaîtront devant le Tribunal pour y répondre des crimes qui leur sont reprochés, ils ne puissent s'exprimer que très brièvement avant la clôture de débats longs de plusieurs années, pour donner au monde entier leur version du conflit et s'expliquer sur l'épuration ethnique, les massacres et les déportations dont ils sont accusés?

[49]Cf. 2(a) Critiques (les fonctions pédagogique et préventive du Tribunal).

[50]Opinion dissidente de M. le juge Martens de l'arrêt "*Saunders c/ Royaume-Uni*", Cour européenne des droits de l'homme (ci-après "CEDH"), 17 décembre 1996, § 9.

[51]Arrêt "*Saunders c/ Royaume-Uni*" (ci-après "arrêt Saunders"), CEDH, 17 décembre 1996, § 68 ; arrêt "*John Murray c/ Royaume-Uni*" (ci-après "arrêt Murray"), CEDH, 8 février 1996, § 45.

[52]Comme le dit F. Kuty, "le droit de tout accusé de ne pas être contraint de contribuer à sa propre incrimination [...] est étroitement lié à la présomption d'innocence consacré notamment par l'article 6 § 2 de la Convention [européenne des droits de l'homme] qui exige non seulement que les juges ne partent pas de l'idée préconçue que l'accusé a commis l'acte incriminé mais également que la charge de la preuve pèse sur l'accusation et que le doute profite à l'accusé" ("L'étendue du droit au silence en procédure pénale", 3 *Revue de droit pénal et de criminologie*, 2000, p. 309. A ce propos, la CEDH a affirmé que "[...] le droit de ne pas contribuer à sa propre incrimination présuppose que, dans une affaire pénale, l'accusation cherche à fonder son argumentation sans recourir à des éléments de preuve obtenus par la contrainte ou les pressions, au mépris de la volonté de l'accusé. *En ce sens, ce droit est intimement lié au principe de la présomption d'innocence consacré à l'article 6 § 2 de la Convention*" (italiques ajoutés) (arrêt Saunders, supra note 51, § 68).

[53]Article 21 § 4, g) du Statut.

[54]Article 14 § 3, g) du Pacte.

"des normes internationales généralement reconnues qui sont au cœur de la notion de procès équitable."[55]

Le statut de l'accusé au procès ne garantit pas toujours au mieux la protection de ses droits. Est-il nécessairement dans l'intérêt de l'accusé d'être représenté en justice – et non pas assisté – par son avocat? Dans les procès à forte dimension politique du Tribunal, où il est parfois difficile d'identifier précisément les intérêts que poursuivent les parties au procès, il convient de se demander s'il n'est pas quelques fois dangereux pour l'accusé d'être entièrement "retranché" pendant toute la durée de la procédure derrière son conseil, seule personne habilitée à s'exprimer en son nom à l'audience.

Par ailleurs, conférer à l'accusé le droit de s'expliquer librement sur les événements criminels très graves qui lui sont reprochés et de donner spontanément sa version de l'histoire au monde entier ne satisferait-il pas ses préoccupations personnelles de justice ? En d'autres termes, n'a-t-il pas un droit à être entendu librement et spontanément à l'audience?

1.2.2 Perspectives

Le rôle et le statut de l'accusé dans le procès devraient être repensés dans une perspective plus conforme aux exigences de la répression pénale internationale.

Premièrement, la portée et la valeur probatoire de la reconnaissance de culpabilité de l'accusé devraient être redéfinies.

La portée. L'accusé ne devrait plus plaider coupable sur les infractions prévues au Statut et les crimes sous-jacents qui les constituent (par exemple, les "persécutions" comme "crimes contre l'humanité"), mais sur des faits précis (par exemple, le meurtre de X), et ce indépendamment de la qualification juridique qu'ils revêtent dans l'acte d'accusation. Ainsi, l'accusé serait-il mieux protégé, puisqu'il n'aurait plus à avouer des crimes dont il ne comprend, par lui-même, que difficilement la signification, mais à se prononcer sur des faits concrets et définis dont il peut plus aisément saisir la portée. Le juge serait, quant à lui, mieux à même d'examiner la valeur du plaidoyer de culpabilité et de se prononcer sur sa validité.

La valeur probatoire. L'aveu de l'accusé ne devrait pas être considéré comme une preuve légale qui, sous réserve de certaines vérifications,[56]

---

[55]Arrêt Saunders, supra note 51, § 69. Dans l'arrêt Murray (supra note 51, § 45), la Cour réunie en grande chambre a affirmé qu' "[i]l ne fait aucun doute que, même si l'article 6 de la Convention ne les mentionne pas expressément, le droit de se taire lors d'un interrogatoire de police et le droit de ne pas contribuer à sa propre incrimination sont des normes internationales généralement reconnues qui sont au cœur de la notion de procès équitable consacré par l'article 6 [...]. En mettant le prévenu à l'abri d'une coercition abusive de la part des autorités, ces immunités concourent à éviter des erreurs judiciaires et à garantir le résultat voulu par l'article 6". Cf. aussi l'arrêt "*Funke c/ France*" (25 février 1993) dans lequel la CEDH a pour la première fois consacré le principe du "droit, pour tout "accusé" au sens autonome que l'article 6 attribue à ce terme, de se taire et de ne point contribuer à sa propre incrimination" (§ 44).

[56]Article 62*bis* du RPP.

entraîne automatiquement sa responsabilité, mais comme un élément de conviction parmi d'autres.[57] En d'autres mots, le juge ne devrait pas déduire du simple aveu de l'accusé – même libre et éclairé – la culpabilité de l'accusé.[58] Au contraire, l'aveu devrait, au même titre que tout témoignage ou expertise, être vérifié[59] et corroboré par d'autres preuves, le cas échéant, débattues par les parties à l'instance. Il en résulterait une plus grande protection des droits de l'accusé, ses quelques mots d'aveu en début de procès perdant leur caractère décisif sur la suite des procédures. Aussi, le juge pourrait-il plus librement évaluer la valeur de la parole de l'accusé selon toutes les circonstances objectives et subjectives de la cause. Et plus essentiellement, pour faire pleinement œuvre de justice,[60] en décidant des suites à réserver aux aveux, il pourrait prendre en compte non seulement leur sincérité, mais aussi la nature et la gravité pour l'ordre public international des crimes perpétrés et, le cas échéant, les impératifs d'efficacité et de célérité des procès.

Deuxièmement, l'accusé devrait pouvoir s'exprimer plus librement au cours de l'instance répressive et être interrogé par le juge.

L'accusé plus libre de s'exprimer spontanément. L'accusé devrait être autorisé à prendre la parole sans devoir prêter serment ni répondre aux questions du procureur, non pas uniquement, comme c'est le cas actuellement, après les déclarations liminaires des parties, mais à tout moment du procès. Celui-ci, libéré du serment et du contre-interrogatoire, serait plus enclin à participer aux débats, et pourrait spontanément contribuer à l'établissement de la vérité des crimes. Son intervention devrait bien entendu se faire sous le contrôle strict du juge, dont les pouvoirs devraient lui permettre de l'écourter lorsque, par exemple, elle prendrait une tournure politique trop marquée ou qu'elle retarderait le déroulement de la procédure. Par ailleurs, comme l'accusé n'aurait pas à choisir entre prendre la parole en tant qu'accusé (c'est-à-dire sans prêter serment, ni répondre aux questions du procureur) ou en tant que témoin, le juge ne pourrait déduire du fait qu'il décide de parler en son nom personnel qu'il cherche à dissimuler la vérité.[61]

L'accusé interrogé par le juge. Le juge devrait pouvoir poser à l'accusé toutes les questions qu'il estime indispensables et confronter ses affirmations avec celles des victimes et des témoins. Cet interrogatoire, lui permettrait, nous l'avons dit, de faire plus complètement la lumière sur les crimes et la personne de leurs auteurs. Ce faisant, le juge ne pourrait toutefois enfreindre les droits fondamentaux de l'accusé, plus spécifiquement le droit au silence,[62] corollaire indispensable du principe de la présomption

---

[57]Cf. G. Levasseur, A. Chavanne, J. Montreuil, B. Bouloc, *Droit pénal général et procédure pénale*, Sirey, 1996, p. 168.

[58]Cf. J. Magnol, supra. note 37, p. 244.

[59]Id.

[60]Cf. 2(a) Critiques (les fonctions pédagogique et préventive du Tribunal).

[61]Cf. 1(b) Fondements.

[62]Pour une étude approfondie sur la notion de droit au silence cf. aussi C. Girard, *Culpabilité et silence en droit comparé*, L'Harmattan, 1997.

d'innocence[63] et des droits à la liberté[64] et à l'intégrité[65] de la personne humaine. En conséquence, l'interrogatoire par le juge devrait être rigoureusement encadré et se faire dans le respect de sept principes essentiels qui, sans faire totalement disparaître le risque psychologique évoqué précédemment (à savoir que le juge présume du silence de l'accusé sa culpabilité),[66] devraient à tout le moins fortement l'atténuer.[67] Premièrement, l'accusé doit pouvoir librement refuser de répondre aux questions du juge.[68] Deuxièmement, s'il décide d'y répondre, l'accusé ne peut être tenu de dire la vérité.[69] Troisièmement, l'accusé ne doit pas prêter serment, afin de ne pas être placé "dans l'alternative soit de s'accuser soit de parjurer".[70] Quatrièmement, le juge doit poser à l'accusé des questions claires et précises dont celui-ci comprend parfaitement le sens et la portée.[71] Cinquièmement, avant de procéder à l'interrogatoire, le juge doit informer l'accusé de son droit de se taire.[72] Sixièmement, aucune présomption de culpabilité ne doit être tirée du silence de l'accusé et aucune sanction résulter de ses mensonges.[73] Septièmement, toute preuve obtenue en

---

[63]J. Hoeffler, supra note 29, no 233, cité dans F. Kuty, supra note 52, no 233.

[64]Cf. Opinion dissidente de M. le juge Martens, supra note 50, § 9.

[65]J. Hoeffler, supra 29, no 233 et F. Kuty, supra note 52, no 233.

[66]Cf. 1(b) Fondements.

[67]Par ses qualités professionnelles, le juge devrait être à même de ne pas préjuger de la responsabilité de l'accusé silencieux. Au demeurant, dans la procédure actuelle, n'existe-t-il pas également un risque psychologique que le juge tire des conclusions hâtives sur la culpabilité du prévenu du fait qu'il ne souhaite pas être entendu à l'audience?

[68]F. Kuty, supra note 52, p. 332.

[69]Id., p. 332.

[70]Id., p. 328.

[71]Selon les mots de F. Kuty, "[d]e manière à garantir l'effectivité de l'exercice du droit au silence, les autorités judiciaires doivent adopter des mesures afin d'empêcher l'utilisation d'artifices destinés à convaincre un inculpé ou un prévenu d'adopter une autre stratégie de défense que celle qu'il a librement choisie" (id., p. 332).

[72]Arrêt Murray, supra note 51, §§ 48, 50, 51 et 56.

[73]F. Kuty, supra note 52, p. 328. Dans l'arrêt Murray rendu en grande chambre le 8 février 1996, la CEDH a toutefois relativisé la portée du droit au silence. Elle a en effet affirmé qu'il n'était pas une notion absolue. Selon ces mots, "[…] il est manifestement incompatible avec [le droit de se taire et de ne pas contribuer à sa propre incrimination] de fonder une condamnation exclusivement ou essentiellement sur le silence du prévenu ou son refus de répondre à des questions ou de déposer. D'autre part, il est tout aussi évident pour la Cour que ces interdictions ne peuvent et *ne sauraient empêcher de prendre en compte le silence de l'intéressé, dans des situations qui appellent assurément une explication de sa part*, pour apprécier la force de persuasion des éléments à charge. […] "*On ne saurait donc dire que la décision d'un prévenu de se taire d'un bout à l'autre de la procédure pénale devrait nécessairement être dépourvue d'incidences une fois que le juge du fond tentera d'apprécier les éléments à charge*" (italiques ajoutés) (arrêt Murray, supra note 51, § 47).

La Cour a cependant affirmé que "[…] le silence ne saurait en soi passer pour un indice de culpabilité", ni constituer une infraction pénale ou un outrage au Tribunal (§ 48). Elle a enfin souligné que le juge ne pouvait tirer des conclusions du silence de l'accusé que lorsqu'il existait un commencement de preuve contre lui (§ 51).

méconnaissance de ces principes ne peut être prise en considération par le juge pour former sa conviction[74] et doit pouvoir être contestée par l'accusé.

2. Conclusion

Elaborer un système de procédure qui permet d'harmoniser parfaitement la protection de l'ordre public international et l'intérêt privé de l'accusé est l'un des défis majeurs du Tribunal.

La procédure de plaidoyer de culpabilité, telle qu'elle est aujourd'hui définie dans les textes fondateurs du Tribunal, non seulement ne favorise pas nécessairement l'intérêt général de la répression pénale internationale, mais encore ne protège pas au mieux l'intérêt privé de l'accusé. Si elle accélère les procès, elle ne répond pas pour autant pleinement à l'intérêt public de la répression internationale, car elle ignore les rôles préventif et "pédagogique" du Tribunal. Elle ne protège pas au mieux l'intérêt privé de l'accusé, parce qu'elle oblige celui-ci à porter un jugement décisif sur son éventuelle responsabilité de crimes particulièrement graves et complexes.

Confier un rôle très réduit à l'accusé lors de son procès ne satisfait pas non plus totalement à l'intérêt public de la répression internationale, ni ne garantit toujours la protection des intérêts légitimes de l'accusé. Il ne satisfait pas totalement à l'intérêt public de la répression internationale, car il ne favorise pas la découverte de la vérité. Il ne garantit pas toujours la protection des intérêts légitimes de l'accusé, car, étranger à la procédure, celui-ci ne peut donner spontanément sa version des événements, ni s'expliquer librement sur les crimes qui lui sont reprochés.

C'est pourquoi il convient de repenser et redéfinir le statut de l'accusé. Ses aveux devraient porter sur des faits précis et, même lorsqu'ils sont libres et éclairés, ne devraient pas conduire à la quasi-suppression du procès. L'accusé devrait pouvoir s'exprimer sans avoir à prêter serment, ni à répondre aux questions du procureur. Il devrait enfin être interrogé par le juge sans, toutefois, qu'il ne soit jamais porté atteinte à ses droits fondamentaux.

---

[74]F. Kuty, supra note 52, p. 332.

PATRICIA WALD[1] and JENNY MARTINEZ[2]

19. Provisional Release at the ICTY: A Work in Progress

Virtually every democratic government in the world has as part of its criminal justice system a procedure for releasing a person accused of crime prior to trial if a judicial officer finds that there is no substantial danger that the suspect will fail to appear for trial or present a danger to the community while awaiting trial. Allowance for pre-trial release is considered an accoutrement of the presumption of innocence; the prosecution must overcome that presumption by demonstrating that the accused is likely to flee or commit a new crime before it may detain him prior to conviction.[3]

1. The Presumption of Pre-Conviction Detention in the International Criminal Tribunal for the Former Yugoslavia

1.1 Evolution of the Current Rule

The statute establishing the International Criminal Tribunal for the Former Yugoslavia ("ICTY"), however, says nothing about pre-trial release. The regimen for allowing violators to be released before, during, or after trial is set forth in the Tribunal's Rule 65. As originally adopted by the Tribunal in plenary session in 1994, this Rule appeared, on its face, to be a dramatic

[1]Judge, International Criminal Tribunal for the Former Yugoslavia; Judge, U.S. Court of Appeals for the District of Columbia Circuit, 1979–1999; Chief Judge, 1986–1991; Yale Law School L.L.B. 1951.

[2]Associate Legal Officer, International Criminal Tribunal for the Former Yugoslavia; Harvard Law School J.D. 1997. The views expressed herein are those of the authors and not of the Tribunal or the UN.

[3]See Daniel Freed and Patricia Wald, Bail in the United States (1964); Bail Reform Act, 18 U.S.C. § 3146. This principle of pre-trial release, along with a guarantee of trial within a reasonable time after arrest, is also a part of the European Convention on Human Rights at Art. 6(1), the International Covenant on Civil and Political Rights at Arts. 9(3) and 14(3)(d), and the African Charter on Human and Peoples' Rights at Art. 7(1)(d).

R. May et al., Essays on ICTY Procedure and Evidence in Honour of Gabrielle Kirk McDonald, 231–246.

departure from the norm. Although amended in several particulars, most notably to provide for a discretionary interlocutory appeal from a grant or denial of release by the trial chamber,[4] the core of the original Rule 65 remained intact until November 1999. Up to that date, the Rule provided:

> (A) Once detained, an accused may not be released except upon an order of a Trial Chamber.
>
> (B) Release may be ordered by a Trial Chamber only in exceptional circumstances, after hearing the host country and only if it is satisfied that the accused will appear for trial and, if released, will not pose a danger to any victim, witness, or other person.
>
> (C) The Trial Chamber may impose such conditions upon the release of the accused as it may determine appropriate, including the execution of a bail bond and the observance of such conditions as are necessary to ensure the presence of the accused for trial and the protection of others.

It is, of course, Rule 65(B) that contains the controlling criteria[5] which distinguish the Tribunal rule from the prevailing international norm. That is, pre-trial detention had been the presumption in the Tribunal and release was allowed only in "exceptional circumstances." Moreover, the Tribunal placed the burden on the accused, not the prosecutor, to demonstrate that he would appear for trial and would pose no substantial danger to victims, witnesses, or others.

When the judges first considered pre-trial release, some thought there should be no mention of it in the Rules at all. They anticipated no immediate problem with bringing suspects to trial quickly. Also, some judges thought that war crimes were akin to murder or other crimes carrying sentences of death or life imprisonment, crimes for which most judicial systems would not allow bail anyway. But judges who wanted the Tribunal's rules to be in conformity with the European Convention on Human Rights ("ECHR"), as well as non-governmental advocacy groups like the Lawyers Committee on Human Rights and Amnesty International, urged that the

---

[4]Rule 65 was amended in January 1995 to add a requirement that the host country be heard from when release was contemplated. In July 1997, the provision for appeal was added, while in November 1997 allowance was made for a stay of release pending appeal at the prosecution's request. An amendment in July 1998 clarified the time for appeal from an oral decision. See John R.W.D. Jones, The Practice of the International Criminal Tribunals for the Former Yugoslavia and for Rwanda (1999) at pp. 146–47.

[5]Although the text of the Rule refers to the "Trial Chamber," the Appeals Chamber has taken the view that it is also empowered to consider requests for provisional release pending appeal, over the dissent of Judge Bennouna. See *Prosecutor v. Delalić ("Čelebići Camp"), Order of the Appeals Chamber on the Motion of the Appellant for a Provisional and Temporary Release*, Case No. IT-96-21-A, A. Ch., 19 Feb. 1999; id., *Dissenting Opinion of Judge Bennouna*, 22 Feb. 1999.

possibility of release be incorporated into the Rules. Examples were cited of war criminals confined in a wheelchair or in need of medical treatment not available in detention. The "exceptional circumstances" requirement would limit the number of prisoners released to such circumstances.

If any doubt existed as to the plain meaning of the original Rule 65(B), such doubt was quickly dispelled once the Tribunal began dealing with defendants' requests for provisional release. In case after case, the various trial chambers adhered unrelentingly to the presumption against release and in favour of detention. As one decision explained:

> The Trial Chamber is cognisant that international standards view pre-trial detention, in general, as the exception rather than the rule. However, both the shifting of the burden to the accused and the requirement that he show exceptional circumstances to qualify for provisional release are justified by the extreme gravity of the offences with which persons accused before the International Tribunal are charged and the unique circumstances under which the Tribunal operates. [...] The International Tribunal only has subject-matter jurisdiction over serious violations of international humanitarian law [...]. It is not in possession of any form of mechanism, such as a police force, that could exercise control over the accused, nor does it have any control over the area in which the accused would reside if released.[6]

But prompted in part by an investigation into the death of two defendants in the detention unit, the judges became increasingly concerned about the depressive effects of lengthy pre-trial detention without regular contact with the court. The Tribunal nevertheless rejected suggestions that the Rule be amended to adopt the ECHR approach in full, with a presumption in favour of release and automatic review of detention every 90 days. Instead, in mid-1999, it adopted a requirement of status conferences every 120 days at which the defendant would be present and asked about the conditions of his detention.[7] In late November 1999, however, a group of United Nations experts still concerned with the length of ICTY trials and pre-trial detention recommended that the Tribunal experiment with granting provisional release more liberally in cases where the defendant had voluntarily surrendered.[8]

---

[6] *Prosecutor v. Delalić ("Čelebići Camp"), Decision on Motion for Provisional Release Filed by the Accused Zejnil Delalić*, Case No. IT-96-21-T, 25 Sept. 1996 ("*Delalić Provisional Release Decision*") at paras. 19–20; see also *Prosecutor v. Aleksovski, Decision Denying a Request for Provisional Release*, Case No. IT-95-14/1-PT, 23 Jan. 1998 ("*Aleksovski Provisional Release Decision*") at p. 4.

[7] See ICTY Rule 65*bis*.

[8] See Report of the Expert Group to Conduct a Review of the Effective Operation and Functioning of the International Tribunal for the Former Yugoslavia and the International Criminal Tribunal for Rwanda, UN Doc. A/54/634 (1999) at p. 96.

As a result, in November 1999, Rule 65(B) was amended to eliminate the requirement of "exceptional circumstances."[9] The full effects of this amendment remain to be seen, though early indications are mixed as to whether it has significantly altered the prior presumption against release. Until the Tribunal's interpretation of the amended rule becomes clearer, decisions under the old Rule provide necessary background for understanding Rule 65 and for predicting the Tribunal's future course.

2. The Justification for the Presumption of Detention

The Tribunal's past justifications for reversing the ordinary presumption in favour of release have been brisk but plausible. They have emphasised the gravity of the crimes charged,[10] a factor that countries with a presumption in favour of release often use as the basis for an exception.[11] It is worth noting in this regard that Article 1 of the Tribunal's statute authorises the prosecution of "serious" violations of international humanitarian law and that the announced policy of every prosecutor so far has been to indict the "big fish," including military and political leaders, along with a few lower echelon figures responsible for particularly atrocious acts. Thus, the bulk of those charged are likely to be subject to long prison terms if convicted.[12] This specialised pool of serious offenders is a distinguishing factor from the more generalised group of criminals with which the international conventions and national laws typically deal.[13]

---

[9]Note that the Statute of the International Criminal Court, Art. 60, basically adopts the current ICTY Rule 65 language requiring the host country be heard, and squarely places the burden on the defendant to show no flight risk or danger to others, and also omits the exceptional circumstances requirement.

[10]See, e.g., *Prosecutor v. Blaškić, Order Denying a Motion for Provisional Release,* Case No. IT-95-14-T, 25 Apr. 1996 ("*Blaškić Provisional Release Decision of April 1996*") at p. 4.

[11]For example, the United States employs a preventive detention scheme in conjunction with a presumption of release in ordinary cases, but changes the presumption in capital cases and legislates a presumption that no conditions will suffice to guarantee against the risk of flight or danger to others when the accused has been charged with a crime of violence and has committed a similar crime in the past or committed one while on release pending trial or is charged with a drug-related crime carrying a punishment of 10 years or more in prison. In all other pre-trial cases the prosecution retains the burden of showing by clear and convincing evidence that no conditions of release will satisfactorily ensure the defendant's appearance at trial as well as the safety of the community. See 18 U.S.C. § 3142(e).

[12]See, e.g., *Prosecutor v. Aleksovski, Judgement*, Case No. IT-95-14/1-A, A. Ch., 24 March 2000 at pp. 75–76.

[13]Thus, civil liberty oriented human rights groups who in general might be expected to favour maximum pre-trial release now find themselves complaining that release for war-related crimes is too liberal. See Lawyers Committee for Human Rights, A Fragile Peace: Laying the Foundations for Justice in Kosovo (Oct. 1999) at p. 20 (criticising 40 percent release rate by Kosovar authorities for offenders apprehended by peacekeeping force).

An allied concern, not mentioned formally by any Trial Chambers, but cited frequently in the Prosecution's perennial opposition to release motions, is a perceived inconsistency in asking UN and national peacekeeping forces to risk their lives to apprehend indicted war criminals[14] only to have them promptly released at arraignment. The Prosecutor has, except in a few humanitarian cases, strongly resisted all release motions brought by defendants.

Another concern that immediately became apparent in applying pre-trial release to ICTY cases was the dilemma of the "host" country to which the accused would be released. Unlike the usual situation inside the frontiers of a single country – for example, a Dutch court releasing a Dutch criminal pursuant to Dutch law – in the case of the ICTY, it would not be the courts of the same country whose legislature passed the release law (or whose judges are enforcing it) who would be freeing the suspect. Rather, it would be an international court that would be releasing suspects from other countries into the local community. Early in the Tribunal's active trial history, this consideration came to the foreground. The Netherlands wrote an official letter expressing serious "practical concerns" about any release of accused into the Hague vicinity, such as the need for residence permits, secure housing, and adequate surveillance, which it was not willing to offer.[15]

The Tribunal amended Rule 65 in 1995 to afford any "host" country to which the accused seeks release the right to be heard. As might be anticipated, no provisional releases into the Netherlands have yet been made.

However, in one case, *Blaškić*, an agreement was reached with the Dutch authorities whereby the accused was allowed to stay under house arrest in the Hague. This was not done as a provisional release under Rule 65, but rather by order of the Tribunal's President under Rule 64 as a modification of the conditions of detention. The order provided that Blaškić's place of residence be designated "by the Netherlands authorities in consultation with the Registrar" and that he be permitted to leave this place of residence only to meet his Counsel, the diplomatic and consular representatives of the Republic of Croatia, and his family and friends, with such meetings to take place in the Detention Unit.[16] Blaškić was required to pay the costs of his house arrest. The main factor in favour of allowing house arrest was that Blaškić had voluntarily surrendered, flying to the Hague on his own initiative. The decision described house arrest as an "intermediate measure [...] milder than incarceration, whilst [...] harsher than provisional release, for house arrest is a form of detention."[17]

---

[14]See, e.g., Charles Truehart, "A Bosnian Serb Leader is Arrested for Genocide," *International Herald Tribune*, 4 Apr. 2000 (describing how NATO troops used explosives to enter the accused's home).

[15]*Prosecutor v. Blaškić, Letter to Registrar*, Case No. IT-95-14-T, 18 July 1996.

[16]*Prosecutor v. Blaškić, Decision on the Motion of the Defence Filed Pursuant to Rule 64 of the Rules of Procedure and Evidence*, Case No. IT-95-14-T, ICTY President, 3 Apr. 1996 at para. 24.

[17]Id., para. 13.

Since the Dutch government is not generally supportive of releasing accused war criminals into the Tribunal's immediate area, provisional releases would have to be to more distant countries, with the attendant difficulties of enforcing or depending upon the guarantees of such countries that they will assure the suspect's return.[18]

This raises a final concern that has often been mentioned in Trial Chamber decisions denying release. That is the lack of sanctions that the Tribunal has at its disposal for violations of release conditions. Unlike a state, the Tribunal has no police force of its own to send to arrest the violator and return him for trial, thus increasing the chance that "once released an accused could escape the International Tribunal's grasp."[19] Additionally, unlike in many countries, such as the United States, there is no separate criminal penalty for failure to appear in the Tribunal.[20] Rule 65(H) authorises the Trial Chamber to issue an arrest warrant to secure the accused's presence if he "has been released or is for any other reason at liberty."[21] But execution of such a warrant would involve substantial difficulties in a country which had guaranteed the accused's return but was now not prepared to carry through on its promise.[22] The Tribunal may also bring a contempt action against an accused who violates the conditions of his release,[23] either by failing to appear or by interfering with a witness. Penalties for contempt may range from fines to imprisonment up to 7 years.[24] And presumably an accused's

---

[18]See, e.g., *Prosecutor v. Kovačević, Decision on Defence Motion for Provisional Release*, Case No. IT-97-24-T, 20 Jan. 1998 ("*Kovačević Provisional Release Decision*") at paras. 25–28. In *Kovačević*, the Trial Chamber pointed out that the Republika Srpska had not arrested or delivered to the Tribunal any of the 48 persons publicly indicted and believed to be living there. "We are also alive to the difficulty of implementing any such guarantee or other conditions of release such as daily reporting to police authorities or home arrest." Id., para. 27; see also *Prosecutor v. Blaškić, Order Denying a Motion for Provisional Release*, Case No. IT-95-14-T, 20 Dec. 1996 ("*Blaškić Provisional Release Decision of December 1996*") at p. 5 (expressing similar doubts about Croatia's assurances of return of suspect).

[19]*Delalić Provisional Release Decision* at para. 20.

[20]See 18 U.S.C. § 314 (wilful failure to appear and obstruction of justice through witness tampering defined as separate offences, penalised by prison terms).

[21]The Rule does not require a violation of release conditions be shown or a hearing be held before the accused is returned to custody.

[22]See ICTY Rules 54 et seq. on arrest warrants.

[23]See ICTY Rule 77 ("Contempt of the Tribunal").

[24]Assuming notice and an opportunity to appear, a finding of contempt may be made in the absence of the physical presence of the contemnor. See ICTY Rule 77(F). The Rules presently do not provide for the trial to proceed in the absence of the defendant if he absconds during trial. Compare U.S. Fed. R. Crim. Proc. 43. The Statute does not allow trials in absentia but many countries which similarly forbid them have not interpreted the ban to include continuing a trial which has commenced with the defendant present when he subsequently flees. The United Nations Expert Group Report recommended a broader rule that would allow provisional release for a defendant who voluntarily surrendered and explicitly waived the right to be present at his trial, should he abscond after his initial appearance. See Report of the Expert Group to Conduct a Review of the Effective Operation and Functioning of the International Tribunal for the Former Yugoslavia and the International Criminal Tribunal for Rwanda, UN Doc. A/54/634 (1999) at p. 96.

violation of release could be considered an aggravating factor at the time of sentencing.[25] But at the end of the day, the risk of non-appearance when an accused is released to a distant country whose co operation is essential to his return poses a greater threat to the integrity of the Tribunal's processes than is normal in domestic courts.

The potential danger to witnesses from the accused's release, especially to the area where the alleged war crimes were originally committed, is also qualitatively different than in ordinary crimes. Attempted intimidations will be more difficult to detect or prevent in faraway places; the witnesses may be more vulnerable both because of what they have already suffered and because of the likely prominence of the accused in his home community, and ironically because the accused himself will know much more about who his accusers are and what they plan to say at trial as a result of the extremely liberal pre-trial discovery rules of the Tribunal.[26]

Ultimately, then, there are strong considerations that may have motivated the Tribunal to adopt a presumption of detention with release only where the defendant can show "exceptional circumstances" in addition to presenting no flight risk or threat to others. We will now examine how the Tribunal applied its "principle of detention."[27]

3. Application of the Presumption of Detention

Even though, until November 1999, the Tribunal's presumption against release was explicit, defendants frequently applied for release, and the trial chambers wrote a number of lengthy judgements analysing the four factors necessary to obtain release under Rule 65: (1) the existence of "exceptional circumstances," (2) whether the accused will appear for trial; (3) whether the accused will pose a danger to any victim, witness, or other person; and (4) the procedural requirement that the host country be heard. It was decided early on that these four requirements were conjunctive, that is that the requirement of proving "exceptional circumstances" was *in addition* to the need for an accused to show that he would appear for trial *and* not pose a danger to others. Over the next several years, the existence of "exceptional circumstances" was found in only two instances – both involving the physical

[25]See ICTY Rule 101(B).

[26]See, e.g., ICTY Rules 65*ter*-68 (requiring prosecution to disclose not only exculpatory evidence but also to turn over statements of all the witnesses it plans to call at trial and a list of exhibits and, if the defendant agrees to reciprocal discovery, to allow the defence to inspect any books, documents, photographs and tangible objects in the Prosecutor's control that are material to the preparation of the defence, or that are intended for use at trial, or that were taken from or belonged to the accused); *compare* U.S. Fed. R. Crim. Proc. 16 (allowing much more limited discovery).

[27]See, e.g., *Aleksovski Provisional Release Decision* at p. 4 ("By considering the extreme gravity of crimes against humanity, the Rules thus establish a presumption of detention according to which detention is the rule and provisional release the exception.")

health of the defendant.[28] As a result, virtually all of the discussions by Trial Chambers on flight and danger to others occurred in the context of decisions already made against the defendant on the first ground, i.e., that no "exceptional circumstances" existed to justify release. Nonetheless, these discussions of the flight and danger risks provide valuable hints as to what release conditions might or might not satisfy the Tribunal in future cases where the exceptional circumstances requirement no longer comes into play.

3.1 What Constituted an Exceptional Circumstance?

3.1.1 Medical Condition of Defendant

The two cases in which defendants met the "exceptional circumstances" test for long-term provisional release featured extreme medical situations.[29] Defendant Simić had surrendered himself to the Tribunal voluntarily; he was in need of intensive daily care not available at the detention facility in the Hague; the Republika Srpska to which he was released offered to put up a U.S. $25,000 bond; and, perhaps most importantly, the prosecution did not object to his release. The conditions of release were strict; among other things, he was required to remain within the municipality of Bosanski Šamac and to meet daily with municipal police.[30]

Defendant Djukić also had serious medical problems. After his trial had begun, Djukić requested the indictment be withdrawn because he was terminally ill.[31] The Chambers found his medical status incompatible with any conditions of detention,[32] and he was allowed to leave the Netherlands to return to his family on conditions similar to those in *Simić*. He died while on release.

In *Kovačević*, by contrast, the court rejected the defendant's request for release based on a health condition that it deemed insufficiently serious to constitute an "exceptional circumstance" since it was treatable in the detention facility and not life-threatening.[33]

---

[28]See *Prosecutor v. Djukić, Decision Rejecting the Application to Withdraw Indictment and Order for Provisional Release*, Case No. IT-96-20-T, 24 Apr. 1996 ("*Djukić Provisional Release Decision*"); *Prosecutor v. Simić, Decision on Provisional Release of the Accused*, Case No. IT-95-9-PT, 26 March 1998 ("*Simić I*"); id., *Decision on the Application of the Accused Mr. Milan Simić to Leave His Residence for Medical Reasons*, 17 Apr 1998 ("*Simić II*"); id., *Decision on the Application of the Accused Mr. Milan Simić to Leave His Residence for Medical Reasons*, 8 May 1998 ("*Simić III*"); id., *Decision on the Application of the Accused Mr. Milan Simić to Leave His Residence for Medical Reasons*, 29 July 1998 ("*Simić IV*"). The later orders permitted Simić to go to Belgrade for treatment on the condition that he file a medical report at the end of his treatment, and that the medical facility and local police verify his whereabouts.

[29]See *Simić I*.

[30]See id.

[31]See *Djukić Provisional Release Decision*.

[32]The Tribunal sent its own medical examiner to verify the defendant's condition. See id.

[33]See *Kovačević Provisional Release Decision* at paras. 13–14.

3.1.2 Non-Existence of a Reasonable Suspicion that the Defendant Committed a Crime

Several chambers considered defendants' arguments that they should be released because there was no longer a reasonable suspicion that they had committed the crimes of which they were accused. Since the existence of a reasonable suspicion of crime was a prerequisite to detention in the first place, they argued, clear and unequivocal refutation of that suspicion would mean that continued detention was unjustified. In *Delalić*, for example, the court agreed to look at new evidence proffered by the defendant to show that he was no longer a reasonable suspect, despite the prosecutor's vigorous objection that such evidence was inadmissible because a judge had already found reasonable suspicion in confirming the indictment and any further excursion into the merits at this stage was unwarranted.[34] But while the chambers were willing to look at the defendant's evidence, they also made clear that they would apply a high threshold before upsetting the confirming judge's conclusion that a reasonable suspicion existed.[35]

3.1.3 Severity of Offence

Another factor frequently considered in evaluating exceptional circumstances was the seriousness of the alleged offences and the defendant's role in them, much as the severity of the alleged conduct weighs against release in many domestic legal systems. In *Delalić*, for example, the severity of the accused's alleged conduct (including significant responsibility for numerous instances of murder, torture, and rape) was found to weigh against release.[36]

3.1.4 Length of Detention

Many chambers have recognised that an unusually long stretch of detention might constitute an "exceptional circumstance," and have considered a variety of factors in this regard: the actual period already served; the relationship of that period to the offence charged and the sentence that might be expected upon conviction; the material and moral effect of detention on the accused; his own conduct which may have contributed to the delay in trial; the difficulties of investigating the crime and how the investigation was conducted; and the conduct of judicial authorities.[37]

Weighing these factors in *Delalić*, the court found that four months in detention was not exceptional.[38] Likewise, in *Aleksovski*, the chamber ruled

[34]See *Delalić Provisional Release Decision* at paras. 24–28.

[35]See id.; see also *Kovačević Provisional Release Decision* at para. 16; *Aleksovski Provisional Release Decision* at p. 3 (noting that reasonable suspicion present); but see *Blaškić Provisional Release Decision of April 1996* at p. 4 ("no questions relating to the evidence on which the charges are based are relevant at this stage of the proceedings [...] and such questions may be reviewed only at a later date, either as part of the preliminary motions or during the trial on the merits").

[36]See *Delalić Provisional Release Decision* at para. 19.

[37]See, e.g., id., para. 30.

[38]See id.

that 577 days was not excessive in light of the severity of his alleged crimes, potential sentence, and his health and family situation.[39] In *Blaškić*, detention of 9 months was not found extraordinary, particularly considering the fact that the many defence motions had contributed to the delay and the fact that the prosecution's investigation was complex and involved extensive on-site excursions. Similarly, in *Kovačević*, the court found that 6 months fell well within international standards, and that weight should be given to the special difficulties faced by the prosecution in terms of investigating crimes away from the Netherlands and without a police force of its own.[40]

3.1.5 Other Factors Deemed Insufficient

Defendant Blaškić argued for his release on two separate occasions in 1996, supporting his plea with references to his voluntary surrender, the prosecution's lack of diligence or productivity in gathering evidence, Croatia's willingness to guarantee his return, his family situation, and his willingness to post a bail bond.[41] None of these were found to constitute "exceptional conditions."[42]

3.1.6 Short-term Humanitarian Release

The Tribunal has on a few occasions allowed short-term release for humanitarian reasons, for example allowing one defendant to attend the funeral of a close relative.[43] The Registrar and authorities of Bosnia and Herzegovina were instructed to co-operate in escorting the defendant to and from the funeral.

3.2 What Kind of Conditions Qualify to Deter Flight and Danger to Others

As recounted, until the 1999 amendment, the Tribunal's evaluation of the effectiveness of proposed conditions has typically come only after a finding that the exceptional circumstances requirement had not been met, and in that sense the discussion of release conditions was technically gratuitous or dicta. These discussions do, however, provide insight into the concerns of the Tribunal judges that are even more important now that the exceptional circumstances requirement has been removed.[44] In *Blaškić*, one of the

[39]See *Aleksovski Provisional Release Decision* at pp. 3–5.

[40]See *Kovačević Provisional Release Decision* at paras. 22–24.

[41]See *Blaškić Provisional Release Decision of April 1996* at p. 3; *Blaškić Provisional Release Decision of December 1996* at p. 3.

[42]However, it should be noted that Blaškić was held under house arrest in the Hague rather than in the UN Detention Unit for a significant part of the period leading up to his trial.

[43]See *Prosecutor v. Kupreškić, Decision on the Motion of Defence Counsel for Drago Josipovic*, Case No. IT-95-16-T, 6 May 1999 (*Request for permission to attend funeral*).

[44]Note also the caveat in *Kovačević* that "even if the Trial Chamber is satisfied in respect of all four conditions, it retains a discretion not to grant provisional release." *Kovačević Provisional Release Decision* at para. 7.

earliest decisions on provisional release, the court indicated that the burden on the defendant to show an absence of danger to others was an almost absolute one in light of the fact "that the knowledge which, as an accused person, he has of the evidence produced by the Prosecutor would place him in a situation permitting him to exert pressure on victims and witnesses and that the investigation of the case might be seriously flawed."[45] In a later decision, although Blaškić had offered to surrender his passport, post a bail bond of DM 1 million, stay in Zagreb, and have Croatia guarantee his return, these conditions were found insufficient "to satisfy that the accused will appear at his trial because of the gravity of the criminal acts of which he stands accused, of the severity of the penalties to which he is liable, and last of his sole offer to reside in his country in Zagreb."[46]

In *Delalić*, the defendant argued that he would reappear if released because he had family and business ties to countries that were co-operative with the Tribunal and would stay in Germany, where his business was, or in Bosnia, where he owned a house. He would not be likely to flee to Serbia because he was wanted for a crime there, and Croatians had threatened his life. Bosnia would stand for his return; all witnesses lived in places inaccessible to him so that he could not intimidate them; and in any event he promised not to contact any.[47] The prosecution, however, protested that he was not precise enough in the details of where he would live or which authorities would guarantee his availability for trial. At the time of arrest, moreover, he had travel and forged ID documents in his possession. In 1992, he had fled from an arrest warrant; he was a man with "influential friends" and financial "connections"; his children were in Serbia and some witnesses were in Bosnia.[48] The court leaned on his 1992 flight in finding that he posed a risk of non-appearance as well as his proximity to states that are "havens" for indictees.[49] It emphasised that it was the defendant's burden to negative the risk of flight and danger.[50] "Although the Trial Chamber is not convinced that the accused would pose a danger to any such victim or witness or other person, it is not necessarily satisfied that he would not."[51]

In *Kovačević*, likewise, the court refused to credit a letter from the Republika Srpska president that it was willing to accept the defendant on release and to post a money bond to assure his reappearance. The Republika Srpska's tainted record in providing a safe refuge for indictees as well as the difficulties in implementing any conditions of daily reporting to local police was found to be fatal.[52]

[45]*Blaškić Provisional Release Decision of April 1996* at p. 5.
[46]*Blaškić Provisional Release Decision of December 1996* at p. 5.
[47]*Delalić Provisional Release Decision* at paras. 6–8.
[48]Id., paras. 15–17.
[49]Id., para. 33.
[50]Id., paras. 32–35.
[51]Id., para. 35.
[52] See *Kovačević Provisional Release Decision*.

Based on the Tribunal's track record, could any conditions qualify for release? Until the 1999 amendment, the two instances in which it was given were based on the extreme physical conditions of the defendant – indeed, one of those defendants in fact died while on release. Even in a close case, the fact that the defendant must prove a negative – that he will not flee or obstruct justice – has tended to control. Thus, until very recently, it was not clear if there were any conditions of release that would satisfy the Tribunal, so long as the defendant himself was still active and healthy.

4. The Elimination of the Exceptional Circumstances Requirement

Rule 65 was adopted at a time when the Tribunal had no live defendants to deal with. By the spring of 2000, however, the situation was much different. Ninety-two individuals had been publicly indicted, and pursuant to Rule 53, additional undisclosed indictments may also have been confirmed. Thirty-seven accused were currently in proceedings before the Tribunal, with 36 actually in the Detention Unit and one released pending appeal. Out of the 37 accused currently in proceedings before the Tribunal, 12 accused were at the appeal stage, 10 accused were in on-going trials, and 15 accused were at the pre-trial stage. Proceedings against four accused had been completed. Other publicly indicted accused remained at large.

Due to the typically lengthy period most trials took – the *Blaškić* trial, for example, took two years – some detainees were spending up to two years or more in detention before their trials could begin. In this atmosphere, the Tribunal revisited Rule 65 and its exceptional circumstances requirement.[53] In the plenary session in November 1999, the Tribunal voted to drop the exceptional circumstances requirement from Rule 65 so that it now reads:

> Release may be ordered by a Trial Chamber only after hearing the host country and only if it is satisfied that the accused will appear for trial and, if released, will not pose a danger to any victim, witness or other person.

The precise impact of this revision in Rule 65 is, however, not immediately apparent. In one of the first decisions under the new rules, the Trial Chamber in *Kvočka* seemed to consider the amendment to have little effect, opining that "the effect of the amendment is not to establish release as the norm and detention as the exception."[54] The Trial Chamber denied Kvočka's

---

[53]See, e.g., H.E. Patrick Robinson, "Ensuring Fair and Expeditious Trials at the International Criminal Tribunal for the Former Yugoslavia," Speech to Leiden University, 30 Sept. 1999 (stressing ICCPR and ECHR guarantees to a trial within a reasonable time or pre-trial release, and the Statute's own Art. 21(4)(c) proclaiming a right to be tried without undue delay).

[54]*Prosecutor v. Kvočka, Decision on Motion for Provisional Release of Miroslav Kvočka*, Case No. IT-98-30-PT, 2 Feb. 2000 ("*Kvočka Provisional Release Decision*") at p. 4.

request for release, rejecting as insufficient his assurances that he would not pose a danger to witnesses and that the government of Republika Srpska had guaranteed his return. In addition, the Trial Chamber considered the fact that trial would commence soon.[55] Likewise, in the *Kupreškić* case, the Trial Chamber denied the motions for release filed after the trial had ended and a few weeks before the judgement was handed down. Despite the defendants' claims that the government of Bosnia and Herzegovina would guarantee their return, the Trial Chamber found that the danger of the accused absconding shortly before the judgement was delivered was too great.[56]

However, a different decision by a different panel a few months later suggested a more dramatic turnabout. In granting provisional release to Miroslav Tadić and Simo Zarić, the Chamber signalled that the deletion of the exceptional circumstances requirement may have had a more serious substantive effect.[57] Provisional release was no longer to be treated as a deviation from the norm, and delay caused by lack of court resources was not viewed as an adequate excuse for keeping an accused in detention for a lengthy pre-trial period.[58] It was not clear whether the Trial Chamber thought that the amendment effected a shift in the burden of persuasion, however, since it said that:

> while Rule 65(B) as amended no longer requires an accused to demonstrate exceptional circumstances before release may be ordered, this amendment does not affect the remaining requirements under this provision.[59]

Its action in granting release, nonetheless, under conditions remarkably similar to those rejected in past cases may speak louder than words. The

---

[55]See id.

[56]*Prosecutor v. Kupreškić, Decision on the Motion for Provisional Release by the Accused Zoran Kupreškić and Mirjan Kupreškić of 15 December 1999*, Case No. IT-95-16-T, 20 Dec. 1999 at p. 2; id., *Decision on the Motion for Provisional Release by the Accused Dragan Papic of 15 December 1999*, 20 Dec. 1999 at p. 2; id., *Decision on the Motion for Provisional Release by the Accused Vladimir Šantic of 15 December 1999*, 20 Dec. 1999, at p. 2; id., *Decision on the Motion for Provisional Release by the Accused Drago Josipovic of 21 December 1999*, 22 Dec. 1999 at p. 2.

[57]*Prosecutor v. Blagoje Simić and Others, Decision on Miroslav Tadić's Application for Provisional Release*, Case No. IT-95-9-PT, 4 Apr. 2000 ("*Tadić Provisional Release Decision*"); *Prosecutor v. Blagoje Simić and Others, Decision on Simo Zarić's Application for Provisional Release*, Case No. IT-95-9-PT, 4 Apr. 2000 ("*Zarić Provisional Release Decision*").

[58]The Trial Chamber noted the accused's citation of a recent European Court of Human Rights Case holding that the right of an accused to be tried within a reasonable time or to be released pending trial under Article 5(3) of the European Convention on Human Rights is violated where the delay is attributable to the judicial system. *Tadić Provisional Release Decision* at p.6 (citing *Affaire Deboub alias Husseini Ali v. France,* Eur. Ct. H. R., Judgement of 9 November 1999); *Zarić Provisional Release Decision* at p. 6 (citing same).

[59]*Tadić Provisional Release Decision* at p. 8; *Zarić Provisional Release Decision* at p. 7.

judgement cited as contributing factors in its release decision the two defendants' voluntary surrender, the expected delay in setting a trial date due to the Tribunal's backlog, and the lengthy period of detention already served.[60] The judges were persuaded, too, by the Republika Srpska's promise to monitor the accused to prevent flight or threats to others, although Chambers in the past had summarily dismissed similar offers as unreliable.[61]

Not unexpectedly, the Prosecutor resisted provisional release for these defendants by arguing that Republika Srpska had not co-operated with the Tribunal in the past, that the defendants were in possession of the summaries of expected testimony from more than 60 witnesses, and that their release would have a chilling effect on getting future victims and witnesses to testify. The Prosecutor sought leave to appeal the Trial Chamber's decision granting release, but the Appeals Chamber rejected the application, finding that the Prosecutor had not shown good cause for appeal by demonstrating an error in the Trial Chamber's decision.[62]

Subsequently, the same Trial Chamber also ordered the release of another of the co-accused, Milan Simić, in the same case, after making similar findings.[63] The Prosecution had earlier alleged that Simić and his attorney had interfered with a witness; however, the Trial Chamber found that those concerns were not credible and, looking to factors such as his voluntary surrender and the guarantees provided for his return, granted release. The Prosecution did not appeal.

It remains to be seen whether other Trial Chambers will follow this lead in granting provisional release more liberally.

---

[60]*Tadić Provisional Release Decision* at p. 8–9; *Zarić Provisional Release Decision* at p. 8. Tadić and Zarić both raised other arguments in favour of release, including the relative gravity of their crimes and, in Tadić's case, his advanced age. But the Trial Chamber did not expressly pass on the strength of these arguments. *Tadić Provisional Release Decision* at p. 3; *Zarić Provisional Release Decision* at p. 6.

[61]In both cases, the release decisions require the accused to abide by and the authorities of Republika Srpska to ensure compliance with a number of conditions: that the accused stay within the confines of the municipality of Bosanki Šamać; surrender their passports; report daily to the local police; consent to having the International Police Task Force check with the local police about their whereabouts or make unannounced visits; not to have contact with co-accuseds or any person who might testify at trial; not to discuss the case with anyone except counsel; and to pay for transport from Schiphol airport to Bosanki Šamać and back. *Tadić Provisional Release Decision* at p. 9–10; *Zarić Provisional Release Decision* at p. 9.

[62]*Prosecutor v. Blagoje Simić and Others, Decision on Application for Leave to Appeal*, Case No. IT-95-9-AR65, A. Ch., 19 Apr. 2000.

[63]*Prosecutor v. Blagoje Simić and Others, Decision on Milan Simić's Application for Provisional Release*, Case No. IT-95-9-PT, 29 May 2000.

5. Conclusion

Before the 1999 amendment went into effect, the Tribunal had turned away virtually all of the petitions for release on failure to meet the exceptional circumstances requirement. Now the heart of the release proceeding is the defendants' ability to convince the judges that there are conditions which will guarantee their return and the safety of victims and witnesses. In this endeavour some of the major concerns of the past Tribunal decisions appear to be abating. The public perception problems of releasing defendants apprehended at the risk of soldiers' lives will remain, but this concern is less compelling where the accused has voluntarily surrendered. Signs of improved co-operation with host governments like those of Republika Srpska and Croatia[64] also appear to enhance the court's perception of the effectiveness of conditions like reporting to local police or house arrest, although only experience will show if that assumption proves to be accurate. Unless the Tribunal cuts back on its liberal pre-trial disclosure Rules, the knowledge factor, so often mentioned by judges as a danger to witnesses, will not change, though this factor did not appear to deter the *Tadić* and *Zarić* releases.

At least one factor in the *Tadić* and *Zarić* decisions must be noted, and that is the Tribunal's inability to bring those apprehended to trial quickly, a factor that will inevitably have wide application unless current attempts to speed up trials are successful. This could result in a cascade of applications from those detainees who have been in the dock for two years or more and still have not had trial dates set.

The real solution to unduly lengthy pre-trial detention, however, may not be pre-trial release but speedier and shorter trials. Recent amendments to the rules are aimed at this goal.[65] There are also proposals for *ad litem* judges and discussions about more flexible assignments of trial judges between the three Trial Chambers in order to increase judicial productivity. Provisional release should ideally not be viewed as an escape valve from the dictates of speedy trials; the stakes for witnesses and victims and for the credibility of the Tribunal and needed co-operation with neighbouring nations and UN peacekeeping forces are too high. The Tribunal recognised at its inception that its circumstances are unique so that the international norm of pre-trial release applicable to ordinary states in ordinary criminal cases cannot

---

[64]See, e.g., Steven Erlanger, "Reformist Croat Leads But He Faces a Runoff", *International Herald Tribune*, 26 January 2000 (discussing new Croatian leadership's avowed intention to co-operate with the Tribunal); see also Report of the Expert Group to Conduct a Review of the Effective Operation and Functioning of the International Tribunal for the Former Yugoslavia and the International Criminal Tribunal for Rwanda, UN Doc. A/54/634 (1999) at para. 52.

[65]See, e.g., Rule 65*bis* and 65*ter* (mandatory system of pre-trial conferencing with a single judge who readies the case for trial); Rule 71 (deposition standards loosened); Rule 71*bis* (video conferencing); Rule 72 (sixty-day time limit for deciding preliminary motions).

be mechanically applied without risk of sacrificing the Tribunal's mission. The elimination of the express exceptional circumstances requirement, certainly as interpreted to cover only extreme illnesses, is all to the good. Particularly if the reliability of the guarantees of other countries to return defendants is proven through experience, the Tribunal can easily make the proper evaluation of the flight and danger criteria on a case-by-case basis, particularly if, as seems likely, the defendant continues to bear the burden of proof. But in the full analysis, the more important problems of overlong detention and too lengthy trials still threaten to dominate the context in which these individual release decisions are made, and quite possibly to colour the results. The fate of Rule 65, in that sense, is inextricably wedded to the Tribunal's ability to process its cases more swiftly, and that, in turn, is very much a work in progress.

PART VII

Evidence

20 Evidence before the ICTY

1 INTRODUCTION

[illegible]

Evidence has been defined as information in the form of personal testimony, documents or material objects [illegible] used to establish facts in a legal investigation. In the context of a criminal trial [illegible] it means the information which is put before the court in order to prove facts in issue [illegible] must establish [illegible] the defendant must [illegible] for the presentation of evidence before the tribunal [illegible] this definition [illegible] the discussion [illegible] scope of evidence before the International Tribunal [illegible] stage of its development.

At the outset [illegible] tribunal are [illegible] different [illegible] before a domestic [illegible] before the International Tribunal [illegible] [illegible]

[illegible]

RICHARD MAY* and MARIEKE WIERDA**

20. Evidence before the ICTY

1. Introduction

1.1 Meaning and Scope of Evidence

Evidence has been defined as information in the form of personal or documented testimony or the production of material objects tending or used to establish facts in a legal investigation.[1] In the context of a common law criminal trial it must be defined more narrowly: "it means the information which is put before the court in order to prove the facts in issue, i.e. those facts which the Prosecution must establish in order to prove their case and the defendant must establish in order to raise a defence".[2] Since the procedures for the presentation of evidence before the Tribunal are essentially adversarial[3] this definition is as good a starting point as any from which to embark on this discussion, the purpose of which is to consider the nature and scope of evidence before the International Tribunal, albeit at a very early stage of its development.

At the outset, it is important to note that trials before the International Tribunal are of a different scope to those before a domestic court. Typically, those before a domestic court deal with an isolated incident, whereas those before the International Tribunal may cover a number of years of conflict and involve many locations and incidents. This was true of the war crimes trials which followed the Second World War. Thus, Robert Jackson, in his

*A Judge of the ICTY since 1997, Presiding Judge Trial Chamber III, formerly a Circuit Judge on the Midland and Oxford Circuit, England.
**Associate Legal Officer (at ICTY since 1997), Trial Chamber III, ICTY. The views expressed herein are those of the author and not of the Tribunal or the United Nations.

[1]The New Shorter Oxford Dictionary (1993).

[2]Richard May, Criminal Evidence (1999) at p. 3.

[3]Each side presents its evidence in the form of examination-in-chief of its witnesses, subject to cross-examination and re-examination: ICTY Rule 85.

R. May et al., Essays on ICTY Procedure and Evidence in Honour of Gabrielle Kirk McDonald, 249–261.

opening speech for the Prosecution before the Military Tribunal at Nuremberg, said that "never before in legal history has an effort been made to bring, within the scope of a single litigation, the developments of a decade, covering a whole continent and involving a score of nations, countless individuals and innumerable events."[4] While the scope of the modern trials may not be as broad, essentially their nature is the same. The result is that the trials are long and complex. For instance, in *Tadić*,[5] 126 witnesses were called and 461 exhibits produced; in *Kupreškić*,[6] 157 witnesses were called and 700 exhibits produced; in *Blaškić*,[7] 161 witnesses were called and 1,423 exhibits produced. This led President McDonald to say that "these are not trials involving ordinary crimes. It is time-consuming to prove, or to respond to, a charge that offences have been committed as part of a widespread or systematic campaign, as is required for establishing crimes against humanity. Similarly, proof that a conflict is international requires considerable evidence that goes beyond proof of the specific crimes with which the accused is charged. Finally, proving or defending an allegation of genocide is more complex than the core crime of murder. All of this is made even more difficult when there are multiple accused".[8]

Thus, in a war crimes trial the Prosecution must prove beyond reasonable doubt, first, that the crimes were committed. This may necessitate the calling of extensive evidence.[9] The crimes themselves may involve numerous offences or attacks.[10] In addition, it may be necessary for the Prosecution to call evidence relating to the historical and political background if these are not familiar to the Trial Chamber. Finally, the Prosecution must establish a link between the accused and the crimes, either by direct evidence of perpetration or indirectly by such means as command responsibility.

It should, at this stage, be noted that the Defence, on the other hand, bears no burden of proof (except when special defences of alibi[11] or

---

[4]Opening Speech of Mr. Justice Robert H. Jackson, Chief Prosecutor for the USA, 21 Nov. 1945, The Trials of German Major War Criminals, HMSO (1946) at p. 4.

[5]*Prosecutor v. Tadić*, Case No. IT-94-1-T.

[6]*Prosecutor v. Kupreškić and Others*, Case No. IT-95-16-T.

[7]*Prosecutor v. Blaškić*, Case No. IT-95-14-T.

[8]Speech of former President Gabrielle Kirk McDonald at the inauguration of new Judges, 16 Nov. 1998.

[9]For example, in order to prove that crimes against humanity occurred the Prosecution must show that the crimes were part of a widespread or systematic attack targeting a civilian population. For grave breaches, the Prosecution is required to show that crimes were committed in the context of an international armed conflict between two sovereign States.

[10]For example, crimes against humanity may involve murder, deportation, or other offences.

[11]An accused will usually call live testimony in support of his alibi; and in one case produced a video recording, made on the day of the crime, to support the evidence of his witnesses: *Prosecutor v. Dokmanović*, Case No. IT 95-13a-T, T. Ch. II.

diminished responsibility[12] are raised).[13] It is the Prosecution who must prove the case. It has been said that the Defence simply has "to lead such evidence as would, if believed and uncontradicted, induce a reasonable doubt about the prosecution case".[14] It can raise such a doubt by attacking the credibility and reliability of the prosecution witnesses by means of cross-examination and by calling its own witnesses. None of this can be intended to cast a burden of proof on the Defence, but evidence called to rebut the prosecution case may nonetheless be extensive.

1.2 The Rules and Relevance

Before discussing the nature of evidence before the Tribunal it is necessary to discuss briefly the rules of evidence, in particular the rule relating to relevance. The ICTY's Rules dealing with evidence are brief and their purpose is "to promote a fair and expeditious trial and Trial Chambers must have the flexibility to achieve this goal."[15] The approach to evidence is liberal and unhindered by technical rules found in national and particularly common law systems. This reflects the real difficulties of proof in a situation where evidence is often difficult to obtain and the challenge to the Tribunal is to establish "incredible facts by means of credible testimony".[16]

Thus Rule 89 of ICTY's Rules provides that "in cases not otherwise provided for [in the Rules], a Chamber shall apply rules of evidence which will best favour a fair determination of the matter before it and are consonant with the spirit of the Statute and the general principles of law". The same rule permits the Chamber to admit any relevant evidence with probative value and to exclude evidence if the probative value is substantially outweighed by the need to ensure a fair trial. Under this regime hearsay evidence is admissible.[17] The general trend is one of liberal

---

[12]In *Prosecutor v. Delalić and Others* the Trial Chamber found that to establish this defence the accused must bring evidence of an abnormality of mind which has substantially impaired his mental responsibility and which has arisen from a condition of arrested or retarded development of the mind, or inherent causes induced by disease or injury. This should be supported by medical evidence: *Prosecutor v. Delalić and Others, Judgement*, Case No. IT-96-21-T, 16 Nov. 1998 at paras. 1166, 1170.

[13]ICTY Rule 67 (ii). Special defences have only to be established on the balance of probability.

[14]*Prosecution v. Delalić and Others, Judgement*, Case No. IT-95-21-T, 16 Nov. 1998 at para. 603.

[15]*Prosecutor v. Aleksovski, Decision on Prosecutor's Appeal on Admissibility of Evidence*, Case No. IT-95-14/1-AR73, A. Ch., 16 Feb. 1999 at para. 19.

[16]*Prosecutor v. Kupreškić and Others, Judgement*, Case No. IT-95-16-T, 14 Jan. 2000 at para. 758.

[17]*Prosecutor v. Tadić, Decision on the Defence Motion on Hearsay*, Case No. IT-94-1-T, 5 Aug. 1996; *Prosecutor v. Blaškić, Decision on Standing Objection of the Defence to the Admission of Hearsay with no Inquiry as to its Reliability*, Case No. IT-95-14-T, 21 Jan. 1998.

admission with weight to be accorded by the Trial Chamber. This was recently reaffirmed in *Blaškić*:[18]

> *Le principe consacré par la jurisprudence de la Chambre en la matière est celui d'une admissibilité extensive des éléments de preuve, les questions de crédibilité ou d'authenticité relevant du poids que les juges accorderont, en temps opportun, à chacun de ces éléments.*

However, the cardinal rule relates to relevance. In order to be admissible, evidence must be relevant to the issues in the trial: if irrelevant, evidence must be excluded. This rule assumes great importance in cases of the size and complexity of those heard by the International Tribunal. An illustration of its operation may be seen in cases where the Defence seeks to adduce evidence of crimes committed by the enemy or evidence tending to suggest that the enemy started the conflict. Thus, in *Kupreškić and Others*, a case which involved conflict between Bosnian Croats and Bosnian Muslims, the Trial Chamber excluded as irrelevant evidence of crimes committed by the "other side".[19] The Trial Chamber also excluded evidence relating to the issue of which side was responsible for starting the conflict unless calling the evidence had a particular purpose relevant to the trial.[20]

In this connection it should however be noted that the Tribunal has institutional functions beyond those of a national criminal court. It was established to contribute to peace in the region by dispensing justice and deterring future breaches of humanitarian law. One of these functions may be the provision of a reliable historical record. A commentator observed about the Nuremberg trials:

> A trial, moreover, would respect the needs of history and provide a record of the Nazi affronts to civilisation [...]. The evidence of the Holocaust was so strong in 1945 that I doubt that anyone then foresaw the so-called Auschwitz lie – the recent denials that the Holocaust actually happened. The trial record surely serves as a corrective of such fantastic revisionism.[21]

---

[18]*Prosecutor v. Blaškić, Judgement*, Case No. IT-95-14-T, 3 March 2000 at para. 34.

[19]The defence of *tu quoque* must be distinguished from self-defence, provided for in Art. 30 (1) of the ICC Statute, on the ground that "in *tu quoque*, the harm is inflicted against persons other than those who committed the original violation": Cherif Bassiouni, "Crimes against Humanity in International Criminal Law", (2nd ed. 1999) at p. 503. The ICTY Statute makes no provision for self-defence as a defence.

[20]*Prosecutor v. Kupreškić and Others, Decision on Evidence of the Good Character of the Accused and the Defence of Tu Quoque*, Case No. IT-95-16-T, 17 Feb. 1999. See also *Prosecutor v. Delalić and Others, Decision on Request of Accused Hazim Delić Pursuant to Rule 68 for Exculpatory Information*, Case No. IT-96-21-T, 24 June 1997.

[21]Bernard D. Meltzer, "War Crimes: The Nuremberg Trial and the Tribunal for the Former Yugoslavia" (The Seegers Lecture), 30 Valparaiso University Law Review (1996), p. 895 at p. 901.

President Antonio Cassese spoke of "an historical record of what occurred during the conflict thereby preventing historical revisionism".[22] Similarly, Judge Gabrielle Kirk McDonald observed after the conclusion of the *Tadić* trial:

> [W]e have begun the task of creating a historical record. In the Judgement that followed the conclusion of our first full trial, over which I presided, we established as a judicial fact what happened in a corner of north-eastern Bosnia in 1992, findings that no amount of revisionism or amnesia will erase.[23]

However, any such result can only be a by-product of the trials where the emphasis must necessarily be in determining whether the Prosecution has established the guilt of the accused beyond reasonable doubt. Thus, the Trial Chamber in *Kupreškić and Others* said:[24]

> Indisputably, what happened on 16 April 1993 in Ahmići has gone down in history as comprising one of the most vicious illustrations of man's inhumanity to man [...] the primary task of this Trial Chamber was not to construct an historical record of modern human horrors in Bosnia and Herzegovina. The principal duty of the Trial Chamber was simply to decide whether the six defendants standing trial were guilty of partaking in this persecutory violence or whether they were, instead, extraneous to it and hence, not guilty.

But, of course, as President McDonald also said:[25]

> By establishing this record we inform the public and help to prevent the recurrence of this tragedy.

2. Direct and Indirect Evidence

The Tribunal's Statute and Rules make no provision for the types of evidence which are to be admissible before it.[26] Rule 90 provides that "witnesses shall, in principle, be heard directly by the Chambers". This emphasis on live testimony does not prevent other forms of evidence being

[22]Address to the General Assembly of the United Nations, IT/127 4 Nov. 1997 at p. 3.

[23]Remarks by former President Gabrielle Kirk McDonald to the Georgetown and George Washington International Law Societies 2nd Annual International Law Weekend Conference on 7 Feb. 1998.

[24]*Prosecutor v. Kupreskić and Others, Judgement*, supra note 16 at paras. 755–756.

[25]Remarks by former President Gabrielle Kirk McDonald to the St. Mary's University's 14th Annual Institute on World Legal Problems, Innsbruck, Austria, 21 July 1999.

[26]This may be contrasted with the Charter of the International Military Tribunal for the Far East which provided for specific forms of evidence admissible before it in Art. 13(c); these included documents, reports of the International Red Cross, affidavits, depositions, signed statements, diaries, letters or other documents including sworn or unsworn statements and copies of documents or any other secondary evidence of its contents.

admitted, e.g. documentary evidence, maps, photographs, video recordings and the occasional physical object.

An important distinction in classification is between direct and indirect evidence (including circumstantial evidence). These two forms of evidence will be first discussed.

2.1 Direct Evidence

The reliance on live evidence has resulted in the calling of a large number of witnesses in the trials, as noted above. The advantage of this form of evidence was stated by the Trial Chamber in *Tadić*:[27]

> The physical presence of a witness at the seat of the International Tribunal enables the Judges to evaluate the credibility of a person giving evidence in the courtroom. Moreover, [it] may help [to] discourage the witness from giving false testimony.

As a matter of law, such evidence does not require corroboration.[28] Thus in *Aleksovski* the Appeals Chamber held that the Trial Chamber had not erred in convicting the accused of physically mistreating certain witnesses on the basis of their own evidence of their injuries and in the absence of medical reports or other scientific evidence.[29]

However, the Trial Chambers have been cautious in their reliance on some forms of evidence, in particular identification evidence.[30] While dock identifications have been allowed (i.e. identification by the witness of the accused in the courtroom), one Trial Chamber said it was appropriate to place little weight upon such an identification and it would assess the credibility of each witness.[31]

---

[27]*Prosecutor v. Tadić, Decision on the Defence Motions to Summon and Protect Witnesses and on the Giving of Evidence by Video-Link*, Case No. IT-94-1-T, 25 June 1996 at para. 11.

[28]*Prosecutor v. Aleksovski, Judgement*, Case No. IT-95-14/1-A, A. Ch., 24 Mar. 2000 at paras. 62–64.

[29]Id.

[30]Due to the nature of the crimes before the ICTY, many witnesses will have suffered a degree of trauma. In *Furundžija* the Trial Chamber had to assess the possible effect of trauma on the memory of the main eye-witness in the case, an alleged victim of rape. Both parties called expert witnesses on whether the witness may have suffered from post-traumatic stress disorder ("PTSD"), and if so, what were the possible effects on her memory. In its judgement the Trial Chamber found that the memory of the witness regarding material aspects of the events was not affected by a disorder, and that "even when a person is suffering from PTSD, this does not mean that he or she is necessarily inaccurate in the evidence given. There is no reason why a person with PTSD cannot be a perfectly reliable witness." *Prosecutor v. Furundžija, Judgement*, Case No. IT-95-17/1-T, 10 Dec. 1998 at para. 109.

[31]*Prosecutor v. Jelisić, Decision on the Motion Concerning Identification Evidence*, Case No. IT-95-10-T, 18 Dec. 1998.

In *Kupreškić and Others* identification evidence was of particular importance. The case concerned an attack on a village in Central Bosnia during which Bosnian Muslims were driven from their homes by Bosnian Croats and many were killed. The six accused were local Bosnian Croats charged with participating in the attack on their neighbours. There were many witnesses to the general attack but few eye-witnesses who could testify as to the role of the accused in it. In the case against the accused Dragan Papić, a witness formerly a member of UNPROFOR testified that some days after the massacre in Ahmići he had met a man who called himself "Dragan" and carried an AK47 rifle. The man indicated that he had killed 32 Muslims by drawing his hand across his throat. The witness subsequently identified the accused in court, stating that "When someone tells you they have killed 32 people, you don't forget their face in a hurry". The Trial Chamber found that it could not be sure that the witness identified the correct man in court five years after the event. The Trial Chamber found that there was reasonable doubt as to whether Dragan Papić participated in the conflict that day.[32] He was acquitted.

In relation to another accused the Trial Chamber heard expert evidence on the effect of distance on identification. A witness had identified the accused as present in a group which was firing on him and his relatives from 50 or 60 meters away. The witness had known the accused his whole life.[33] The Defence called a professor of experimental psychology who gave his expert opinion on how distance affected identification: he said that the likelihood of a witness making a mistake at 60 meters was higher than 50 percent.[34] The Trial Chamber concluded that "in the absence of confirmation of the correctness of this identification, the Trial Chamber is not able to be sure that it is correct. Accordingly, the allegation that Vlatko Kupreškić was present when these crimes were committed is not made out."[35]

The video-conference link provides a modern way in which evidence may be obtained as near "live" as possible. In the early practice of the Tribunal, video-conference link was only available in exceptional circumstances.[36] This

---

[32]*Prosecutor v. Kupreškić and Others, Judgement*, supra note 16 at paras. 356, 368.

[33]Id., para. 449.

[34]Id., para. 457.

[35]Id., para. 469. The Trial Chamber went on to find that Vlatko Kupreškić did play a part in the attack on Ahmići and convicted him of persecution.

[36]Prior to its amendment, Rule 90(A) permitted a Trial Chamber "in exceptional circumstances and in the interests of justice" to authorise the receipt of testimony via video-conference link. Evidence was received in this way in the *Tadić* case (and on several occasions since). However, the Trial Chamber noted that the evidentiary value of testimony of a witness who is physically present is weightier than testimony given by video-link and said that the "hearing of witnesses by video-link should therefore be avoided as much as possible". The Trial Chamber attached two conditions to the use of such evidence: (1) that the testimony of a witness is shown to be sufficiently important to make it unfair to proceed without it; and (2) that the witness is unable or unwilling to come to the International Tribunal. *Prosecutor v. Tadić, Decision on the Defence Motions to Summon and Protect Defence Witnesses, and on the Giving of Evidence by Video-Link*, supra note 27 at para. 21.

practice has been relaxed and a new rule now provides that at the request of either party a Trial Chamber may, in the interests of justice, order that testimony be received via video-conference link.[37] This follows the rule change in relation to depositions,[38] and is intended to provide for flexibility and to expedite trials. Its use may be most appropriate for evidence on the background of the conflict or for evidence which is undisputed or corroborative.

2.2 Indirect Evidence

Many cases depend on indirect or circumstantial evidence. For instance, in order to prove command responsibility the Prosecution must establish that a commander "knew or had reason to know that the subordinate was about to commit [crimes] or had done so and the superior failed to take the necessary and reasonable measures to prevent the acts or to punish the perpetrators."[39] A Trial Chamber held that the *mens rea* of the accused in such cases can be inferred from the general circumstances; however, it "cannot be presumed, but must be established by way of circumstantial evidence".[40] However, as stated in an English case: "[I]t is no derogation of evidence to say that it is circumstantial."[41] The individual items of such evidence may by themselves be insufficient to establish guilt but, taken together, the effect may be telling. This effect has been described in this way in another English case:

> It has been said that circumstantial evidence is to be considered as a chain, and each piece of evidence as a link in the chain, but that is not so, for then, if any one link broke, the chain would fall. It is more like the case of a rope comprised of several cords. One strand of the cord might be insufficient to sustain the weight but three stranded together may be quite of sufficient strength. Thus it may be in circumstantial evidence – there may be a combination of circumstances, no one of which would raise a reasonable conviction or a mere suspicion, but the whole taken together may create a conclusion of guilt with as much certainty as human affairs can require or admit of.[42]

3. Other Forms of Evidence

The length of trials before the International Tribunal has made it impossible to rely purely on live evidence and has led Trial Chambers, increasingly, to

[37]ICTY Rule 71*bis*.
[38]See below.
[39]ICTY Statute, Art. 7 (3).
[40]*Prosecutor v. Delalić and Others, Judgement*, supra note 12 at para. 386.
[41]*Taylor, Weaver and Donovan* [1928] 21 Cr. App. R. 20,21 *per* Lord Hewart C.J.
[42]*Exall* (1866) 4 E. & F. 922 at 929.

admit alternative forms of evidence involving hearsay, in order to expedite trials. Such alternative forms include documentary evidence (including transcripts from related trials and affidavits), depositions, and compilations of evidence by experts, a form of evidence peculiar to the Tribunal. The treatment of these forms of evidence is considered below.

3.1 Documentary Evidence

In the post-Second World War trials documentary evidence played a crucial role. As Brigadier-General Telford Taylor said in his Report on the trials under Control Council Law No. 10 (for which he was Chief Prosecutor):

> Few of the defendants committed atrocities with their own hands, and in fact they were rarely visible at or within many miles of the scenes of their worst crimes. They made plans and transmitted orders, and the most compelling witnesses against them were the documents which they had drafted, signed, initialled, or distributed.[43]

Documentary evidence is also capable of playing an important part in trials before the International Tribunal. Documents are liberally admitted. Factors such as authenticity and proof of ownership are of greater significance in relation to the weight to be attributed to evidence rather than their admissibility. The Trial Chamber in *Delalić and Others* said that the threshold for admission of documents should not be excessively high, as often documents are not the ultimate proof of guilt or innocence, but merely shed light on the context in which the crimes occurred.[44]

There is no reason for the International Tribunal to be bound by common law rules such as those which require all exhibits to be produced by a witness. Thus, the practice has developed of allowing the admission of documents and other exhibits without entering them through the intermediary of a witness. In *Blaškić* this procedure was adopted on the grounds that the Trial Chamber, composed of professional judges, was able to assess the evidence and accord it its proper weight in light of all the evidence presented during the trial. This procedure has the advantage of limiting the calling of witnesses purely for the submission of documents, thus expediting the trial, while respecting "*le caractère équitable du procès et en contribuant à la manifestation de la vérité*".[45]

[43]Telford Taylor, *Final Report to the Secretary of the Army on the Nuernberg War Crimes Trials under Control Council Law No. 10*, at 86 (G.P.O., Aug. 15, 1949).

[44]*Prosecutor v. Delalić and Others, Decision on Motion of Prosecution for Admissibility of Evidence*, Case No. IT-96-21-T, 19 Jan. 1998. However, there are occasions where the Prosecution case may rest substantially on documents, for instance if they are orders to attack. This was the case in *Blaškić* where several such orders, issued by the accused shortly before the attack by Bosnian Croats on Ahmići on 16 April 1993, were entered into evidence.

[45]*Prosecutor v. Blaškić, Judgement*, supra note 18 at para. 35.

In a similar vein, the Trial Chamber sitting in *Kordić and Čerkez* has accepted numerous exhibits without the intermediary of a witness, including a number of "village binders" and materials on the character of the conflict. The history of the "village binders" is instructive as indicating the general approach of a Trial Chamber towards evidence put before it. It began with the submission by the Prosecution of a "dossier" relating to an attack on a particular village.[46] The dossier contained a variety of materials, including maps, videos, witness statements, transcripts, exhumation reports and photographs. It also contained the report of an investigator who had compiled these materials. The Trial Chamber held that "the investigator is not reporting as a contemporary witness of fact, he has only recently collated statements and other materials [...]. He could, in reality, only give evidence that material was or was not in the Dossier."[47] The Trial Chamber concluded that it would not be assisted by the report and excluded it.

The Trial Chamber also excluded witness statements, on the ground that they lacked probative value. In doing so, the Trial Chamber drew attention to the procedure available under Rule 94*ter*, which provides for the admissibility of affidavits or formal statements.[48]

On the other hand, the Trial Chamber admitted transcripts from related cases. This was consistent with a decision in *Aleksovski*, where the Appeals Chamber held that the transcript of the evidence of a witness, together with a video recording of the evidence and accompanying exhibits, was admissible as hearsay; "i.e. the statement of a person made otherwise than in the proceedings in which it is being tendered, but nevertheless being tendered in those proceedings in order to establish the truth of what that person says".[49]

[46]Dossiers are, of course, common in the civil law system where they are usually prepared by an investigating judge.

[47]*Prosecutor v. Kordić and Čerkez, Decision on the Prosecution Application to Admit the Tulića Report and Dossier into Evidence*, Case No. IT-95-14/2-T, 29 July 1999 at para. 20.

[48]Rule 94*ter*: To prove a fact in dispute, a party may propose to call a witness and to submit in corroboration of his or her testimony on that fact affidavits or formal statements signed by other witnesses in accordance with the law and procedure of the State in which such affidavits or statements are signed [...]

[49]*Prosecutor v. Aleksovski, Decision on Prosecutor's Appeal on Admissibility of Evidence*, supra note 15 at para. 14. The Appeals Chamber also stated that "[T]he fact remains that, if the evidence is admitted on a hearsay basis, this accused will be denied the opportunity of cross-examining the witness. However, this is the case with the admission of any hearsay evidence: the opposing party loses the opportunity to cross-examine the witness. The disadvantage is tempered in this case by the cross-examination in *Blaškić* [...] (para. 27)." The Trial Chamber in *Kordić and Čerkez* later admitted around 40 transcripts, most of them from the related *Blaškić* case. Most of these related to background issues such as attacks on particular villages. Defence objections relating to hearsay, speculation by the witnesses, inconsistency of the evidence, and relevance were deemed to go to the weight of the evidence rather than providing grounds for exclusion. However, certain transcripts were excluded on the grounds that they were repetitive of testimony already heard. Where the transcript related directly to the accused the Trial Chamber determined that the witness should be called (*Prosecutor v. Kordić and Čerkez*, Case No. IT-95-14/2-T, Transcript, 18 Feb. 2000 at pp. 14612–14621).

The remaining materials, including documentary evidence, photographs, and exhumation reports were also admitted; the total compilation became known as a "village binder." Village binders, affidavits, and transcripts from related cases all have the potential to expedite trials.

3.2 Deposition Evidence

Rules of the ICTY have always provided for evidence to be given by way of deposition. As originally drafted Rule 71 provided that depositions could only be taken in exceptional circumstances and in the interests of justice. In fact Trial Chambers began making use of this Rule when one of their number was temporarily indisposed through illness, holding that this was an "exceptional circumstance", so as not to delay the trial. Usually the accused consented but on one occasion an accused objected and the matter went to appeal. This led the Appeals Chamber to state that the Rule must be construed strictly and in accordance with its original purpose of providing an exception to the general rule that witnesses be heard directly by the Trial Chamber.[50] This restriction has not prevented the use of the rule to allow for the taking of deposition evidence in other cases where both parties have given their consent to this course.[51]

Meanwhile, the rule has been amended to make it more flexible and to serve the purpose of expediting trials. The need to demonstrate exceptional circumstances has been removed, but it must still be in the interests of justice to order the taking of depositions. This requirement will cover such issues as the importance of the evidence and whether it is in dispute. Depositions may now be taken either at the seat of, or away from, the Tribunal and may be initiated by a party or by the Trial Chamber acting *proprio motu*. The witness is subject to examination and cross-examination by the parties under a Presiding Officer who must ensure that the deposition is taken in accordance with the rules (although there is no mention in the rule that the accused need be present). Objections to the admissibility of evidence are reserved for the Trial Chamber.

Depositions may be a useful means of recording evidence in particular relating to the background and context of the crimes. This process can take place prior to, or simultaneously with, the trial thus expediting the

[50]*Prosecutor v. Kupreškić and Others, Decision on Appeal by Dragan Papić against Ruling to Proceed by Deposition*, Case No. IT-95-16-AR73.3, A. Ch., 15 July 1999.

[51]For instance, in one case a Trial Chamber ordered depositions to be taken from around 70 witnesses by a Presiding Officer noting that "exceptional circumstances exist to warrant the use of deposition evidence under Rule 71 [...] namely, the length of pre-trial detention of the accused and the complexity of the cases currently assigned to this Trial Chamber, which precludes it from setting a date for trial for the commencement of this trial". The parties had agreed to the witnesses as they were not critical but would testify to the background of the case. *Prosecutor v. Kvočka and Others, Decision to Proceed by Way of Deposition Pursuant to Rule 71*, Case No. IT-98-30-PT, 15 Nov. 1999.

proceedings and allowing the Trial Chamber to review the evidence without having to convene.

3.3 Compilations by Experts

The Prosecution has on occasion called a witness who has studied the conflict and compiled a report and who is thus able to give an overview. The practice has generally been to admit such reports if they deal with general events and assist the Trial Chamber. They have normally been excluded where they draw conclusions about the role of the accused, or generally fail to assist the Trial Chamber.

For instance, in the case of *Kovačević*, the Prosecution called a former member of the United Nations Commission of Experts, established pursuant to the United Nations Security Council Resolution 780. In the course of her testimony the Prosecution sought to enter into evidence her report about events in the Prijedor region of Bosnia-Herzegovina, based on around 400 witness statements (taken by others) and media reports. Defence counsel objected on the ground that (a) this was hearsay evidence which was not subject to cross-examination and (b) that witnesses "cannot merely summarise evidence and introduce it under the guise of being an expert".[52] However, the Trial Chamber admitted the evidence on the basis that the witness was an expert who had made a study of the material and was qualified to give evidence about it, her status being analogous to that of a contemporary historian. In so doing, the Trial Chamber stated that it had in mind that the evidence was hearsay, the Defence would not be able to cross-examine the makers of the witness statements and, accordingly, there was no question of the defendant being convicted on any count based on this evidence alone and other evidence would be required.[53]

In another case the Prosecution sought to call as an expert a political and military analyst of the conflict in Bosnia-Herzegovina. He had written a report that the Prosecution sought to introduce as his examination-in-chief. In the report the witness made direct references to the accused, drawing conclusions about his responsibility as a civilian and military superior.[54] The Trial Chamber excluded the evidence on the basis that the witness indeed was drawing conclusions on the very matters upon which the Trial Chamber

[52]Official Transcript, *Prosecutor v. Kovačević*, Case No. IT-97-24-T, 6 July 1998 at p. 71.

[53]Id. at p. 75.

[54]The Prosecution argued that an expert's conclusions on mixed questions of fact and law, such as command responsibility, are admissible, as they are in the case of "diminished responsibility" in domestic criminal trials. The Defence submitted that the witness was drawing inferences which were in fact the duty of the Trial Chamber to draw, and that in so doing he was in effect being called as a substitute for the Prosecution's closing submissions, or becoming the "fourth judge".

was required to rule, thus invading its province. It also found that the witness's evidence would not assist it in this task.[55]

4. General Conclusions

The following conclusions can be drawn on the nature and scope of evidence before the Tribunal:

(1) In relation to general background and to some extent general elements of crimes, alternative forms of evidence, which have not been subject to cross-examination, may be relied on. The absence of formal technical rules of admission and the general tendency to liberal admission is mitigated by the Trial Chamber's evaluation of the weight of the evidence if there has been no confrontation or cross-examination.
(2) Hearsay evidence such as affidavits or transcripts from related cases may also be relied on to establish whether a particular crime was committed. Such evidence is less likely to be relied on for determining the participation of the accused in the crime, although it may be used to corroborate witness testimony on that point.
(3) In general, evidence which relates directly to the accused is more stringently evaluated in terms of weight, as can be seen from the way Trial Chambers have dealt with identification evidence. In general, hearsay evidence will not form the sole basis for a conviction.
(4) Finally, trials before the Tribunal are long and complex; unnecessary repetition of evidence must be avoided. Different forms of evidence may be a substitute for testimony and speed up the trial. In cases of command responsibility, where certain crimes may not be in dispute, prosecution evidence in relation to them may be given in the form of transcripts from related cases or compilations of evidence such as reports or village binders.

[55]Official Transcript, *Prosecutor v. Kordić and Čerkez*, Case No. IT-95-14/2-T, 28 Jan. 2000 at pp. 13268–13306.

GIDEON BOAS*

21. Admissibility of Evidence under the Rules of Procedure and Evidence of the ICTY: Development of the 'Flexibility Principle'

The ICTY was the first international criminal tribunal since the Nuremberg and Tokyo tribunals. In creating the ICTY, the Security Council granted its judges the unique power of drafting and amending its own Rules.[1] Article 15 of the ICTY Statute reads:

> The judges of the International Tribunal shall adopt rules of procedure and evidence for the conduct of the pre-trial phase of the proceedings, trials and appeals, the admission of evidence, the protection of victims and witnesses and other appropriate measures.

The Secretary-General's Report stated that "the judges of the International Tribunal as a whole should draft and adopt the rules of procedure and evidence".[2] This, along with Security Council Resolution 827 and Article 15 of the Statute, clearly laid down the framework for the manner of the creation of the Rules of the ICTY.

The Tribunal was little assisted by any available precedent in the drafting of its Rules. In particular, the most important procedures by which the admission of evidence were to be dealt with was an area of relatively new terrain in the trying of international crimes by an international tribunal. The only tribunals punishing similar crimes under an international jurisdictional

---

*Associate Legal Officer, ICTY Chambers. The views expressed are solely those of the author and do not necessarily reflect those of the United Nations or ICTY.

[1]See para. 3 of SC Res 827, UN Doc S/Res/827 (3 May 1993) in which the Security Council:
"*Requests* the Secretary-General to submit to the judges of the International Tribunal, upon their election, any suggestions received from States for the rules of procedure and evidence called for in Article 15 of the Statute of the International Tribunal."

[2]Secretary-General's Report, appended to SC Res 827, UN Doc S/Res/827 (3 May 1993), para. 83.

R. May et al., Essays on ICTY Procedure and Evidence in Honour of Gabrielle Kirk McDonald, 263–274

mandate were the Nuremberg and Tokyo Tribunals. The Nuremberg Tribunal had dealt with the admissibility and taking of evidence in an extremely truncated way. Article 18 of the Charter of the Nuremberg Tribunal required an expeditious hearing, with irrelevant issues and statements which would cause unreasonable delay to be ruled out.[3] Article 19 stated that the Tribunal should not be bound by technical rules of evidence, and should adopt and apply "to the greatest possible extent an expeditious and non-technical procedure" and "admit *any* evidence which it deems to be of probative value".[4]

Like the Charter of the Nuremberg Tribunal, the Tokyo Tribunal was not to be bound by technical rules of evidence. It was required to apply "to the greatest extent possible expeditious and non-technical procedure" and was to admit evidence deemed to have probative value.[5] The Rules of Procedure of the Tokyo Tribunal were also extremely brief, constituting only nine rules in all.[6]

It was stated in a recent article that

> The procedural framework of the ICTY is laid out in its Statute and Rules of Procedure and Evidence. The Rules, drafted by the Judges, essentially amounts to a code of procedure for international criminal law, and the amendments reflect the experience gained by the Tribunal. The Rules are based on general principles underlying the major legal systems of the world, striking a balance between the common law and civil law systems.[7]

The Rules of the ICTY provide the Trial Chambers with flexibility in deciding the admissibility of evidence and regulating the examination and cross-examination of witnesses. What has developed as standard practice within the ICTY is an extremely open approach to the admissibility of evidence in its proceedings. This system has led one critic to conclude that the Tribunal is a "rogue court with rigged rules".[8] However, misconceived hyperbole aside, what in fact this openness of admissibility has led to is what will be referred to as the "flexibility principle".

---

[3]Charter of the International Military Tribunal, Articles 18–21, annexed to 'Agreement for the Prosecution and Punishment of the Major War Criminals of the European Axis Powers', August 8, 1945, 59 Stat. 1544, 82 UNTS, 284. See also Judge Richard May and Marieke Wierda, "Trends in International Criminal Evidence: Nuremberg, Tokyo, The Hague, and Arusha" Vol. 37, No. 3 *Columbia Journal of Transnational Law* 729.

[4]Id. Emphasis added.

[5]Charter of the International Military Tribunal for the Far East, Article 13, Jan. 19, 1946, TIAS No. 1589, 4 Bevans 20 (as amended April 26, 1946), 4 Bevans 27. See also Judge Richard May and Marieke Wierda, supra note 3, p. 730 ff.

[6]Charter of the International Military Tribunal for the Far East, Id.

[7]Judge Richard May and Marieke Wierda, supra note 3 at p. 735.

[8]Letter to *The Times* entitled "The anomalies of the International Criminal Tribunal are legion", 17 June 1999.

1. The relevant provisions of the Rules of Procedure and Evidence

The principal provisions dictating the admissibility of evidence in proceedings before the ICTY fall under Rule 89:

> (A) The rules of evidence set forth in this Section shall govern the proceedings before the Chambers. The Chambers shall not be bound by national rules of evidence.
>
> (B) In cases not otherwise provided for in this Section, a Chamber shall apply rules of evidence which will best favour a fair determination of the matter before it and are consonant with the spirit of the Statute and the general principles of law.
>
> (C) A Chamber may admit any relevant evidence which it deems to have probative value.
>
> (D) A Chamber may exclude evidence if its probative value is substantially outweighed by the need to ensure a fair trial.
>
> (E) A Chamber may request verification of the authenticity of evidence obtained out of court.

It is clear that the principle of *la liberté de la preuve* understood in the French criminal law system, allowing the court to rule any form of evidence admissible, is to an extent present in the Rules and practice of the ICTY. Rule 89(C) is the pivotal provision concerning the admissibility of evidence, allowing in *any* evidence which may be deemed to have probative value. The evidence must be relevant and capable of authentication, and may be excluded if its probative value is substantially outweighed by the need to ensure a fair trial. This key requirement of fairness, especially in a Tribunal in which the triers of fact are professional judges, grants a Chamber a great deal of leeway in determining what evidence before it is admissible, certainly more so than that available to courts in common law criminal jurisdiction, in particular where lay jurors are the triers of fact.

In looking at the flexibility of the Tribunal in the admissibility of evidence, it is important to note that Rule 89(A) dictates that the Chambers will not be bound by national rules of evidence. However, the applicability of general principles of law, as well as the dearth of experience of evidentiary procedure in such a jurisdiction as the ICTY, open the door on the contemplation of national rules of evidence by Trial Chambers.

In the First Annual Report of the ICTY, then-President Cassese stated:

> Based on the limited precedent of the Nürnberg and Tokyo Trials, the statute of the Tribunal has adopted a largely adversarial approach to its procedures,

rather than the inquisitorial system prevailing in continental Europe and elsewhere.[9]

In saying this, the President made it clear that this analysis was based on the fact that the Prosecutor has the sole task of inquiring into allegations of the commission of offences under the Statute, and obtaining the necessary evidence to secure a conviction.[10] The Prosecutor is the only one who can submit an indictment to a judge for confirmation and subsequently argues the case before a Trial Chamber.[11]

This is familiar territory for lawyers of an adversarial system of criminal justice, in which it is common for the court not to interfere significantly in the preparation or indeed, to a great degree, in the prosecution of the case. On the other hand, in the civil law criminal system, the court is involved in the process from the investigatory phase onward.

In this limited sense, the basis of the statement by President Cassese that the ICTY has adopted a largely adversarial approach to its procedures can be understood. The Statute of the ICTY envisages such a process for the investigation and prosecution of crimes which form the subject matter of its jurisdiction.

On the other hand, President Cassese went on to note two important deviations from rules governing the admissibility of evidence in the adversarial systems. First, as noted above, the ICTY is not constrained by restrictive rules with regard to the admissibility of evidence, and consequently all relevant evidence may be admitted unless its probative value is substantially outweighed by the need to ensure a fair trial.[12] Secondly, the Tribunal may *proprio motu* order the production of new or additional evidence, not relying upon the evidence placed before it by the parties.[13]

2. General principles of law and the applicability of national laws of evidence

The idea of national law helping to shape the international law of nations was first formally introduced at the 1907 Hague Peace Convention in relation to discussions on the formation of a World Court.[14] Furthermore, "there is a well established consensus that 'general principles' are to be derived

---

[9]First Annual Report, para. 71; ICTY Yearbook 1994 at p. 99.

[10]See Rules 39–43 of the Rules of the ICTY.

[11]See Rules 47, 84 and 85 of the Rules of the ICTY.

[12]Rule 89 of the Rules of the ICTY; see also ICTY Yearbook 1994 at para. 72.

[13]Rule 98 of the Rules of the ICTY; ICTY Yearbook 1994 at para. 73.

[14]Hermann Mosler, "General Principles of Law", in Encyclopedia of Public International Law, 94 vol. II (1984). See also, Lauterpacht, Private Law Sources and Analogies of International Law 67–68 (1927), and L. Oppenheim, International Law 29–30 (8th ed. 1955).

from national legal systems".[15] It is clear, therefore, that the domestic laws of nations play a significant role in shaping international law.

This is reflected in the statute of the International Court of Justice (ICJ), which lists "general principles of law recognised by civilised nations" as one of four sources of international law guiding its decisions.[16] The drafters of the Statute of the ICJ[17] included this general provision, as a means of ensuring that international law would always reflect those "basic principles embodied in national legal systems which, because of their commonality, rise to an internationally enforceable level".[18] It was therefore acknowledged that while conventional and customary international law might address many international disputes, some might be properly resolved through the application of "general principles".[19] This is increasingly important as a source of international law, especially in the prosecution of serious violations of international humanitarian law.

Rule 89(B) of the Rules of the ICTY provides for the application of general principles of law in cases not otherwise provided for in the relevant section of the Rules.[20] In relation to what constitutes "general principles of law", Judge Stephen has stated:

> [W]here a substantial number of well-recognised legal systems adopt a particular solution to a problem it is appropriate to regard that solution as involving some quite general principle of law such as is referred to in Sub-rule 89(B).[21]

As an example of the application of these general principles, in the *Tadić* case, the Trial Chamber was faced with the question as to the standard and nature of proof required for conviction on a count the underlying crime for which is the killing of a human being. It stated the following:

> The Trial Chamber is cognisant of the fact that during the conflict there were widespread beatings and killings and indifferent, careless and even callous treatment of the dead. Dead prisoners were buried in makeshift graves and

[15]M. Cherif Bassiouni, "A Functional Approach to 'General Principles of International Law'", Vol. 11 *Michigan Journal of International Law*, (1990) 768, at 816–817.

[16]Article 38(1)(b) of the Statute of the ICJ.

[17]These are the drafters of the statute of the League of Nations' Permanent Court of International Justice (PCIJ). Article 38 of the PCIJ is essentially the same as the ICJ Statute.

[18]Bassiouni, supra note 15 at p. 817.

[19]Bin Cheng, General Principles of International Law as Applied by International Courts and Tribunals, (1987). See also Lauterpacht, supra note 14, at pp. 68–69: "[t]he will of states as expressed in treaties, or failing that in international custom, remains thus the primary source of law. If, however, these sources are silent, the Court, far from having to declare its incompetence, is bound to pronounce on the basis of general principles of law which are thus definitely recognised as a subsidiary source of international law."

[20]Section 3 of Part Six of the Rules of the ICTY.

[21]*Prosecutor v. Tadić, Separate Opinion of Judge Stephen on Prosecution Motion for Production of Defence Witness Statements*, Case No. IT-94-1-T, 27 Nov. 1996 at p. 6.

> heaps of bodies were not infrequently to be seen in the grounds of the camps. Since these were not times of normalcy, it is inappropriate to apply rules of some national systems that require the production of a body as proof to death. However, there must be evidence to link injuries received to a resulting death. This the Prosecution has failed to do. Although the Defence has not raised this particular inadequacy of proof, it is incumbent upon the Trial Chamber to do so. When there is more than one conclusion reasonably open on the evidence, it is not for this Trial Chamber to draw the conclusion least favourable to the accused, which is what the Trial Chamber would be required to do in finding that any of the four prisoners died as a result of their injuries or, indeed, that they are in fact dead.[22]

The Trial Chamber found that the Prosecution had failed to establish beyond reasonable doubt that any of the four persons in question had died as a result of the injuries they had received, and the accused was therefore acquitted on charges of having killed them.[23]

However, whilst the Tribunal is guided by general principles of law, it is so guided only when a question of evidence arises which is outside of the perimeters of the Rules themselves. Furthermore, whilst the Tribunal has been willing to consider national rules of evidence in proceedings before it, it has also been clear in maintaining strictly the position that it is bound primarily by its own Statute and Rules, and to the applicable international law.

In a recent decision, Trial Chamber III stated:

> The Trial Chamber has heard the arguments of the parties with regard to these matters. Furthermore, the Trial Chamber has heard the parties regarding the applicability of common and civil law evidentiary procedures. Whilst the International Tribunal may look to municipal criminal law and procedure for assistance in its work, it is bound first and foremost by its own Statute and Rules, and to international law as it applies to its particular mandate to try persons alleged to have committed serious violations of international humanitarian law.[24]

The Appeals Chamber has also stated clearly the proposition that the Tribunal is not bound by national rules of evidence, and confirms the

---

[22]*Prosecutor v. Tadić, Judgment,* Case No. IT-94-1, 7 May 1997 at para. 240. See also Judge Richard May and Marieke Wierda, supra note 3 at p. 754 (citing the decision in the *Flick* case from the Nuremberg Military Tribunal): "If from the credible evidence two reasonable inferences may be drawn, one of guilt and the other of innocence, the latter must be drawn".

[23]This finding has been overturned by the Appeals Chamber, however the principle remains untouched. *Prosecutor v. Tadić, Judgment*, Case No. IT-94-1-A, A. Ch., 15 July 1999.

[24]*Prosecutor v. Kordić and Čerkez, Decision on the Prosecution Application to Admit the Tulića Report and Dossier into Evidence*, Case No. IT-95-14/2-T, 29 July 1999 ("*Tulića Decision*") at para. 12.

principles of fairness and flexibility in the determination of evidentiary matters before it. In the *Aleksovski* Appeals Decision,[25] it was considered whether the Trial Chamber had erred in admitting a transcript of the testimony by a witness in the *Blaškić* case. In doing so, the Appeals Chamber stated:

> [T]he Appellant refers to the sometimes elaborate rules in national jurisdictions covering the circumstances when courts are entitled to hold that witnesses are unavailable to give evidence. However, there is no reason to import such rules into the practice of the Tribunal, which is not bound by national rules of evidence. The purpose of the Rules is to promote a fair and expeditious trial, and Trial Chambers must have the flexibility to achieve this goal.[26]

This overriding principle of flexibility is the cornerstone of the Tribunal's approach to the admissibility of evidence in proceedings before it.

The ICTY, as well as by the Tokyo and Nuremberg Tribunals, have justified the admission of evidence which would, in a common law jurisdiction, be ruled inadmissible, on the basis that where that evidence is less credible or reliable the Chamber will simply apportion it less weight when considering all the evidence before it.

3. Hearsay Evidence[27]

One Judge of the ICTY has stated:

> A significant practice in all the international tribunals is their refusal to be hindered by a technical approach to the admission of evidence in their search for truth. This is best illustrated by their approach to hearsay evidence, but is also reflected in the admission of documents and affidavits. In all these matters the tribunals have adopted a liberal approach, not fettered by common law rules.[28]

It is trite to mention that, subject to a growing number of exceptions, hearsay evidence is ordinarily inadmissible in common law systems.[29] However, the

---

[25]*Prosecutor v. Aleksovski, Decision on Prosecutor's Appeal on Admissibility of Evidence*, Case No. IT-95-14/1-AR73, A. Ch., 16 Feb. 1999.

[26]Id. para. 19, quoted with approval by Trial Chamber III in *Prosecutor v. Kordić and Čerkez*, supra note 24, at para. 7

[27]It is not the purpose of the author to analyse in depth the hearsay rule as interpreted by the Tribunal, as this will be the subject of another chapter in this book. The purpose of this analysis is simply to place in context the rule as it relates to the overriding principle of flexibility in the Tribunal's approach to the admissibility of evidence.

[28]Judge Richard May and Marieke Wierda, supra note 3 at p. 745.

[29]Colin Tapper, Cross on Evidence (1990), see generally Chapter XIV; Evidence Act 1995 of Australia (Cth), Part 3.2.

ICTY has adopted the view and has clearly stated on numerous occasions that the fact that evidence is hearsay is not in itself a basis for its exclusion.

Hearsay is commonly defined as an out-of-court statement tendered in court to prove the truth of its contents. Cross defines it as "an assertion other than one made by a person while giving oral evidence in the proceedings".[30] In the *Aleksovski* Appeals Decision, hearsay is defined as the

> [S]tatement of a person made otherwise than in the proceedings in which it is being tendered, but nevertheless being tendered in those proceedings in order to establish the truth of what the person says.[31]

Hearsay statements are not excluded under the Tribunal's Rules. The Trial Chamber in the *Tadić* case stated:

> Under our Rules, specifically Sub-rule 89(C), out-of-court [hearsay] statements that are relevant and found to have probative value are admissible.[32]

This position was further clarified by the Appeals Chamber in the *Aleksovski* Appeals Decision, in which it was stated:

> It is well settled in the practice of the Tribunal that hearsay evidence is admissible. Thus relevant out of court statements which a Trial Chamber considers probative are admissible under Rule 89(C). This was established in 1996 by the Decision of Trial Chamber II in *Prosecutor v. Tadić* and followed by Trial Chamber I in *Prosecutor v. Blaškić*. Neither Decision was the subject of appeal and it is not now submitted that they were wrongly decided. Accordingly, Trial Chambers have a broad discretion under Rule 89(C) to admit relevant hearsay evidence. Since such evidence is admitted to prove the truth of its contents, a Trial Chamber must be satisfied that it is reliable for that purpose, in the sense of being voluntary, truthful and trustworthy, as appropriate; and for this purpose may consider both the content of the hearsay statement and the circumstances under which the evidence arose; or, as Judge Stephen described it, the probative value of a hearsay statement will depend upon the context and character of the evidence in question. The absence of the opportunity to cross-examine the person who made the statements, and whether the hearsay is "first-hand" or more removed, are also relevant to the probative value of the evidence. The fact that the evidence is hearsay does not necessarily deprive it of probative value, but it is acknowledged that the weight or probative value to be afforded to that evidence will usually be less than that given to the testimony of a witness who has given it under a form of oath and who has been cross-

---

[30]Id., p. 509.

[31]Supra note 25 at para. 27.

[32]*Prosecutor v. Tadić, Decision on the Defence Motion on Hearsay*, Case No. IT-94-1-T, 27 Aug. 1996 at para. 7.

> examined, although even this will depend upon the infinitely variable circumstances which surround hearsay evidence.[33]

The crucial aspect of the Tribunal's treatment of hearsay evidence is that it is, generally speaking, a question not of admissibility but of *weight*. In this respect, the Chambers of the Tribunal will admit hearsay evidence on the basis that the weight to be attributed to it would obviously be less than the weight attributed to direct testimony of events witnessed first-hand.

4. Admissibility versus Weight

The Tribunal has consistently adopted the approach that where objections to the admission of evidence in substance goes to questions of the weight to be attributed to the evidence, that evidence will, subject to questions of relevance, prejudice and authenticity, be admitted. In this respect, documentary evidence which would be inadmissible in a domestic common law jurisdiction has been admitted with reservations concerning the weight to be attributed to it.

In the *Kordić* case, for example, the Trial Chamber ruled on an application by the Prosecution to admit a package of material comprising various forms of documentary evidence.[34] The Chamber excluded the report of an investigator of the Office of the Prosecutor on the basis that he would not be giving evidence as a contemporary witness of fact, as he had merely collected the materials for the immediate purpose of the Application. The Chamber therefore found that

> He could, in reality, only give evidence that material was or was not in the *Dossier*. The Report therefore is of little or no probative value and will not be admitted into evidence.[35]

The Chamber also excluded witness statements tendered by the Prosecution as part of the *dossier*. The Prosecution argued that the statements were merely documentary forms of hearsay, which the Chamber had clearly emphasised was an admissible form of evidence before the Tribunal. The Chamber, however, stated:

> It is proposed that the witness statements should be produced by the Investigator, and would not be subject to cross-examination by the accused unless the Defence could justify the need to do so. The Trial Chamber is of the view that whilst it could admit the witness statements under Rule 89(C), this is not an appropriate case for the exercise of its discretion under that provision,

---

[33]Supra note 25 at para. 15.
[34]*The Tulića Decision*, supra note 24.
[35]Id., para. 20.

> as it would amount to the wholesale admission of hearsay untested by cross-examination, namely the attack on Tulića, and would be of no probative value. The Trial Chamber therefore declines to admit the witness statements into evidence, however, draws attention to Rule 94 *ter* of the Rules.[36]

In doing so, the Trial Chamber showed that the flexibility principle is not a vehicle for wholesale admission of documentary evidence not consistent with the fundamental rules of admissibility under Rule 89. In particular, it shows that there are circumstances in which such little weight could legitimately be attributed to a piece of evidence that there is no value in its admission, and it must therefore be excluded.

However, a number of categories of evidence were admitted by the Chamber in the *Tulića Decision*. Most notably, transcripts of evidence given by a witness in another trial before the Tribunal, which were also relevant to the instant proceedings, were admitted. Having quoted the principle set out in the *Aleksovski* Appeals Decision, the Chamber stated:

> [T]he Trial Chamber holds that the transcripts…are admissible since the witnesses have been cross-examined in *Blaškić*, a case in which the Defence have a common interest with the Defence in this case. However, this ruling will not preclude the application by the Defence to cross-examine the witnesses on the ground that there are significant relevant matters not covered by cross-examination in *Blaškić* which ought to be raised in this case.[37]

The Trial Chamber therefore admitted testimony from another trial whilst providing the Defence with the opportunity to apply to cross-examine the witness on matters not covered adequately in the cross-examination in the other case. It is noteworthy that the Trial Chamber rejected the Defence's proposition that such admission of material violated the fundamental right of the accused to confrontation and cross-examination guaranteed by the Statute and Rules of the ICTY.[38]

Other documentary evidence admitted in the *Tulića Decision* included exhumation documents (a report by an Investigating Judge of the Sarajevo Cantonal Court, photographs and death certificates);[39] documentary evidence relating to the destruction of property;[40] and photographs, video footage and maps.[41]

This admission of transcript material in the *Tulića Decision* led to the subsequent application by the Prosecution to introduce into evidence the testimony of more then fifty witnesses via this method. On the principle set

[36]Id., para. 23.
[37]Id., para. 28.
[38]Id., para. 25.
[39]Id., para. 32.
[40]Id., para. 34 – admitted subject to challenges made to the authenticity.
[41]Id., para. 36 – admitted subject to challenges made to the authenticity.

out in the *Tulića Decision* and the *Aleksovski* Appeals Decision, the Trial Chamber admitted over thirty transcripts.[42]

An important aspect of the admission of these transcripts was the denial of the Defence's opportunity to cross-examine these witnesses on the testimony relied upon. Judge May, delivering the Chamber's ruling, referred to the *Aleksovski* Appeals Decision, in which the Appeals Chamber noted that the disadvantage of a party not being able to cross-examine a witness whose transcript was admitted is tempered by the cross-examination in another case. In particular, it was noted that the background issues in this case were significantly similar to those in the *Blaskić* case, and that no particular areas of cross-examination had been raised by the Defence to warrant rejection of the transcripts which were in fact admitted or indeed to warrant cross-examination of the witnesses.[43]

In relation to the admission of documentary evidence in general, Trial Chamber III of the Tribunal has taken an inclusive approach in the *Kordić* trial. The presiding Judge of the Chamber, in admitting a significant number of documents tendered by the Prosecution on the issue of internationality of the armed conflict in central Bosnia, stated that in admitting the documents:

> [W]e are applying the same principles in relation to admissibility as those we apply to the admissibility of the documents when ruling on the outstanding exhibits. The objections that related to hearsay, lack of foundation, and authenticity, signature, or relevance, or indeed other objections, are all matters which go to the weight of the evidence and not to its admissibility. However, only legible exhibits will be admitted and those with translations in one of the languages of the Tribunal.[44]

This position emphasises the operation of the flexibility principle in the Tribunal's contemplation of the admissibility of evidence.

5. Conclusion

The rules of admissibility of evidence of the Tribunal, and the expansive application of these rules, display a commitment on the part of the Tribunal to what has been described above as the flexibility principle. The fact that the weighing of evidence before the Tribunal is undertaken by professional judges means that the damage that is often contemplated in the rules of evidence in common law jurisdictions is avoided. Evidence which is quite prejudicial or of marginal credibility can be given the weight which it deserves, and the Chambers need not be burdened with technical rules of

[42]Oral ruling in *Prosecutor v. Kordić and Čerkez*, Case No. IT-95-14/2-T, 18 Feb. 2000, at Transcript Pages 14612–14621.

[43]Id., Transcript Pages 14614–15.

[44]*Kordić* case, supra note 24, 10 March 2000, at Transcript Pages 16449–16450.

evidence designed to protect the accused from unreliable or overly prejudicial material being given undue consideration.

The evolving approach to the admissibility of evidence by the Tribunal provides a flexible yet realistic framework for a system of evidence and procedure befitting the trying of international criminal cases.

PATRICIA VISEUR SELLERS*

22. Rule 89(C) and (D): At Odds or Overlapping with Rule 96 and Rule 95?

1. Introduction

Part Six of the ICTY Rules, "*Proceedings before the Trial Chamber*", sets forth the general provisions of admission and exclusion of evidence in Rule 89. Consistently interpreted as "embodying a flexible standard that presumes admissibility in order to permit the development of the law",[1] Rule 89(C) and (D) state:

> (C) A Chamber may admit any relevant evidence which it deems to have a probative value
>
> (D) A Chamber may exclude evidence if its probative value is substantially outweighed by the need to ensure a fair trial.

Unbound by national rules of procedure, judges *may* admit evidence that is relevant and deemed probative, yet conversely, *may* exclude evidence whose probative value undermines the conduct of a fair trial. During the drafting stage, governments urged the Secretary General to adopt elastic admissibility rules due to foreseeable constraints on gathering evidence in the

*Ms. Sellers, a member of the Legal Advisory Section, is the Legal Advisor for Sexual Assault Crimes in the Office of the Prosecutor of the ICTY. She was a trial attorney in the *Furundžija* case, co-counsel in *Akayesu* and is the legal advisor in *Kunarac* (the *Foča* case). Ms. Sellers is a graduate of the University of Pennsylvania Law School. The opinions expressed in this article are solely those of the author and are not intended to represent the official views or policies of the Office of the Prosecutor of the ICTY nor those of the United Nations.

[1] *Prosecutor v. Bagasora and Others, Decision on the Defence Motion for Pre-Determination of Rules of Evidence*, Case No. ICTR-96-7-T, 8 Jul. 1998.

R. May et al., Essays on ICTY Procedure and Evidence in Honour of Gabrielle Kirk McDonald, 275–290.

course of an on-going armed conflict and because the subsequent trials would depend largely upon eyewitness testimony and "*viva voce evidence*."[2]

Another rationale for Rule 89's flexible admissibility standard lies in the Tribunal's reliance upon judges not juries, to hear and weigh evidence. International tribunals, traditionally composed of judges, tend to enact broad admissibility rules and to display little interest in excluding evidence.[3] Even though the procedural rules applied at the Nuremberg and Tokyo International Military Tribunals offer limited guidance[4] to the ICTY Rules, the IMT's reliance upon judges, similarly, drove the presumption of admissibility. Justice Jackson, a prosecutor at the Nuremberg Tribunal, explained that:

> The rules of evidence which should govern the [IMT] Tribunal might have caused serious disagreement if we had insisted on our own. Continental lawyers regard our common-law rules of evidence with abhorrence. Since they were evolved in response to the particularities of trial by jury, we saw no reason to urge their use in an international tribunal before professional judges. They have not generally been followed by international tribunals. We settled, therefore, upon one simple rule: that the Tribunal shall admit any evidence that it deems to have probative value. [...][5]

However "wide and liberal" the latitude vested in ICTY judges to admit or exclude evidence under Rule 89(C) and (D), their discretionary powers are not limitless.[6] Rule 89's general provisions are directly followed by specialised evidentiary rules. Among these, Rule 95 excludes evidence obtained by methods that are antithetical to the integrity of the proceeding while Rule 96 excludes evidence of prior sexual conduct and controls the admission of evidence concerning a sexual assault victim's consent. This note examines the extent that Rules 95 and 96 overlap or are at odds with Rule 89. The author suggests that if the precepts of Rule 89(C) and (D) are interpreted broadly, then the specialised rules primarily serve to re-enforce the general provisions, albeit with pronounced exceptions. However, when

---

[2] *Prosecutor v. Delalić and Others, Decision on the Prosecutor's Motion for the Redaction of the Public Record*, Case No. IT-96-21-T, 5 June 1997 at para 41.

[3] W. Michael Reisman and Eric E. Freedman, "The Plaintiff's Dilemma: Illegally Obtained Evidence and Admissibility in International Adjudication", 76 *AJIL* 4 (Oct. 1982), pp. 739–743.

[4] *Prosecutor v. Tadić, Decision on the Prosecutor's Motion for Protective Measures for Victims and Witnesses*, Case No. IT-94-1-T, 10 Aug. 1995 at para. 20.

[5] Robert H. Jackson, "Nuremberg in Retrospect", *27 Can. B. Rev. 769 (1949)* cited in Evan J. Wallach, "The Procedural And Evidentiary Rules of the Post-World War II Crimes Trials: Did They Provide An Outline For International Legal Procedure?", 37 Columbia Journal of Transnational Law, p. 851 at 854.

[6] *Prosecutor v. Simić and Others, Decision on the Prosecution Motion Under Rule 73 for a Ruling Concerning the Testimony of a Witness*, Case No. IT-95-9-PT, 27 July 1999 at para. 42.

constructed narrowly, Rule 89 and the Trial Chamber's discretion risk being proverbially swallowed by the specialised rules of admission and exclusion, especially by the residual function of Rule 95.

2. RULE 89(C) AND (D)

Rule 89(C) governs admissibility and is arguably the most frequently used provision in the Rules. The *Delalić* Trial Chamber held that Rule 89(C) was "clear and unambiguous" and emphasised the "plain, fair, literal meaning of it words." Its essential elements address the relevancy and the probative value of evidence.[7] Simply stated, admissibility under 89(C) requires the "establishment in the evidence of *some* relevance and some probative value."[8]

The connotation of relevancy is well settled among commentators. Lilly[9] stipulates that relevant evidence is evidence that must tend to prove or disprove a factual proposition.[10] May[11] contends, that in a criminal trial, relevant evidence is evidence that "make[s] more or less probable the existence of any fact" or that "form[s] part of the story."[12] Correspondingly, the *Delalić* Trial Chamber cited with approval the Canadian Supreme Court's ruling in *Cloutier*, that held a fact is relevant to another fact when there is "a connection or nexus between the two which makes it possible to infer the existence of one from the other".[13]

The relationship between relevancy and probative value is less tangible. Lilly posits that the factual proposition supported by relevant evidence must be "consequential" under the substantive law and therefore consequential to the outcome of the trial.[14] May observes that the more or less probable fact refers to a fact that is at "issue, i.e. upon which guilt or innocence depends."[15] Judge Stephen, in his Separate Opinion to the *Decision on the Defence Motion on Hearsay* underscored the difficulty in precisely defining probative value, suggesting that it is a "quality of necessarily very variable content and [that] much will depend on the character of the evidence in question".[16] Likewise, the Appeals Chamber, in determining whether the *Aleksovski* Trial Chamber properly exercised their discretion when admitting

---

[7]*Prosecutor v. Delalić and Others, Decision on the Prosecutor's Oral Request for the Admission of Exhibit 155 into Evidence and for an order to Compel the Accused, Zdravko Mucić, To Provide a Handwriting Sample*, Case No. IT-96-21-T, 19 Jan. 1998 at para. 29.

[8]*Prosecutor v. Musema, Judgement,* Case No. ICTR-96-13-T, 27 Jan. 2000 at para. 56.

[9]Graham C. Lilly, An Introduction to the Law of Evidence (1987).

[10]Id., p. 23.

[11]Richard May, Criminal Evidence (1995).

[12]Id., pp. 8–9.

[13]Supra note 7, para. 29.

[14]Supra note 9, p. 23.

[15]Supra note 11, p. 8.

[16]*Prosecutor v. Tadić, Decision on the Defence Motion on Hearsay, Separate Opinion of Judge Stephen*, Case No. IT-94-IT, 5 Aug. 1996 at p. 3.

hearsay evidence, observed that probative value depended upon the content and character of the evidence in question.[17]

Another admissibility factor, not explicitly expressed in Rule 89(C), is reliability. The *Hearsay Decision* issued by the *Tadić* Trial Chamber ruled that reliability was an inherent and implicit component of relevance and probative value under Rule 89.[18] The *Delalić* Trial Chamber, concurred with the *Hearsay Decision* and further opined that reliability is the invisible golden thread that runs through all components of admissibility.[19] Hence, evidence that is relevant, in that it tends to prove a fact, and evidence that has probative value, meaning it concerns a fact that is at issue or that is consequential to the outcome, may be admitted under Rule 89(C). Moreover, relevant and probative evidence must possess inherent reliability.

The corollary to Rule 89(C) is Rule 89(D) – the exclusion of evidence. Rule 89(D) permits Tribunal judges to exclude evidence whose probative value is substantially outweighed by the need to ensure a fair trial. Probative value, as meant under than Rule 89(C), is assumed to retain its ordinary meaning under Rule 89(D).[20] Likewise, the notion of fair trial as embodied in Articles 20[21] and 21[22] of the Statute should be interpreted as consonant with the provision in Rule 89(D). Under the Tribunal's jurisprudence, a fair trial is owed to the prosecution[23] as well as to the defence and accordingly, the ICTY Rules comply with the fundamental rights of both the accused and victims.[24]

Rule 89(D) has not occasioned extensive jurisprudence; however, it clearly excludes evidence if the defence has had inadequate time to examine

---

[17]*Prosecutor v. Aleksovski, Decision on Prosecutor's Appeal on Admissibility of Evidence*, Case No. IT-95-14/1-A73, A. Ch., 16 Feb. 1999 at para. 15.

[18]Supra note 16, para. 15. See also, *Prosecutor v. Musema, Judgement*, supra note 8, para. 30, that held: "[R]eliability of evidence does not constitute a separate condition of admissibility; rather it provides the basis for the finding of relevance and probative value required under 89(C)."

[19]Supra note 7, para. 32.

[20]Art. 31 of the Vienna Convention on the Law of Treaties provides that "[a] treaty shall be interpreted in […] in accordance with the ordinary meaning to be given to the terms of the treaty […]". Vienna Convention on the Law of Treaties, 23 May 1969, 1155 U.N.T.S. 331.

[21]ICTY Statute Art. 20. Sub-section (1) provides that "The Trial Chamber shall ensure that a trial is fair and expeditious and that the proceeding are conducted in accordance with the rules of procedure and evidence with full respect for the rights of the accused and due regard for the protection of victims and witnesses."

[22]ICTY Statute Art. 21 provides in sub-section (2) that: "In determination of the charges against him, the accused shall be entitled to a fair and public hearing, subject to article 22 of the Statute."

[23]*Prosecutor v. Tadić, Decision on the Prosecutor's Motion: Protective Measures for Victims and Witnesses*, Case No. IT-94-I-T, 10 Aug. 1995 at para. 55.

[24]*Prosecutor v. Tadić, Decision on the Prosecutor's Motion for Protective Measures for Victims and Witnesses*, Case No. IT-94-1-T, 10 Aug. 1995 at para. 25.

its content and to prepare a proper defence.[25] It follows that Rule 89(D) would disallow the introduction of evidence that infringed upon any rights of an accused's expressly preserved in Article 21 of the Statute.

By way of contrast, evidence that is barred in certain domestic systems, such as hearsay, is not *per se* excludable[26] under Rule 89(D), although the inability to cross-examine witnesses to test their veracity will be considered when attributing weight to the evidence.

As such, Rule 89(D) excludes even probative evidence that is consequential or in issue, if it were to breach the safeguards of a fair trial. To that end Judge Robinson succinctly averred that, "no matter how relevant and probative a particular piece of evidence is, it will be excluded [...] under Rule 89(D)."[27]

A final factor affecting the interpretation of Rule 89 merits mention. Customary law binds the interpretation of the Rules as well as the Tribunal Statute. The Trial Chamber in *Prosecutor v. Simić*, noted that "the discretionary power to admit relevant evidence with probative value may not be exercised where the admission of such evidence is prohibited by a rule of customary law."[28] This author would add that customary law similarly binds the exclusion of evidence.

Therefore, in order to decipher whether Rules 95 or 96 overlap or are at odds with Rule 89(C) and (D), the latitude of the specialised rules must be measured against the precepts of relevancy, probative value, inherent reliability, fair trial and adherence to customary law as ascribed to in the general provisions. This note first examines Rule 96 for reasons that will become apparent in the Rule 95 discussion.

3. Rule 96 – Evidence in Cases of Sexual Assault

Attentive to the allegations of sexual violence raised in the Secretary General's Report,[29] the judges adopted Rule 96 to address the "unique concerns of victims in cases of sexual assault".[30] Rule 96 incorporates "special provisions as to the standard of evidence, and matters of credibility of

---

[25]*Prosecutor v. Delalić and Others, Decision on Motion by the Defendants on the Production of Evidence by the Prosecution*, Case No. IT-96-21-T, 8 Sept. 1997 at para. 9.

[26]*Prosecutor v. Aleksovski, Decision on Prosecutor's Appeal on Admissibility of Evidence*, Case No.IT-95-14/1-AR73, A. Ch., 16 Feb. 1999 at para. 15.

[27]*Prosecutor v. Aleksovski, Decision on Prosecutor's Appeal on Admissibility of Evidence*, Judge Robinson Dissenting Opinion, Case No.IT-95-14/1-AR73, A. Ch., 16 Feb. 1999 at para. 6.

[28]Supra note 6, para. 42

[29]Secretary General's Report, paras. 9, 11, and 48.

[30]*Prosecutor v. Tadić, Decision on the Prosecutor's Motion for Protective Measures for Victims and Witnesses*, Case No. IT-94-1-T, 10 Aug. 1995 at para. 49.

witnesses which may be raised by the defense in cases of sexual assault"[31] to guide the Trial Chambers in the adjudication of sex based crimes. In its present form[32] Rule 96 reads:

> In cases of sexual assault:
> (i) No corroboration of the victim's testimony shall be required;
> (ii) consent shall not be allowed as a defense if the victim
> (a) has been subjected to or threatened with or has reason to fear violence, duress, detention or psychological oppression, or
> (b) reasonably believed that if the victim did not submit, another might be so subjected.
> (iii) before evidence of the victim's consent is admitted, the accused shall satisfy the Trial Chamber in camera that the evidence is relevant and credible;
> (iv) prior sexual conduct of the victim shall not be admitted in evidence.[33]

3.1 Rule 96(i)

Rule 96(i) is neither an admissibility nor an exclusionary rule. It rather concerns reliability and the assessment of evidence. In *Tadić*, the defense invoked Rule 96(i) to attack the uncorroborated testimony of prosecution witnesses, asserting that Rule 96 implicitly required corroboration for all witness testimony, except that of sexual assault victims. The Trial Chamber took an opposite view. It first noted that the general principles for the admissibility and exclusion of evidence under Rule 89(C) and (D) and then observed that the function of Sub-rule 96(i) was to accord "the testimony of a sexual assault victim the same presumption of reliability as the testimony of victims of other crimes, something which has long been denied."[34] The Trial Chamber furthermore opined that Sub-rule 96(i) did not justify any inference that crimes other than sexual assaults required corroboration and more importantly, it held that no grounds exist to conclude that a "requirement of corroboration is any part of customary international law [...]".[35] The

[31] Id., para. 24.
[32] For the amendments to ICTY Rule 96, see UN Doc. IT/32 (1 Feb. 1994), UN Doc. IT/32/Rev. 3 (1994) and UN Doc. IT/32/Rev.3/Corr. 3 (1995).
[33] ICTR Rule 96 is substantially identical to its ICTY counterpart, with the exception that sub-section 96(i) under the ICTR Rules starts with the phrase, "Notwithstanding Rule 90(C) [...]" By overriding Rule 90(C), the ICTR Rule 96 allows a child's testimony to be the basis of a conviction for sexual assault, if the Trial Chamber is satisfied that the child understands the duty to tell the truth and is sufficiently mature to report upon facts, even if the child cannot appreciate the nature of a solemn oath.
[34] *Prosecutor v. Tadić, Judgement*, Case No. IT-94-1-T, 7 May 1997 at para. 536.
[35] Id., para. 539.

Akayesu[36] and *Rutaganda*[37] Judgements concurred with *Tadić's* interpretation of the correlation of Rule 96(i) to the general principles of admissibility. In *Rutaganda*, the Trial Chamber again recited the non-corroboration premise accorded all witness testimony, then stressed that it would rely on the evidence of a single witness provided that such evidence were relevant, admissible and credible. Rule 89, it held, allowed a Chamber to "assess all relevant evidence which it deems to have probative value."[38] The *Aleksovski* Appeals Chamber subsequently confirmed the Trial Chambers' holdings of non-corroboration when it ruled that under Rule 89(C) "the testimony of a single witness on a material fact does not require, as a matter of law, any corroboration."[39]

Rule 96(i) and Rule 89(C) have different, but wholly compatible functions. Rule 96(i) merely affirms a customary law principle – uncorroborated testimony can possess inherent reliability and therefore be admissible evidence – as applied to sexual assault victims. As a consequence, Rule 89(C) treats sexual assault victim testimony on par with that of any other witness.

3.2 Rule 96(ii) and (iii)

Rule 96(ii) disallows consent as a defence to sexual assaults if a victim has been subjected to or threatened with or has reason to fear violence, duress, detention, or psychological oppression. When an accused nevertheless raises consent as a defence, Rule 96(ii) functions in tandem with sub-section (iii) to require an *in camera* hearing to evaluate the relevance and credibility of the *victim*'s consent evidence prior to its admission. To determine whether Rule 96(ii) and (iii) overlap or are at odds with Rule 89(C) or (D) two inquiries will be pursued. First, what are the customary norms that apply to Rule 96(ii)'s exclusion of a consent defence? Second, are the admissibility criteria under Rule 96(iii) decidedly different from that of Rule 89(C)?

The *Furundžija* Trial Chamber, after deliberation upon evidence of rape as outrages upon personal dignity under Article 3 of the Statute, opined that "[c]onsent was not raised by the Defence, and in any case, [the victim] was in captivity. Further, it is the position of the Trial Chamber that any form of captivity vitiates consent."[40] *Furundžija* emphasised that it was the victim's situational context that disallowed a consent defence. What the drafters of Rule 96 intended to illustrate in sub-sections (ii)(a) and (b) were situations that were inherently threatening or coercive and that preclude the victim's

---

[36]*Prosecutor v. Akayesu, Judgement*, Case No. ICTR-96-4-4-T, 2 Sept. 1998 at paras. 133–135.

[37]*Prosecutor v. Rutaganda, Judgement and Sentence*, Case No. ICTR-96-3-T, 6 Dec. 1999 at para. 18.

[38]Id.

[39]*Prosecutor v. Aleksovski, Judgement*, Case No. IT-95-14/1-A, A. Ch., 24 March 2000 at para. 62.

[40]*Furundžija* at para. 271.

consent.[41] It is suggested that the "situational" rational of Rule 96(ii) has a basis in conventional law and customary law.

Post-World War II prosecutions for war crimes did not bequeath jurisprudence relating to a defence of consent to sexual assaults, simply because those accused of sexual violence never raised the defence.[42] A few cases that dealt with the prohibition of medical and scientific experiments under humanitarian law however did deliberate upon evidence of the victim's consent.

In the *Trial of Karl Brandt and Others*[43] a subsequent Nuremberg proceeding under Control Council Law No. 10,[44] the accused, a doctor, was tried for conducting medical experiments on concentration camp detainees. The Decision held that absent voluntary consent medical experiments constituted war crimes or crimes against humanity and that:

> 1. The voluntary consent of the human subject is absolutely essential. This means that the person involved should have legal capacity to give consent; *should be so situated as able to exercise free power of choice, without the intervention of any element of force, fraud, deceit, duress, overreaching or other form of constraint or coercion*.[45] (Emphasis added).

The *Milch*[46] and the *Pohl*[47] cases upheld the voluntary consent principles of the *Trial of Karl Brandt and Others* Judgement.

---

[41]Morris and Scharf, An Insider's Guide to the International Criminal Tribunal for the Former Yugoslavia (1995). The authors explained the genesis of Rule 96. They state that, "[t]he initial [unpublished] proposal for this provision contained a detailed description of the situations in which a victim could not possibly have freely consented to the act in question and the defence was therefore precluded from raising the defence of consent. [...] In response to criticism [of the published rule] by governments, the judges decided to return to the original approach amending the rule to identify the inherently threatening or coercive situations which preclude the possibility of consent by the victim and consequently the possibility of the defense counsel raising the issue at trial." (at p. 263.)

[42]See, e.g., *Trials of Takashi*, Case No. 83, XIV Law Reports of Trials of War Criminals 1 (1946), *Trial of Awochi*, XIII Law Reports of Trials of War Criminals 122 (1946), *The Trial of Josef Kramerz & 44 Others*, II Law Reports of Trials of War Criminals 1 (1947).

[43]*Trial of Karl Brandt and 22 Others*, Vol. II p. 55 ff, Trial of War Crimes before the Nuremberg Military Tribunal.

[44]Allied Control Council Law No. 10, Punishment of Persons guilty of War Crimes, Crimes Against Peace and Against Humanity, 20 Dec. 1945, Official Gazette of the Control Council of Germany, No. 3, Berlin, 31 Jan. 1946.

[45]See, *United States v. Erhard Milch*, Vol. II, p. 623, Trial of War Crimes before the Nuremberg Military Tribunal.

[46]Id. The tribunal found Milch not guilty of medical experiments because the accused was found not to have possessed knowledge of the nature, and thus the illegality of the experiments.

[47]*The Trial of Oswald Pohl and Others*, Vol. V, Trial of War Crimes before the Nuremberg Military Tribunal.

Erratum: ***Essays on ICTY Procedure and Evidence: In Honour of Gabrielle Kirk McDonald.*** **Edited by Richard May *et al.* (ISBN 90-411-1482-3)**

Correction within the Text on page 282, to be inserted after Footnote 42.

Rule 89 (C) and (D): At Odds or Overlapping with Rule 96 and 95

Post-World War II prosecutions for war crimes did not bequeath lengthy jurisprudence relating to a defense of consent to sexual assaults **(footnote 42)**. An exception was the *Batavia*[1] case that examined the notion of "voluntariness". The *Batavia* trial convicted Japanese military officers and Japanese civilians of rape and of the forced prostitution of female Dutch citizens who were interred in detention camps during the Japanese military occupation of Indonesia. Based on the evidence, the judges determined that the women and girls had been beaten, threaten with death and the death of their interred relatives, and then forced to sign documents in Japanese stating that they agreed to be transferred from the detention camps to the Japanese military brothels. The judges stipulated that the ranking officer should have "satisfied himself that the women had been fully informed and that their voluntariness was beyond any doubt." [2] Somewhat contrary to that proviso, the court strongly intoned that the circumstances of the women and girls indeed prevented any voluntary acquiescence to forced prostitution or rape. The Judges found the ranking officer guilty, holding that:

> ...[B]y obeying the order to go and select women and girls in the camps in the way as has been established, he therefore knew that he was assisting in the execution of a serious, universally punishable act, which – as he could have realized- must certainly result in an act contrary to the laws and customs of war, especially when the act was committed against a group of women and girls who were completely in the hands of the Japanese and who were wholly at the mercy of the Occupying power.
>
> ...[H]e should have known that the selection did not meet the principle of "making a decision in full liberty."[3]

The rationale, that lack of full liberty endured by the Batavia detainees, undermines evidence of voluntariness, is similar to the "situational context" construction of Rule 96 (iii).[4]

---

[1] The Temporary Court-Martial in Batavia in the case of the Judge-Advocate ratione officii, versus: Unnamed Accused. No. 72/1947 Verdict 231 (Handwritten) 14-2-48. Batavia is the Indonesian name for Jakarta.

[2] Id.

[3] Id.

[4] In the post-war period, the international community reaffirmed that even if the consent of a victim were secured for purposes of trafficking or exploitation of the prostitution of other, such consent is legally irrelevant to the guilt of the accused. See discussion *infra*.

In an apparent "legislative" response, drafters of Article 12 common to the First[48] and Second[49] Geneva Conventions and Article 13 of the Third Geneva Convention of 1949 emphatically prohibited medical experiments "of any kind"[50] on the wounded, sick, shipwrecked or prisoners of war. Subsequently, Article 11(2) of Additional Protocol I to the Geneva Convention, reiterated the Geneva Conventions' interdiction of medical experiments and stressed the lack of recourse to a consent defence, stating:

> [I]t is, in particular, prohibited to carry out on such persons, *even with their consent*: (a) physical mutilations; (b) medical or scientific experiments; (c) removal of tissue or organs for transplantation, except where these acts are justified in conformity with the conditions provided for in paragraph 1.[51] (Emphasis added).

The Commentary notes that Article 11(2) erects a "*strict prohibition*",[52] permitting but a limited exception set forth in Article 11(3):

> 3. Exceptions to the prohibition in paragraph 2(c) may be made *only* in the case of donations of blood for transfusion or of skin for grafting, provided that they are given *voluntarily and without any coercion or inducement*.[53] (Emphasis added).

The Commentary to Article 11(3) observes that in regard to blood donations and skin grafts:

> the will must be expressed voluntarily, and any coercive measures (threats, discriminatory measures, punishments etc.) and even inducements (promises of important advantages, pressure on those who hold out) were explicitly prohibited.[54] (Emphasis added).

---

[48]Convention for the Amelioration of the Condition of the Wounded and Sick in Armed Forces on the Field, 12 Aug. 1949, 75 U.N.T.S. 31.

[49]Convention for the Amelioration of the Condition of the Wounded Sick and Shipwrecked members of the Armed Forces at Sea, 12 Aug. 1949, 75 U.N.T.S. 85, Art. 12 reads in pertinent part: "in particular, they shall not be subjected to [...] biological experiments [...]".

[50]Convention Relative to the Treatment of Prisoners of War, 12 Aug., 1949, 75 U.N.T.S. 287, Art. 13. Art. 13 reads in part: "In particular, no prisoner may be subjected to physical mutilation or to medical or scientific experiments of any kind which are not justified by the medical, dental or hospital treatment of the prisoner concerned and carried out in his interest."

[51]Protocol Additional I to the Geneva Conventions of 12 August 1949, and Relating to the Protection of Victims of International Armed Conflicts, 8 June 1977, 1125 U.N.T.S. 3, Art. 11(2).

[52]Commentary to the Additional Protocols of 8 June 1977 to the Geneva Conventions of 1949, ICRC, 1987, commentary to Article 11, para. 485.

[53]Supra note 51, Art. 11(3).

[54]Supra note 52, para. 486.

By contrast, physical mutilations, medical and scientific experiments, and organ and tissue transplantation are never "cured" by consent, even if expressed voluntarily and without inducement.

Humanitarian law, concerned with the regulation of armed conflict, purposely places great value on a victim's circumstances. Article 11(2) and (3) of Additional Protocol I and the *Furundžija* Trial Chambers both evince the relevance of the situational context. The presumption is that persons *hors de combat* or who fall into enemy hands are fundamentally incapable of rendering credible consent to scientific or medical experiments or to other inhumane treatment. Rule 96(ii)'s resonates with the reasoning of the post-World War II cases of *Batavia Karl Brandt and Others, Milch* and *Pohl*, and the codified customary law of Geneva Conventions and Additional Protocol I. Rule 96(ii) probably restates a general exclusionary tenet of humanitarian law as applied to sexual violence. To that end, the provision is at odds with Rule 89(D), but more accurately can be seen to side step Rule 89(D)'s rationale. Rule 89(D) excludes evidence that admittedly has probative value but substantially prejudices the conduct of a fair trial. Under Rule 96(ii) exclusion is justified because the inherently coercive circumstances are presumed to fatally taint the evidentiary value of consent.

However tailored to respond to circumstances occasioned by the armed conflict in the former Yugoslavia, Rule 96 (ii)'s emphasis on the victim's situational context might not be the sole criterion by which to analyse the admission or exclusion of consent evidence. Given that the Secretary General incorporated the customary bases of the crimes genocide[55] torture,[56] enslavement[57] and into the ICTY Statute and that the Rules are bound by custom, it is proffered that Rule 96(ii) and (iii) must respect the customary norms, *jus cogens* status, and intrinsic character of these crimes as applied to sexual assault conduct.

The *Furundžija* Trial Chamber was not called upon to rule on a consent defence to the crime rape.[58] More importantly and correctly so, the Trial Chamber did not entertain the plausibility of a consent defence to sexual torture,[59] presumably because it was the offence of torture and not of rape. The Trial Chamber in a lengthy exposition found that over and beyond the prohibition of torture in times of armed conflict, international law assiduously "supress[ed] any manifestation of torture"[60] at the interstate and individual level and left "no legal loopholes."[61] The *jus cogens* status of torture, the Trial Chamber observed, invalidated treaties or customs that

---

[55]Art. 4 of the ICTY Statute.

[56]Arts. 2(b), 5(f) and 3 of the ICTY Statute, as recognised by article 3(a) common to the Geneva Conventions of 1949.

[57]Art. 5(c) of the ICTY Statute.

[58]*Furundžija* at para. 271.

[59]Id., paras. 264–269.

[60]Id., para. 146.

[61]Id.

were contrary to the prohibition and necessarily voided any State measures to authorize, condone or absolve perpetrators *via* amnesty laws[62] or erect statutes of limitation. The international community's true interest lies in eradicating torture by reviling the perpetrator's acts. "The torturer has become like the pirate and the slave trader, before him, *hostis humani generis*, enemy of all mankind."[63]

The Trial Chamber attributed similar principles to the peremptory norms of genocide, slavery, and racial discrimination. Higher than "ordinary" customary rules,[64] *jus cogens* norms prevail, procedurally and substantively, over other, lesser international law canons. It is therefore inconceivable that perpetrators who knowingly commit *jus cogens* crimes like slavery, torture or genocide could avoid liability by entreating the victim's consent and subvert the highest collective value of the international community. Even if the perpetrator obtained a victim's consent, it could only be viewed as having *de minimus* legal relevance.

The intrinsic character of a crime could indicate the appropriateness of defences. For example, humanitarian law's proscription of consent as a defence to physical mutilation, the disallowance of superior orders or *tu quoque* as defences to war crimes or even municipal law's bar of consent as a defence to statutory or under-aged rape derives from the intrinsic character of these crimes. International criminal conventions that explicitly or implicitly proscribe sexual assaults might, due to the intrinsic character of the crimes, evince norms concerning consent as a defence. The Genocide Convention,[65] for example, does not refer to consent as a defence to acts of genocide. The Torture Convention bars superior orders or "exceptional circumstances whatsoever" as justifications of torture[66] and explicitly requires establishment of the consent or acquiescence of officials to prove torture, but not that of a victim to excuse acts of torture.[67] The Slavery Convention of 1926[68] is silent about defences to slavery or the slave trade. The Supplementary Convention on the Abolition of Slavery[69] does not provide for any defence, but in order to prevent the slavery-like practice of forced marriages, urges the State to encourage the "use of facilities whereby the consent of both parties to a marriage may be freely expressed in the

---

[62]Id., para. 155.

[63]Id., citing *Filartiga v. Pena-Irala*, 630 F.2d. 876 (2d. Cir. 1980).

[64]Id., para. 153.

[65]Convention on the Prevention and Punishment of the Crime of Genocide, 1949, 78 U.N.T.S. 277.

[66]Convention against Torture and other Cruel Inhuman or Degrading Treatment or Punishment, 1984, 23 I.L.M. 1027, Art. 2.

[67]Id., Art. 1.

[68]The Slavery Convention of 1926, U.K.T.S. 12, (1927), (As amended by Protocol of 23 Oct. 1953), 212 U.N.T.S. 17.

[69]The Supplementary Convention on the Abolition of Slavery, the Slave Trade, and Institutions and Practices Similar to Slavery, (7 Sept. 1956), 266 U.N.T.S. 40.

presence of competent civil or religious authority".[70] The International Convention on the Suppression and Punishment of the Crime of Apartheid likewise does not refer to defences.[71] The Convention for the Suppression of the Traffic in Persons and the Exploitation of the Prostitution of Others[72] specifically holds the procurer liable even if the victim consents.[73]

Yet Rule 96(ii)'s declaration that consent *shall not be a defence*, when certain circumstances are present, augurs that the defence is therefore unavailable not because of the intrinsic character of a crime but because of the situational context. This author would posit that defences to sexual violence charged as genocide, enslavement, or torture most likely reside not in the failure to establish the coercive circumstances or evidence of the victim's consent, but upon the failure to prove an essential element of the crime. The *Furundžija* Trial Chamber when it examined the underlying facts and elements of torture appeared to signal an understanding of how the intrinsic character of the crime limited recourse to a consent defence.

If an accused were to assert a victim's evidence of consent, to a charge of rape, he or she would have to show either in the absence of the Rule 96(ii) circumstances or that notwithstanding those circumstances, that the consent evidence was relevant and credible under Rule 96(iii). And if the plain language of Rule 96(ii) permits an accused to raise evidence of a victim's consent to challenge genocide, torture, or enslavement, it too must traverse the admissibility test of Rule 96(iii).

Rule 96(iii) provides that if relevant and credible, evidence of the victim's consent can be admitted into the proceeding. Relevant evidence, coupled with inherent reliability is assumed to carry its ordinary meaning as noted in the Rule 89(C) discussion. Credibility can be defined as "worthy of belief."[74] Credibility is usually assessed at the deliberation stage of proceedings along with weight. The *Musema* judgement clearly held in reference to Rule 89(C) that "determination of admissibility does not go to *credibility*, but merely *reliability* [...] [l]ater, that same [reliable] evidence may be found, after examination by the Trial Chamber, not to be credible."[75]

After the *in camera* hearing, the Trial Chamber must be satisfied that the victim's consent evidence was relevant to the crime rape. Under municipal law rape has traditionally been challenged by evidence of the victim's

---

[70]Id., Art. 2

[71]International Convention on the Suppression and Punishment of the Crime of Apartheid of Nov. 30, 1973, GAOR 28th Sess., Res. 3068; UNTS Vol. 1015, p. 243.

[72]Convention for the Suppression of the Traffic in Persons and of the Exploitation of the Prostitution of Others, G. A. Res. 317(IV), 2 Dec. 1949.

[73]Id., Art. 1(1)(2).

[74]Black's Law Dictionary (Abridged 1991), p. 255.

[75]*Prosecutor v. Musema, Judgement*, Case No. ICTR-96-13-T, 27 Jan. 2000 at para. 57. See also, *Prosecutor v. Kunarac and Others, Decision on Motion for Acquittal*, Case No. IT-96-23-T & IT-96-23/1-T, 3 July 2000 at paras. 4–6.

consent. Relevant evidence that is material or, according to May, "forms part of the story," would have to be credible, worthy of belief, to overcome the circumstances detailed of Rule 96(ii). Under that same test, a victim's consent to sexual mutilation, indicted as an act of genocide, might not satisfy the Trial Chamber that it is relevant to any part of the "story" since it is neither a material fact to be proved nor would it, according to Lilly, support a fact proposition that is consequential under the substantive law. Consent evidence would not negate any elements of genocide, particularly the *mens rea* element.

The Rule 96(iii) admissibility test whereby the Trial Chamber must be satisfied that the victim's consent is relevant and credible, despite the compelling situational context of Rule 96(ii), is a higher admissibility standard than Rule 89(C). Rule 96(iii)'s credibility threshold alone, substantially narrows Rule 89(C)'s presumption of admissibility. The author suggests that Rule 96(iii) is *lex specialis*, yet not necessarily at odds with Rule 89(C).

However in practice, the general provisions of Rule 89(C) and Rule 96(iii) could overlap each other. Due to a lack of legal relevance evidence of consent offered as a defence to torture, genocide, and enslavement, Rule 96(iii) and Rule 89(C) could arrive at consistent conclusions and exclude such evidence. Therefore, even in the absence of Rule 96(iii), evidence of consent for sexual assaults indicted as *jus cogens* crimes should be inadmissible under Rule 89(C) criteria.

3.3 Rule 96(iv)

Rule 96 (iv) declares that evidence of prior sexual conduct *shall* not be admitted. The provision was extensively discussed in *Delalić, Decision on the Prosecutor's Motion for the Redaction of the Public Record*.[76] During cross-examination the defence elicited from a sexual assault witness testimony that she had undergone an abortion. The prosecution relied on Rule 96(iv) to request that the Chamber redact the testimony of the victim's abortion from the public record. In its decision, the Chamber held that, "(i)n contrast to the general presumption of admissibility which governs the Rules, evidence concerning past sexual conduct of the victim is inadmissible under sub-rule 96(iv)".[77] The Trial Chamber emphatically ruled that, "Sub-rule 96(iv) is an exclusionary rule which totally forbids the introduction of evidence concerning prior sexual conduct and [...] the rule is not susceptible to waiver."[78]

---

[76] *Prosecutor v. Delalić & Others, Decision on the Prosecutor's Motion for the Redaction of the Public Record*, Case No. IT-96-21-T, 5 June 1996.

[77] Id. para. 43.

[78] Id. para. 58.

Rule 96(iv) is not a privilege. Privileges protect communications stemming from certain societal relations, such as the lawyer/client privilege. The holder can waive his or her privileges. Rule 96 (iv) is not susceptible to waiver. Presumptions of admissibility yield and the "prime objective [...] to adequately protect the (sexual assault) victims from harassment, embarrassment and humiliation by the presentation of evidence that relates to past sexual conduct,"[79] is allotted priority. Prior sexual conduct, whether relevant or possessing probative value, or indeed whether insubstantial, is inadmissible. Rule 96(iv)'s exclusion is based on policy that overrides and is at odds with Rule 89(C) admissibility criteria. The same is not true in regard to Rule 89(D). If under Rule 89(D) due regard to witness interests leads to excluding evidence of prior sexual conduct because its admission would substantially prejudice a fair trial, then Rule 96(iv) re-enforces and overlaps this part of the general provisions.

4. Rule 95 – Exclusion of Certain Evidence

Rule 95 is a two-part exclusionary rule that states:

> No evidence shall be admissible if obtained by methods which cast substantial doubt on its reliability or if its admission is antithetical to, and would seriously damage the integrity of the proceedings.

The original version of Rule 95 excluded evidence obtained directly or indirectly by means that constituted a violation of internationally protected human rights, but was amended to "broaden the rights of suspects and accused persons."[80]

In practice Rule 95 has upheld an accused's standing to challenge the admissibility of evidence captured in an armed search and seizure operation[81] and another accused's standing to challenge transcripts derived from irregular investigation procedures,[82] yet, in the interest of justice, Rule 95 admitted evidence obtained by a mere breach in the procedural rules of the Tribunal.[83]

---

[79]Id. para. 48.

[80]For rule change prior to amendment, on 30 Jan. 1995, Second Annual Report, para. 26, fn. 9.

[81]*Prosecutor v. Kordić and Čerkez, Decision Stating Reasons for Trial Chamber's Ruling of 1 June 1999 Rejecting Defence Motion to Suppress Evidence*, Case No. IT-95-14/2-T 25 June 1999 at pp. 3–5.

[82]*Prosecutor v. Delalić and Others, Decision on the Motion for the Exclusion of Evidence and Restitution of Evidence by the Accused Zejnil Delalić*, Case No. IT-96-21-T, 25 Sept. 1997 at para. 45.

[83]*Prosecutor v. Delalić and Others, Decision on the Tendering of Prosecution Exhibits 104–108*, Case No. IT-96-21-T, 9 Feb. 1998 at para. 20.

The *Delalić* ruling that granted an accused's motion to exclude statements elicited contrary to ICTY Rule 42[84] delineated the tenets of Rule 95. Reliability, the golden thread coursing through relevant and probative evidence, is subjected to further tests under Rule 95. While Rule 89 focuses upon reliability to determine whether evidence is relevant and probative in and of itself, Rule 95 scrutinises reliability to determine the source and circumstances that produced the evidence. "For evidence to be reliable, it must be [...] obtained under circumstances which cast no doubt on its nature and character."[85] A torture-extracted confession would be excluded under Rule 95 because the method used to obtain the statement destroys its fundamental reliability. Rule 95 excludes the evidence because of its source.

Rule 95 also excludes evidence to preserve the integrity of the proceeding. The *Delalić* Chamber further held that certain fair trial rights as understood by international and regional conventions are incorporated into Rule 42. Violation of an accused's rights under Rule 42 finds recourse under Rule 95,[86] therefore, clearly, standards of fair trial are subsumed within the phrase, integrity of the proceedings.[87] Independent of "source reliability," the admission of evidence extracted by confession would be antithetical to the integrity of the Tribunal proceedings. To "admit" evidence of the accused's statement under Rule 95, the Chamber held that the prosecution would have to prove "convincingly and beyond a reasonable doubt" the voluntary character of the statements.[88] The Trial Chamber's admissibility test imposed the same burden of proof as that required in proving the elements of a crime. This test is plainly higher than and at odds with the Rule 89(C) admissibility thresholds.

The *Delalić* Chamber then, in a noteworthy conclusion, said that, "[w]e read Rule 95 as a summary of the provisions in the Rules which enable exclusion of evidence [...] We regard it as a residual exclusionary provision."[89] Rule 95 is thus a repository of all the provisions that enable exclusion, or the author suggests, that narrow admissibility under the Rules.

Rule 95's broader focus on source reliability and integrity of proceedings, overlaps completely with the Rule 89(C) and (D) precepts and is at odds

---

[84]*Prosecutor v. Delalić and Others, Decision on Zdravko Mucić's Motion for the Exclusion of Evidence*, Case No. IT-96-21-T, 2 Sept. 1997 at para. 55. The ICTY Rule 42 embodies the rights of a suspect during investigation.

[85]Id., para. 41.

[86]Id., para. 43.

[87]*Prosecutor v. Barayagwiza, Decision*, Case No. ICTR-97-19-AR72, A. Ch., 3 Nov. 1999 at paras. 73, 108. Preservation of the integrity of the proceedings is not limited to the introduction of evidence, but applies to the transfer, pre-trial detention, conveyance of indictment to an accused and scheduling of initial appearance. It appears that the integrity of proceedings can be seriously damaged separately or jointly by any of the three organs of the Tribunal.

[88]Supra note 85, para. 41.

[89]Id., paras. 43 and 44.

only to the extent that it extends and supplements their rationales beyond the capabilities of the general provisions.

Similarly, and importantly, Rule 95 also overlaps and at times exceeds the Rule 96 provisions, assuming that Rule 95's regard for the integrity of the proceedings encompasses Article 20's regard for victims and witnesses and that it safeguards the ability of the prosecution to have a fair trial.

By way of example, Rule 96(i)'s restatement of reliability and non-corroboration as pertains to victim testimony is fully compatible with Rule 95. Rule 95's scrutiny of the source and circumstances that produces evidence also serves to re-enforce and to offer another avenue to exclude "consent evidence" tainted by its Rule 96(ii) "situational context." The Rule 95 narrow admissibility test of "convincingly and beyond a reasonable doubt" for reliable and therefore relevant evidence appears to be a tougher standard that the Rule 96(iii) test of relevant and credible evidence. If the burden is attributed to the moving party, and can be placed on the defence, Rule 95 could shelter the evidence of consent more effectively than Rule 96(iii). Lastly, Rule 95's stance on antithetical evidence conceivably could require a Trial Chamber to exclude evidence of a victim's consent to *jus cogens* crimes, finding that they seriously damage the integrity of the proceedings.

5. Conclusion

Rule 89(C) and (D) are flexible general provisions that presume admissibility of relevant and probative evidence, but that exclude evidence that violates fair trial norms. The expressed admissibility test under Rule 96(iii) and implied test under Rule 95 as well as the non-waivable exclusion of evidence under Rule 96(iv) are indeed at odds with admissibility under Rule 89(C). However, in most instances, overlap between the specialised rules and the general provisions exist and any conflicting posture originates from how broadly a Trial Chamber is willing to interpret the precepts of relevancy, reliability, probative value and the norms of a fair trial included in the general provisions.

Beyond overlap or stances that are at odds, Rule 95's exclusionary role supplements the general provisions by extending to the accused, and the author suggests to the prosecution and witnesses, two additional safety nets. To be admitted or to avoid exclusion, evidence must have source reliability and maintain respect for the integrity of proceedings before the Tribunal.

ALMIRO RODRIGUES and CÉCILE TOURNAYE*

23. Hearsay Evidence

Hearsay evidence is evidence for which some national systems, generally those categorised as common law systems, devote specific rules regarding the conditions for their admissibility. It is defined as a "statement, other than one made by the declarant while testifying at the trial or hearing, offered in evidence to prove the truth of the matter asserted".[1] This statement may be verbal, written, or even consist in non-verbal conduct intended as an assertion. The rule excluding hearsay varies in its scope from one domestic system to another but it can be so broad as to cover any written document, including expert reports and official documents,[2] which is not adduced by its author while testifying, as well as any behaviour carried out and words uttered by a person other than the witness who reports them in court to establish the truth of the matter.

While the Tribunal's procedure is rather fashioned upon the accusatorial model, none of the ICTY Rules cater specifically for hearsay evidence and the jurisprudence has found that it may in principle be found admissible.

Although the Tribunal is not bound by national rules of evidence,[3] it may nevertheless be instructive to consider the position taken by national legal systems with respect to this form of evidence. This preliminary study will assist in our understanding the reason behind the general exclusion of this type of evidence and how it has been considered in the context of the Tribunal. In particular, jurisprudence related to hearsay illustrates how the Tribunal's interpretation of basic principles of criminal procedure can differ from that to be found in national systems. We will first describe the rationale underlying the exclusionary rule adopted in some domestic systems. We will

---

*Judge Almiro Rodrigues is the presiding Judge of Trial Chamber I at the ICTY; Cécile Tournaye is an Associate Legal Officer at the ICTY. The views expressed herein are those of the authors and not of the United Nations.

[1]Black's Law Dictionary, 6th edition, at p. 722.

[2]Public documents are usually considered an exception to hearsay rule.

[3]Rule 89(A) provides that : "The Chambers shall not be bound by national rules of evidence".

R. May et al., Essays on ICTY Procedure and Evidence in Honour of Gabrielle Kirk McDonald, 291–303.

thereafter analyse the position adopted by the Tribunal with respect to hearsay evidence. Finally, some suggested guidelines for assessing the reliability of evidence will be presented.

1. The Rationale behind Admissibility or Inadmissibility in Domestic Systems

Many features of criminal procedure stem from two basic values: the search for truth in order to protect society from crime, and the need to protect the innocent from conviction. While those requirements are common to any legal system, methods and procedures used to strike a balance between them differ from one system to another. Barriers to the admission of certain evidence can be interpreted as being necessary to protect the innocent against conviction and are primarily evident in common law jurisdictions. A comparative look at criminal procedure within both common law and civil law jurisdictions illustrates why these are more frequently found in the former.

One should be warned at the outset that the following presentation aims at providing an overview of both model systems although clearly a close review of national practice shows that overlap often occurs. There is considerable variation between common law (or primarily accusatorial) systems themselves and some domestic systems which as a general rule one would class as civil law (or primarily inquisitorial) systems, do provide for a rule excluding admission of hearsay evidence (one could cite *e.g.*, Portugal or Italy). This presentation indeed does not intend to give an accurate description of any national system, but rather tries to bring to the fore the elements that justify the existence, or otherwise, of the exclusionary rules against hearsay evidence.

Criminal procedure in common law systems is characterised by the adversarial nature of the trial and the intervention of the jury in the factual findings. The trial in an adversarial system is rather organised as a contest between two parties. The judges have no real control over the issues debated by the jury when reaching its verdict and cannot control the jury's evaluation of the evidence. In addition, the jury is not required to justify its findings. Under such conditions, it was found necessary to entrust the judges with some preliminary control over the evidence to be presented to the jury in order to ensure that the latter only considered reliable evidence in reaching its verdict. Rules governing admissibility of evidence are the main tool created for that purpose. It is, as a result, an important and well-developed feature in the criminal procedure of common law jurisdictions.

The thinking behind the exclusion of hearsay evidence is initially to ensure that the opposing party is provided with the opportunity to cross-examine the declarant. In a system where presentation of evidence is in the hands of the parties, cross-examination by the opposing party is the main tool available to test reliability of evidence. The right of confrontation is thus considered of the utmost importance to a fair trial and one of the main principles underlying the rules regulating admission. It is also thought that the general admission of such evidence would lead to a proliferation of evidence directed to proving or negating the hearsay rather than being directly relevant to the case in hand. To admit hearsay is thus seen to threaten the right to a fair and expeditious trial.

On the other hand, the judge in a non-adversarial system actively participates in the search for evidence. Evidence is marshalled at the pre-trial stage by a judge or a public officer. It is then transmitted in a *dossier* to the trial judge well before the trial starts. During trial, the judge, who is already acquainted with the evidence through the *dossier*, questions the witnesses and can summon additional witnesses and experts if he/she deems it necessary to discover the truth. Finally, he/she is always involved in the final evaluation of the evidence even when the trial is conducted in the presence of a jury.[4] The chance that the reliability of evidence will be improperly evaluated is thus considered to be minimal. The risk of proliferation of evidence, on the other hand, is non-existent given the control exercised by the judges over the proceedings. These specific features of the non-adversarial proceedings explain why rules of evidence are far less stringent than those found in an adversarial system.

According to Mirjan Damaska,[5] these differences in procedure also lead to differing methods in evaluating evidence: "[p]robative force [in an accusatorial system] is attributed to distinct items of evidence and discrete inferential sequences, and the final determination is made by aggregating these separate probative values through some sort of additive process".[6] The inquisitorial system, on the other hand, "reflects a holistic approach to evidence in that the probative force of any item of information arises from interaction among elements of the total information output".[7] Under the latter approach, the probative value of any item of evidence can never be determined in advance. Taking the example of hearsay, the author states that in American practice, "the judge, prior to hearing all the evidence in the case, is expected to weigh whether a particular hearsay item nevertheless possesses sufficient guarantees of trustworthiness to be admissible. Under a holistic model such indicia of reliability can be established only in interaction with all other evidence in the case, suggesting that the typical Anglo-American ruling on admissibility is premature".[8]

Nevertheless, the need to protect the innocent from conviction requires that the manner in which evidence is adduced must not infringe the rights of

---

[4]If so, the judge(s) participate(s) in, and even preside(s) over, the debate with the jurors.

[5]Mirjan Damaska, "Atomistic and Holistic Evaluation of Evidence: A Comparative View", in David S. Clark (Ed.), Comparative and Private International Law Essays in Honour of John Merryman (1990), pp. 91–104 at p. 91.

[6]Id., 91.

[7]Id., 92.

[8]Id., 93.

the accused even in jurisdictions which apply a free system of evidence.[9] The right to confront witnesses is one of these rights.[10] Indeed it holds a place as being a generally recognised principle of criminal procedure evident in its inclusion in most international instruments on human rights.[11] In particular, it is one aspect of the general requirement of fairness embodied in Article 6 of the European Convention Human Rights (ECHR) and derives from the principle of "equality of arms" pursuant to which both parties should be treated in a manner ensuring their procedurally equal position during the course of a trial. The provisions of Article 6(3)(d),[12] however, do not include any specific restrictions as to the nature of evidence used and the value to be attached thereto. In particular, it does not specify that the right to examine or have examined witnesses should extend to the initial declarant. Jurisprudence of the European Court of Human Rights has consistently emphasised that the scope and interpretation of this right is primarily a matter for national regulation[13] and has to be assessed in light of the overall proceedings in order to take due count of the specific features of each national system.[14] While requiring that the accused have, at some stage of the proceedings, an "adequate and proper opportunity to challenge a witness against him",[15] the Court did not infer from this principle that hearsay

[9]See for example under French law, Crim. 19 June 1989, Bull. Crim. Nº 261, where the *Cour de cassation* specified that although breaches can be pursued by any means, those means must nevertheless abide by the rules of procedure and be consistent with the rights of the defence.

[10]Under a civil law system, confrontation first occurs at the pre-trial stage. Evidence enclosed in the *dossier* that is considered important is also usually brought before the court in order for the accused or his counsel to be able to challenge it in the context of a public hearing.

[11]Article 14(3)(e) of the International Covenant of Civil and Political Rights; Article 8 of the American Convention on Human Rights; Article 6(3)(d) of the European Convention on Human Rights.

[12]Article 6(3)(d) reads as follows: "Everyone charged with a criminal offence has the following minimum rights: […] (d) to examine or have examined witnesses against him and to obtain the attendance and examination of witnesses on his behalf under the same conditions as witnesses against him".

[13]Eur. Court H. R., *Schenk v. Switzerland*, Judgment of 12 July 1988, Series A, No. 140-A at 29.

[14]"The admissibility of evidence is primarily a matter for regulation by national law, and, as a general rule, it is for the national courts to assess the evidence before them. Accordingly, the Court's task under the Convention is to ascertain whether the proceedings considered as a whole, including the way in which evidence was taken, were fair", Eur. Court H. R., *Delta v. France*, Judgment of 19 December 1990, Series A, No. 191-A, para. 35 at 15.

[15]Eur. Court H. R., *Kostovski v. Netherlands*, Judgment of 20 November 1989, Series A, No. 166 at 20. See also Eur. Court H. R., *Unterpertinger v. Austria*, Judgment of 24 November 1986, Series A, No. 110–A at 14-15; Eur. Court H. R., *Delta v. France*, Judgment of 19 December 1990, Series A, No. 191-A; Eur. Court H. R., *Schenk v. Switzerland*, 145 Eur. Ct. H.R. (ser. A) 29 (1988), Eur. Court H. R., *Ludi v. Switzerland*, Judgment of 15 June 19, Series A, No. 238-A; Eur. Court H. R., *Windish v. Austria*, Judgment of 27 Sept. 1990, Series A, No. 186-A. Eur. Court H.R, *Van Mechelen and others v. the Netherlands*, Judgment of 23 April 1997, Reports of Judgements and Decisions 1997-III.

statements should be excluded. Rather, it has found a violation of Article 6(3)(d) only when conviction of the accused had solely or decisively been based upon evidence that was not submitted to confrontation. Thus, the Court not only takes into account the technical aspects of the presentation of evidence, but also considers the weight eventually attached to the evidence in question.

Despite the above-mentioned differences between what we have generally discussed as common law and civil law systems, the result reached under both systems does not necessarily differ. As Donald Piragoff states, "the two systems are often not that dissimilar in the types of evidence that are finally considered, but rather differ in the manner and the timing of how unreliable evidence is disregarded or weeded-out".[16] Moreover, it can be found that the differences between both systems more recently have become less marked. The rule against hearsay is subject to an increasing number of exceptions in many common law systems[17] and some authors even argue that the rule should be dropped.[18]

2. The Admissibility of Hearsay Evidence Before the Tribunal

2.1 A free system of evidence

Although the procedure before the Tribunal is *sui generis*, presentation of evidence is more akin to the adversarial system than that in the inquisitorial

[16]Donald K. Piragoff, "Article 69, Evidence", in Otto Triffterer (Ed.), Commentary on the Rome Statute of the ICC (1999), pp. 889–916 at p. 904.

[17]The United States Federal Rules of Evidence lists a large number of exceptions, including a "catch all" provision that is one the most significant examples of the decrease in importance of the exclusionary rule against hearsay. The United States Federal Rule of Evidence 807 reads as follows: "A statement not specifically covered by any of the [enumerated] exceptions but having equivalent circumstantial guarantees of trustworthiness, is not excluded by the hearsay rule, if the court determines that (A) the statement is offered as evidence of a material fact; (B) the statement is more probative on the point for which it is offered than any other evidence which the proponent can procure through reasonable efforts; and (C) the general purpose of these rules and the interests of justice will best be served by admission of the statement into evidence. However, a statement may not be admitted under this exception unless the proponent of it makes known to the adverse party sufficiently in advance of the trial or hearing to provide the adverse party with a fair opportunity to prepare to meet it, his intention to offer the statement and the particulars of it, including the name and address of the declarant". In Canada, hearsay is declared admissible as soon as it is found "necessary and reliable" (*R. v. Finta* (1994) 28 CR (4th) 265, 329 per Cory J. See also *R. v. Kahn* (1990) 79 CR (3d) 1.

[18]A. A. S. Zuckerman, The Principles of Criminal Evidence (1989), at p. 217, suggests that "trial judges should have the power to admit hearsay whenever it is of sufficient probative value" provided that the declarant is not available and that notice be given to the opposite side so that it may prepare a case against its reception. See also Andrew L-T Choo, Hearsay and Confrontation in Criminal Trials (1996) at pp. 192–193; Consultation Paper No. 138 of the Law Commission (1995), *Criminal Law – Evidence in Criminal Proceedings: Hearsay and Related Topics*.

one. The parties control the evidence adduced and they can agree on the issues they want to debate at trial. Yet, the ICTY Rules have adopted a free system of evidence, both with regard to admissibility and evaluation, characteristic of the civil law model. In particular, Rule 89(C) states that "a Chamber may admit any relevant evidence which it deems to have probative value".[19]

This practice is common to most evidentiary procedures before international tribunals. As shown by the rules of the International Military Tribunal in Nuremberg,[20] or of the International Court of Justice, bodies establishing international tribunals are careful not to be bound by strict rules of evidence. The Tribunal does not depart from this trend. In fact, consideration was given, while drafting the relevant rules, to the specific difficulties that the Tribunal would encounter in gathering evidence.[21] The Tribunal is dependent on States' co-operation, and documentary evidence is hard to collect. In that respect, the situation of the Tribunal differs from that of the Nuremberg and Tokyo trials.[22] In addition, the Tribunal primarily deals with massive crimes that led to extensive displacement of the population and victims can be hard to reach. The investigation conducted against the Kosovo Liberation Army is an example of these difficulties encountered; the Serbian population of Kosovo has massively fled the region and resettled in Serbia, where they cannot be reached by the office of the Prosecutor. Furthermore, victims often fear for their safety or may find it emotionally unbearable to testify. To adopt strict rules on admissibility of evidence in these circumstances would complicate the task of the Tribunal tremendously when its lack of coercive powers already makes gathering of evidence very difficult. A further reason to adopt a free system of evidence in the context of the Tribunal lies in its goals: the Tribunal is not only entrusted with the task of trying the individuals responsible for serious violations of humanitarian law, but it is also intended that it will "contribute to the restoration and maintenance of peace".[23] The search for the historical truth

---

[19]Article 69 of the ICC Statute reproduces *verbatim* this provision.

[20]Agreement for the Prosecution and Punishment of the Major War Criminals of the European Axis, 8 August 1945, 82 U.N.T.S. 280, Articles 19 ("the Tribunal shall admit any evidence which it deems to have probative value") and 20 ("the Tribunal shall not be bound by technical rules of evidence. It may require the parties to inform it of the nature of the evidence before ruling on its relevance").

[21]See for instance 2d Plenary, PM 15 at 72 (28 January 1994).

[22]As Christian Tomuschat mentions, "(b)ack in 1945, ample factual evidence was available. The victorious Allied powers had access to all the archives of Germany and Japan, where much of the illegal activities of the two regimes had been carefully documented. The International Tribunal for the Former Yugoslavia, in contrast, is constrained to act outside the territory of the former Yugoslavia. Its main source of evidence will therefore be testimony of witnesses. Thus, over and beyond the problem of arresting any intellectual authors, there is a tremendous risk that acts of planning, organizing, and incitement may not be capable of being proven at the level of proof required for conviction", Christian Tomuschat, "International Criminal Prosecution: the Precedent of Nuremberg Confirmed", *Criminal Law Forum*, Vol. 5, No. 2–3 (1994), at 243.

[23]SC Res 808, UN Doc. S/Res/ 808 (22 February 1993).

is central to meet this goal. Many victims or their relatives, years later, are still carrying out investigations with a view to discovering how and where their friends, neighbours or relatives disappeared. Their relentless quest for truth must be addressed as a prerequisite to peace and the Tribunal, notably through its procedure, has to take this into account.

2.2 The Tribunal's case-law on hearsay evidence

In both the *Tadić*[24] and the *Blaškić* cases, the Defence objected to the unlimited admission of hearsay evidence. None of their arguments however contended that hearsay should be inadmissible as a matter of principle. Rather, they requested that the trial judges should follow specific procedural steps in order to ensure that the statements admitted were reliable. Both motions claimed that to admit hearsay statements without further safeguards would "deprive the Defence of any ability to investigate the statements in issue and meaningfully challenge the credibility of the out-of-court declarant".[25] This would amount to a violation of the right of the accused to cross-examine the declarant provided in Article 21(4)(e) of the Statute.[26]

The Defence in the *Tadić* case requested that the Chamber decide on admissibility before hearing the content of the out of court statement and on the sole basis of the circumstances under which the evidence was received. Likewise, the Defence in the *Blaškić* case contended that the Trial Chamber should exclude hearsay statements that are not *prima facie* reliable or whose admission would be procedurally unfair to the accused, *e.g.* in a case where it has not been shown that the original declarant is unavailable to testify.[27] The Defence claimed that to rule otherwise would carry the risk that the Prosecution would call derivative witnesses, rather than direct witnesses, to prevent the Defence from cross-examining the declarant. The Defence therefore first requested that hearsay evidence be admitted only if the unavailability of the declarant was established and, if so, under the condition that specific information be given to the Trial Chamber, with respect to the identity of the alleged speaker and, to the extent known, the time, place and

[24] *Prosecutor v. Tadić, Decision on the Defence Motion on Hearsay*, Case No. IT-94-I-T, 5 Aug. 1996 ("*Tadić Decision*").

[25] *Prosecutor v. Blaškić, Defense's reply to Prosecutor's Response to the Defence's Standing Objection to the Admission of Hearsay with no Foundational Requirements and with no Inquiry as to its Reliability*, Case No. IT-95-14-T, 19 Nov. 1997 at 3.

[26] Article 21(4)(e) provides: "In the determination of any charge against the accused pursuant to the present Statute, the accused shall be entitled to the following minimum guarantees, in full equality": (e)"to examine, or have examined, the witnesses against him and to obtain the attendance and examination of witnesses on his behalf under the same conditions as witnesses against him".

[27] *Prosecutor v. Blaškić, Defense's reply to Prosecutor's Response to the Defence's Standing Objection to the Admission of Hearsay with no Foundational Requirements and with no Inquiry as to its Reliability*, Case No. IT-95-14-T, 19 Nov. 1997, at 5.

circumstances surrounding the alleged statement. The Defence considered those indications necessary not only for the Chamber to decide on admission but also to assess the weight that should be attached to this piece of evidence if admitted.[28]

Both Trial Chambers first asserted that the admission of hearsay evidence was not excluded by the Statute or the ICTY Rules. With respect to the Statute, Trial Chamber I specified that "the right to cross-examination guaranteed by Article 21(4)(e) of the Statute applies to the witness testifying before the Trial Chamber and not to the initial declarant whose statement has been transmitted to this Trial Chamber by the witness".[29] Both Chambers further noted that the only provision dealing with admission of evidence in the ICTY Rules, namely Rule 89(C), did not exclude hearsay evidence as a matter of principle. They concluded that hearsay should not be treated any differently from other types of evidence and was admissible, subject to its relevance and probative value, as set forth in Rule 89(C) of the ICTY Rules.[30]

Both Trial Chambers also concurred in finding that no further procedural safeguards were necessary to ensure that the reliability of hearsay statements would be properly assessed. Trial Chamber II rejected the procedure suggested by the Defence on the ground that, "while possibly appropriate if trials before the International Tribunal were conducted before a jury, [it was] not warranted [in these cases] for the trials are conducted by Judges who are able, by virtue of their training and experience, to hear the evidence in the context in which it was obtained and accord it appropriate weight".[31] Likewise, Trial Chamber I in the *Blaškić* case stated that it would be down to the parties in a particular case to determine what elements should be presented in order for the Chamber to properly assess the reliability of the particular item of evidence.[32]

Both Chambers additionally referred to Rule 89(D) under which "a Chamber may exclude any relevant evidence if its probative value is substantially outweighed by the need to ensure a fair trial". They both found that this provision allowed the Defence "to demonstrate that a hearsay testimony which was declared admissible must, in the end, be excluded because its probative value is insufficient".[33] The Defence is thus free to adduce further evidence intended to challenge the credibility of the declarant or the content of his/her statement.

---

[28] Id., 3.

[29] *Prosecutor v. Blaškić, Decision on Standing Objection of the Defence to the Admission of Hearsay with no Inquiry as to its Reliability*, Case No. IT-95-14-T, 21 Jan. 1998 ("Blaškić Decision") at para. 12.

[30] *Tadić* Decision at para. 7; *Blaškić* Decision at para. 9.

[31] *Tadić* Decision, para. 17.

[32] *Blaškić* Decision, para. 14.

[33] *Blaškić* Decision, para. 14. See also the *Tadić* Decision, para. 18.

The Appeals Chamber confirmed this position in its decision of 16 February 1999,[34] when it was seized by the Prosecutor on the question as to whether a Trial Chamber could admit as evidence the transcript of the testimony given by a witness in another related case before the Tribunal.[35] The Appeals Chamber first noted that transcripts coming from other ongoing proceedings before the Tribunal qualified as hearsay evidence. It then stated that "it is well settled in the practice of the Tribunal that hearsay is admissible. Thus relevant out-of-court statements which a Trial Chamber considers probative are admissible under Rule 89(C)".[36] The Appeals Chamber did not add any further condition to the requirement of relevance and probative value. In particular, it rejected the argument submitted by the appellant pursuant to which hearsay evidence should be admitted only if the declarant is unavailable. Following the arguments previously presented by the Defence in other cases, the Prosecutor claimed that Rule 90(A)[37] set out the principle of oral and direct examination and that, accordingly, indirect evidence was admissible only if it was proven that direct evidence could not be obtained. The Appeals Chamber rejected this interpretation, Judge Robinson dissenting,[38] and considered that Rule 90(A) was not intended to establish a preference for direct and oral evidence but rather dealt with technicalities relating to reception of testimony. Rule 90(A) did not in itself prevent the Trial Chamber from admitting derivative evidence that would meet the requirements of Rule 89(C). An out-of-court statement made by a person, who is available to testify in person, is admissible if the Trial Chamber decides, in its discretion, that it is relevant and of sufficient probative value, pursuant to Rule 89(C). Under those circumstances, the Trial Chamber can either order the witness to testify before it or admit the hearsay statement under Rule 89(C). The Appeals Chamber specified that "the Trial Chamber was entitled to take account of the stage of the trial, the length of time the

---

[34]*Prosecutor v. Aleksovski, Decision on Prosecutor's Appeal on Admissibility of Evidence*, Case No. IT-95-14/1-AR73, A. Ch., 16 Feb. 1999 ("*Aleksovski Decision*").

[35]The Trial Chamber (*Prosecutor v. Aleksovski, Decision Granting for the Admission of Evidence*, Case No. IT-95-14/1-T, 22 Oct. 1998) admitted as evidence the transcript of a testimony heard in the *Blaškić* case, on the ground that: 1. the evidence in question had indisputable probative value; 2. the situation was exceptional as the witness concerned was not available to testify until later in the year and the trial was at its final stage. To request appearance of the witness would thus have unduly delayed the proceedings; and 3. the right of the opposing party to cross-examine the witness was not infringed as the office of the Prosecutor was one single entity and had already had the opportunity to cross-examine the witness in the context of another proceedings.

[36]*Aleksovski Decision*, para. 15.

[37]Rule 90 (A) reads as follows: "Witnesses shall, in principle, be heard directly by the Chambers unless a Chamber has ordered that the witness be heard by means of a deposition as provided for in Rule 71 or where, in exceptional circumstances and in the interest of justice, a Chamber has authorised the receipt of testimony via video-conference link".

[38]Judge Robinson considered that Rule 90(A) intended to give primacy to direct and oral evidence. *Prosecutor v. Aleksovski, Dissenting Opinion of Judge Patrick Robinson*, Case No. IT-95-14/1-AR73, A. Ch., 16 Feb. 1999 at para. 10.

accused had been in custody and its finding that the witness was not immediately available in exercising its discretion to admit the evidence".[39] As for the right to confront witnesses, the Appeals Chamber, noting the common interest shared by the parties in both cases (*Aleksovski* and *Blaškić*), stated that the need for the Prosecutor or the Defence to cross-examine a witness already subjected to cross-examination in the previous case on the same issue, does not arise. Therefore the transcript of that testimony can be admitted as evidence.[40]

Thus trial judges have a very broad discretion to decide on the admission of hearsay statements. They have invoked this discretion in different ways, depending on the legal tradition which they come from.

Trial Chamber I tends to adopt a civil law or "holistic" approach: reliability cannot be properly assessed at the stage of admissibility and is rather considered at the stage of weighing all the evidence presented. In the *Blaškić* Decision, Trial Chamber I indicated that "the absence of cross-examination is not related to admissibility but to the weight given to the evidence",[41] an evaluation that "can logically be made only *a posteriori* once the Parties have presented all their claims".[42] Likewise, Trial Chamber I*bis* specified in the *Aleksovski* case that the question of weight of the evidence will be settled "at the close of trial", taking into account "all the evidence in their possession and the manner it was presented to them".[43] This position was reasserted in the *Blaškić* Judgement: "[t]he principle embodied by the case-law of the Trial Chamber on the issue is the one of extensive admissibility of evidence – questions of credibility or authenticity being determined according to the weight given to each of the materials by the Judges at the appropriate time".[44] It further specified that "Sub-rule 89(C) of the Rules authorises the Trial Chamber to receive any relevant evidence which it deems has probative value and [...] the indirect nature of the testimony depends on the weight which the Judges give to it and not its admissibility".[45]

Trial Chambers II and III on the other hand have adopted a common-law or "atomistic" approach. In the *Tadić* Decision, Trial Chamber II found that the hearsay nature of the evidence should be considered at the stage of admissibility, as one element that impacts upon its reliability. Hence reliability was found by Trial Chamber II to be one element to consider in assessing the probative value.[46] In doing so, Trial Chamber II acknowledged that

---

[39] *Aleksovski Decision*, para. 19.

[40] *Aleksovski Decision*, para. 27.

[41] *Blaškić Decision*, para. 11.

[42] Id., para. 13.

[43] *Prosecutor v. Aleksovski, Decision Granting for the Admission of Evidence*, Case No. IT-95-14/1-T, 22 Oct. 1998 at p. 4.

[44] *Prosecutor v. Blaškić, Judgement*, Case No. IT-95-14-T, 3 March 2000 ("*Blaškić Judgement*") at para. 34.

[45] Id., para. 36.

[46] *Tadić Decision*, paras. 9, 15 and 16.

reliability could be evaluated *a priori* and that a hearsay statement could be excluded at the stage of admission for lack of probative value.

Trial Chamber III, in the case against *Kordić and Cerkez,* followed this approach in its *Decision on the Prosecution Application to Admit the Tulića Report and Dossier into Evidence*.[47] It considered "each category of material submitted by the Prosecution for admission into evidence"[48] and inquired *a priori* whether, for each of them, there was enough guarantee that the reliability of the information so tendered would be properly debated at trial, notably through cross-examination. This reasoning led the Chamber to reject some hearsay evidence for lack of probative value.

The Prosecutor intended to adduce, through an investigator from the Office of the Prosecutor, a *dossier* of documentary evidence including maps, video footage, witness statements, court transcripts, exhumation documents and photographs, as well as a report prepared by the investigator that summarised the evidence contained in the *dossier*.

With regard to the report, the Prosecutor claimed that it was admissible hearsay and would not violate Article 21(4)(e) since the Defence would have the opportunity to cross-examine the Investigator. Trial Chamber III considered however that cross-examination of the investigator could not provide the Court with any proper indication as to the reliability of the material contained in the report. The Investigator had been neither a contemporary witness of fact nor heard the witnesses himself. The report thus amounted to second-hand or third-hand hearsay whose reliability could not be properly tested by cross-examination. The report was rejected for lack of probative value.

The Chamber also rejected the admission of seven witness statements contained in the *dossier*, on the ground that, although admissible under Rule 89 (C), "it would amount to a wholesale admission of hearsay untested by cross-examination [...] and would be of no probative value".[49]

Except for one witness who had already testified in the *Kordić and Cerkez* case,[50] testimony of witnesses received in a related case, namely the *Blaškić* case, was found admissible. Following the Appeals Chamber's Decision,[51] it considered that cross-examination by the Defence in the *Blaškić* case, "a case in which the Defence have a common interest with the Defence in this case", was sufficient to meet the right of the accused to confront witnesses.[52] The Chamber nevertheless added that the Defence could apply for cross-examination of the witnesses concerned if it deemed that matters relevant to this case had not been covered by cross-examination in the *Blaškić* case.

---

[47]Hereinafter "*Tadić Decision*", Case No. IT-95-14/2-T, 29 July 1999.
[48]*Tulića Decision*, para. 13.
[49]*Tulića Decision*, para. 23.
[50]*Tulića Decision*, para. 26.
[51]*Aleksovski Decision*, para. 27.
[52]Id., para. 28.

3. Suggested Guidelines to Assess Reliability of Evidence

Trial judges are vested with considerable discretion in determining reliability of the evidence presented and it is unlikely that the Appeals Chamber would quash their findings on admission of hearsay evidence.[53] However, some guidelines as to how trial judges should exercise this power could be drawn both from the specific features of the Tribunal's procedure and the context in which it carries out its task.

The rather adversarial nature of the procedure and the ensuing limited control by the judges over the evidence presented is the first element to be considered. As seen earlier, cross-examination is the main tool used to test the reliability of evidence tendered under such a procedure. Live testimony and direct evidence should therefore be favoured as much as possible as they obviously constitute the best evidence of any facts asserted. In fact, it is the case that limitations to the right to cross-examine are usually confined to cases either agreed upon by the parties[54] or admitted by reason of a common interest shared by the Defence or the Prosecutor in a different but related case.

Nevertheless, although live testimony is the goal, it must be acknowledged that limitations necessarily occur for the following reasons. First, the Tribunal must take account of both the emotional trauma which victims endure in reliving their experiences through live testimony as well as the risk they take in coming forward to give evidence. In addition, the Tribunal is limited by the lack of coercive powers it possesses in compelling witnesses to attend court. The need to ensure an expeditious trial is also one element to be considered. Hearsay evidence might well be an important source of information under these circumstances and the ICTY Rules even expressly cater for the use of affidavits in place of live testimony to corroborate prior testimony, as a tool to address those practical constraints.[55]

Furthermore, it is in the nature of the cases that come before the Tribunal that live testimony itself will often contain hearsay statements. Trial Chamber I stated in that regard that "thousands of people were displaced, detained or even killed. Under such conditions, it can be expected that the witnesses will refer to events which others, and not they themselves, experienced".[56] All

---

[53]An appeal is currently awaiting consideration by the Appeals Chamber in the case of Kordić and Cerkez, related to the statement of a deceased witness admitted as evidence by the Trial Chamber. The same statement was admitted in the Blaškić case where the decision was not appealed (*Prosecutor v. Blaškić, Decision on the Defence Motion to Admit into Evidence the Prior Statement of Deceased Witness Midhat Haskić*, Case No. IT-94-T, 29 Apr. 1998).

[54]See Rule 94*bis* related to testimony of expert witnesses, or Rule 94*ter* dealing with affidavit evidence.

[55]Rule 94*ter* of the ICTY Rules. An appeal is currently awaiting related to the admission of prior statements of witnesses in the *Kordić and Cerkez* case and touches upon the issue of the interpretation of Rule 94*ter*.

[56]*Blaškić Decision*.

domestic systems express reservations to evidence that have not been directly seen by the person who testifies and these reservations obviously apply to the Tribunal as well.[57] All efforts should thus be made to obtain as much information as possible on the origin and circumstances of the hearsay statements produced in the course of live testimony, in order to rebuild the chain of communication. Questioning by the parties and the judges is the tool available for that purpose. To exclude admission of such statements, however, appears both impracticable and inadvisable. It is impracticable because those statements will often be entwined with direct evidence considering the nature of the crimes adjudicated by the Tribunal. It is neither advisable as in crimes of this scale, particularly in relation to crimes against humanity and genocide, often hearsay evidence, if considered in light of all evidence presented, can assist in establishing a pattern of conduct. In these circumstances, it is suggested that it is more appropriate to assess the evidence at the conclusion of the trial and at that point to consider what weight should be attributed to it. This solution would be consistent with the free system of evidence that the Tribunal has adopted in view, among others, of its specific task.

Nevertheless, as it is felt that as a general rule one should have the right to confront a witness, it follows from this that a hearsay statement should never be given such a weight as to be the only evidence relied upon to convict an accused. Lack of corroboration would amount to a violation of the right of the accused and it is suggested that corroboration should be a prerequisite. This would be consistent with the case law of the European Court of Human Rights described above, together with the practice of the International Court of Justice.[58]

---

[57]Psychological studies have shown that a message is always altered in the process of being transmitted from one person to another. The information is distorted even where there is no intention to do so and as a mere result of being transmitted. Factors such as the sex, age, education of the persons involved in the transmission, as well as the length and content of the message transmitted, impact upon the type of transformation affecting the original message. But chain transmission invariably alters the original message. Indeed, experiments in this field have shown that the process of receiving information is not merely passive but involves both a conscious and unconscious activity from the part of the receptor. The meaning of the message received is consequently "rebuilt" out of the elements that are significant to the receptor's subjectivity.

[58]Professor Rosenne explains that the ICJ would consider hearsay as "'allegations' falling short of conclusive evidence" in The Law and Practice of the International Court (1985) at p. 558.

RENEE PRUITT*

24. Discovery: Mutual Disclosure, Unilateral Disclosure and Non-Disclosure under the Rules of Procedure and Evidence

Because they govern access to information by a person accused of violations of international humanitarian law, discovery rules in the ICTY are of supreme importance. Instead of leaving it to the parties to decide what to reveal or allowing the Trial Chambers to order disclosure of material completely on a case-by-case basis, the Rules provide structure and guidelines with respect to the obligations of the Prosecution and the Defence in this regard. The rules governing discovery are rooted at least in part in Article 21 of the ICTY Statute, which addresses the rights of the accused. Specifically, pursuant to this Article, an accused person is allowed to "examine, or have examined, the witnesses against him and to obtain the attendance and examination of witnesses on his behalf under the same conditions as witnesses against him".[1] This Article also guarantees an accused the right "to have adequate time and facilities for the preparation of his defence".[2] The discovery rules contained in Rules 66, 67 and 68, which provide for prosecutorial disclosure, reciprocal disclosure and disclosure of exculpatory evidence, respectively, help ensure that these guarantees are met.

1. Overview of the Rules

In its current formulation, Rule 66 provides that the Prosecution must provide to the Defence all supporting material that accompanied the indictment and

*Currently working as a Litigation Attorney in New York City. Formerly worked as an Associate Legal Officer at the ICTY and is a 1993 graduate of Harvard Law School. The views expressed herein are those of the author alone and do not necessarily reflect the views of the United Nations or the ICTY.

[1]ICTY Art. 21(e).

[2]ICTY Art. 21(b).

R. May et al., Essays on ICTY Procedure and Evidence in Honour of Gabrielle Kirk McDonald, 305–314.

all prior statements of the accused within thirty days of the accused's initial appearance. The Prosecution must also tender to the Defence copies of statements of all witnesses that the Prosecution intends to call at trial within a time set forth by the Trial Chamber or Judge.[3] In addition, paragraph B of this Rule provides that where the Defence so requests, the Prosecution must allow the inspection of "books, documents, photographs and tangible objects in the Prosecutor's custody or control" which (i) the Prosecution will use as evidence in the trial, (ii) belonged to or were obtained from the accused, or (iii) are material to the Defence's preparation for trial.[4] However, this Rule also allows the Prosecution to apply to the Trial Chamber to be relieved from this obligation where the evidence, if disclosed, would prejudice other ongoing investigations, would be contrary to the public interest, or would affect the security interests of any State.[5]

Rule 67 dovetails with Rule 66, providing that, where the Defence has requested disclosure pursuant to Rule 66(B), the Prosecution is then entitled to "inspect any books, documents, photographs and tangible objects" in the custody and control of the Defence that are intended for use at trial.[6] This Rule also imposes upon the Defence the obligation to notify the Prosecution of the specifics of any special Defence and its claim, if any, of alibi, including the names and addresses of witnesses the Defence will call at trial and any evidence the accused will rely on to establish the alibi.[7] In response to this information, the Prosecution is required to notify the Defence of the names of witnesses it intends to call to rebut the claims of the accused.[8] Interestingly, Rule 67 explicitly provides that the Defence's failure to comply with this Rule "shall not limit the right of the accused to testify on the above defences", although it leaves open the question of whether the Defence can present any additional evidence, including witness testimony, with respect to these defences.[9] Instead, the Rule implies that such determinations are to be made on a case-by-case basis, with the parties mandated to promptly notify the other party and the Trial Chamber on the discovery of material that should have been produced "pursuant to the Rules".[10]

The final disclosure obligation on the Prosecution is that found in Rule 68, which mandates the disclosure to the Defence, "as soon as practicable", of evidence that "in any way tends to suggest the innocence or mitigate the guilt of the accused or may affect the credibility of prosecution evidence".

These Rules impose a unilateral burden of disclosure on the Prosecution, particularly with respect to exculpatory evidence and information accompanying the indictment, both of which are necessary for the accused to

[3]ICTY Rule 66(A).
[4]ICTY Rule 66(B).
[5]ICTY Rule 66(C).
[6]ICTY Rule 67(C).
[7]ICTY Rule 67(A)(ii).
[8]ICTY Rule 67(A)(i).
[9]ICTY Rule 67(B).
[10]ICTY Rule 67(E).

adequately defend himself against charges he faces. The Defence, by contrast, faces no unilateral burden of disclosure. Instead, for every case in which the Defence is required to produce evidence or other information, the Prosecution faces a corresponding obligation. For example, when the Defence presents information regarding an alibi or special defence, the Prosecution is required to provide information on that which it will use to rebut the Defence case. Similarly, the Defence is only required to allow the Prosecution access to its files if it asks the Prosecution for access to the Prosecution files. Because of this, the Defence is able to withhold damaging information while the Prosecution has no such entitlement. In such a case, if the Defence has something very damaging in its files, it can avoid the Prosecution gaining access to it simply by not making a request under 66(B). Thus, the Defence may choose whether to invoke the mutual obligations, but if it does so, Prosecution compliance is mandatory. With respect to non-disclosure, the Rules allow for the Trial Chambers to excuse the Prosecution from its disclosure obligation.[11]

2. Issues Not Specifically Addressed by the Rules

Although quite extensive, these Rules do not cover all situations, leaving several questions open for determination by the Trial and Appeals Chambers with respect to each case in which they become an issue. For example, how broadly will the ICTY construe the term "within the custody and control" with respect to Rules 66(B) and 67(C)? Who determines, and how, whether certain information is "material" to the Defence as noted in Rule 66(B)? How is the Prosecutor regulated to ensure that it in fact provides information called for by the Rules, particularly with respect to witnesses it later decides to call to testify at trial? With respect to Rule 66(C), will the provision of information to the Trial Chamber, albeit in camera, also prejudice potential ongoing investigations, and if so, what steps can the Trial Chamber take to counteract any prejudice? An additional question is whether it is appropriate that the defence does not have the opportunity to argue against an assertion by the Prosecution that it cannot disclose the required information due to ongoing investigation or based on security interests. While not fully answering each of these issues, the Trial Chambers have rendered decisions that address some of these concerns and that have further established the responsibilities of the parties with respect to discovery.

---

[11] In addition, ICTY Rule 70 provides that work product such as "reports, memoranda, or other internal documents prepared by a party, its assistants or representatives in connection with the investigation or preparation of the case, are not subject to disclosure".

2.1 Prior Statements

One of the first questions by an accused regarding the Prosecutor's responsibility under these Rules was raised in the case of *Prosecutor v. Delalić*, wherein Trial Chamber II determined that the obligation on the Prosecution to provide all prior statements of an accused does not end after the Prosecution has complied initially with this Rule. Instead, this is a "continuing obligation" and the Prosecution must provide statements that enter in its possession at any time.[12] In a later decision in response to a Defence motion for discovery from the Prosecution, Trial Chamber I held that not only is the obligation a continuing one, but the Prosecution is obligated to disclose all statements regardless of the form or source of the statement. In coming to this decision, the Trial Chamber cited the United States rules and referred to French law to support this conclusion:

> 35. The reference to the legal standards in effect in developed legal systems – such as those of the United States or France – leads to the same conclusion, namely, that the accused must have access to his own statements no matter how the Prosecution has obtained them.
>
> [...]
>
> 37. The principles identified in support of the interpretation of Sub-rule 66(A) lead the Trial Chamber to the decision that all the previous statements of the accused which appear in the Prosecutor's file, whether collected by the Prosecution or originating from any other source, must be disclosed to the Defence immediately.

The same interpretation of Sub-rule 66(A) leads the Trial Chamber to draw no distinction between the form or forms which these statements may have. Moreover, nothing in the text permits the introduction of the distinctions suggested by the Prosecution between "the official statements taken under oath or signed and recognised by the accused" and the others.[13]

The Trial Chamber went on to note that the Prosecution could avoid disclosure of certain information, referring to Rule 66(C), which allows the Prosecution to request relief from the obligation from the Trial Chamber, and Rule 70(A), which provides that reports, memoranda and other internal documents prepared by a party or on behalf of a party in connection with the case are not subject to disclosure.[14]

---

[12] *Prosecutor v. Delalić and Others, Decision on Motion by the Accused Zejnil Delalić for the Disclosure of Evidence*, Case No. IT-96-21-PT, 27 Jan. 1997 at para. 4.

[13] *Prosecutor v. Blaškić, Decision on the Production of Discovery Materials*, Case No. IT-95-14-T, 27 Jan. 1997 at paras. 35–37.

[14] Id., para. 39.

While this holding reveals the Trial Chamber's understanding that the term "prior statements" is to be given a broad reading, Trial Chamber I later made it clear in this same case that the term does not include every statement by an accused. In refusing to designate orders issued by the accused military commander as "prior statements" within the ambit of this Rule, the Trial Chamber held that the term "must be understood to refer to all statements made by the accused during questioning in any type of judicial proceeding which may be in the possession of the Prosecutor, but only such statements".[15]

2.2 Exculpatory Material

With respect to another obligation of the Prosecution – that to provide the Defence with exculpatory material – Trial Chamber decisions also have helped to clarify the parameters of this Rule, first by providing a definition of "exculpatory material". According to a Trial Chamber, exculpatory material is "material which is known to the Prosecutor and which is favourable to the accused in the sense that it tends to suggest the innocence or mitigate the guilt of the accused or may affect the credibility of prosecution evidence".[16] Such material is not limited to that found only in the files relating to the accused; instead it includes all information, including that in case files in the custody or control of the Prosecution of other accused or suspected persons. However, it appears that requests to inspect such files of other accused persons will be denied based on confidentiality concerns,[17] although the information contained therein presumably would be available otherwise.

Trial Chamber I has also addressed that which does not fall within the category of exculpatory material: a lack of evidence. This determination was made with respect to a motion by the Defence, which argued that because a "lack of inculpatory evidence constitutes exculpatory evidence", the Prosecution should reveal the insufficiency of its case. The Trial Chamber denied the Defence request for such an acknowledgement on the basis that the

> time and place to raise the possible question of the lack of evidence can only be at the trial on the merits. Possible evaluation of the exculpatory nature of this lack of evidence can take place at that time only.[18]

Accordingly, the Trial Chamber found no basis for mandating that the Prosecution acknowledge any shortcomings in its case against an accused.

---

[15] *Prosecutor v. Blaškić, Decision on the Defence Motion for Sanctions for the Prosecutor's Failure to Comply with Sub-rule 66(a) of the Rules and the Decision of 27 January 1997 Compelling the Production of All Statements of the Accused*, Case No. IT-95-14-T, 15 July 1998.

[16] *Prosecutor v. Blaškić*, supra note at para. 12.

[17] *Prosecutor v. Blaškić*, supra note at paras. 26–30.

[18] *Prosecutor v. Blaškić*, supra note at para. 8.

Also with respect to exculpatory material, the Trial Chamber assumed that the Prosecution would employ good faith in complying with this rule, although it recognised that there is some subjectivity in determining what information or evidence will be exculpatory.[19]

It appears that there was some effort to counter the effects of any potential subjectivity on the part of the Defence in the implementation of Rule 66(B). This Rule allows the Defence to inspect items that are material to its preparation and the jurisprudence has established that in order to do so, the Defence is required to show by a *prima facie* case that the requested items are material and that the Prosecution has custody or control of the evidence.[20] Thus, where the Defence requested access to all documents and objects within the Prosecution's custody or control having to do with the accused or the camp in which the accused was alleged to have been involved, but failed to specifically allege why such evidence would be material to its preparation, the Trial Chamber denied access to the material.[21] The Trial Chamber found that it was "inappropriate for the Trial Chamber to intervene" "[g]iven the absence of a specific identification of material evidence that the defence alleges the Prosecution withheld".[22]

Considering that in most cases, the Defence will not know what evidence is in the custody of the Prosecution that may aid in the defence of the charges, this holding imposes a difficult standard on the Defence. In order to find out what information is available, it would appear necessary to issue a broad request for information. However, absent some knowledge of information in the Prosecution's custody, it seems that it would be difficult for the Defence to make this *prima facie* showing of materiality, putting the Defence in a quandary.

This same situation presents itself with respect to Rule 68, which requires the disclosure of exculpatory material. This is revealed by a Trial Chamber decision in which the Trial Chamber queried the standard for a Defence request for disclosure of materials not made in reliance on Rule 66(B) but based on Rule 68:

> Does the Defence which does not base its Motion on Sub-rule 66(B) – which would entail the obligation of mutual disclosure as required by Sub-rule 67(C) – have a general and unilateral right to inspect the Prosecutor's file by demanding and obtaining extensive and unrestricted disclosure?

The Trial Chamber answered that where the Defence believes that the Prosecution has not complied, not only must the Defence establish that the requested information is indeed in the possession of the Prosecution, but it

[19] *Prosecutor v. Blaškić, Decision*, Case No. IT-95-14-T, 29 April 1998.

[20] *Prosecutor v. Delalić and Others, Decision on Motion by the Accused Zejnil Delalić for the Disclosure of Evidence*, Case No. IT-96-21-PT, 26 Sept. 1996 at para. 9.

[21] Id., para. 10.

[22] Id.

must also "present a *prima facie* case which would make probable the exculpatory nature of the materials sought".[23]

The Trial Chambers have not cleared up this difficulty, but the manner in which the Defence can establish that evidence is in the possession of the Prosecution has been explained somewhat. In this same case, the Trial Chamber held that where the Defence moved for disclosure of exculpatory material, the Prosecution was obligated to state, with respect to each item of evidentiary material mentioned by the Defence, whether the Prosecution in fact had the material in its possession, whether the material contained exculpatory evidence, and whether the Prosecution believed that the confidentiality of the materials, if exculpatory, needed to be protected pursuant to Rule 66(C).[24] The Trial Chamber explicitly found that the initial response given by the Prosecutor that she "recognises her obligations under the Rule and has complied with them" was inadequate.

2.3 Notification Obligations for Witness Testimony

The Trial Chambers also have more clearly defined the responsibility of the parties with respect to notification regarding the witnesses that will testify at trial. The obligation of Rule 67(A) that the Prosecution give the names of its witnesses requires more than just informing the Defence of the witness names; in fact, it requires a "comprehensive document" containing a list of witnesses. Specifically, the Trial Chamber held that despite the acknowledgement of the Defence that the Prosecution had transmitted to the Defence the identify of over 100 witnesses names, more was needed:

> The Trial Chamber notes that Sub-rule 67(A) does not refer to an official list. However, by stipulating that the Prosecution has the obligation to inform the Defence of the names of the prosecution witnesses "as early as reasonably practicable and in any event prior to the commencement of the trial", the Rules support the idea that all the names of the prosecution witnesses must be disclosed at the same time in a comprehensive document which thus permits the Defence to have a clear and cohesive view of the Prosecution's strategy and to make the appropriate preparations.[25]

Another Trial Chamber declined to impose any additional obligation not articulated by this Rule on the Defence by its failure to require the Defence to present a list of witnesses prior to trial. After issuing a scheduling order in which it directed both the Prosecution and the Defence to present witness lists to the other side prior to trial, the Trial Chamber amended the order. This amendment was based on the Trial Chamber's determination that the

---

[23] *Prosecutor v. Blaškić*, supra note 13 at para. 49.
[24] Id., para. 47.
[25] Id., para. 22.

Rules did not impose such an obligation on the Defence absent an intent to present a special defence, holding that because the accused had "not given notice of its intent to offer any of the defences contemplated by Sub-rule 67(A)(ii)", the Defence was not obligated to provide a witness list to the Prosecution.[26] However, the Trial Chamber stopped short of holding that the Defence need never present a list of planned witnesses to the Prosecution. Indeed, the Trial Chamber in this same case later required the Defence to provide the name of each planned witness to be presented at trial "in writing at least seven working days prior to" that witness's testimony.[27] This Rule was not extended in another case, where a Trial Chamber explicitly held that the Defence need not disclose its intended witnesses. However, because this decision was limited to while the Prosecution was still presenting its case, it is unclear whether any additional obligation would be imposed during the Defence case.[28] Nonetheless, as the Rules clearly indicate, where the Defence alleges an alibi or special defence, the requirement that it provide the names and addresses of planned witnesses is "clear and unambiguous".[29] The disclosure obligation of the Defence beyond this has so far depended on the specific circumstances of each case.

2.4 Additional Obligations with respect to Disclosure

Another issue that has arisen is the timing of the disclosure obligations. The obligations found in Rules 66, 67 and 68 do not register until after the initial appearance of an accused, so despite the potential utility of such evidence in any proceedings that occur prior to that time, there is no entitlement to that information.[30] After that time, as noted above, the obligations are continuing.

---

[26]*Prosecution v. Delalić and Others, Decision on the Applications filed by the Defence for the Accused Zejnil Delalić and Esad Landžo on 14 February 1997 and 18 February 1997 Respectively*, Case No. IT-96-21-PT, 21 Feb. 1997 at paras. 10–11.

[27]*Prosecutor v. Delalić and Others, Decision on the Prosecutor's Motion for an Order Requiring Advance Disclosure of Witnesses by the Defence*, Case No. IT-96-21, 4 Feb. 1998. Instead of basing this decision on the disclosure obligations of Rule 67, the Trial Chamber relied on Rule 54 allowing orders "necessary for the conduct of the trial".

[28]*Prosecutor v. Blaškić, Decision of Trial Chamber I on the Prosecutor's Motion for Clarification of Order Requiring Advance Disclosure of Witnesses and for Order Requiring Reciprocal Advance Disclosure by the Defence*, Case No. IT-96-21-PT, 29 Jan. 1998.

[29]*Prosecutor v. Delalić and Others, Decision on the Motion to Compel the Disclosure of the Addresses of the Witnesses*, Case No. IT-96-21-T, 13 June 1997 at para. 11. While the Trial Chamber noted that the parties could not challenge their obligation under this Rule, it did note that the Defence could apply for protective measures that could stop the release of information about a witness, including name, address, or other identifying information.

[30]*Prosecutor v. Karadžić, Decision Partially Rejecting the Request Submitted by Mr. Igor Pantelić, Counsel for Radovan Karadžić*, Case. No. IT-95-5-R61/IT-95-18-R61, 27 June 1996, refusing a request for information at a Rule 61 hearing, holding instead that "access to the relevant documents and case files ... could only be granted as part of a trial following an initial appearance of the accused in person, pursuant to Rule 66".

A major issue of concern is the effect of the failure to comply with these obligations. While the Rules call for prompt notification of the Trial Chamber and the opposing party where it is believed that a party has not complied with its disclosure obligations, the Rules leave open the penalty or remedy for such situations. If an insufficient penalty were imposed, then there would be no incentive for the parties, particularly the Prosecution, to comply with these mandates. This is of special concern when one considers that it is likely that the Defence would not be aware of a lack of compliance absent some leak of information from the Prosecutor's office in the case that the Prosecution has information that it does not use at trial. While a potential solution could include sanctions or disallowing testimony or the presentation of evidence that the Prosecution failed to disclose, the Trial Chambers have so far declined to take such measures. For example, in the *Furundžija* case, wherein the Trial Chamber found that the Prosecution failed to comply with the disclosure obligations, the Trial Chamber merely noted its "grave concern" at the Prosecution's action and found this inaction "deplorable" and "unjustifiable".[31] Similarly, another Trial Chamber acknowledged that it would not seek a "sanctions approach" where the Prosecution failed to comply with Rule 68. Instead, that Trial Chamber held that it would evaluate the evidence presented and the extent to which the opposing party had the opportunity to contest the evidence, thereby making its decision as to the guilt or innocence of the accused on the merits.[32]

Perhaps the most severe reaction by a Trial Chamber to prosecutorial failure to abide by the disclosure obligations occurred later in the *Furundžija* case, where the Trial Chamber found that the Prosecution had failed to reveal that one of its witnesses had received psychological treatment following her rape that was the subject of her testimony. Based on the assertion that this information went to her credibility, the Defence argued for the Trial Chamber to strike her testimony or order a new trial. While agreeing that the Prosecution should have revealed the information, the Trial Chamber declined to take such harsh remedies. Instead, it re-opened the trial proceedings only on this issue.[33]

3. Conclusion

As can be seen from these decisions, the Trial Chambers of the ICTY have significantly expanded on and clarified the discovery obligations contained in the Rules of Procedure and Evidence. While many questions about these

[31] *Prosecutor v. Furundžija, Scheduling Order and Decision on Motion of Defendant Anto Furundžija to Preclude Testimony of Certain Prosecution Witnesses*, Case No. IT-95-17/1-T, 29 Apr. 1998.

[32] *Prosecutor v. Blaškić, Decision on the Defence Motion for Sanctions for the Prosecutor's Continuing Violation of Rule 68*, Case No. IT-95-14-T, 28 Sept. 1998.

[33] *Prosecutor v. Furundžija, Decision*, Case No. IT-95-17/1-T, 16 July 1998. See also *Prosecutor v. Furundžija, Scheduling Order*, Case No. IT-95-17/1-T, 17 July 1998.

Rules and their application remain, the continuing cases will present more issues arising in this context which will result in further explanations of the rights and responsibilities of the parties. Finally, with respect to the heightened disclosure obligations of the Prosecution, appropriate measures by the Trial Chambers in an event of non-compliance will have the effect of deterring future misconduct in this regard. Whether re-opening proceedings alone – as opposed to imposing sanctions – is enough remains to be seen. Because of the importance of the rights of the accused at stake, the seriousness of the crimes before the ICTY, and the key part discovery plays in an accused's defence, this is an area that requires special consideration by the Judges.

MARK B. HARMON and MAGDALINI KARAGIANNAKIS[1]

25. The Disclosure of Exculpatory Material by the Prosecution to the Defence under Rule 68 of the ICTY Rules

1. INTRODUCTION

A fundamental tenet of international criminal law is that trials should be fair. Rule 68 is an important procedural rule of the ICTY that gives expression to this fundamental requirement of fairness. This rule requires that the prosecution disclose to the defence the existence of evidence known to it which tends to suggest the innocence of the accused or mitigate his guilt or affect the credibility of prosecution evidence. The purpose of this article is to provide an analysis of the scope of this rule.

This paper will commence with some general comments regarding: the rationale of Rule 68; what this rule implies about the role of the Prosecutor; and its place in the context of the other main disclosure provisions under the ICTY Rules. The discussion will then turn to an analysis of the jurisprudence that has interpreted the rule and the manner in which it is to be

[1]Mark Harmon, B.A. J.D., Hastings College of Law, University of California. The author is a Senior Trial Attorney in the Office of the Prosecutor of the ICTY. In this capacity he prosecuted General Tihomir Blaškić and is currently prosecuting General Radislav Krstić for genocide, crimes against humanity and war crimes in relation to the events surrounding the fall of Srebrenica in July 1995. Prior to his current position he was employed by the United States Department of Justice, firstly as a Federal Prosecutor in the civil rights division and subsequently as a Federal Prosecutor and Unit Chief in the Environmental Crimes Section. In this capacity he prosecuted Exxon Corporation for the Exxon Valdez oil spill. Magdalini Karagiannakis, B.Ec.LLB LLM.(Monash University) and LLM Public International Law *cum laude* (Leiden University). The author is an Associate Legal Officer in the Trial Section of the Office of the Prosecutor currently working on the trial of General Radislav Krstić. Prior to her current position she was an Associate Legal Officer in the Judges Chambers of the ICTY and has previously worked for the Deputy Agent for Bosnia and Herzegovina in the genocide case of Bosnia and Herzegovina v Yugoslavia (Serbia and Montenegro) before the International Court of Justice. The views expressed herein are those of the authors and not of the United Nations or the Office of the Prosecutor of the ICTY.

R. May et al., Essays on ICTY Procedure and Evidence in Honour of Gabrielle Kirk McDonald, 315–328.

applied. Further, some suggestions as to the general manner in which Rule 68 should be interpreted will be made. Finally, there will be a discussion as to how the defence can contribute to better disclosure under Rule 68. The decisions which will be referred to in this paper, bar one decision of the ICTY Appeals Chamber, have been handed down by various Trial Chambers of the ICTY. They indicate the judicial conceptualisation of this rule and may constitute persuasive authority for other Trial Chambers.

2. General Comments

2.1 Underlying rationale of the rule and implications for the role of the Prosecutor

Rule 68 provides that the Prosecutor:

> shall, as soon as practicable, disclose to the defence the existence of evidence known to the Prosecutor which in any way tends to suggest the innocence or mitigate the guilt of the accused or may affect the credibility of prosecution evidence.

This is a broad definition that is intended to ensure that the rights of the accused, as enshrined in Articles 20 and 21 are maintained.[2] The disclosure of exculpatory evidence should be seen in the broader context of the role of the Prosecutor in the administration of international criminal justice. In a *Decision* rendered in *Kupreškić* on 21 September 1998, the Trial Chamber interpreted this role and stated that,

> the Prosecutor of the Tribunal is not, or not only, a Party to adversarial proceedings but is an organ of the Tribunal and an organ of international criminal justice whose object is not simply to secure a conviction but to present the case for the Prosecution, which includes not only inculpatory, *but also exculpatory evidence, in order to assist the Chamber to discover the truth in a judicial setting.*[3] (Emphasis added.)

This view was most recently expressed by Judge Shahabuddeen in his Separate Opinion appended to the ICTR Appeals Chamber Decision on the

---

[2]Rule 68 was amended at the suggestion of the International Law Committee of the Association of the Bar of the City of New York, at the fifth plenary session in January 1995, "to broaden the rights of suspects and accused persons" by adding the last eight words (second Annual Report, para. 26: "Rule 68 was amended so that the Prosecutor's obligation to disclose to the defence exculpatory evidence which tended to suggest the innocence or mitigate the guilt of the accused now extends to any evidence which may affect the credibility of prosecution evidence").

[3]*Prosecutor v. Kupreškić and Others, Decision on Communication Between the Parties and Their Witnesses*, Case No. IT-95-16-T, 21 Sept. 1998 at p. 3, para. (ii).

Prosecutor's Request for Review or Reconsideration in *Barayagwiza*, where he stated:

> The Prosecutor [...] is not required to be neutral in a case; she is a party. But she is not of course a partisan. This is why, for example, the Rules of the Tribunal require the Prosecutor to disclose to the defence all exculpatory material. The implications of that requirement suggest that, while a prosecution must be conducted vigorously, there is room for the injunction that prosecuting counsel "ought to bear themselves rather in the character of ministers of justice assisting in the administration of justice."[4] (Footnote omitted.)

Therefore it may be said that, as well as securing the right of the accused to a fair trial, Rule 68 is a provision which demonstrates that the role of the Prosecutor is one of a party to the proceedings representing the international community and as an officer of the court assisting in the proper administration of international criminal justice.

2.2 Rule 68 in the context of other disclosure provisions in the Rules of the ICTY

The ICTY is not a jurisdiction where the whole of the prosecution's file is automatically provided to the defence. Rather it is a system which requires the prosecution to disclose certain specified material to the defence. In addition to discovery obligations under Rule 68, Rule 66 requires the disclosure to the defence of: the supporting material which accompanied the indictment when it was confirmed by a Judge, prior statements obtained by the Prosecutor from the accused, statements of all the witnesses whom the Prosecutor intends to call at trial and copies of affidavits and formal statements that will be used to corroborate a witnesses' testimony pursuant to Rule 94*ter*. Another relevant provision is Rule 65*ter*(E) which requires the prosecution to include in its pre-trial filing a list of witnesses[5] that it intends to call and a list of exhibits. In addition, a full statement of any expert witness must be disclosed to the opposing party pursuant to Rule 94*bis*. Finally, Rule 70(B) requires that information disclosed to the Prosecutor on a confidential basis and used solely for the purpose of generating new evidence may be introduced into evidence if the person or entity providing the information has consented, and only if disclosed to the accused prior to its introduction into evidence.

---

[4]*Barayagwiza v. Prosecutor, Decision (Prosecutor's Request for Review of Reconsideration)*, Case No. ICTR-97-19-AR72, A. Ch., 31 March 2000, Separate Opinion of Judge Shahabuddeen at para. 68.

[5]Pursuant to Rule 65*ter*(E)(iv) this list must include: the name and pseudonym of each witness, a summary of the facts on which each witness will testify, the points in the indictment as to which each witness will testify and the estimated length of the testimony.

As can be seen from the forgoing description, of all of these disclosure rules, Rule 68 is the least specific in its description of what must be provided to the defence. This reflects that fact that its application is heavily dependent upon the particular facts of each case.

If the defence wishes to inspect any books, documents, photographs and tangible objects in the Prosecutor's custody or control which is material to the preparation of the defence or is intended for use by the Prosecutor at trial or which was obtained or belonged to the accused, it may do so by making a request pursuant to Rule 66(B). By doing so the defence triggers reciprocal discovery which entitles the prosecution, by virtue of Rule 67(C), to inspect any books, documents, photographs and tangible objects, which are within the custody or control of the defence and which it intends to use as evidence at trial.

3. The scope of Rule 68

3.1 The meaning of exculpatory evidence

A general definition of what constitutes exculpatory evidence under Rule 68 was first provided in the *Decision on the Request of the Accused Pursuant to Rule 68 for Exculpatory Information* rendered on 24 June 1997 in *Delalić*. The Chamber defined such evidence as:

> material which is known to the Prosecutor and which is favourable to the accused in the sense that it tends to suggest the innocence or mitigate the guilt of the accused or may affect the credibility of prosecution evidence.[6]

This definition is very general and largely repeats the expression of the rule itself. This generality in definition is understandable given that the issue of what evidence may be exculpatory evidence is primarily a facts based judgement and is therefore difficult to define in the abstract.

Further clarification on this issue was most recently provided by Judge Hunt acting as Pre-Trial Judge in *Krnojelac*, when he found that, in the context of Rule 68:

> The expression "evidence" is intended to include any material which may put the accused on notice that material exists which may assist him in his defence, *and is not limited to material which is itself admissible in evidence*.[7] (Emphasis added.)

---

[6] *Prosecutor v. Delalić and Others, Decision on the Request of the Accused Pursuant to Rule 68 for Exculpatory Information*, Case No. IT-96-21-T, 24 June 1997 at para. 12.

[7] *Prosecutor v. Krnojelac, Record of Rulings Made in Status Conference*, Case No. IT-97-25-PT, 14 Sept. 1999 at p. 2 para. 1. A record of rulings so made does not constitute a written decision of the Pre-Trial Judge but is simply a record of oral orders made.

This is arguably an even broader definition than that posited in *Delalić* in that the final phrase of this definition explicitly extends Rule 68 obligations to any material notwithstanding any issues of admissibility. There is a question as to whether this finding would substantially broaden the pool of material that must be considered for the purposes of Rule 68 given the very broad rules of admissibility of evidence before the ICTY.[8]

Further, with respect to documents not in the public domain, it has been held by one Trial Chamber that pursuant to Rule 68, the Prosecutor is obliged to disclose "certain documents, with no distinction made which is based on their non-public nature".[9] This accords with the plain meaning of the rule that requires the disclosure of all material "known to the Prosecutor". In practice, this phrase requires the Prosecutor to search the evidence known to her in order to identify which evidence may be exculpatory under Rule 68. As will be discussed below, Trial Chamber I has stated that the obligation to disclose exculpatory information lies solely with the Prosecutor because "if for no other reason she is the one in possession of the materials."[10] This reasoning may be considered to imply that the reason that the Prosecutor carries the burden under Rule 68 is because she has a monopoly on certain materials that may be exculpatory. If the defence has equal access to certain materials which the Prosecutor also has access to, for example material in the public domain, then she is no longer the only entity which is in this position. Therefore the rationale for imposing this obligation on the prosecution falls away and arguably, so should the obligation to disclose. This issue will be discussed further in the specific context of whether public materials should be included in the possible pool of evidence which should be subject to Rule 68.

In addition to these general comments, it is helpful to consider specific categories of material which have been held to be exculpatory by Trial Chambers of the Tribunal. These include:

- evidence in a document or written form or included in a database,[11]
- evidence in the case files of other accused persons,[12]

[8]Rule 89(C) provides that a Chamber may admit any relevant evidence which it deems to have probative value. Other rules relevant to the admissibility of evidence are Rules 89(D) and 95.

[9]*Prosecutor v. Aleksovski, Opinion Further to the Decision of the Trial Chamber seized of the Case the Prosecutor v. Dairo Kordić and Mario Čerkez dated 12 November 1998*, Case No. IT-95-14/1-T, 8 Feb. 1999 ("*Aleksovski Decision*") at p. 4 and *Prosecutor v. Blaškić, Opinion Further to the Decision of the Trial Chamber seized of the Case the Prosecutor v. Dairo Kordić and Mario Čerkez dated 12 November 1998*, IT-95-14-T, 16 Dec. 1998 ("*Blaškić Decision*") at p. 4.

[10]*Prosecutor v. Blaškić, Decision on the Production of Discovery Materials*, Case No. IT-95-14-T, 27 Jan. 1997 ("*Blaškić Discovery Decision*") at para. 47.

[11]Id., para. 54.

[12]Id., paras. 26–30.

- testimony of witnesses made in another case and associated exhibits. In this scenario the fact that a witness is subject to protective measures in one case does not relieve the prosecution of its obligation under Rule 68; it is for the prosecution to seek further protective measures,[13]
- a redacted certificate and a witness statement from a psychologist concerning the treatment that a prosecution witness had received on the basis that the evidence "clearly had the potential to affect the "credibility of prosecution evidence".[14] In this case the Trial Chamber reasoned that the witnesses' testimony was pivotal to the prosecution case and the defence had been conducted on the basis that the witnesses' memory was flawed. Therefore, any evidence relating to the medical, psychiatric or psychological treatment of the accused was clearly relevant to the accused's defence,
- material which impugns the evidence of a person whose statement is to be introduced as hearsay. Under Rule 66(A) a hearsay declarant is not a witness whose prior statements must be disclosed to the defence, however prior statements must be disclosed if they are exculpatory pursuant to Rule 68.[15]

There are materials that are not considered exculpatory, or if considered as such, need not be disclosed upon a lawful basis. For example, a lack of evidence is not considered exculpatory.[16] Further, information that has been disclosed to the prosecution on a confidential basis and has been used solely for the purpose of generating new evidence pursuant to Rule 70(B) may be considered exempt from disclosure under Rule 68 if the information is not at issue in the case in point and the person or entity providing it objects to its disclosure.

There does not appear to be any case law regarding the issues of whether work product, documents in the public domain and documents which are inculpatory of co-accused, are subject to Rule 68 disclosure. There may be valid arguments that militate both for and against the consideration of these categories of evidence as falling within the purview of Rule 68. For example, the work product of the prosecution may properly be considered as material prepared for the purposes of conducting litigation and therefore confidential. However, in this case the decision regarding disclosure will depend on the nature of the work product. For example, an analysis of evidence may rightly be considered as confidential whereas investigators' notes disclosing the name of an alibi witness may be considered as exculpatory. In the latter

---

[13]*Aleksovski Decision*, supra note 9, at p. 4 and *Blaškić Decision*, supra note 9, at p. 3.
[14]*Prosecutor v. Furundžija*, Decision, Case No. IT-95-17/1-T, 16 July 1988 at p. 6.
[15]*Prosecutor v. Blaškić, Decision on the Defence Motion to Compel the Disclosure of Rule 66 and 68 material relating to statements made by a Person known as "X"*, Case No. IT-95-14-T, 15 July 1998.
[16]*Blaškić Discovery Decision* supra note 10, at para. 25.

case, whilst the work product itself should not be disclosed, the existence of a possible alibi witness should be disclosed.

Another as yet undecided general question is whether documents in the public domain fall within the terms of Rule 68. The terms of Rule 68 state that the scope of this rule extends to "evidence known to the Prosecutor". Thus the rule does not on its terms make any distinction between public evidence and non-public evidence. However if, in order to comply with Rule 68, the Prosecutor must search through the information known to her and this evidence is considered to include materials in the public domain, for example material which is readily accessible on the internet or in public libraries, then this could be viewed as amounting to an obligation to search material establishing both its case and the case for the defence.

Whilst the Prosecutor is an officer of the court with an obligation to assist in the conduct of a fair trial, her obligations and role cannot be said to extend to that of investigator for the defence. Therefore, the term "known to the Prosecutor" should not be construed so widely as to impose upon the Prosecutor an obligation to search and/or disclose possibly exculpatory information from public sources equally available to the defence. That task, rightly and more appropriately, belongs to the defence itself, which is in the best position to assess the evidence which is helpful to it.

This issue has recently arisen in *Blaškić* where the appellant alleged that the prosecution had "withheld" witness testimony given in another case which ought to have been disclosed to the appellant under Rule 68. One argument in response to this allegation may be that the prosecution did not withhold this testimony because each of these witness testified in open session, so that their testimony was as freely available to the defence as it was to any staff of the Office of the Prosecutor. This matter is pending before the Appeals Chamber.

Information which is inculpatory of other accused allegedly involved in the same cluster of offences is a more difficult category of evidence to consider in this context. However, evidence that indicates that another person may have been responsible for the commission of an offence for which the accused is charged could justifiably be considered as exculpatory.

However, this view ought to be tempered by the reality of the manner in which crimes were committed in the Former Yugoslavia. These crimes usually involve a cluster of offences committed by or with the involvement of numerous individuals. These perpetrators may range from those at the top of a military chain of command or a political structure, who may order the commission of crimes, all the way through to the individuals who actually commit them. This is reflected in indictments that name multiple defendants in relation to the same criminal transaction but charge each accused in accordance with their alleged involvement. In these circumstances, it cannot fairly be said that any evidence inculpating one accused or a third party is *ipso facto* evidence which is exculpatory of another accused. In this situation a judgement must be made based on the facts of each case.

3.2 Form of disclosure under Rule 68

Even if evidence can be considered exculpatory, Rule 68 only requires the prosecution to disclose to the defence "the *existence* of evidence" to which the rule applies. The prosecution is not required to actually *provide* the defence with all of the evidence in question according to the plain ordinary meaning of the rule.

In practice however, the prosecution has adopted a mixed approach. On some occasions it has informed the defence of the existence of exculpatory evidence and on others it has exercised its discretion to go beyond its legal obligation by actually providing the exculpatory evidence. Again, such judgements will of course depend on the circumstances of each case and the nature of the evidence to be disclosed.

If the evidence itself is to be disclosed, pursuant to an exercise of prosecutorial discretion or a court order, then Rule 68 only requires the disclosure of the portions of the Prosecutor's documentation that are exculpatory and not all or an entire section of the Prosecutor's documentation. The prosecution is able to redact from the documents it discloses the passages that are confidential and constitute neither incriminating nor exculpatory evidence.[17] If redacted evidence is disclosed or ordered to be disclosed, it should be "sufficiently cohesive, understandable and usable".[18] For example, if exculpatory material is contained in a few paragraphs of a 70-page witness statement, there is no obligation to disclose the entire statement. Only the sections that contain the exculpatory material should be provided to the defence. The justification for this is clear: the other sections may not be relevant or may contain sensitive material that relates to other investigations or may identify confidential sources.

3.3 Temporal scope of Rule 68

It is important to note that the terms of Rule 68 do not contain any explicit temporal restrictions, although it has been stated by at least one Trial Chamber that the obligations under this rule are of a continuous nature.[19]

The issue as to whether Rule 68 applies after the close of trial has recently arisen before the ICTY Appeals Chamber in *Blaškić* where the appellant submitted that Rule 68 imposes a continuing obligation to which the Prosecutor remains subject even after the end of trial proceedings. The prosecution accepts that its obligation continues throughout the trial

---

[17]*Prosecutor v. Blaškić, Decision on the Defence Motion for Sanctions for the Prosecutor's Repeated Violations of Rule 68 of the Rules of Procedure and Evidence*, Case No. IT-95-14-T, 29 Apr. 1998 ("*Blaškić Sanctions Decision*") at para. 20.

[18]Id., para. 19.

[19]*Prosecutor v. Kordić and Čerkez, Order on Motion to Compel Compliance by the Prosecutor with Rules 66(A) and 68*, Case No. IT-95-14/2-PT, 26 Feb. 1999 at p. 5.

proceedings but does not continue after they have concluded. Once trial proceedings have concluded, the prosecution argues, if it became aware of the existence of evidence which cast serious doubt on the correctness of the Trial Chamber's judgement, it would so inform the defence. However it would not do so by operation of Rule 68 but by virtue of its role as an organ of the Tribunal and of international criminal justice. This obligation is different from that imposed by Rule 68. Rule 68 may be considered broader in the sense that it applies to evidence which may not be likely to affect the verdict but may be material to the defence such as evidence which points to inconsistency in some aspect of the prosecution case or affects the credibility of some prosecution evidence. Further, once the judgement has been handed down the principle of finality dictates that the Judgement must be taken to be correct, subject to appeal, review or the presentation of additional evidence which of itself would be sufficient to affect the verdict. This matter is currently pending before the ICTY Appeals Chamber.

4. Obligations of the Prosecution

The prosecution bears sole responsibility for disclosure under Rule 68 subject to the supervision of the Trial Chamber.[20] This obligation arises out of necessity and has been recognised as being tinged with subjectivity. However there may be a presumption that the Prosecutor has acted in good faith.[21] This last point may be interpreted as being related to the Prosecutor's understanding that, as well as being a party to the proceedings, she is an officer of the court as discussed above.

In the recent oral order made in *Krnojelac*, Judge Hunt acting as Pre-Trial Judge imposed upon the prosecution an obligation to file an affidavit of its analyst in which he or she testifies that:

(a) a full search has been conducted through the materials in the possession of the prosecution or otherwise within its knowledge for the existence of such evidence; and
(b) he or she is aware of the continuing nature of the obligation pursuant to Rule 68.[22]

In a subsequent decision this order was modified to require, *inter alia*, a report to be signed by a member of the prosecution team. In the decision modifying the order Judge Hunt explained that the reason for requiring certification was:

[20] *Blaškić Discovery Decision*, supra note 10, at paras. 47 and 50(1) and *Blaškić Sanctions Decision*, supra note 17, at para. 14.
[21] *Blaškić Sanctions Decision*, supra note 17, at para. 21.
[22] Supra note 7, at p. 2 para. 2.

> [...] to impose some type of additional onus on the prosecution to ensure compliance with the rule, so that one person would take responsibly for giving such an assurance. Having to swear an affidavit is an effective way of focussing the mind of the deponent upon his or her responsibilities [...] [and is] a practical way of avoiding that person having to give oral evidence in the interlocutory proceedings under solemn declaration [...].[23]

The issue as to whether it is proper to require such certification has recently arisen in *Blaškić* where the appellant sought further discovery under, *inter alia*, Rule 68 after the end of trial, and requested that the prosecution provide the appellant with a signed certification that the prosecution had complied with the request for further discovery and was aware of its continuing obligation under, *inter alia*, Rule 68. The prosecution recognised that certification had been required in *Krnojelac* but considered that such an order was inappropriate in this case because it did not reflect the common practice in cases before the Tribunal. In addition disclosure obligations are imposed directly by the Rules and no signed certification is necessary to ensure observance of these obligations. In addition it can be said that as officers of the court prosecution counsel are clearly aware of their obligations and discharge them in good faith. This matter is currently pending before the ICTY Appeals Chamber.

5. Process to be undertaken in the event of a defence motion for the disclosure of exculpatory material

If the prosecution considers that it has fulfilled its disclosure obligations but the defence considers that there is further evidence which should be disclosed, the defence must make a motion indicating the specific material it regards as exculpatory and presenting a *prima facie* case that would tend to make it likely that the evidence is exculpatory and is in the Prosecutor's possession.[24]

Trial Chamber I has more fully specified the procedure to be followed if the defence meets this requirement. It has held that in this event the prosecution should reply, in respect of all the materials mentioned by the defence,

---

[23] *Prosecutor v. Krnojelac, Decision on Motion by Prosecution to Modify order for Compliance with Rule 68*, Case No. IT-97-25-PT, 1 Nov. 1999 at para. 9.

[24] *Blaškić Discovery Decision* supra note 10, at para. 50(2); *Blaškić Sanctions Decision*, supra note 17, at para. 14; *Prosecutor v. Delalić and Others, Decision on Motion by the Accused Zejnil Delalić for the Disclosure of Evidence*, Case No. IT-96-21-T, 26 Sept. 1996 at para. 49; supra note 6, at para. 18. In this case the motion was denied by the Chamber, which, following the test laid down in *Blaškić Discovery Decision*, concluded "that the Defence has failed to indicate the specific material it regards as exculpatory and which should be disclosed pursuant to Rule 68. Moreover, the Defence has failed to show prima facie that the information it seeks to be disclosed is in fact exculpatory".

- whether the materials are in fact in her possession;
- whether the materials contain exculpatory evidence;
- whether she believes that although she does possess exculpatory materials, Sub-rule 66(C) or any other relevant provision require that their confidentiality be protected.

In these circumstances it is not considered sufficient that the Prosecutor declares that she "recognises her obligations under the Rule and has complied with them."[25]

The Trial Chamber may then, exercising its powers of supervision over disclosure, make further orders, such as an order for the verification of materials in its possession and possibly for the actual disclosure of materials.[26]

6. Sanctions for Prosecutor's failure to comply with Rule 68

Trial Chamber I sitting in the *Blaškić* case has said that it does not take a "sanctions approach" to non-compliance by the Prosecutor with Rule 68, but rather it examines in each case whether or not the defence has been prejudiced by that non-compliance and then acts accordingly.[27] This is a sound approach.

If there has been a failure to comply with Rule 68 a Trial Chamber may order that a trial be reopened. In the *Furundžija Decision* dated 16 July 1998, the Trial Chamber found "serious misconduct on the part of the Prosecution" in failing to disclose to the defence evidence to the effect that a prosecution witness, who was an alleged rape victim, had received psychological treatment following the rape. The Trial Chamber held that the prosecution should have disclosed the evidence in question as it clearly affected the credibility of prosecution evidence, and stated that if the prosecution had wished to withhold disclosure for public policy reasons, it should have followed the procedure laid down in Rule 66(C),[28] which states:

> (C) Where information is in the possession of the Prosecutor, the disclosure of which may prejudice further or ongoing investigations, or for any other reasons may be contrary to the public interest or affect the security interests of any State, the Prosecutor may apply to the Trial Chamber sitting *in camera* to be relieved from the obligation to disclose pursuant to Sub-rule (B). When making

[25] *Blaškić Discovery Decision,* supra note 10, at paras. 47 and 56.

[26] *Blaškić Discovery Decision*, supra note 10, at para. 47 and *Blaškić Sanctions Decision*, supra note 17, at para. 19.

[27] *Prosecutor v. Blaškić, Decision on the Defence Motion for Sanctions for the Prosecutor's Continuing Violation of Rule 68*, Case No. IT-95-14-T, 28 Sept. 1998 at p. 3.

[28] Supra note 14, at paras. 18 and 19.

> such application the Prosecutor shall provide the Trial Chamber (but only the Trial Chamber) with the information that is sought to be kept confidential.

Despite the defence request that the evidence of the witness be struck from the record or that a new trial be ordered in this case, the Trial Chamber simply re-opened the trial to deal with this specific issue.

7. The manner in which Rule 68 should be interpreted

As noted above Rule 68 is one of the most important and general discovery provisions under the ICTY Rules. In interpreting the scope of this rule emphasis must be put on its position in the context of the other discovery provisions under the Rules and the maintenance of the balance between them, which would consequently affect the balance of the trial.

Before the *Blaškić* trial was due to commence, the Trial Chamber was faced with a very broad request for discovery by the defence. This was characterised as a request for a "general right of inspection" of the Prosecutor's material under Rule 68. In responding to this request the Trial Chamber noted that the border between Rule 66(B) and Rule 68 was tenuous. It refused the defence request on the basis that:

> The Trial Chamber [...] has the responsibility of ensuring that the balance of the respective rights of the parties in this matter be honoured. Thus, if the Trial Chamber notes that the Defence does not wish to honour the need for balanced reciprocal disclosure provided for in Sub-rules 66(B) and 67(C), it must then be particularly vigilant as to limiting the nature and extent of the request for exculpatory evidence from the Prosecutor's file [...].[29]

In this case the Trial Chamber was mindful of expanding the application of Rule 68 to the extent that it would give the defence extensive access to the prosecutor's files and thereby render the reciprocal discovery provision under the Rules redundant. This seems to be a sound approach to the application of Rule 68 as it maintains the relationship between the different discovery provisions under the Rules. It is therefore an approach which should, it is submitted, be adopted by other Trial Chambers.

8. The defence can facilitate Rule 68 disclosure

As noted above, the main purpose of Rule 68 is to ensure a fair trial. This right is enshrined in Articles 20 and 21 of the Statute. Closely linked to the right to a fair trial is the fundamental right to be tried expeditiously (Article

---

[29] *Blaškić Discovery Decision*, supra note 10, at paras. 47–49.

20) and without undue delay (Article 21(c)). The disclosure duty imposed on the Prosecutor by Rule 68 contributes to achieving these fundamental goals of international justice. However, one must not ignore that the defence can, in the context of Rule 68 disclosure, contribute to the fulfilment of these objectives.

Pursuant to Rule 65*ter*(F)(i), the defence is required to disclose the general nature of the accused's defence quite late in the pre-trial stage, specifically, after the receipt of the Prosecutor's Rule 65*ter*(E) filing which contains the pre-trial brief addressing legal and factual issues and witness summaries. However, there is nothing sacrosanct about the timing of this disclosure. Instead, if the defence were to disclose the general nature of the defence as early as practicable, and well before the time embedded in the Rule 65*ter*(F)(i), this would permit the Prosecutor to focus her searches for exculpatory material and avoid large, time-consuming and speculative inquiries. Such focused searches would lead to early disclosure of exculpatory material and would permit the defence to more thoroughly benefit from the fruits of this disclosure by allowing them to properly investigate the nature of the exculpatory material and by developing possible investigative leads from it.

In evaluating whether the Prosecutor has discharged her responsibilities under Rule 68 in the face of a claim by the defence that exculpatory material has not been disclosed in a timely fashion, the Trial Chamber should include in its evaluation whether the Prosecutor has requested that the defence identify the general nature of the defence and whether the defence has refused to provide it. The defence should not be permitted to simply refuse to take modest steps that will ensure the best and earliest Rule 68 disclosure possible and later seek to sanction the Prosecutor if this does not occur.

9. Conclusion

Rule 68 can be described as one of the regulatory cornerstones of fairness under the ICTY Rules. Its application can be critical for the preparation and conduct of the defence case and hence it is broad in its scope. It, more than any other discovery rule, contains the most general description of what must be disclosed because its application depends so significantly on the facts of each case. The fact that this obligation falls on the Prosecutor indicates that her role in criminal proceedings is one of an officer of the court and international criminal justice. In applying this Rule the Trial Chambers of the Tribunal have taken a generally balanced attitude. They have interpreted the definition of the term "exculpatory evidence" broadly, thereby properly ensuring the rights of the accused to have access to information which may assist them in their defence. However there are also indications that at least one Trial Chamber has been careful in maintaining a balance between providing exculpatory evidence and allowing the defence to be granted broad access to the Prosecutor's files thereby allowing the defence to avoid the reciprocal obligations it would have pursuant to Rules 66 and 67 and consequently disturbing the balance of the trial.[30] Finally, the defence can also play a role in ensuring a fair and expeditious trial through Rule 68 disclosure. It can do so by disclosing the general nature of the accused's defence as early as practicable, and well before the time embedded in the Rule 65*ter*(F)(i), thus permitting the Prosecutor to focus her searches in order to produce the best and earliest Rule 68 disclosure possible.

POSTSCRIPT: On 26 September 2000 the Appeals Chamber of the ICTY handed down the *Decision on the Appellant's Motion for the Production of Material, Suspension or Extension of the Briefing Schedule, and Additional Filings*, (Prosecutor v. Blaškić Case No. IT-95-14-A). In this decision it was held that the Prosecution is under a continuing obligation under Rule 68 to disclose exculpatory evidence at the post-trial stage, including appeals (para. 42). In reaching this decision the Appeals Chamber considered that the Prosecution could be relieved of its Rule 68 obligation if the existence of relevant exculpatory evidence is known and the evidence is accessible to the Appellant (para. 38). Further, the Appeals Chamber opined that without proof that the Prosecution abused its discretion in deciding what evidence fell within the ambit of Rule 68, it would not be inclined to intervene in the way such discretion was exercised (para. 39). Finally, the Appeals Chamber held that the Prosecution need not provide a certificate acknowledging, *inter alia*, its compliance with Rule 68 as a matter of course, on the basis that the Prosecution is expected to fulfil its obligations in good faith (para. 45).

[30] *Blaškić Discovery Decision*, supra note 17, at para. 20.

EUGENE O'SULLIVAN[1]

26. Judicial Notice

This paper examines the interpretation and application by the International Tribunal of the concept of judicial notice under Rule 94 of the Rules of Procedure and Evidence ("RPE").[2] Rule 94 is found in Section Three of Part Six of the RPE, which contains Rules 89 to 98, the ten rules of evidence which are used in proceedings before the International Tribunal. Rule 94 reads as follows:

Rule 94

Judicial Notice

(A) Trial Chamber shall not require proof of facts of common knowledge but shall take judicial notice thereof.

(B) At the request of a party or *proprio motu*, a Trial Chamber, after hearing the parties, may decide to take judicial notice of adjudicated facts or documentary evidence from other proceedings of the Tribunal relating to matters at issue in the current proceedings.[3]

---

[1]The author is a Professor of Law at Laurentian University in Sudbury, Canada, a Researcher at L'Institut des sciences criminelles in Poitiers, France and a member of the Law Society of British Columbia, Canada. At trial before the International Criminal Tribunal for the former Yugoslavia, he represented the accused Zejnil Delalić in the case of the *Prosecutor v. Delalić and Others* and Milojica Kos in the case of the *Prosecutor v. Kvočka and Others*.

[2]IT/32/REV.17 (7 Dec. 1999).

[3]See also Rules of Procedure and Evidence of the International Criminal Tribunal for Rwanda ("ICTR"), Rule 94 which reads, as follows: "A Trial Chamber shall not require proof of facts of common knowledge but shall take judicial notice". There is no equivalent to Rule 94(B) in the Rules of the ICTR.

R. May et al., Essays on ICTY Procedure and Evidence in Honour of Gabrielle Kirk McDonald, 329–339.

A Trial Chamber may take judicial notice of three types of evidence: facts of common knowledge pursuant to Rule 94(A), adjudicated facts or documentary evidence from other proceedings of the Tribunal pursuant to Rule 94(B). A Trial Chamber may take judicial notice of a fact on its own initiative or at the request of a party. Judicial notice may be taken over the objection of a party; however, a Trial Chamber may only take judicial notice after hearing the parties if the facts in question are adjudicated facts or documentary evidence within the meaning of Rule 94(B).

In regards to the interpretation and application of the rules of evidence contained in Rules 89 to 98 of the RPE, the jurisprudence of the International Tribunal has recognised as a general proposition that the terms used therein carry their own specific meaning, suited for an international criminal court and that a Trial Chamber is not bound by national rules of evidence.[4] Furthermore, pursuant to Rule 89(B), a Trial Chamber is required to apply rules of evidence which best favour a fair determination of an evidentiary issue in a manner that is consonant with the spirit of the Statute and the general principles of law, including the general principles of municipal law.[5] As discussed below, judicial notice is a well-established legal concept in many countries around the world and as such reflects general principles of law which may form the basis for the interpretation and application of the RPE. For this reason, it seems appropriate to turn to those legal regimes as an interpretative aid in determining the definition and scope of judicial notice under Rule 94. In addition, although analogy is normally inadmissible with regard to substantive rules of international criminal law, it may be warranted to fill lacunae in the interpretation and application of international rules of criminal procedure.[6] This view is qualified with the proviso that resorting to analogy should not lead to results contrary to the intent of the law-making body or fall afoul of the basic *ratio* behind the enactment, nor should it result in infringements or unjust restrictions of fundamental human rights.[7]

---

[4]*Prosecutor v. Blaškić, Decision on the Objection of the Republic of Croatia to the Issuance of Subpoenae Duces Tecum*, Case No. IT-95-14-PT, 18 July 1997 at paras. 60–61; and *Prosecutor v. Tadić, Separate and Dissenting Opinion of Judge McDonald on Prosecution Motion on Defence Witness Statements*, Case No. IT-94-1-T, 27 Nov. 1996.

[5]See, *Prosecutor v. Tadić, Separate Opinion of Judge Stephen on Prosecution Motion for Production of Defence Witness Statements*, Case No. IT-94-1-T, 27 Nov. 1996 at p. 6; *Prosecutor v. Delalić and Others, Decision on the Motion to Allow Witness K, L and M to Give Their Testimony by Means of Video-link Conference*, Case No. IT-92-21-T, 28 May 1997 at paras. 8–10; and *Prosecutor v. Kupreškić and Others, Judgement*, Case No. IT-95-16-T, 14 Jan. 2000 at para. 539.

[6]*Prosecutor v. Delalić and Others, Decision of the President on the Prosecutor's Motion for the Production of Notes Exchanged between Zejnil Delalić and Zdravko Mucić*, Case No. IT-96-21, 11 Nov. 1996 at para. 24.

[7]Id.

Judicial notice is a rule of judicial convenience which is known in virtually all Common Law jurisdictions.[8] In Civil Law criminal systems, on the other hand, the concept of judicial notice does not exist.[9] Taking judicial notice is an exception to the general rule that all facts in issue or relevant to the issue in a given case must be proved by evidence – testimony, statements, documents or things.[10] As the review of the authorities surveyed in this part of the paper suggests, the ability of a Trial Chamber to take judicial notice of adjudicated facts or documentary evidence from other proceedings of the Tribunal under Rule 94(B) broadens the scope of the doctrine of judicial notice as it is generally understood in municipal law.

Black's Law Dictionary (1990) defines judicial notice in the following way:

> The act by which a court, in conducting a trial, or framing its decision, will of its own motion or on request of a party, and without the production of evidence, recognize the existence of the truth of certain facts, having a bearing on the controversy at bar, which, from their nature, are not properly the subject of testimony, or which are universally regarded as established by common notoriety, e.g., the laws of the state, international law, historical events, the constitution and course of nature, main geographic features, etc. The cognizance of certain facts which judges and jurors may properly take and act upon without proof, because they already know them. Hutchison v. State, Ind,. 477 N.E. 2nd 850, 854. Fed. Evid. Rule 201.[11]

There is no strict definition about the category or class of facts which may be noticed. However, it is clear that a court may only notice, without proof, facts which can be described as being too notorious to be the subject of serious dispute[12] or that are known to everyone.[13] Here are a few examples

---

[8]See, for example, United Kingdom: Rupert Cross et al., Cross on Evidence (1990); P.J. Richardson, Archbold: Criminal Pleading, Evidence and Practice (1999); Peter Murphy (Ed.-in-Ch.), Blackstone's Criminal Practice 1998 (1998); U.S.A.: J.B Weinstein et al., Evidence (1997); Canada: John Sopinka et al., The Law of Evidence in Canada (1992); New Zealand: Cross on Evidence (1989); Hong Kong: Andrew Bruce, Criminal Evidence in Hong Kong (1991); Malaysia and Singapour: Janab's Key to the Law of Evidence in Mayalsia and Singapour (1994).

[9]See, for example, in French Criminal Law, Jean Pradel et Francis Carsola, Code de procédure pénal (1997–1998) at p. 508: Articles 427 et sui. "Peut être annulé le jugement non fondé sur des renseignements puisés dans l'instruction de la cause et sur les débats, mais sur la notoriété publique ou sur la connaissance personnelle que le juge de police aurait du fait, objet de la poursuite; ou sur la connaissance personnelle d'éléments de preuve puisés dans d'autres procédures". See, also the decision of the Criminal Chamber of the Cour de Cassation, 30 Nov. 1993, *Bulletin civil*, no. 221, p. 429: "Il n'est pas permis de procéder par simple référence aux appréciations d'une précédente décision rendue entre autres parties, ni de donner comme motifs des affirmations qui ne sont que d'une telle référence".

[10]Cross on Evidence, supra note 8, p. 62.

[11]Black's Law Dictionary (1990).

[12]Cross on Evidence, supra note 8, p. 63.

[13]The Law of Evidence in Canada, supra note 8, pp. 976–977.

of facts which have been noticed judicially: international boundaries, location of cities, rivers, lakes, and the normal period of gestation.[14]

Furthermore, facts may be judicially noticed after inquiry. A court may act on information supplied by an official organ of the Government with regard to what may be described as political matters; historical facts; various customs and matters of professional practice. Examples include certificates from Government or State bodies (i.e. whether a country is at war or at peace, whether a person is an ambassador with diplomatic privileges, etc.), historical facts, times, measures and weights, natural and scientific facts. It must be noted, however, that even these kinds of facts may be at the heart of litigation and disputed by the parties, in which case, judicial notice cannot be taken of the facts.[15]

There are at least two reasons for taking judicial notice: it may expedite the hearing of a case and it can produce uniformity of decision on certain matters.[16] However, any taking of judicial notice of a fact must be consistent with procedural fairness. In the context of criminal proceedings, this means that if the accused is adversely affected, he must have the chance to challenge facts which are to be noticed. The ultimate principle is that extra-record facts should be assumed as a matter of convenience, except that convenience should always yield to the requirement of procedural fairness that the accused should have the opportunity to meet in the appropriate fashion all facts that influence the disposition of the case.[17] When a fact relates to a matter which is a legitimate matter of dispute between the parties, judicial notice of the fact should not be taken.

The doctrine of judicial notice is not foreign to public international law. The practice of the International Court of Justice reveals that when faced with issues dealing with establishing a factual situation, such as relevant periods, critical dates and subsequent developments relevant to events being litigated, it is central to the determination of these issues whether they are in dispute and whether there exists conflicting evidence on the matter at issue.[18] In addition, one learned author points out that general principles of law, as applied by international courts and tribunals, recognise, *inter alia*, that a party alleging a violation of international law giving rise to international responsibility has the burden of proving its assertion and allegations of the truth of which a tribunal does not take judicial notice or which are not presumed by it, unless they are admitted by the other party.[19]

In the practice of the International Tribunal, one of the first instances where the issue of judicial notice was addressed was in the context of the

[14] The Law of Evidence in Canada, supra note 8, pp. 979–983.

[15] Id., pp. 979–983.

[16] Cross on Evidence, supra note 8, p. 71.

[17] Evidence, supra note 8, pp. 1238–12139.

[18] Repertory of Decisions of the International Court of Justice (1947–1992), Volume II, pp. 793, 795, 797.

[19] Bin Cheng, General Principles of Law as applied by International Courts and Tribunals (1987), pp. 303–309.

Decision on the Defence Motion for Interlocutory Appeal on Jurisdiction in the Tadić case ("*Tadić* Jurisdictional Decision").[20] Although the question of judicial notice did not form any significant part of the Decision,[21] this matter was raised and argued extensively during oral submissions before the Appeals Chamber. In particular, the Prosecutor advocated that the International Tribunal take a conservative approach to the issue of judicial notice in the context of criminal proceedings dealing with the former Yugoslavia. He stated:

> In this interlocutory appeal we would ask the court, and we have in the appeal brief, to take notice particularly of Security Council resolutions and other notorious state acts which were affected [sic] by parties, states in the former Yugoslavia at the relevant time... We would respectfully support the broader approach of the Trial Chamber in not having regard to all of the facts that were presented by both of the parties as having been proven where they are subject to proof... [I]t would not be proper to deal with the preliminary motion on facts which are disputed, on facts which are not notorious. To the extent that they need to be proved, that is a matter for the Trial Chamber and not a matter fit for preliminary motion. To the extent that the Defence relies on those facts, the preliminary motion must fail. It does not mean that the Prosecutor will not have the burden of proof at the trial, but by the same token it certainly does not mean that the Defence can simply, as it were, by way of preliminary motion put in dispute facts which require proof at a trial.[22]

To date, Trial Chambers have not relied on judicial notice to a significant extent in rendering final judgement.[23] For instance, in the *Tadić Opinion and Judgement*, the Trial Chamber took notice of two facts in relation to the issue of protected persons under Article 2 of the Statute:

> The first is the conclusion inherent in the Appeals Chamber Decision and in the statements of the Security Council in relation to the conflict in the former Yugoslavia that that conflict was of a mixed character, and the Appeals Chamber's implicit deference to this Trial Chamber on the issue of whether the victims were "protected persons" in the present case. It is thus for the Trial Chamber to characterize the exact nature of the armed conflict, of which the events in opština Prijedor formed a part, when applying international humanitarian law to those events. The second fact is the nature of the conflict in the Republic of Bosnia and Herzegovina as understood by the parties to that conflict, which was made clear by the signing, on 22 May 1992, just two days before the

[20]*Prosecutor v. Tadić* , Case No. IT-94-1-AR72, A. Ch., 2 Oct. 1995.

[21]See, however, *Prosecutor v. Tadić, Separate Opinion of Judge Sidhwa on the Defence Motion for Interlocutory Appeal on Jurisdiction*, Case No. IT-94-1-AR72, 2 Oct. 1995 at paras. 121–123.

[22]Transcript, *Prosecutor v. Tadić*, Case No. IT-94-1-AR72, 7 Sept. 1995, p. 110.

[23]See also, *Prosecutor v. Akayesu, Judgement*, Case No. ICTR-96-4-T, 2 Sept. 1998, paras. 157, 165, 627 and the reference to Rule 94 of the ICTR.

> attack on Kozarac, of an agreement by the representatives of Alija Izetbegović (President of the Republic of Bosnia and Herzegovina and the SDA), Radovan Karadzić (President of the SDS) and Miljenko Brkić (President of the Croatian Democratic Community) to abide by the substantive rules of armed conflict not of an international character prescribed by Common Article 3 of the Geneva Conventions. It was also agreed, on the basis of paragraph 3 of Common Article 3, to apply certain provisions of the full Geneva Convention regime concerning international conflicts. This agreement was supported by the ICRC. In accordance with the terms of Common Article 3, the signing of such agreements does not in any way affect the legal status of the parties to the conflict and does not in any way affect the independent determination of the nature of that conflict by this Trial Chamber.[24]

Similarly, in the *Čelebići case*, the Trial Chamber made the following observations in regards to judicial notice in connection with background and preliminary factual findings:

> The Trial Chamber has heard extensive witness testimony and been presented with many documents and written reports. For the purposes of this background, particular reliance is placed on the evidence presented through the historical, political and military expert witnesses of both the Prosecution and the Defence. In addition, we have taken notice of many public documents which bear substantial authority – in particular, resolutions of the United Nations Security Council and General Assembly, the Final Report of the United Nations Commission of Experts, reports of the United Nations Secretary-General, and declarations and statements from the European Community and the Conference on Security and Cooperation in Europe (CSCE).[25]

In these early judgements in the history of the International Tribunal, taking notice of statements and documents emanating from the organs of the United Nations or their representatives as well as agreements between Government representatives is clearly within the commonly understood parameters of the doctrine of judicial notice.

Recently, as the body of case law of the International Tribunal has grown, decisions have been handed down which serve to highlight the role which Rule 94 may play in subsequent proceedings. In the case of the *Prosecutor v. Simić and Others* ("*Bosanski Samac* case"), the Trial Chamber dismissed a pre-trial motion by the Prosecution brought under Rule 94 to take judicial notice of the international character of the conflict in Bosnia and Herzegovina.[26]

---

[24]*Prosecutor v. Tadić, Opinion and Judgement,* Case No. IT-94-1-T, 7 May 1997, para. 583, footnotes omitted.

[25]*Prosecutor v. Delalić and Others, Judgement*, Case No. IT-96-21-T, 16 Nov. 1998 at para. 90, footnotes omitted.

[26]*Prosecutor v. Simić and Others, Decision on the Pre-Trial Motion by the Prosecution Requesting the Trial Chamber to Take Judicial Notice of the International Character of the Conflict in Bosnia-Herzegovina*, Case No. IT-95-9, 25 March 1999.

In this case, the Prosecution was requesting the Trial Chamber to take judicial notice of the international character of the conflict in Bosnia and Herzegovina either as a fact of common knowledge under Rule 94(A) or an adjudicated fact under Rule 94(B), based on the findings in the *Tadić*[27] and *Čelebići*[28] judgements. The request was aimed at having the Trial Chamber take judicial notice of the international character of the conflict in relation to Article 2 of the Statute which requires the Prosecution to prove *inter alia* the existence of an international armed conflict. The Prosecution sought an order by which the taking of judicial notice of the international character of the conflict meant that the Trial Chamber did not warrant examining any further evidence in relation to this matter.

The Defence opposed the request by the Prosecution on two main grounds. First, it was argued that the issue of judicial notice in criminal proceedings should be approached with great caution, particularly when a fact is a matter of reasonable dispute between the parties or incapable of immediate and accurate demonstration by resorting to readily accessible sources of indispensable accuracy. Second, it was argued that judicial notice of the international character of the conflict would jeopardise the rights of the accused under Article 21 of the Statute,[29] in particular the right to examine or have examined the evidence presented by the Prosecutor and the right to an independent determination of the facts at issue.

The Trial Chamber observed that in applying Rule 94, a balance must be struck between judicial economy and the right of the accused to a fair trial. The purpose of judicial notice under Rule 94 was considered to be judicial economy and it should be interpreted as covering facts which are not subject to reasonable dispute. The Trial Chamber held that Rule 94 is intended to cover facts and not legal consequences inferred from those facts. In other words, judicial notice may only be taken of factual findings but not of a legal characterisation as such.

The Trial Chamber rejected the submission under Rule 94(A) that the international character of the conflict in Bosnia and Herzegovina was a fact of common knowledge, as an historical fact of common knowledge or that it was a fact of common knowledge within the Tribunal, simply because the jurisprudence of the Tribunal had found an international armed conflict to exist as a matter of fact in other cases. However, pursuant to Rule 94(A), the Trial Chamber, *proprio motu*, took judicial notice of the following facts. The proclamation of independence of Bosnia and Herzegovina from the Socialist Federal Republic of Yugoslavia on 6 March 1992 and the recognition of the independence of Bosnia and Herzegovina as a State by the European Community on 6 April 1992 and by the United States on 7 April 1992.

---

[27]Footnote 23.
[28]Footnote 24.
[29]As amended 13 May 1998.

Subsequently, in the case of the *Prosecutor v. Kvočka and Others* ("*Omarska* case"),[30] pursuant to Rule 94(B), the Trial Chamber took judicial notice of 444 facts from the *Tadić*[31] and *Čelebići*[32] judgements which the parties had agreed were adjudicated facts.[33] In addition, on the basis of these facts, the Trial Chamber found certain elements of Article 3 (Violations of the Law and Customs of War) and Article 5 (Crimes Against Humanity) of the Statute had been proven beyond reasonable doubt and that no further evidence needed to be adduced in regards to these issues at trial. The Trial Chamber decided that at the times and places alleged in the indictment, there existed an armed conflict, which included widespread and systematic attack against notably the Muslim and Croat civilian population and that there was a nexus between this armed conflict and the widespread and systematic attack on the civilian population and the existence of the Omarska, Keraterm and Trnopolje camps and the mistreatment of the prisoners therein.[34] This finding by the Trial Chamber, on the basis of adjudicated facts, did not mean that the accused were responsible for the commission of any offences alleged in the indictment. The Trial Chamber emphasised that the Prosecution maintained the burden of proving the guilt of the accused beyond reasonable doubt under Article 7(1) and Article 7(3), as charged in the indictment.[35]

The importance of these two decisions seems to lie in the approach each Trial Chamber took to the application of the rule of judicial notice and the consequences of taking judicial notice of certain facts. In the *Bosanski Samac* case, the Trial Chamber declined to take judicial notice of the international character of the armed conflict on the request of the Prosecution. Relying upon the *Tadić* Jurisdictional Decision,[36] the Trial Chamber found that different conflicts of different nature took place in the former Yugoslavia and that it would be for each Trial Chamber, depending on the circumstances of each case, to make its own determination on the nature of the armed conflict, based upon the specific evidence presented to it. The Trial Chamber stated that these findings have no binding force except as between the parties in respect of a particular case ("*effet relatif de la chose jugée*"), that the circumstances of each case are different, and that as regards the controversial issue of the nature of the conflict, which involves an interpretation of facts, both parties should be able to present arguments and evidence on them.

---

[30]*Prosecutor v. Kvočka and Others, Decision on Judicial Notice*, Case No. IT-98-30/1-T, 8 June 2000.

[31]Footnote 23 and, *Prosecutor v. Tadić, Judgement*, IT-94-1-A, A. Ch., 15 July 1999.

[32]Footnote 24.

[33]See, also, *Prosecutor v. Kvočka and Others, Prosecutor's Motion for Judicial Notice of Adjudicated Facts*, Case No. IT-98-30-PT, 11 Jan. 1999 and *Prosecutor v. Kvočka and Others, Decision on Prosecutor's Motion for Judicial Notice of Adjudicated Facts*, Case No. IT-98-30-PT, 19 March 1999.

[34]Footnote 30, p. 7.

[35]Id., p. 6.

[36]Footnote 19.

In the *Omarska* case, the parties had agreed to a large number of adjudicated facts from prior cases before the International Tribunal. The question which faced the Trial Chamber was whether, on the basis of those adjudicated facts, certain elements of the charges could be considered proven beyond reasonable doubt. In ruling that certain legal conclusions could be drawn based on those facts, the Trial Chamber did not appear to be departing from the decision handed down in the *Bosanski Samac* case. Indeed, in the instance of the *Omarska* case, the agreement by the parties to adjudicated facts from prior cases amounted to admissions by the parties or a statement of matters which are not in dispute.[37] Once the parties had agreed to certain facts contained in prior judgements of the International Tribunal, nothing precluded the Trial Chamber from drawing legal conclusions based on those facts.

To sum up, under Rule 94, judicial notice of certain facts may be taken within the exercise of the powers conferred on a Trial Chamber, as a matter of law, as part of the process of determining the facts upon which it may render a final decision on the merits of a case. One way of formulating whether the fact in question can be noticed, without proof, is to ask whether the fact under consideration is not a matter of reasonable dispute between the parties and thought to be capable of immediate and accurate demonstration by reference to an indisputable source of information. The jurisprudence of the International Tribunal indicates that Rule 94 has been relied upon to take judicial notice of official statements or documents from international organisations or governments or in regard to background matters which the parties admit or agree are not in dispute.

Furthermore, Rule 94(B) expands the scope of judicial notice to include adjudicated facts or documentary evidence from other proceedings of the Tribunal. This provision may be seen as an example of a rule incorporating a concept which is specific to the prosecution of cases before the International Tribunal. It sets parameters on the way in which evidence from other proceedings in the Tribunal may be treated in subsequent trials and confines this peculiar species of judicial notice to facts or documentary evidence that have been adjudicated in the system established by the Statute. This includes facts or documentary evidence in respect of which there has been a final determination by a Trial Chamber, where there is no appeal or, in the case of an appeal, by the Appeals Chamber.[38] Without final judicial determination of the facts and documentary evidence from other proceedings of the Tribunal, it would be unsafe and imprudent to admit them without proof in a trial before a Chamber.

[37]See, Rule 65*ter* of the RPE.

[38]See, *Prosecutor v. Aleksovski, Dissenting Opinion of Judge Patrick Robinson on the Decision on Prosecutor's Appeal on Admissibility of Evidence*, Case No. IT-95-14/1-A, 16 Feb. 1999, paras. 13–15. Pursuant to Article 25 of the Statute, the Appeals Chamber may hear appeals on matter of law or fact.

In keeping with the rationale which underpins the concept of judicial notice, the types of facts falling under Rule 94(B) must be confined to those which are so notorious as to be beyond any reasonable dispute between people of good faith. Nonetheless, certain adjudicated facts may be disputed and be central to litigation between the parties *inter se* in subsequent proceedings, in which case no judicial notice of those facts can be taken. In those circumstances, those facts are limited to the acknowledgement that a certain finding of fact has been made in other proceedings, without comment or concession as to its correctness or underlying justice.[39]

A review of the case law of the International Tribunal indicates that a Trial Chamber may not only take judicial notice of certain facts, but also enter a ruling that certain legal conclusions may be made at any point in the proceedings. However, where a Trial Chamber takes judicial notice of certain facts and does not decide upon the legal characterisation of those facts, the parties to the proceedings must determine whether further evidence must be adduced in order to establish the point which is suggested or inferred by the judicially noticed facts. For example, the Prosecution must assess whether those facts which are relevant to an ingredient of an offence are sufficient for it to meet its burden of proving guilt beyond reasonable doubt or whether it must present additional evidence on that point.

One of the outstanding issues in relation to judicial notice before the International Tribunal is the question of successive indictments and trials which arise out of common geographic or temporal events from the conflicts in the former Yugoslavia, where the parties dispute findings of fact from previous cases. As has been seen, Rule 94(B) broadens the usual parameters of judicial notice by referring to adjudicated facts or documentary evidence from other proceedings of the Tribunal relating to matters at issue in a subsequent trial. However, a defendant who was not a party in the original

---

[39]See, for example, the *Prosecutor v. Delalić and Others, Judgement*, Case No. IT-96-21-T, 16 Nov. 1998, para. 228 where the Trial Chamber made the following observations which seem apposite to the application of the interpretation and application of Rule 94(B). The Trial Chamber held that the principle of *res judicata* (a thing adjudicated is received as the truth) only applies *inter partes* in a case where a matter has already been judicially determined within that case itself. The Trial Chamber observed that as in national criminal systems which employ a public prosecutor in some form, the Prosecution is clearly always a party to cases before the International Tribunal. The doctrine of *res judicata* is limited, in criminal cases, to the question of whether, when the previous trial of a particular individual is followed by another of the same individual, a specific matter has already been fully litigated. In national systems where a public prosecutor appears in all criminal cases, the doctrine is clearly not applied so as to prevent the prosecutor from disputing a matter which the prosecutor has argued in a previous, different case. The Trial Chamber added that it is certainly not bound by the Decisions of other Trial Chambers in past cases and must make its findings based on the evidence presented to it and its own interpretation of the law applicable to the case at issue. The circumstances of each case differ significantly and thus also the evidence presented by the Prosecution. The Trial Chamber concluded by pointing out that even should the Prosecution bring evidence which is largely similar to that presented in a previous case, the Trial Chamber's assessment of it may lead to entirely different results.

proceeding, where the adjudication took place, should not be bound by those facts where it can be said that there exists a reasonable basis to dispute the facts in question. For example, certain facts in earlier proceedings may not have been contested by a party or the parties at trial for a variety of reasons, including the fact they were secondary to the ultimate issue of guilt or innocence of the particular accused. The judgement rendered in such a case will make findings of fact based on the evidence presented to it by the parties *inter se*, not in anticipation of subsequent proceedings. In a later trial, however, those very facts may be central to the determination of the guilt or innocence of the accused, in which case those facts are likely to be disputed by the parties and it would be inappropriate to take judicial notice of those facts. This particular issue can only be determined on a case by case basis, for the approach and strategy of a party in a subsequent trial may be entirely different from those advocated by the parties in earlier proceedings.

CLAIRE HARRIS*

27. Precedent in the Practice of the ICTY

The issue of precedent in the International Tribunal – or the way in which Chambers of the Tribunal treat previous decisions of other Chambers in their own judicial decision-making – is one of recurring significance in the practice of the Tribunal. It is an issue which is not dealt with explicitly in the Statute of the Tribunal, nor its Rules of Procedure and Evidence, and only recently, almost seven years after the adoption of the Tribunal's Statute, has it been the subject of a definitive consideration by the Appeals Chamber.[1] The related question of how decisions of courts and tribunals in other jurisdictions are used by the Tribunal, although not strictly one of precedent, was also examined in a recent judgement[2] and is briefly considered here.

1. Status of Judicial Decisions from Other Jurisdictions

Jurisprudence of international and national courts and tribunals is frequently referred to in Tribunal decisions.[3] Reference to such jurispru-

*Associate Legal Officer, International Criminal Tribunal for the Former Yugoslavia, B.A./LL.B (Hons) (Monash University); LL.M (Cantab), Barrister and Solicitor of the Supreme Court of Victoria. The views expressed herein are those of the author and do not represent the views of the ICTY or the United Nations.

[1]*Prosecutor v. Aleksovski, Judgement*, Case No. IT-95-14/1-A, A. Ch., 24 March 2000 ("*Aleksovski Appeal Judgement*").

[2]*Prosecutor v. Kupreškić, Judgement*, Case No. IT-95-16-T, 14 Jan. 2000 ("*Kupreškić, Judgement*").

[3]See, eg, *Prosecutor v. Tadić, Judgement*, Case No. IT-94-1-A, A. Ch., 15 July 1999, paras. 255–270 (use of case-law in determining whether crimes against humanity can be committed for "purely personal reasons"); *Prosecutor v. Delalić and Others, Judgement*, Case No. IT-96-21-T, 16 Nov. 1998, para. 424, fn. 435 (on elements of wilful killing) para. 600 (on burden of proof); *Prosecutor v. Furundžija, Judgement*, Case No. IT –95-17/1-T, 10 Dec. 1998 ("*Furundžija, Judgement*") at paras. 180–181, (on the elements of rape); *Prosecutor v. Tadić, Judgement on Allegations of Contempt Against Prior Counsel, Milan Vujin*, Case No IT-94-1-A-R77, A.Ch., 31 Jan. 2000, ("*Tadić Contempt Judgement*"), paras. 14–17 (whether the Tribunal's powers include the power to punish contempt of court, and nature and scope of contempt).

R. May et al., Essays on ICTY Procedure and Evidence in Honour of Gabrielle Kirk McDonald, 341–356.

dence is necessary in part because of the generality with which the ICTY Statute identifies some of the offences within the Tribunal's jurisdiction. The elements of the offences are not provided in the Statute and other matters, such as the exact requirements of crimes of complicity such as aiding and abetting, are not defined.[4] As Trial Chamber II has observed:

> The Tribunal's need to draw upon judicial decisions is only to be expected, due to the fact that both substantive and procedural criminal law is still at a rudimentary stage in international law. In particular, there exist relatively few treaty provisions on the matter. By contrast, especially after World War II, a copious amount of case-law has developed on international crimes.[5]

The jurisprudence of the post-World War II military tribunals is of obvious assistance on the basis that those institutions "operated under international instruments laying down provisions that were either declaratory of existing law or which had been gradually transformed into customary international law."[6] Some caution is, however, exercised in using this jurisprudence in the unique context of the Tribunal. One reason for this, referred to early in the *Tadić* proceedings, is that the trials conducted by these tribunals have been described as "victor's justice".[7] It has also been observed that although the Charter of the International Military Tribunal and Control Council Law No. 10 could be regarded as declaratory of customary international law, this does not necessarily extend to the tribunals' jurisprudence on matters not provided for in those instruments, for the determination of which the tribunals "invariably drew on the jurisprudence of their own *national* jurisdictions".[8]

In relation to procedural and evidentiary law, the Rules of Procedure and Evidence, as supplemented and revised over the life of the Tribunal and interpreted by the growing body of Tribunal decisions, limit the need to look to judicial decisions of other jurisdictions. In practice the chambers do use such external jurisprudence – principally decisions of national courts – in interpreting some of the more open-textured Articles or Rules or in cases

---

[4]See the discussion of the definition of "aiding and abetting" in the *Furundžija Judgement*, para. 191: "Since no treaty law on the subject exists, the Trial Chamber must examine customary international law in order to establish the content of this head of criminal responsibility."

[5]*Prosecutor v. Kupreškić, Judgement*, Case No. IT-95-16-T, 14 Jan. 2000 ("*Kupreškić Judgement*"), para. 537.

[6]Id., para. 541.

[7]*Prosecutor v. Tadić, Decision on the Prosecutor's Motion Requesting Protective Measures for Victims and Witnesses*, Case No. IT-94-1-T, 10 Aug. 1996 ("*Tadić Protective Measures Decision*"), para. 21: "only the vanquished were charged with violations of international humanitarian law and the defendants were prosecuted and punished for crimes expressly defined in an instrument adopted by the victors".

[8]*Prosecutor v. Erdemović, Judgement*, Case No. IT-96-22-A, A. Ch., 7 Oct. 1997 ("*Erdemović Appeal Judgement*"), *Joint Separate Opinion of Judge McDonald and Judge Vorah*, paras. 49–54, at 54 (emphasis added).

where issues arise which are not dealt with in the Rules.[9] Use is also made of the jurisprudence of international human rights tribunals, particularly the European Court of Human Rights, in elaborating provisions relating to matters such as the rights of the accused,[10] again bearing in mind that the unique circumstances of the Tribunal must be considered when using such decisions.[11]

The conceptual basis of the Tribunal's use of judicial decisions from other jurisdictions, and their exact status in the corpus of international law applied by the Tribunal, was analysed in the recent *Kupreškić judgement*.[12] Trial Chamber II observed that as the Security Council established the Tribunal as an "international court proper" the body of law to be applied by the Tribunal is international law, although

> [...] the Tribunal may be well advised to draw upon national law to fill possible *lacunae* in the Statute or in customary international law. For instance, it may have to peruse and rely on national legislation or national judicial decisions with a view to determining the emergence of a general principle of criminal law common to all major systems of the world. Furthermore, the Tribunal may have to apply national law *incidenter tantum*, i.e. in the exercise of its incidental jurisdiction.[13]

An example of such incidental use is the relevance of national laws in determining the nationality of a victim to ascertain whether he is a protected

---

[9]See, eg, *Prosecutor v. Krnojelac, Decision on the Defence Preliminary Motion on the Form of the Indictment*, Case No. IT-97-25-PT, 24 Feb. 1999, para. 12, where decisions of national courts were referred to for assistance in determining the necessary particularity of the Indictment. See also the Appeals Chamber's consideration of decisions of international tribunals and national courts on the question of whether "national security" claims of privilege can be reviewed, in *Prosecutor v. Blaškić, Judgement on the Request of the Republic of Croatia for Review of the Decision of Trial Chamber II of 18 July 1997*, Case No. IT-95-14-AR108*bis*, A. Ch., 29 Oct. 1997, paras. 139–146.

[10]See, e.g., *Prosecutor v. Mrksić and Others, Decision on the Motion for Release by the Accused Slavko Dokmanović*, Case No. IT-95-13a-PT, 22 Oct. 1997, paras. 28; 58–65 (the meaning of arrest and legality of a particular method of arrest); *Prosecutor v. Blaškić, Order Denying a Motion for Provisional Release*, Case No. IT-95-14-T, 20 Dec. 1996, pp. 6–7 (whether the pre-trial detention of the accused "exceeds the reasonable time period pursuant to international principles and particularly those of the European Convention as interpreted by the Commission and the European Court"); *Tadić Protective Measures Decision*, para. 12, and *Separate Opinion of Judge Stephen*, pp. 16–19 (scope of the accused's right to examine witnesses against him – discussion of jurisprudence on Article 6(3)(d), European Convention on Human Rights).

[11]See e.g., the *Tadić Protective Measures Decision*, para. 27: the Trial Chamber is not bound by other judicial bodies' interpretations of international human rights standards reflected in the Statute (in this case, the Article 20 right to a fair trial). While jurisprudence of other international judicial bodies is relevant, the Tribunal must interpret the Statutes and the Rules within the Tribunal's own unique legal framework.

[12]*Kupreškić Judgement*, paras. 537–542.

[13]Id., para. 513.

person for the purposes of Article 2 of the Statute. In exercising its principal jurisdiction, however, the Trial Chamber regarded judicial decisions as being relevant only as "subsidiary means for the determination of rules of law", using the expression from Article 38(1)(d) of the Statute of the International Court of Justice. Therefore, "subject to the binding force of decisions of the Tribunal's Appeals Chamber upon the Trial Chambers, the International Tribunal cannot uphold the doctrine of binding precedent (*stare decisis*) adhered to in common law countries."[14] Decisions of other international criminal tribunals are not precedents for the Tribunal. Their value is in demonstrating the possible existence of an international practice as evidence of a customary rule, insofar as they indicate the existence of international practice and *opinio juris sive necessitatis* on a given matter, or as an indication of the emergence of a general principle of international law. Alternatively a prior decision may act as persuasive authority that a particular interpretation is the correct understanding of the international law on an issue. This is particularly the case with decisions of the International Court of Justice.[15] Decisions of national courts, which primarily apply national law, or interpret international law "through the prism of national legislation", require stricter scrutiny before being used in this way.[16]

2. Internal precedent

The ICTY Statute, unlike the Statute of the International Criminal Court,[17] contains no provisions which directly govern the issue of precedent or the

[14] Id., para. 540.

[15] See the Separate Opinion of Judge Shahabuddeen in *Laurent Semanza c. Le Procureur, Décision*, ICTR-97-20-A, A. Ch., 31 May 2000 ("*Semanza Decision*") where Judge Shahabuddeen, at paras 29–36, discusses the relationship between the Tribunal and the International Court of Justice and "the responsibility (of the Tribunal) to show deference to the views of the ICJ as to what is customary international law [...]" (para. 29).

[16] *Kupreškić Judgement*, para. 540.

[17] Article 21(2) of the Rome Statute of the International Criminal Court states: "The Court may apply principles and rules of law as interpreted in its previous decisions." The Statute of the International Court of Justice provides in Article 38(1)(d) that, subject to Article 59, the Court shall apply "judicial decisions and the teachings of the most highly qualified publicists of the various nations, as subsidiary means for the determination of rules of law." This has been interpreted to include decisions of the Court itself: see Dissenting Opinion of Judge Read in *Anglo-Iranian Oil Co.*, ICJ Rep 1952, p. 143. Article 59 states that "The decision of the Court has no binding force except between the parties and in respect of that particular case." There is some controversy as to whether Article 59 bars the operation of binding precedent in the Court. Judge Mohamed Shahabuddeen states in his authoritative work on the subject that "Article 59 is not concerned one way or another with the precedential effect of decisions": Mohamed Shahabuddeen, Precedent in the World Court (1996) at p. 97. Judge Shahabuddeen observes that although *stare decisis* is inapplicable in the ICJ, the Court regards its decisions as authoritative expositions of the law and, although free to depart, will generally follow them – at pp. 238–9.

status generally of decisions of chambers of the Tribunal before other chambers. The Statute does provide indirect assistance in that it partially defines the relationships between Trial Chambers, and between the Trial Chambers and the Appeals Chamber, thereby giving some indication as to the view each chamber should take to the decisions of the others. Article 25 of the Statute provides for the Appeals Chamber to hear appeals from the Prosecutor or convicted accused, and to affirm, reverse or revise the decisions taken by the Trial Chambers. The ability of the Appeals Chamber to reverse or revise Trial Chamber decisions gives it the final determination in any given case of what the applicable law is. Once the Appeals Chamber has expressed its opinion on the law it could give rise to needless re-litigation of issues if Trial Chambers were not obliged to follow that determination of the law in other cases, given the probability that the Appeals Chamber will (applying its previously stated view of the law) reverse Trial Chamber decisions inconsistent with those stated views.

In the *Aleksovski Appeal Judgement*, the Appeals Chamber referred to Article 25 and the hierarchical structure established by the Tribunal's Statute, pursuant to which the Appeals Chamber has the function of definitively settling questions of law and fact arising from Trial Chamber decisions.[18] The Appeals Chamber gave two additional reasons, based more indirectly on the construction of the Statute, for its conclusion that the *ratio decidendi* of Appeals Chamber decisions is binding on Trial Chambers.[19] It regarded the mandate of the Tribunal to prosecute persons responsible for serious violations of international humanitarian law as requiring the assurance of certainty and predictability in the application of the relevant law. Secondly, it viewed the right to a fair trial as giving rise to a right of the accused to have like cases treated alike. If each Trial Chamber were free to disregard decisions of law of the Appeals Chamber, it would be

> [I]nconsistent with the intention of the Security Council, which, from a plain reading of the Statute and the Report of the Secretary General, envisaged a tribunal comprising three trial chambers and one appeals chamber, applying a single, unified, coherent and rational corpus of law.[20]

[18]*Aleksovski Appeal Judgement*, para. 112.

[19]This conclusion was consistent with most Trial Chamber statements on the issue; which (although the issue had never been considered at length) indicated the view that Trial Chambers are generally bound by Appeals Chamber decisions: see e.g., *Prosecutor v. Kordić, Decision on the Joint Defence Motion to Dismiss the Amended Indictment for Lack of Jurisdiction Based on the Limited Jurisdictional Reach of Articles 2 and 3*, Case No. IT-95-14/2-AR108*bis*, A. Ch., 2 March 1999 para. 12; *Prosecutor v. Delalić and Others, Judgement*, Case No. IT-96-21-T, 16 Nov. 1998, para. 167.

[20]Id., par. 113. In an appended Declaration, Judge Hunt agreed, "largely for the reasons given", that a Trial Chamber is bound by Appeals Chamber decisions but that it should be permitted to express a reasoned disagreement with the decision for the later consideration of the Appeals Chamber: *Declaration of Judge David Hunt*, ("*Declaration*") para. 10.

There is less obvious guidance in the Statute as to how the Appeals Chamber should approach its own previous decisions. This is an important question in view of the fact that the Appeals Chamber is, for a number of practical reasons,[21] frequently composed of different benches of judges. This was a key issue in the *Aleksovski Appeal Judgement*. A prosecution ground of appeal in those proceedings was that the majority of the Trial Chamber applied the wrong legal tests for determining when acts of persons or groups could be imputed to a foreign government, thus rendering a prima facie internal conflict international, and on the circumstances in which victims can be considered to be protected persons within the meaning of Article 4 of Geneva Convention IV. After the rendering of the *Aleksovski* trial judgment, the judgement in the *Tadić* appeal, in which the Appeals Chamber gave its views on both issues, was delivered. The Appeals Chamber in *Aleksovski* then invited the parties to make further submissions on "the doctrine of *stare decisis*, its applicability, if at all, to proceedings before the International Tribunal and in particular to this case".[22] The prosecution submissions refer to the use of precedent in various domestic jurisdictions, and emphasise that in the criminal law generally there is a particular need for certainty and predictability. It submitted that although "*stare decisis*" per se is not a general principle of law, the Appeals Chamber should follow its previous decisions unless it concludes that a previous decision was clearly erroneous and cannot stand.[23] The defence submissions took a different approach, treating the question of the status of Appeals Chamber decisions as essentially one of sources of law.[24] It was submitted, relying on the Report of the Secretary-General, that the Tribunal may apply only rules of international humanitarian law which are beyond any doubt part of customary law, and the Report makes no mention of judicial precedent as a source of law.[25]

The Appeals Chamber essentially accepted the prosecution submissions. The judgement refers to various common law jurisdictions which recognise (with narrow exceptions) a system of binding precedent, and observes that although civil systems do not recognise a principle of *stare decisis*, their highest courts generally follow their previous decisions.[26] The Appeals Chamber noted that the European Court of Human Rights, although not bound by its previous judgements, describes its own practice as usually following and applying its own precedents in the interests of legal certainty

[21]Including the judge's participation in various earlier phases of the proceedings – but see now Rule 15(C) in relation to the ability of the judge who confirms the indictment to sit in the Appeals Chamber in relation to the matter – and the occasional disqualification for other reasons of the regular Appeals Chamber judges.

[22]*Scheduling Order*, 8 Dec. 1999, p. 2.

[23]*Prosecution Response to the Scheduling Order of 8 December 1999*, 11 Jan. 2000. See also *Brief in Reply of the Prosecution*, 10 Nov. 1999, paras. 1.9–1.12.

[24]*The Appellant's Additional Submissions on the Doctrine of Stare Decisis and Defence of "Necessity"*, 11 Jan. 2000, ("*Appellant's Submissions*") para. 3.

[25]Id., paras. 4–5.

[26]*Aleksovski Appeal Judgement*, paras. 92–94.

and orderly development of case-law, but departing from an earlier decision if there are "cogent reasons" for doing so.[27] The Appeals Chamber also observed that despite the non-operation of *stare decisis* in the International Court of Justice, its previous decisions are accorded considerable weight.[28] The principles underlying this tendency among the highest courts of respect for previous decisions were identified as the need for consistency, certainty and predictability. These needs are particularly acute in the criminal law where the liberty of the individual is implicated.[29]

The Appeals Chamber observed, however, that the law and practice in national jurisdictions and international institutions are not determinative and that the answer must ultimately be found in the ICTY Statute and Rules. It referred to the Appeals Chamber's appellate role pursuant to Article 25 of the Statute, and the accused's right to a fair trial under Article 21, which incorporates the right of appeal. It also considered that the fundamental purpose of the Tribunal of prosecuting persons responsible for violations of international humanitarian law, described in Article 1, required "an approach which, while recognising the need for certainty, stability and predictability in criminal law, also recognises that there may be instances in which the strict, absolute application of that principle may lead to injustice."[30] The Appeals Chamber concluded:

> [A] proper construction of the Statute, taking due account of its text and purpose, yields the conclusion that in the interests of certainty and predictability, the Appeals Chamber should follow its previous decisions, but should be free to depart from them for cogent reasons in the interests of justice.[31]

The Appeals Chamber gave, as examples of such "cogent reasons", cases where the previous decision was decided on the basis of a wrong legal principle or was given per incuriam.[32] In applying this principle to the facts of the appeal, the Appeals Chamber determined that it would follow the exposition of the applicable law in the *Tadić Appeal Judgement* "since, after careful analysis, it is unable to find any cogent reason to depart from it".[33]

The Appeals Chamber also emphasised that relying on previous judicial decisions in this way does not mean that the previous decisions are treated as a source of law. Aleksovski had argued that reliance on previous judicial decisions contradicts the principle of legality or *nullem crimen sine lege*. In particular, it was submitted that the Appeals Chamber could not follow the statement of the law in the *Tadić Appeal Judgement* as it had not been deliv-

---

[27] *Cossey* Judgement of 27 September 1990, Series A, vol. 184, para. 35, cited id. at para. 95

[28] *Aleksovski Appeal Judgment*, para. 96.

[29] Id., para. 97.

[30] Id., para. 101.

[31] Id., para. 107.

[32] Id., para. 108.

[33] Id., para. 134.

ered when the Aleksovski judgement was rendered.[34] The Appeals Chamber described this argument as being "based on a misconception", and said:

> The Appeals Chamber wishes to clarify that when it interprets Article 2 of the Statute, it is merely identifying what the proper interpretation of that provision has always been, even though not previously expressed that way.[35]

It described the principle of *nullem crimen sine lege* as meaning that a person might be found guilty of a crime only if the relevant acts constituted a violation of the law at the time of their commission.[36] The principle "does not prevent a court relying on previous decisions which reflect an interpretation as to the meaning to be ascribed to particular ingredients of a crime".[37]

The Appeals Chamber therefore clearly sees itself as identifying, rather than stating or making the law, which is really the only assessment of its role which could be consistent with the established understanding of sources of international law expressed in Article 38 of the Statute of the International Court of Justice. Of course, the view that the Tribunal is declaring rather than making law may possibly be optimistic in cases where there are very limited conventional or customary sources from which to determine the law, or where the existing sources do not provide a clear-cut answer, a situation to which the Tribunal may be tempted to respond by stating the law in a way which goes beyond what the limited state practice on an issue strictly permits.[38]

A separate Declaration of Judge Hunt on the issue of precedent was appended to the *Aleksovski Appeal Judgement*. Judge Hunt agreed that the Appeals Chamber should generally follow its decisions and depart from them only exceptionally, but expressed different reasoning for that conclusion. He first observed that in general, judicial decisions do not play an important part in international law but constitute subsidiary means for determining what the law is.[39] Because of the unique nature of the Tribunal, as the only international court with its own appellate structure and the only existing international criminal court, Judge Hunt considered that the resolution of the issue of precedent was not to be found "in the practices of other international courts (which are necessarily not criminal courts) or in the

---

[34]Appellant's Submissions, para. 8.

[35]*Aleksovski Appeal Judgment* para. 135.

[36]Id., para. 126.

[37]Id., para. 127.

[38]See, e.g., the observation of Professor Christopher Greenwood, in relation to *Prosecutor v. Tadić, Decision on the Interlocutory Appeal on Jurisdiction*, Case No. IT-94-1-AR-72, 2 Oct. 1995, ("*Tadić Jurisdiction Decision*"), that it was "doubtful" whether the practice relied on by the Appeals Chamber for a particular proposition "really sustains some of the inferences drawn from it": Christopher Greenwood, "International Humanitarian Law and the *Tadić* Case" 7 *European Journal of International Law* (1996) 265 at p. 278.

[39]Id., para. 2.

doctrine of judicial precedent in the domestic courts where the situation in which those courts operate is quite different [...]".[40] He relied more directly on the established principles underlying criminal law – the need for certainty in the criminal law, and the counterbalancing need for flexibility where adherence to a previous decision would create injustice – and placed greater emphasis on the need for flexibility than did the Judgement. This emphasis is evident from two matters referred to in the Declaration. The Tribunal, unlike domestic courts, is not subject to a legislative body which is readily able to "fine-tune" its Statute if an Appeals Chamber decision is seen subsequently to have produced an injustice, and it is unrealistic to expect the Security Council to do so. The second matter is that the Statute "is not a self-contained code of the nature adopted in the civil law systems" and thus requires constant interpretation for its continuing application.[41] Judge Hunt observed that the need for certainty in the law means that "the Appeals Chamber should never disregard a previous decision simply because the members of the Appeals Chamber do not personally agree with it" and concluded that "a departure from a previous decision is justified only when the interests of justice require it".[42]

Although the Appeals Chamber regarded the law and practice in national jurisdictions and in international institutions as not being determinative of the issue, it did use the practices of other, principally domestic, courts as its starting point in the *Aleksovski Appeal Judgement* and thereby appeared to conceptualise the issue in terms of whether the doctrine of precedent, in the sense in which it has developed in other contexts, should be applied by the Tribunal. Given the paucity of guidance on the subject in the Tribunal's Statute this reference to other systems is understandable. While the Statute provisions referred to by the Appeals Chamber do provide some indication of the approach to be taken, it is only in a framework of existing principles of judicial decision-making that provisions so general in nature can really be understood as indicating how the Appeals Chamber should regard its own previous decisions. Judge Hunt's Declaration treats the issue of judicial precedent as touching on the issues of sources of law in international law (as conceptualised in the Appellant's submissions) and of the applicability of a system of precedent as that concept is known in national systems (which was emphasised by the prosecution). However, like the majority, he found certain fundamental principles to be the ultimate source of the answer to the issue. The differences between the analyses in the Judgement and the Declaration

---

[40] Id., para. 7.

[41] Id., para. 6.

[42] Id., para. 8. He referred, as examples of when such a departure is justified, to situations where a previous decision "has led to an injustice, or would lead to an injustice if its principle is applied in a subsequent case, or where a subsequent decision of the International Court of Justice, the European Court of Human Rights or a senior appellate court within a domestic jurisdiction has demonstrated an error of reasoning in the previous decision, or where, in the light of subsequent events, the previous decision can be seen to be plainly wrong, or [...] was given *per incuriam*."

are therefore not substantial – indeed, Judge Hunt emphasised that the differences "lie in emphasis rather than in substance"[43] – as both opinions ultimately relied on long-developed legal *principles* to determine the issue, albeit with differing emphases on those principles.

The *Aleksovski Appeal Judgment's* statement of the practice the Appeals Chamber considers appropriate in relation to its previous decisions was adopted by the Appeals Chamber in the International Criminal Tribunal for Rwanda in a decision in the *Semanza* proceedings.[44] Judge Shahabuddeen, in an appended Separate Opinion, cautiously supported the adoption of the *Aleksovski* statement subject to certain considerations as to its exact legal status. Judge Shahabuddeen's detailed consideration of the issues merit a closer examination than is possible here; however his observations on the nature of the Appeals Chamber's legal obligations in relation to its previous decisions should briefly be noted.

Judge Shahabuddeen first considered whether the *Aleksovski Appeals Chamber* regarded itself as being *required* by the Statute to follow its previous decisions subject to a limited power of departure – making it an obligation "in the nature of a super norm directing the Appeals Chamber how it should select the rule of substantive case-law to be applied in a particular matter" – or simply that it was *enabled* by the Statute to adopt this practice.[45] He regarded the Statute as *not* imposing such a principle, as such a super norm could only be laid down with an explicitness not present in the Statute's text,[46] and emphasised that nothing in the Statute obliges or binds the Appeals Chamber to follow its previous decisions.[47] Because the *Aleksovski* Appeals Chamber's view on previous decisions resulted from an *interpretation* of the Statute, it was itself a statement which could be reconsidered and departed from by future Appeals Chambers, as that Chamber could not deprive itself of the competence to reverse a previous interpretation.[48] He therefore expressed the view that "it is difficult to see what the earlier decision achieves".[49] Presumably – and as is implicitly recognised later in the Separate Opinion – the *Aleksovski* Appeals Chamber regarded itself as attempting, in the interests of the imperatives of consistency, predictability and certainty in the criminal law which it discusses in its judgement, to give to parties subject to the Tribunal's jurisdiction an indication of the judicial

---

[43]Declaration, para. 1.

[44]*Semanza Decision*, par. 92: "La Chambre d'appel reprend les conclusions de la Chambre d'appel du TPIY dans l'affaire *Aleksovksi,* et rappelle que dans l'intérêt de la sécurité et de la prévisibilité juridiques, la Chambre d'appel doit suivre ses décisions antérieures mais reste libre de s'en écarter si des raisons impérieuses lui paraissent le commander dans l'intérêt de la justice", citing paras. 107 to 109 of the *Aleksovski Appeal Judgement*.

[45]*Separate Opinion of Judge Shahabuddeen*, paras. 6–10.

[46]Id., para. 10.

[47]Id., paras. 13, 17.

[48]Id., para. 11.

[49]Id., para. 12.

method which it regards as consistent with principles of criminal law and international law generally and therefore the appropriate practice. Judge Shahabuddeen was in fact able to agree with the *Aleksovski* statement on the basis that it did not state a legal requirement, but a *practice* which the Appeals Chamber would adopt.[50]

Ultimately, Judge Shahabuddeen's views on the subject matter of the status of previous decisions do not appear to differ substantially from those expressed in *Aleksovski*. As noted by Judge Shahabuddeen,[51] the *Aleksovski* Appeals Chamber did not at any point express itself to be *bound* by previous decisions but pointed to the practice which it believed, in the Tribunal's unique context, it was appropriate to adopt. In relation to the circumstances in which departure would be appropriate, Judge Shahabuddeen emphasised the obligation of the Tribunal to apply customary international law even if this might be at variance with previous decisions of the Appeals Chamber.[52] He reiterated the consideration that there is no institution corresponding to a domestic legislature which has the general competence to amend a statement by the courts as to what is the law.[53] He ultimately cautioned that the Tribunal must, in identifying customary international law take account of (while *not* being bound by) judicial pronouncements of other international judicial bodies as to what is the law. This is both because decisions of other such bodies must provide obvious guidance as to what that law is and because, given the Tribunal's place in the international judicial system, it is obliged to take account of the interest of achieving coherence within that system. The ultimate effect of these considerations is that the Appeals Chamber must retain a certain flexibility in relation to its own previous decisions when considering what constitute appropriate reasons to exercise the power of departure.[54]

2.1 Appeals Chamber Practice

In light of the limited number of Appeals Chamber decisions on substantive issues to date, it is not possible to discern a meaningful trend in Appeals Chamber decisions to determine whether the principles on precedent in the *Aleksovski Appeal Judgement* reflect the prior practice of the Appeals Chamber. The Appeals Chamber has certainly considered itself bound by its determinations of the law in interlocutory phases of the same proceedings. The Appeals Chamber in *Tadić*, for example, considered itself bound by the

---

[50] Id., para. 17. He did, however, appear to question the wisdom of announcing such a practice in relation to a temporary body such as the Tribunal: Id. para. 15.

[51] Id., para. 14.

[52] Id., para. 20.

[53] Id., para. 22. Judge Hunt had referred to this consideration in his Separate Opinion in *Aleksovski* – see para. 5. Judge Shahabuddeen discussed the legal reasons why it would not even be open to the Security Council to perform the task of correcting any statements by the Tribunal as to what is the law – see *Separate Opinion of Judge Shahabuddeen*, para. 23.

[54] Id., paras. 25–28.

earlier interlocutory decision of a differently composed Appeals Chamber that Article 2 applies only in the context of international armed conflicts.[55] An example of the Appeals Chamber not considering itself bound by a previous Appeals Chamber decision in *different* proceedings is provided by the *Tadić Judgement in Sentencing Appeals*.[56] One of Tadić's grounds of appeal was that the Trial Chamber had erred in holding that crimes against humanity should attract a higher sentence than war crimes. The Trial Chamber had followed the holding of the majority of the Appeals Chamber in *Erdemović* that an act committed as part of a crime against humanity is, all things being equal, a more serious offence than an ordinary war crime and should ordinarily entail a higher penalty.[57] In the *Tadić* proceedings, the Appeals Chamber stated that it had taken account of the parties' arguments "and the authorities to which they refer, inclusive of previous judgements of the Trial Chambers and the Appeals Chamber" and that after full consideration it was of the view that there is no legal distinction between the seriousness of a war crime and that of a crime against humanity. The reasons given for this conclusion were brief:

> The Appeals Chamber finds no basis for such a distinction in the Statute or the Rules of the International Tribunal construed in accordance with international customary law; the authorized penalties are also the same, the level in any particular case being fixed by reference to the circumstances of the case. The position is similar under the Statute of the International Criminal Court, Article 8(1) of the Statute, in the opinion of the Appeals Chamber, not importing a difference.[58]

---

[55] *Prosecutor v. Tadić, Judgement*, Case No. IT-94-1-A, A. Ch., 15 July 1999, para. 80: "According to the interpretation given by the Appeals Chamber in its decision on a Defence Motion for interlocutory appeal on jurisdiction in the present case, the international nature of the conflict is a prerequisite for the applicability of Article 2." The language used by the Appeals Chamber suggested it may not necessarily have taken the same view if it had regarded the question as being open to it to determine – the Appeals Chamber also observed subsequently (para. 83) that the requirement of an *international* conflict had not been contested by the parties. It is unclear what position would have been taken if such a challenge had been made.

[56] *Prosecutor v. Tadić, Judgement*, Case No. IT-94-1-A and IT-94-1-A*bis*, 26 January 2000 ("*Tadić Sentencing Appeals Judgement*").

[57] *Prosecutor v. Erdemović, Joint Separate Opinion of Judge McDonald and Judge Vohrah*, Case No. IT-96-22-A, Judgement, 7 Oct. 1997: Their Honours held that the accused's plea was not informed, in part because he did not appreciate "the true legal distinction" between war crimes and crimes against humanity (para. 19). They identified the relevant distinction as being that all things being equal, a crime against humanity is "more serious and should ordinarily entail a higher penalty" than a war crime. Judge Stephen agreed with Judge McDonald and Judge Vohrah that the plea was not informed for the reasons they expressed: *Separate and Dissenting Opinion of Judge Stephen*, para. 5. The majority's finding was followed in *Prosecutor v. Tadić, Sentencing Judgement*, Case IT-94-T*bis*-R117, 11 Nov. 1999, paras. 28–9. (Judge Robinson in a Separate Opinion, disagreed that crimes against humanity should attract a higher penalty but considered himself bound by the majority's decision in Erdemović: *Separate Opinion of Judge Robinson*, 11 Nov. 1999, p. 2.)

[58] *Tadić Sentencing Appeals Judgement*, para. 69.

There was no express reference to the holding of the majority in *Erdemović*. Nor did the Appeals Chamber provide express reasoning as to why it disagreed with the particular *reasons* provided by the *Erdemović* majority for its different conclusion. It is possible that the Appeals Chamber did not consider the majority's views to form part of the *ratio decidendi* of the decision.[59] It did not express such a view. In any case, the publication of the reasons for its disagreement – if, for example, the *Tadić* Appeals Chamber believed that the *Erdemović* majority had erred in its interpretation of the cases relied on – would have contributed to a clear understanding of the issue and prevent similar errors or misinterpretations[60] occurring in future. Because of the Appeals Chamber's statement in the *Aleksovski Appeal Judgement* that it will only (and then exceptionally) depart from its previous decisions for "cogent reasons" in the interests of justice, it may be expected that future departures from previous decisions will make explicit these reasons.

3. Previous Factual Findings

In domestic systems which recognise a doctrine of binding precedent, the only part of a previous decision which is binding in future is the *ratio decidendi*, essentially the *legal* principle on which the decision depends. Determinations of factual matters are not binding except upon the parties to that decision. Given the unique nature of the elements of certain crimes in the Tribunal's jurisdiction, which require fact findings on large scale matters going beyond events directly involving the accused – such as the requirement that an international armed conflict must be proved for Article 2 offences – it has been suggested that Appeals Chamber decisions on certain factual matters should be binding in subsequent cases. Such a submission has been made by the prosecution in the proceedings in *Prosecutor v Brđanin and Talić*.[61] The prosecution refers to the finding of the Appeals Chamber in the *Tadić* proceedings[62] that the armed forces of the *Republika Srpska* were, at the relevant time, acting under the overall control of and on behalf of the Federal Republic of Yugoslavia with the result that the armed conflict in Bosnia and Herzegovina at that time must be classified as an *international*

---

[59]Views already expressed in other Trial Chambers – both in the Tadić judgement under appeal (supra fn. 44), and in the *Separate Opinion of Judge Shahabuddeen* in *Prosecutor v. Erdemović*, Case No. IT-96-22-T-*bis*, 5 March 1998, at p. 7, indicate that those judges believed that it was indeed part of the *ratio decidendi* of the decision of the *Erdemović* majority. However, recent Prosecution submissions have disagreed with this view: *Prosecutor v. Delalić and Others, Prosecution Response to the Appellants' Supplementary Brief*, filed 25 April 2000, paras. 5.2–5.13.

[60]Unless some sort of error or misinterpretation existed, the Appeals Chamber surely could not have felt free to depart from its previous decision.

[61]Prosecution Response to 'Motion for Dismissal of the Indictment' filed by Counsel for Brđanin and Talić, 28 Feb. 2000, para. 21.

[62]*Judgement*, Case No. IT-94-1-A, A. Ch., 15 July 1999, para. 162.

armed conflict. It was submitted that because the time frame and area in the *Tadić* case is "echoed" in the *Brđanin* and *Talić* proceedings, and because Trial Chambers are bound by Appeals Chamber decisions,[63] for the purposes of Article 2 charges there was an international armed conflict during the relevant period.

A number of arguments can be made in favour of regarding factual decisions on the nature of the conflict as binding. It may appear artificial and inconsistent to have different conclusions on the one issue of whether the conflict in a given area was internal or international. One commentator has observed that the *Tadić Jurisdiction Decision*, where it was determined that the conflict in the former Yugoslavia had both international and internal aspects, leaving it to Trial Chambers to determine the nature of the conflict in each case,[64]

> [...] is unfortunate in that it complicates unnecessarily the further work of the Tribunal by suggesting that each prosecution will have to involve arguments and decisions as to the characterization of the armed conflict in which the alleged offenses occurred and, if the finding is that the conflict is internal, then further arguments and decisions as to the consequences.[65]

In the *Aleksovski* judgment Judge Rodrigues referred to this commentary in his conclusion that the case by case approach, with the possibility that two Trial Chambers hearing different cases which relate to the same conflict may reach different conclusions as to its nature, is undesirable.[66]

The undoubted difficulty of establishing the existence of an international armed conflict makes the charging of Article 2 offences an onerous option for the prosecution. It has been observed that after the *Tadić Jurisdiction Decision* which affirmed the international armed conflict requirement for Article 2 offences, the Prosecutor began to withdraw Article 2 charges from some indictments.[67] Given the growing case load of the Tribunal, the length of trials and the imperative for the Tribunal to ensure expeditious trials,[68]

---

[63]The prosecution relied on the *Separate Opinion of Judge Robinson* in *Prosecutor v. Tadić, Sentencing Judgement*, Case No. IT-94-1-T*bis*-R117, 11 Nov. 1999, p. 2: "The decision of the Appeals Chamber in *Erdemović* ... is, of course, binding on Trial Chambers as to the relative gravity of crimes against humanity and war crimes [...]." The *Aleksovski Appeal Judgement*, with its discussion of precedent, had not been delivered at the time.

[64]*Tadić Jurisdiction Decision*, para. 77.

[65]George H Aldrich, "Jurisdiction of the International Criminal Tribunal for the Former Yugoslavia", 90 *AJIL* 64 (1996) at 68.

[66]*Prosecutor v. Aleksovski, Dissenting Opinion of Judge Rodrigues*, Case No. IT-95-14/1-T, 25 June 1999, para. 27.

[67]Sean D. Murphy, "Progress and Jurisprudence of the International Criminal Tribunal for the Former Yugoslavia", 95 *AJIL* 57 (1999) at 68. The author identifies the cases affected as the "*Furundžija, Jelisić, Kunarac*, and *Kupreškić* cases."

[68]See Article 20 of the Tribunal Statute: "The Trial Chambers shall ensure that a trial is fair and expeditious...".

the attractions of adopting or following previous determinations of other Chambers are obvious.

However, there are also compelling reasons why each Trial Chamber should be required to determine itself all factual questions which go to the very elements of the crimes upon which it is called to adjudicate. As Professor Christopher Greenwood has observed, the answer to the question of the characterisation of the conflict determines the substantive law against which the defendant's conduct must be judged, and "[i]n a criminal trial it would be wholly inappropriate for a question of this importance to be determined without full consideration of the evidence."[69]

If Trial Chambers were bound by an Appeals Chamber finding that the conflict in a particular area was international, it is also hard to see where the limits of such a principle – of the binding nature of factual determinations – would lie. There is little to distinguish decisions as to the character of the conflict from determinations of matters such as the existence of a widespread and systematic attack on the civilian population, one of the preliminary elements of crimes against humanity under Article 5 of the Statute. More significantly, it is also unclear how these examples would be distinguished as a matter of principle from other more fundamental matters such as, for example, an Appeals Chamber finding,[70] or endorsement of a Trial Chamber's finding, in one trial that particular crimes – such as participation in an attack on a civilian population – were committed by a particular accused. It could be argued that the finding that these crimes were committed is binding on the Trial Chamber in the subsequent trial of any superior of that accused who is charged with superior responsibility for offences including the criminal acts of the subordinate. This example starts to touch on matters at the core of the criminal responsibility of each accused. It may then be contended that any principle that Trial Chambers are bound by factual decisions of the Appeals Chamber could be limited to more "objective" issues such as the international character of the conflict. However, it is difficult to draw a clear line between the nature of issues such as the characterisation of the conflict (which itself may require subsidiary fact findings on a number of issues) and questions of whether more specific events (such as might be the subject of an individual's criminal responsibility) occurred, as similar types of evidence and similar fact findings may be involved in each case.

It was not necessary for the Appeals Chamber to express a view on this particular issue in its discussion of precedent in the *Aleksovski Appeal Judgement*. However, both the Judgement and Judge Hunt's Declaration both stress that it is the *ratione decidendi*, or legal principle, of Appeals Chamber

---

[69]Supra note 36 at 275.

[70]See the *Aleksovski Appeal Judgement*, para. 172, for an example of the Appeals Chambers making its own factual findings on whether the accused was responsible for given acts.

decisions which is to be followed.[71] It would be surprising if a subsequent Appeals Chamber came to a different conclusion.

In relation to the specific issue of the characterisation of the conflict, it is possible that compromises might be found by the cautious use of Rule 94.[72] In cases relating to an area and time frame which has been the subject of a previous determination, judicial notice could be taken of adjudicated facts or documentary evidence from other proceedings on various of the factual issues involved in a determination of the nature of the conflict – as distinct from the ultimate legal question of how the conflict should be characterised[73] – and the parties permitted to adduce any additional evidence which may point to a different conclusion. Rule 94 has already been used in circumstances where the parties were agreed on a number of adjudicated facts to be the subject of judicial notice,[74] and where Trial Chamber II decided, *proprio motu*, to take judicial notice of certain facts of relevance to the characterisation of the conflict in Bosnia and Herzegovina.[75] The extent to which Trial Chambers may be willing to take notice of adjudicated facts in the absence of agreement of both parties remains to be seen.

[71]Id, paras. 110 and 113; *Declaration*, para. 9.

[72]Rule 94(B) provides: "At the request of a party or *proprio motu*, a Trial Chamber, after hearing the parties, may decide to take judicial notice of adjudicated facts or documentary evidence from other proceedings of the Tribunal relating to matters at issue in the current proceedings."

[73]See *Prosecutor v. Simić and Others, Decision on the Pre-Trial Motion by the Prosecution Requesting the Trial Chamber to take Judicial Notice of the International Character of the Conflict in Bosnia-Herzegovina*, Case No. IT-95-9-PT, 25 March 1999 ("*Simić Judicial Notice Decision*") where an application pursuant to Rule 94 to take judicial notice of the international character of the conflict as a fact adjudicated in other proceedings (and as a "fact of common knowledge" under Rule 94(A)) was rejected, *inter alia*, because such findings "have no binding force except between the parties in respect of a particular case" and that this is a controversial issue upon which the parties must be able to present evidence and argument: p. 4.

[74]*Prosecutor v. Kvočka, Decision on Prosecutor's Motion for Judicial Notice of Adjudicated Facts*, Case No. IT-98-30-PT, 19 March 1999: "CONSIDERING that it would be in the interests of judicial economy and would promote an expeditious trial for the Trial Chamber to take judicial notice of the adjudicated facts upon which the parties are agreed…" p. 2.

[75]*Simić Judicial Notice Decision*, p. 5: having rejected the application to take judicial notice of the international character of the conflict, the Trial Chamber *proprio motu* took judicial notice of (1) Bosnia and Herzegovina's proclamation of independence from the Socialist Federal Republic of Yugoslavia on 6 March 1992, and (2) the recognition of this independence by the European Community on 6 April 1992 and by the United States on 7 April 1992.

PART VIII

Victims and Witnesses

FLORENCE MUMBA*

28. Ensuring a Fair Trial whilst Protecting Victims and Witnesses – Balancing of Interests?

1. Introduction

The ICTY Statute emphasises the right of the accused to a fair and public trial. The ICTY Statute also acknowledges the need for protection of victims and witnesses. During the trial, measures for protection of victims and witnesses, could potentially affect the right of the accused to a fair and public trial. This note addresses the need for protection of victims and witnesses, the balancing of the interests of an expeditious trial and protection of victims and witnesses against the interests of a fair and public trial for the accused.

A large number of witnesses testifying before the Tribunal are themselves victims of crimes for which the accused are being prosecuted. Many were themselves driven from their homes and subjected to torture, rape or other forms of inhuman treatment. Others saw their family, friends or close relatives being mistreated and killed.

In the following paragraphs, I will discuss the need for the protection of these witnesses and the balancing of interests of such witnesses with those of the accused to a fair and public trial.

*Judge Florence Mumba LLB, Zambia, Vice-President of the International Criminal Tribunal for the former Yugoslavia; Judge Trial Chamber II. Formerly, Judge of the High Court, Investigator-General, Zambia; Vice-President of the International Ombudsman Institute Board; member, UN Commission on the Status of Women. The author wishes to express her gratitude to Jorunn Gjostein for her assistance in the research of this contribution.

R. May et al., Essays on ICTY Procedure and Evidence in Honour of Gabrielle Kirk McDonald, 359–371.

2. The Need for Protection of Witnesses Testifying Before the Tribunal

The conflict in the former Yugoslavia, in which the atrocities which are the subject of the trials at the Tribunal took place, was a conflict between basically three ethnic or religious groups: the Serbs, the Croats and the Muslims. Although the armed conflict in the former Yugoslavia has come to an end, there is still much tension, bitterness and hatred in the region. The bitterness of the peoples of the former Yugoslavia follows ethnic lines.

As mentioned above, witnesses testifying before this Tribunal are, in the main, survivors of these atrocities. In most of the trials, witnesses belong to a different religious or ethnic group from that of the accused. The aim of the testimony of a witness is to prove that the accused committed the crimes, with which he is charged. As a result of the lingering animosities between the various ethnic groups, not only the witness, but also his or her family, and in some cases, a whole local community may be the object of acts of revenge, not only from the accused himself, but also from other individuals belonging to his ethnic or religious group, who are interested in his welfare and are opposed to his being prosecuted.

After their appearance before the Tribunal, most witnesses return to the former Yugoslavia. The need for protection of the witnesses is therefore very real, especially after the witness' appearance before that Tribunal. The fact that there have been reports of cases where witnesses have been threatened proves that the fear of the witnesses is well founded.[1]

The higher an accused was in the hierarchy during the conflict in the former Yugoslavia, the greater is the danger for the witnesses who testify against him, as more individuals will care about the welfare of the accused. The need for protecting the witness' identity for reasons of security is therefore, in general, greater in cases where the accused held a high position in the former Yugoslavia. Due to the situation in the former Yugoslavia, there should be no need for witnesses who testify before the Tribunal to justify their fear or provide evidence of the dangers they face by testifying. Judges are well informed by the Victims and Witnesses Unit. Thus, the trial chambers may assume that the witnesses' fear is well founded.

The protection measures available to the Tribunal are mainly limited to the time before and during the witness' appearance before the Tribunal. Unlike national judicial systems, the Tribunal does not have its own police

[1]See *Prosecutor v. Tadić, Decision on Appellant's Motion for the Extension of the Time-limit and Admission of Additional Evidence*, Case No. IT-94-1-A, A. Ch., 15 Oct. 1998 at para. 9: "The Appellant submits that witness and documentary evidence was not available at trial for a number of reasons, including […] difficulty faced by Appellant in obtaining and collecting evidence in Republica Srpska at the time of the trial, as well as other investigatory difficulties, which meant that […] some witnesses would not come forward due to threats or intimidation, in particular by Simo Drljača (now deceased) and/or Mišo Daničič." See also paras. 59 and 62.

force to protect witnesses on the ground after their testimony. The protection measures available to the Tribunal are therefore to a great extent aimed at minimising the risks to the safety of the witness after returning to his or her country of residence.[2]

In the *Tadić* case, the protective measures sought were divided into five categories: those seeking confidentiality, whereby the victims and witnesses would not be identified to the public and the media (1); those seeking protection from retraumatisation by avoiding confrontation with the accused (2); those seeking anonymity, whereby the victims and witnesses would not be identified to the accused (3); miscellaneous measures for certain victims and witnesses (4); and, finally, general measures for all victims and witnesses who may testify before the Tribunal in the future (5).[3]

Witness anonymity has only been used for the protection of the safety of a witness, whereas confidentiality measures can be aimed at protecting both the safety and the privacy of witnesses. Protection of the witness' privacy through confidentiality measures is particularly relevant in cases of rape and sexual assault, where victims could feel it as an extra burden if it becomes known in their home community that they were raped or sexually assaulted. In many communities, in particular, the Muslim community, a woman known to have been raped will most likely become a social outcast and, if single, she may not have any suitors.

3. Balancing the Protection of Witnesses with the Right of the Accused to a Fair Trial

After having identified the witnesses, their need for protection and the various protective measures available to the Tribunal, we will now look at the accused. What are the rights of the accused and how should the Tribunal balance the rights of the accused *vis-à-vis* the need for protection of witnesses?

Judge Stephen put the problem in his Separate Opinion in the *Tadić* case as "how to respond to the very natural concern of witnesses while at the same time according justice to the accused and ensuring a fair trial".[4]

---

[2] Åsa Rydberg, "The Protection of the Interests of Witnesses – The ICTY in comparison to the Future ICC," 12 *Leiden Journal of International Law* (1999) at p. 470.

[3] *Prosecutor v. Tadić, Decision on the Prosecutor's Motion Requesting Measures for Victims and Witnesses*, Case No. IT-94-1-T, 10 Aug. 1995.

[4] *Prosecutor v. Tadić, Separate Opinion of Judge Stephen on the Prosecutor's Motion Requesting Protective Measures for Victims and Witnesses*, Case No. IT-94-1-T, 10 Aug. 1995 at p. 2.

3.1 Relevant sources of law

The major instruments in determining the balance between the rights of the accused and protection of victims and witnesses, are the basic documents of the Tribunal: the ICTY Statute and the ICTY Rules, and as the Tribunal gradually develops its own practice, the jurisprudence of the Tribunal. In interpreting the ICTY Statute and the ICTY Rules, however, the relevant Security Council resolutions[5] and the Secretary General's Report provide useful guidelines.

The rights of the accused are outlined in various international and regional human rights instruments, such as the Universal Declaration on Human Rights (UDHR), the UN Covenant on Civil and Political Rights (ICCPR), the European Convention on Human Rights (ECHR), the African Charter on Human and Peoples Rights and the American Convention on Human Rights.

One question which has been an issue both in decisions by the Tribunal and in legal literature, is the weight which is to be given to the above mentioned instruments. To what extent is the Tribunal bound by other Human Rights Instruments and the practice of other international bodies?[6]

The question was discussed by the Trial Chamber in the *Tadić* case: "A fundamental issue raised by this motion is whether, in interpreting and applying the Statute and the Rules of the International Tribunal, the Trial Chamber is bound by interpretations of other judicial bodies or whether it is at liberty to adapt those rulings to its own context."[7]

The Trial Chamber further stated:

> Although Article 14 of the ICCPR was the source for Article 21 of the Statute, the terms of that provision must be interpreted within the context of the "object and purpose" and unique characteristics of the Statute. Among those unique considerations is the affirmative obligation to protect victims and witnesses. [...] This affirmative obligation to provide protection to victims and witnesses must be considered when interpreting the provisions of the Statute and Rules of the International Tribunal. In this regard it is also relevant that the International Tribunal is operating in the midst of a continuing conflict and is without a police force or witness protection program to provide protection for victims and witnesses. These considerations are unique: neither Article 14 of the ICCPR nor Article 6 of the European Convention on Human Rights ("ECHR"), which concerns the rights to a fair trial, list the protection of victims and witnesses as one of its primary considerations. As such, the interpretation given by other

[5]SC Res 808, UN Doc. S/Res/808 (22 February 1993); SC Res 827, UN Doc. S/Res/827 (3 May 1993).

[6]This question was examined in an article by Natasha A. Affolder: "*Tadić*, The Anonymous Witness and the Sources of International Procedural Law," 19 *Michigan Journal of International Law* (No. 2 1998) at p. 445.

[7]Supra note 3 at para. 17.

judicial bodies to Article 14 of the ICCPR and Article 6 of the ECHR is only of limited relevance in applying the provisions of the Statute and Rules of the International Tribunal, as these bodies interpret their provisions in the context of their legal framework, which do not contain the same considerations. In interpreting the provisions which are applicable to the International Tribunal and determining where the balance lies between the accused's right to a fair and public trial and the protection of victims and witnesses, the Judges of the International Tribunal must do so within the context of its own unique legal framework.[8]

This is more so that this Tribunal cannot offer witness and victims support on the ground.

In the *Delalić* case however, the Trial Chamber stated: "[D]ecisions on the provisions of the International Covenant on Civil and Political Rights ("ICCPR") and the European Convention on Human Rights ("ECHR") have been found to be authoritative and applicable. This approach is consistent with the view of the Secretary General that many of the provisions in the Statute are formulations based upon provisions found in existing international Instruments (See paragraph 17 of the Report)."[9]

I fully support the ruling of the Trial Chamber in the *Delalić* decision. If the International Tribunal should not feel bound by the standards set out in international human rights instruments, how can one expect states to do so? It is crucial to the work of the Tribunal that it has credibility and support in the world community. In order to achieve and uphold such credibility, the Tribunal must hold on to the highest standards of human rights, and as a tribunal created by the United Nations, it must at least feel bound by instruments created by its parent organ.

In any case, judges of the Tribunal, even though acting independently, are nationals of member states of the UN or state parties to these international instruments, or, by the principle of *jus cogens* are bound by the said instruments.

The Secretary General's Report paragraph 106 reads as follows:

It is axiomatic that the International Tribunal must fully respect internationally recognized standards regarding the rights of the accused at all stages of its proceedings. In the view of the Secretary General, such internationally recognized standards are, in particular, contained in article 14 of the International Covenant on Civil and Political Rights.

I agree with these sentiments. However, the Trial Chamber in interpreting the ICTY Statute and relevant human rights instruments is entitled to take

---

[8]Id., paras. 26–27.

[9]*Prosecutor v. Delalić and Others, Decision on the Motions by the Prosecutor for Protective Measures for the Prosecution Witnesses pseudonymed "B" through "M"*, Case No. IT-96-21-T, 28 Apr. 1997 at para. 27.

into consideration the unique situation of the Tribunal, the situation of the witnesses and the lack of means for protecting the witnesses on the ground. This does not mean that these instruments and their interpretation by other organs, is less relevant to the Tribunal. It merely means that the legal instruments should be interpreted in the factual context of each case before the Tribunal, as in any other case before any other judicial body given the task to interpret legal instruments.

3.2 The balancing of interests

The contrast in the language of Article 20(1) of the ICTY Statute indicates that the right of the accused to a fair trial has priority:

> The Trial Chamber shall ensure that a trial is fair and expeditious and that proceedings are conducted in accordance with the rules of procedure and evidence, with *full respect* for the rights of the accused and *due regard* for the protection of victims and witnesses. (emphasis added)

Rule 75(A) further indicates such a priority:

> A Chamber may [...] order appropriate measures for the privacy and protection of victims and witnesses, *provided that the measures are consistent with the rights of the accused*. (emphasis added)

Article 22 of the Statute requires that "[t]he International Tribunal *shall provide* in its rules of procedure for the protection of victims and witnesses". The Secretary General's Report states in paragraph 99 that "[t]he Trial Chamber should also provide appropriate protection for victims and witnesses during the proceedings", and further in paragraph 108:

> In the light of the particular nature of the crimes committed in the former Yugoslavia, it will be necessary for the International Tribunal to ensure the protection of victims and witnesses. Necessary protection measures should therefore be provided in the rules of procedure and evidence for victims and witnesses, especially in cases of rape or sexual assault. Such measures should include, but should not be limited to the conduct of *in camera* proceedings, and the protection of the victim's identity.

Although the ICTY Statute and the Secretary General's Report emphasise the need for protective measures for witnesses, the relevant articles of the ICTY Statute give no room for undermining the fairness of the trial. Besides, ICTY Rules are secondary legislation and as such cannot override the spirit of the ICTY Statute.

Among the rights of the accused provided for in the ICTY Statute are: the right to a fair and public hearing (Article 21.2), subject to Article 22;

adequate time for the preparation of his defence (Article 21.4 (b)); the right to be present at his trial (Article 21.4 (d)); and the right to examine the witnesses against him (Article 24.4 (e)).

In the following, I will go through some of the most important protective measures and discuss whether they are likely to affect the rights of the accused.

(a) Closed sessions and other confidentiality measures

Both the ICTY Statute (Arts. 20.4 and 22), the Secretary General's Report (paragraph 108) and the ICTY Rules (Rules 75(B) and 79) mention explicitly the conduct of *in camera* proceedings and the protection of the victim's identity as necessary protective measures. The question whether to allow various measures of confidentiality has been raised before the Trial Chambers in numerous motions.[10] The practice of the Tribunal is that such measures are only to be taken when absolutely necessary.

Closed sessions and non-disclosure to the public and the media of the identity of witnesses are measures that are well known to national legal systems. In many national systems it is more the rule than the exception that, cases of rape or sexual assault and other cases, where there is a special need for protection of the privacy of victims and witnesses, are held *in camera*. *In camera* hearings do not, however, affect the fairness of the trial. Nor is the use of closed hearings to protect vulnerable witnesses considered to be in violation of the right to a public trial as secured in Article 14 of the ICCPR or Article 6 of the ECHR or other similar instruments, even if an entire trial is held *in camera*. Thus, these instruments allow exceptions from the principle of public trial under such circumstances.[11]

The public nature of a trial is mainly for education purposes. It is important that people generally understand how the law is applied to facts that constitute crimes. It is also important that people identify the accusations and the accusers to avoid 'framed' trials. The public is also offered an opportunity to assist the administration of justice as they have a choice to respect the law or to suggest changes to the law or the system of justice. This is more true of trials at national level. Having said that, lack of publicity still does not affect the rights of the accused to a fair trial.

In the *Tadić* case, the Trial Chamber stated:

> With regard to the limitation on the accused's right to a public trial, this Trial Chamber has to ensure that any curtailment of the accused's right to a public

---

[10] See for example *Prosecutor v. Tadić, Decision on the Prosecutor's Motion Requesting Protective Measures for Witness "R"*, Case No. IT-94-1-T, 31 July 1996; *Prosecutor v. Furund'ija, Decision on Prosecutor's Motion Requesting Protective Measures for Witnesses "A" and "D" at Trial,* Case No. IT-95-17/1-T, 11 June 1998.

[11] ICCPR Art. 14. 1: "[…] The press and the public may be excluded from all or part of a trial for reasons of morals, public order ("*ordre public*") or national security in a democratic society, or when the interest of the private lives of the parties so requires, or to the extent strictly necessary in the opinion of the court in special circumstances where publicity would prejudice the interests of justice […]" (emphasis added).

> hearing is justified by a genuine fear for the safety of witness R and/or the members of witness R's family. [...] In balancing the interests of the accused, the public and witness R, this Trial Chamber considers that the public's right to information and the accused's right to a public hearing must yield in the present circumstances to confidentiality in light of the affirmative obligation under the Statute and the Rules to afford protection to victims and witnesses.[12]

As the application of protective measures is open to the accused and his witnesses, the use of confidentiality measures does not affect the right to equality of arms.

(b) Measures aimed at protecting witnesses from retraumatisation

One-way closed circuit television, allowing the witness to testify without seeing the accused, and restrictions on the questions that the parties may ask the witness are aimed at protecting the witness from the trauma of reliving the atrocities. Such measures are in particular relevant for witnesses who have been victims of sexual violence and other forms of personal violence.

ICTY Rule 96 deals with evidence in cases of sexual assault:

> In cases of sexual assault:
> (i) no corroboration of the victim's testimony shall be required;
> (ii) consent shall not be allowed as a defence if the victim
> (a) has been subjected to or threatened with or has had reason to fear violence, duress, detention or psychological oppression, or
> (b) reasonably believed that if the victim did not submit, another might be so subjected, threatened or put in fear;
> (iii) before evidence of the victim's consent is admitted, the accused shall satisfy the Trial Chamber *in camera* that the evidence is relevant and credible;
> (v) prior sexual conduct of the victim shall not be admitted in evidence.

ICTY Rule 75(C) states: "A Chamber shall, whenever necessary, control the manner of questioning to avoid any harassment or intimidation."

The restrictions on consent as a defence and evidence regarding prior sexual conduct are stronger in the ICTY Rules than in many national legal systems. These restrictions are, however, well founded, as they help minimise the trauma for one of the most vulnerable groups of witnesses with a minimum of effect on the accused's right to defend himself. The pattern of sexual violence during the war in the former Yugoslavia shows that the defence of consent and evidence of prior sexual conduct is less relevant in cases before the Tribunal than in most cases before national courts. Women of all ages and also young girls were raped indiscriminately, some being subjected to gang rapes, circumstances under which evidence of prior sexual conduct and consent as a defence is very unlikely to be relevant. Limitations on the defence of consent and evidence of prior sexual conduct are,

[12] Supra note 3 at para. 6.

therefore, unlikely to affect the right of the accused to defend himself.[13] As regards ICTY Rule 75(C), this rule does not affect the right of the accused to a fair trial, as the guarantee of a fair trial does not contain a right to intimidate or harass witnesses.

(c) Anonymity – non-disclosure of the identity of witnesses to the Defence

Rule 69(A) provides for non-disclosure to the defence of a witness' identity until such person is brought under the protection of the Tribunal. This rule is only to be used in exceptional circumstances. The identity shall however, be disclosed in sufficient time prior to the trial to allow adequate time for preparation of the defence pursuant to Rule 69(D). The non-disclosure of the identity of a witness until a short period before commencement of trial proceedings does not violate the right of the accused to prepare his defence, as most of the defence can be prepared without knowledge of the identity of a witness. When the identity, within a reasonable time before the trial, is disclosed to the Defence, there should be sufficient time to prepare the remainder of the defence case. What constitutes a reasonable time does, however, differ from case to case, depending among other things on the role of the witness.

A different situation occurs, however, if the Prosecutor applies for complete non-disclosure to the accused and his counsel of the identity of a witness. The question whether to allow anonymous witnesses to testify before the Tribunal was discussed in the *Tadić* case[14], the *Blaškić* case[15] and the *Delalić* case[16].

Only in one decision has a Trial Chamber granted complete anonymity for a witness during trial. This was in the *Tadić* case, decision of 10 August 1995, to which Judge Stephen gave a separate opinion.[17]

In the majority ruling, the Trial Chamber stated that: "[t]he situation of armed conflict that existed and endures in the area where the alleged atrocities were committed is an exceptional circumstance *par excellence*."[18]

[13]The Cross-Examination Right before the ICTY was examined in an article by Alex C. Lakatos, "Evaluating the Rules of Procedure and Evidence for the International Tribunal in the Former Yugoslavia: Balancing Witnesses' Needs Against Defendants' Rights," 46 *Hastings Law Journal* (No. 3 March 1995), at pp. 932–937.

[14]Supra notes 3 and 4.

[15]*Prosecutor v. Blaškić, Decision on the application of the Prosecutor dated 17 October 1996 requesting protective measures for victims and witnesses*, Case No. IT-95-14-T, 5 Nov. 1996.

[16]*Prosecutor v. Delalić and Others, Decision on the motions by the Prosecutor for protective measures for the protection of witnesses pseudonymed "B" through "M"*, Case No. IT-96-21-T, 28 Apr. 1997.

[17]The decision has been examined and commentated in the following articles: Monroe Leigh, "The Yugoslav Tribunal: Use of Unnamed Witnesses Against Accused," 90 *AJIL* (1996) 235; Christine M. Chinkin, "Due Process and Witness Anonymity," 91 *AJIL* (1997) 75; Monroe Leigh, "Witness Anonymity Is Inconsistent with Due Process," 91 *AJIL* (1997) 80; and Affolder, supra note 6 at p. 445.

[18]Supra note 3 at para. 61.

The Trial Chamber then listed five conditions, which the Prosecutor needs to satisfy before a measure of anonymity would be granted: real fear for the safety of the witness or his or her family (1); the testimony of the particular witness must be important to the Prosecutor's case (2); the Trial Chamber has to be satisfied that there is no prima facie evidence that the witness is untrustworthy (3); ineffectiveness or non-existence of a witness protection program (4); and, finally, any measures taken should be strictly necessary. If less restrictive measures can secure the required protection, that measure should be applied.[19]

In the *Blaškić* case, Trial Chamber I, referred to the ruling by Trial Chamber II in the *Tadić* decision regarding exceptional circumstances and stated: "But it is public knowledge that this situation no longer exists and the Prosecutor cannot benefit from it. This Trial Chamber is not satisfied that the case-file demonstrates the existence of an "exceptional case," the pre-requisite for taking into consideration the five conditions which might lead to the granting of the protective measures the Prosecutor has requested."[20] Trial Chamber I, however, seems to support the five categories set out by Trial Chamber II in the *Tadic* decision.

In my view, however, the legal instruments of this Tribunal do not allow anonymous witnesses at trial. The ICTY Statute states in Arts. 20(1) and 21(2) the right of the accused to a "fair trial". Article 21(4) (e) specifically guarantees the accused the right to "examine, or have examined, the witnesses against him".

Article 22 of the ICTY Statute states that "the International Tribunal shall provide in its rules of procedure and evidence for the protection of victims and witnesses". Rule 75(B) lists protective measures that a Chamber may order. Non-disclosure of the witness' identity to the accused and his counsel is not among the listed protective measures. The ICTY Rules so far do not provide for non-disclosure of the identity of a witness to the accused during the trial. In my view, in order for a Trial Chamber to order such non-disclosure, this would have to be provided for through amendment of the Rules, because I think it is such a drastic step, since it may hamper fair cross-examination of the unknown witness.

Further, ICTY Rule 69(A) and (C) state:

> In *exceptional circumstances*, the Prosecutor may apply to a Trial Chamber to order the non-disclosure of the identity of a victim or witness who may be in danger or at risk *until such person is brought under the protection of the Tribunal.* [...] Subject to Rule 75, the identity of the victim or witness *shall be disclosed in sufficient time prior to the trial to allow adequate time for the preparation of the defence*. (emphasis added)

---

[19]Id. paras. 62–66.
[20]Supra note 15 at para. 45.

First, ICTY Rule 69(A) states that non-disclosure may only be ordered in 'exceptional circumstances'. Second, it states that the identity must be disclosed when the person is brought under the protection of the Tribunal. And third, Rule 69(C) states that the identity of the victim or witness shall be disclosed in sufficient time prior to the trial to allow adequate time for preparation of the defence. The disclosure discussed here is to the accused, not to the public.

In my view, granting of witness anonymity during trial is inconsistent with the ICTY Rules. In his Separate Opinion in the *Tadić* decision, Judge Stephen stated: "But as to any general anonymity in the case of witnesses who have had dealings with the defendant and are known to him, I would regard it as curious indeed for the Rules, after such specific and elaborate provisions for full disclosure, to introduce so radical a concept of anonymity by such indirect and ambiguous wording,"[21] and further: "I can conclude my survey of the Rules by saying, in sum, that they give no support for anonymity of witnesses at the expense of fairness of the trial and the rights of the accused spelt out in Article 21."[22] In the *Blaškić* case Trial Chamber I unanimously concurred with the above quoted opinion.[23]

Further, witness anonymity is only consistent with the ICTY Statute and the ICCPR and other relevant human rights instruments if it does not affect the accused's right to a fair trial, to prepare his defence and to cross-examine the witnesses against him. I believe that it is rare to find situations where witness anonymity does not affect these fundamental rights.

In his Separate Opinion, Judge Stephen stated: "My conclusion therefore is that the Statute does not authorise anonymity of witnesses where this would in a real sense affect the rights of the accused specified in Article 21 and in particular the "minimum guarantee" in (4)."[24]

Judge Stephen further stated about the combination of an anonymous witness and other protective measures:

> The consequence could be that to the defence the accuser would appear as no more than a disembodied and distorted voice transmitted by electronic means. Yet this could be the means of bringing before the Chamber evidence which the prosecution has described as either very important or important, evidence which could lead to the accused's conviction on very serious charges.[25]

In *Kostovski v. The Netherlands*, the European Court of Human Rights stated: "How can one conceive of the accused being afforded an equitable trial, adequate time for preparation of his defence, and intelligent cross-

[21]Supra note 4 at para. 13.
[22]Id. p. 15.
[23]Supra note 15 at para. 34.
[24]Supra note 4 at p. 11.
[25]Id., p. 12.

examination of the Prosecution witnesses if he does not know from where and by whom he is accused?"[26]

Judge Stephen seems to leave open the possibility for witness anonymity in two situations, in which he finds that the right of the accused to a fair trial is not threatened: under-cover police witnesses, where the accused has known the witness in the past but only under a false name, the false name can be revealed; and where the witness has been a mere chance observer who is not known to the accused at all. Judge Stephen found that for these categories of witnesses, different considerations apply. Although the non-disclosure of the witness' identity may prevent the defence from conducting prior inquiry, Judge Stephen concluded that such non-disclosure is not problematic, as he found that it does not prevent the defence from conducting a proper cross-examination of the witness.[27]

I do not fully agree with Judge Stephen that allowing anonymous mere chance observer witnesses does not affect the cross-examination. In cases where the defence wishes to question whether an alleged eyewitness was present at the crime scene, it could be necessary for the defence to know the witness's identity in order to disprove the whereabouts of the witness. Further, if the defence finds reason to examine the credibility of a witness, this could be difficult without the knowledge of the witness identity, especially as such investigations could require knowledge of the witness' past and other identifying information.

Concerning the argument that witnesses who were victims of sexual violence have a special need for protection, Judge Stephen stated: "What does make their case special is the combination of possible social consequences of it becoming generally known in communities in the former Yugoslavia that a woman has been a rape victim and also the often acute trauma facing one's attacker in court and being made to relieve the experience of the rape. The customary protection measures to guard against these two possible consequences are *in camera* proceedings, devices to avoid confrontation with the accused in court and careful control of cross-examination. That being so, it leads me to the conclusion that it is measures such as those, and not any wholesale anonymity of witnesses, that Article 22 primarily contemplates."[28]

---

[26]*Kostovski v. Netherlands*, 1989 Series A No. 166, The European Court of Human Rights, para. 25.

[27]Supra note 4 at pp. 13–14.

[28]Id., p. 11.

4. CONCLUDING REMARKS

It is clear from the discussions above that the Tribunal has to apply unusual measures to discharge its mandate without undermining the established doctrines of criminal law. It has an unusual status, consequently it can only operate taking into account its uniqueness while at the same time remaining credible as an instrument of international justice for all: victims, witnesses and accused persons.

SUSANNE MALMSTRÖM[1]

29. Restitution of Property and Compensation to Victims

1. Introduction

In international law restitution and compensation are concepts usually based on the principle of State responsibility.[2] However, the Tribunal only has jurisdiction over natural persons; its Statute and Rules focusing on the individual's responsibility and liability. Therefore, the term restitution in the ICTY Rules does not relate to State responsibility; the State' role is to enforce the Tribunal's orders on restitution. Such restitution is to individuals from another individual; the term thereby reflects principles in national legal systems.

Genocide, crimes against humanity and war crimes often occur in the context of a general breakdown of order in a State. In such situations individuals as well as States may be responsible for the crimes and thus liable for compensation. Compensation in the ICTY Rules only relates to compensation which is awarded by national courts to the victims. The Tribunal does not have any authority to award compensation.

Restitution of property and compensation to victims are addressed in two separate Rules in the ICTY Rules and will therefore be treated separately below. As the two Rules do not relate to compensation claims against the ICTY and the United Nations, such claims are not covered in this paper.[3]

---

[1]Associate Legal Officer, Appeals Chamber ICTY. The views expressed herein are those of the author and not of the Tribunal or United Nations.

[2]See for example, *Chorzow Factory Case*, PCIJ, Series A, no. 17, 1928; *Trial Smelter Arbitration Case*, (*US v. Canada*) UNRIAA 1905; *Iran Case*, ICJ Reports (1980); *Rainbow Warrior Case*, 74 ILR.

[3]With regard to compensation from the United Nations, see for example *Barayagwiza v. Prosecutor*, Decision, Case No. ICTR-97-19-AR72, A. Ch., 3 Nov. 1999; *Barayagwiza v. Prosecutor, Decision* (*Prosecutor's Request for Review or Reconsideration*), Case No. ICTR-97-19-AR72, A. Ch., 31 March 2000; *Semanza v. Prosecutor, Decision,* Case No. ICTR-97-20-A, A. Ch., 31 May 2000.

R. May et al., Essays on ICTY Procedure and Evidence in Honour of Gabrielle Kirk McDonald, 373–384.

2. Restitution of property

With regard to restitution of property the International Tribunal is entitled, pursuant to Article 24(3) of the ICTY Statute, to "order the return of any property and proceeds acquired by criminal conduct, including by means of duress, to their rightful owners."[4] An identical provision is found in the ICTR Statute.[5] The provision in the ICTY Statute is expanded in more detail in the ICTY Rules, more specifically in Rule 105, which reads:

> (A) After a judgement of conviction containing a specific finding as provided in Sub-rule 98 *ter*, the Trial Chamber shall, at the request of the Prosecutor, or may, *proprio motu*, hold a special hearing to determine the matter of the restitution of the property or the proceeds thereof, and may in the meantime order such provisional measures for the preservation and protection of the property or proceeds as it considers appropriate.
> (B) The determination may extend to such property or its proceeds, even in the hands of third parties not otherwise connected with the crime of which the convicted person has been found guilty.
> (C) Such third parties shall be summoned before the Trial Chamber and be given an opportunity to justify their claim to the property or its proceeds.
> (D) Should the Trial Chamber be able to determine the rightful owner on the balance of probabilities, it shall order the restitution either of the property or the proceeds or make such other order as it may deem appropriate.
> (E) Should the Trial Chamber not be able to determine ownership, it shall notify the competent national authorities and request them so to determine.
> (F) Upon notice from the national authorities that an affirmative determination has been made, the Trial Chamber shall order the restitution either of the property or the proceeds or make such other order as it may deem appropriate.
> (G) The Registrar shall transmit to the competent national authorities any summonses, orders and requests issued by a Trial Chamber pursuant to Sub-rules (C), (D), (E) and (F).[6]

The original version of this Rule was adopted at the Second Plenary Session in 1994.[7] The Rule was changed substantially at the Fifth Plenary Session[8]

---

[4] Art. 24(3) ICTY Statute reads: "In addition to imprisonment, the Trial Chambers may order the return of any property and proceeds acquired by criminal conduct, including by means of duress, to their rightful owner."

[5] Art. 23(3) ICTR Statute.

[6] Rule 105 ICTY Rules, Rev. 17.

[7] The original ICTY Rules were adopted on 11 Feb. 1994 at the Second Plenary Session pursuant to Article 15 of the ICTY Statute. The ICTY Rules entered into force on 14 March 1994.

[8] On 30 Jan. 1995, the following sub-paragraphs were amended; sub-paragraph (D), "as appropriate" was replaced with, "or make such other order as it may deem appropriate"; a new sub-paragraph (F) was introduced which reads: "Upon notice from the national authorities that an affirmative determination has been made, the Trial Chamber shall order the restitution either of the property or the proceeds or make such other order as it may deem appropriate." Former sub-paragraph (F) became (G).

and small technical changes were made at the Thirteenth[9] and Eighteenth[10] Plenary Sessions. The ICTR Rules has a provision with the same content.[11]

In order to interpret the application of the Rule, guidance may be found in the Report of the Secretary-General,[12] but on this issue it is not very informative or complete. However, read in conjunction with the Statute and the Rules, an indication is given that the principle underlying this Rule is the same as may be found in many national systems, namely the principle against unjust enrichment, whereby a perpetrator of a crime should not profit from the crime and property acquired by criminal conduct should be returned.

Rule 105 together with Rule 98*ter*(B) set out three requirements to allow for the restitution of property.[13] First, the conviction of an accused is required. Second, a connection must exist between the crime and the property taken, that is the unlawful taking of property must be "associated with" the crime.[14] The third criterion is that a request of the Prosecutor or action of the Chamber *proprio motu* is required for restitution. The second and third requirements will be discussed below.

The Rules require an association with the crime, but what constitutes such association is not exactly defined in the Rules. As the crimes under the Tribunal's jurisdiction are extremely serious and complex in nature, the requirement of "associated with" may be difficult to interpret. Crimes may have occurred over the timeframe of several years and over a large geographical area. It is submitted, however, that the Rule is applicable regardless of which crime the accused is convicted of under the Tribunal's jurisdiction. The accused does not have to be convicted of the crime of looting or plunder. For example, a person convicted of persecution, as a crime against humanity where the persecution involves the "emptying" of a village where houses and businesses were taken over or a person convicted of wilful killing as grave breaches of the Geneva Conventions also steals the victim's property, the requirement of association is likely to be fulfilled as

---

[9]25 July 1997, sub-paragraph (A) was amended so that, "at its own initiative" was replaced with "*proprio motu*."

[10]10 July 1998, as Rule 88 was deleted, a reference to Rule 88 was changed to Rule 98*ter*.

[11]Rule 105 ICTR Rules.

[12]Secretary General's Report pursuant to Security Council Resolution 808, para. 114 states; "[i]n addition to imprisonment, property and proceeds acquired by criminal conduct should be confiscated and returned to their rightful owners. This would include the return of property wrongfully acquired by means of duress. In this connection the Secretary-General recalls that in resolution 779 (1992) of 6 October 1992, the Security Council endorsed the principle that all statements or commitments made under duress, particularly those relating to land and property, are wholly null and void".

[13]Rule 98*ter*(B) ICTY Rules, reads; "If the Trial Chamber finds the accused guilty of a crime and concludes from the evidence that unlawful taking of property by the accused was associated with it, it shall make a specific finding to that effect in its judgement. The Trial Chamber may order restitution as provided in Rule 105."

[14]Rule 98*ter* ICTY Rules.

there is unlawful taking of property associated with the crimes. Thus, the person may be convicted of any crime and restitution of property is not depending on which crime the convicted person is found liable. It must only be possible to conclude the unlawful taking of the property from the evidence in the case.

Further, the language of "unlawful taking of property by the accused" requires a link between the accused and the property taken. However, it is submitted that the phrase does not limit the application of the Rule in the sense that the convicted person has to be involved personally in the unlawful taking or has to have the property in his possession. The provision should be interpreted to be equally applicable when the person is found guilty as an aider or abettor or as a commander, as the crime is still "associated with" the property. The underlying principle is that there should not be any gain from criminal conduct, and a conviction for aiding or abetting, in which the crime committed is associated with unlawful taking of property, should result in such property being returned to the rightful owner.

Further, the Rule does not require the accused to be in possession of the property and the Tribunal can order the restitution of property in the hands of third parties.[15] The authority to order the return of property in the hands of third party, is a far-reaching authority, which is not unusual in national jurisdictions. Sub-Rule 105(C) implies consideration of good-faith acquisition, as it provides that third parties shall be summoned and be given an opportunity to justify their claims to the property and proceeds.[16]

In determining if a third party has acted in good faith, it is submitted that the International Tribunal will be required to establish its own definition and determination of the concept. This might be difficult as the standards and definitions in national systems, where existing at all, are inconsistent. The definition of good faith is especially problematic in relation to enforcement, as the Tribunal's concept of good faith may contravene the national legislation in the State where the orders will be enforced.

With regard to the third criterion, as stated above, a request of the Prosecutor or action of the Chamber *proprio motu* is required for restitution. An individual does not have *locus standi* before the Tribunal, and therefore cannot make a claim for restitution of property. It is only the Prosecutor or the Chamber that may initiate the restitution of property. There is not any requirement that the beneficiaries must be witnesses in the Tribunal's proceedings. To date the Prosecutor has made no such request in any case before the ICTY or the ICTR, nor have any of the Chambers acted *proprio motu*, and thus the Rule has never been applied.[17]

---

[15]Rule 105(B) ICTY Rules.

[16]Art. 109 of the Rome Statute states that "[a] forfeiture of proceeds, property and assets derived directly or indirectly from that crime, without prejudice to the right of bona fides third parties."

[17]As of 25 May 2000.

However, there have been cases before the Tribunal in which it has been established by the evidence in the case that property was illegally taken from the victims of the crime. For example in the *Aleksovski* Judgement, the Trial Chamber found that:

> seven witness [sic] reported thefts during the search while the accused was present. According to Witness L, the thefts were committed on orders from the accused. Witnesses Osmancević, E, I, J, L, Garanović and Meho Sivro explained that the guards ordered the detainees to empty their pockets and that their belongings were seized. Some witnesses even said that they were robbed of their clothes and shoes.[18]

The accused Aleksovski was found guilty with regard to these acts, with the Trial Chamber finding that he "aided and abetted in the commission of these acts. In his capacity as prison warden he was clearly in charge of organising the body-searches of detainees and of supervising them."[19] This aspect of the judgement was upheld on appeal.[20]

Before the ICTR, the Rwandan Government has expressed its dissatisfaction with the handling of the issue of restitution of property in the *Bagosora* case[21] where it has requested to appear as *amicus curiae* before the ICTR. The request asks the Tribunal "to order the restitution of property stolen, looted and taken away by the accused; to return the property and any proceeds derived from them to their real owners."[22] The Trial Chamber heard the motion in May 2000 but a decision is currently pending.

If there is a conviction, unlawful taking of property associated with the crime and a request from the Prosecutor, or an initiative from the Trial Chamber, a spccial hearing shall be convened to determine the matter of the restitution of property. At the hearing the Trial Chamber should determine the rightful owner of the property. This determination is done in accordance with Rule 105(D) on the balance of probabilities. It means that the standard of proof is lower than in the judgements of the Tribunal, where an accused has to be found guilty beyond reasonable doubt in order to be convicted. The Rules do not offer a definition of balance of probabilities. It is submitted that, if it is probable that certain property belongs to another person than the convicted person, the Tribunal should order the restitution of such property, provided the other requirements of Rule 105 are met. In instances where the Chamber is not in the position to identify the rightful owner, Rule 105(A) provides it shall request the assistance of the competent national authorities in identifying the rightful owner.[23]

---

[18] *Prosecutor v. Aleksovski, Judgement*, Case No. IT-95-14/1/T, 25 June 1999 at p. 72, para. 186.
[19] Id., pp. 34–35 para. 87.
[20] *Prosecutor v. Aleksovski Judgement*, Case No. IT-95-14/1-A, A. Ch., 24 March 2000.
[21] *Prosecutor v. Bagosora and Others*, Case No. ICTR-98-37.
[22] Fondation Hirondelle – Hirondelle Press Agency in Arusha. International Criminal Tribunal for Rwanda. News May 11th 2000. ICTY/Bagosora. Rwandan Government asks to appear in Bagosora case.
[23] Rule 105(E) ICTY Rules.

Following a conviction, while awaiting such special hearing, the Tribunal has the authority to order "such provisional measures for the preservation and protection of the property or proceeds, as it considers appropriate."[24] The intention is to hinder the convicted person and third parties from selling or in other ways disposing of the property. However, as the Rule is only applicable after conviction, its impact may be limited.

The Tribunal may, however, when issuing an international arrest warrant order provisional measures to freeze the assets of an accused,[25] which are aimed at limiting the accused's possibilities of avoiding arrest. The Prosecutor has recently suggested that such "frozen assets" should be used for compensation to the victims.[26] However, such a solution will require changes to the Statute as the Tribunal does not have the mandate to award compensation. However, the Tribunal has the mandate to order restitution of property but it is also unclear if the Tribunal may order the restitution of such "frozen assets" without changes to the Statute and the Rules. There is currently no provision regulating the continued freezing of the accused's assets during trial nor any provisions on how such assets should be distributed following a conviction. Further, all the frozen assets of an accused may not be associated with the crime under the Tribunal's jurisdiction.

Rule 109 of the Statute of ICC provides that if the state party is not in a position to return the property, it shall take measures to recover the value of the property.[27] The ICTY Rules do not provide for this explicitly, but provide that the Trial Chamber may make "such other order it may deem appropriate."[28] There is therefore nothing precluding the Tribunal from making an order requesting the restitution of the value of the property if the property as such cannot be returned. The Registry of the ICTY has the

---

[24]Rule 105(A) ICTY Rules.

[25]Rule 61(D) ICTY Rules.

[26]Security Council Minutes from 4150th meeting, UN Doc. S/PV.4150, (2 June 2000), p. 5. The Prosecutor Carla Del Ponte stated " [...] This is a very important aspect of our activities. If we cut off the funding – that is, the bank accounts – of the inductees, not only will we make their escape more difficult, but the money, according to the Chamber judges' decision, will also be used to provide compensation to the victims. [...] It would be regrettable were we are unable to obtain such a decision from the judges. There is a problem, however. There is a loophole in our law. Our procedural rules do not provide access to confiscated sequestered funds. That is why we would request that a change be made in the rules."

[27]Art.109 of the Rome Statute reads: "(1) State Parties shall give effect to fines or forfeitures ordered by the Court under part 7, without prejudice to the rights of bona fide third parties, and in accordance with the procedure of their national law. (2) If a State party is unable to give effect to an order for forfeiture, it shall take measures to recover the value of the proceeds, property or assets ordered by the Court to be forfeited, without prejudice to the rights of bona fide third parties. (3) Property, or the proceeds of the sale of real property or, where appropriate, the sale of other property, which is obtained by a State Party as a result of its enforcement of a judgement of the Court shall be transferred to the Court."

[28]Rule 105(F) ICTY Rules.

responsibility of transmitting orders to the competent national authorities, which are then responsible for the enforcement of the orders received.

The ICTY Rules on restitution of property provide a unique mechanism, whereby an International Tribunal may order restitution of property from one individual to another under international law, but outside the concept of state responsibility.

3. Compensation to Victims

Traditionally in international law compensation is awarded to States. There is no international mechanism in place where individual victims of armed conflicts may claim compensation. However, there is a trend towards providing compensation not only to states but also to individuals based on state responsibility.[29] One recent example is the United Nations Compensation Committee ("UNCC"),[30] where individuals have a possibility to be awarded compensation based on Iraq's legal responsibility,[31] for what in many instances are human rights violations and breaches of humanitarian law.[32]

States may also be found liable to pay compensation granted to individuals under regional human rights treaties. For example Article 50 of the European Convention on Human Rights and Fundamental Freedoms,[33] provides:

---

[29]A/51/10, at p. 125, Report of the International Law Commission on the work of its forty-eighth session, 6 May–26 July 1996. The International Law Commission in its draft articles on State responsibility provides unlike the situation in traditional international law, the violating States' duty to provide reparation for the breach if not owed primarily to other Contracting States but to the injured individual.

[30]SC Res. 687, UN Doc. S/RES/687 (8 April 1991).

[31]It was established in 1991 by the Security Council with the mandate to process claims and pay compensation for losses resulting for the Iraq's unlawful invasion and occupation of Kuwait. There are three categories of claimants, individuals, corporations and governments. The claims of individuals and corporations are submitted through the respective governments. Governments may submit claims on behalf of their national and of other persons resident in their territory. Article 5 (1) Rules for Claims Procedure. See further, Norbert Wühler, "The United Nations Compensation Commission", in Albrecht Randelzhofer and Christian Tomuschat (Eds.), State responsibility and the Individual Reparation in Instances of Grave Violations of Human Rights (1999) at pp. 213–231.

[32]Governing Council decision 11, UN Doc. S/AC.26/1991/1, (2 Aug. 1991). Claims by members of the Allied Coalition Armed Forces, as a consequence of their involvement in coalition military operations against Iraq, are excluded, except if they are for loss or injury that is otherwise compensable before the Commission, if the claimant that been a prisoner of war, and if the loss or injury resulted from mistreatment in violation of international humanitarian law (including the Geneva Conventions of 1949).

[33]European Convention for the Protection of Human Rights and Fundamental Freedoms, adopted by the Council of Europe on 4 Nov. 1950, Rome, entered into force 3 Sept. 1953. Art. 50.

> If the Court finds that a decision or a measure taken by a legal authority or any other authority of a High Contracting party is completely or partially in conflict with the obligations arising from the present Convention, and if the internal law of the said party allows only partial reparation to be made for the consequences of this decision or measure, the decision of the Court shall, if necessary, afford just satisfaction to the injured party.

Further, the International Covenant on Civil and Political Rights ("ICCPR"),[34] sets forth provisions calling for a national regime of compensation in the event a person is unlawfully arrested or detained, in Article 9(5) which reads that "Anyone who has been a victim of unlawful arrest or detention shall have an enforceable right to compensation."

Further, victims of miscarriages of justice should have a right to compensation, which is provided for in Article 14 (6) of the ICCPR, which states:

> When a person has by a final decision been convicted of a criminal offence been pardoned on the ground that a new or newly discovered fact shows conclusively that there has been a miscarriage of justice, the person who has suffered punishment as a result of such conviction shall be compensated according to law, unless it is proved that the non-disclosure of the unknown fact in time is wholly or partly attributable to him.

Under the ICCPR compensation is not awarded to the individual victims; the treaty is merely providing for an obligation for State Parties to establish a national compensation scheme with regard to certain violations of human rights.

The title of Rule 106 of the ICTY Rules, "Compensation to Victims," is misleading to the extent that it implies that the Tribunal can award compensation to victims. In the context of the ICTY Rules compensation is a term which relates to one individual being liable to pay compensation to another individual based on individual criminal responsibility and is therefore different from the above-mentioned examples. The Tribunal does not have the authority to decide on an amount to be awarded to a victim nor can it direct States to award compensation. The victims are those who have suffered the consequences of a substantive crime under the ICTY jurisdiction and not those potential victims of violations of their rights by the Tribunal.

The Security Council when adopting the ICTY Statute decided that "the work of the International Tribunal shall be carried out without prejudice to the right of the victim to seek, through appropriate means, compensation for damages incurred as a result of violations of international humanitarian law."[35] Nonetheless, there is no provision in the Statute, which addresses the

[34] International Covenant on Civil and Political Rights, 999 UNTS 171 (16 Dec. 1966).
[35] SC Res 827, UN Doc. S/Res/827 (1993), (25 May 1993), at para. 7.

issue of compensation to victims. It is therefore unclear whether the Security Council considered the issue to be within the Tribunal's mandate.

However, the Rule as adopted by the judges of the ICTY provides:

> (A) The Registrar shall transmit to the competent authorities of the State concerned the judgement finding the accused guilty of a crime which has caused injury to a victim.
>
> (B) Pursuant to the relevant national legislation, a victim or person claiming through the victim may bring an action in a national court or other competent body to obtain compensation.
>
> (C) For the purposes of a claim made under Sub-rule (B) the judgement of the Tribunal shall be final and binding as to the criminal responsibility of the convicted person for such injury.[36]

The original Rule was adopted at the Second Plenary Session and only a minor revision of the text was adopted at the Thirteenth Session.[37] The ICTR has a similar provision.[38] Former ICTY President Cassese described the background to the adoption of the Rule as follows:

> We decided to adopt provisions in Rule 106 of our Rules of procedure whereby the Tribunal has the right to transmit the judgement to the relevant national authorities deciding that somebody, say, has been raped or has been the victim of physical atrocities, and then we also go on to say that under the national legislation the victim, or person claiming through the victim, may bring action in a national court. This is a sort of hint to the victim: please go to the national court and try to get some sort of vindication of your rights.[39]

Rule 106 provides that the Registry of the ICTY shall transmit the judgement to the concerned State. Further, it requires that the crime cause injury to the victim, but it does not specify what type of injury. 'Victim' is not defined in the Rules.[40] The only guidance given is that the Rule is equally applicable for persons claiming through the victim, without defining if the

---

[36]Rule 106 ICTY Rules.

[37]25 July 1997, sub-paragraph (B) was amended; "him" was replaced with "the victim".

[38]Rule 106 ICTR Rules.

[39]Albrecht Randelzhofer and Christian Tomuschat (Eds.), State Responsibility and the Individual, Reparation in Instances of Grave Violations of Human Rights (1999) at p. 48.

[40]To determine the notion of victim, both individually and collectively, it is useful to refer to the UN Declaration of Basic Principles of Justice for Victims of Crime and Abuse of Power, Annex to GA Res 40/34 of 29 Nov. 1985, at paras. 1 and 2, which reads: "'Victim' means persons who, individually, or collectively, have suffered harm, including physical or mental injury, emotional suffering, economic loss or substantial impairment of their fundamental rights [...]". "[...] The term 'victim' also includes, where appropriate, the immediate family or dependants of the direct victim and persons who have suffered harm in intervening to assist victims in distress or to prevent victimization."

person has to be related or may be a representative of an organisation, etc. Rule 106 does not preclude collective claims. However, as the claim has to be brought before a national court, the issue of who is entitled to bring claims, will be dependent upon the respective national laws. The relevant national jurisdiction may not allow claims by anyone else than the victim and may not allow standing for relatives or family. Rule 106 does not provide for an obligation of the respective State to provide compensation and the scope of the compensation will depend on the respective national jurisdictions.

Rule 106 allows, in addition to action in a national court, claims to be brought before an "other competent body to obtain compensation." Presently, there is no international scheme or body providing compensation for victims of the conflict in the former Yugoslavia. However, the Rule does not limit the application of the Rule to national courts in the former Yugoslavia. Compensation claims may be brought in any national legal systems. One example of a national law which has jurisdiction is the US Alien Tort Claims Act, under which a claim has been brought against Radovan Karadzić who is indicted by the Tribunal.[41] However, to date no victim has been awarded compensation based on a judgement from the Tribunal.[42]

The Rule states that "the judgement of the Tribunal shall be final and binding as to the criminal responsibility of the convicted person for such injury". It is doubtful what impact this provision has, as a judgement of the Tribunal in certain countries for example Germany, is not enforceable in the domestic legal system unless the judgement has been transformed into a domestic judgement. The provision in the ICTY Rules will in such circumstances be of little value.

It is important to consider the context in which these crimes are committed; genocide or crimes against humanity do not occur one day and disappear the next, usually they are committed in the state of general breakdown of law, leaving thousands of victims. It is difficult to see how the Rule in any effective way may assist these victims in receiving compensation. In the ICTY Rules claims are limited to claims connected with a crime under the ICTY jurisdiction. Those entitled to reparation or compensation depend on those convicted. Thus, it is those whose crimes have been successfully prosecuted who may be able to recover. The victim whose crime is unadressed, however, will not be entitled to financial compensation or property restitution.

The Tribunal was established to prosecute serious violations of humanitarian law. However, with the limited resources available and the mandate entrusted to it, the ICTY is not intended or in the position to prosecute all crimes committed, neither to be the solution for compensation issues. The jurisdiction of the Tribunal has pursuant to Article 9 of the ICTY Statute concurrent jurisdiction with national courts, but the Tribunal has primacy.

---

[41]*Karadzić v. Kadic et al.*, 70 F.3d 232, 64 USLW 2231.

[42]As of 25 May 2000.

Realistically, many perpetrators of these crimes will have no or very limited financial resources available to compensate for their crime. Therefore, it is important to find a solution for individuals to receive access to compensation not only from the convicted person, or in the alternative also from States or trust funds.

The Statute of the ICC has addressed the issue of compensation to victims more extensively than the ICTY Statute and Rules. The ICC has the mandate pursuant to Article 75[43] to grant compensation to victims and to determine the scope and extent of any damage, loss and injury;[44] further a trust fund has been created.[45] The ICC will be in a better position than the ICTY to address the questions of compensation in a more satisfactory way for the victims.

---

[43]It reads: "(1) The Court shall establish principles relating to reparation to, or in respect of victims, including restitution, compensation and rehabilitation. On this basis, in its decision the Court may, either upon request or on its own motion in exceptional circumstances, determine the scope and extent of any damage, loss and injury to, or in respect of, victims and will state the principles on which it is acting. (2) The Court may make an order directly against a convicted person specifying appropriate reparations to, or in respect of, victims, including restitution, compensation and rehabilitation. Where appropriate, the Court may order that the award for reparations be made through the Trust fund provided for in article 79. (3) Before making an order under this article, the Court may invite and shall take into account of representations from or on behalf of the convicted person, victims, other interested persons or interested States. (4) In exercising its power under this article, the Court may, after a person is convicted of a crime within the jurisdiction of the Court, determine whether, in order to give effect to an order which it may make under this article, it is necessary to seek measures under article 93, paragraph 1. (5) A State Party shall give effect to a decision under this article as if the provisions of article 109 were applicable to this article. (6) Nothing in this article shall be interpreted as prejudicing the rights of victims under national law or international law."

[44]For further reading concerning victims and witnesses see for example, Muttukumaru, "Reparations to victims" in Roy S. Lee (Ed.), The International Criminal Court, The making of the Rome Statute, Issues, Negotiations, Results (1999); Åsa Rydberg, "The Protection of the Interests of Witnesses: The ICTY in Comparison to the Future ICC", 12 Leiden Journal of International Law (1999), pp. 455–478; Claude Jorda and Jérôme de Hemptinne, Status and Role of the Victims, to be published in "The Statute of the International Criminal Court and International Law, Oxford University Press; Theo van Boven, "The Position of the Victim in the Statute of the International Court", in Reflections on the International Criminal Court, essays in Honour of Adriaan Bos (1999); Gudmundur Alfredsson, "Human Rights and Victims' Rights in Europe", in Yael Danieli, Elsa Stamatopoulou, Clarence J. Dias (Eds.), The Universal Declaration of Human Rights: Fifty years and beyond (1999).

[45]Art. 79 of the Rome Statute provides: "(1) A Trust Fund shall be established by decision of the Assembly of States parties for the benefit of victims of crimes within the jurisdiction of the Court, and of the families of such victims. (2) The court may order money and other property collected through fines or forfeiture to be transferred, by order of the Court, to the Trust Fund. (3) The Trust Fund shall be managed according to criteria to be determined by the Assembly of States Parties."

4. Conclusion

Prosecution is but one means of redress. Recovering one's home or receiving compensation may mean as much to the victims and survivors of a conflict. It is therefore important that the Tribunal affirm the principle that there should be no individual gain from criminal conduct and make use of the mandate entrusted to it with regard to restitution of property.

The victims of the conflict in the former Yugoslavia cannot rely only on the Tribunal for compensation, as the ICTY Rules have limited applicability. Unless a general international scheme for compensation is established for the region, the victims of the crimes committed will be dependent on national legal systems to be awarded compensation, which to date has proven not to be an efficient way for the victims. However, it should be kept in mind that the Tribunal was established with the primary function to prosecute persons responsible for serious violations of international humanitarian law and not to address the question of compensation.

PART IX

Power of Chambers to Control Proceedings

GABRIËL OOSTHUIZEN*

30. Of Misconduct, Contempt, False Testimony, Rule Mutations and other Interesting Powers: A Potpourri of Questions and Notes

1. Introduction

The ICTY can carry out its primary judicial function – prosecuting individuals alleged to have committed serious violations of international humanitarian law in the former Yugoslavia – only if it is able to effectively deal with parties, witnesses or others who interfere with its primary work. The ICTY faces some peculiar difficulties in this respect, mainly because it is a maturing, *ad hoc* creature in an underdeveloped system of international criminal justice, with a Statute providing only a skeletal framework for its primary and ancillary functions.

*Associate Legal Officer in Chambers, ICTY; BLC LLB (University of Pretoria, South Africa) LLM Public International Law *cum laude* (Leiden University). He has previously worked for the Deputy Agent for Bosnia and Herzegovina in the genocide case of *Bosnia and Herzegovina v Yugoslavia (Serbia and Montenegro)* before the International Court of Justice. The views expressed herein are those of the author and not of the Tribunal or the United Nations.

R. May et al., Essays on ICTY Procedure and Evidence in Honour of Gabrielle Kirk McDonald, 387–402.

The Rules of Procedure and Evidence ("Rules") currently[1] contain five Rules ("subject Rules") that could assist a Judge or a Chamber to solve problems like a witness being abusive in court, counsel ignoring an order or somebody bribing potential witnesses to lie in court.[2] Rule 46 concerns misconduct of counsel,[3] Rule 80 a Trial Chamber's power to control proceedings[4] and Rule 91 false testimony given under oath.[5] Rule 77 deals with

---

[1]IT/32/Rev. 17, 7 Dec. 1999.

[2]For the text of the ICTY Statute and the latest version of the ICTY Rules, as well as the judgments and other information, see *http://www.un.org/icty*. Also see, as a guide to the jurisprudence of the ICTY and International Criminal Tribunal for Rwanda ("ICTR") and the development of the Rules, John R.W.D. Jones, The Practice of the International Criminal Tribunals for the Former Yugoslavia and Rwanda (2000) ("Practice").

[3]Rule 46 ("Misconduct of Counsel") provides: "(A) A Chamber may, after a warning, refuse audience to counsel if, in its opinion, the conduct of that counsel is offensive, abusive or otherwise obstructs the proper conduct of the proceedings. (B) A Judge or a Chamber may also, with the approval of the President, communicate any misconduct of counsel to the professional body regulating the conduct of counsel in the counsel's State of admission or, if a professor and not otherwise admitted to the profession, to the governing body of that counsel's University." Compare this Rule to the slightly different corresponding ICTR Rule 46. Also see the Statute of the International Criminal Court ("ICC Statute") Art. 71.

[4]Rule 80 ("Control of Proceedings") provides: "(A) The Trial Chamber may exclude a person from the courtroom in order to protect the right of the accused to a fair and public trial, or to maintain the dignity and decorum of the proceedings. (B) The Trial Chamber may order the removal of an accused from the courtroom and continue the proceedings in the absence of the accused if the accused has persisted in disruptive conduct following a warning that such conduct may warrant the removal of the accused from the courtroom." See the identical corresponding ICTR Rule 80. Also see ICC Statute Art. 63.

[5]Rule 91 ("False Testimony under Solemn Declaration") provides: "(A) A Chamber, *proprio motu* or at the request of a party, may warn a witness of the duty to tell the truth and the consequences that may result from a failure to do so. (B) If a Chamber has strong grounds for believing that a witness has knowingly and wilfully given false testimony, it may direct the Prosecutor to investigate the matter with a view to the preparation and submission of an indictment for false testimony. (C) The rules of procedure and evidence in Parts Four to Eight shall apply *mutatis mutandis* to proceedings under this Rule. (D) No Judge who sat as a member of the Trial Chamber before which the witness appeared shall sit for the trial of the witness for false testimony. (E) The maximum penalty for false testimony under solemn declaration shall be a fine of Dfl. 200,000 or a term of imprisonment of seven years, or both. The payment of any fine imposed shall be paid to the Registrar to be held in the account referred to in Sub-rule 77 (I). (F) Sub-rules (B) to (E) apply *mutatis mutandis* to a person who knowingly and willingly makes a false statement in an affidavit or formal statement which the person knows or has reason to know may be used as evidence in proceedings before the Tribunal." Compare this Rule to the slightly different corresponding ICTR Rule 91 (which, *inter alia*, has no provisions similar to ICTY Rules 91(D) and (F)). Also see ICC Statute Art. 70.

contempt[6] and Rule 77*bis* with the payment of fines imposed pursuant to Rules 77 and 91, but it also provides for a finding of contempt in case of wilful failure to pay such fines.[7]

---

[6]Rule 77 ("Contempt of the Tribunal"), in pertinent part, provides: "(A) Any person who (i) being a witness before a Chamber, contumaciously refuses or fails to answer a question, (ii) discloses information relating to those proceedings in knowing violation of an order of a Chamber, or (iii) without just excuse fails to comply with an order to attend before or produce documents before a Chamber, commits a contempt of the Tribunal. (B) Any person who threatens, intimidates, causes any injury or offers a bribe to, or otherwise interferes with, a witness who is giving, has given, or is about to give evidence in proceedings before a Chamber, or a potential witness, commits a contempt of the Tribunal. (C) Any person who threatens, intimidates, offers a bribe to, or otherwise seeks to coerce any other person, with the intention of preventing that other person from complying with an obligation under an order of a Judge or Chamber, commits a contempt of the Tribunal. (D) Incitement to commit, and attempts to commit, any of the acts punishable under this Rule are punishable as contempts of the Tribunal with the same penalties. (E) Nothing in this Rule affects the inherent power of the Tribunal to hold in contempt those who knowingly and wilfully interfere with its administration of justice. (F) When a Chamber has reason to believe that a person may be in contempt of the Tribunal, it may, *proprio motu*, initiate proceedings and call upon that person that he or she may be found in contempt, giving notice of the nature of the allegations against that person. After affording such person an opportunity to appear and answer personally or by counsel, the Chamber may, if satisfied beyond reasonable doubt, find the person to be in contempt of the Tribunal. (G) Any person so called upon shall, if that person satisfies the criteria for determination of indigency established by the Registrar, be assigned counsel in accordance with Rule 45. (H) The maximum penalty that may be imposed on a person found to be in contempt of the Tribunal: (i) under Sub-rules (A) and (E) above is a term of imprisonment not exceeding twelve months, or a fine not exceeding Dfl. 40,000, or both; (ii) under Sub-rules (B), (C) or (D) above is a term of imprisonment not exceeding seven years, or a fine not exceeding Dfl. 200,000, or both. (I) Payment of a fine shall be made to the Registrar to be held in a separate account. (J) Any decision rendered by a Trial Chamber under this Rule shall be subject to appeal in cases where leave is granted by a bench of three Judges of the Appeals Chamber, upon good grounds being shown [...]" Compare this Rule to the different corresponding ICTR Rule 77. Also see ICC Statute Art. 70.

[7]Rule 77*bis* ("Payment of Fines") provides: "(A) In imposing a fine under Rule 77 or Rule 91, a Judge or Chamber shall specify the time for its payment. (B) Where a fine imposed under Rule 77 or Rule 91 is not paid within the time specified, the Judge or Chamber imposing the fine may issue an order requiring the person on whom the fine is imposed to appear before, or to respond in writing to, the Tribunal to explain why the fine has not been paid. (C) After affording the person on whom the fine is imposed an opportunity to be heard, the Judge or Chamber may make a decision that appropriate measures be taken, including: (i) extending the time for payment of the fine; (ii) requiring the payment of the fine to be made in instalments; (iii) in consultation with the Registrar, requiring that the moneys owed be deducted from any outstanding fees owing to the person by the Tribunal where the person is a counsel retained by the Tribunal pursuant to the Directive on the Assignment of Defence Counsel; (iv) converting the whole or part of the fine to a term of imprisonment not exceeding twelve months. (D) In addition to a decision under Sub-rule (C), the Judge or Chamber may find the person in contempt of the Tribunal and impose a new penalty applying Rule 77 (H)(i), if that person was able to pay the fine within the specified time and has wilfully failed to do so. This penalty for contempt of the Tribunal shall be additional to the original fine imposed.

These Rules raise a plethora of questions, some important, others merely interesting. Only a handful of the more salient of these will be highlighted briefly in this contribution. The first question to be looked at, is what are the legal bases of in particular Rules 77, 77 *bis* and 91. The focus will then fall on misconduct of counsel, shifting, third, to false testimony under oath, with particular emphasis falling on the Rule mutations that the Latin maxim *mutatis mutandis* could present. Fourth, some comparative notes in respect of Rules 77, 77 *bis* and 91 will be made. Finally, some concluding remarks will be ventured on what has gone before. Rule 80, seeing that it appears to be relatively simple, will not be commented on.[8]

2. A PRELIMINARY NOTE ON THE TRANSCENDENT INHERENT POWERS OF THE TRIBUNAL

The Judges of the Tribunal adopted the five subject Rules pursuant to Article 15 of the Statute.[9] Given the fairly rudimentary terms of that Article and the enormous powers that Rules 77, 77 *bis* and 91 express, probably the most important question is what the legal basis for these Rules is, whether the Tribunal has jurisdiction to deal with these 'secondary' matters. Extending the ruling of the Appeals Chamber on Rule 77 in the *Judgment on Allegations of Contempt Against Prior Counsel, Milan Vujin* in *Prosecutor v. Tadić* ("*Tadić* Contempt Judgment") to the other subject Rules, it would appear as if the answer is the Tribunal's "inherent power to deal with conduct

(E) The Judge or Chamber may, if necessary, issue an arrest warrant to secure the person's presence where he or she fails to appear before or respond in writing pursuant to an order under Sub-rule (B). A State or authority to whom such a warrant is addressed, in accordance with Article 29 of the Statute, shall act promptly and with all due diligence to ensure proper and effective execution thereof. Where an arrest warrant is issued under this Sub-rule, the provisions of Rules 45, 57, 58, 59, 59 *bis*, and 60 shall apply *mutatis mutandis*. Following the transfer of the person concerned to the Tribunal, the provisions of Rules 64, 65 and 99 shall apply *mutatis mutandis*. (F) Where under this Rule a penalty of imprisonment is imposed, or a fine is converted to a term of imprisonment, the provisions of Rules 102, 103 and 104 and Part Nine shall apply *mutatis mutandis*. (G) Any finding of contempt or penalty imposed under this Rule shall be subject to appeal as allowed for in Rule 77 (J)." The ICTR Rules does not have a corresponding provision.

[8]At the time of writing, the Tribunal has not yet applied this Rule.

[9]Statute Art. 15 ("Rules of procedure and evidence") provides: "The judges of the International Tribunal shall adopt rules of procedure and evidence for the conduct of the pre-trial phase of the proceedings, trials and appeals, the admission of evidence, the protection of victims and witnesses and other appropriate matters."

which interferes with its administration of justice" ("inherent power").[10] By similar extension, the subject Rules probably share two other traits as well. First, these Rules do not constitute new offences[11] – although one may reasonably wonder whether this is not a convenient assertion, in light of the rather serious penalties provided for under especially Rules 77, 77 *bis* and 91. Second, the inherent power of the Tribunal to deal with such matters necessarily existed ever since its creation and the existence of that inherent power does not depend upon a reference being made to it in the Rules.[12]

---

[10]Case No. IT-94-1-A-R77, A. Ch., 31 Jan. 2000. ICTY Rule 77(E) of course makes explicit reference to the "inherent power of the Tribunal to hold in contempt those who knowingly and wilfully interfere with its administration of justice", which is not the case under Rules 77 *bis* and 91. On the Tribunal's inherent powers, see *Tadić* Contempt Judgment at para. 13: "There is no mention in the Tribunal's Statute of its power to deal with contempt. The Tribunal does, however, possess an inherent jurisdiction, deriving from its judicial function, to ensure that its exercise of the jurisdiction which is expressly given to it by that Statute is not frustrated and that its basic judicial functions are safeguarded. As an international criminal court, the Tribunal must therefore possess the inherent power to deal with conduct which interferes with its administration of justice. The content of that inherent power may be discerned by reference to the usual sources of international law." In terms generally more pertinent to all of the subject Rules, it was held in the same Judgment that "A power in the Tribunal to punish conduct which tends to obstruct, prejudice or abuse its administration of justice is a necessity in order to ensure that its exercise of the jurisdiction which is expressly given to it by its Statute is not frustrated and that its basic judicial functions are safeguarded. Thus the power to deal with contempt is clearly within its inherent jurisdiction." (para. 18). In footnote 25 of the same Judgment, the Appeals Chamber in fact stated that Rule 91 is another provision of the rules concerning the conduct of a matter falling within the inherent jurisdiction of the Tribunal. Also see, for references to other Tribunal cases that deal with inherent powers and other authorities on this, the *Tadić* Contempt Judgment at paras. 12–29; *Prosecutor v. Blaškić, Judgment on the Request of the Republic of Croatia for Review of the Decision of Trial Chamber II of 18 July 1997*, Case No. IT-95-14-AR108*bis*, A. Ch., 29 Oct. 1997 ("*Blaškic Subpoena Decision*"); *Prosecutor v. Kunarać and Others, Decision on the Request of the Accused Radomir Kovać to Allow Mr. Milan Vujin to Appear as Co-counsel Acting Pro Bono*, IT-96-23-PT & IT-96-23/1-PT, 14 March 2000; and *Prosecutor v. Simić and Others, Separate Opinion of Judge David Hunt on Prosecutor's Motion for a Ruling Concerning the Testimony of a Witness*, Case No. IT-95-9-PT, 27 July 1999.

[11]*Tadić* Contempt Judgment at para. 24: "[The power under Article 15 of the Statute to adopt only rules of procedure and evidence] does not permit rules to be adopted which constitute new offences, but it does permit the judges to adopt *rules of procedure and evidence* for the conduct of matters falling within the inherent jurisdiction of the Tribunal as well as matters within its statutory jurisdiction."

[12]Id., para. 28.

The rather intricate issues of whether the Tribunal actually possesses such far-reaching inherent powers and whether the Rules do not express limits to those inherent powers, will be skirted for lack of space. What is noteworthy for current purposes is the apparent implication of, in particular, the *Tadić* Contempt Judgment that what the subject Rules state, is but a mirage of the corresponding or even broader inherent powers, of the "underlying law".[13] What follows has to be understood in that light – the questions to be raised, the notes to be made, all might very well be solved and qualified with reference to the omnipresent inherent power of the Tribunal. In the main body of this contribution, an attempt will be made to limit what is suggested to the terms of the Rules.[14]

3. Misconduct of counsel

Three questions arising from Rule 46,[15] dealing with misconduct of counsel,[16] will be highlighted here.[17]

What constitutes "misconduct of counsel"? During a hearing in *Prosecutor v. Kolundžija* the Trial Chamber issued a formal warning to a counsel under Rule 46(A) due to his absence from a duly scheduled hearing, which left his client unrepresented and caused "grave inconvenience".[18] In *Prosecutor v. Delalić and Others*, the Trial Chamber warned another counsel twice pursuant to Rule 46(A).[19] The first warning resulted from a Defence filing

[13] Id., para. 25. See also, for example, Art. 1(4) of the Code of Professional Conduct for Defence Counsel Appearing before the International Tribunal, IT/125, 12 June 1997 ("Code of Conduct for Defence Counsel"), which provides: "While Counsel is bound by this Code, it is not, and should not be read as if it were, a complete or detailed code of conduct for Counsel. Other standards and requirements may be imposed on the conduct of Counsel by virtue of the Tribunal's inherent jurisdiction [...]"

[14] What is expressed in the Rules has to fall within the inherent powers of the Tribunal: *Tadić* Contempt Judgment at para. 28.

[15] See Practice supra note 2 at p. 264.

[16] The use of "counsel" appears to be restrictive, in that it excludes, for example, assistants or investigators of a party, or any other person, who may obstruct the proceedings without their conduct amounting to contempt; "counsel" probably includes co-counsel.

[17] Rule 44(B) provides: "In the performance of their duties counsel shall be subject to the relevant provisions of the Statute, the Rules, the Rules of Detention and any other rules or regulations adopted by the Tribunal, the Host Country Agreement, the Code of Conduct and the codes of practice and ethics governing their profession and, if applicable, the Directive on the Assignment of Defence Counsel." Also see the Directive on Assignment of Defence Counsel, IT/73/Rev. 6, in particular Art. 17 ("Applicable law"), which is a restatement of Rule 44(B); the Code of Professional Conduct for Defence Counsel Appearing before the International Tribunal, IT/125, 12 June 1997 ("Code of Conduct for Defence Counsel"), in particular Arts. 20, 21 and 22; and the Standards of Professional Conduct for Prosecution Counsel, Prosecutor's Regulation No. 2 (1999), 14 Sept. 1999 ("Code of Conduct for Prosecution Counsel"), in particular paras. 2(e) and 4.

[18] Case No. IT-95-8-PT ("*Kolundžija* case"), transcript, pp. 135–136 and 144 (28 Sept. 1999).

[19] *Judgement*, Case No. IT-96-21-T, 16. Nov. 1998 ("*Delalić* case") at para. 75.

in response to a scheduling order. The response was "inappropriate and insufficient in fulfilling the obligations of the Defence" and "unacceptable as a document filed with the International Tribunal, in the quality of its language, its attacks on the Office of the Prosecutor and its impuning (sic) of the proceedings of the International Tribunal itself".[20] The second warning followed the failure of the same counsel to provide the Chamber with a revised witness list in response to an oral order.[21] It may also be that a Judge or a Chamber may, in considering what constitutes misconduct under Rule 46, be guided by the misconduct provisions of the Code of Conduct for Defence Counsel.[22] Article 20 of that Code sets out what kind of conduct might constitute professional misconduct and Article 21 of the Code provides for a counsel to inform a Judge or a Chamber of another counsel's misconduct.

The second question relates to a procedural problem. Does Rule 46(A) cover conduct of counsel that is offensive, abusive or otherwise obstructs the proper conduct of proceedings before, for example, a pre-trial Judge during a Status Conference?[23] Rule 46(A), providing for the discretionary power to refuse audience to counsel, following a warning, only refers to "[a] Chamber".[24] It might be that a pre-trial Judge, sitting alone, could act under Rule 46(A), since the Judge acts on behalf of, or in the words of the relevant Rule, "under the authority and supervision" of the Trial Chamber.[25] Another, preferable way might be for the pre-trial Judge to refer the matter to the Trial Chamber for consideration,[26] since the power to act against counsel is

---

[20] *Order*, Case No. IT-96-21-T, 18 May 1998.

[21] *Order*, Case No. IT-96-21-T, 9 June 1998.

[22] Art. 20 ("Misconduct") of the Code of Conduct for Defence Counsel provides: "It is professional misconduct for Counsel, *inter alia*, to: (a) violate or attempt to violate this Code or to knowingly assist or induce another person to do so through the acts of another person; (b) commit a criminal act which reflects adversely on Counsel's honesty, trustworthiness or fitness as Counsel; (c) engage in conduct involving dishonesty, fraud, deceit or misrepresentation; (d) engage in conduct which is prejudicial to the proper administration of justice before the Tribunal; or (e) attempt to influence an officer of the Tribunal in an improper manner." Art. 21 ("Reporting Misconduct") of the same Code provides for one Counsel to inform a Judge or a Chamber of another counsel's misconduct. Presumably, where necessary, such misconduct may also be brought to a Judge's or Chamber's attention by the Registrar. Also see para. 4 of the Code of Conduct for Prosecution Counsel, which provides: "Failure by prosecution counsel to observe the above standards will be dealt with by the Prosecutor, in the exercise of her discretion, and subject to the staff rules of the United Nations, apart from any sanctions that may exceptionally be imposed upon prosecution counsel pursuant to Rules 46 or 77 of the [Rules of both the ICTY and ICTR] (or other provisions of the Statutes and Rules)."

[23] See Rules 65*bis* and 65*ter*.

[24] 46(B) refers to "[a] Judge or a Chamber".

[25] Rule 65*ter* (B).

[26] See Rule 65*ter* (J): "The pre-trial Judge shall keep the Trial Chamber regularly informed, particularly where issues are in dispute and may refer such disputes to the Trial Chamber."

not expressly mentioned in the Rules as a pre-trial function with which a pre-trial Judge may be entrusted.[27]

In the *Kolundžija* case the Trial Chamber, after having issued a formal warning to counsel under Rule 46(A), reported this "serious matter"[28] to the Registrar "for her to take what action she thinks fit".[29] This example gives rise to the fourth question. What follows a warning to counsel, refusing counsel audience and reporting the matter to the Registrar and the relevant professional body or university?

In the *Delalić* case, following the failure of counsel to comply with the order in which the second warning was issued, the Chamber, referring to the "obstructive conduct" of counsel, issued an order compelling compliance and reminding counsel "that he has already been warned twice pursuant to Sub-rule 46(A) of the Rules and that, should the present Order not be complied with in full, to the satisfaction of the Trial Chamber, counsel will be refused audience, the necessary consequence thus being that that he will be withdrawn from representing [his client] and the defence case will be continued by co-counsel, with the assistance of such other counsel as the Registrar shall assign."[30] In this respect, Article 20(B) of the Directive on Assignment of Defence Counsel provides that the Registrar "*shall* withdraw the assignment of counsel: (i) upon the decision by a Chamber to refuse audience to assigned counsel for misconduct under Rule 46(A) [...]."[31] However, where a Chamber decides upon other measures, it might be that the Registrar should not withdraw the assignment of counsel. Such other measures might include for a Judge or Chamber to require an explanation or apology from counsel before again granting him or her audience. A Chamber could also interpret "refuse audience" to exclude the continued filing of the usual written filings by the relevant counsel.[32] Whether a Judge or a Chamber can demand counsel to pay a fine before being allowed to appear again is doubtful, since Rule 46 does not expressly provide for it, like, for example, Rules 77 and 91 do. Where a Chamber considers it appropriate or necessary to impose a fine on counsel, the misconduct would in any case probably be serious enough to amount to contempt under Rule 77. The

---

[27]Rule 65*ter* (D). Another, similar example is where the misconduct is committed before a Presiding Officer, who need not be a Judge, during the taking of a deposition under Rule 71. Notwithstanding the possible argument that the Presiding Officer also acts on behalf of the Trial Chamber since the latter appoints the former for the purpose of deposition taking, the preferable course of action would appear to be for the misconduct to be referred to the Trial Chamber, especially where the Presiding Officer is not a Judge.

[28]Supra note 18 at p. 136.

[29]Id., pp. 136 and 144.

[30]*Order*, Case No. IT-96-21-T, 16 June 1998.

[31]Emphasis added. Art. 20(B)(iii) of the same Directive further provides that "Under such circumstances, the Registrar may strike counsel off the list of defence counsel [...]."

[32]In would not seem improper that the Chamber in the *Delalić* case implicitly interpreted "proceedings" broadly to include misconduct manifested in the written filings. Such filings are part and parcel of the proceedings before the Tribunal.

Code of Conduct for Defence Counsel is not of much assistance in this regard – the relevant general provision states that "[c]ounsel must abide by and voluntarily submit to any enforcement and disciplinary procedures as may be established by the Tribunal in accordance with the Rules."[33]

4. False testimony under solemn declaration

Rule 91[34] raises some difficult and important questions. Some of these will be discussed with reference to a specific case where this Rule was put into effect.

4.1 The false testimony of a witness in the Tadić *case*

In *Prosecutor v. Tadić*, the Trial Chamber had strong grounds for believing that a certain witness lied to the Chamber while under oath.[35] Pursuant to Rule 91(B), the Chamber directed the Prosecutor to investigate the matter with a view to the preparation and submission of an indictment against the witness for false testimony.[36]

The Prosecutor's investigation related to two aspects of the purported false testimony of Dragan Opacić, only the first of which is relevant here.[37] With respect thereto, the Prosecutor informed the Trial Chamber through the Registrar that the witness did knowingly and willingly give false testimony in relation to his father.[38] She indicated, however, that she did not consider the matter as appropriate for prosecution under Rule 91. The Prosecutor's reasons for not prosecuting included: (a) the false testimony was "not sufficiently material to the proceedings to justify prosecution", (b) sentencing Dragan Opacić to a further term of imprisonment[39] would not have served

---

[33]Art. 22. If the phrase "in accordance with the Rules" qualifies the procedures and not the compliance with the procedures, the question arises whether counsel can ignore procedures which have not been adopted in accordance with the Rules.

[34]See Practice supra note 2 at p. 424.

[35]*Prosecutor v. Duško Tadić, Order for the Prosecution to Investigate the False Testimony of Dragan Opacić*, Case No. IT-94-1-T, 10 Dec. 1996 ("*Order to Investigate*").

[36]Id. Also see *Prosecutor v. Duško Tadić, Opinion and Judgment*, Case No. IT-94-1-T, 7 May 1997 at para. 33.

[37]Publicly filed internal memorandum from the Prosecutor, Justice Louise Arbour, addressed to the Registrar, Ms. Dorothee de Sampayo Garrido, *Dragon Opacić* [sic] – *Proceedings for False Testimony*, IT-95-7-Misc.1, dated 8 May 1997, filed 9 May 1997 ("Prosecutor's Memorandum").

[38]Id.

[39]Dragan Opacić was convicted of genocide and war crimes by the Higher Court of Sarajevo and was sentenced to 10 year's imprisonment. He was transferred to the ICTY to testify as a witness following an agreement with the Government of Bosnia and Herzegovina that he would be returned to that Government's custody upon completing his participation as witness before the ICTY: see *Prosecutor v. Duško Tadić, Order for the Return of a Detained Witness*, IT-94-1-T/IT-95-7.Misc.1, 27 May 1997 ("*Order for Return*").

any significant sentencing purpose and he did not have the capacity to pay a fine; and (c) such a "collateral prosecution" would have a minimal deterrent effect and would contribute very little to the overall objectives of the Tribunal.

4.2 Questions and mutant answers

Rules 91(B) and (F) give a Chamber a discretionary power, if it has strong grounds for believing that a witness gave false testimony or a person made a false statement,[40] to "direct the Prosecutor to investigate the matter with a view to the preparation and submission of an indictment for false testimony". Rule 91(C) provides that parts four to eight of the Rules shall apply *mutatis mutandis* to proceedings under this Rule.[41] As will be seen, some of the problems raised here flow from this Latin phrase, which literally means "things being changed that have to be changed".

The first question to be considered is whether the phrase "may *direct* the Prosecutor to investigate the matter *with a view to*" obliges the Prosecutor to prepare and submit an indictment for false testimony.[42] In other words, is it within the Prosecutor's discretion not to prepare and submit such an indictment?[43] In the *Tadić* case, the question was answered in the affirmative. This is evident from the *Order to Investigate* – in which the Trial Chamber directed the Prosecutor to "investigate the matter of the presentation of false testimony [...] and evaluate the *possibility* of the preparation and submission of an indictment"[44] – as well as the Chamber's acceptance of the Prosecutor's decision not to prosecute, in subsequently ruling that "[...] under Rule 91 of the Rules, the decision as to whether to prosecute for false testimony rests solely with the Prosecutor and not with the Trial Chamber".[45] Is it not, however, possible to also reasonably construe the phrase to mean that once the Chamber itself "has strong grounds" for believing that false testimony was given or a false statement was made, the Prosecutor has to prepare and submit an indictment for false testimony? As a policy matter, should a Chamber leave the Prosecutor with such discretion? Is a conflict of

---

[40]Hereafter, references to Rule 91(B) include Rule 91(F), unless indicated otherwise.

[41]Parts four to eight are respectively headed: "Investigations and rights of suspects"; "Pre-trial proceedings"; "Proceedings before Trial Chambers"; "Appellate proceedings"; and "Review proceedings". These parts include Rules 39 to 122.

[42]Emphasis added. It is assumed that the Prosecutor has to investigate the matter, once so directed by a Chamber.

[43]It is assumed that a Chamber does not have the power to directly refer – bypassing the Prosecutor – a matter for trial for false testimony to another Chamber, that a trial for false testimony may be held only on the basis of an indictment for false testimony, prepared by the Prosecutor.

[44]Supra note 35.

[45]*Order for Return* supra note 39.

interest not imaginable where, for example, the Prosecutor is loath to prosecute because the relevant false testimony will impinge on or prejudice her case?

The second salient question is whether the decision of a Chamber to direct the Prosecutor to investigate the matter might be subject to interlocutory appeal? Rule 91 does not expressly provide for such a right. However, the *mutatis mutandis* provision might mean that where the requirements of Rule 73(B)[46] are met, it will apply *mutatis mutandis* to proceedings under Rule 91, so that such a decision, in principle, can be subject to interlocutory appeal. The Rules do not rule an interlocutory appeal out. There also does not appear to be a good reason for not allowing for such a possibility – is not even the mere direction to the Prosecutor to investigate such a matter a potentially very serious matter for a witness?[47]

The third question is whether an "indictment for false testimony" is subject to the provisions pertaining to an indictment against a person suspected of having committed serious violations of international humanitarian law. In particular, does "*mutatis mutandis*" here mean, first, that the Prosecutor has to determine that a prima facie case exists before preparing an indictment for false testimony, and, second, does that indictment have to be submitted for review?[48] As to the former issue, to argue that the

---

[46]Rule 73(B) provides: "(B) Decisions on such motions are without interlocutory appeal save with the leave of a bench of three Judges of the Appeals Chamber which may grant such leave (i) if the decision impugned would cause such prejudice to the case of the party seeking leave as could not be cured by the final disposal of the trial including post-judgement appeal; (ii) if the issue in the proposed appeal is of general importance to proceedings before the Tribunal or in international law generally."

[47]Whether such a directive by the Appeals Chamber can be the basis of an interlocutory appeal will not be discussed here.

[48]Statute Arts. 18 and 19 and Rule 47 are relevant here. Art. 18 ("Investigation and preparation of indictment") provides, in pertinent part: "(1) The Prosecutor shall initiate investigations [...] The Prosecutor shall assess the information received or obtained and decide whether there is sufficient basis to proceed [...] (4) Upon a determination that a prima facie case exists, the Prosecutor shall prepare an indictment containing a concise statement of the facts and the crime or crimes with which the accused is charged under the Statute. The indictment shall be transmitted to a judge of the Trial Chamber." ICTY Statute Art. 19 ("Review of the indictment") provides: "(1) The judge of the Trial Chamber to whom the indictment has been transmitted shall review it. If satisfied that a prima facie case has been established by the Prosecutor, he shall confirm the indictment. If not so satisfied, the indictment shall be dismissed. (2) Upon confirmation of an indictment, the judge may, at the request of the Prosecutor, issue such orders and warrants for the arrest, detention, surrender or transfer of persons, and any other orders as may be required for the conduct of the trial." ICTY Rule 47 ("Submission of Indictment by the Prosecutor") provides: "(A) An indictment, submitted in accordance with the following procedure, shall be reviewed by a Judge. [...] (B) The Prosecutor, if satisfied in the course of an investigation that there is sufficient evidence to provide reasonable grounds for believing that a suspect has committed a crime within the jurisdiction of the Tribunal,

Prosecutor should employ the prima facie test under Article 18(4) of the Statute[49] where she is bound to prosecute, following a directive from a Chamber, makes no sense. Assuming for the moment, therefore, that the Prosecutor is not bound to prosecute, it would appear as if she still may not have to employ that test. This may be so if one is to regard the basis for a Chamber's direction to investigate – the "strong grounds test" under Rule 91(B) – as replacing or constituting the prima facie test. As to the review issue, there does not appear to be a good reason for not submitting the indictment for false testimony for review to a Judge. Article 19 of the Statute and Rule 47 of the Rules should then, presumably, be applied *mutatis mutandis*. Or would such a course be anomalous, on the view that a *single Judge* would apply the "strong grounds test", which replaced the prima facie test and has already been applied by *a Chamber*?

Finally, it is presumed that the *mutatis mutandis* provision means that a Chamber's judgment following a trial for false testimony may be appealed or reviewed in accordance with the Statute and the Rules.[50] Equally, there are strong arguments to be made for allowing an implicated witness to have the right to lodge preliminary motions, in particular challenging the jurisdiction of the Tribunal to stage trials for false testimony or alleging defects in the indictment for false testimony.[51]

---

shall prepare and forward to the Registrar an indictment for confirmation by a Judge, together with supporting material. (C) The indictment shall set forth the name and particulars of the suspect, and a concise statement of the facts of the case and of the crime with which the suspect is charged [...] (E) The reviewing Judge shall examine each of the counts in the indictment, and any supporting materials the Prosecutor may provide, to determine, applying the standard set forth in Article 19, paragraph 1, of the Statute, whether a case exists against the suspect. [...] (H) Upon confirmation of any or all counts in the indictment, (i) the Judge may issue an arrest warrant, in accordance with Sub-rule 55 (A), and any orders as provided in Article 19 of the Statute, and (ii) the suspect shall have the status of an accused [...]"

[49] It is assumed that the prima facie test is the relevant test, and not the apparently looser and possibly *ultra vires* test under Rule 47(B).

[50] See Statute Art. 25 and Rules 107–122.

[51] See Rule 72 ("Preliminary Motions").

5. Rules 91, 77 and 77 *bis* compared

No attempt will be made here to comprehensively deal with Rules 77[52] and 77*bis* – both Rules raise many an interesting and intricate question.[53]

One of the more striking differences between these Rules concerns the composition of the Chamber authorised to conduct the false testimony and contempt proceedings. Under Rule 91, a Judge who sat as a member of the Trial Chamber before which a witness allegedly gave false testimony under oath is barred from sitting for the trial for false testimony. However, in the case of contempt under Rule 77 the same Chamber before which the alleged contempt was committed, may sit for the trial of contempt. Under Rule 77*bis*, the position is even more interesting. Not only may the same Chamber before which the alleged contempt was committed, sit for the trial of contempt, but even a single Judge may find a person who wilfully failed to pay

---

[52]The Tribunal has had to deal with a handful of contempt cases. See, for example, *Prosecutor v. Zlatko Aleksovski, Decision*, Case No. IT-95-14/1-T, 11 Dec. 1998 ("*Aleksovski* case") (Counsel Anto Nobilo was found to be in contempt of the Tribunal for divulging in public session in the *Blaškić* hearings the identity of a protected witness in violation of a protective measures order in the *Aleksovksi* case. The decision is presently under appeal.); *Prosecutor v. Duško Tadić, Judgment on Allegations of Contempt Against Prior Counsel, Milan Vujin*, Case No. IT-94-1-A-R77, A. Ch., 31 Jan. 2000 (Counsel Milan Vujin was found to be in contempt of the Tribunal for, *inter alia*, having manipulated witnesses to avoid identification by them of persons who may have been responsible for crimes for which Duško Tadić had been convicted. Mr. Vujin has appealed the judgment. The question whether a finding of contempt made by the Appeals Chamber, as is the case with the judgment on Mr. Vujin, can be appealed, is, at the time of the writing of this contribution, *sub iudice*, as is the question whether counsel who have been found to be in contempt of the Tribunal can be refused audience. On the latter issue, see *Prosecutor v. Kunarać and Others, Decision on the Request of the Accused Radomir Kovać to Allow Mr. Milan Vujin to Appear as Co-counsel Acting Pro Bono*, Case No. IT-96-23-PT & IT-96-23/1-PT, 14 March 2000 and *Prosecutor v. Kunarać and Others, Separate Opinion of Judge David Hunt on Request by Radomir Kovać to Allow Milan Vujin to Appear as Counsel Acting Without Payment by the Tribunal*, Case No. IT-96-23-PT & IT-96-23/1-PT, 24 March 2000); and *Prosecutor v. Simić and Others, Judgement in the Matter of Contempt Allegations Against an Accused and His Counsel*, Case No. IT-95-9-R77, 30 June 2000 (The Trial Chamber found that the allegations levelled by the Prosecutor – relating to the bribery, intimidation of witness and suborning perjury of witness – against Milan Simić and his counsel, Mr. Branislav Avramovic, had not been established beyond reasonable doubt.) Also see Practice supra note 2 at pp. 391–395.

[53]A few other questions that will not be dealt with here, are the following. First, what is the meaning of "knowing and wilfully" under Rules 91(B) and (F) and 77(E). Are the two terms to be understood conjunctively or disjunctively? Second, why, in light of the seriousness of both processes, does Rule 91(B) refer to "strong grounds for believing" whilst Rule 77(F) refers to "reason to believe"? Third, why, under Rule 91, is the Prosecutor accorded a role in the process, whereas, under Rules 77 and 77 *bis*, no express reference to any role for the Prosecutor is made? Regardless of this, the practice of the Tribunal with respect to contempt proceedings, is to, where appropriate, ask the Prosecutor, especially where she brought a complaint, to effectively lead the case of contempt.

a fine to be in contempt,[54] or, may convert a fine to a term of imprisonment.[55] As an aside, the references in Rule 77*bis* to a "Judge" are rather strange. Does it not seem as if only a Chamber may impose fines under both Rules 77 and 91? Anyhow, in light of the tremendous powers vested in the Chambers by these Rules, the difference in the composition of the various Chambers authorised to deal with these matters is hard to explain.

The next apparent difference concerns the standard of proof required for the various possible findings under Rules 77, 77*bis* and 91. Proof beyond reasonable doubt is required under Rule 77(F) for a finding of contempt. However, under Rule 77*bis*, were a Judge or a Chamber to convert a fine to a term of imprisonment,[56] no express mention is made of the standard of proof required. The power to imprison a person, without proof beyond reasonable doubt of some wilful failure to do so, would be rather unusual. Similarly, under Rule 77*bis*(D), the required standard of proof for a finding of contempt for wilful failure to pay a fine imposed under Rules 77 or 91 is not expressly mentioned. The argument for a standard of proof beyond reasonable doubt in this instance could lie in the apparent incorporation of the contempt Rule (Rule 77) by reference to the word "contempt". Under Rule 91, Rule 87(A), which provides for the standard of proof beyond reasonable doubt for findings of guilt for primary crimes, would probably apply by virtue of the *mutatis mutandis* provision, for a finding of false testimony under oath.

Another apparent difference concerns the right of appeal. It would appear as if under Rule 91, a person found to have given false testimony under oath has an automatic right of appeal: part seven of the Rules, which applies *mutatis mutandis*, provides for that right. The same is however not the case under Rules 77 and 77*bis*. Rule 77(J) clearly states that leave to appeal has to be sought from a bench of three Judges, and Rule 77*bis* (G) provides that "[a]ny finding of contempt or penalty[57] imposed under this Rule shall be subject to appeal as allowed for in Rule 77(J)". In light of the similar and potentially serious consequences flowing from adverse findings under these Rules – in fact, the penalty for contempt under Rule 77*bis* is in addition to the original fine imposed – this difference is difficult to explain.

Rule 77*bis*(E) raises a contentious issue, namely, whether a State, in light of Article 29[58] of the Statute, is bound to comply with the terms of an arrest

[54]Rule 77*bis*(D).

[55]Rule 77*bis*(C)(iv).

[56]Rule 77*bis*(C)(iv).

[57]Whether this includes the "measures" under Rule 77*bis*(C)(iii) and (iv) is unclear.

[58]Statute Art. 29 ("Cooperation and judicial assistance") provides: "(1) States shall cooperate with the International Tribunal in the investigation and prosecution of persons accused of committing serious violations of international humanitarian law. (2) States shall comply without undue delay with any request for assistance or an order issued by a Trial Chamber, including, but not limited to: (a) the identification and location of persons; (b) the taking of testimony and the production of evidence; (c) the service of documents; (d) the arrest or detention of persons; (e) the surrender or the transfer of the accused to the International Tribunal."

warrant addressed to it under that Rule. Does a State not have to co-operate with the Tribunal only insofar as persons accused of having committed serious violations of international humanitarian law are concerned? Does a State have to comply with an arrest warrant issued under Rule 77*bis*(E), which clearly does not involve an accused being suspected of having committed serious violations of international humanitarian law? Furthermore, Rules 77 and 91 do not contain similar provisions, although by virtue of the *mutatis mutandis* provision under Rule 91(C), one may be able to argue that those Rules providing for State co-operation, like Rule 56 ("Cooperation of States"), will apply, raising the same question with respect to Article 29.

6. Final remarks

It would appear that the Judges and Chambers possess the varied powers necessary to safeguard the Tribunal's primary judicial function, based on the seemingly all-encompassing inherent powers of the Tribunal and the provisions of Rules 46, 80, 77, 77*bis* and 91.[59] There is of course no gainsaying that the Tribunal needs like powers to effectively carry out its primary judicial function. What is less clear, however, is whether these powers are satisfactory.

Concentrating first on the subject Rules, it has been suggested that they raise a number of inconsistencies and uncertainties. Some of these inconsistencies and uncertainties are too important to be papered over, in particular those with respect to Rules 77, 77*bis* and 91. It is trite that it is impossible to foresee, at the time of the drafting of a Rule, all possible problems that may arise therefrom, as to a large extent the Tribunal's rule-making process is reactive. It is often claimed that a certain degree of flexibility needs to be maintained to develop the Rules. However, it would appear that not all the inconsistencies and uncertainties are to be explained away by these observations, and that an argument may be made out for clarifying and correcting some of the more important problems suggested.

As far as the Tribunal's inherent powers are concerned, the present state of affairs similarly raises some concerns. It is stating the obvious to maintain that the Tribunal needs such powers. Whether the Tribunal, however, possesses such broad powers, as defined in its jurisprudence, is another matter, as is the nature of the propounded relationship between the Rules and the inherent powers. A questionable degree of uncertainty, with respect to not only procedural and evidentiary but substantive matters as well, may result from placing undue emphasis on the broad and overriding nature of the Tribunal's inherent powers.

---

[59]As was noted under Section B supra, the legal basis of these Rules appears to be the inherent power of the Tribunal.

The reliance by the Chambers on the inherent powers of the Tribunal might be a result of the skeletal nature of the Statute. The Rules, and where the Rules fail or are silent, the inherent powers, acquire greater importance where the constituent instrument is as basic and vague, in respect of procedural and evidentiary matters, as the Statute. The danger of assuming powers or creating Rules, some of which seemingly result in effect in constituting new offences, consequently also increases. In this respect the more detailed and circumscribed provisions in the ICC Statute may be preferable.[60]

Relative to the corresponding law in national systems, the procedural and evidentiary law of the Tribunal is still in its infancy. That does not, however, mean that the law with respect to the subject Rules is wholly unsatisfactory or that it will not be developed and refined in the years to come.

---

[60]See ICC Statute Art. 71 ("Sanctions for misconduct before the Court"), which provides: "(1) The Court may sanction persons present before it who commit misconduct, including disruption of its proceedings or deliberate refusal to comply with its directions, by administrative measures other than imprisonment, such as temporary or permanent removal from the courtroom, a fine or other similar measures provided for in the Rules of Procedure and Evidence. (2) The procedures governing the imposition of the measures set forth in paragraph 1 shall be those provided for in the Rules of Procedure and Evidence."; Art. 70 ("Offences against the administration of justice"), which provides: "(1) The Court shall have jurisdiction over the following offences against its administration of justice when committed intentionally: (a) Giving false testimony when under an obligation pursuant to article 69, paragraph 1, to tell the truth; (b) Presenting evidence that the party knows is false or forged; (c) Corruptly influencing a witness, obstructing or interfering with the attendance or testimony of a witness, retaliating against a witness for giving testimony or destroying, tampering with or interfering with the collection of evidence; (d) Impeding, intimidating or corruptly influencing an official of the Court for the purpose of forcing or persuading the official not to perform, or to perform improperly, his or her duties; (e) Retaliating against an official of the Court on account of duties performed by that or another official; (f) Soliciting or accepting a bribe as an official of the Court in conjunction with his or her official duties. (2) The principles and procedures governing the Court's exercise of jurisdiction over offences under this article shall be those provided for in the Rules of Procedure and Evidence. The conditions for providing international cooperation to the Court with respect to its proceedings under this article shall be governed by the domestic laws of the requested State. (3) In the event of conviction, the Court may impose a term of imprisonment not exceeding five years, or a fine in accordance with the Rules of Procedure and Evidence, or both. (4) (a) Each State Party shall extend its criminal laws penalizing offences against the integrity of its own investigative or judicial process to offences against the administration of justice referred to in this article, committed on its territory, or by one of its nationals; (b) Upon request by the Court, whenever it deems it proper, the State Party shall submit the case to its competent authorities for the purpose of prosecution. Those authorities shall treat such cases with diligence and devote sufficient resources to enable them to be conducted effectively."; and Art. 63 ("Trial in the presence of the accused"), which provides: "(1) The accused shall be present during the trial. (2) If the accused, being present before the Court, continues to disrupt the trial, the Trial Chamber may remove the accused and shall make provision for him or her to observe the trial and instruct counsel from outside the courtroom, through the use of communications technology, if required. Such measures shall be taken only in exceptional circumstances after other reasonable alternatives have proved inadequate, and only for such duration as is strictly required." For a commentary on these Articles, see Otto Triffterer (ed.), Commentary on the Rome Statute of the International Criminal Court: Observers' Notes, Article by Article (1999).

STUART BERESFORD*

31. Non-Compliance with the Rules of Procedure and Evidence

1. Introduction

Although non-compliance with the Rules of Procedure and Evidence of the Tribunal (the "Rules") will not automatically invalidate the act concerned, a party to the proceedings – pursuant to Rule 5 thereto[1] – may seek to nullify the act by decision of a Trial Chamber. Such an objection may relate to an act or omission by the Prosecution during the investigation or pre-trial stages or to some procedural or evidentiary aspect of the judicial proceedings. In order for the objection to be upheld and the appropriate relief granted, the Chamber must be satisfied that the alleged non-compliance is proved and that it caused material prejudice to the objecting party.

Given that the investigation and pre-trial stages of the proceedings receive only modest judicial supervision, the ability of a party to refer acts of non-compliance to the Trial Chambers is essential. Nevertheless, while the granting of appropriate relief may be at times necessary, to avoid the relationship between the parties deteriorating, the objecting party should, where possible, exhaust all reasonable avenues before moving for relief. Conversely, the Chambers should maintain a high level of judicial oversight and control over the proceedings thus avoiding unnecessary interlocutory

*Associate Legal Officer, Registry, ICTY. LLB, BSc (majoring in psychology), LLM *with distinction*, University of Otago. Formerly: Temporary Legal Officer, Secretariat, ECHR. Member of the Bar Association of New Zealand. The views expressed herein are those of the author alone and do not necessarily reflect the views of the United Nations or the ICTY.

[1]ICTY Rule 5 also permits the Defence to refer acts of non-compliance with any Regulations issued by the Prosecutor – pursuant to Rule 37 of the Rules – to the Chamber. Such regulations govern the functions of the Prosecutor as provided by the Statute. See John Jones, The Practice of the International Criminal Tribunals for the former Yugoslavia and Rwanda (2000) at 223.

R. May et al., Essays on ICTY Procedure and Evidence in Honour of Gabrielle Kirk McDonald, 403–417

litigation and the collateral effects that may follow. The purpose of this chapter is, therefore, to analyse the reasons why acts of non-compliance occur and the conditions that need to be satisfied in order for a Chamber to invalidate an act of a party. Through an examination of the jurisprudence of the Tribunal, and, where appropriate, the case-law of the International Criminal Tribunal for Rwanda (the "Rwanda Tribunal"),[2] the chapter will discuss the meaning of the phrases "material prejudice" and "relief", and will examine whether the decision of the Chamber may be challenged.

2. The Need to Ensure Compliance

Although the Rules, as a whole, strike a balance between the common law adversarial system and the civil law inquisitorial system of dealing with criminal proceedings, there is little, if any, judicial supervision over the investigation stage of the proceedings.[3] Following the arrest of persons charged with committing offences coming within the jurisdiction of the Tribunal, the level of judicial oversight and control increases dramatically. Accused persons must be brought immediately before a Trial Chamber which shall read the indictment to them, ensure that their rights are respected, confirm they understand the indictment and instruct them to enter a plea.[4] As the case proceeds to trial the Chamber may convene status conferences to organise exchanges between the parties,[5] and may designate one of its

[2]ICTR Rule 5 also allows a party to the proceedings to refer acts of non-compliance with the Rules to the Chambers. Such objections shall be upheld if the act was inconsistent with the fundamental principles of fairness and had occasioned a miscarriage of justice.

[3]Articles 18 and 19 of the Statute of the Tribunal, read in conjunction with Rules 39 through 43 of the Rules, entrusts the responsibility for initiating investigations on the Prosecutor. During such investigations, the Prosecutor has the authority to question suspects, victims and witnesses, collect evidence and conduct on-site investigations. To ensure that investigations are not thwarted by the escape of suspects to jurisdictions hostile to the Tribunal, the Prosecutor may request a State to temporarily arrest suspects and, in exceptional circumstances, transfer them to the premises of the United Nations Detention Unit.

[4]ICTY Rule 62.

[5]ICTY Rule 65*bis*. During the pre-trial phase, the Prosecutor is required to make available to the accused copies of the supporting material that accompanied the indictment when it was confirmed, along with "all prior statements obtained by the Prosecutor from the accused or from prosecution witnesses." The Prosecutor must also permit the defence to inspect any books, documents, photographs and tangible objects in his custody or control, unless the disclosure may prejudice further or ongoing investigations, or for any reason may be contrary to the public interest or affect the security interests of any state. See ICTY Rule 66. The Prosecutor is further required to disclose to the defence any evidence that tends in any way to exculpate the accused or may affect the credibility of prosecution evidence. See ICTY Rule 68. Conversely, the defence must notify the Prosecutor of its intent to offer the defence of alibi or any other special defence, including that of diminished or lack of mental responsibility and provide the necessary details thereof. See ICTY Rule 67.

members as a pre-trial Judge to assist the parties reach agreement on facts, issues, witnesses, exhibits and scheduling.[6] Nevertheless, responsibility for ensuring compliance with their procedural and evidentiary obligations rests primarily with the parties themselves. In this connection, it has been opined that the Trial Chambers:

> [...] should not have to remind or prompt the [parties] of [their] obligations, nor should it have to pursue the (parties(in order to ensure that deadlines are kept and that orders or decisions are complied with in their entirety.[7]

While the Chambers endeavour to promote fairness, honesty and professional courtesy between the parties,[8] a reduction in the level of judicial oversight and control – caused by excessive case-loads or other commitments – may cause a decrease in the effectiveness of case management, resulting in an unintentional upsurge in the number of acts of non-compliance. On the other hand, the stakes involved in and the pressures generated by the cases that come before the Tribunal may lead some parties to knowingly and intentionally violate the Rules. It is, therefore, essential that the parties have the ability to refer acts of non-compliance to a Trial Chamber. Nonetheless, given that the resulting proceedings may be "disruptive, costly and may create personal antagonism inimical to an atmosphere of co-operation",[9] the objecting party should, where possible, exhaust all reasonable avenues before moving for relief.

3. Material Prejudice

The appropriate timing for granting relief necessitates that objections based on non-compliance with the Rules should be raised by the objecting party at the earliest opportunity.[10] In the majority of cases, the relief granted by the Trial Chambers will be most effective when imposed promptly after the non-compliance has occurred. In addition to maximising its deterrent effect, prompt imposition allows the Chambers to resolve the problem by imposing less severe forms of relief before resorting to more extreme measures should they become necessary.[11] Certain acts of non-compliance or the extent of their consequences may not, however, become apparent until the proceedings

[6]ICTY Rule 65*ter*.

[7]*Prosecutor v. Blaškić, Decision on the Production of Discovery Materials*, Case No. IT-95-14-PT, 27 Jan. 1997 ("*Blaškić Discovery Decision*") at para. 47.

[8]*Prosecutor v. Furundžija, The Trial Chamber's Formal Complaint to the Prosecutor Concerning the Conduct of the Prosecution*, Case No. IT-95-17/1-T, 11 Dec. 1998 ("*Furundžija Formal Complaint*") at para. 7.

[9]See Federal Judicial Center, Manual for Complex Litigation (1995) ("Manual for Complex Litigation") at p. 18.

[10]ICTY Rule 5 (B).

[11]See Manual for Complex Litigation, supra note 9, at p. 23.

have moved on. Accordingly, sub-Rule 5 (B) allows the Chamber to review, at its discretion, an objection based on non-compliance raised otherwise than at the earliest opportunity.

The decision of a Trial Chamber to secure compliance with the Rules should not be taken without giving the offending party an opportunity to be heard. Moreover, appropriate relief should only be granted if the Chamber is satisfied that the alleged non-compliance is proved and that it has caused material prejudice to the objecting party. When making such a determination, the Trial Chamber should not deny the relief requested on the mere basis that the objecting party has failed to comply with its own obligations.[12] The decision of the Chamber, however, should be governed "less by a system of 'sanctions' than by the Judges' definitive evaluation of the evidence presented by either party and the possibility which the opposing party will have had to contest it."[13]

These principles are applicable particularly to the Rules relating to the discovery, inspection and production of documents and other material in the possession of the parties. In the case of *Prosecutor v. Furundžija*, the Prosecution failed to make available to the Defence sixty days before the date set for trial copies of the statements of all the witnesses whom they intended to call to testify as mandated by sub-Rule 66 (A)(ii). Trial Chamber II – Judges Mumba, Cassese and May – expressed grave concern at the unjustifiable failure of the Prosecution to comply with its disclosure obligations. Nevertheless, since the Prosecution agreed to disclose the statements to the Defence within two days, the Chamber dismissed the Defence's request to have the testimony of the witnesses in question precluded.[14] Despite the fact that the Prosecution was late in complying with its discovery obligations, such conduct did not overly prejudice the preparation of the defence of the accused.

The *Furundžija* case was notable for the Prosecution's continued and repeated failure to comply with its discovery obligations. Critical of the approach taken by the Prosecution and after having expressed dismay at what it considered to be conduct close to negligence in the Prosecution's preparation of the case,[15] on 5 June 1998 the Trial Chamber issued a formal complaint to the Prosecutor concerning the conduct of the Prosecution.[16]

---

[12] *Prosecutor v. Blaškić, Decision on the Defence Motion for Sanctions for the Prosecutor's Continuing Violation of Rule 98*, Case No. IT-95-14-T, 28 Sept. 1998.

[13] In the *Blaškić* case, it was alleged that the Prosecution had failed in its obligations to disclose to the defence evidence which might exculpate the accused that it had obtained as part of another case pending before the Tribunal. Without considering the merits of the claim, Trial Chamber I – Judges Jorda, Riad and Shahabuddeen – denied the relief sought on the basis that the defence did not intend to seize the Chamber of the matter. Id.

[14] *Prosecutor v. Furundžija, Decision on Motion of Defendant Anto Furundžija to Preclude Testimony of Certain Prosecution Witnesses*, Case No. IT-95-17/1-PT, 29 Apr. 1998.

[15] *Prosecutor v. Furundžija, Decision*, Case No. IT-95-17/1-PT, 2 June 1998.

[16] Furundžija Formal Complaint, supra note 7. The Chamber was particularly disturbed by the fact that a witness statement from the main witness against the accused was only disclosed to the defence seventeen days before the commencement of the trial, even though it had been in their possession for almost seven months.

Despite such a strong condemnation, the Prosecution continued to breach its obligation to disclose to the Defence, in a timely manner, documents and other material in its possession. On 29 June 1998 – seven days after the close of the proceedings against the accused – the Prosecution submitted to the Defence a redacted certificate and a witness statement from a psychologist working at the Medica Women's Therapy Centre ("Medica") in Zenica, Bosnia and Herzegovina, concerning Witness A, the victim of the rape which was the subject of the allegations against the accused, and the treatment she had received at Medica following the rape. The Defence alleged that the Prosecution had deprived the accused of a fair trial by knowingly and intentionally failing to disclose evidence that cast doubt on the reliability of the memory of the witness. They maintained that such non-compliance could only be remedied by striking the witness's testimony or, in the event that the accused was convicted, by ordering a new trial.[17] The Prosecution objected to the contention that it had deprived the defence of certain lines of cross-examination, arguing that the Defence had adequate opportunity and, in fact, pursued many lines of inquiry relating to Witness A's mental condition, mental stability and ability to recollect events accurately.[18]

Having heard the oral submissions of the parties, the Trial Chamber found serious misconduct on the part of the Prosecution in breach of its discovery obligations.[19] In its opinion, the documents had the potential to affect the credibility of prosecution evidence and, therefore, the Prosecution was obliged to either advise the Defence that they had these documents in their possession or provide them with copies as part of the disclosure process.[20] Referring to the fact that the accused's defence had been conducted on the basis that Witness A's memory was flawed, the Chamber found that "prejudice was suffered by the Defence, which was unable to fully cross-examine relevant Prosecution witnesses and to call evidence to deal with any medical, psychiatric or psychological treatment or counselling that may have been received by Witness A."[21]

One of the fundamental principles of criminal law is that "material which is known to the Prosecution and which is favourable to the accused in the sense that it tends to suggest the innocence or mitigate the guilt of the accused or may affect the credibility of Prosecution evidence" must be

---

[17]*Prosecutor v. Furundžija, Defendant's Motion to Strike the Testimony of Witness A due to Prosecutorial Misconduct or, in the Event of a Conviction, for a New Trial*, Case No. IT-95-17/1-PT, 9 July 1998.

[18]*Prosecutor v. Furundžija, Prosecutor's response to defence motion to strike testimony of witness "A" or order new trial, dated 9 July 1998*, Case No. IT-95-17/1-PT, 13 July 1998.

[19]*Prosecutor v. Furundžija, Decision,* Case No. IT-95-17/1-T, 16 July 1998 ("*Furundžija Decision*") at para. 16.

[20]Id., para. 17.

[21]Id., para. 18.

disclosed to the Defence.[22] This principle is reflected in Rule 68 of the Rules, which requires the Prosecution to disclose, as soon as practicable, exculpatory evidence to the defence.[23] Nevertheless, on several occasions the Trial Chambers have been called upon to resolve disputes relating to the alleged failure on the part of the Prosecution to comply with its obligations thereto. Responding to a motion by the defence of the accused, Tihomir Blaškić requesting an order compelling the Prosecution to produce information, documents and other items of potential evidentiary value, including, inter alia, statements of the accused, Trial Chamber I asserted:

> There is no doubt that the obligation to disclose evidence which might exculpate the accused is the responsibility of the Prosecutor alone, if for no other reason than the fact that she is the one in possession of the materials.[24]

However, if the Prosecution – to the satisfaction of the Trial Chamber – complies with its obligation to disclose exculpatory evidence but the Defence maintains that evidence is still in the possession of the Prosecution which might prove exculpatory for the accused:

> [...] it must submit to the Trial Chamber all *prima facie* proofs tending to make it likely that the evidence is exculpatory and was in the Prosecutor's possession. Should it not present this *prima facie* proof to the Trial Chamber, the Defence will not be granted authorisation to have the evidence disclosed.[25]

Shortly after the commencement of the *Čelebići* trial, Trial Chamber II - Judges Karibi-Whyte, Odio-Benito and Jan – was called upon by the accused, Hazim Delić, to order the Prosecution to disclose material in its possession which would demonstrate that the victims of the crimes which the accused was alleged to have committed were not protected under the Geneva Prisoners of War Convention of 1949.[26] The Chamber, following the test laid down in the *Blaškić* Case, denied the motion, concluding "that the Defence has failed to indicate the specific material it regards as exculpatory and which should be disclosed pursuant to Rule 68. Moreover, the Defence

[22] *Prosecutor v. Delalić and Others, Decision on the Request of the Accused Pursuant to Rule 68 for Exculpatory Information*, Case No. IT-96-21-T, 24 June 1997 at para. 12.

[23] Rule 68 provides "[t]he Prosecutor shall, as soon as practicable, disclose to the defence the existence of evidence known to the Prosecutor which in any way tends to suggest the innocence or mitigate the guilt of the accused or may affect the credibility of prosecution evidence."

[24] *Blaškić Discovery Decision*, supra note 7. The Chamber considered that the Prosecution's obligation under Rule 68 to disclose exculpatory evidence could in principle extend to such evidence contained in case-files of other accused (at paras. 26–30).

[25] Id., para. 49.

[26] See *Prosecutor v. Delalić and Others, Request Pursuant to Rule 68 for Exculpatory Information*, Case No. IT-96-21-T, 21 Apr. 1997.

has failed to show *prima facie* that the information it seeks to be disclosed is in fact exculpatory."[27]

Although objections based on non-compliance with the Rules have primarily centred on issues of discovery, the ability of one party to have an act of the other party declared null and void is not confined to such matters. In the case of *Prosecutor v. Barayagwiza*, the Defence challenged the legality of the arrest and provisional detention of the accused by the authorities of Cameroon prior to his transfer to Arusha, the seat of the Rwanda Tribunal. Although the primary area of dispute focused on alleged violations of the fair trial rights of the accused as prescribed by Article 20 of the ICTR Statute, the Defence contended, inter alia, that the Prosecution failed to comply with its obligations under Rule 40*bis* of the ICTR Rules to promptly charge the accused – who was a suspect at the time of his arrest. Furthermore, the Defence argued that a delay of ninety-six days between his transfer to Arusha and his initial appearance violated the statutory requirement, as mandated by Rule 62 of the ICTR Rules, that the initial appearance be held without delay.[28]

On 3 November 1999, the ICTR Appeals Chamber – Judges McDonald, Shahabuddeen, Vohrah, Wang and Nieto-Navia (who had been seized of the matter following the decision of Trial Chamber II – Judges Sekule, Ostrovsky and Khan – to reject the complaints of the Defence *in toto*[29]) – found, inter alia, that the length of time the accused was detained in Cameroon at the behest of the Prosecution without being indicted violated the limitation on the detention of suspects as laid down in Rule 40*bis*.[30] In their opinion, such a limitation was consistent with established human rights jurisprudence governing the detention of suspects.[31] The Chamber also found that the Prosecution had failed to ensure that the accused was

[27] *Decision on the Request of the Accused Pursuant to Rule 68 for Exculpatory Information*, supra note 22 at para. 18.

[28] *Prosecutor v. Barayagwiza, Extremely Urgent Motion by the Defence for Orders to Review and/or Nullify the Arrest and Provisional Detention of the Suspect*, Case No. ICTR-97-19-I, dated 19 Feb. 1998, filed 24 Feb. 1998. See also *Prosecutor v. Barayagwiza, Notification of Appeal of Decision of Trial Chamber II*, Case No. ICTR-97-19-AR72, dated 27 Nov. 1998, filed 4 Dec. 1998; *Prosecutor v. Barayagwiza, Memorandum of Appeal*, Case No. ICTR-97-19-AR72, dated 27 Nov. 1998; *Prosecutor v. Barayagwiza, The Defence Memorial in Support of the Accused Person's Appeal of the Decision of Trial Chamber II on the Extremely Urgent Motion by the Defence for Orders to Review and/or Nullify the Arrest and Provisional Detention of the Suspect*, Case No. ICTR-97-19-AR72, dated 2 Feb. 1999; and *Prosecutor v. Barayagwiza, Amended Version of Appellant's Brief*, Case No. ICTR-97-19-AR72, dated 23 Feb. 1999.

[29] See *Prosecutor v. Barayagwiza, Decision on the Extremely Urgent Motion by the Defence for Orders to Review and/or Nullify the Arrest and Provisional Detention of the Suspect*, Case No. ICTR-97-19-I, 17 Nov. 1998.

[30] *Prosecutor v. Barayagwiza, Decision*, Case No. ICTR-97-19-AR72, A. Ch., 3 Nov. 1999 ("*Barayagwiza Decision*") at para. 67.

[31] Id.

promptly brought before a judicial authority and formally charged.[32] Rejecting the Prosecution's contention that a thirty-one day holiday recess could somehow justify the delay between the transfer of the accused to the Rwanda Tribunal on 19 November 1996 and his initial appearance which took place on 23 February 1997[33], the Chamber further found that the ninety-six day delay denied the accused the opportunity to mount an effective defence.[34]

Arguing that new facts had been discovered which justified a reopening of the case, on 19 November 1999 the Prosecution requested and was granted permission to seek a review of the Appeals Chamber's decision.[35] The new facts which the Prosecution sought to introduce and relied on in its *Motion for Review* fell within two categories: new facts which were not known or could not have been known to the Prosecution at the time of the argument before the Appeals Chamber and facts which although they "may have possibly been discovered" by the Prosecution at the time were not known to be part of the factual dispute or relevant to the issues subsequently determined by the Appeals Chamber.[36]

After construing that the condition laid down in ICTR Rule 120 governing the submission of motions for review – namely, that the fact be unknown to the moving party at the time of the proceedings before a Chamber, and not discoverable through the exercise of due diligence – was directory in nature[37], the Appeals Chamber – then comprising Judges Jorda, Vohrah, Shahabuddeen, Nieto-Navia and Pocar[38] – concluded that "to reject the facts presented by the [Prosecution], in the light of their impact on the [decision reached by the Appeals Chamber], would [...] be to close one's eyes to reality."[39] These facts demonstrated, inter alia, that the accused knew the general nature of the charges against him eighteen days after his arrest

[32] Id., para. 71.

[33] Id., para. 68. In the opinion of the Appeals Chamber, the accused should have had his initial appearance well before the holiday recess even commenced.

[34] Id., para. 70.

[35] See *Prosecutor v. Barayagwiza, Notice of Intention to File Request for Review of Decision of the Appeals Chamber of 3 November 1999*, Case No. ICTR-97-19-AR72, 19 Nov. 1999.

[36] The Prosecution alleged that numerous factual issues were raised for the first time on appeal by the Appeals Chamber, *proprio motu*, without a full hearing or adjudication of the facts by the Appeals Chamber and contended, therefore, that it could not be faulted for failing to comprehend the full nature of the facts required by the Appeals Chamber. In this connection, the Prosecution argued that the questions raised did not correspond in full to the subsequent determinations by the Appeal Chamber. See *Prosecutor v. Barayagwiza, Motion for Review*, Case No. ICTR-97-19-AR72, 1 December 1999.

[37] *Prosecutor v. Barayagwiza, Decision (Prosecutor's Request for Review or Reconsideration)*, Case No. ICTR-97-19-AR72, A. Ch., 31 March 2000 ("*Barayagwiza Review Decision*") at para. 65.

[38] The change in composition was necessitated by the departure of Judges McDonald and Wang Tieya, who resigned from the ICTY (and the ICTR Appeals Chamber) as of 17 November 1999 and 2 April 2000 respectively. See ICTY Press Releases JL/PIU/385-E (16 March 1999) and CC/P.I.S./486-E (3 April 2000).

[39] *Barayagwiza Review Decision*, supra note 37, para. 69.

at latest. Although such a time period violated the right of the accused to be informed of the charges against him without delay, the Chamber found this violation to be of a different magnitude than the one it had identified in its previous decision – whereby the accused was without any information for eleven months.[40] The facts also demonstrated to the satisfaction of the Chamber that the defence counsel of the accused had assented to deferring the initial appearance until 3 February 1997, thus reducing to 20 days the period during which the right of the accused to be brought before a judicial authority and formally charged was violated.[41] Although it found this delay to be substantial, the Chamber considered the intensity of the violation of the right of the accused to be less severe than it appeared at the time of its original decision.[42]

4. Relief

According to sub-Rule 5 (C), the form of the relief imposed shall be "such remedy as the Trial Chamber considers appropriate to ensure consistency with the fundamental principles of fairness". Since the relief imposed should provide a complete and proportionate remedy for the non-compliance in question,[43] the Chamber should, therefore, take into account several factors including, inter alia, what prejudice was caused to the objecting party, was the act deliberate or inadvertent, were there any extenuating circumstances and what was the impact of the act on the Chambers and the integrity of the Tribunal as a whole.[44] The Chamber should also consider the purpose to be served by the relief – to protect the objecting party, to remedy prejudice caused, to deter future non-compliance or to punish the offending party – and whether it should be imposed promptly or delayed until the end of the trial.[45] Finally, the Chamber should consider what is the least severe form of relief that will accomplish the intended purpose.[46]

In the vast majority of cases where non-compliance by a party has been adjudged to have prejudiced the case of the objecting party, the Trial Chambers have imposed less severe forms of relief. For most minor violations, particularly a first infraction, they have merely issued oral warnings to the offending party. However, on occasions, as illustrated above

---

[40] Id., paras. 54–55.

[41] Id., paras. 60–61.

[42] Id., para. 62.

[43] See *Prosecutor v. Furundžija, Prosecutor's Response to the Formal Complaint of the Trial Chamber issued on 5 June 1998*, Case No. IT-95-17/1-T, 11 Dec. 1998 at para. 7.

[44] Federal Judicial Center, Manual for Litigation Management and Cost & Delay Reduction (1992) at p. 35.

[45] Id.

[46] See Manual for Complex Litigation, supra note 9, at p. 20.

in the *Furundžija* Case,[47] a written reprimand has been deemed to be more appropriate. Where delays to disclose, in a timely manner, documents and other material in the possession of a party have been found to be unacceptable, the Chambers have awarded the objecting party additional time for discovery or other matters or denied requests from the offending party for extension of time.[48] In this connection, the author notes that, although such sanctions have yet to be imposed, it is conceivable that the Chambers may order defence counsel not to charge their clients, or instruct the Registrar to decline to remunerate assigned counsel, for any costs or reimbursements they occur through dilatory or otherwise improper conduct or in proceedings brought by such conduct.[49]

In the view of the author, more extreme forms of relief, such as dismissal, default or preclusion of a claim or evidence should be imposed only in egregious circumstances. In the case of the *Prosecutor v. Bagilishema*, the Prosecution was ordered to remove four witnesses from its witness list because it failed to disclose their testimonies to the Defence within sixty days of the start of the trial.[50] Since the case of the Prosecution had already commenced, this ruling should be distinguished from the *Decision on the Motion by the Defence Counsel for Disclosure* rendered by ICTR Trial Chamber II in the *Bagosora* Case. The Chamber found that pendency of a motion for protective measures for its witnesses did not exonerate the Prosecution of its discovery obligations, and, accordingly, directed the Prosecution to fulfil its obligations and disclose the statements in question to the Defence within two weeks.[51] Further relief was not granted, however, as the Chamber did not consider that the Defence had been overly prejudiced by the failure to disclose, especially as the trial date had been postponed and that the Defence would, consequently, have sufficient time to prepare for trial.[52]

---

[47]See supra note 15 and accompanying text.

[48]Prior to the commencement of the *Furundžija* trial, the defence brought to the attention of Trial Chamber II the fact that the Prosecution had not complied with all of its discovery obligations. Expressing grave concern and deploring that the Prosecution had failed to comply with its obligation to disclose to the Defence "no later than sixty days before the date set for trial, copies of the statements of all witnesses whom the Prosecutor intends to call to testify at trial" the Trial Chamber ordered the Prosecution to provide full disclosure to the Defence within two days. The Defence was also requested to inform the Chamber whether in consideration of the need to ensure an expeditious trial, it would be in a position to waive its right to timely disclosure and to proceed with the trial, keeping in mind that in the circumstances, postponement of the trial date would not be attributed to the Defence. *Prosecutor v. Furundžija, Scheduling Order*, Case No. IT-95-17/1-T, 29 Apr. 1998.

[49]See Manual for Complex Litigation, supra note 9, at p. 21.

[50]Reported on the web-site of Fondation Hirondelle at *http://www.wcw.org* on 2 Feb. 2000.

[51]*Prosecutor v. Bagosora, Decision on the Motion by the Defence Counsel for Disclosure*, Case No. ICTR-96-7-PT, 27 Nov. 1997.

[52]Id.

As mentioned above, in its *Decision* of 16 July 1999, Trial Chamber II held that the Prosecution had made a serious procedural error by not disclosing to the Defence of the accused, Anto Furundžija, material that may have affected the credibility of the main witness against the accused.[53] In order to avoid any prejudice to the accused and to prevent the occurrence of a miscarriage of justice, the Chamber ordered the re-opening of the proceedings against the accused insofar as the medical, psychological and psychiatric treatment or counselling of Witness A was concerned. Furthermore, the Prosecution was ordered to disclose to the Defence any other document in its possession which related to this issue.[54]

The Defence had sought to strike the testimony of Witness A, or, in the event of a conviction, an order for a new trial. Although it considered that there had been a "serious procedural error" on the part of found "that the relevant witness, who in this instance is also a victim, should not be made to suffer as a the Prosecution, the Trial Chamber consequence of such misconduct by 'striking her evidence'".[55] In connection to the alternative remedy sought by the Defence, the Chamber stated that since the accused had not been convicted and as the date for the delivery of judgement had not been set, such a remedy was inappropriate. In any event, it was not within the power of the Chamber to order a re-trial.[56]

Such a restriction on the form of relief that may be imposed has also been recognised by the Rwanda Tribunal. Although highly critical of the failure of the Prosecution to comply with its disclosure obligations, ICTR Trial Chamber I – Judges Kama, Aspegren and Ostrovsky – held, in the case of *Prosecutor v. Kayishema*, that it was estopped from imposing the sanction of annulment of the indictment as proposed by the Defence as such sanction was not provided for by the Rules.[57]

Although the relief imposed must be provided for by the Rules (or lie within their inherent powers), the Trial Chambers should ensure that it is effective and accomplishes adequately the intended purpose. Moreover, the Chambers should guarantee that it does not place the objecting party in a worse position than it would have been in had it not sought relief from the Chamber. In the aforementioned *Barayagwiza* Case, the Appeals Chamber initially determined – having found the actions of the Prosecution to be 'egregious' – that the failure of the Prosecution to prosecute the case against the accused was tantamount to negligence. It therefore concluded that "the only remedy available for such prosecutorial inaction and the resultant

---

[53]See supra notes 17 to 21 and accompanying text.

[54]*Furundžija Decision*, supra note 19, at para. 21.

[55]Id., para. 20.

[56]Id. Referring to Rule 117 (C) of the Rules the Chamber stated that such a measure lies exclusively in the power of the Appeals Chamber.

[57]*Prosecutor v. Kayishema*, *Decision on the Preliminary Motion filed by the Defence*, Case No. ICTR-95-1-T, 6 Nov. 1996.

denial of his rights is to release the [accused] and dismiss the charges against him."[58] In its opinion:

> This finding is consistent with Rule 40 *bis* (H), which requires release if the suspect is not charged within 90 days of the commencement of the provisional detention and Rule 40(D) which requires release if the Prosecutor fails to issue an indictment within 20 days after the transfer of the suspect.[59]

Believing that to proceed with the accused's trial when such violations have been committed, would cause irreparable damage to the integrity of the judicial process, the Appeal Chamber further ordered that the dismissal of the indictment be with prejudice to the prosecution.[60] In the Chamber's view, such a remedy was the only effective relief for the cumulative breaches of the rights of the accused.[61] Were the Appeals Chamber to dismiss the charges without prejudice "the strict 90-day limit set forth in sub-Rule 40*bis*(H) could be thwarted by repeated release and re-arrest, thereby giving the [Prosecution] a potentially unlimited period of time to prepare and submit an indictment for confirmation.[62] In such a situation, to allow the accused to stand trial on the charges for which he was belatedly indicted would amount to a travesty of justice and would result in "loss of public confidence in the [Rwanda] Tribunal."[63]

However, after reviewing its decision in light of new facts presented by the Prosecution,[64] the Appeals Chamber concluded that these facts diminished "the role played by the failings of the Prosecutor as well as the intensity of the violation of the right of the [accused]."[65] Since the cumulative nature of violations had been thus reduced, the Chamber considered that the reparation ordered appeared "disproportionate in relation to the events".[66] The Chamber, therefore, dismissed the accused's claim to be released and ordered that, should he subsequently be found not guilty, the accused should receive financial compensation. In the event that he is found guilty, the eventual sentence of the accused should be reduced to take account of the infringements of his rights.[67]

---

[58] *Barayagwiza Decision*, supra note 30, at para. 106.

[59] Id. The Appeals Chamber also found that such a limitation on the period of provisional detention was consistent with international human rights jurisprudence.

[60] Id., para. 108.

[61] Id.

[62] Id., para. 109.

[63] Id., para. 112.

[64] See supra notes 37 to 42 and accompanying text.

[65] *Barayagwiza Review Decision*, supra note 37, at para. 71.

[66] Id.

[67] Id. para. 75.

5. Appeal

Since an objection based on the ground of non-compliance with those sections of the Rules relating to the arrest and detention of an accused persons may be considered an objection based on lack of personal jurisdiction over the accused, the parties may challenge the decision of the Trial Chamber, as such an appeal lies as of right under sub-Rule 72(B)(i).[68] However, in other cases the decision of the Trial Chamber is without interlocutory appeal, except where it has been established by the party seeking leave to the satisfaction of a bench of three Judges of the Appeals Chamber that the decision would cause such prejudice to its case as could not be cured by the final disposal of the trial including post-judgement appeal, or the issue in the proposed appeal is of general importance to proceedings before the Tribunal or in international law generally.[69] In such cases,

---

[68]In the *Barayagwiza* Case, following the rejection of the request of the defence to nullify his arrest and provisional detention, the accused sought leave to appeal the decision of Trial Chamber II, see supra notes 28–29 and accompanying text. Concluding that an objection challenging the legality of his detention raised the issue of whether the Tribunal had personal jurisdiction over the accused, the Appeals Chamber determined that the Decision of the Trial Chamber may be appealed as of right under sub-Rule 72(D) of the ICTR Rules. *Prosecutor v. Barayagwiza, Decision and Scheduling Order*, Case No. ICTR-97-19-AR72, A. Ch., 5 Feb. 1999.

[69]See ICTY Rule 73 (B) (i) and (ii). Arguing that to reopen the proceedings solely in relation to the medical, psychological and psychiatric treatment of Witness A would cause serious harm to the fair trial rights the accused, Anto Furundžija, and that such harm could not be cured on post-judgement appeal, on 23 July 1998 the Defence requested leave to appeal the Trial Chamber II's order of 16 July 1998. The defence also contended that the issues raised by the appeal – namely, what remedy should be afforded an accused if the Trial Chamber makes a specific finding that there has been "serious prosecutorial misconduct" that threatens to cause "a miscarriage of justice" if not remedied and whether a Trial Chamber has the authority to "re-open" the case after the hearing has been closed – were of general importance to the proceedings before the Tribunal. See *Prosecutor v. Furundžija, Defendant's Request for Leave to Appeal Trial Chamber II's Order of 16 July 1998*, Case No. IT-95-17/1-AR73, 23 July 1998; and *Prosecutor v. Furundžija, Defendant's Proposed Appeal of Trial Chamber II's Order of 16 July 1998*), Case No. IT-95-17/1-AR73, 23 July 1998. In response the Prosecution requested the Appeals Chamber to deny the request of the Defence for leave to appeal on the basis that the requirements of sub-Rule 73(B)(i) were not met. Referring to the inherent power of the Trial Chamber to issue a broad range of orders and decisions to insure the judicial flexibility needed to remedy gaps within the trial process, the Prosecution maintained that "the Trial Chamber's Decision to reopen the case is neither extraordinary nor controversial, and does not require interlocutory review for confirmation of a very basic right of every sitting trial court." *Prosecutor v. Furundžija, Prosecutor's Response to the Defence Request for Leave to Appeal in Accordance with Appeals Chamber Scheduling Order of 29 July 1998*, Case No. IT-95-17/1-AR73, 5 Aug. 1998. The Bench of the Appeals Chamber agreed and decided, unanimously, to refuse to grant leave to appeal as sought in the Defence's request. *Prosecutor v. Furundžija, Decision on Defendant's Request for Leave to Appeal Trial Chamber II's Order of 16 July 1998*, Case No. IT-95-17/1-AR73, A. Ch., 24 Aug. 1998.

application for leave to appeal must be filed within seven days of the filing of the impugned decision.[70]

6. Concluding Remarks

The ability of a party to refer acts of non-compliance to the Trial Chambers and to be granted appropriate relief, serves a number of purposes: to protect a party, to remedy prejudice caused, to deter future non-compliance and to punish the offending party. Although the Chambers should only impose the least severe form of relief appropriate to accomplish the intended purpose, the imposition of such measures should not be a means for effective case management or a substitute for it. Often the need to impose appropriate relief arises when a case has not been managed in a clear, specific and reasonable manner. In such cases, the parties do not know what is expected of them or the consequences of failing to comply with their obligations. On the other hand, effective case management cannot anticipate acts of misconduct on the part of the parties or control them when they occur. While the imposition of appropriate relief may, therefore, be at times necessary, the Chambers should maintain high level of judicial control and oversight over the proceedings thus avoiding unnecessary interlocutory litigation and the collateral effects that may follow.

The recent adoption of a provision allowing the Presiding Judge of the Trial Chamber to designate from among its members a Judge responsible for the pre-trial proceedings will improve significantly the level of judicial supervision over the pre-trial proceedings.[71] In particular, since "the pre-trial may be entrusted by the Trial Chamber with all or part of any pre-trial functions set forth in Rule 73,"[72] the pre-trial Judge will be able to resolve promptly disputes relating to the discovery obligations of the parties, particularly those that may be time-consuming or require immediate action. However, as highlighted by the Expert Group to Conduct a Review of the Effectiveness Operation and Functioning of the International Criminal Tribunal for the Former Yugoslavia and the International Criminal Tribunal for Rwanda (the

[70] ICTY Rule 73 (C).

[71] See Rule 65*ter*. This Rule was adopted at the eighteenth plenary session of the Tribunal held on 9 and 10 July 1998. See Jones, supra note 1, at 332.

[72] ICTY sub-Rule 65*ter* (D).

"Expert Group")[73], the pre-trial Judge is not empowered with the ability "to issue rulings on behalf of the Trial Chamber requiring action by the parties."[74] Instead, the function of the pre-trial Judge "seems to be more in the nature of an attempt to persuade [the parties] to agree."[75] In the view of the author, this approach should change. The Judges should take a more interventionist approach in controlling the proceedings by allowing the pre-trial Judge to hear objections based on acts of non-compliance with the Rules and impose appropriate relief where appropriate. In this connection, although as a general rule the imposition of relief should not be a means of case management, the pre-trial Judge needs to make clear his or her willingness to resort to such measures, *sua sponte* if necessary, to ensure compliance with the Rules.[76]

---

[73]The Expert Group was established in 1999 to prepare an evaluation of the functioning and operation of the International Criminal Tribunal for the former Yugoslavia and the International Criminal Tribunal for Rwanda with the objective of enhancing the efficient use of the resources allocated to the Tribunals. After meeting with the Judges and various staff members of the two Tribunals as well as other interested persons, the Expert Group prepared its report, which was submitted to the Secretary-General of the United Nations on 11 November 1999. See *Identical letters dated 17 November 1999 from the Secretary-General addressed to the President of the General Assembly and to the Chairman of the Advisory Committee on Administrative and Budgetary Questions*, UN Doc. A/54/634 of 22 November 1999.

[74]Id., para. 83.

[75]Id.

[76]In reaching its decision to dismiss the indictment against the accused, Jean-Bosco Barayagwiza, with prejudice, the Appeals Chamber stated that "this disposition may very well deter the commission of such serious violations in the future. *Barayagwiza Decision*, supra note 30, at para. 108.

PART X

State Co-operation and Compliance Issues

DARYL A. MUNDIS*

32. Reporting Non-Compliance: Rule 7*bis*

1. Introduction

Every developed criminal justice system in the world relies on effective means of compliance in order to enforce judicial orders, decisions and judgements. Such methods of compliance typically include moral as well as physical means of ensuring that such judicial orders are enforced. Ultimately, national systems have police forces to implement the decisions of the courts. The evolving international criminal justice system, including the International Criminal Tribunal for the former Yugoslavia ("Tribunal"), lacks such enforcement mechanisms, however.[1] Consequently, the Tribunal must rely on the actions of the international community and individual States in order to be effective.[2] In the event that States fail to comply with the orders and decisions of the Tribunal, the Tribunal possesses no independent police or military force to ensure compliance. Rather, as a subsidiary organ of the Security Council, the Tribunal must look to that body to enforce its orders in the event of non-compliance by States.

---

*Associate Legal Officer, ICTY Office of the Prosecutor (formerly Associate Legal Officer in the Chambers of President McDonald); LLM *with Merit* (London), MIA (Columbia), JD *with Honors in Foreign and Comparative Law* (Columbia), BA *magna cum laude* (Manhattanville); former Judge Advocate, US Navy. The views expressed herein are solely those of the author and are not to be imputed to the United Nations or the ICTY.

[1]The lack of effective enforcement mechanisms is not unique to the international *criminal* legal system. The lack of effective enforcement and compliance mechanisms in international law in general leads some critics to conclude that international law as a whole, fails to meet the traditional definition of a legal system.

[2]For example, it is States that: (1) arrest the individuals indicted by the Tribunal; (2) comply with discovery requests or undertake searches for evidence; and (3) agree to incarcerate individuals convicted and sentenced by the Tribunal.

R. May et al., Essays on ICTY Procedure and Evidence in Honour of Gabrielle Kirk McDonald, 421–438.

When the Security Council created the Tribunal, the potential problem of State non-compliance was evident, and consequently Article 29 of the Statute sets forth the obligations of States to comply with requests for assistance or orders issued by the Trial Chambers of the Tribunal.[3] The Appeals Chamber has indicated that Article 29 sets forth an obligation *erga omnes*.[4] Moreover, pursuant to Article 9(2) of the Statute, the Tribunal has primacy over national courts, with the consequence that States may not avoid their obligations to the Tribunal on the basis of pending judicial activity by their domestic judiciary system.[5] In order to give effect to these statutory provisions, there are several Rules which set forth obligations with which States must comply, and which require the President to report such States to the Security Council in the event of non-compliance.[6]

[3]ICTY Article 29, subtitled, "Cooperation and judicial assistance," reads as follows: "(1) States shall comply with the International Tribunal in the investigation and prosecution of persons accused of committing serious violations of international humanitarian law. (2) States shall comply without undue delay with any request for assistance or an order issued by a Trial Chamber, including, but not limited to: (a) the identification and location of persons; (b) the taking of testimony and the production of evidence; (c) the service of documents; (d) the arrest or detention of persons; (e) the surrender or the transfer of the accused to the International Tribunal." Moreover, as is clear from the Secretary-General's Report (UN Doc. S/25704) appended to Security Council Resolution 827, establishing the Tribunal, "[A]n order by a Trial Chamber for the surrender or transfer of persons to the custody of the International Tribunal shall be considered to be the application of an enforcement measure under Chapter VII of the Charter of the United Nations." UN Doc. S/25704 at para. 126. Such Chapter VII enforcement mechanisms are binding on all Member States of the UN.

[4]*Prosecutor v. Tihomir Blaškić, Judgement on the Request of the Republic of Croatia for Review of the Decision of Trial Chamber II of 18 July 1997*, Case No. IT-95-14-AR108*bis*, A. Ch., 29 Oct. 1997 ("*Blaškić Subpoena Judgement*") ("Article 29 imposes an obligation on Member States towards all other Members or, in other words, an 'obligation *erga omnes partes*'." Id., para. 26.)

[5]The Tribunal has primacy despite the fact that concurrent jurisdiction exists between the Tribunal and national courts as ICTY Article 9, subtitled "Concurrent jurisdiction," makes clear: "(1) The International Tribunal and national courts have concurrent jurisdiction to prosecute persons for serious violations of international humanitarian law committed in the territory of the former Yugoslavia since 1 January 1991. (2) The International Tribunal shall have primacy over national courts. At any stage of the procedure, the International Tribunal may formally request national courts to defer to the competence of the International Tribunal in accordance with the present Statute and the Rules of Procedure and Evidence of the International Tribunal." See also, Bartram S. Brown, "Primacy or Complementarity: Reconciling the Jurisdiction of National Courts and International Criminal Tribunals," 23 Yale J. Intl. L. 383 (1998).

[6]See for example, Rule 11 (under which the President may report failure to comply with a request for deferral to the Tribunal's competence pursuant to Rule 9 and Rule 10); Rule 13 (under which the President may report a State's failure to permanently discontinue its proceedings against an individual already tried by the Tribunal in accordance with the principle of *Non Bis in Idem*); Rule 59 (under which the President may report a State's failure to execute a warrant of arrest or order for transfer); and Rule 61 (under which the President, after consulting with the Presiding Judges of the Chambers, shall report non-compliance in the event that a Trial Chamber certifies that a State has failed or refused to effectuate personal service on an indicted individual).

In addition to these provisions, however, Rule 7*bis* sets forth a mandatory scheme for reporting non-compliance to the Security Council, if certain "triggering" events occur.[7] Rule 7*bis*(A)[8] establishes a residual reporting requirement for any matter falling outside the scope of Rule 11, Rule 13, Rule 59 or Rule 61, whenever a Judge or Trial Chamber is satisfied that a State is in non-compliance with its obligations and so advises the President. Pursuant to Rule 7*bis*(B),[9] the Prosecutor may request the President to make a finding of State non-compliance with Article 29, and if the President makes such a finding, the Security Council must be notified. Upon receipt of the President's report, the Security Council has discretion with respect to what action, if any is necessary to bring the recalcitrant State into compliance with its obligations. As will be clear from the repeated reports concerning the same underlying facts and circumstances, the Security Council has largely failed to effectively respond to reports of non-compliance, typically issuing Presidential Statements in response to reports of non-compliance by the President.

This essay will analyse the scheme under which the President of the Tribunal reports State non-compliance to the Security Council, with special emphasis on Rule 7*bis*. On three occasions, the Prosecutor has invoked Rule 7*bis*(B) in requesting the President to report non-compliance. Before analysing these Rule 7*bis*(B) requests, it is necessary to briefly discuss reports

[7]Rule 7*bis* was adopted at the 13th Plenary, on 25 July 1997. In the *Blaškić Subpoena Judgement*, the Appeals Chamber (at para. 34) held that "the adoption of Rule 7*bis* is clearly to be regarded as falling within the authority of the International Tribunal." The same substantive Rule was adopted earlier by the ICTR at the 4th ICTR Plenary on 2–6 June 1997. See ICTR Rule 7*bis*.

[8]ICTY Rule 7*bis*(A) states: "In addition to cases to which Rule 11, Rule 13, Rule 59 or Rule 61 applies, where a Trial Chamber or a Judge is satisfied that a State has failed to comply with an obligation under Article 29 of the Statute which relates to any proceedings before that Chamber or Judge, the Chamber or Judge may advise the President, who shall report the matter to the Security Council." Since its adoption, Rule 7*bis*(A) has not been invoked in reporting non-compliance to the Security Council.

[9]ICTY Rule 7*bis*(B) provides: "If the Prosecutor satisfies the President that a State has failed to comply with an obligation under Article 29 of the Statute in respect of a request by the Prosecutor under Rule 8, Rule 39 or Rule 40, the President shall notify the Security Council thereof." ICTY Rule 8 governs "Requests for Information." Pursuant to this Rule, when the Prosecutor determines that a crime within the jurisdiction of the Tribunal has been committed or is the subject of an investigation or criminal proceeding in the courts of any State, the Prosecutor may request that State to forward all relevant information regarding that investigation or proceeding. The State is required to transmit such information in accordance with Article 29. ICTY Rule 39 sets forth the "Conduct of Investigations," and permits the Prosecutor to, *inter alia*, summon and question suspects, collect evidence, seek the assistance of any State or international body, and request such orders as may be necessary from a Trial Chamber or Judge. Rule 40 governs "Provisional Measures" and in the event of urgency, authorises the Prosecutor to request any State to provisionally arrest a suspect or accused, to seize any physical evidence and to take all necessary measures to prevent the escape of the suspect or accused, injury to or intimidation of any victim or witness, or the destruction of evidence.

to the Security Council prior to the adoption of Rule 7*bis* and the *Blaškić Appeals Chamber Subpoena Judgement*, as it relates to non-compliance.[10] The essay will conclude with some comments on whether Rule 7*bis* is the best mechanism for reporting State non-compliance with orders and decisions of the Tribunal.

2. Reports of Non-Compliance to the Security Council Prior to the Adoption of Rule 7*bis*

The President of the Tribunal has made 11 written reports[11] to the Security Council concerning a failure by a State or an Entity[12] to comply with its international obligations under Article 29. Several of these reports cover the same repeated failure to comply and were made pursuant to Rule 61. President Antonio Cassese made five reports to the Security Council, all of which related to the failure of States to arrest and transfer individuals indicted by the Tribunal. Four of these reports followed Trial Chamber reviews pursuant to Rule 61.[13]

President Cassese's first report was made on 31 October 1995 and concerned the failure or refusal of the Bosnian-Serb Administration in Pale[14] to

[10] To date, this is the only judicial decision that has discussed Rule 7*bis*.

[11] These reports have been made at the request of a Trial Chamber, *proprio motu*, or at the request of the Prosecutor pursuant to Rule 7*bis*(B). There have also been instances where the President, in orally addressing the Security Council, has raised instances of non-compliance that were also the subject of the written requests.

[12] As used by the Tribunal, the term "Entity" typically refers to the Bosnian Serb Republic (Republika Srpska), the Bosnian Serb component of the Republic of Bosnia and Herzegovina.

[13] The fifth report apparently was the result of information provided informally to the President by the Prosecutor. See note 18, infra.

[14] This term was used in the President's report to refer to what would become the Bosnian Serb Republic upon the signing of the General Framework Agreement for Peace in Bosnia and Herzegovina ("Dayton Agreement") on 14 December 1995. See UN Doc. A/50/79C and S/1995/999, reprinted at 35 ILM 223 (1996). It should be pointed out that the Dayton Agreement also contained several obligations upon the Parties to co-operate with the Tribunal, thereby supplementing Article 29 and the Rules. See, for example, Article IX of the Dayton Agreement (requiring the Parties to co-operate fully with all entities involved in the peace process, specifically including co-operation in the investigation and prosecution of war crimes and other violations of international humanitarian law); Article X of Annex 1-A: Agreement on Military Aspects of the Peace Settlement (specifically requiring co-operation with the Tribunal in relation to the arrest or detention of, and surrender to, the Tribunal of prisoners of war indicted by the Tribunal); Article XIII(4), Annex 6: Agreement on Human Rights (providing the Tribunal with unrestricted access to areas over which the Parties exercise control); Article IX(3), Annex 4: Constitution of Bosnia and Herzegovina (prohibiting the holding of public office by persons indicted by the Tribunal, but who have refused to comply with orders to appear before it); and Article III(2), Annex 7: Agreement on Refugees and Displaced Persons (allowing all International Organisations full and unrestricted access to all refugees and displaced persons).

co-operate with the Tribunal concerning the execution of an arrest warrant issued by Trial Chamber I for Dragan Nikolić.[15] In his second report, on 24 April 1996, President Cassese informed the Security Council of the failure of the Federal Republic of Yugoslavia (Serbia and Montenegro) ("FRY") to arrest the "Vukovar Three."[16] On the basis of information provided by the Prosecutor, President Cassese submitted his third report on 22 May 1996 to the Security Council when he reported that General Mladić[17] and Colonel Šljivančanin were present in Belgrade on the previous day attending the

[15]President's Report of 31 October 1995, UN Doc. S/1995/910, reprinted in ICTY Yearbook 1995 at p. 288. The indictment against Nikolić had been confirmed on 4 November 1994 and an international arrest warrant issued on 7 November 1994. The Republic of Bosnia and Herzegovina had informed the Tribunal that Nikolić was "residing in territory outside their control and therefore they could not carry out the Tribunal's request." President's Report of 31 October 1995, UN Doc. S/1995/910. The Bosnian-Serb Administration in Pale failed to respond to the Tribunal's request and on 20 October 1995, Trial Chamber I rendered a Decision pursuant to Rule 61 which *inter alia*, requested the President to report the matter to the Security Council. *Prosecutor v. Nikolić, Review of Indictment Pursuant to Rule 61 of the Rules of Procedure and Evidence*, Case No. IT-94-2-R61, 20 Oct. 1995. Simultaneously, the Trial Chamber issued a second International Warrant of Arrest and Order for Surrender directing all States to "search for and promptly arrest and transfer" the accused to the custody of the Tribunal. Both documents are reprinted in ICTY Yearbook 1995 at pp. 295 and 291, respectively. In response to President Cassese's Report, the Security Council adopted Resolution 940 and demanded all States, and in particular those of the former Yugoslavia, to comply with "requests for assistance or orders issued by a Trial Chamber under Article 29 of the Statute of the Tribunal." UN Security Council Resolution 940 (9 November 1995), UN Doc. S/RES/940 (1995). Dragan Nikolić was arrested on 21 April 2000 and transferred to the custody of the ICTY on the following day. See ICTY Press Release CC/PIS/496-E, 26 April 2000, available on the ICTY website at: *http://www.un.org/icty*.

[16]President's Report of 24 April 1996, UN Doc. S/1996/319, reprinted in ICTY Yearbook 1996 at p. 212. This was the first of what would be several reports to the Security Council concerning these individuals. On 7 November 1995, the Tribunal indicted three individuals, Mile Mrkšic, Miroslav Radić and Colonel Veselin Šljivančanin, for the murder of 260 unarmed men following the fall of Vukovar in November 1991. A warrant for their arrest and transfer was transmitted to *inter alia* the FRY, as the accused were believed to be residing on the territory of that State. On 3 April 1996, Trial Chamber I, in accordance with Rule 61, certified that the failure to effect service of the indictment was due to the failure of the FRY to co-operate with the Tribunal. Consequently, the Trial Chamber requested the President to report the matter to the Security Council. In response to President Cassese's Report, the President of the Security Council issued a Presidential Statement on 8 May 1996. Presidential Statement, 8 May 1996, UN Doc. S/PRST/1996/23. In this Statement, the President indicated that, "The Security Council deplores the failure to date of the Federal Republic of Yugoslavia to execute the arrest warrants issued by the Tribunal against the three individuals referred to in the letter of 24 April 1996, and calls for the execution of those warrants without delay.

[17]An indictment for genocide, crimes against humanity and war crimes was confirmed against Radovan Karadžić and Ratko Mladić on 25 July 1995. (An amended indictment was submitted and confirmed on 16 November 1996.) International arrest warrants were transmitted to all States shortly after both the original and the amended indictments were confirmed. Both individuals were believed to be residing in Republika Srpska.

funeral of General Djukić.[18] The fourth report followed a Rule 61 Review by Trial Chamber I regarding the indictments against Radovan Karadžić and Ratko Mladić. The Trial Chamber concluded that the Security Council should be notified of the failure of Republika Srpska and the FRY to cooperate with the Tribunal in arresting these two individuals,[19] and President Cassese reported this non-compliance to the Security Council on 11 July 1996.[20] In his letter, President Cassese informed the Security Council that on a number of occasions Karadžić and Mladić had been on the territory of the FRY and had not been arrested and transferred to the custody of the Tribunal.[21] In his

[18]President's Report of 22 May 1996, UN Doc. S/1996/364, reprinted in ICTY Yearbook 1996 at p. 213. President Cassese noted in this report that the Prosecutor, Richard Goldstone, had drawn his attention to the attendance of these indicted individuals at the funeral. In his letter, President Cassese also noted that, "It is self-evident that General Mladić entered and left Belgrade unhindered." Moreover, President Cassese characterized the actions of the FRY as a "blatant failure of that State to comply with its clear and overriding legal obligation to execute orders of this Tribunal [...]" There was no specific response from the Security Council to this report.

[19]In this review, the Trial Chamber concluded that: "[T]he Trial Chamber considers that the failure to effect personal service of the indictments and to execute the warrants of arrest issued against Radovan Karadžić and Ratko Mladić may be ascribed to the refusal of Republika Srpska and the Federal Republic of Yugoslavia to cooperate with the Tribunal. Accordingly, the Trial Chamber so certifies for the purposes of notifying the Security Council." *Prosecutor v. Karadžić and Mladić, Review of the Indictments Pursuant to Rule 61 of the Rules of Procedure and Evidence*, Case No. IT-95-5-R61/IT-95-18-R61, 11 July 1996 at para. 101. (Relevant extracts reprinted in ICTY Yearbook 1996 at p. 214.)

[20]President's Report of 11 July 1996, UN Doc. S/1996/556, reprinted in ICTY Yearbook 1996 at p. 214.

[21]Id. In this letter, President Cassese indicated to the Security Council that he had written four letters to Yugoslav President Slobodan Milošević complaining of the failure of the FRY to arrest and transfer these individuals to the custody of the Tribunal. As a result of this refusal to comply, the Security Council, in the form of a Presidential Statement, condemned Republika Srpska and the FRY for failure to comply. Presidential Statement, 8 August 1996, UN Doc. S/PRST/1996/34. See also, UN Doc. S/6253, 3687th meeting (PM).

fifth and final report on non-compliance,[22] President Cassese notified the Security Council on 16 September 1996 that Trial Chamber II had certified that the Republic of Croatia and the Federation of Bosnia and Herzegovina had failed to execute an arrest warrant against Ivica Rajić.[23]

Following President Cassese's 16 September 1996 report, a two-year period elapsed during which there were no reports from the President of the Tribunal to the Security Council concerning issues of non-compliance. In the interim, Rule 7*bis* was adopted in July 1997, the Appeals Chamber rendered the *Blaškić Subpoena Judgement* on 29 October 1997, and President McDonald succeeded President Cassese on 19 November 1997.

[22]President's Report of 16 September 1996, UN Doc. S/1996/763, reprinted in ICTY Yearbook 1996 at p. 219. In reporting this non-compliance to the Security Council, President Cassese noted that: "[T]he failure to cooperate in the arrest of Ivica Rajić is not an isolated incident, but forms part of a general pattern of failure in respect of matters concerning the Tribunal. As I have informed the Security Council and General Assembly on a number of occasions, notably in the Tribunal's annual reports, the Federation and Croatia are systematically failing to comply with the Tribunal's orders for the arrest of accused. In particular, the following Bosnian Croats have not been arrested by either the Federation or Croatia: Dario Kordić, Mario Čerkez, Ivan Santić, Pero Skopljak, Zoran Marinić, Zoran Kupreškić, Mirjan Kupreškić, Vlatko Kupreškić, Vladimir Santić, Stipo Aliović, Drago Josipović, Marinko Katava and Drago Papić. Arrest warrants for some of these accused have now been outstanding for more than 10 months." Several of these individuals subsequently surrendered or were arrested. President McDonald would later use the same approach in taking the opportunity to report a specific act of non-compliance to list all outstanding examples of State non-compliance in an effort to persuade the Security Council to take forceful action. See discussion, infra. On 20 September 1996, the President of the Security Council issued a Presidential Statement on Croatia, which briefly referred to President Cassese's report. Presidential Statement, 20 September 1996, UN Doc. S/PRST/1996/39. This Presidential Statement deplored Croatia's failure to comply and reminded that State of its international obligations. The bulk of this Presidential Statement, however, concerns the Report of the Secretary-General of 23 August 1996 (UN Doc. S/1996/691) that was submitted pursuant to Security Council Resolution 1019 (1995) regarding the overall humanitarian and human rights situation in Croatia.

[23]*Prosecutor v. Rajić, Review of the Indictment Pursuant to Rule 61 of the Rules of Procedure and Evidence*, Case No. IT-96-12-R61, 13 Sept. 1996. See also the attached *Rule 61 Decision Separate Opinion of Judge Sidhwa*. Based upon its review, the Trial Chamber "entrusts the responsibility of so informing the Security Council to the President of the International Tribunal, pursuant to Sub-rule 61(E)."

3. The Blaškić Appeals Chamber Subpoena Judgement and Non-Compliance

In the *Blaškić Subpoena Judgement* of 29 October 1997, the Appeals Chamber was seized with the issue of the validity of a subpoena *duces tecum* issued by Judge McDonald to the Republic of Croatia and its Defence Minister. Although the full scope of the *Blaškić Subpoena Judgement* is beyond the scope of this essay, the Appeals Chamber did address the issue of State non-compliance with "binding" orders of the Tribunal.[24] Moreover, the *Blaškić Subpoena Judgement* was issued shortly after the adoption of Rule 7*bis*, and during the course of its analysis of legal remedies available in the event of State non-compliance, the Appeals Chamber discussed Rule 7*bis* at length.[25]

The Appeals Chamber noted that, because the Tribunal was not vested with any enforcement power *vis-à-vis* States, any sanctions imposed on "recalcitrant States" must be imposed by the Security Council, under the conditions provided for in Chapter VII of the UN Charter. This fact, however, does not render the Tribunal powerless to act in the event a State fails to comply with an order of the Tribunal. The Appeals Chamber concluded that the Tribunal has an inherent power to make judicial findings, and is empowered to report these judicial findings to the Security Council.[26] Thus, because the Security Council established the Tribunal pursuant to its Chapter VII powers, the Tribunal is entitled to report to the Security Council any non-compliance by a State with its international obligations under Article 29 of the Tribunal's Statute.

The Appeals Chamber determined that these inherent powers were incorporated into Rule 7*bis*, concluding that the adoption of Rule 7*bis* was "within the authority of the Tribunal."[27] In support of this proposition, the *Blaškić Subpoena Judgement* cited to the fact that following the previous

---

[24]In the *Blaškić Subpoena Judgement* the Appeals Chamber determined that a subpoena cannot be issued to States. (*Blaškić Subpoena Judgement* at para. 25) Rather, only binding "orders" or "requests" may be addressed to States. In analysing whether the Tribunal may issue such binding orders or requests, the Appeals Chamber determined that, although the Tribunal has primary jurisdiction over individuals only, it had ancillary (or incidental) jurisdiction over States. (Id., paras. 26–31) The Appeals Chamber set forth four guidelines that must be followed in addressing such binding orders or requests to States: (1) The order must identify specific documents; (2) The order must set forth succinctly why such documents are relevant for trial; (3) The order must not be unduly onerous; and (4) The order must allow the requested State reasonable time to comply. (Id. at para. 32). The Appeals Chamber then addressed whether the Tribunal has the authority to issue binding orders to State officials acting in their official capacity and whether the Tribunal could issue binding orders or subpoenas to State officials qua private individuals.

[25]Id., pp. 23–27.

[26]Id., para. 33. The Appeals Chamber found that the inherent power to make such judicial findings is crucial for the Tribunal "in order that its basic judicial function may be fully discharged and its judicial role safeguarded."

[27]Id., para. 34.

instances of reports of non-compliance by the President of the Tribunal, the Security Council did not object to this procedure. Rather, the Security Council normally responded to such reports "with a statement made, on behalf of the whole body, by the President of the Security Council and addressed to the recalcitrant State or Entity."[28]

4. Reports of Non-Compliance to the Security Council After the Adoption of Rule 7*bis*

Nearly one year would elapse after the issuance of the *Blaškić Subpoena Judgement* before the President of the Tribunal would issue another report to the Security Council on non-compliance. However, from 8 September 1998 through 8 December 1998, President McDonald would make five reports to the Security Council of non-compliance by the FRY. The Vukovar

[28] Id., para. 34. The Appeals Chamber then discussed the power of the Tribunal to make such judicial findings and compared a judicial finding with findings made by the Security Council or other political or quasi-political bodies. The *Blaškić Subpoena Judgement* concludes that findings by a political or quasi-political body: "[M]ay undoubtedly constitute an authoritative statement of what has occurred in a particular area of interest to the Security Council; it may set forth the views of the relevant body on the question of whether or not a certain State has breached international standards." (Id., para. 35). Judicial findings, the Appeals Chamber held, are different: "By contrast, the International Tribunal (i.e., a Trial Chamber, Judge or the President) engages in a judicial activity proper: acting upon all the principles and rules of judicial propriety, it scrutinises the behaviour of a certain State in order to establish formally whether or not that State has breached its international obligation to cooperate with the International Tribunal." (Id.). Additionally, the conclusions of political or quasi-political bodies may include suggestions or recommendations for action by the Security Council, whereas judicial findings by the Tribunal "must not include any recommendations or suggestions" as to which source of action the Security Council may wish to pursue." (Id., paras. 35–36). Finally, in considering Rule 7*bis*, the Appeals Chamber noted that: "[A]part from the cases provided for in Rule 7*bis*(B), the President of the International Tribunal simply has the role of *nuncius*, that is to say, he or she shall simply transmit to the Security Council the judicial finding of the relevant Judge or Chamber."(Id., para. 37). Based upon this analysis and its earlier finding that Article 29 of the Statute sets forth an obligation *erga omnes* (see note 4, supra.), the Appeals Chamber proceeded to set forth what actions the international community could take when faced with a judicial finding and report to the Security Council by the Tribunal that Article 29 had been breached. First, States could take unilateral action, such as requesting the offending State to "terminate its breach of Article 29." Second, the Appeals Chamber envisaged a "collective response through other intergovernmental organizations." The Appeals Chamber cautioned to emphasise that such collective action may be undertaken only after the Tribunal has made a judicial finding; and that such collective action may take several forms, such as political or moral condemnation, a collective request to cease the breach, or economic or diplomatic sanctions. Finally, "collective action would be warranted in the case of repeated and blatant breaches of Article 29 by the same State; and provided the Security Council had not decided that it enjoyed exclusive powers on the matter, the situation being part of a general condition of threat to the peace." (*Blaškić Subpoena Judgement* at para. 36)

Three[29] and the refusal of the FRY to recognise the Tribunal's jurisdiction over alleged crimes in Kosovo were the main focus of these reports.

On 1 September 1998, the Prosecutor, Louise Arbour, wrote a letter requesting President McDonald to report the continuing refusal of the FRY to arrest and transfer the Vukovar Three.[30] On 8 September 1998, President McDonald reported this non-compliance to the Security Council in a letter in which she also set forth other examples of the refusal of the FRY to cooperate with the Tribunal and comply with its international obligations.[31] President McDonald also took note of the impending humanitarian disaster in Kosovo, informing the Security Council that "recent events there threaten to destabilise further the Balkan region."[32]

President McDonald again reported to the Security Council that the FRY was refusing to arrest and transfer the Vukovar Three on 23 October 1998. Perhaps more importantly, she also reported that the FRY was reserving for its domestic judicial system "the right to investigate, prosecute and try

---

[29]See note 16, supra. See also ICTY Press Release CC/PIU/344-E, 9 September 1998, available on the ICTY website: *http://www.un.org/icty*.

[30]The Prosecutor was prompted to write to President McDonald by a Security Council Resolution concerning Libya and the Lockerbie case, in which the Security Council unanimously called upon Libya to honour its pledges to transfer the two suspects in the Lockerbie bombing case. See UN Security Council Resolution 1192 (27 August 1998), UN Doc. S/RES/1192 (1998). In her letter to President McDonald, the Prosecutor wrote, "This Resolution stands in stark contrast with the lack of action by the Council regarding the [Vukovar] case which offers much similarity to the Lockerbie case." ICTY Press Release CC/PIU/344-E, note 29, supra.

[31]President's Report of 8 September 1998, UN Doc. S/1998/839. In discussing the failure of the FRY to meet its obligations, President McDonald wrote: "The persistent and continuing rejection of orders to arrest Mile Mrkšic, Miroslav Radić and Veselin Šljivanćanin is but the most blatant example of the refusal of the FRY to cooperate with the International Tribunal. Such intransigence has formed a consistent pattern since the International Tribunal was established by the Security Council in Resolution 827 of 27 May 1993. Notable in this regard is failure to take measures necessary under domestic law to implement the provisions of Resolution 827 and the Statute of the International Tribunal, as required by paragraph 4 of the Resolution. Indeed, the FRY remains the only signatory to the Dayton Agreement that has neither adopted legislation to facilitate cooperation with the International Tribunal, nor taken steps to transfer to the International Tribunal's custody those indictees on its territory."

[32]Id. She characterised the conduct of the FRY as "illegal" and closed with the following plea: "I respectfully submit that it is imperative that the reprehensible conduct of the Government of the FRY in violating the United Nations Charter, Resolutions of the Security Council and the Dayton Agreement, should no longer be tolerated." In response to this report, President McDonald was invited to address the Security Council, which she did on 2 October 1998. Repeating many of the themes set forth in the 8 September 1998 letter, she reiterated her demand that the "threat posed by the non-compliance of the FRY must be dealt with once and for all." See also ICTY Press Release CC/PIU/349-E, 2 October 1998, available on the ICTY website: *http://www.un.org/icty*.

offences committed in Kosovo that may fall within the jurisdiction of the International Tribunal."[33]

5. Requests by the Prosecutor Pursuant to Rule 7*bis*(B)

Within two weeks, President McDonald's fears regarding FRY intransigence concerning Kosovo were realised when FRY officials refused to issue visas for investigators of the Office of the Prosecutor to enter Kosovo to pursue their investigation into alleged criminal activity within the purview of the Tribunal's Statute. In failing to issue such visas, the FRY stated that it "does not accept any investigation of the ICTY in Kosovo and Metohija."[34] Consequently, on 5 November 1998, the Prosecutor relied on Rule 7*bis*(B) (for the first time) and requested the President to report the matter to the Security Council.

Without referring specifically to Rule 7*bis*(B), President McDonald submitted a report to the Security Council on 6 November 1998, in which she outlined the FRY's obligations to cooperate with the Tribunal in its investigation of alleged atrocities in Kosovo.[35] In this letter, President McDonald reminded the Security Council of the Presidential Statements issued in response to previous reports of non-compliance by the Tribunal. In so doing, she noted that such Presidential Statements had "failed to bring

---

[33]President's Report of 22 October 1998, UN Doc. S/1998/990. President McDonald duly noted that in two Security Council Resolutions, the FRY was bound to comply with orders of the Tribunal with respect to events occurring in Kosovo. See Security Council Resolution 1160 (31 March 1998), UN Doc. S/RES/1160 (1998) and Security Council Resolution 1199 (23 September 1998), UN Doc. S/RES/1199 (1998). Additionally, at the time, an agreement had recently been reached between the FRY, OSCE and NATO for a peaceful resolution of the crisis in Kosovo. President McDonald expressed her concerns that this agreement, brokered by US special envoy Richard Holbrooke, lacked any explicit reference to the FRY's obligations under international law to comply and cooperate with the Tribunal. President McDonald wrote: "I am, therefore, gravely concerned that the agreements concluded on the situation in Kosovo lack an explicit recognition of the FRY's obligations towards the International Tribunal. While they do require, *inter alia*, the FRY to comply with the provisions of Resolution 1199, there is no express commitment from the Government of the FRY to cooperate with the International Tribunal. In this regard, I note with alarm that the Statement of the President of Serbia declares that 'no persons will be prosecuted in state courts for crimes related to the conflict in Kosovo except for crimes against humanity and international law.' This expression of the view of the Government of Serbia does not include a reference to the International Tribunal. I fear, therefore, that it represents an implicit attempt to deny the primacy of the International Tribunal and to disregard the legal requirement that Serbia, as part of the FRY, should facilitate the work of the International Tribunal." Id. As the following reports of non-compliance indicate, President McDonald's fears were well-grounded.

[34]President's Report of 6 November 1998, UN Doc. S/1998/1040.

[35]Id.

about the required cooperation with the Tribunal."[36] Consequently, she requested the Security Council provide "measures which are sufficiently compelling to bring the Federal Republic of Yugoslavia into the fold of law-abiding nations."[37] Responding to this report, and noting the two previous reports to the Security Council,[38] the Security Council adopted Resolution 1207 on 17 November 1998 – undoubtedly the strongest response of the Security Council to any of the reports made by the President of the Tribunal. However, three weeks later, President McDonald appeared before the Security Council to inform the Council about the implementation of Resolution 1207.[39] In her remarks, President McDonald reported that the FRY was failing to comply with its obligations under Resolution 1207, specifically its failure to issue visas for investigators to enter Kosovo.[40]

On 1 February 1999, the Prosecutor submitted her second Rule 7*bis*(B) Request to President McDonald. This Request concerned the continuing failure of the FRY to meet its obligations under Article 29 with respect to alleged criminal activity in Kosovo within the jurisdiction of the Tribunal. What set this request apart from the previous Rule 7*bis*(B) Request was the lengthy documentation attached to the Request and the scope of what the Prosecutor was requesting. In her request, the Prosecutor wrote:

---

[36]Id.

[37]Id.

[38]President's Report of 8 September 1998, UN Doc. S/1998/839 and President's Report of 22 October 1998, UN Doc. S/1998/990. Resolution 1207 (17 November 1998) UN Doc. S/RES/1207 (1998), *inter alia*, reiterates earlier demands that all states comply with orders of the Tribunal, calls upon the FRY to bring its domestic legislation in conformity with its international obligations under Resolution 827 and the Statute of the Tribunal, condemns the failure of the FRY to arrest and transfer the Vukovar Three and reminds the authorities of the FRY and leadership of the Kosovo Albanian community of their obligation to "cooperate fully with the Prosecutor in the investigation of all possible violations within the jurisdiction of the Tribunal."

[39]Address of President McDonald to the Security Council, 8 December 1998. See also ICTY Press Release JL/PIU/371-E, 8 December 1998, available on the ICTY website: *http://www.un.org/icty*.

[40]Additionally, she reported that Trial Chamber I was seized of a proposal from the Prosecutor formally requesting the FRY to defer to the Tribunal's competence in accordance with Rule 9 with respect to the Vukovar Three. The FRY had initiated proceedings against the Vukovar Three before the Belgrade Military Court. Thus, despite having these three individuals in custody, the FRY continued its refusal to transfer them to the Tribunal, despite an explicit demand in Resolution 1207 that they be transferred. Moreover, the Belgrade Military Court, twisting the primacy provisions of Article 9(2) of the Statute, requested the Tribunal to transfer the case file and all evidence regarding the Vukovar Three to the Belgrade Military Court. In effect, the Belgrade Military Court was asserting that it had primacy over the Tribunal, an assertion that is contradictory to the plain meaning of Article 9(2) of the Statute. The Trial Chamber requested the FRY to defer to the Tribunal's competence on 10 December 1998. See *Prosecutor v. Mile Mrkšic, Veselin Šljivančanin and Miroslav Radić, Decision on the Proposal of the Prosecutor for a Request to the Federal Republic of Yugoslavia (Serbia and Montenegro) to Defer the Pending Investigations and Criminal Proceedings to the Tribunal*, Case No. IT-95-13-R61, I, 10 December 1998.

> Assuming the Prosecutor's decision to initiate an investigation is reviewable, the decision could only be challenged on the ground that it was arbitrary and capricious. To conclude the decision was arbitrary and capricious, the reviewer would have to find that no reasonable person could have decided to initiate an investigation. Such is not the case here. [41]

Nevertheless, President McDonald interpreted this request as requiring her to review, pursuant to Rule 7*bis*(B), the decision to initiate the investigation. More important, however, than the request for the President to review her decision to commence an investigation in Kosovo, was her request that the President determine that an armed conflict existed in Kosovo at the time.[42]

President McDonald declined to review the Prosecutor's decision that there was a sufficient basis to initiate an investigation on the basis that such a determination was within the sole discretion of the Prosecutor to make, pursuant to Article 16(2) of the Statute.[43] Furthermore, she declined to find that an armed conflict existed.[44] Nevertheless, she did conclude that the Request included sufficient evidence of FRY non-compliance to warrant a report to the Security Council, which was made on 16 March 1999.[45]

On 28 July 1999, the Prosecutor filed her third Request pursuant to Rule 7*bis*(B).[46] This eight page Request (with 34 additional pages of annexes and attachments) concerned the Republic of Croatia and raised three issues for

---

[41]*Request by the Prosecutor, Pursuant to Rule 7bis(B), that the President Notify the Security Council that the Federal Republic of Yugoslavia has Failed to Comply with its Obligations Under Article 29*, 1 February 1999 (on file with the author). Notwithstanding this assertion, and in support of her position, the Prosecutor set forth, in great detail, five points: (1) the basis for initiating the investigation in Kosovo; (2) the "nature" of the FRY's non-compliance; (3) the threshold determination necessary to commence the investigation; (4) the FRY's jurisdictional objections to the investigation; and (5) why those objections had no merit. Letter from President McDonald to Prosecutor Arbour, dated 16 March 1999. Attached to ICTY Press Release JL/PIU/386-E, 18 March 1999. ("President McDonald's 16 March 1999 Letter".)

[42]President's Report of 16 March 1999, UN Doc. S/1999/383. President McDonald invited the FRY to respond – an invitation that the authorities in Belgrade ignored.

[43]President McDonald's 16 March 1999 Letter.

[44]As President McDonald correctly noted in declining to make such a finding, "This is quintessentially a judicial determination that should be made in the context of an ongoing case; it is not necessary for the President to make such a determination to find non-compliance under Rule 7bis(B)." President McDonald's 16 March 1999 Letter.

[45]President's Report of 16 March 1999, UN Doc. S/1999/383. In her report, President McDonald indicated that the reason for filing the report was "the continuing and additional instances in which the Federal Republic of Yugoslavia has refused to permit the Prosecutor and her investigators to enter Kosovo, in order to initiate investigations into alleged crimes committed in that territory."

[46]*Request by the Prosecutor Under Rule 7bis(B) that the President Notify the Security Council of the Failure of the Republic of Croatia Under Article 29*, Case No. IT-99-35-misc 4, 28 July 1999.

the President to consider.[47] President McDonald declined to make a finding with respect to the requests for evidence and other information sought by the Prosecutor. Her rationale for declining was that the Prosecutor had failed to utilise Rule 39(iv) to request a binding order from a Judge. Moreover, she concluded that the Prosecutor had failed to exhaust the methods set forth in the *Blaškić Subpoena Judgement*.[48]

Regarding the Prosecutor's assertions that the Republic of Croatia was refusing to accept the Tribunal's jurisdiction over Operations "Flash" and "Storm," President McDonald noted that the Prosecutor was not seeking a review of the decision to initiate such an investigation.[49] She also noted that "the eventual determination of whether the alleged crimes committed during the course of these operations is within the jurisdiction of the Tribunal is obviously for a Trial Chamber to make."[50] Relying on a teleological approach to the Statute and Rules, however, she concluded that:

> [T]he Statute and Rules of Procedure and Evidence clearly do not permit a State to thwart the conduct of an investigation simply by asserting that the Tribunal has no jurisdiction. Article 18(2) of the Statute allows the Prosecutor to seek the assistance of the State authorities concerned as she collects evidence. Article 29(1) imposes an obligation on States to cooperate with the Tribunal in its investigations and prosecutions.[51]

---

[47]The three issues were: (1) the alleged failure of the Republic of Croatia to respond to numerous requests for evidence and information; (2) the alleged refusal of the Republic of Croatia to accept the Tribunal's jurisdiction over crimes committed during and in the aftermath of Operations "Flash" and "Storm;" and (3) the alleged failure of the Republic of Croatia to arrest and transfer two individuals indicted by the Tribunal. Letter from President McDonald to Prosecutor Arbour, 25 August 1999, Annex to UN Doc S/1999/912. Also filed as ICTY document IT-99-35-misc 4, on 26 August 1999. ("President McDonald's 25 August 1999 Letter".) Unlike the Request concerning the FRY, President McDonald did not specifically invite the Republic of Croatia to respond, although they did submit two letters for her consideration, dated 23 July 1999 and 30 July 1999. See President McDonald's 25 August 1999 Letter.

[48]In reaching this conclusion, President McDonald wrote: "This approach is also consistent with the approach you advanced before the Appeals Chamber in the *Blaškić [Subpoena] Judgement* case, in which you stated that '[A]s a matter of policy and in order to foster good relations with States, ...cooperative processes should wherever possible, be used, ...they should be used first, and [...] resort to mandatory compliance powers expressly given by Article 29(2) should be reserved for cases in which they are really necessary.'" (*Blaškić Judgement* at para. 31, citing to Prosecutor's Brief at p. 15). See President McDonald's 25 August 1999 Letter.

[49]President McDonald noted that, consistent with her findings in the FRY Rule 7*bis(B)* matter, she had no authority to conduct such a review: "I agree and reiterate that it is neither necessary nor appropriate for the President to review, in the context of Rule 7*bis*(B), the Prosecutor's decision that there is a sufficient basis to initiate an investigation under Article 18 of the Statute. [...] I do not have the authority to conduct a review of the appropriateness of your decision to investigate Operations "Flash" and "Storm" – or any other investigation." Id.

[50]Id.

[51]Id.

Consequently, she found the Republic of Croatia to be in non-compliance with its international obligations to provide evidence relating to Operations "Flash" and "Storm."

The third issue raised by the Prosecutor in her Request was the alleged failure of the Republic of Croatia to arrest and transfer two individuals indicted by the Tribunal. One of these individuals, Vinko Martinović (aka "Štela"), was arrested and transferred to the Tribunal after the Request was made but prior to the President's findings. Regarding the second individual, Mladen Naletilić (aka "Tuta"), the President found that the Republic of Croatia was in non-compliance regarding its failure to arrest and transfer him to the Tribunal.[52]

In conclusion, President McDonald found the Republic of Croatia in non-compliance on two of the three grounds asserted by the Prosecutor: the failure to provide evidence relating to Operations "Flash" and "Storm" and the failure to arrest and transfer Mladen Naletilić. President McDonald reported these findings to the Security Council on 25 August 1999.[53]

Prior to the expiration of her term on 16 November 1999, President McDonald sent a final report to the Security Council concerning outstanding issues of State non-compliance.[54] In this report, President McDonald made a special plea regarding the failure of certain States to arrest and transfer indicted individuals to the custody of the Tribunal:

> On the verge of the twenty-first century, it is simply unacceptable that territories have become safe-havens for individuals indicted for the most serious offences against humanity. It must be made absolutely clear to such States that this behaviour is legally – as well as morally – wrong. The Security Council has the authority and wherewithal to rectify this situation. For the benefit of all the peoples of the former Yugoslavia, I urge you to act.[55]

---

[52]Id. Naletilić was subsequently transferred to the custody of the Tribunal on 21 March 2000. See ICTY Press Release JL/PIS/480-E, 21 March 2000, available on the ICTY website: *http://www.un.org/icty*.

[53]President's Report of 25 August 1999, UN Doc. S/1999/912. Also filed with the Registry of the Tribunal on 26 August 1999, as IT-99-35-misc 4. In response to this report of non-compliance, the Croatian Government issued a "White Paper on Cooperation with the International Criminal Tribunal for the Prosecution of Persons Responsible for Serious Violations of International Humanitarian Law Committed in the Territory of the Former Yugoslavia Since 1991." (Zagreb: September 1999) (Copy on file with the author.)

[54]Letter from President McDonald to the President of the Security Council Concerning Outstanding Issues of State Non-Compliance, 2 November 1999, UN Doc S/1999/1117. See also ICTY Press Release JL/PIS/444-E, 2 November 1999, available on the ICTY website: *http://www.un.org/icty*.

[55]Id. To date, the Security Council has not responded to President McDonald's letter.

6. Conclusion: Is Rule 7*bis*(B) Necessary?

Rule 7*bis*(B) was undoubtedly adopted with good intentions, based on the important need to inform the Security Council of examples of State non-compliance. However, several factors indicate that Rule 7*bis*(B) may not be the best mechanism to ensure that such reports are made. First, Rule 7*bis*(B) may unnecessarily restrict the independence of the Prosecutor. Although the Prosecutor herself may communicate State non-compliance directly to the Security Council (as has been done on several occasions[56]), Rule 7*bis*(B) could be interpreted, in accord with the principle of *expressio unius*, as setting forth the exclusive method for reporting such non-compliance. Such an interpretation could hinder the independence of the Prosecutor.

---

[56]The most recent example being on 10 November 1999, when Madame Del Ponte, in addressing the Security Council, stated that in order to do her job effectively, she needed the Security Council's strong support, especially in coercing the FRY and Republic of Croatia to arrest and surrender those individuals indicted by the Tribunal. (See "Initial Report on War Crimes in Kosovo says 2,108 People were Killed," Elizabeth M. Lederer, Associated Press, 11 November 1999.) See also UN Doc S/1998/1124, a letter from Prosecutor Arbour to the President of the Security Council dated 27 November 1998. In this letter, submitted in rebuttal to a letter from the Yugoslav Chargé d'affaires (UN Doc. A/53/653 and UN Doc. S/1998/1051) regarding the President's Report of 6 November 1998 (UN Doc. S/1998/1040), the Prosecutor drew to the attention of the Security Council the failure of the FRY to provide her staff with visas to investigate alleged crimes in Kosovo. Moreover, there is nothing in the Statute or Rules that require communications between the independent organs of the Tribunal and the Security Council to be funneled through the President. When the Prosecutor directly reports such acts of State non-compliance, there are no illusions that such conclusions have the imprimatur of the President or that the President has provided legitimacy to the Prosecutor's request by making a "finding." By their very nature, Rule 7*bis*(B) requests require a quasi-judicial finding by the President, which raises several troubling questions. For example, in the context of on-going investigations is it wise to place the President in a position of determining the responsiveness of what are, in effect, discovery requests of the Prosecutor? Doesn't this necessitate an analysis of the relevance of the evidence submitted? Or is the President simply to examine the Prosecutor's request to the State for assistance, compare it with the Prosecutor's analysis of whether the State complied or not, and then make a finding? What standards are to be applied in making this determination? In the event that discovery becomes an issue at trial, what effect, if any, will the President's finding pursuant to Rule 7*bis*(B) have upon the trial? Will such a finding bind the Trial Chamber? If not, what are the consequences of a Trial Chamber finding that contradicts that of the President? Moreover, because the Rules do not permit a State to be a party before the trial proceedings (see Rule 2), how are the interests of States to be preserved at trial following a finding of non-compliance? Additionally, this does not place the President in the difficult position of making quasi-judicial determinations in the context of findings of non-compliance by States. There is simply no satisfactory reason for the Rules to formalize a procedure, whereby the President of the Tribunal, acting in an *extra-judicial* capacity, is required to report non-compliance to the Security Council upon being "satisfied" by a request from the Prosecutor.

Second, there is nothing in either the Statute or Rules that prohibit the Prosecutor from informally calling instances of State non-compliance to the attention of the President.[57] The President may then determine whether to relay this information to the Security Council.

Third, in practice, this procedure may lead to abuse, thereby harming the integrity of the Tribunal. Rule 7*bis*(B) does not provide for the State that is the target of the Request to be heard on the merits of the Request.[58] This is problematic on two levels. First, decision-making without the full benefit of input from both sides can be difficult at best, and can lead to wrong decisions at worst. Second, it provides the State with a good defence if the President reports non-compliance to the Security Council. Namely, the State will claim that it wasn't given an opportunity to be heard and that its due process rights were abused.

Fourth, the *ex parte* Rule 7*bis*(B) procedure is detrimental to the Tribunal's outreach efforts in the former Yugoslavia. The Tribunal is devoting resources to demonstrate to the peoples of the region that the Tribunal is fair, with an independent judiciary. Such a procedure harms the Tribunal's integrity by fostering an appearance of collusion between the President and Prosecutor in reporting non-compliance to the Security Council.

In conclusion, until all members of the international community comply with the Tribunal's orders, reports to the Security Council of non-compliance will periodically continue to be necessary. States will be more willing to comply if the entire judicial system is perceived to be fair. The key to achieving this goal is a strong and independent judiciary. As the head of the judiciary, the acts of the President must be beyond reproach.[59] Reporting State non-compliance to the Security Council by the President is a serious matter and should be reserved for those occasions when a Judge or Trial Chamber has found a State has failed to meet its obligations. The President

---

[57]This approach has been utilised in conveying information to the President for purposes of notifying the Security Council of non-compliance. See note 18, supra.

[58]Although President McDonald specifically sought the views of the FRY concerning the Rule 7*bis*(B) Request regarding that State, she did not solicit the Republic of Croatia's views with respect to the Request of that State.

[59]This is not to imply that the President has no role in reporting non-compliance to the Security Council. On the contrary, there are several Rules, such as Rules 11 and 61, that either permit or require the President to report such non-compliance. However, the important distinction between these Rules and Rule 7*bis*(B), is that under the former, the Trial Chamber (or a Judge) is involved and it is the Trial Chamber (or Judge) that makes the requisite findings relating to State non-compliance. The President then reports these findings to the Security Council for possible action. Under Rule 7*bis*(B), the President, on the basis of a request from the Prosecutor, makes the necessary finding and then reports this finding to the Security Council. By removing the safeguards inherent in Trial Chamber proceedings, the potential for the appearance of collusion between the President and Prosecutor is detrimental to the Tribunal's integrity.

should not place the judiciary's imprimatur on such reports until a Judge or Trial Chamber has made the requisite finding of non-compliance. In other instances, the proper recourse should be for the Prosecutor, as an independent organ of the Tribunal, to report such non-compliance directly to the Security Council. This is the only effective means of ensuring that judicial integrity is maintained, thus increasing the willingness of recalcitrant States to bring their actions into conformity with their obligations. It is only when all States so act that the need for such Presidential reports will diminish.

SAM MULLER*

33. Immunities of ICTY Staff Members, Assets and Archives before the ICTY

1. INTRODUCTION

The fuel in the engine of a criminal judicial process is proof: proof with the help of witness statements, proof in the form of transcripts, letters, reports, faxes, and other documents. And proof must be obtained. In this contribution, we look at how the Tribunal has dealt with obtaining such proof in cases where the witness or the information material originates from the Tribunal itself, and, more in particular, Chambers and the Registry. What rules apply to an ICTY staff member who is requested to appear before the Tribunal? What status do ICTY assets and archives have in this regard?

It has taken a while before any serious case law was developed in this regard, but the rudiments of a system within which such issues of immunity can be looked at have now emerged. Firstly, an outline will be given of the most significant immunity questions that can arise before the Tribunal for the United Nations, and more in particular, ICTY Staff. After that, an overview will be given of the law that applies to those cases. With that framework in mind, the case law of the Tribunal which deals with the immunities of ICTY Staff and assets will be examined. We end with a conclusion.

2. ISSUES OF PRIVILEGES AND IMMUNITIES BEFORE THE ICTY

By way of illustration, two hypothetical cases are set out below.

In the first case, a United Nations High Commissioner for Refugees ("UNHCR") protection officer stationed in Bosnia Herzegovina during the dark years of the war in the former Yugoslavia comes across an armed military convoy of one of the warring factions during one of his field trips.

*Dr. A.S. Muller, Legal Adviser, Registry Legal Advisory Section, ICTY. The views expressed herein are those of the author and not of the Tribunal or the United Nations.

R. May et al., Essays on ICTY Procedure and Evidence in Honour of Gabrielle Kirk McDonald, 439–455.

The troops prevent him from continuing his journey as planned and turn him back. On his retreat, he runs into small groups of people, clearly refugees fleeing the area. Later in the day, he hears reports from local staff of a shooting which allegedly occurred, not far from the place where he ran into the military convoy. In line with his job description, he writes a report that evening of what he saw and submits that to his superiors. Two years later, the Office of the Prosecutor ("OTP") traces down this diligent UN staff member as part of its investigations into an alleged massacre. The investigators determine that the staff member would be a good witness in court, and the OTP indicates that it would like to submit the report that was written by him as evidence in Court. Soon thereafter, the Prosecutor files a request for an order under Rule 54 to have the staff member appear as a witness, and to have the UNHCR produce the report to the Chamber.

The second hypothetical scenario takes place within the premises of the Tribunal. It is assumed that, immediately after the formal ending of an interview of a detainee by the OTP, an ICTY security officer – a staff member of the Registry – overhears pertinent things that are said as the detainee prepares to leave the interview room. In order to cover himself, the security officer writes a short note to his superior, informing him of the somewhat unusual ending of the interview. The note is subsequently noted and filed. Months later, a contentious issue arises before a Chamber in connection with that interview. The Defence Counsel considers it essential that the officer in question testify regarding the last few minutes of the interview, and files a request to the Chamber for a Rule 54 order to have the officer appear in Court. Somehow, the Defence Counsel also finds out that a note was written on the topic, and a further request is submitted to order the Registry to submit that document.

These two hypothetical cases show that there are privileges and immunities issues which involve UN staff members, and there are such issues which involve UN staff members which are also ICTY staff members. They also demonstrate that cases involving such immunities can involve two types of requests: one directed at persons (to testify as a witness), the other directed at assets/archives (submission of some form of archived information). What law applies to such cases? Two sources of law appear to present themselves.

The first source is the general principles of law. All national jurisdictions have rules – statutory or based on case law – which grant a privileged status to certain categories of persons who possess certain information. Well known privileges are the information privileges in the doctor-patient relationship, and the sacerdotal privilege granted to religious representatives. It is important to keep in mind that in such instances (and unlike in the case of a person with diplomatic immunities), the person in question cannot claim an immunity against the obligation to appear in court. He or she must appear, but can, in respect of some of the information he/she is requested to provide claim that it is privileged, a question on which, ultimately, the court in question will decide.

The second source of law is more concrete. A year after the signing of the Charter, the UN General Assembly adopted the General Convention on the Privileges and Immunities of the United Nations. That convention – hereinafter referred to as the General Convention – provides a special legal status for the UN within the territory of its member States[1] i.e. those privileges and immunities which are necessary for the effective fulfilment of its mandate.[2] Within the context of this contribution, the immunity from legal process granted to the Organisation and its staff, and the inviolability of its assets and archives are most relevant.[3] As a subsidiary organ of the Security Council, the ICTY and its staff have the full benefit of the General Convention.[4]

Section 2 of the General Convention provides that:

> The United Nations, its property and assets wherever located and by whomsoever held, shall enjoy immunity from every form of legal process except insofar as in any particular case it has expressly waived its immunity. [...]

Section 3 adds that:

> [...] The property and assets of the United Nations shall be inviolable. The property and assets of the United Nations, wherever located and by whomsoever held, shall be immune from search, requisition, confiscation, expropriation,

---

[1]Convention on the Privileges and Immunities of the United Nations, adopted by the General Assembly on 13 Feb. 1946 (1 UNTS 15).

[2]The so-called 'doctrine of functional necessity'. See in this connection also the following decisions by the International Court of Justice: *Reparation for Injuries Suffered in the Service of the United Nations, Advisory Opinion of 11 April 1949*, 1949 ICJ Rep. 178; *Applicability of Article VI, Section 22, of the Convention on the Privileges and Immunities of the United Nations, Advisory Opinion of 15 December 1989,* 1989 ICJ Rep. 177 (also known as the *Mazilu* case); *Difference Relating to Immunity from Legal Process of a Special Rapporteur of the Commission on Human Rights, Advisory Opinion of 29 April 1999*, 1999 ICJ Rep. 62 (also known as the *Cumaraswamy* case). For a more elaborate background on the framework of the General Convention, see A.S. Muller, International Organizations and their Host States: Aspects of their Legal Relationship (1995) at 26 et seq. See also H.G. Schermers and N.M. Blokker, International Institutional Law (1995) at 235, et seq. and 975, et seq.

[3]The following privileges and immunities have been considered necessary for the UN to function effectively in a member state: inviolability of assets and archives, immunity from legal process connected with official acts, a favourable and privileged treatment of its official communications, an exemption from currency controls, taxation and customs duties, a privileged status for the representatives of members to the Organisation, and a privileged status for those persons through which the Organisation does its work. On the rationale behind the privileges and immunities of the Organisation, see Muller, id.; as regards specific privileges and immunities granted to persons working for and with the Organisation, see D.B. Michaels, International Privileges and Immunities (1971), A. Pellet and R. Ruzié, Les Fonctionnaires Internationaux (1993).

[4]Article 29 UN Charter. As to the applicability of the General Convention to the International Tribunal, see Secretary General's Report at paras. 128–129, and Article 30 ICTY Statute.

> and any other form of interference, whether by executive, administrative, judicial or legislative action.

Finally, Section 4 states:

> The archives of the United Nations, and in general all documents belonging to it or held by it, shall be inviolable wherever located.

Pursuant to Article V of the General Convention, "Officials" of the United Nations are granted immunity from legal process "in respect of words spoken or written and all acts performed by them in their official capacity".[5] For the highest UN officials, including the Secretary-General, the privileges and immunities that are commonly granted to diplomatic envoys have been set out.[6]

The functional limitation to the privileges and immunities granted to UN officials is made clear in Section 22 of the General Convention, which states that:

> Privileges and immunities are granted to officials in the interests of the United Nations and not for the personal benefit of the individuals themselves. The Secretary-General shall have the right and the duty to waive the immunity of any official in any case where, in his opinion, the immunity would impede the course of justice and can be waived without prejudice to the interests of the United Nations. [...][7]

Thus, there is a wide immunity from jurisdiction for the UN and its officials, which includes all its assets (moveable, immovable, and wherever located)

---

[5]"Experts on Mission" are granted the same immunity for all "words spoken and acts done by them in the course of their mission." For this category, it is added that this immunity from legal process will continue to apply after the working relationship with the UN has ended. The rationale behind this is that the Expert on Mission status is used to grant privileges and immunities to persons who temporarily work for the organization, without an employment contract in the strictest sense. In most cases persons who fall under this category are experts who provide specific expertise to the organization, often with some involvement of their national Government (for example, the special rapporteurs of the UN Commission on Human Rights or a special envoy of the Secretary-General).

[6]This includes, amongst others, personal inviolability from arrest and detention, the inviolability and right to protection of the private residence, inviolability of papers and correspondence, full immunity from criminal jurisdiction, a limited immunity from civil and administrative jurisdiction, exemption from social security provisions, fiscal exemptions, customs exemptions, and the similar immunities for the members of the family of the official. Section 19 General Convention. See, Articles 29, 30, 31, 33, 34, 36, and 37 of the 1961 Vienna Convention on Diplomatic Relations. The Judges of the International Tribunal also fall under this category.

[7]For a similar provision of Experts on Mission, see Section 23 General Convention. Section 21 adds to that a general obligation on the part of the UN to co-operate at all times with the appropriate authorities of member states to facilitate the proper administration of justice.

and its officials have immunity from jurisdiction for official acts. In both cases, there is an obligation on the UN to waive the immunity if "the proper administration of justice" is at stake. The question that is not explicitly answered when looking at the provisions set out above, is immunity *vis à vis* whom?

Taking a traditional state sovereignty viewpoint, the drafters of the Convention sought to protect the Organisation against certain aspects of the exercise of state jurisdiction.[8] Little would they have thought that 47 years, 2 months and 20 days after its adoption, an international tribunal would come into being with jurisdictional powers comparable to that of a court of a member state. Does the General Convention also apply in respect of that Tribunal?

Let us go back to the first of the two hypothetical cases. Do the official acts of the UNHCR staff member summoned by the International Tribunal fall under an immunity provided for in the General Convention?[9] An answer to that question requires an answer to a more general, underlying question: can a convention, drafted to protect an international organisation from the exercise of jurisdiction of member states, also be deemed to apply in respect of a judicial organ set up by that organisation?

The UN Secretariat has taken the position that, in respect of the Tribunal, the General Convention does apply to UN staff members and in respect of UN archives and assets.[10] This means that if an order of the Tribunal relates to testimony connected with an official act of a UNHCR staff member, a waiver by the Secretary-General of the immunity from legal process is required.[11] Since orders of the Tribunal are binding on states and international organisations, the Secretary-General would, on the basis of Section 22 of the General Convention, be under a duty to waive the immunity if this can be done without prejudice to the United Nations.[12]

---

[8]In the preambular paragraphs of the Convention, reference is made to Article 105 of the Charter, and it is recalled that the privileges and immunities are necessary for the fulfilment of the Organisation's purposes, "in the territory in each of its Members".

[9]The UNHRC is a subsidiary body of the General Assembly, established in 1951 pursuant to Article 22 of the UN Charter. On its relationship with the UN, see Schermers and Blokker, supra note 2, at 1059–1060, and B. Simma (Ed.), The Charter of the United Nations (1994) at 381–391.

[10]As an example, the immunity of General Philippe Morillion, former Commander of UNPROFOR, was waived before he could testify in *Prosecutor v. Blaškić* regarding matters relating to his functions as Force Commander.

[11]Section 18(a) and Section 20 of the General Convention.

[12]See, for example, *Prosecutor v. Blaškić, Decision of Trial Chamber I on Protective Measures for General Philippe Morillon, Witness of the Trial Chamber*, Case No. IT-95-14-T, 12 May 1999. Here, the Chamber expressly made it clear that it wanted to exert ultimate control by stating that "pursuant to Article 29 of the Statute, States are bound to cooperate with the Tribunal [...]; that this obligation is of a general nature; that the Tribunal could accept only that the limits to such cooperation be established unilaterally under conditions other than those set down by the Judges within the context of the Statute and the Rules".

Does this also apply to UN archives and assets if they are ICTY archives and assets, or to UN officials if they are ICTY officials? The Tribunal seems to have taken the position that it does not, at least not in respect of archives and officials of Chambers and the Registry. Faced with the choice of who has the ultimate say as regards the application of immunities which are connected with the innermost workings of the Tribunal, the Secretary-General or the Judges, a clear choice appears to have been made. As shall be demonstrated below, the Tribunal has developed its own framework to deal with issues of immunity of its own officials and, in that sense, it has created a special category of UN official and archives. In examining that framework, we come across some of the same concepts used in the General Convention, although we never see full reliance on the instrument itself.

3. Cases before the Tribunal

3.1 Čelebicí *(first instance)*

In March 1996, one of the accused in the case of the *Prosecutor v. Delalić and Others*,[13] Zdravko Mucić, was interviewed by the Prosecution without a lawyer being present. The Defence alleged that the consent by Mr. Mucić to be interviewed without a lawyer present resulted from pressure applied by the Prosecution in a conversation that took place just before the interview began. Besides the Defendant and the investigators of the Office of the Prosecutor, the only other person who was present just before, during, and immediately after the interview was an ICTY interpreter, a staff member from the Registry.[14] As the informal conversations before and immediately after the interview were not included in the records of the proceedings, the Defence, in an *ex parte* motion, sought a subpoena to have the interpreter testify as to what was said, in order to determine with certainty under which circumstances Mr. Mucić agreed to be interviewed without legal representation.

In reaching its decision on the motion,[15] the Trial Chamber based much of its reasoning on a test of necessity, which had been formulated in the *Decision of the President on the Prosecutor's Motion for the Production of Notes Exchanged Between Zejnil Delalić and Zdravko Mucić* of 11 November

---

[13]*Prosecutor v. Zejnil Delalić, Zdravko Mucić also known as "Pavo", Hazim Delić, and Esad Landžo also known as "Zenga"*, (IT-96-21-T) Hereafter referred to as the *Čelebicí* case, after the name of the camp at which the crimes relating to this case took place.

[14]In the organisational structure of the ICTY, interpreters fall under the Conference and Language Services Section, a section of the Registry. Thus, they fall under the 'servicing' functions of the Registry, as defined in Article 17(1) Statute and Rule 33.

[15]*Prosecutor v. Delalić and Others, Decision on Motion Ex Parte by the Defence of Zdravko Mucić Concerning the Issue of a Subpoena to an Interpreter*, Case No. IT-96-21-T, 8 July 1997 ("*Čelebicí, Decision on Motion Ex Parte*").

1996.[16] That Decision dealt with a controversy between two organs of the Tribunal, the Prosecutor and the Registry, and an issue of disclosure, not so much with an issue of immunity.

In her capacity as head of the Detention Unit, the Registrar had confiscated notes that had been exchanged between two of the accused in this case, Delalić and Mucić, within the confines of the Detention Unit.[17] The Prosecutor wanted the contents of the notes disclosed to him and had filed a request thereto.[18] The Trial Chamber in question requested the Registrar to provide the notes to the President of the Tribunal, for his determination as to whether they should be disclosed or not. In respect of the general question whether in a specific case the Registrar must disclose confiscated material to the Prosecutor, the President formulated the following test:

> Is it necessary (not simply useful or helpful) for the purposes of the investigation for the preparation or conduct of the trial that the Registrar be ordered to produce the notes in question?[19]

The President elaborated that this test required the meeting of two conditions: (a) the order that is sought must be necessary for the Prosecutor to obtain such material (i.e., there must be no other, less compelling way), and (b) the material being sought must be relevant for the investigation or prosecution in question. In relation to the second condition – the one most relevant for this contribution – the President added that "[a]s with any search or seizure warrant, the Prosecutor cannot simply conduct a 'fishing expedition' through the Registrar's records".[20] In other words, he must make

---

[16]IT-96-21-T ("*Čelebicí, Decision of the President*").

[17]See, Rule 2, Rules of Detention, and the following Regulations issued by the Registrar pursuant to those Rules: Regulations for the Establishment of a Complaints Procedure for Detainees (April 1995); Regulations for the Establishment of a Disciplinary Procedure for Detainees (April 1995); Regulations to Govern the Supervision of Visits to and Communications with Detainees (Amended 1999); House Rules for Detainees (Amended June 1995).

[18]*Prosecutor's Motion for the Production of Notes exchanged between Detainees Delalić and Mucić*, 26 Aug. 1996 (RP 1130–1115).

[19]*Čelebicí, Decision of the President*, para. 38. The test is formulated on the basis of Rule 39(iv) and Rule 54, which both require an element of necessity.

[20]Id., paras. 39 and 41. As part of the parameters within which to examine this question, the President used those set out by the Trial Chamber in *Decision on the Motion by the Accused Zejnil Delalić for the Disclosure of Evidence*, in which United States federal court decisions were used to support that "[t]he requested evidence must be 'significantly helpful to an understanding of important inculpatory or exculpatory evidence'; it is material here if there 'is a strong indication that [...] it will' play an important role in uncovering admissible evidence, aiding witness preparation, corroborating testimony, or assisting impeachment or rebuttal" (26 Sept. 1996, IT-96-21-T at para. 7; it must be kept in mind however, that these parameters, though of relevance, dealt with an issue of disclosure, and not immunity). To this, the President added that "the fundamental rights of the accused" play a pivotal role as well (in this case, the right to privacy of communication).

it clear to the Judges that *specific* information sought after is pivotal for answering a *specific* question in the case at hand. In this case, the President concluded that the first condition had been met[21] and as regards the second condition, that no 'fishing expedition' was taking place.[22] Hence, he ordered total disclosure of the notes to the Prosecutor.[23]

The 'necessity test' as it was developed by President Cassese for assessing whether an order for the disclosure of documents is called for resembles the functional necessity criterion that is so central in the general law of privileges and immunities of international organisations. The concept is applied in much the same way as the notion of functional necessity is used, first as the yardstick with which to assess whether on the most general level an immunity exists (i.e. is it necessary for the functions of the organisation), and subsequently on a more specific level whether, if it exists, it should or should not be waived. In his Decision, the notion of 'necessity' was first used to assess whether a court order is required at all, or whether the request in question can be dealt with in another, less intrusive way. The same yardstick was subsequently used on a very specific level (*this* investigation, *this* particular question).

We now turn back to the Chamber's consideration of the question whether the Registry interpreter could be called to testify. Using the President's necessity test, the Trial Chamber in its *Decision on Motion Ex Parte*, stated that "it is not persuaded by the contention of the defence counsel that the only way to fill the gap created by omissions in the proceedings is through testimony of the interpreter."[24] In fact, it concluded that it did not consider that the Defence had established that an 'informal conversation' before the actual start of the interview had taken place at all. Accordingly, the Chamber found that an order for the investigation into the evidence that there had indeed been an 'informal conversation' was *not necessary*. Therefore, and "*pursuant to Rule 54*",[25] the motion seeking the order to compel the interpreter to testify was rejected.

The Trial Chamber in an *obiter dictum*[26] entitled "The Position of the Interpreter" stated in general that "judicial functionaries such as clerks or registrars of courts should be protected from matters arising from their

---

[21]Id., para. 42: "The Registrar has been held to be acting properly in withholding the notes and thus cannot be compelled to disclose them without further order."

[22]Id.: "after reading the notes and having carefully considered the matter, applying the test and parameters set out above, and taking into account also the fundamental rights of the accused, I hold that the notes warrant total disclosure to the Prosecutor."

[23]Id., para. 43. The President even went further, and also upheld another request that had been made by the Prosecutor before the Trial Chamber (a request on which the Chamber had not passed judgement), and ordered disclosure of the report on the circumstances of the exchange of notes.

[24]Id., para. 15.

[25]Emphasis added.

[26]Black's Law Dictionary (1990) at 1072: "Words of an opinion entirely unnecessary for the decision of the case". With the gate already closed at Rule 54, i.e. rejection of the need for an order, any further ruling on the issue of immunity was unnecessary.

official duties."[27] The Chamber based that general statement on the principle that: "the stream of justice should be kept pure and undefiled from extraneous factors or fear or prejudice arising from the transaction between the parties."[28] This overly poetic phraseology appears to say that, in order to maintain an effective system for the administration of justice, those involved directly in the process should not have to fear that they will become embroiled in the very matter they are helping to adjudicate.[29] However, the Trial Chamber did not go as far as saying that court functionaries can *never* be compelled to testify. The Decision uses much softer language, and concludes that it would be "undesirable" and "invidious" to "compel an interpreter into the arena of conflict on behalf of either party to the proceedings".[30] Such action should, according to the Chamber, "not be encouraged where other ways exist for the determination of the issue".[31]

3.2 Čelebicí *(Appeal Part I)*

The *Čelebicí* case has acted as a magnet for more issues involving the immunity of ICTY officials and archives. After the President's Decision of November 1996, the Trial Chamber's Decision of July 1997, the issue resurfaced in April 1999 with the rendering of the *Decision of the Appeals Chamber on Motion to Preserve and Provide Evidence*.[32] After having been found guilty of grave breaches of the Geneva Conventions, Esad Landžo appealed his conviction on grounds, *inter alia*, that his right to a fair trial under the Statute had been violated because the verdict and sentence had been rendered by a Trial Chamber whose Presiding Judge had been permitted to sleep through much of the proceedings. By a Motion filed on 4 February 1999, the appellant sought an order to preserve the daily video record of the trial and the production of a copy to his counsel in order to assist him in founding his appeal.

In its response to the Motion, the Prosecution used the 'necessity test' formulated by President Cassese to argue that, in the case at hand, an order to preserve the recordings was not necessary, as Rule 81(A) required the

[27] *Čelebicí, Decision on Motion Ex Parte*, para. 18. See note 15, supra.

[28] Id.

[29] In this connection, the Trial Chamber Decision explicitly referred to the privileged status between client and counsel, and amongst jurors.

[30] *Čelebicí case, Decision on Motion Ex Parte*, para. 20. See note 15, supra.

[31] Id.

[32] *Čelebicí, Decision on Motion to Preserve and Provide Evidence*, Case No. IT-96-21-A, A. Ch., 22 Apr. 1999.

Registrar to preserve the video tape as a record of the trial proceedings.[33] In his Reply, the appellant accepted that submission and withdrew that part of his application, leaving the request to supply his counsel with a copy of the video standing. The Prosecutor's response to that request was short: by not raising the conduct of the Presiding Judge during the trial, the appellant had effectively waived his right to do so on appeal. The appellant countered that the matter had been raised, albeit informally, with the Legal Officer in the Judges' Chambers, and with the then President of the Tribunal, President Cassese.[34]

Understandably, the Appeals Chamber was careful not to be drawn into any determination of the appeal itself,[35] and kept its focus on the issue at hand: should the Registry be requested to provide a copy of the video to the appellant's counsel? Although not by explicit reference, the Chamber reverted to the second part of President's Casesse's "necessity test" when considering this question, and required "first-hand and detailed evidence citing specific instances" before access can be considered. In other words, the Chamber forbade a "fishing expedition":

> [I]f the Appellant files a fresh motion, supported by evidence of a first-hand (that is, not hearsay) and detailed nature which demonstrates that access to the video recording is likely to materially assist in the presentation of his case on appeal, and if the Appeals Chamber (after considering the submissions of the parties) considers that the evidence falls within that description, relief will be granted.

The standard set by the Appeals Chamber is quite high; first-hand evidence of a detailed nature is required. At the same time, there is a tone of consolation: if the standard is met, the Chamber seems to indicate that

[33]*Čelebići, Prosecution's Submissions Concerning Motion to Preserve and Provide Evidence*, Case No. IT-96-21-A, A. Ch., 26 Feb. 1999. Rule 81 provides as follows: "(A) The Registrar shall cause to be made and preserve a full and accurate record of all proceedings, including audio recordings, transcripts and, when deemed necessary by the Trial Chamber, video recordings. (B) The Trial Chamber may order the disclosure of all or part of the record of closed proceedings when the reasons for ordering its non-disclosure no longer exist. (C) The Registrar shall retain and preserve all physical evidence offered during the proceedings subject to any Practice Direction or any order which a Chamber may at any time make with respect to the control or disposition of physical evidence offered during proceedings before that Chamber. (D) Photography, video-recording or audio-recording of the trial, otherwise than by the Registrar, may be authorised at the discretion of the Trial Chamber."

[34]*Čelebići, Response of the Appellant, Esad Landžo, to Prosecution's Submissions Concerning Motion to Preserve and Provide Evidence*, Case No. IT-96-21-A, A. Ch., 11 March 1999.

[35]The Chamber ruled that: "The absence of any complaint at the trial concerning the Judge's alleged conduct does no more than raise the issue as to whether, by the Appellant's silence during the trial, he waived his right to complain of that alleged conduct on appeal. Whether such a waiver should be implied is a matter to be determined in the Appeal.": *Čelebići*, note 32 supra, at 4.

access to the archives containing the videos will be granted. One must however be careful here not to interpret the court's anticipatory benevolence too widely, and conclude that (once the high standard has been met) access will always be granted to all Registry archives. An important distinguishing factor in the case at hand is the fact that the video in question constituted part of the official record of the trial, explicitly referred to in the Rules. That would not necessarily be the case for other segments of the archives maintained by the Registry.

Of final interest in this decision is a statement, not relating to the archives and files of the Registry, but to its personnel. While discussing the issue of waiver and the appellant's allegation that the alleged sleeping of the Presiding Judge had been raised informally with the Legal Officer of the Chamber and the then President of the Tribunal, the Appeals Chamber used the same criteria which had previously been used by the Trial Chamber in its *Decision on Motion Ex Parte*:

> [...] they [the former President and the Legal Officer] *cannot be subpoenaed to testify* as witnesses on matters relating to their official duties or functions because their work is *integral to the operation of the Tribunal* which must be protected by confidentiality. [emphasis added]

In sum, it can be said that the Appeals Chamber applied roughly the same parameters as the Trial Chamber in considering the case. Similarly set on preventing "fishing expeditions" into the Registry's archives, the Chamber set a high bench-mark for determining whether there was reason to grant the requesting party's request for access. It could be argued that the Appeals Chamber has opened the door a little wider than the Trial Chamber by saying that it will most likely grant relief when its rather strict "necessity test" has been passed. However, it could be countered that that may be implying too much, as the Decision related to parts of the official records of the trial. As regards the Chambers and Registry personnel involved in this case, the Appeals Chamber formulated the same rule (i.e., that judicial functionaries of the court should not be subpoenaed to testify), but based on slightly different wording. Whereas the Trial Chamber based the rule on the principle that it would be detrimental to the judicial process if those servicing it could be drawn into the area of conflict, the Appeals Chamber makes that general principle a bit more specific, by linking it to the notion of "confidentiality". On a final note, the absence of any reference to the General Convention by the Appeals Chamber is noticeable.

3.3 The Simić *case*

The *Simić* case[36] dealt primarily with immunity of Registry archives and is the first decision on this topic that explicitly deals with the question of the

[36] *Prosecutor v. Simić and Others, Order for Limited Access to Registry Files*, Case No. IT-95-9-R77, 1 Nov. 1999 ("*Simić* case").

application of the 1946 General Convention on the Privileges and Immunities of the United Nations. As part of investigations into allegations of contempt of court against the accused Milan Simić and his defence counsel, Branislav Avramović, the Prosecutor sought to have the Trial Chamber direct the Registry to provide the Chamber with copies of billing records of Mr. Avramović, on the assumption that such billing records could provide an insight into certain events connected with the contempt proceedings.[37] Two alternatives were proposed by the Prosecutor: either to allow the Prosecution direct access to the billing records, or, alternatively, to have the personnel of the Defence Counsel Unit (DCU)[38] submit to the Trial Chamber those parts of the billing records which directly related to the contempt allegations. At its request, the Registry was granted leave to provide the Chamber with its views on the matter. In its submission, it opposed both alternatives on grounds that the archives of Registry were inviolable and that the personnel of the DCU enjoy privileged status as witnesses, without there being any special circumstances that would warrant lifting of those immunities in the case at hand.[39] The Registry based the immunities it invoked on general principles of law, similar immunities provided in national legal systems, and the 1946 General Convention.

In reaching a decision, the Trial Chamber went back to the very basics of the structure of the Tribunal, and took the "the fundamental responsibility" of prosecuting persons for the most serious violations of international humanitarian law as the basis for its decision. According to the Trial Chamber, a Registry has been provided to the Tribunal to assist in the discharge of that "fundamental" function, whose task it is to service the Chambers and to provide them with "information and material as it may receive that is relevant to [the Chamber's] work".

The Chamber appears to open up the Registry's archives to Chambers quite significantly. The following ruling was based on the 'fundamental' foundation set out above:

> [T]here being no issue taken as to the application generally of the Convention on the Privileges and Immunities of the United Nations of 13 February 1946 to proceedings of the International Tribunal, the principle of the inviolability of archives of the United Nations (Article II, section 4, of the 1946 Convention,

[37] The following facts connected with the billing records were considered non-confidential by the Trial Chamber, and pertinent to the contempt proceedings: records that would help establish that Mr. Avramović "met with anyone in Sremska Mitrovca between July 1998 and April 1999; (b) that he or an employee of his law firm made a telephone call to Srmeska Mitrovca between these dates; or (c) that he met with anyone in Bosanski Šamac between those dates".

[38] Now known as the Office for Legal Aid and Detention Matters (OLAD); the office has remained part of the Registry.

[39] *Simić* case, *Comments of the Registrar on the Prosecution's Request For an Order Granting Limited Access to Registry Files and the Alternative Proposals of the Defence*, Case No. IT-95-9-PT-R77, 24 Sept. 1999.

referred to in Article 30 of the Statute of the Tribunal) is directed primarily at national authorities and other bodies external to the United Nations, and is not applicable *to the International Tribunal* in respect of information and material in the possession of the Registry relevant to the discharge of its fundamental purpose, [...], this being without prejudice to the non-disclosure of information or material that is confidential in accordance with the general principles of international law.[40]

Thus, the Chamber declared the General Convention non-applicable to "*the International Tribunal*", which, in line with Article 11 of the Statute, would mean that the General Convention does not protect the inviolability of the archives of the Registry *vis à vis* Chambers and, in theory, the Prosecutor. Non-disclosure of material that is contained in the archives of the Registry is made dependent on that information or material being "confidential in accordance with the general principles of international law". We have come across the notion of "confidentiality" before (see paragraph 3.2, above), and have already pointed to the fact that its use is a specification of the phraseology used in *Čelebići, Decision on Motion Ex Parte*.

The Chamber did not entertain the question whether, in the alternative, DCU staff could be ordered to submit billing records to the Chamber. Instead, it opted for proposing a pragmatic solution that "a person designated by the Trial Chamber" examine the billing records on "behalf of the Trial Chamber" and prepare a report on the matter.[41] Through this indirect route, many of the concerns raised by the Registrar in her submission were taken into account, while the Chamber retained ultimate control over the decision to disclose the documents or not. That the ultimate control rests with the Tribunal makes judicial sense, and, in this regard, there is reason to be pleased with that part of the decision which declared the General Convention not applicable.[42]

3.4 Čelebići *(Appeal, Part II)*

A little less than a month later, on 7 December 1999, the Appeals Chamber handed down an order in the *Čelebići* case, the *Order on Motion of the*

---

[40]Id. Emphasis added.

[41]The person designated in the Order was the Senior Legal Officer of the Trial Chamber, who was also ordered to prepare a confidential report, providing copies to Milan Simić and his counsel (not to the Prosecutor). That report was submitted to the Chamber on 4 Nov. 1999. Judgement in the contempt proceedings was issued on 30 June 2000 (*Judgement in the Matter of Contempt Allegations Against an Accused and his Counsel*, 30 June 2000, (IT-95-9-R77)). The Trial Chamber unanimously decided that the allegations of contempt against both Branislav Avramović and Milan Simić had not been proven beyond reasonable doubt, and that therefore neither of them were in contempt of the Tribunal.

[42]As set out above, in the structure of the General Convention, it is the Secretary-General of the United Nations who makes the final decision to waive or not to waive.

Appellant, Esad Landžo, for Permission to Obtain and Adduce Further Evidence on Appeal.[43] The issue at hand was whether the appellant could obtain and adduce further evidence to help establish that he had not waived his right to raise the issue of fair trial by not raising the alleged sleeping of the Presiding Judge during the trial proceedings. The appellant asserted that he had raised the matter and sought evidence to support that from the former President of the Tribunal, Judge Cassese (testimony and written records)[44] the Registrar (testimony and written records), and the Senior Legal Officer of the Trial Chamber (testimony). More concretely, the Appellant sough a motion that would:

> (i) [...] order or request the appropriate official to waive any privilege and immunity in respect of the Former President, the Registrar, and the Senior Legal Officer [...];
>
> (ii) [...] order or request the proposed witnesses to testify by deposition, and
>
> (iii) [...] order or request the Former President and the Registrar to produce documents.

One of the arguments raised by the Prosecution in this case was that the evidence of the proposed witnesses was "not necessary" for the disposition of the matter. Further, the Prosecutor accepted certain facts without further contention.[45] Hence, the Chamber was able to conclude that "much of the testimony of the proposed witnesses is rendered unnecessary as a substantial number of the facts sought to be established by the Appellant may be established by the undertakings offered by the Prosecution."[46]

However, a determination regarding the 'left-overs' was still necessary, and, in doing so, the Chamber reverted to the 'necessity test' drafted by one of the proposed witnesses, Judge Cassese. It was considered that there was "no indication" that the Appellant would be unable to provide the evidence in respect of those left-overs "otherwise than by testimony of the proposed witnesses". Hence, the request did not pass the first test.

The Chamber was not quite as unequivocal as the Judges in *Simić* in declaring the 1946 General Convention inapplicable, and, in fact, appeared

[43]IT-96-21-A.

[44]At the time this decision was rendered, Former President Cassese was a Judge. On 8 February 2000, he resigned from the Tribunal after having been a Judge since its establishment in 1993.

[45]Namely (i) "certain undertakings from counsel then appearing for the Appellant that she met separately with each of the proposed witnesses" (without being prepared to accept the particulars of the conversations which took place in these meetings)"; (ii) that "the letter dated 18 August 1997 [...] was sent to the Former President by the Appellant [...] and that the letter in response dated 3 September 1997 [...] was sent by the Former President"; and (iii) "that the counsel for the Appellant prepared the documents 'Motion on Mistrial' and 'Cynthia McMurrey's Resignation under Protest' [...]".

[46]See note 43, supra.

to have wanted to distance itself somewhat from the *Simić* Decision. In this instance, the Chamber thought it "unnecessary" to consider the possible application of the General Convention, and preferred instead to revert to "wider legal grounds", by stating "that a survey of the relevant jurisprudence of municipal legal systems indicates that the general principles of law recognise an *adjudicative privilege* or *judicial immunity* from compulsion to testify in relation to judicial deliberations and certain other related matters."[47] The Chamber was not prepared to declare the General Convention inapplicable, but, at the same time, it was not prepared to apply it either. It went on to say that:

> it is an inherent quality of an independent judicial institution such as the International Tribunal that it be able to maintain confidentiality in relation to its basic judicial functions, that the independence of judges and other officers of the Tribunal exercising judicial functions should be safeguarded from being drawn into the controversies before it by being compelled to testify on behalf of any of the parties to the proceedings before it [...][48]

Based on these "fundamental considerations", the Chamber concluded that the possible testimony of the Former President or the Senior Legal Officer is covered by the 'judicial privilege'. The Appeals Chamber concluded that, as "the relevant evidence is available from other sources, and consistently with the fundamental consideration already referred to, it is [...] inappropriate to request the witnesses [the Former President and the Senior Legal Officer] to testify."

The immunity of the Registrar was somewhat more qualified. The Registrar, the Chamber concluded, "in view of her official role at the International Tribunal, [...] should not be drawn into proceedings before the International Tribunal to give evidence for either of the parties unless such evidence is not available from another source and is otherwise necessary".[49] The Appeals Chamber concluded that "the evidence of the Registrar [...] is not necessary to establish any of the matters sought to be established by the appellant."[50] Two judges seem to set the standard for the Registrar giving evidence a little differently, by only allowing such evidence "in exceptional circumstances", as opposed to the majority view, which allowed testimony in cases where "such evidence is not available from another source and is

---

[47]Id. note 43, supra. Emphasis added.
[48]Id.
[49]Id.
[50]Id.

otherwise necessary".[51] The latter view is more in line with the previous case law cited above.

4. Conclusion

Overall, it is fair to say that there is reasonable consistency in the case law which the Tribunal has developed to deal with the requests for ICTY Registry and Chambers staff members to testify or produce documents, although, there are slight nuances which cause some divergence.

The foundation for many of the decisions appears to be President Cassese's decision, which set three criteria for determining whether a UN staff member who is also an ICTY court functionary can be compelled to testify before the Tribunal. Notably lacking in the formulation of those criteria is any reference to the General Convention.

Firstly, it must be *necessary* (not simply useful or helpful) that an order be made to testify and/or to produce documents; both from a perspective of the Statute/Rules (i.e. within the framework of the Statute/Rules, it takes an 'order' to obtain what is being sought) and from a perspective of the investigation or prosecution in question (i.e., it must be established that the specific information that is being sought after is essential for a specific question in a specific case). This last condition aims to prevent frivolous "fishing expeditions" into the Registry's archives and official acts by its personnel.[52]

If no order is *necessary* within the framework of the Statute/Rules, the story, in principle, ends. If, however, it has been established that an order is necessary, the rule is that interpreters or other court functionaries of the Tribunal should be shielded from becoming involved in judicial proceedings in respect of matters arising from their official duties.

There is one exception to this rule, more or less constantly left open in the Tribunal's case law, and also borne out of 'necessity': if there is no other way to determine the issue but through testimony of the court functionary in question, then access may have to be granted, in spite of the fundamental reasons for shielding Registry personnel or archives.

---

[51]Id. The conclusion regarding the Registrar was reached by majority, Judges Riad and Nieto-Navia considering that: "the Registrar, in view of her official role at the International Tribunal which includes assisting Chambers and certain functions of a judicial nature, should not be drawn into proceedings before the International Tribunal to give evidence for either of the parties except in exceptional circumstances, and that no such circumstances have been established which would make it appropriate for the Registrar to give evidence in this case."

[52]If this test is applied to most of the staff of the OTP, one would conclude that an order to have them testify is not "necessary", as the official functions of the majority functions of those staff (investigators, legal advisers, trial attorneys) would include having to appear in court.

The author would interpret the relationship between the various criteria of necessity as one of generality versus specificity. The 'necessity test' as formulated by President Cassese refers directly to Rule 54, and asks questions regarding *means* (order or no order?) and *specificity* (why is this specific information necessary in this specific case?). The criteria formulated in the *Čelebići* Decision on July 1997 also pose a question of necessity, but here the question is much more specific. When the time has come to ask this question, it is already clear that we are not dealing with a 'fishing expedition'. In such cases it has, in principle, been decided that an order to disclose or testify is called for. The Judges are now faced with the question whether the Rule that court functionaries should not be compelled to produce official documents or testify regarding official functions is applicable, and, if it is, whether the exception to the rule applies.

In developing its case law in this area, the Judges have paid little or no attention to the General Convention on the Privileges and Immunities of the United Nations. That Convention has only been used in cases where non-ICTY UN staff members were requested to testify or where other UN organisations were requested to produce documents (UNHCR, UN Secretariat, etc). For matters that come closer to the inner workings of the Tribunal, the Judges have rightly chosen to keep matters in their own hands, even when doing so has meant giving general principles of law more weight than a written convention without much explanation. That, however, one must probably simply explain away by the simple fact that the ad hoc tribunal for the former Yugoslavia is a unique institution, set up within the UN mould, but not always fitting in that mould. It has adapted well.

PART XI

Appeals

JOHN HOCKING*

34. Interlocutory Appeals before the ICTY

1. Introduction

The ICTY is the first international criminal court to have been established with an Appeals Chamber. Although not specifically provided for in its Statute, the ICTY has, through its Rules, developed a regime for determining appeals from interlocutory decisions of Trial Chambers in specific and limited circumstances.

This chapter will look at the development of this appeals regime, its legal basis and, through an examination of the Tribunal's jurisprudence, set out the circumstances in which an interlocutory decision of a Trial Chamber may be brought before the Appeals Chamber of the ICTY.

2. Current Rules

Interlocutory appeals before the ICTY Appeals Chamber may arise from decisions of Trial Chambers on four specific types of matters: 1) preliminary motions; 2) other motions; 3) applications for provisional release; and 4) state requests for review.[1]

---

*John Hocking, Senior Legal Officer, Appeals Chamber ICTY; BSc, LLB, LLM with merit (London School of Economics, University of London); formerly Associate to Justice Kirby (currently Judge of High Court of Australia); Barrister, Lincoln's Inn, London; legal and policy adviser to Organisation for Economic Co-operation and Development (OECD) and Australian Government Broadcaster (SBS); and legal assistant to Geoffrey Robertson QC. The views expressed herein are those of the author and do not necessarily represent those of the United Nations, ICTY or ICTR.

[1]There is also a provision under Rule 54*bis* for appeals from decisions rejecting an application by a party for a State to produce documents or information. As this Rule is yet to be considered by the Appeals Chamber, it will not be discussed in this Chapter.

R. May et al., Essays on ICTY Procedure and Evidence in Honour of Gabrielle Kirk McDonald, 459–472.

2.1 Preliminary Motions

Rule 72 of the ICTY Rules of Procedure and Evidence ("Rules") defines four categories of preliminary motions. These are motions which:

(i) challenge jurisdiction
(ii) allege defects in the indictment
(iii) seek severance of counts or separate trials
(iv) raise objections based on the refusal of a request for the assignment of counsel.[2]

Preliminary motions are by their very nature, motions which need to be dealt with prior to the commencement of proceedings. They are, therefore, required to be brought before the Trial Chamber within thirty days of the Prosecutor meeting her disclosure obligations under sub-Rule 66(A)(i).[3] Rule 72 obligates the Trial Chamber to dispose of all preliminary motions no later than sixty days after their filing and at latest before the commencement of the trial.[4]

Sub-Rule 72(B) establishes an appeals regime for decisions on preliminary motions. Either party has an automatic right of appeal from decisions on preliminary motions challenging jurisdiction. This provision recognises the importance of challenges to jurisdiction by allowing a direct right of appeal to the Appeals Chamber. For the other three categories of preliminary motions, an interlocutory appeal may only be pursued where a bench of three Judges of the Appeals Chamber grants leave to appeal. The test to be applied by the bench of the Appeals Chamber in determining whether to grant leave is that "good cause" be shown.

2.2 Other Motions

Other motions before a Trial Chamber are governed by Rule 73 of the Rules.[5] Pursuant to sub-Rule 73(A), either party may at any time, either by writing or orally, move before the Trial Chamber "by way of motion, not being a preliminary motion, for appropriate ruling or relief."

Sub-Rule 73(B) contains two exceptions to a general bar on interlocutory appeals from decisions on motions other than preliminary motions. The sub-Rule provides that decisions "on such motions are without interlocutory appeal save with the leave of a bench of three Judges of the Appeals

---

[2]Sub-Rule 72(A) of the Rules.

[3]Sub-Rule 66(A) provides that the Prosecutor shall make available to the defence in a language which the accused understands "(i) within thirty days of the initial appearance of the accused, copies of the supporting material which accompanied the indictment when confirmation was sought as well as all prior statements obtained by the Prosecutor from the accused".

[4]Sub-Rule 72(A) specifically provides "before the commencement of the opening statements provided for in Rule 84."

[5]Except for applications for provisional release discussed below.

Chamber which may grant such leave" if one or both of the following tests are satisfied:

(i) if the impugned decision would cause such prejudice to the case of the party seeking leave as could not be cured by the final disposal of the trial including post-judgement appeal;

(ii) if the issue in the proposed appeal is of general importance to proceedings before the Tribunal or in international law generally.

2.3 Applications for Provisional Release

Although Rule 73 specifically refers to "other motions", Rule 65 provides a separate procedure for applications for provisional release and for appeals from those decisions. Pursuant to sub-Rule 65(D), such decisions "shall be subject to appeal in cases where leave is granted by a bench of three Judges of the Appeals Chamber, upon good cause being shown."

2.4 State Requests for Review

A final provision for interlocutory appeal is contained in Rule 108*bis*. This Rule permits a state "directly affected by an interlocutory decision of a Trial Chamber" to request a review of the decision by the Appeals Chamber if the decision concerns "issues of general importance relating to the powers of the Tribunal."[6]

3. History of the Rules

The original Rules were adopted at the Tribunal's Second Plenary Session on 11 February 1994.[7] The general provision for motions was set out in Rule 72 and preliminary motions were defined in Rule 73, the converse of their current structure. Preliminary motions by the accused were defined to include the four categories set out in the current Rule 72 plus applications for the exclusion of evidence obtained from the accused. But the wording of the Rule was not exclusionary and clearly envisaged the possibility of other types of preliminary motions.[8] Rule 65 dealt with provisional release. None of the three Rules as originally drafted made any reference to appeal proceedings from decisions by Trial Chambers pursuant to those Rules.

It was in January 1995 at the Tribunal's fifth Plenary Session that a limited right of interlocutory appeal from decisions on preliminary motions was introduced. Rule 72 was amended to permit interlocutory appeals as of right

[6]Sub-Rule 108*bis*(A).
[7]Rules of Procedure and Evidence IT/32, entered into force on 14 March 1994.
[8]Rule 73 then provided that preliminary "motions by the accused shall include…".

but only in respect of a decision of a Trial Chamber dismissing a challenge to jurisdiction.[9] It was not until June 1996 at the Eleventh Plenary Session, that the interlocutory appeal regime was expanded to include other preliminary motions. These appeals were not as of right, however, but required "serious cause" to be shown to a bench of three Judges of the Appeals Chamber.[10]

This new test of serious cause was later applied to decisions on applications for provisional release by the Judges at their Thirteenth Plenary Session in July 1997. The amendment allowed an appeal under Rule 65 when a bench of three Judges of the Appeals Chamber was satisfied that serious cause had been shown. At the same Plenary, Rule 108*bis* was introduced.[11]

The major revision of Rules 72 and 73, which created their current structure, occurred at the Fourteenth Plenary Session in October and November 1997.[12] Preliminary motions were moved to Rule 72 and limited to their current four specified categories.[13] The wording of the Rule was now exclusionary with no other type of preliminary motions contemplated. "Other motions" were brought under Rule 73.

The right to an interlocutory appeal on preliminary motions was also amended in two respects. First, appeals from decisions on challenges to jurisdiction remained as of right but were expanded to become a right for both parties. It was no longer limited to those decisions of a Trial Chamber which had dismissed an objection based on lack of jurisdiction. Secondly, the test for the granting of leave to appeal for the remaining three categories of preliminary motions was changed from "serious cause" to "good cause".

This re-arrangement of the Rules was clearly designed to differentiate between those specifically defined "preliminary motions" and "other motions". In so doing, the Judges acknowledged the importance of bringing preliminary motions as early as possible during the pre-trial phase. The issues raised by preliminary motions: challenges to jurisdiction; alleged defects in the form of the indictment; severance of counts or separation of a trial; and refusal of a request for assignment of counsel on the basis of indigency; are matters which should be finally resolved before the commencement of trial.

The amendments to Rule 73 also introduced for the first time an avenue of appeal from decisions on "other motions". The Judges at Plenary thereby recognised that in certain circumstances it may be more beneficial to finally resolve an issue rather than waiting for the completion of both the trial and final appeal processes. However the right was limited, as decisions on other motions may only be subject to appeal if a bench of three Judges of the

---

[9]Rules of Procedure and Evidence IT/32 Rev. 3, issued 30 January 1995. Rule 77 (contempt of court) was also amended to provide that any "judgement rendered under this Rule shall be subject to appeal".

[10]Rules of Procedure and Evidence IT/32 Rev. 9, issued 5 July 1996.

[11]Rules of Procedure and Evidence IT/32 Rev. 11, issued 25 July 1997.

[12]Rules of Procedure and Evidence IT/32 Rev. 12, issued 12 November 1997.

[13]One category, "applications for the exclusion of evidence obtained from the accused or having belonged to him", was deleted.

Appeals Chamber determines that one of two tests is satisfied. The first test deals with matters that are important to resolve early on in the proceedings as they "would cause such prejudice" to the party seeking leave to appeal that could not be cured by final appeal.[14] The second test, raises issues of general importance to proceedings before the Tribunal or to international law generally and reflects the burgeoning stage of development of the Tribunal (and of international criminal law in general). It recognises that it is in the interests of justice and judicial efficiency, and fairness to the parties in subsequent cases, to resolve certain issues as they arise during a trial rather than waiting for their resolution at the final appeal.

It was also at the Fourteenth Plenary that the serious cause requirement for appeals from decisions on provisional release under Rule 65 was amended to its current wording of "good cause".[15]

4. Interlocutory Appellate Jurisprudence of the Tribunal

4.1 Statutory Basis for Interlocutory Appeals

The Tribunal's appellate jurisdiction is established by Article 25 of the Statute. The Article makes no reference, however, to interlocutory appeals.[16] The jurisdictional basis for interlocutory appeals was first considered by the full bench of the Appeals Chamber in the *Tadić* case.[17] In that case, the Judges expressed the Tribunal's Statute to be "general in nature" and that the Security Council had "surely expected that it would be supplemented, where advisable, by the rules which the Judges were mandated to adopt".[18] The Appeals Chamber noted that it is in the interests of the administration of justice and in fairness to the accused that certain issues should not be kept for a final decision until the end of potentially "lengthy, emotional and expensive" trials.[19]

In adopting a broad interpretation of the concept of jurisdiction, the Appeals Chamber was of the view that "in a court of law, common sense ought to be honoured not only when facts are weighed, but equally when

[14]Sub-Rule 73(B)(i) of the Rules.

[15]Id. Rule 77 was also amended to remove the right of appeal and introducing a preliminary requirement of leave to appeal from a bench of three Judges of the Appeals Chamber upon "good cause" being shown. At the Nineteenth Plenary, this was amended to "good grounds", IT/142 Rev. 14, 17 December 1998.

[16]Article 25 provides: "1. The Appeals Chamber shall hear appeals from persons convicted by the Trial Chambers or from the Prosecutor on the following grounds: (a) an error on a question of law invalidating the decision; or (b) an error of fact which has occasioned a miscarriage of justice. 2. The Appeals Chamber may affirm, reverse or revise the decisions taken by the Trial Chambers."

[17]*Prosecutor v. Tadić, Decision on the Defence Motion for Interlocutory Appeal on Jurisdiction*, Case No. IT-94-1-AR72, A. Ch., 2 Oct. 1995.

[18]Id., para. 4.

[19]Id., para. 6.

laws are surveyed and the proper rule is selected. In the present case, the jurisdiction of this Chamber to hear and dispose of [the] Appellant's interlocutory appeal is indisputable."[20]

It would appear to be well settled that the International Tribunal has jurisdiction to entertain interlocutory appeals. Similarly, the legality of the establishment of a bench of three Judges of the Appeals Chamber to consider applications for leave to appeal has also been confirmed.[21]

However, the jurisdiction of the Appeals Chamber to hear an interlocutory appeal presupposes that the impugned decision was made by a Trial Chamber during the course of a pending case. Thus, an application for leave to appeal an interlocutory decision in a case where the accused had died was held to be outside the jurisdiction of the Appeals Chamber.[22]

4.2 Rule 72 – Jurisdiction

With the introduction of a limited right of interlocutory appeal for decisions dismissing challenges to jurisdiction in January 1995, the first decision of the Appeals Chamber under the amended Rule 72 was in the *Tadić* case.[23] The appeal challenged a decision of the Trial Chamber where the defence had alleged that the Tribunal: had been unlawfully established; wrongfully had primacy over domestic courts; and lacked subject matter jurisdiction under Articles 2, 3 and 5 of the Statute.[24] The Appeals Chamber revised the decision of the Trial Chamber[25] but affirmed the jurisdiction of the Tribunal. In doing so, the Appeals Chamber confirmed that the issues raised in the appeal were indeed challenging the jurisdiction of the Tribunal and that it was properly seized of the matter.

Since the *Tadić* decision, a number of other cases have, however, unsuccessfully attempted to classify issues as jurisdictional before the Appeals Chamber. In *Brđanin*, an alleged substantive error in the *prima facie* assess-

[20]Id. See also *Prosecutor v. Tadić, Separate Opinion of Judge Sidhwa on the Defence Motion for Interlocutory Appeal on Jurisdiction*, Case No. IT-94-1-AR72, A. Ch., 2 Oct. 1995 at pp. 2 to 8.

[21]*Prosecutor v. Delalić and Others, Decision on Application for Leave to Appeal (Provisional Release) by Hazim Delić*, Case No. IT-96-21-AR72.4, A. Ch., 22 Nov. 1996, p. 7.

[22]*Prosecutor v. Kovačević, Order Refusing Leave to Appeal*, Case No. IT-97-24-AR73(B).3, A. Ch., 24 Sept. 1998.

[23]*Prosecutor v. Tadić, Decision on the Defence Motion for Interlocutory Appeal on Jurisdiction*, Case No. IT-94-1-AR72, A. Ch., 2 Oct. 1995.

[24]The basis for this allegation was that the subject-matter jurisdiction under Article 2 (grave breaches of the Geneva Conventions of 1949), Article 3 (violations of the laws or customs of war) and Article 5 (crimes against humanity) was limited to crimes committed during an international armed conflict. The appellant alleged that at most the conflict was internal in nature or alternatively that there was no conflict at all in the region where the crimes were allegedly committed, id., para. 65.

[25]The Trial Chamber had ruled that it was not competent to decide on the legality of the Tribunal's establishment. The Appeals Chamber held that it was empowered to pronounce on this plea (Judge Li dissenting) and held that the Tribunal had been "established by law", id., para. 47.

ment of the material before a Judge confirming an indictment was held not to constitute a challenge to jurisdiction.[26] In *Simić*, a request by the defence for an evidentiary hearing and for the Prosecution to make available material relating to the circumstances of the arrest of the accused *Todorović* and his delivery to the Tribunal was held not to constitute a challenge to jurisdiction.[27]

It is interesting to contrast this position with that before the ICTR[28] Appeals Chamber. Until recently, the ICTR Rules of Procedure and Evidence ("ICTR Rules") did not permit any interlocutory appeals except "in the case of dismissal of an objection based on lack of jurisdiction" where an appeal lay as of right.[29] In the five years since the ICTR was established, there had been 27 applications for interlocutory appeal pursuant to this Rule. Only four of these having been accepted as challenges to jurisdiction under Rule 72 of the ICTR Rules. As a consequence, at the Seventh Plenary Session of the ICTR in February 2000, the Judges amended Rule 72 and inserted a definition of jurisdiction and a preliminary requirement that a bench of three Judges of the Appeals Chamber of the ICTR first determine whether an application does in fact fit within that definition.[30]

4.3 Rules 65 & 72 – Serious/Good Cause

The first decision by a bench of three Judges of the Appeals Chamber was in October 1996. The then version of Rule 72 provided that appeals from decisions on preliminary motions, apart from challenges to jurisdiction, obtain leave to appeal by showing "serious cause". The Judges in that case stated that the Rule was created as a filter for appeals other than those relating to

---

[26] *Prosecutor v. Brđanin and Talić, Decision on Interlocutory Appeal from Decision on Motion to Dismiss Indictment filed under Rule 72*, Case No. IT-99-36-AR72, A. Ch., 16 Nov. 1999. See also *Prosecutor v. Delalić and Others, Decision on Application for Leave to Appeal by Hazim Delić (Defects in the form of the Indictment)*, Case No. IT-96-21-AR72.5, A. Ch., 6 Dec. 1996.

[27] *Prosecutor v. Simić and Others, Decision and Scheduling Order*, Case No. IT-95-9-AR72, A. Ch., 18 May 1999.

[28] International Criminal Tribunal for the Prosecution of Persons Responsible for Genocide and Other Serious Violations of International Humanitarian Law Committed in the Territory of Rwanda and Rwandan Citizens responsible for genocide and other such violations committed in the territory of neighbouring States between 1 January and 31 December 1994 ("ICTR").

[29] Rule 72, ICTR Rules as amended at 1 July 1999.

[30] Rule 72 of the ICTR Rules (as amended on 21 February 2000) now provides, *inter alia,*: "(H) For the purposes of Rule 72(B)(i) and (D) an "objection based on lack of jurisdiction" refers exclusively to a motion which challenges an indictment on the ground that it does not relate to: (i) any of the persons indicated in Articles 1, 5, 6 and 8 of the Statute; (ii) the territories indicated in Articles 1, 7 and 8 of the Statute; (iii) the period indicated in Articles 1, 7 and 8 of the Statute; or (iv) any of the violations indicated in Articles 2, 3, 4 and 6 of the Statute. (I) An appeal brought under Rule 72(D) may not be proceeded with if a bench of three Judges of the Appeals Chamber, assigned by the Presiding Judge of the Appeals Chamber, decides that the appeal is not capable of satisfying the requirements of paragraph (H), in which case the appeal shall be dismissed."

jurisdiction and that the bench of three was to undertake a preliminary scrutiny.[31] "Clearly, the purpose of this "sifting" device is to prevent the Appeals Chamber from being flooded with unimportant or unnecessary appeals which unduly prolong pre-trial proceedings. The "filter" was not considered necessary for questions of jurisdiction, because of the intrinsic importance and preliminary nature of such questions: therefore, they must be decided upon prior to any consideration of the merits".[32]

In determining the merits of the application, the three Judges considered it necessary to first ensure that the application was indeed covered by the relevant rule. Secondly, the Judges would exclude any applications which were "frivolous, vexatious, manifestly ill founded, an abuse of the process of court or so vague and imprecise as to be unsusceptible of any serious consideration".[33] If these two preliminary hurdles were overcome, then the bench would turn to consider the issue of serious cause.

In determining serious cause, the bench held that it was necessary to show one of two things. Either, a "grave error" on the part of the Trial Chamber which would cause "substantial prejudice to the accused" or be contrary to the interests of justice. Alternatively, the applicant needed to raise issues which were not only of general importance but also "directly material to the future development" of the trial proceedings such that the decision of the Appeals Chamber "would seriously impact upon further proceedings before the Trial Chamber".[34] It is interesting to see that the two tests set out in this case are a narrower version of what was ultimately incorporated into Rule 73 for "other motions".

This assessment process was followed in a number of other decisions under Rule 72 as it was then worded.[35] In one matter, an application by a witness was held to be clearly outside the provisions of Rule 72 in that the applicant lacked standing. Specifically, in rejecting the application, the bench requested the Registrar not to reimburse any sums incurred by the

---

[31] *Prosecutor v. Delalić and Others, Decision on Application for Leave to Appeal (Separate Trials)*, Case No. IT-96-21-AR72.1, A. Ch., 14 Oct. 1996 (Judges Cassese, Li and Deschênes).

[32] Id., para 16.

[33] Id., para 19.

[34] Id., para 20.

[35] *See Prosecutor v. Blaškić, Decision on Application for Leave to Appeal (Protection of Victims and Witnesses)*, Case No. IT-95-14-AR72, A. Ch., 14 Oct. 1996; *Prosecutor v. Delalić and Others, Decision on Application for Leave to Appeal (Provisional Release),* Case No. IT-96-21-AR72.2, A. Ch., 15 Oct. 1996; *Prosecutor v. Delalić and Others, Decision on Application for Leave to Appeal (Form of the Indictment)*, Case No. IT-96-21-AR72.3, A. Ch., 15 Oct. 1996; *Prosecutor v. Delalić and Others, Decision on Application for Leave to Appeal (Provisional Release) by Hazim Delić*, Case No. IT-96-21-AR72.4, A. Ch., 22 Nov. 1996; *Prosecutor v. Delalić and Others, Decision on Application for Leave to Appeal by Hazim Delić (Defects in the Form of the Indictment)*, Case No. IT-96-21-AR72.5, A. Ch., 6 Dec. 1996; *Prosecutor v. Dokmanović, Decision on Application for Leave to Appeal by the Accused Slavko Dokmanović*, Case No. IT-95-13a-AR72, A. Ch., 11 Nov. 1997.

defence in respect of it.[36] The seven other applications for leave to appeal under that Rule were rejected, *inter alia*, for failing to show "serious cause".

Since the significant re-drafting of Rules 72 and 73 in November 1997, there has been only one application under Rule 72 for leave to appeal preliminary motions other than challenges to jurisdiction.[37] In that case, the defence sought leave to appeal the denial by the Trial Chamber of its application for a separate trial. In rejecting the application, the bench of three Judges determined that no error on the part of the Trial Chamber had been shown and that, therefore, good cause had not been established.[38]

There have, however, been a number of decisions under Rule 65 on applications for provisional release and the definition of serious/good cause under that Rule. The decisions under Rule 65, although not excluding the first two preliminary hurdles in assessing serious cause set out above, have followed the definition of serious cause in the earlier cases under Rule 72 to the extent that it is necessary for the applicant to show that the Trial Chamber may have erred in making its decision. Thus in an application by the accused Dragoljub Kunarać who had been denied provisional release by the Trial Chamber, the bench of three Judges rejected his application for leave to appeal on the basis that he had "failed to state precisely why the decision erred under applicable legal principles".[39]

Similarly in an application by the Prosecutor against a decision of the Trial Chamber granting provisional release to two accused who had voluntarily surrendered to the Tribunal, the bench rejected the application on the basis that it had not demonstrated that the Trial Chamber may have erred in making the decision.[40] In fact, not one of the eleven applications for leave to appeal filed under Rule 65 has been successful.[41]

Although not an interlocutory appeal, sub-Rule 77(J) provides that decisions of a Trial Chamber under this Rule, which relates to contempt of the

---

[36]*In the case of Dragan Opačić, Decision on Application for Leave to Appeal,* Case No. IT-95-7-Misc.1, A. Ch., 3 June 1997.

[37]*Prosecutor v. Brđanin and Talić, Decision on Request to Appeal,* Case No. IT-99-36-AR72.2, A. Ch., 16 May 2000.

[38]Id. See also *Prosecutor v. Brđanin and Talić, Decision on Interlocutory Appeal from Decision on Motion to Dismiss Indictment filed under Rule 72,* Case No. IT-99-36-AR72, A. Ch., 16 Nov. 1999, where an interlocutory appeal filed by the defence against a decision of the Trial Chamber dismissing a challenge to the confirmation of the indictment was held by the full Appeals Chamber to be neither a challenge to jurisdiction nor any of the other types of preliminary motions and was dismissed without further consideration.

[39]*Prosecutor v. Kunarać and Kovać, Order Rejecting Application for Leave to Appeal,* Case No. IT-96-23-AR65, A. Ch., 25 Nov. 1999.

[40]*Prosecutor v. Simić and Others, Decision on Application for Leave to Appeal,* Case No. IT-95-9-AR65, A. Ch., 19 Apr. 2000. See also *Prosecutor v. Kupreškić and Others, Decision on Application for Leave to Appeal,* Case No. IT-95-16-AR65.4, A. Ch., 1 Dec. 1999; *Decision on Application for Leave to Appeal,* Case No. IT-95-16- AR65.3, A. Ch., 29 Sept. 1999; *Decision on Application for Leave to Appeal,* Case No. IT-95-16-AR65.2, A. Ch., 18 Aug. 1999; and *Decision on Application for Leave to Appeal,* Case No. IT-95-16-AR65, A. Ch., 18 Aug. 1999.

[41]As at 8 June 2000.

Tribunal, are subject to appeal where a bench of three Judges of the Appeals Chamber grants leave upon "good grounds" being shown. The only decision under this Rule referred interchangeably to both good grounds and good cause and applying a somewhat broader definition than in the serious/good cause cases discussed above, held the application admissible as the issues of law raised were "matters of general importance to proceedings before the International Tribunal or in international law generally".[42] In so doing, it would appear that the bench was applying the second of the two tests set out in Rule 73 rather than the interpretation given to good or serious cause adopted by other benches determining applications for leave to appeal.[43]

4.4 Rule 73 – Two Tests

The Appeals Chamber, in interpreting the first test under Rule 73, has stated that the applicant "must establish that the impugned decision is so prejudicial to the case that the detrimental effect could not be rectified by the Trial Chamber in its judgement or by the Appeals Chamber in post-judgement appeal."[44] In fact, it has proved extremely difficult for an applicant to successfully argue leave to appeal under the first test of Rule 73 and only one application to date has succeeded.[45] In that case, one of the accused challenged the legality of his arrest and had brought a motion before the Trial Chamber seeking an evidentiary hearing and discovery from the Prosecution as a preliminary step to having the indictment against him dismissed. The bench of the Appeals Chamber, in granting leave to appeal, held that the Trial Chamber's denial of the accused's requests "could not be cured by the final disposal of the trial including post-judgement appeal".[46]

The second test under Rule 73 would appear to have a wider ambit than the first test. In the second test, the issues raised in the proposed appeal must be either of general importance to proceedings before the Tribunal or of general importance in international law generally. The second test was considered in the first decision rendered by a bench of three Judges under the new Rule 73. In that case, the Prosecution appealed a decision of the Trial Chamber which refused its application to call an additional expert

---

[42]*Prosecutor v. Aleksovski, Decision on Application of Mr. Nobilo for Leave to Appeal the Trial Chamber finding of Contempt*, Case No. IT-95-14/1/AR77, A. Ch., 22 Dec. 1998.

[43]An application under Rule 77 for leave to appeal a finding of contempt committed before the Appeals Chamber is currently pending before a bench of three Judges of the Appeals Chamber: *Prosecutor v. Tadić, Application for Leave to Appeal against Judgement on Allegations of Contempt against prior Counsel Milan Vujin IT-94-1-A-R77, Case No. IT-94-1-A-AR77*, A. Ch., 7 Feb. 2000.

[44]*Prosecutor v. Delalić and Others, Decision on Application of Defendant Zejnil Delalić for Leave to Appeal against the Decision of the Trial Chamber of 19 January 1998 for the Admissibility of Evidence*, Case No. IT-96-21-AR73.2, A. Ch., 4 March 1998 at para. 9.

[45]*Prosecutor v. Simić and Others, Decision on Application by Stevan Todorović for Leave to Appeal against the Oral Decision of Trial Chamber III of 4 March 1999*, Case No. IT-95-9-AR73.2, A. Ch., 1 July 1999.

[46]Id., p. 4.

witness to testify as to the handwriting of one of the accused.[47] The bench, in considering whether the application raised an issue of general importance to proceedings before the Tribunal or in international law generally, stated that the intention behind the introduction of this test reflected the function of the "jurisprudence of this International Tribunal which has a pioneering role in the development of international criminal law".[48]

The bench considered the application to be of general importance to both proceedings before the Tribunal and to international criminal law "because at its heart are issues of fairness to the accused and the proper conduct of international criminal proceedings."[49] However, the bench did not consider this in itself sufficient to grant leave under Rule 73 and went on to consider the merits of the application itself. The bench rejected the application on the basis that the Prosecution had failed to demonstrate a possible error on the part of the Trial Chamber.[50] This is consistent with the discretionary wording of sub-Rule 73(B) which provides that the "bench of three Judges of the Appeals Chamber *may*" grant leave and recognises the filtering role of the bench. Thus, although an application may satisfy one or both of the tests under Rule 73, it may still be rejected if it fails to show an error on the part of the Trial Chamber.

The second decision under the new Rule was also in the *Delalić* case. One of the accused appealed an oral decision of the Trial Chamber which required the defence to disclose a list of the witnesses it intended to call seven days prior to their hearing.[51] Although finding that the application had been filed out of time, the bench went on to consider its merits. In rejecting the application, the bench stated that the two Rules in question[52] were not ambiguous and that their interpretation had "achieved sufficient consistency in the practice of the International Tribunal".[53] Therefore, their interpretation would not raise an issue of general importance to proceedings before the Tribunal or in international law generally.

There have been seven successful applications under the second test in Rule 73. They are: whether a decision denying leave to amend an indictment was contrary to the jurisprudence of the Tribunal or internationally recognised legal standards;[54] whether the confirmation of an indictment after the

---

[47]*Prosecutor v. Delalić and Others, Decision on Prosecution's Application for Leave to Appeal Pursuant to Rule 73*, Case No. IT-96-21-AR73, A. Ch., 16 Dec. 1997.

[48]Id., para. 6.

[49]Id.

[50]Id., pp. 4–7.

[51]*Prosecutor v. Delalić and Others, Decision on Application of Defendant Zejnil Delalić for Leave to Appeal against the Oral Decision of the Trial Chamber of 12 January 1998 Requiring Advance Disclosure of Witnesses by the Defence*, Case No. IT-96-21-AR73.3, A. Ch., 3 March 1998.

[52]Rule 54 and sub-Rule 67(A).

[53]Supra footnote 51 at para. 14.

[54]*Prosecutor v. Kovačević, Decision on Application for Leave to Appeal by the Prosecution*, Case No. IT-97-24-AR73, A. Ch., 22 Apr. 1998.

initial appearance of an accused is an *ex parte* or *inter partes* proceeding;[55] equality of arms and the right to a fair trial for both the Prosecution and the Defence;[56] interpretation of the Rules governing the conduct of proceedings during the illness of a Judge;[57] once a Trial Chamber orders that oral arguments will be heard on a pending matter can it then issue a decision solely on the basis of the written submissions;[58] the admission of a statement from a deceased person;[59] and the ambit of a Trial Chamber's authority in admitting affidavit evidence.[60]

Since the introduction of an appeal process for decisions on other motions in November 1997, 27 applications for leave to appeal have been filed under Rule 73.[61] Of these, eight have been granted leave, 17 have been rejected and two withdrawn. This jurisprudence suggests that it is more difficult for an appellant to successfully argue an application under the first test of Rule 73 than the second. Of the seven successful applications under the second test, four have been granted leave for having raised issues of general importance to proceedings before the Tribunal only. None, however, have been granted leave for raising only an issue of general importance in international law generally.[62] Finally, although an issue may be considered

---

[55] *Prosecutor v. Kovačević, Decision on Defense's Request for Leave to Appeal Trial Chamber Decision of 3 July 1998*, Case No. IT-97-24-AR73(B).2, A. Ch., 14 July 1998.

[56] *Prosecutor v. Aleksovski, Decision on Application of the Prosecution for Leave to Appeal: (1) the Trial Chamber's Decision to Admit Further Defence Evidence; and (2) the Trial Chamber's Decision to Deny the Prosecutor's Motion to Admit Further Evidence in Reply*, Case No. IT-95-14/1-AR73, A. Ch., 18 Dec. 1998.

[57] *Prosecutor v. Kupreškić and Others, Decision on Request of the Defence Counsel for Dragan Papić for Leave to Appeal against the Oral Decision dated 24 February 1999*, Case No. IT-95-16-AR73.3, A. Ch., 12 March 1999.

[58] *Prosecutor v. Simić and Others, Decision on Application by Mirslav Tadić for Leave to Appeal against Decision on Provisional Release*, Case No. IT-95-9-AR73, A. Ch., 8 June 1999.

[59] *Prosecutor v. Kordić and Čerkez, Decision on Application for Leave to Appeal and Scheduling Order*, Case No. IT-95-14/2-AR73.5, A. Ch., 28 March 2000.

[60] *Prosecutor v. Kordić and Čerkez, Decision on Application for Leave to Appeal and on Request for Leave to File a Supplementary Response*, Case No. IT-95-14/2-AR73.6, A. Ch., 28 Apr. 2000.

[61] As at 8 June 2000.

[62] See *Prosecutor v. Kovačević, Decision on Defense's Request for Leave to Appeal Trial Chamber Decision of 3 July 1998*, Case No. IT-97-24-AR73(B).2, A. Ch., 14 July 1998; *Prosecutor v. Aleksovski, Decision on Application of the Prosecution for Leave to Appeal: (1) the Trial Chamber's Decision to Admit Further Defence Evidence; and (2) the Trial Chamber's Decision to Deny the Prosecutor's Motion to Admit Further Evidence in Reply*, Case No. IT-95-14/1-AR73, A. Ch., 18 Dec. 1998; *Prosecutor v. Kupreškić and Others, Decision on Request of the Defence Counsel for Dragan Papić for Leave to Appeal against the Oral Decision dated 24 February 1999*, Case No. IT-95-16-AR73.3, A. Ch., 12 March 1999; and *Prosecutor v. Simić and Others, Decision on Application by Mirslav Tadić for Leave to Appeal against Decision on Provisional Release*, Case No. IT-95-9-AR73, A. Ch., 8 June 1999. The three other decisions were held to raise either an issue of general importance to proceedings before the Tribunal or in international law generally.

of general importance, if there is no error demonstrated on the part of the Trial Chamber then the application will fail.

4.5 State Requests for Review

There have been only two applications under Rule 108*bis* by a state (in both instances Croatia) requesting the review of a decision of a Trial Chamber. In both applications, the Appeals Chamber first determined that Croatia was directly affected by the decisions. In the first application, the Appeals Chamber held that whether the Tribunal has the power to subpoena States and high officials of States was an issue "of general importance relating to the powers of the Tribunal".[63] In the second application, "questions regarding the meaning and intent of Article 29 of the Statute" of the Tribunal, was similarly held to be an issue of general importance relating to the powers of the Tribunal.[64]

5. CONCLUSION

Criminal appeal processes in domestic legal systems have developed over hundreds of years. The ICTY is the first international criminal court established since the war crimes tribunals of the Second World War and has the first ever international criminal appeal court. It has been functioning for a little over six years. Yet in that short period of time, its appeals process has become fully operational developing both an effective and fair system for dealing with interlocutory appeals, and a solid body of jurisprudence. The

[63]*Prosecutor v. Blaškić, Decision on the Admissibility of the Request for Review by the Republic of Croatia of an Interlocutory Decision of a Trial Chamber (Issuance of Subpoenae Duces Tecum) and Scheduling Order*, Case No. IT-95-14-AR108*bis*, A. Ch., 29 July 1997 at para. 13.

[64]*Prosecutor v. Kordić and Čerkez, Order on Admissibility of State Request for Review of Order to the Republic of Croatia for the Production of Documents Issued by Trial Chamber III on 4 February 1999 and Request for Suspension of Execution of Order*, Case No. IT-95-14/2-AR108*bis*, A. Ch., 26 March 1999.

Appeals Chamber has been able to safeguard the rights of the accused and the interests of justice by striking a balance between interlocutory decisions that need to be finally resolved during the pre-trial and trial proceedings, and those which can be left for resolution during the final appeal from judgement. The Tribunal's appeals regime is a harbinger to that which has been established for the permanent International Criminal Court under the Rome Statute.[65] The Tribunal's interlocutory appeal decisions will form an important part of the jurisprudence for the International Criminal Court to consider when it becomes operational.

---

[65]The Statute of the International Criminal Court was adopted at Rome on 17 July 1998 ("Rome Statute"). Although there are procedural differences, the Rome Statute provides for appeals from similar interlocutory decisions to those before the ICTY, such as appeals from decisions with respect to jurisdiction and applications for provisional release (Rome Statute Article 82(1)). The Rome Statute also allows for appeals from a "decision that involves an issue that would significantly affect the fair and expeditious conduct of the proceedings or the outcome of the trial" (Rome Statute Article 82(1)(d)). Although, there is no requirement for leave to appeal, such an application requires first that the pre-trial or trial chamber concerned be of the opinion that its "immediate resolution by the Appeals Chamber may materially advance the proceedings" (Rome Statute Article 82(1)(d)).

RAFAEL NIETO-NAVIA and BARBARA ROCHE*

35. The Ambit of the Powers under Article 25 of the ICTY Statute: Three Issues of Recent Interest

1. Introduction

According to Article 25 of the ICTY Statute:[1]

1. The Appeals Chamber shall hear appeals from persons convicted by the Trial Chambers or from the Prosecutor on the following grounds:
   (a) an error on a question of law invalidating the decision; or
   (b) an error of fact which has occasioned a miscarriage of justice.
2. The Appeals Chamber may affirm, reverse or revise the decisions taken by the Trial Chambers.

This Article provides for appeals by both parties to the Appeals Chamber on questions of law and fact. This should entail on a plain reading of the Statute[2] that a convicted person could appeal against conviction, the Prosecution could appeal against an acquittal and both could appeal against sentence. To complete the process, the Appeals Chamber, in considering an appeal, is

*Judge and Associate Legal Officer respectively, of the ICTY. The views expressed herein are those of the authors and do not represent the views of the ICTY, ICTR or the United Nations.

[1]ICTR Statute Art. 24 mirrors the terms of ICTY Statute Art. 25.

[2]See Vienna Convention on the Law of Treaties, 1155 U.N.T.S. 331 (23 May 1969) at Art. 31.1: "A treaty shall be interpreted in good faith in accordance with the ordinary meaning to be given to the terms of the treaty in their context and in the light of its object and purpose". In the case of *Prosecutor v. Tadić, Decision on the Prosecutor's Motion Requesting Protective Measures for Victims and Witnesses*, Case No. IT-94-1-T, 10 Aug. 1995 at para. 18, the Trial Chamber found that "[a]lthough the Statute of the International Tribunal is a *sui generis* legal instrument and not a treaty, in interpreting its provisions and the drafters' conception of the applicability of the jurisprudence of other courts, the rules of treaty interpretation contained in the Vienna Convention on the Law of Treaties appear relevant".

R. May et al., Essays on ICTY Procedure and Evidence in Honour of Gabrielle Kirk McDonald, 473–494.

accorded broad powers to make an immediate decision on the merits and either "affirm, reverse, or revise" the Trial Chamber decision.

It is the case to date, in the history of the ICTY and the ICTR, that both the Prosecution and Defence have filed appeals against decisions rendered by a Trial Chamber, alleging errors on both questions of law and fact.[3] These appeals continue to raise interesting issues for consideration by the Appeals Chamber as is particularly evident in the most recent jurisprudence seen to emerge. We shall however see this pattern continue in the months to come and it is our intention to consider in this paper, three issues of recent interest. In doing so, for practical purposes, we will divide our analysis into three main sections:

Prosecution appeals against acquittals;
The right of an acquitted person to 'appeal against an acquittal'; and
The doctrine of *Stare Decisis*.

2. Prosecution Appeals against Acquittals

As stated, the Prosecution and the Defence have filed appeals following final judgement of a Trial Chamber, on questions of both fact and law. In light of the principle of *non bis in idem*, which provides that a person "shall not be twice tried for the same crime",[4] it would appear on the face of it, that despite the fact that the Statutes of both the ICTY and ICTR provide an express right of appeal to the Prosecution; nevertheless, Prosecution appeals against acquittals, may be in contravention of this legal doctrine.

The principle is in its origins based on a civil law doctrine, with the corresponding common law principle of double jeopardy protecting the accused from being twice put in jeopardy for the same offence. In this paper, we will discuss to what extent (if any) the provisions of ICTY Statute Article 25 may violate a doctrine, which it has been said was:

> designed to prevent the state from repeatedly subjecting a person to prosecution for offences arising out of the same event until the desired results are achieved. It derives from a sense of fairness and can be analogised to the civil law concept of *res judicata*.[5]

---

[3]Indeed, contrary to the plain interpretation of the provision, recently more unusual steps have been taken in certain cases before the ICTY, which attempt to persuade the Appeals Chamber to interpret the ICTY Statute and Rules in a manner which takes them beyond their plain meaning. These cases will be explored below.

[4]Blacks Law Dictionary (1990) at p. 1051.

[5]M. Cherif Bassiouni, "Human Rights in the Context of Criminal Justice: Identifying International Procedural Protections and Equivalent Protections in National Constitutions", 3 Duke Journal of Comparative and International Law (1993), 235 at p. 288.

In considering this issue, a starting point must be to analyse if it can be said that there exists a general principle of law recognised by civilised nations,[6] or a general rule of law,[7] which provides that the Prosecution can or cannot appeal against an acquittal. If it can be said that there is such a principle, are ICTY Statute Article 25 and ICTR Statute Article 24 consistent with this principle?

There is no detailed analysis of the right of the Prosecution to appeal against an acquittal in either the Secretary-General's Report on the ICTY Statute[8] nor in that on the ICTR Statute,[9] the former simply stating that:

---

[6]As a source of international law as provided in Art. 38 (1)(c) of the Statute of the International Court of Justice, ICJ Acts and Documents, No. 5: "1. The Court, whose function is to decide in accordance with international law such disputes as are submitted to it, shall apply: [...] (c) the general principles of law recognised by civilised nations; [...]" In the Appeals Chamber decision of 7 Oct. 1997, it was affirmed that "[t]he sources of international law are generally considered to be exhaustively listed in Article 38 of the Statute of the International Court of Justice". *Prosecutor v. Erdemović, Judgement, Joint Separate Opinion of Judge McDonald and Judge Vohrah*, Case No. IT-96-22-A, A. Ch., 7 Oct. 1997 at para. 40. International jurisprudence, mainly of the PCIJ, the ICJ and the PCA, does not "define" general principles of law. However, as it is possible to infer from some decisions and separate or dissenting opinions, general principles of law are those which are commonly recognised (constituting a common denominator) by the laws of civilised nations as binding in *foro domestico*, reference being made to Art. 38 aforesaid. See *Reservations to the Convention on the Prevention and Punishment of the Crime of Genocide, Advisory Opinion*, 1951 ICJ Reports 15 at p. 23. See also *South-West Africa Cases*, 1966 ICJ Reports at p. 298 (Dissenting Opinion by Judge Tanaka); *Interpretation of Judgements Nos. 7 and 8 (the Chorzów factory)*, PCIJ Series A, No. 13 at p. 27 (Dissenting Opinion by M. Anzilotti); *The Diversion of the Water from the Meuse*, PCIJ Series A/B, No. 70 at p. 50 (Dissenting Opinion by M. Anzilotti); *Lighthouses in Crete and Samos*, PCIJ Series A/B, No. 71 at pp. 137–138 (Separate Opinion by M. Séfériadès); *International Status of South-West Africa*, 1950 ICJ Reports 128 at p. 148 (Separate Opinion of Sir Arnold McNair); *Voting Procedure on Questions Relating to Reports and Petitions Concerning the Territory of South-West Afrcia* 1955 ICJ Reports 67 at p. 105 (Separate Opinion of Judge Lauterpacht); *Case Concerning the Temple of Preah Vitear*, 1962 ICJ Reports 6 at pp. 42–43 (Separate Opinion of Vice-President Alfaro); *South West Africa Cases*, 1962 ICJ Reports 319 at p. 510 (Joint Dissenting Opinion of Sir Perry Spender and Sir Gerald Fitzmaurice); *North Sea Continental Shelf Cases*, 1969 ICJ Reports, p. 4 at p. 134 (Separate Opinion of Judge Fouad Ammoun). Authors agree with the same idea: See H. Lauterpacht, Private Law Sources and Analogies of International Law (1927) at p. 71; P. Guggenheim, "Contribution à l'Histoire des Sources du Droit des Gens, Recueil des Cours" 1958, II, at p. 78. Also see B. Cheng, General Principles of Law as Applied by International Courts and Tribunals (1987) at pp. 24 and 25.

[7]While general principles of law are "maxims of law" as defined by Lord Phillimore (PCIJ, Advisory Committee of Jurists, *Procès-verbaux of the Proceedings of the Committee, June 16–July 24 1920 with Annexes*, The Hague, 1920 at p. 335), rules are essentially practical.

[8]Report of the Secretary-General pursuant to paragraph 2 of Security Council Resolution 808 (1993) (S/25704).

[9]Report of the Secretary-General pursuant to paragraph. 5 of Security Council Resolution 955 (1994) (S/1995/134).

116. The Secretary-General is of the view that the right of appeal should be provided for under the Statute. Such a right is a fundamental element of individual civil and political rights and has, inter alia, been incorporated in the International Covenant on Civil and Political Rights. For this reason, the Secretary-General has proposed that there should be an Appeals Chamber.

117. The right of appeal should be exercisable on two grounds: an error on a question of law invalidating the decision or, an error of fact which has occasioned a miscarriage of justice. The *Prosecutor should also be entitled to initiate appeal proceedings on the same grounds.*[10]

2.1 International recognition of the right of appeal

International conventions and agreements on this issue vary, although it must be acknowledged that international opinion has indeed developed considerably over the years. The right of appeal *per se*, is a well-settled human right in domestic legislation and as such, is recognised in both international and regional human rights treaties. However, despite this generalisation, the nature and extent of the right accorded both on the national level (which will be considered below) and internationally, continues to vary. In terms of the latter, one can turn to several human rights conventions for guidance. E.g., although Article 14(5) of the United Nations International Covenant on Civil and Political Rights (1966) ("ICCPR")[11] provides that "[e]veryone convicted of a crime shall have the right to his conviction and sentence being reviewed by a higher court according to law", this right is clearly only accorded to the convicted person and hence the Prosecution have no recourse should they wish to appeal against an acquittal. Similarly, Article 2 of Protocol No. 7 to the European Convention[12] provides, *inter alia*: "Everyone convicted of a criminal offence by a tribunal shall have the right to have his conviction or sentence reviewed by a higher tribunal". Finally, Article 8 (2)(h) of the American Convention[13] is limited to according a "right to appeal the judgement to a higher court" solely to the accused, as is Article 7(a) of the African Charter on Human and People's Rights.[14]

However, until now, no international tribunal has recognised the right of a party to appeal against their decisions. The International Military Tribunals at Nuremberg and Tokyo, the courts established to prosecute the major war criminals after the Second World War, (being criminal tribunals similar to

[10]Supra note 8 at paras. 116 and 117 (emphasis added).

[11]999 UNTS 171 (16 Dec. 1966).

[12]Protocol No. 7 to the Convention for the Protection of Human Rights and Fundamental Freedoms ("European Convention") was adopted in Strasbourg on 22 Nov. 1984.

[13]The American Convention on Human Rights ("American Convention") was adopted at the Inter-American Specialised Conference on Human Rights, San José, Costa Rica, 22 Nov. 1969.

[14]The African Charter on Human and People's Rights was adopted at the 18th Conference of Heads of State and Government, Nairobi, Kenya on 27 June 1981.

the ICTY and ICTR), provided no right of appeal against conviction or acquittal for either the Prosecution or the Defence (convicted or acquitted person).[15] Similarly, the judgements of the International Court of Justice, are "final and without appeal",[16] while analogous provisions appear in the legislation promulgated to govern some of the other main international tribunals.[17] Nevertheless, both the ICTY and ICTR Statutes expressly provide the Prosecution with a right of appeal and this precedent has been followed in the Rome Statute, pursuant to Article 81.[18]

2.2 Domestic recognition

It now falls to consider if it can be said that there is a general principle or a rule of law according a right of appeal, ascertainable through a survey of the general practice of national domestic systems. On review, it is clear that generally in domestic systems a right of appeal to a higher court against decisions rendered, has been accorded. However, it is also apparent that there is a clear dichotomy in the practice of the main legal systems of the world, between those, which clearly accord a right of appeal against acquittals to the Prosecution, and those which do not. It can also be said that these systems may be generally divided into those, which may be classified as common law jurisdictions on the one hand, and those, which may be classified as civil law jurisdictions on the other hand.

2.2.1 Common law jurisdictions

In the United States, the Supreme Court has interpreted the double jeopardy clause of the Fifth Amendment of the Constitution[19] to mean that

---

[15]Art. 17 of the Charter of the International Military Tribunal for the Far East, Tokyo, 19 January 1946 and Art. 26 of the Charter of the International Military Tribunal at Nuremberg, Germany, 8 Aug. 1945, the latter providing that its decisions were final and not subject to review. Therefore neither party had a right of appeal against a decision rendered.

[16]ICJ Statute, Art. 60. It should however be noted that this Statute does provide for a right of review of a judgement on the emergence of a fact of a decisive nature, which was, when the judgement was given, unknown to the Court and also to the party claiming revision, provided this ignorance was not due to negligence (Art. 61(1)).

[17]See Art. 67 of the American Convention, Art. 52 of the European Convention and Art. 33.1 of the Statute of the International Tribunal for the Law of the Sea, Annex VI to the United Nations Convention on the Law of the Sea, adopted on 10 Dec. 1982. These provisions determine that the decisions of the respective tribunals are final, there being no right of appeal, while at the same time providing for the right for either party to apply for interpretation of the judgement rendered.

[18]Rome Statute of the International Criminal Court, PCNICC/1999/INF/3 (adopted at Rome on 17 July 1998). It should be noted that the exact terms of this article, during the preparatory phases, was the subject of much deliberation. See e.g.: Report of the Preparatory Committee on the Establishment of an International Criminal Court, (Proceedings of the Preparatory Committee during March–April and August 1996): General Assembly Official Records, 51st Session Supp No 22 (A/51/22) at para. 295.

[19]The Fifth Amendment of the United States Constitution reads: "nor shall any person be subject for the same offence to be twice put in jeopardy of life or limb".

the Prosecution cannot appeal against a verdict, whether on an error on a question of law or fact.[20] This finality accorded to criminal judgements has been interpreted as being intended to protect the acquitted or convicted person against "Prosecution oppression". On the other hand, double jeopardy does not bar the convicted person from appealing because he or she personally chooses to put him or herself at risk once more.

Similarly, in the United Kingdom the application of the double jeopardy principle precludes the Prosecution from appealing against acquittals[21] save in two cases: where the appeal challenges an acquittal tainted by bribery, threats or other interference with a witness or juror;[22] or, where the appeal is from an acquittal in the Magistrates' Court by way of case stated to the Divisional Court of the Queen's Bench Division on the grounds that it was rendered in error of law or alternatively, in excess of jurisdiction.[23]

Although very rarely employed, a further protection offered in the United Kingdom to an accused protecting against ongoing jeopardy and repeated prosecution for the same offence, are what have become known as the pleas of *autrefois acquit and autrefois convict*, together with the plea of pardon. Essentially referred to as pleas in bar, they bar any further proceedings on an indictment. They are in fact rarely required, as it is generally accepted that the Prosecution will not commence proceedings if they are aware that a person has already been acquitted or convicted of the proposed offence. The leading authority in this regard is that of *Connelly v. DPP*,[24] wherein Lord Morris of Borth-y-gest is generally treated as laying down the nine propositions which form the foundation of the modern law, including the main

---

[20]See *United States v. DiFrancesco*, 449 U.S. 117 (1980); *Sanabria v. United States*, 437 U.S. 54 (1978); *Green v. United States*, 355 U.S. 184 (1957); *Kepner v. United States*, 195 U.S. 100 (1904). In the latter case however, it should be noted that Justice Holmes, dissenting, advocated the adoption of the concept of "continuing jeopardy", a concept familiar to the German civil law tradition (infra). He argued that "a man cannot be said to be more than once in jeopardy on the same cause however often he may be tried. The jeopardy is one continuing jeopardy from its beginning to the end of the cause". The majority, however, rejected this argument and concluded that the verdict at trial terminated the initial jeopardy.

[21]Section 1 Criminal Appeals Act 1968 provides for the right of appeal of a convicted person who may appeal to the Court of Appeal against his conviction. See, Archbold 2000 at para. 7–36.

[22]Section 54 Criminal Procedure and Investigations Act 1996. See, Archbold 2000 at para. 4–128a.

[23]Section 111(1) of the Magistrates' Courts Act 1980 provides that "Any person who was a party to any proceeding before a magistrates' court or is aggrieved by the conviction, order, determination, or other proceeding of the court may question the proceeding on the ground that it is wrong in law or is in excess of jurisdiction by applying to the [magistrates] to state a case for the opinion of the High Court on the question of law or jurisdiction involved". Most appeals by way of case stated are aimed at overturning either a summary conviction or a summary acquittal. See, Archbold 2000 at para. 2–174.

[24]Connelly v. DPP [1964] A.C. 1254, HL.

tenet that a man may not be tried for a crime in respect of which he has previously been acquitted or convicted.[25]

Recent moves have been made in the United Kingdom to propose legislation which in limited circumstances, would permit a second prosecution following acquittal. These circumstances would be solely in case of serious offences (presumably defined), when substantial new evidence emerges which could not have been discovered or was not available before but which would have had a decisive effect on the original decision reached so that conviction is likely.[26] The current position is that if a person is found not guilty or a case is not proven, under the principle of double jeopardy, the acquitted person cannot be re-charged with the offence. The concern is that this blanket prohibition fails to account for situations whereby substantial new evidence could arise in the future. If such were the case, why not re-try?[27] This would however, remove the very clear sense of finality and certainty, which currently underlies the legal position.

It should also be noted, that in the United Kingdom, similar to the provision in Australia,[28] the Attorney General has the right to refer a point of law to the Court of Appeal following an acquittal for an opinion on that point of law.[29] However, if the Attorney General makes such a referral, this will not affect the trial in relation to which reference was made or any acquittal in that trial and is used rather for future purposes.[30]

In South Africa, the Prosecution cannot appeal against an acquittal on the facts. However, the Attorney General does have the right to ask the trial court to state a case to the Court of Appeal if the decision was given by the trial court in favour of the accused on a question of law.[31]

In Australia, the Prosecution has no right of appeal against a jury's verdict of acquittal. If the accused is however convicted by the jury and this is reversed by an Appellate Court, then it is open to the Prosecution to seek an appeal against that decision to the High Court of Australia. The

---

[25]Archbold 2000 at paras. 4–116 et seq.

[26]On 25 Jan. 2000 a joint proposal was due to be put to the Commons Home Affairs Commission by the Crown Prosecution Service (CPS) and the police. This proposal was largely provoked by the public condemnation following the handling of the Stephen Lawrence affair when four youths were acquitted of murder in circumstances where the general public opinion was that they were guilty of the offence.

[27]E.g., in the case of sexual offences as scientific skills increase and improve, DNA testing looks closer and at smaller samples. The thinking is that one should be able to take advantage of these significant improvements.

[28]Infra.

[29]Section 36(1) Criminal Justice Act 1972: "Where a person tried on indictment has been acquitted (whether in respect of the whole or part of the indictment) the Attorney General may, if he desires the opinion of the Court of Appeal on a point of law which has arisen in the case, refer that point to the court, and the court shall, in accordance with this section, consider the point and give their opinion on it." See Archbold 2000, at paras. 7–296 to 7–298.

[30]Id., Section 36(7).

[31]Section 310, Criminal Procedure Act 51 of 1977.

Prosecution may also refer any point of law, which arose during the case to the full Court of Appeal for its opinion.[32] Although this is heard in the form of a normal appeal, the decision given is simply for future purposes. It has no effect on the accused's acquittal and is therefore known as an "academic appeal".[33] It should be noted that Australia also provides additional protection with similar pleas to those in the United Kingdom, of *autrefois acquit* and *autrefois convict*.

Thus it seems that the common law gives special weight to acquittals. In the United Kingdom the Prosecution does not have the right to appeal against an acquittal, save for appeals permitted in certain very limited and clearly circumscribed instances. In the United States there is a complete bar on appeals against acquittals.[34]

2.2.2 Civil law jurisdictions

In the civil law tradition, generally appeals against decisions made at first instance are permitted for both parties although decisions rendered by the second-tier courts can be appealed by way of *cassation* only on errors of law.

In France in particular,[35] criminal procedure is rather distinct to that found in common law traditions. Criminal legal proceedings generally commence by alerting the Prosecutor ("*Ministère Public*") of the commission of a crime.[36] The *Ministère Public* considers whether or not to commence an investigation and, if it decides in the affirmative,[37] will refer the case to the *Juge d'Instruction* who will commence investigation proper of the crime and consider whether or not there is a case to answer.[38] This constitutes the first level of proceedings. The file can be subject to a second review by the *Chambre d'Accusation*,[39] before being finally forwarded to the *Cour d'Assises* for trial.[40] There is no right of appeal as such from decisions rendered before the second tier criminal courts in France. However, decisions can be appealed by way of "*Pourvoi en Cassation*". Both parties have the right to file a *pourvoi* on points of law only and the motion is heard before the *Chambre Criminelle de la Cour de Cassation*. If it quashes all or part of the previous decision, the case is returned to another *Cour d'Assises* for a final decision on the case.[41]

---

[32]Section 450A, Crimes Act 1958 (Vic), Section 5A, Criminal Appeal Act 1912 (NSW), ss 350–1, Criminal Law Consolidation Act 1935 (SA) .

[33]Waller and Williams, Criminal Law Text and Materials (1997).

[34]See however, supra note 20 for the dissenting opinion of Justice Holmes in *Kepner v. United States*.

[35]Generally considered as the model civil law tradition.

[36]Art. 19 of the Code de Procédure Pénale (CPP).

[37]Id., Art. 40.

[38]Id., Arts. 49, 51 and 80.

[39]Id., Arts. 191 et seq.

[40]Id., Art. 214.

[41]Id., Arts. 567 et seq.

In Germany, Prosecution appeals against acquittals are not considered to violate the principle of *non bis in idem*, because the judgement at trial is not seen to constitute the end of the criminal proceedings.[42] It seems that in the German legal system jeopardy attaches with the criminal charge and continues throughout the duration of all proceedings that arise from the original charge. Hence a Prosecution appeal from acquittal is seen as another step in the criminal proceedings.

In Belgium, according to Article 202 of the *Code d'Instruction Criminelle*,[43] the right of appeal belongs to both the convicted person and the Prosecution, while in Denmark, although the issue has been the subject of recent debate,[44] currently a lower court judgement may be appealed to the High Court by both parties on all questions without exception,[45] i.e. on questions of formality, fact, law or sentence.

2.3 General principle or rule of law?

Following this short survey, it can be said that it is quite clear that one cannot draw a general principle or rule of law from either domestic or international law in relation to the right (or prohibition) of the Prosecution to appeal against an acquittal. There is no common denominator or clear thread and the rules and legislation adopted in each domestic jurisdiction considered are largely inconsistent. Unlike the Anglo-American common law system, the civil law system does not construe Prosecution appeals against acquittals to compromise the principle of *non bis in idem*.

In light of this, it appears that it can also be concluded that Articles 25 and 24 of the ICTY and ICTR Statutes respectively and indeed Article 81 of the Rome Statute, each of which provide for the right of appeal by the Prosecution against an acquittal, reflect a civil law tradition rather than a common law tradition. The rationale which underpins the common law's vigorous approach to protect against double jeopardy (the desire to prevent a government, possessed of vast superior resources and power, from abusing its power to prosecute persons by re-prosecuting them until it manages to obtain a conviction), is absent in the context of prosecutions before both the ICTY and ICTR and indeed those which will soon take place before the International Criminal Court. Before these Tribunals, although admittedly the Prosecution does prosecute on behalf of the international community, similar resources to those which are abundant within national jurisdictions

[42] SS 312 and 333 of the German Criminal Code.

[43] Art. 202 of the *Code d'Instruction Criminelle*, 17 Apr. 1878, original title being *Code de Procédure Pénale* (M.B. 25.IV.1878).

[44] Recent debate has been taking place on the possible abolition of the right currently held by the Prosecutor to file an appeal against an acquittal. It also appears that the Prosecution in practice do not often exercise their right of appeal and that only one in ten appeals originate from them. See, Lars Bo Langsted, Peter Garde and Vagn Greve, "Denmark", in International Encyclopaedia of Laws (1998), Volume 2, at pp. 190 et seq.

[45] Section 963, Administration of Justice Act 1916 (in force from 1919).

are not available. It must rely, together with the Defence, on the resources of the United Nations and therefore the risk in every case of repeated prosecution following appeals against acquittals cannot arise.

2.4 Examination of the right before the ICTY

It has been seen that the governing legislation of both Tribunals provides for appeals against acquittals by the Prosecution. Such appeals have been filed by the Prosecution for both the ICTY and ICTR in several cases to date, including in the first final decision rendered by the Appeals Chamber on an appeal from a final judgement of a Trial Chamber, in the case of *Tadić*.[46] In this case, the Defendant had been found guilty by the Trial Chamber on nine counts on the Indictment, guilty in part on two counts and not guilty on twenty counts.[47] The Prosecution appealed against the acquittals and by decision of 15 July 1999, the Appeals Chamber allowed the appeal in part. In doing so, it reversed the Trial Chamber's findings of acquittal on nine counts and immediately substituted its own verdict, finding the Defendant guilty. The matter was returned to the Trial Chamber for sentence. On 11 November 1999 the Trial Chamber increased the sentence originally imposed from the original range of 6 to 20 years' imprisonment, to 6 to 25 years' imprisonment. This sentence was appealed and thereafter revised by the Appeals Chamber on 26 January 2000,[48] returning it to a maximum of 20 years imprisonment.

Nevertheless, such a finding could sit uncomfortably for many jurists who may have difficulty in accepting the resulting 'jeopardy' to the Defendant. It would appear to some that the apparent ease by which the Appeals Chamber may substitute their verdict for a Trial Chamber decision of acquittal, directly contravenes a principle which is designed to protect a person who has already been subjected to a lengthy trial. Of course in these cases the Appeals Chamber must apply appropriate standards of review in reaching a decision to substitute their own verdict. Indeed as it pointed out:

> The task of hearing, assessing and weighing the evidence presented at trial is left to the Judges sitting in a Trial Chamber. Therefore, the Appeals Chamber must give a margin of deference to a finding of fact reached by a Trial Chamber. It is only where the evidence relied on by the Trial Chamber could not reasonably have been accepted by any reasonable person that the Appeals Chamber can substitute its own finding for that of the Trial Chamber.[49]

[46] *Prosecutor v. Tadić, Judgement*, Case No. IT-94-1-A, A. Ch., 15 July 1999 ("*Tadić Appeals Chamber Judgement*"). Previous to this, the Appeals Chamber had rendered only one other final decision in the case of *Prosecutor v. Erdemović, Judgement*, Case No. IT-96-22-A, 7 Oct. 1997, wherein the accused had entered a guilty plea to one count.

[47] *Prosecutor v. Tadić, Opinion and Judgment,* Case No. IT-94-1-T, 7 May 1997.

[48] *Prosecutor v. Tadić, Judgement in Sentencing Appeals*, Case No. IT-94-1-A and IT-94-1-A*bis*, A. Ch., 26 Jan. 2000.

[49] *Tadić Appeals Chamber Judgement* at para. 64.

Nevertheless, the power accorded pursuant to ICTY Statute Article 25 is broad and allows for changes, which can substantially alter a Defendant's position.

These changes are most apparent in the area of sentencing. The risk of sentence being increased following such an appeal became a live issue in the case under discussion and indeed at this stage a separate Declaration highlighting the point was appended to the *Tadić Appeals Chamber Judgement* which *inter alia*, initially reversed the acquittals.[50] However, the Appeals Chamber did not consider the issue in depth in its reasoning in either this decision nor indeed in the subsequent decision on sentence,[51] despite the fact that it reinstated the original sentence imposed. The justification for doing so, was rather, substantive considering the nature of the charges involved and the Appellant's relative position in the hierarchy during the war:

> In the opinion of the Appeals Chamber, the Trial Chamber's decision, when considered against the background of the jurisprudence of the International Tribunal [...] fails to adequately consider the need for sentences to reflect the relative significance of the role of the Appellant in the broader context of the conflict in the former Yugoslavia. Although the criminal conduct underlying the charges of which the Appellant now stands convicted was incontestably heinous, his level in the command structure, when compared to that of his superiors, i.e. commanders, or the very architects of the strategy of ethnic cleansing, was low. In the circumstances of the case, the Appeals Chamber considers that the sentence of more than 20 years' imprisonment for any count of the Indictment on which the Appellant stands convicted is excessive and cannot stand.[52]

However, to an accused, the final outcome on appeal is clearly of central importance if, e.g., an accused has been acquitted on all charges and in addition has even already been released from custody (this will be considered in greater depth below in the context of the pending case of Zejnil Delalić). Should a Prosecution appeal against an acquittal succeed, the consequences for an accused can be immense, in that they could find themselves immediately convicted of one or more offences on which they had previously been acquitted, the wording of ICTY Statute, Article 25 being that the "Appeals Chamber may affirm reverse or revise the decisions taken by the Trial Chambers". The ultimate (and to the Defendant, most detrimental) consequence is an increased sentence. Hence, as seen above, when finally sentenced by the Trial Chamber, the sentence imposed on Duško Tadić was increased from periods ranging from 6 to 20 years to 6 to 25 years. The implications can be so extreme that it is accordingly felt that this should be

---

[50] *Declaration of Judge Nieto-Navia*, appended to the *Tadić Appeals Chamber Judgement* at p. 146.

[51] Infra.

[52] *Prosecutor v. Tadić, Judgement in Sentencing Appeals*, Case No IT-94-1-A and IT-94-1-A*bis*, A. Ch., 26 Jan. 2000 at paras. 55–57.

an issue actively considered by the Appeals Chamber on sentencing in the event of a reversal of an acquittal.

The recent decision by the Appeals Chamber on 9 February 2000[53] in the case of *Aleksovski* illustrates the consequences to an accused perfectly. By decision of the Trial Chamber on 25 June 1999,[54] Aleksovski had been found not guilty of "Grave Breaches of the Geneva Conventions of 1949" but guilty of "Violations of the laws or customs of war."[55] Although sentenced to two and a half years imprisonment on the same day, having already served more time in custody than the sentence imposed, he was entitled to credit and was released immediately.[56] Following a successful Prosecution appeal,[57] the Appeals Chamber immediately returned him to custody pending a final decision on the sentence to be imposed. This was despite the fact that he had been at liberty for over seven months since the final decision of the Trial Chamber and no decision had yet been taken on the appeal. The Appeals Chamber finally issued its full reasoned decision, including its decision on revision of appropriate sentence, which should be imposed and although it did not reverse the acquittals on the two counts appealed by the Prosecution,[58] in making an additional finding in respect of the Prosecution second ground of appeal, it stated that "the additional finding is, strictly, a matter to be taken into account, when [...] the Appeals Chamber comes to impose a revised sentence upon Count 10."[59] Despite this, it found that the "additional finding makes no difference to the revised sentence [...] [and] does not of itself warrant any heavier sentence than would have been imposed without it."[60]

[53]*Prosecutor v. Aleksovski, Order for Detention on Remand*, Case No. IT-95-14/1-A, A. Ch., 9 Feb. 2000.

[54]*Prosecutor v. Aleksovski, Judgement,* Case No. IT-95-14/1-T, 25 June 1999.

[55]ICTY Statute Arts. 2 and 3 respectively.

[56]ICTY Rule 101(D) provides that "[c]redit shall be given to the convicted person for the period, if any, during which the convicted person was detained in custody pending surrender to the Tribunal or pending trial or appeal".

[57]In fact both parties had appealed against the Trial Chamber written judgement of 25 June 1999. The Prosecution filed its notice of appeal against both the acquittals (seeking a substitution of the findings of not guilty with findings of guilt) and sentence, on 19 May 1999, while the Defendant filed his notice of appeal on 19 May 1999 seeking a reversal of each finding of guilt. The Appeals Chamber denied each of the Defendant's grounds but allowed the Prosecution appeal in part against judgement, although refusing to reverse the acquittals, while also allowing the appeal against sentence.

[58]The Prosecution appealed against acquittals on Counts 8 and 9 of the Indictment and although the Appeals Chamber found that the ground of appeal succeeded to the extent that the Trial Chamber applied the wrong test for determining the nature of the armed conflict and the status of protected persons within the meaning of Art. 2 of the Statute, it found that as the material acts underlying the charges were the same as those for which the Defendant was convicted in Count 10, it would not be appropriate to either reverse the acquittals or increase the sentence. *Prosecutor v. Aleksovski, Judgement*, Case No. IT-95-14/1-A, A. Ch., 24 March 2000 at paras. 153 and 154.

[59]Id., para. 173.

[60]Id., para. 189.

Thus, it became clear that the Appeals Chamber has now begun to recognise the risks to the accused attendant on Prosecution appeals. And although it did revise the sentence imposed on the accused following trial, to one of seven years imprisonment from the day of the decision (subject to deductions for time served in detention), it did so on the basis that the Trial Chamber had erred in not having sufficient regard to the gravity of the accused's conduct. In considering the sentence to be imposed, it specifically stated:

> In imposing a revised sentence the Appeals Chamber bears in mind the element of double jeopardy in this process in that the Appellant has had to appear for sentence twice for the same conduct, suffering the consequent anxiety and distress, and also that he has been detained a second time after a period of release of nine months. Had it not been for these factors the sentence would have been considerably longer.[61]

Hence, the risks involved were apparent and the relevance of the attendant principle of "*reformatio in pejus*" was confirmed.[62] The questions remain however as to whether or not a successful Prosecution appeal should put the subject in a worse position than that in which he found himself at the end of trial.

Several more cases are currently pending before the Appeals Chamber,[63] notably those of *Jelisić* and *Delalić*, and in both cases the Prosecution has continued to utilise the right accorded by ICTY Statute Article 25, filing notices of appeal against, *inter alia*, the acquittals. Zejnil Delalić, one of four charged in the so-called "*Čelebići'*case",[64] was acquitted of all charges faced, by a decision of the Trial Chamber on 16 November 1998.[65] This case in particular raises novel and interesting issues for consideration by the Appeals Chamber, as both parties have in fact now filed notices of appeal.[66] But, particularly, in relation to the appeal by the Prosecution, should it be successful, the consequences for Mr. Delalić, are clearly drastic, entailing conviction and detention for the most serious of offences. The Prosecution has also

---

[61]Id., para. 190 (footnote omitted).

[62]It is thought that the Appeals Chamber should consider and analyse, based on the particular case before it and therefore only if relevant, if at the sentencing stage a successful Prosecution appeal should put the person in a worse position than at the end of the trial ("*reformatio in pejus*")". Supra note 50 at p. 148.

[63]At the time of writing this article, April 2000.

[64]The case acquired this name as allegations concerned offences, which took, place in the detention facility in the village of Čelebići, in central Bosnia and Herzegovina. The other three indictees were Zdravko Mucić, Hazim Delić and Esad Landžo.

[65]*Prosecutor v. Delalić and Others, Judgement,* Case No. IT-96-21-T, 16 Nov. 1998 ("*Čelebicí* Judgement").

[66]Notice of Appeal of the Prosecution against the acquittal was filed on 26 Nov. 1998, with the Prosecution Appeal Brief filed on 2 July 1999. Notice of Cross-Appeal was filed by Zejnil Delalić against the Trial Chamber's Judgement on 1 Dec. 1998, with his Cross Appellant's brief filed on 2 July 1999.

appealed against the acquittal of Goran Jelisić on charges of Genocide, despite the fact that he has already been convicted of 31 other counts and sentenced to a period of 40 years imprisonment.[67] If one considers the precedent established in, particularly the case of *Tadić*, it is clear that the implications of an Appeals Chamber decision to reverse an acquittal were not so marked, given he already stood convicted of many offences and had already been sentenced to serve a substantial period of time in detention. Indeed one could state that the implications of the outcome in the case of *Jelisić* are comparable in that any additional sentence, which may be imposed following appeal, could hardly have an extremely tangible impact on the Defendant. In the case of *Delalić* the situation is quite different. Clearly if the Prosecution appeal succeeds, he will find himself in a position undeniably worse than that in which he found himself at the end of trial. However, if the Prosecution is accorded the right to appeal against an acquittal, as it clearly is, this is surely the inevitable consequence.

If this were not the case, the alternative would be for such appeals to become simply academic exercises, whereby the Prosecution could appeal against an acquittal but solely with a view to obtaining a ruling from the Appeals Chamber on an issue of law, for guidance in future cases. This would fall outside the scope of ICTY Statute Article 25(1), whose intent was for the Appeals Chamber to hear appeals on particular questions of law or errors of fact, following which they would make a decision such that the verdict would be effected. On a plain reading, the Statute does not provide for such 'academic appeals'. Nevertheless, despite this, the Appeals Chamber has in fact already considered such cases and justified doing so on the basis that the questions raised, were "matters of general significance for the Tribunal's jurisprudence" and that it was "therefore appropriate for the Appeals Chamber to set forth its view" on the matter.[68]

However, in any event and as seen, in light of the implications to an accused, the possible impact on sentence, should a Prosecution appeal succeed, should be carefully considered by the Appeals Chamber in its deliberations, as was the case in the aforementioned case of Zlatko Aleksovski.

---

[67] *Prosecutor v. Jelisić, Judgement*, Case No. IT-95-10-T, 14 Dec. 1999. Goran Jelisić also filed a Notice of Cross-Appeal on 26 Oct. 1999, "from (1) the Judgement of the Trial Chamber delivered orally on 19 Oct. 1999; and (2) that certain *PROSECUTION'S NOTICE OF APPEAL*, dated 21 October 1999, should such Notice be deemed to be sufficient".

[68] *Tadić Appeals Chamber Judgement*, paras. 247 and 281. In this matter, the Appeals Chamber acknowledged the fact that the grounds of appeal being considered did not fall within the express terms and scope of the ICTY Statute, Art. 25(1), but nevertheless carried out an in-depth analysis of the issues raised: whether or not a crime against humanity may be committed for purely personal motives and whether or not such crimes require a discriminatory intent.

3. The Right of an Acquitted Person to Appeal Against an Acquittal

As seen above, ICTY Statute, Article 25,[69] expressly provides for a right of appeal by both the Prosecution and the Defendant. One would be forgiven for assuming that such a right, in normal circumstances, would entail a Defendant (convicted person) appealing against conviction and the Prosecution appealing against an acquittal. Indeed the wording of the Statute is clear. In reality, however, it appears that recently the Appeals Chamber has been requested to extend the scope of this right and permit the Defendant to effectively appeal or cross-appeal an acquittal, thereby exceeding the plain meaning of the provision.

In the case of *Jelisić*, the issue was specifically highlighted for consideration by a Prosecution motion seeking clarification of the right of the Appellant, to file a specific notice of appeal against his acquittal.[70] It therefore fell to the Appeals Chamber to consider whether or not it is indeed appropriate for an acquitted person to utilise this facility and file such an appeal against his acquittal; whether a person acquitted of a crime, in fact has *locus standi* to do so.[71] The thinking behind such appeals would appear to be that it is taken as a precautionary measure to ensure that the Appeals Chamber is fully apprised of the surrounding circumstances and facts of the case which may not have been raised as part of the Prosecution appeal. This would ensure that the Appeals Chamber, in reaching a decision, is not confined to the issue(s) raised by the Prosecution but on the contrary has the benefit of knowledge of surrounding issues which may be crucial in the final consideration.

---

[69]ICTY Statute Art. 24.

[70]In this case, the Trial Chamber had returned a mixed verdict, unanimously finding the accused not guilty of genocide but guilty of 31 counts of "violations of the laws or customs of war" and "crimes against humanity" (ICTY Statute, Arts. 4, 3 and 5(a) respectively), following a guilty plea by the Appellant. The Appellant first indicated his intention to enter a guilty plea to the 31 counts prior to the amendment of the indictment by the Prosecution on 19 Oct. 1998. On 29 Oct. 1998 he confirmed that this guilty plea was to be retained in accordance with the Agreed Factual Basis of 9 Sept. 1998. Pursuant to Rule 73 of the Rules of Procedure and Evidence, the Prosecution filed the Prosecution Motion for Clarification of the Right of the Appellant Goran Jelisić to File two Notices of Appeal And for a Scheduling Order in Relation to the Appeal, filed on 20 Dec. 1999, in which the Prosecution challenged the right of the Defendant to appeal against his acquittal on the count of genocide.

[71]The procedure to be followed on appeal is set down in Part Seven of the ICTY Rules: "Appellate Proceedings". Rule 108 provides that both parties shall file notices of appeal within fifteen days from the date of pronouncement of judgement. Rule 111 provides that the Appellant's brief of argument shall be filed within ninety days of filing of the notice of appeal, Rule 112 provides that the Respondent's brief of argument shall be filed within thirty days of filing of the Appellant's brief and Rule 113 provides that the Appellant's brief in reply shall be filed within fifteen days after filing of the Respondent's brief.

Both parties made submissions as to the interpretation to be taken.[72] The Appellant in particular submitting that as the Appeals Chamber had the power to overturn an acquittal and substitute a verdict of conviction,[73] an appellant should "as a matter, at the very least, of natural justice, have the right to challenge the legal and factual bases in respect of matters of which he has been acquitted."[74]

The matter was resolved by the Appeals Chamber in its Order of 21 March 2000. It decided that "under Article 25 of the Statute of the International Tribunal an acquitted person has no right of appeal from acquittals and that the Prosecutor alone has that right" but, "that if the Prosecutor in her Appellant's Brief relies on a particular ground to reverse the acquittal, the Defence in its Respondent's Brief may seek to support the acquittal on additional grounds".[75] By adopting this interpretation, the Appeals Chamber clearly gave Article 25 its plain meaning but at the same time, preserved the right of the Defence to put forward his position and clarify the issues brought by the Prosecution. In doing so, it ensured that it did not limit the Appellant as to the issues which it may raise, but rather provided that he could ensure that the Appeals Chamber is fully apprised of the surrounding circumstances and facts which may not have been raised as part of the Prosecution appeal, in the Respondent's Brief. This would thereby ensure that the Appeals Chamber, in reaching a decision, has the benefit of knowledge of issues which may be crucial in the final consideration and is not confined to the selected issue(s) raised by the Prosecution.

It is clear however that the ICTY Rules also contain a mechanism which contributes to meeting this concern of the Defence. The "Record on Appeal", although certified by the Registrar, is done so with full co-operation and input of both parties to the appeal: "The parties, within thirty days of the certification of the trial record by the Registrar, may by agreement designate the parts of that record which, in their opinion are necessary for the decision on the appeal."[76] Should the parties fail to reach an agreement, they may then inform the Registrar of "the parts of the trial record which each

[72]The Prosecution submitted that there is no provision permitting an acquitted person to file a notice of appeal or cross-appeal against an acquittal. In particular, Art. 25 only authorises either the Prosecution or a *convicted person* to file an appeal, no right of appeal is conferred on a person who has been acquitted and therefore neither a notice of appeal nor appellant's brief can be filed addressing the acquittal. The Prosecution submitted that an appeal is brought against the judgement of the Trial Chamber not against a notice of appeal filed by another party and that the correct avenue for challenging the issues raised by the Prosecution is via a response to the Prosecution's notice of appeal against acquittal. The Appellant submitted that as he was in fact convicted on several other counts of the Indictment which in themselves clearly raised a right of appeal, his appeal therefore falls within the ambit of Art. 25.

[73]See above, in *Tadić Appeals Chamber Judgement*.

[74]Response to Prosecution Motion Filed 20 December 1999, filed by the Defence on 21 Jan. 2000.

[75]*Prosecutor v. Jelisić, Order*, 21 March 2000, p. 4.

[76]Rule 109(B) ICTY Rules.

considers necessary for the decision on the appeal."[77] Clearly both parties have every opportunity to contribute and ensure that information is before the Appeals Chamber on the issues each feel will be relevant to their deliberations. In addition, as was confirmed in the above decision, the acquitted person has every opportunity to advise the Court of the issues considered relevant by means of the Respondent's Brief, with the Rules expressly providing that "[a] Respondent's brief of argument and authorities shall be served on the other party and filed with the Registrar within thirty days of the filing of the Appellant's brief."[78] Nothing in the Rules appears to confine either party to the issues expressly raised in the Notice of Appeal or Briefs and indeed Rule 115 also makes provision for both parties to apply to present additional evidence not available at trial, before the Appeals Chamber, which may admit it "if it considers that the interests of justice so require."[79]

4. The Doctrine of *Stare Decisis*

Stare Decisis is a principle of central importance in common law jurisdictions. It is defined in Black's Law Dictionary as the "[p]olicy of courts to stand by precedent and not to disturb [a] settled point" on questions of law.[80] The corresponding practice in civil law systems, although not so central to their legal process, generally leads to the same results.[81] The doctrine is founded on the thesis of legal certainty so that accepted and established legal principles are followed if at all possible. This is subject to the proviso, that although a point of law already decided should generally be adhered to and followed, "there are occasions when departure is rendered necessary to vindicate plain, obvious principles of law and remedy continued injustice."[82] This allows the Court to retain its inherent discretion to depart from a decision where necessary.

Both the ICTY and ICTR are striving for the continuing development of International Humanitarian Law, and are therefore precedent setting venues of prime importance. It could be argued that to depart from precedent so recently established by the Appeals Chambers in what is still essentially the infancy of the Tribunals could divest them of any credibility they had already

---

[77]Rule 109(C) ICTY Rules.

[78]Rule 112 ICTY Rules.

[79]Rule 115: "(A) A party may apply by motion to present before the Appeals Chamber additional evidence which was not available to it at the trial. Such motion must be served on the other party and filed with the Registrar not less than fifteen days before the date of the hearing. (B) The Appeals Chamber shall authorise the presentation of such evidence if it considers that the interests of justice so require."

[80]Black's Law Dictionary (1990) at p. 1406.

[81]Rabel in *RabelsZ* 16 (1951) 340, at 345, as cited in the Prosecution Response to the Scheduling Order of 8 December 1999 filed on 11 Jan. 2000 in the case of the *Prosecutor v. Aleksovski*, Case No. IT-95-14/1-A at p. 3.

[82]Supra note 80.

gained. It is clear that Trial Chambers have followed precedent established in the Appeals Chambers[83] but it recently fell to the Appeals Chamber to consider the extent to which it was bound by its own previously rendered decisions.

The case of *Tadić* has already been referred to above, but on 26 January 2000, the Appeals Chamber rendered its final decision in respect of the substantive case in its *Judgement in Sentencing Appeals*.[84] The issue had been raised in the Appeals Chamber as to the implications of the classification of an offence as either a violation of the laws or customs of war (ICTY Statute, Article 3) or a crime against humanity (ICTY Statute, Article 5). Was the severity of the penalty on conviction dependent on this classification? In the decision of the Trial Chamber in the same case, it had previously been held that:

> A prohibited act committed as part of a crime against humanity, that is with an awareness that the act formed part of a widespread or systematic attack on a civilian population, is, all else being equal, a more serious offence than an ordinary war crime. This follows from the requirement that crimes against humanity be committed on a widespread or systematic scale, the quantity of the crimes having a qualitative impact on the nature of the offence which is seen as a crime against more than just the victims themselves but against humanity as a whole.[85]

The Appeals Chamber in a subsequent decision in October 1997 confirmed this finding in the joint separate opinion of Judge McDonald and Judge Vohrah:

> [...] all things being equal, a punishable offence, if charged and proven as a crime against humanity, is more serious and should ordinarily entail a heavier penalty than if it were proceeded upon on the basis that it were a war crime.[86]

---

[83]E.g. in the case of *Prosecutor v. Aleksovski, Judgement*, Case No IT-95-14/1-T, 25 June 1999, the Trial Chamber clearly followed the precedent which had been set in the Appeals Chamber in the case of *Prosecutor v. Tadić, Decision on the Defence Motion for Interlocutory Appeal on Jurisdiction*, Case No. IT-94-1-AR72, A. Ch., 2 Oct. 1995 at paras. 67 and 70 in establishing the existence of an armed conflict for the purposes of ICTY Statute Arts. 2 and 3 (paras. 43 and 44).

[84]*Prosecutor v. Tadić, Judgement in Sentencing Appeals*, Case No. IT-94-1-A and IT 94-1-A*bis*, A. Ch., 26 Jan. 2000. It should be noted that although this judgement disposed of the case in respect of the appellant, in fact the Appeals Chamber was still seized of the matter of the allegations of contempt which had been made against his former counsel, Milan Vujin, a matter on which they ruled on 31 Jan. 2000, *Judgement on Allegations of Contempt against prior Counsel Milan Vujin*, Case No. IT-94-1-A-R77, A. Ch.

[85]*Prosecutor v. Tadić, Sentencing Judgement*, Case No. IT-94-1-T, 14 July 1997 at para. 73.

[86]*Prosecutor v. Erdemović, Joint Separate Opinion of Judge McDonald and Judge Vohrah, Judgement*, Case No. IT-96-22-A, 7 Oct. 1997 at para. 20.

Despite this trend, when the Appeals Chamber came to reconsider the question in the *Judgement in Sentencing Appeals* in the case of *Tadić*, with Judge Cassese dissenting on the particular point,[87] it decided to depart from this precedent and accordingly ruled that: "[…] there is in law no distinction between the seriousness of a crime against humanity and that of a war crime."[88]

It is not suggested that the Appeals Chamber should never depart from its previous decisions. On the contrary, the Appeals Chamber should do so if an appropriate situation should arise. But this should only occur, when it is faced with a situation which clearly merits departure and where good reason to do so can be shown. The alternative is that the jurisprudence of the Tribunal will essentially become devoid of legal effect and its law making abilities will become to an extent, negligible. It is clearly not advisable for decisions of the Tribunal to be dependent on exterior factors and there is a practical need for consistency together with a need for the creation of binding jurisprudence.

The matter was touched on for the first time in an ICTY Trial Chamber decision in the case of *Kupreskić* (and others).[89] The Trial Chamber stated that:

> The Tribunal's need to draw upon judicial decisions is only to be expected, due to the fact that both substantive and procedural criminal law is still at a rudimentary stage in international law.

The Trial Chamber continued by examining the body of law it should apply. It concluded that in terms of judicial decisions, although they were bound to apply international law (subject to drawing on national law to fill any gaps), judicial decisions should only be used as a "subsidiary means for the determination of rules of law."[90] It stated that "generally speaking, and subject to

---

[87]*Judgement in Sentencing Appeals, Separate Opinion of Judge Cassesse.*

[88]Id., para. 69.

[89]*Prosecutor v. Kupreskić and Others, Judgement,* Case No. IT-95-16-T, 14 Jan. 2000 at paras. 537–542.

[90]Judicial decisions are considered "as subsidiary means for the determination of rules of law" in Art. 38.1(d) of the Statute of the ICJ. However, the ICJ normally follows its own precedent in a consistent manner. Judge Mohamed Shahabuddeen wrote an excellent book on the Precedent in the World Court, Hersh Lauterpacht Memorial Lectures, Cambridge (reprinted 1997), in which we can read: "*Stare decisis* does not apply. This fact is generally taken as a feature which radically separates the Court's practice from that in common law systems. But there have been interesting developments in both sides. On the side of the Court, its jurisprudence has developed in the direction of a strong tendency to adhere closely to previous holdings. On the common law side, courts of last resort have come to accept that they are not obliged to follow their previous decisions; within careful bounds, they may depart. The World Court may do likewise. Naturally, it will not do so except with caution. The Court has not had occasion to consider whether its decisions create law. It may incline towards avoiding the question; if it has to give an answer, it would probably do so in the negative. But, on balance, it is possible to hold that the arguments, which run both ways, support the view that the Court has a power of limited creativity" (p. 238).

the binding force of decisions of the Tribunal's Appeals Chamber upon the Trial Chambers, the International Tribunal cannot uphold the doctrine of binding precedent (*stare decisis*) adhered to in common law countries".

It appears from this that although the Trial Chamber felt unable to commit itself fully to a system of binding precedent, nevertheless it held that decisions of the Appeals Chamber were "binding" on a Trial Chamber. This does not however clarify the issue in terms of the binding nature of decisions of the Appeals Chamber on itself.

However, despite the fact that as seen above, the Appeals Chamber has departed from its own precedent in the past, clearly this was not indicative of the future practice of the Appeals Chamber, as can be seen in the most recent decision rendered in the case of *Aleksovski*.[91] The issue was specifically highlighted for consideration by the Appeals Chamber in its Scheduling Order of 8 December 1999, wherein both parties were ordered to file submissions on, *inter alia*, "the doctrine of *Stare Decisis*, its applicability, if at all, to proceedings before the International Tribunal and in particular to this case."[92] It was considered that issues were under consideration which had already been determined by the Appeals Chamber in their decision in the case of *Tadić*, notably determination of the proper test to establish the existence of an international armed conflict and the interpretation of the nationality requirement for civilians under Geneva Convention IV to be considered protected persons. Accordingly, for the first time, the Appeals Chamber ruled on what it considered should be the future impact of its own decisions.

The Appeals Chamber commenced with a review of various jurisdictions to consider whether or not they consider themselves bound by their previous decisions:

> The Appeals Chamber recognises that the principles which underpin the general trend in both the common law and civil law systems, whereby the highest courts, whether as a matter of doctrine or of practice, will normally follow their previous decisions and will only depart from them in exceptional circumstances, are the need for consistency, certainty and predictability.[93]

It acknowledged that although there is no provision in the ICTY Statute dealing expressly with the question of the binding force of Appeals Chamber decisions,[94] "[a]n aspect of the fair trial requirement is the right of an

---

[91] *Prosecutor v. Aleksovski, Judgement*, Case No. IT-95-14/1-A, A.Ch., 24 March 2000.

[92] The submissions filed were the "Prosecution Response to the Scheduling Order of 8 December 1999", filed on 11 Jan. 2000 and the Appellant's Additional Submissions on Doctrine of *Stare Decisis* and Defence of "*necessity*", filed on 11 Jan. 2000.

[93] Supra note 91, para. 97.

[94] Id., para. 99.

accused to have like cases treated alike, so that in general, the same cases will be treated in the same way."[95] It concluded by stating:

> The Appeals Chamber, therefore, concludes that a proper construction of the Statute, taking due account of its text and purpose, yields the conclusion that in the interests of certainty and predictability, the Appeals Chamber should follow its previous decisions, but should be free to depart from them for cogent reasons in the interests of justice [...]. It is necessary to stress that the normal rule is that previous decisions are to be followed, and departure from them is the exception.[96]

In applying these principles to the case under consideration, the Appeals Chamber considered that the Trial Chamber applied the wrong test for determining the nature of the armed conflict and the status of protected persons within the meaning of ICTY Statute Article 2[97] and that it should on the contrary apply the relevant tests as were fully reasoned and enunciated in the *Tadić Appeals Chamber Judgement*.

The importance of the *ratio decidendi*, which has emerged from the Appeals Chamber on this particular issue of precedent, cannot be over-stated. It is an issue which is very much alive before both Tribunals and will be of the utmost importance in forthcoming Appeals Chamber decisions which are due to consider matters which have, to a certain extent been examined before.[98]

5. Conclusion

The matters discussed above are just some of the many interesting issues which have confronted both the Trial Chambers and Appeals Chamber of the ICTY and ICTR. The forthcoming months and years promise to continue in the development of its jurisprudence and the principles which will be applied by, in particular, the Appeals Chamber, the 'highest' court and point of final appeal, whose decisions have recently been confirmed as having binding effect.

---

[95] Id., para. 105.

[96] Id., paras. 107 and 109.

[97] Id., para. 154.

[98] E.g., the appeals filed in the case of *Čelebicí*, raise issues and questions on the applicability of both ICTY Statute Arts. 2 and 3, both of which were examined at length in the *Tadić Appeals Chamber Judgement.*

(Select Bibliography: M Cherif Bassiouni, Human Rights in the Context of Criminal Justice: Identifying Procedural Protections and Equivalent Protections in National Constitutions, 3 Duke Journal of Comparative and International Law, (1993), 235; Virginia Morris and Michael P. Scharf: The International Criminal Tribunal for Rwanda (1995); Vriginia Morris and Michael P. Scharf: An Insider's Guide to the International Criminal Tribunal for the Former Yugoslavia (1995); John R.W.D. Jones, The Practice of the International Criminal Tribunals for the Former Yugoslavia and Rwanda (Second Edition, 2000); M.Cherif Bassiouni and Peter Manikas: The Law of the International Criminal Tribunal for the Former Yugoslavia (1996); Editors: André Klip and Göran Sluiter, "Annotated Leading Cases of International Criminal Tribunals"(1999); Editor: Otto Triffterer, "Commentary on the Rome Statute of the International Criminal Court, Observers' Notes, Article by Article" (1999).)

YVONNE M.O. FEATHERSTONE*

36. Additional Evidence in the Appeals Proceedings and Review of Final Judgement

1. Introduction

Both the ICTY and the ICTR have provisions permitting the review of judgements and admission of additional evidence in appeals proceedings. A review of a decision under ICTR Rule 120 was recently conducted for the first time by the Appeals Chamber in the *Barayagwiza* case.[1] The provision concerning additional evidence in appeals proceedings (ICTR and ICTY Rule 115), has been applied in two proceedings, in the *Tadić* case[2] before the ICTY in October 1998 and, most recently, in the *Semanza* case[3] before the ICTR in May 2000.

In addition to the general appellate power both as to an error on a question of law and as to an "an error of fact which has occasioned a miscarriage of justice", contained in Article 24 of the ICTR Statute and Article 25 of the ICTY Statute, the specific power to review a decision is also enshrined in both the ICTY and the ICTR Statutes. Article 25 of the ICTR Statute and Article 26 of the ICTY Statute provide:

---

*Yvonne M.O. Featherstone; Senior Legal Officer, ICTY Chambers, 1994 to present; B.A. Hons (Law); Solicitor, England and Wales; Barrister and Solicitor, Victoria, Australia. The views expressed herein are those of the author and not those of the International Tribunal or of the United Nations.

[1]*Barayagwiza v. Prosecutor, Decision*, Case No. ICTR-97-19-AR72, A. Ch., 31 Mar. 2000 ("*Barayagwiza Review Decision*").

[2]*Prosecutor v. Tadić, Decision on Appellant's Motion for the Extension of the Time-limit and Admission of Additional Evidence*, Case No. IT-94-1-A, A. Ch., 15 Oct. 1998 ("*Tadić Rule 115 Decision*").

[3]*Semanza v. Prosecutor, Decision*, Case No. ICTR-97-20-A, A. Ch., 31 May 2000 ("*Semanza Appeals Decision*").

R. May et al., Essays on ICTY Procedure and Evidence in Honour of Gabrielle Kirk McDonald, 495–508.

Article 25 (ICTR)/Article 26 (ICTY)

Review proceedings

> Where a new fact has been discovered which was not known at the time of the proceedings before the Trial Chambers or the Appeals Chamber and which could have been a decisive factor in reaching the decision, the convicted person or the Prosecutor may submit to the International Tribunal [for Rwanda] an application for review of the judgement.

The application of these provisions of the Statutes is then set out in more detail in Part Eight of the Rules of Procedure and Evidence ("Rules") of each International Tribunal,[4] governing Review Proceedings. The operative Rules of that part are as follows:

Rule 120 (ICTR)/Rule 119 (ICTY)

Request for Review

> Where a new fact has been discovered which was not known to the moving party at the time of the proceedings before a [Trial Chamber or the Appeals] Chamber, and could not have been discovered through the exercise of due diligence, the defence or, within one year after the final judgement has been pronounced, the Prosecutor, may make a motion to that Chamber, [if it can be reconstructed or, failing that, to the appropriate Chamber of the Tribunal] for review of the judgement.

Rule 121 (ICTR)/Rule 120 (ICTY)

Preliminary Examination

> If [a majority of Judges of] the Chamber which rules on the matter decides [that pronounced the judgement agree] that the new fact, if [it had been] proved, could have been a decisive factor in reaching a decision, the Chamber shall review the judgement, and pronounce a further judgement after hearing the parties.

The possibility of review of a previous decision is familiar both on the international and national level. Article 61 of the Statute of the International Court of Justice permits the Court to entertain an application for revision of a judgement "based on the discovery of some fact of such a nature as to be a decisive factor, which fact was, when the judgment was given, unknown to the Court and also to the party claiming revision, always provided that such ignorance was not due to negligence."[5] Protocol No. 7 to the European

[4] The language of the two provisions is very similar but not identical. Text in [...] is that of the ICTR provision.

[5] Statute of the International Court of Justice as annexed to the Charter of the United Nations, 26th June 1945, I.C.J. Acts and Documents No. 5.

Convention for the Protection of Human Rights and Fundamental Freedoms (1950) also provides for the reopening of cases upon evidence of "new or newly discovered facts".[6] Furthermore, the International Law Commission has stated that such a provision is a "necessary guarantee against the possibility of factual error relating to material not available to the accused and therefore not brought to the attention of the Court at the time of the initial trial or of any appeal."[7] Revision of a decision is also permitted by the Rome Statute of the International Criminal Court if new evidence has been discovered that was not available at the time of trial (where such unavailability is not attributable to the party making the application) and the material is sufficiently important that it is likely to have resulted in a different verdict.[8] At the national level, the possibility of review is often supported by legislation, especially in civil law countries.[9] The criteria to be fulfilled differ from country to country and the procedures vary but the underlying concept of a power of review remains constant.

By way of contrast to the well-established power of review of a judgement, with its source in the Statutes and detailed provisions in the Rules of the two Tribunals themselves, there is no specific reference in either Statute to the power to admit additional evidence on appeal. This power is codified only in the Rules themselves. Rule 115 of both sets of Rules reads:

Rule 115

Additional Evidence

(A) A party may apply by motion to present before the Appeals Chamber additional evidence which was not available to it at the trial. Such motion must be served on the other party and filed with the Registrar not less than fifteen days before the date of the hearing.

(B) The Appeals Chamber shall authorise the presentation of such evidence if it considers that the interests of justice so require.

The admission of additional evidence on appeal is recognized in a number of common law systems. In civil code systems, however, the *Cour d'appel* (as opposed to the *Cour de cassation*) conducts a complete re-examination of the case, which may include the consideration of additional evidence. As the appellate jurisdiction of the two Tribunals specifically includes the ability to revise decisions of fact taken by the Trial Chambers, and is not limited to review of questions of law, in the unique circumstances of the ICTY and the ICTR, the power to admit additional evidence of the facts on which those

[6] 22 Nov. 1984, 24 ILM 435 at 436.

[7] Report of the International Law Commission on the work of its 46th session. Official Records, 49th Session. Supplement number No. 10 (A/49/10) at p. 128.

[8] Rome Statute of the International Criminal Court, Art. 84, 17 Aug. 1999, PCNICC/1999/INF/3.

[9] For example, France and Italy.

decisions are made may be regarded as a natural concomitant of that jurisdiction. The presentation of additional evidence is not a ground of appeal in its own right and, as stated in Rule 115, such material is admissible only in the interests of justice.

The precise nature of the distinction between Rule 115 and ICTY Rule 119 and ICTR Rule 120 may not immediately be apparent. Article 26 of the ICTR Statute and Article 25 of the ICTY Statute specifically require that the material for consideration for review be both "new" and that it was not known at the time the impugned decision was made; these requirements are then reflected in ICTY Rule 119 and ICTR Rule 120. With this in mind, the concept of a "new fact", that is, something that did not exist at the time of the trial, and which could be a decisive factor for the Chamber that originally made the decision, can be distinguished from the notion of additional evidence, i.e., material that was in existence at the time of the decision but, for some reason, was not presented to the Trial Chamber. Such material then falls to be considered by the Appeals Chamber in connection with, or in support of, an appeal against the decision of the Trial Chamber. Another issue for consideration is whether evidence of a new fact, that could be the basis for an application for review, may, instead, be admitted as additional evidence under Rule 115.

The nature of the distinction between the two types of proceedings was considered in the *Tadić Rule 115 Decision*. During the briefing stage of the proceedings, Tadić, the appellant, sought leave to introduce additional evidence that fell into five categories:

(a) Material not in existence at the time of the trial;
(b) Material the existence of which the appellant was unaware;
(c) Material the appellant was unable to adduce at trial because, e.g., witnesses felt intimidated and refused to testify;
(d) Material the appellant's lawyers had failed to seek out or obtain, whether negligently or not; and
(e) Material the appellant's lawyers had failed to call other than with the agreement of the appellant.[10]

The appellant submitted that the material he sought to present was admissible as additional evidence under Rule 115. If, however, the Appeals Chamber were to determine that the material sought to be introduced should more properly be considered a matter for review by the original Chamber, rather than appellate proceedings, then the appellant asked that his motion be remitted to the Trial Chamber as an application for review.[11] The Prosecution contended that the standard for admission is the same under both Rule 115 and Rule 119 but that the discovery of a new fact after judgement is a matter for review under Rule 119, rather than admission of additional evidence under Rule 115, asserting that there would be potential duplication of

[10] *Tadić Rule 115 Decision*, supra note 2, at para. 8.
[11] Id., para. 23.

proceedings if the discovery of new evidence after trial could give rise to grounds for both appeal and review.[12]

Disposing of these arguments, the Appeals Chamber confirmed that there is indeed a distinction between the two Articles of the Statute and the related Rules.[13] The Appeals Chamber held that, where an applicant seeks to present a new fact which only becomes known after trial, despite the exercise of due diligence during the trial, then Rule 119 is the governing provision. The reason, as explained by the Appeals Chamber, is that in such a case, the applicant is not seeking to admit additional evidence of a fact that was considered at trial, but a new fact.[14] Thus it is not the evidence that is new, it is the underlying fact that the evidence seeks to establish that is new. The proper venue for such a review is the Chamber that rendered the decision and it is for that Chamber to determine whether the new fact, if proved, could have been a decisive factor in reaching a decision.

Pursuing the distinction between a fact and evidence of that fact, the Appeals Chamber held that the subsequent discovery of additional evidence of a fact that was known at trial is not itself a new fact within the meaning of Rule 119 but is additional evidence of facts in issue at the trial which thus falls for consideration under Rule 115.[15]

The Appeals Chamber went on to consider the requirements of Rule 115 for admission and determined that the material sought to be admitted must meet two requirements: the material must be shown not to have been available at trial and, once that is established, it must be shown that its admission is required in the interests of justice.[16] The need for judicial certainty and the principle of finality mitigate against the introduction of additional evidence on appeal except in circumstances where to do otherwise would best serve the interests of justice. The Appeals Chamber noted, however, that "the principle of finality must be balanced against the need to avoid a miscarriage of justice; when there could be a miscarriage the principle of finality will not operate to prevent the admission of additional evidence that was not available at trial, if that evidence would assist in the determination of guilt or innocence."[17] As will be seen later, the need to avoid a miscarriage of justice was indeed used by the Appeals Chamber in the *Semanza* case as a basis for admitting material under Rule 115 which would otherwise have been excluded.

This exception to the principle of finality, based on the need to avoid a miscarriage of justice, has its roots in the general appellate power of the Appeals Chamber pursuant to Article 24 of the ICTR Statute and Article 25 of the ICTY Statute which empowers the Appeals Chamber to hear appeals

[12]Id., para. 24.
[13]Id., para. 29.
[14]Id., para. 30.
[15]Id., para. 32.
[16]Id., para. 34.
[17]Id., para. 35.

concerning an error of fact which has occasioned a miscarriage of justice. If the exclusion of facts that were not placed before the Chamber that made the decision would lead to or continue a miscarriage of justice, the Appeals Chamber may consider those facts, irrespective of whether or not they were known to the party seeking to introduce them. It must be stressed, however, that such a situation should be seen to be exceptional, and that usually, the question of availability at trial will be dispositive of the matter.

The issue of the availability of evidence at trial was treated extensively in the *Tadić Rule 115 Decision*. Although Rule 115, unlike Rule 119, does not specifically refer to a requirement of due diligence on the part of the applicant in discovering the material before trial, the Appeals Chamber went on to construe the reference to "an error of fact" in Article 25 of the Statute to mean "an incorrectness of fact disclosed by relevant material, whether or not erroneously excluded by the Trial Chamber".[18] Justice requires correction of such an error but also requires the accused to demonstrate why the additional evidence was not presented to the Trial Chamber. The burden of proof falls on the applicant and failure to meet it will result in the material being excluded.[19] The Statute provides certain guarantees to an accused as to the preparation and presentation of his defence, which have the effect of imposing a duty to be reasonably diligent. If an accused fails to utilise all of the rights under the Statute, he cannot then complain of unfairness if material is excluded.[20]

In the *Tadić Rule 115 Decision* the Appeals Chamber had to consider various categories of additional evidence presented for admission and that analysis provides guidance as to what may, or may not, be considered to have been unavailable at trial. It is important to bear in mind here that, as discussed above, Rule 115 concerns the admission of "additional evidence", that is, the underlying fact which it goes to prove was known and considered at trial, but there is now further evidence of that fact, which evidence may be considered by the Appeals Chamber. A helpful example of the application of this principle is the first category of material which the Appeals Chamber found to have been unavailable at trial in this case: material not in existence at the date of the trial, such as voter registration figures complied after trial. The underlying fact, the ethnic composition of the region, had been discussed at trial, and so the material in question was not a new fact giving rise to review, but was additional evidence which could assist the Appeals Chamber in determining whether the Trial Chamber was correct in its factual determination of the issue. The Appeals Chamber also held that evidence of litigated events from witnesses who were unknown to the party or who could not have been identified with due diligence, perhaps because the witnesses themselves were not aware of the trial and so did not volunteer themselves, and of relevant witnesses who had fled the region and could not

[18] Id., para. 38.
[19] Id., paras. 52–53.
[20] Id., paras. 36–45.

be located, again despite due diligence, was unavailable at trial and thus potentially admissible on appeal.[21]

Having found that certain of the material sought to be admitted had not been available at trial, the Appeals Chamber then had to determine whether or not to admit any of those materials "in the interests of justice". The Appeals Chamber determined that the appropriate test is not whether the proposed evidence does or does not disclose "an error of fact which has occasioned a miscarriage of justice" within the terms of Article 25 of the ICTY Statute, this being left for decision at a later stage[22] but, rather, to apply the more flexible formula of Rule 115 and to admit the material only if: (a) it is relevant to a material issue; (b) the evidence is credible; and (c) the evidence would probably show that the conviction is unsafe.[23] Applying these principles to the case at hand, the Appeals Chamber simply stated that it was not satisfied in this case that "any material which was not available at trial is required by the interests of justice to be presented at the hearing of the appeal."[24] The Appeals Chamber did not find it necessary to give details of how it had applied the criteria for admission in respect of each of the items of additional evidence found not to have been available at trial. The application of the criteria for admission "in the interests of justice" therefore remains open for further elucidation in other matters.

Turning now to the *Barayagwiza Review Decision*, this, naturally, examines the relationship between the two types of proceedings from the perspective of review. The Appeals Chamber stated:

> [I]t is clear from the Statute and the Rules that, in order for a Chamber to carry out a review, it must be satisfied that four criteria have been met. There must be a new fact; this new fact must not have been known by the moving party at the time of the original proceedings; the lack of discovery of the new fact must not have been through the lack of due diligence on the part of the moving party; and it must be shown that the new fact could have been a decisive factor in reaching the original decision. (Footnote omitted.)[25]

It appears from both this statement and the subsequent language of the *Barayagwiza Review Decision* that the Appeals Chamber has interpreted the language of the first part of Article 25 of the ICTR Statute ("a new fact [...] which was not known at the time of the proceedings"), to apply solely to the state of knowledge of the Chamber at the time of its original decision.[26] Thus the first criterion, the existence of "a new fact", refers to a fact that is new to the Chamber in its consideration of the matter; the state of knowledge of

[21] Id., paras. 54–68.
[22] Id., para. 70.
[23] Id., para. 71.
[24] Id., para. 74.
[25] *Barayagwiza Review Decision*, supra note 1, at para. 41.
[26] See, e.g., id., paras. 54 and 61.

the party seeking to admit the material being irrelevant to meeting this first requirement. The second and third requirements, that a fact "was not known to the moving party at the time of the proceedings" and "could not have been discovered through the exercise of due diligence", are separate and distinct from the statutory requirement that the fact not be known to the Chamber at the time of the original proceedings. As was considered by the Appeals Chamber later in the *Barayagwiza Review Decision*, these two criteria derive not from the Statute but from the Rules.

The Appeals Chamber then endorsed and adopted the test established in the *Tadić Rule 115 Decision* to distinguish between a genuinely new fact and additional evidence of a fact that is already known and thus to determine the applicable Rule.[27] In his Separate Opinion, Judge Shahabuddeen (who was also a member of the Chamber in the *Tadić Rule 115 Decision*), discussed the distinction in some detail, noting that a "new fact is generically in the nature of additional evidence".[28]

The Appeals Chamber also considered the argument of the appellant that something that occurred before the trial could not be characterised as "new". The Chamber held that the crucial aspect is not the date of occurrence of the fact at issue but whether that fact satisfies the four criteria set out above. If it does, and could have been a decisive factor in reaching the decision, then the Chamber may review the decision.[29]

The *Barayagwiza Review Decision* arose not at the completion of trial but upon application by the Prosecutor for review of an Appeals Chamber Decision on interlocutory appeal as to jurisdiction, based on a challenge to the legality of the arrest of the appellant and of his subsequent detention. Rule 115 was therefore no longer available to the Prosecutor as the appellate proceedings had already been completed.[30] Arguing against the exercise of the power of review in these circumstances, the appellant asserted that Article 25 of the ICTR Statute applies only after a conviction has been handed down, relying on the reference in that Article to a "convicted person". The Appeals Chamber rejected this argument, noting that appeals from acquittals have been allowed in ICTY proceedings. The language of Article 25 of the ICTR Statute merely indicates that each of the parties has the right to seek review of a decision.[31] The Appeals Chamber went on to note that only a final judgement, being a judgement which terminates the proceedings, may be reviewed in this way.[32]

---

[27]Id., para. 43.

[28]Id., Separate Opinion of Judge Shahabuddeen, para. 47.

[29]Id., para. 44.

[30]The *Barayagwiza Review Decision* does not address the issue of why evidence of these new facts was not presented to the Appeals Chamber under Rule 115 in the initial stage of the appellate proceedings, the procedure used subsequently by the Prosecutor in *Semanza*.

[31]*Barayagwiza Review Decision*, supra note 1, at paras. 45–48.

[32]Id., para. 49.

The Appeals Chamber then applied the four criteria set out above to the various facts presented to it, before going on to consider whether any facts that met the criteria could have been a decisive factor in reaching its decision. First, the Appeals Chamber determined that, although some of the material being presented by the Prosecutor was evidence rather than facts, that evidence disclosed facts that were new to the Chamber. As noted by Judge Shahabuddeen, the newness has to be in relation to the facts previously before the court, not to whether the fact was in existence at the time of trial.[33] This material included transcripts evidencing the position taken by the defence in proceedings in the detaining State, leading to the presumption that the appellant had been informed of the nature of the crimes for which he was wanted and of the charges against him;[34] reports from responsible officials demonstrating the lack of ability or preparedness of the detaining State to effect transfer of the appellant at an earlier date;[35] and correspondence indicating the consent of defence counsel to deferral of the initial appearance of the appellant before the ICTR Tribunal.[36]

Having found that there were new facts not known to the Chamber at the time of its decision, and that the first requirement of the test had been met, the Appeals Chamber then concluded that certain of those new facts may have been known to the Prosecutor or could have been discovered.[37] Thus the second and third criteria were not met with regard to these particular items. Considering these items, the Chamber noted that Rule 120 introduces an additional consideration which is not in Article 25 of the Statute, namely that the new fact "could not have been discovered through the exercise of due diligence". In the face of a possible miscarriage of justice and in the "wholly exceptional circumstances of this case", the Appeals Chamber went on to construe this requirement as being directory in nature, rather than mandatory.[38] In so doing, the Chamber had regard both to the fact that the condition does not derive from the Statute itself and that, while not providing direct authority for the Tribunal, there is precedent for such an approach to similar problems in a number of national jurisdictions. Whilst it is clearly not in the interests of justice to encourage parties to proceed in a less than diligent manner, "courts cannot close their eyes to injustice on account of the facility of abuse"[39] and that "[t]o reject the facts presented by the Prosecutor, in light of their impact on the Decision, would indeed be to close ones eyes to reality."[40] Judge Shahabuddeen also addressed this point in his Separate Opinion, concluding: "Here, the overriding purpose of the provision

---

[33]*Barayagwiza Review Decision*, supra note 1, Separate Opinion of Judge Shahabuddeen, para. 47.

[34]Id., para. 54.

[35]Id., paras. 57–58.

[36]Id., para. 61.

[37]Id., para. 64.

[38]Id., para. 65.

[39]Id., para. 66, quoting *Berggren v. Mutual Life Insurance Co.*, 231 Mass. at 177.

[40]Id., para. 69.

is to achieve justice. Justice is denied by adopting a mandatory interpretation of the text; a directory approach achieves it."[41]

Having concluded that the new facts diminished both the role played by the failings of the Prosecutor in this case and the intensity of the violation of the rights of the appellant, and given that the original remedy ordered by the Appeals Chamber had been based on a cumulation of elements, the Chamber found that such remedy now appeared disproportionate to the events. As the new facts were therefore facts which could have been decisive in reaching its decision, thus satisfying the fourth criterion of the applicable test, the Appeals Chamber upheld the application for review, ruling that the remedy must be modified.[42] The Chamber then proceeded to review its original decision, confirming its finding that the appellant's rights had been violated but varying the remedy.[43] Judge Shahabuddeen addressed the question of the proper venue for such review in his Separate Opinion, noting that the review was being conducted by the same Chamber that had rendered the final judgement and so was fully capable of assessing the impact of these new facts.[44]

Until the end of May 2000, these two Decisions were the only two Decisions directly interpreting the provisions of these Articles of the Statutes and Rules. In *Prosecutor v. Furundžija*, the Appeals Chamber noted in an Order that ICTY Rules 115 and 119 did not apply to the material sought to be admitted, as it related to a ground of appeal concerning an issue of law (the alleged partiality of a trial judge) and not to the guilt or innocence of the appellant.[45]

This line of reasoning, that Rule 115 applies only in relation to material that goes to the guilt or innocence of the accused, being the matter litigated by the Trial Chamber, rather than to grounds of appeal such as the fairness of the trial, has been continued by the Appeals Chamber in three Orders in *Prosecutor v. Delalić and others*.[46] In the first of those Orders, the Appeals

[41]Id., Separate Opinion of Judge Shahabuddeen, paras. 48–54, at para. 53.

[42]Id., paras. 71–72.

[43]Id., para. 74. In the original decision the Appeals Chamber had dismissed the indictment and ordered the release of the appellant. On review this was revised to uphold the indictment and the detention of the appellant but to provide for financial compensation in case of an acquittal or a reduction of sentence on conviction.

[44]Id., Separate Opinion of Judge Shahabuddeen, para. 55.

[45]*Prosecutor v. Furundžija, Order on Defendant's Motion to Supplement Record on Appeal*, Case No. IT-95-17/1-A, A. Ch., 2 Sept. 1999.

[46]*Prosecutor v. Delalić and Others, Order on Esad Landžo's Motion (1) to Vary in part Order on Motion to Preserve and Provide Evidence, (2) to be Permitted to Prepare and Present Further Evidence, and (3) that the Appeals Chamber take Judicial Notice of Certain Facts, and on his Second Motion for Expedited Consideration of the Above Motion,* Case No. IT-96-21-A, A. Ch., 4 Oct. 1999 *("Landžo First Order"); Prosecutor v. Delalić and Others, Order in Relation to Witnesses on Appeal*, Case No. IT-96-21-A, A. Ch., 19 May 2000 ("*Landžo Second Order*"); *Prosecutor v. Delalić and Others, Order on Motion of Appellant, Esad Landžo, to Admit Evidence on Appeal, and for Taking of Judicial Notice*, Case No. IT-96-21-A, A. Ch., 31 May 2000 ("*Landžo Third Order*").

Chamber (now in a different composition to that which considered the *Tadić Rule 115 Decision*) held that "Rule 115 is not applicable to the material sought to be admitted, which relates to the [...] fairness of the trial and not [...] the guilt or innocence of [the accused]."[47] In the second Order, the Chamber stated that while Rule 115 "limits the extent to which evidence upon matters relating to the guilt or innocence of the accused may be given before the Appeals Chamber (being the issue litigated in the Trial Chamber)", the Appeals Chamber may, when hearing evidence which relates to matters other than the issues litigated in the Trial Chamber, admit relevant or probative evidence pursuant to ICTY Rule 89 by utilising the *mutatis mutandis* power granted to the Appeals Chamber by ICTY Rule 107.[48] The Chamber admitted one item (an expert report as to the law of a foreign State) pursuant to that Rule on the basis that "without prejudice to the determination of the weight to be afforded to the views expressed [...] it offers a degree of relevance and probative value to the issues raised" on appeal.[49] In the third Order issued in the matter, the Chamber then admitted certain categories of evidence in the appeals proceedings pursuant to ICTY Rule 107, subject to the Appeals Chamber's determination of its relevance to the issues raised.[50]

At the end of May 2000, a further application for admission of additional evidence pursuant to Rule 115 was determined by the Appeals Chamber in the ICTR in the *Semanza* case,[51] in similar procedural circumstances to those in the *Barayagwiza* case. In this case, the Prosecutor sought to admit 21 categories of additional evidence relating to pre-trial detention which were not before the Trial Chamber but which, it was argued, would form a proper factual basis for the Appeals Chamber determination in light of the decisions taken in *Barayagwiza*. The Prosecutor was thus seeking admission under Rule 115 of "additional evidence" on appeal[52] of facts similar to those which, in *Barayagwiza*, were admitted by the Appeals Chamber as new facts justifying review of the final appellate decision under ICTR Rule 120.

In *Semanza*, the Appeals Chamber (sitting in the same combination as in *Barayagwiza*), again noted with approval the interpretation of Rule 115 in the *Tadić Rule 115 Decision*. The Chamber noted that, as a general principle, the non-availability of the material is a pre-condition to consideration of whether admission of the material would be in the interests of justice, save in exceptional circumstances, where it may be overridden by the need to avoid a miscarriage of justice.[53]

---

[47]*Landžo First Order*, supra note 46 at p. 4.

[48]*Landžo First Order*, supra note 46, at p. 3.

[49]Id., p. 4.

[50]*Landžo First Order*, supra note 46, at p. 4 *et seq*.

[51]*Semanza Appeals Decision*, supra note 3.

[52]As the decision of the Trial Chamber was interlocutory in nature and did not terminate the proceedings, it was not open to the Prosecutor to apply to the Trial Chamber for review of that decision.

[53]*Semanza Appeals Decision*, supra note 3, at paras. 40–41.

Applying the principles of the *Tadić Rule 115 Decision* to the case at hand, the Appeals Chamber rejected five of the categories of additional evidence presented by the Prosecutor for procedural reasons, as not having been formally presented as additional evidence.[54] Of the remaining 16 categories, the Appeals Chamber found that they failed to meet the first test set out in the *Tadić Rule 115 Decision*, that of non-availability at trial, in that the Prosecutor had not proved that they were not available at the time of the original proceedings, and would therefore fall to be excluded.[55] The Appeals Chamber rejected the argument of the Prosecutor that the intervening decision in *Barayagwiza* was a reason for non-availability. The Appeals Chamber stated that the development of jurisprudence in one case could not constitute either grounds or a factor in the availability or otherwise of an item of evidence.[56] The material could only be admitted if failure to do so could lead to a miscarriage of justice.

The Appeals Chamber took note of the fact that, in *Barayagwiza*, the Chamber had reviewed its determination in order to correct a miscarriage of justice that had become apparent in the light of new facts. Consequently, the Chamber would now be in error if refusal to admit the additional evidence would lead to a miscarriage of justice. In these exceptional circumstances, the Appeals Chamber could therefore admit those items of additional evidence fundamental to the arguments on which the interlocutory appeal was based.

The Appeals Chamber then reviewed the various categories of additional evidence sought to be adduced for relevance. Four categories were admitted on the basis that they were essential to the analysis of the right of the accused to be informed of the charges against him, while six other categories were admitted as they were relevant to the evaluation of the possible negligence of the Prosecutor, as alleged by the accused.[57] Two further categories, evidencing the development of the proceedings involving the accused in the national courts and the underlying political situation in the country of detention were admitted on similar grounds.[58] One category, relating to the motion for *habeas corpus*, was rejected on the basis that it was not necessary, the Chamber having already accepted that such a motion existed and the five remaining categories were excluded on the ground that that they did not go to fundamental aspects of the appeal and therefore their admission would not prevent a miscarriage of justice.[59]

The Decisions discussed above do provide guidance to parties where before there was none. However, the invocation in both *Barayagwiza* and *Semanza* of exceptional circumstances, and the need to avoid a possible

[54]Id., para. 42.
[55]Id., paras. 43–44.
[56]Id., para. 43.
[57]Id., para. 46.
[58]Id., paras. 48–49.
[59]Id., paras. 47 and 50.

miscarriage of justice, has led the Appeals Chamber to take into account facts that, it acknowledges, in different circumstances would have been excluded. A number of questions of interpretation are thus left open and are yet to be resolved. These include matters such as the application of the criterion of "interests of justice", especially with regard to material that meets the first requirement of Rule 115, and the balance to be struck between the interests of justice and finality of proceedings in connection with review of judgement. In addition to the substantive issues still to be resolved, practical difficulties, especially those associated with review proceedings, will also arise with increasing frequency. For example, at present, only the ICTR Rules make any provision for the situation where the original Chamber cannot be reconstituted, a situation which will surely arise at some time.

It is submitted that the *Barayagwiza Review Decision* should be treated as an exceptional case; as the material was known to, or could have been discovered by, the Prosecution, it could have sought to have this material admitted in the original appeals proceedings under Rule 115, rather than awaiting final determination and then seeking review. The *Barayagwiza Review Decision* should not be taken as encouragement for a party to withhold evidence and then seek review: the Appeals Chamber has made it clear that, because this material was not new to the party seeking its admission, it was only admitted in order to avoid a miscarriage of justice, a situation that, it is hoped, will be exceptional. The fact that it concerned review of an interlocutory (albeit final) Appeals Chamber decision, rather than a review by a Trial Chamber of its judgement after the conclusion of a trial, further complicates analysis and has led to the filing of other requests for review of ICTR interlocutory appeals decisions.

As the various Orders in *Prosecutor v. Delalić and others* demonstrate, the Appeals Chamber has the power to admit relevant evidence on appellate issues other than the facts litigated by the Trial Chamber. The *Semanza Appeals Decision* continues the conventional approach that additional evidence of a matter already raised before and litigated by the Trial Chamber falls to be considered by the Appeals Chamber under Rule 115, rather than being remitted to the original Chamber under ICTY Rule 119 or ICTR Rule 120.

Even material that might, at first glance, appear to be new, may be considered by the Appeals Chamber as additional evidence, provided it relates to the issues litigated by the Trial Chamber. In many situations, it seems that the same material may be categorised as additional evidence if presented during the appellate stage, or as a new fact if presented after the close of all proceedings. An example of this is the material accepted in the *Barayagwiza Review Decision* as new facts relating to the "first period" from April 1996 to February 1997. The transcripts produced in support of the review indicated that the period that the accused was detained without being informed of the reasons therefor was, at most, 18 days, rather than the 11 months found in the previous decision. Although the Appeals Chamber held this to be a new fact, it could also be argued that this was further evidence of the period of detention. If the initial finding had been made by a Trial Chamber, rather than by the Appeals Chamber itself, it would then have been additional evidence of a matter already considered in the original decision and could have been admitted to show that the original Chamber had made an error of fact. Thus a newly discovered fact may be capable of admission either as a new fact in review proceedings under ICTY Rule 119 or ICTR 120, or as additional evidence in appellate proceedings under Rule 115, depending upon the particular circumstances. The ability to categorise material in this way is particularly helpful if the remedy of review is not available, for example, because the decision in question does not terminate the proceedings.

Finally, the exception demonstrated in the *Semanza Appeals Decision* permitting admission of material in circumstances where to do otherwise would lead to a miscarriage of justice allows the Appeals Chamber, in certain circumstances, the necessary flexibility to admit material it would normally have to reject. It would indeed seem perverse for the Appeals Chamber not to be able to admit material as additional evidence on appeal simply because it relates to a fact not discussed at first instance, where the Chamber is aware that to do so would lead to a miscarriage of justice.[60]

Clearly, applications for the admission of additional evidence on appeal and for the review of judgements will increase as more cases proceed to the Appeals Chamber. From a practical perspective, it would seem preferable for newly discovered material to be dealt with by the Appeals Chamber wherever possible, and for the review process to be retained solely for those situations where the material discloses a completely new fact after all proceedings have been completed.

---

[60] See also *Semanza Appeals Decision*, supra note 3, at para. 45.

CHRISTIAN ROHDE*

37. Are Administrative Decisions from the Registry Appealable?

1. The Position and Functions of the Registry in the International Tribunal

The Registry at the International Tribunal is a court administration organ, which would not necessarily be found in a national judicial system.[1] To be administered by a Registry, separate from the judiciary itself, is however very common for international courts, be they courts adjudicating on State disputes or criminal courts.[2] Article 17 of the ICTY Statute ("Statute")[3] establishes that the Registry shall be responsible for the administration and servicing of the Tribunal. In this connection it is worth while mentioning that the Registrar and her staff are UN employees appointed by the Secretary-General.[4]

Pursuant to its Statute,[5] the Tribunal is composed of the Chambers and its officers,[6] responsible for the adjudication of the Tribunal's cases; the

---

*1st State Exam (Munich); 2nd State Exam, Assessor (Munich), Ph.D. International Law (Greifswald); Legal Officer, Registry, Chief of the Office for Legal Aid and Detention Matters. The views expressed herein are those of the author and do not necessarily reflect the views of the United Nations.

[1]Judicial administration called "Registry" or in French "Greffe" with functions comparable to the Registry at the ICTY in (examples): Belgium, France; no independent judicial administration of such kind in Bosnia & Herzegovina, Croatia, Federal Republic of Yugoslavia, Germany, Italy, Spain, United Kingdom and the USA.

[2]International Courts with a Registry (examples): International Court of Justice (Art. 21 II ICJ Statute), European Court of Justice (Art. 9 *et seq.* ECJ Statute), European Court of Human Rights (Art. 11 *et seq.* Rules of Procedure II), ICTR (Art. 16 ICTR Statute), the future International Criminal Court (Art. 43 ICC Statute), International Tribunal for the Law of the Sea (Art. 36 ITLOS Statute).

[3]Annex to SC Res. 827, UN Doc. S/Res/827 (25 May 1993).

[4]Art. 17 (2)–(4) Statute.

[5]Art. 11 Statute.

[6]Art. 14 Statute.

R. May et al., Essays on ICTY Procedure and Evidence in Honour of Gabrielle Kirk McDonald, 509–521.

Prosecutor,[7] responsible for the investigation and prosecution of persons responsible under the Statute; and the Registry, in charge of making judicial and administrative arrangements for the functioning of the Tribunal by supporting the Chambers, the Prosecutor and, to a certain extent, the defence of accused and legal representation of suspects.[8]

The Rules of Procedure and Evidence ("Rules", "RPE") of the Tribunal are more specific on the functions of the Registry. Rule 33 establishes that the Registrar shall, under the authority of the President, not only be responsible for the administration and servicing of the Tribunal, including assistance with plenary meetings of the Judges, but also serve as the communications channel of the Tribunal. Having been amended recently,[9] Rule 33 (B) permits the Registrar to make oral and written representations to Chambers on any issue arising in the context of a specific case which affects or may affect the discharge of her functions, including issues relating to the implementation of judicial decisions.

While this new Rule 33(B) identifies the implementation of judicial decisions as a key task of the Registrar, the Rule also permits submissions to be made relating to any of the Registrar's functions. This can be understood as recognition of the Registrar's important judicial functions, but also shows that these are partly exercised under the overall authority of the Chambers. This partition of overall authority between the President and Chambers reflects the various functions of the Registrar, which range from providing a "UN administrative" basis for the work of all Tribunal offices, to taking judicial decisions in legal aid and detention matters, recommending protective measures for witnesses,[10] and to promulgating certain rules of the Tribunal.[11] Therefore, the tasks of the Registrar are generally administrative, but, as an analysis of the Rules will show, also reach into the field of judicial administration.

2. Types and nature of administrative decisions of the Registrar

2.1 Decisions with internal character

The decision-making powers of the Registrar can be divided into two areas, namely, decisions with effects within the ICTY and decisions with effects for

[7]Art. 16 Statute.

[8]Rule 44 *et seq*. Rules; Directive on Assignment of Defence Counsel (IT/73 Rev. 7).

[9]7 Dec. 1999 (IT 32 Rev. 17). Further background on Registry tasks at the Tribunal's Yearbooks 1994, 1995, 1996, and the latest for 1997 at pp. 15, 112 and 171; and the Annual Reports to the General Assembly, the most recent A/54/187 at pp. 138 *et seq*.

[10]Rule 34 Rules.

[11]Directive on Assignment of Defence Counsel; Code of Conduct for Counsel Appearing before the Tribunal (IT 125); Detention Regulations (IT 98/Rev. 3), etc.

third parties.[12] For the purposes of this article, decisions obviously having no effect on or no direct relation to the criminal judicial procedures before the Tribunal shall be referred to as being of internal character. Examples of those are (in no particular order): provision of facilities and equipment for the Tribunal including the detention facility; human resources management, including the recruitment and dismissal of staff, contractual arrangements for consultants and other outside experts; budgetary and financial management; procurement administration; provision of security and prison guard services; provision of court management arrangements such as the filing of documents, recording of procedures/exhibits, provision of transcripts and video footage; provision of travel for prosecution and defence investigators and other persons; public information services; assistance to victims and witnesses; conclusion of agreements with States regarding the enforcement of sentences, witness protection, host country matters etc.

These are merely examples of the Registrar's decision and policy-making competencies with regard to the internal organisation of the Tribunal. When acting in connection with these matters, the Registrar is exclusively under the authority of the President as established in Rule 33(A). Nevertheless, the mentioned areas are managed on the basis of UN administrative and financial regulations.[13]

Appeals against decisions of the Registrar in these fields would be possible in accordance with the above-mentioned UN rules and regulations. Should these provide for the possibility of an appeal, e.g. in personnel matters, it may be submitted to the relevant organ. Otherwise, decisions of the Registrar in relation to these internal matters hardly have effects on third parties, thereby not giving rise to the question of an appeal.

As an example, even in a case where the Registrar decides to conclude an agreement of enforcement of sentences with a State, this decision does not directly affect a person found guilty by a Chamber. Only the decision of the President designating a country in which the convict is to serve his or her sentence has such an effect.[14]

2.2 Decisions with external effects

Obviously, an array of decisions of the Registrar may have indirect effects for third parties by creating policies or practices which influence the operations and functioning of the ICTY. But what constitutes an administrative decision in the sense of this article's topic? The following criteria are suggested to distinguish such decisions from acts internal to the

[12]Regarding this distinction see De Smith and Brazier, Constitutional and Administrative Law (1998) at pp. 507 *et seq*.

[13]This important feature of the Tribunal administration is not clearly stated in a comprehensive provision, but follows from various provisions, e.g. Arts. 17(3) and (4), 30, 32 and 34 Statute.

[14]Rule 103 Rules.

organisation. It is implied that only decisions taken on the basis of the Tribunal's Rules constitute decisions in the sense of this essay, and that in accordance with the above-mentioned functions of the Registry, all its decisions are of an administrative nature.

3. Legal Features of Decisions with External Effect

3.1 Formal character

A strong indication of whether an act by the Registrar is a decision or not, is the formality of its legal basis and systematic position in the Rules of the Tribunal. Where a competence of the Registrar is described with the explicit possibility of an appeal, e. g. in Rule 66 of the Detention Rules on contact restrictions between detainees, a formal decision is foreseen.[15] In practice this is also expressed by the filing of decisions in the recording file of the relevant cases.[16]

3.2 Subordination

Another feature of a decision, I suggest, would be that it is taken on the basis of a subordinate relationship between the Registrar and the addressee, whereby the Registrar is able to directly set regulations or conditions. Here again, Rule 66 of the Detention Rules is a good example of such a competence of the Registrar. Contrary to this, a subordinate relationship does not prevail when the Registrar deals with States regarding enforcement agreements.[17] As the ICTY Statute indicates, States may voluntarily offer to enter into an agreement with the Tribunal, but are not obliged to do so, and could not be so obliged by a decision on an appeal of any party.

3.3 Possible contents of decisions

Decisions of the Registrar may regulate various matters. They could contain a regulation including a prohibition,[18] an order,[19] the granting or denial of a right or privilege,[20] or even the expression of a legal opinion.[21] All other acts cannot be regarded as containing a regulation sufficient to qualify them as a decision.

---

[15]See Directive for the Registry (IT 121), Art. 10(a)(ii), e. g. *stamping* a decision.
[16]See Art. 11 Directive for the Registry.
[17]Art. 27 Statute.
[18]E.g. restrictions of contacts between detainees, Rules 66 Detention Rules.
[19]E.g. the assignment of counsel, Article 11 Directive on Assignment of Defence Counsel.
[20]E.g. the granting or denial of travel authorisations for the defence.
[21]De Smith and Brazier, Constitutional and Administrative Law (1998) at p. 508.

3.4 Individuality

For the purposes of this essay, only decisions addressed to individual parties are dealt with. Where the regulations contained in an administrative act of the Registrar are more general and concern multiple addressees, it would be more appropriate to speak of administrative norms, not individual decisions.

3.5 External effect

An important feature qualifying an act of the Registrar as a decision, is the nature of its effect. In order to be characterised as having external effects, an act would either need to be addressed to a third party or, it would have to directly affect that party.

In light of the independence of the Registry as a Tribunal organ, a third party could be any other organ of the Tribunal, such as the President, a Trial or Appeals Chamber, the Bureau of Judges. It could also be the prosecution, the defence, an individual detainee, a defence counsel, witnesses, State representatives appearing in Court etc. However, the authority of the Registrar to make formal decisions, which generally relate to the status of and conditions for defendants and defence counsel, is provided by the Rules. These persons are external parties not forming part of the Tribunal and decisions addressed to them or affecting them in a substantial manner may therefore be classified as of an external character.

According to the Rules, the President, a Chamber, the Bureau or the prosecution may not be the addressee of a decision. Decisions of the Registrar may effect other Tribunal organs, but it would be meaningless to assume a right for the President or a Chamber, because a number of Rules[22] name the President and the Chambers as appeal organs for recourse against the Registrar's decisions. The Bureau is an organ which organises the work of the Chambers of the Tribunal, and would hardly be affected by the Registrar's decisions in a substantive manner.

It is not impossible that the prosecution may be affected by decisions of the Registrar. If one assumed that the Registrar has the authority to verify not only the proper form, but also the substance of requests of the Prosecutor under Rule 66 of the Detention Rules, and the Registrar refused to decide in accordance with one such request, it might be reasonable to assert a right of appeal for the prosecution, as such a refusal may affect her substantive functions. However, it would be argued here that, in light of the wording of Rule 66, the Registrar is not competent to verify the substance

[22]See the overviews infra.

matter of a request by the Prosecution.[23] Therefore it also appears that a right of the Prosecutor to appeal negative decisions is not necessary, and is consequently not mentioned in the Rules.

On another matter, decisions on the allocation of legal aid to defendants affects the strength of the prosecution's trial counterpart. However, it would be difficult to acknowledge that this could amount to a substantial effect on the prosecution's position resulting in a right to appeal such a decision.

It is unsure whether only rights or only interests must be affected. It is argued here that generally procedural or substantive rights have to be affected, not only mere peripheral interests,[24] as only rights of parties entitle them to gain procedural or substantive advantages. Only in exceptional cases should the effect on mere interests lead to a right to recourse for a party which is not the addressee of a decision. In sum, a decision has an external effect if a decision is addressed to a third party and negatively affects the rights of that party, or if the decision negatively affects the rights of a third party in a substantial manner.[25]

4. Examples from the Tribunal's Rules

We should now turn to the explicit references to decisions of the Registrar in the Rules of the Tribunal and the available remedies.[26] The Rules and other rules of the Tribunal such as the Detention Rules address decisions of the Registrar in more detail:

---

[23]It could though be argued that the Registrar is competent to weigh certain rights of detainees against a request.

[24]Interests which have been quoted are economical, corporate or private image and reputation, relating to the functions of an affected party.

[25]See De Smith and Brazier, Constitutional and Administrative Law (1998) at p. 555, who afford appeals rights to "a person aggrieved" by a decision; Galligan, Due Process and Fair Procedures (1996) at p. 191.

[26] In general on recourse in administrative or judicial procedures Galligan, Due Process and Fair Procedures (1996) at p. 392.

Registrar's Competence	*Matter*	*Recourse*	*Legal Ground*
Arts. 11 and 11*bis*, 22 Directive (DI), Rule 45 (D) Rules	Determination of ability of suspects and accused to finance their defence	*For suspects:* Request for review of Registrar's decision to *President*, can confirm Registrar's decision or decide a counsel must be assigned	Art. 13 DI
		Accused, for initial appearance: Motion to *Trial Chamber*, can confirm Registrar's decision or decide a counsel must be assigned	
		Accused, after initial appearance: Objection against denial must be made as preliminary motion to Trial Chamber no later than 60 days after first appearance and before the hearing on the merits	
	Right of otherwise detained persons to obtain counsel	*Accused, after beginning of the hearings on the merits:* Article 13 is silent, but the practice of the Tribunal supports responsibility of a Trial or Appeals Chamber	
		Other detained persons' rights: Rule 45*bis* RPE	
Arts. 11 and 11*bis*, 16(C), 22 DI, Rule 45 (D) Rules	Assignment of a counsel	See supra.	Art. 13 DI
Rule 44 Rules (private counsel) Rule 45 Rules Articles 14, 15 Directive (assigned counsel)	Admission of persons to practice before the Tribunal, retained privately or assigned	Rules are silent, *possible*: application of Article 33 Directive, new decision of the Registrar after consultation with the President	Possible: Art. 33 DI *analogue*
Arts. 19, 20 DI	Withdrawal/ Replacement of assigned counsel	*Related to financial situation, Article 19*: See supra regarding determination of ability of suspects and accused to finance their defence	Arts. 13, 19(D) DI
		Re other situations, Article 20: Review by the President	Art. 20(E) DI
Rule 45 Rules Arts. 23 *et seq.* 18 DI	Payment of fees/expenses of assigned counsel	Review by the Registrar, who is under obligation to *consult* the President	Art. 33 DI

4.1 Defence counsel and legal aid system

A number of explicit decision-making competencies are provided to the Registrar in the areas of qualification of counsel and legal aid.

4.2 Detention matters

The authority of the Registrar to take decisions on detention matters, are well described in the Rules of the Tribunal:

Registrar's Competence	*Matter*	*Recourse*	*Legal Ground*
36*ter* Detention Rules	Monitoring of Cell	Request for reversion of decision to *President*	36*ter*(C) Detention Rules
45(A)(ii), (iii) Detention Rules	Isolation of a detainee	Request to *President*	48(B) Detention
63, 65, 67, 68 & 69 Detention Rules, Regulation 33(A), (B) Detention Regulations	Visit permits	Request to *President* for reversal of denial of permit	Regulation 35
66 Detention Rules	Contact restrictions inside/outside UNDU	Request to *President* for denial or reversion of restriction	66(C) Detention Rules
76 Detention Rules	Restrictions for access to news	Request to *President* for denial or reversion of restriction	76(C) Detention Rules
5 Detention Regulations	Mail cost limit of indigent detainees	Request to *President* for variation of order	5(C) Detention regulations
21 Detention Regulations	Phone monitoring	Request to *President* for reversal of decision	44 Detention regulations
44 Detention Regulations	Recording of communications of detainee with visitors	Request to *President* for reversal of decision	45 Detention regulations
Para. 1 *et seq.* Disciplinary Procedure (Commanding Officer)	Disciplinary offences of detainees	Appeal to *President* against determination of both offence and punishment	Para. 9 Disciplinary Procedure

5. Discussion of remedies as provided by the Rules

5.1 Competent appeals organ

When looking at the Rules it is obvious that for most decisions of the Registrar affecting the rights of suspects or accused, the President of the International Tribunal is the competent organ for a remedy. In detention matters, the President is exclusively responsible for determining any remedies.

In legal aid questions, judging by the two applicable Rules, Article 23 and 20(E) of the Directive, the picture is somewhat mixed. Article 13 of the Directive appears to relate more to the determination of indigency than to the choice of a person as counsel. Here, the President is competent regarding remedies of suspects, but for accused expecting their initial appearance the relevant Trial Chamber is the organ for recourse against decisions of the Registrar. This is so until the beginning of the hearings on the merits.[27] While Article 13 is silent on decisions made by the Registrar during the trial or appeals phase, it appears that once a Chamber is seized of the matter it remains in charge of recourse against decisions related to the provision of legal aid. This view is supported by the practice of the ICTY.[28]

For decisions relating to withdrawal of counsel made upon the request of the accused or counsel, according to Article 20(E) of the Directive, the President is competent to decide on a recourse. It appears therefore that legal aid matters fall somewhat between characterisation as administrative or judicial; the question whether legal aid will be granted or not and the initial choice of counsel falling under the authority of the Chambers, the withdrawal or change of counsel for other reasons under the authority of the President.

However, it could be argued that the determination whether a suspect or accused is indigent or not appears to be a decision of an administrative nature, and not linked closer to the criminal case itself or the rights of the accused than the withdrawal of counsel for other reasons. It is in the hands of the Registrar as the head of the judicial administration of the Tribunal.

---

[27]Art. 13 Directive.

[28]Regarding Art. 20(E) Directive see *Prosecutor v. Delalić and Others, Decision of Vice-President Shahabuddeen on request of defendant Zdravko Mucić for reversion of the Deputy Registrar's decision on his request for replacement of lead counsel*, Case No. IT-96-21-T, 5 Aug. 1998. Regarding Art. 13(C) Directive see *Prosecutor v. Dokmanović and Others, Decision on Defence Preliminary Motion on the Assignment of Counsel*, Case No. IT-95-13a-I, 30 Sept. 1997; *Prosecutor v. Naletilić and Martinović, Decision on the Appeal of the Accused Martinović against the Registry's refusal of his request for assignment of counsel*, Case No. IT 98-34-PT, 30 Nov. 1999; *Prosecutor v. Kordić and Čerkez, Decision on the Registrar's withdrawal of the assignment of defence counsel*, Case No. IT-95-14/2-T, 3 Sept. 1999; *Prosecutor v. Kupreškić and Others, Decision on the Registrar's withdrawal of the assignment of defence counsel*, Case No. IT-95-16-T, 3 Sept. 1999.

The President, according to his position in the Tribunal's organisation, is the highest judicial administrative authority of the Tribunal, also overseeing the Registrar's management, particularly in matters relevant to the rights of the accused.

Fulfilling a different task, Chambers are mainly dealing with the procedural and substantive treatment of cases. They are also concerned with procedural fairness, which includes the right of indigent accused to a proper defence in accordance with Article 21 of the Statute. However, it may be more appropriate for the President to deal with these matters.

Assignment of counsel matters contain strong administrative elements. The determination of the financial status of accused is a matter requiring an equal approach to all applicants.[29] Individual Chambers may also not always be in the best position to exercise this approach. I suggest that rather the President, also being the supervisor of the financial administration of the Tribunal and familiar with the expertise necessary to assess the financial status of persons, might be better placed to rule on indigency appeals.

5.2 Appeal rights for the Prosecutor

It is debatable whether a party who may not be directly affected by the foregoing administrative decisions of the Registrar, like the Prosecutor, may have a right of appeal concerning these decisions. Obviously, no rights of appeal are mentioned. Nevertheless, the Prosecution is affected to an extent by most decisions of the Registrar concerning the defence or a detainee.

In the absence of substantive rights of the prosecution, such as fair trial or the like, a right to appeal should be considered only for situations where procedural rights are affected in a significant manner. In matters relating to assignment of counsel, the prosecution may only very remotely be affected. An assignment provides substantial defence assistance, however, even if assignment is granted to an accused of which the prosecution believes that he is not indigent, it would be difficult to argue that the prosecution would be substantially affected in the exercise of their duties.

In detention matters, and particularly in those areas where the Registrar sets restrictive measures for detainees upon request of the prosecution,[30] a right of appeal for the prosecution is not mentioned by the Rules and is, *prima facie*, not necessary. This is because the Detention Rules, if interpreted correctly, do not provide a right for the Registrar to question the substance of the prosecution's request.[31]

---

[29]Art. 21(1) Statute, declaring that all persons are equal before the Tribunal.
[30]See Rules 66 and 76 Detention Rules.
[31]See supra 3.5.

5.3 General right of detainees, suspects and accused to a remedy against decisions of the Registrar?

From a brief analysis of the Rules it can easily be concluded that comprehensive remedies are provided for against decisions of the Registrar having a potential for affecting the rights of suspects and accused. The Rules set out the possible form of application for a remedy, the Tribunal organ authorised to deal with it and the applicable procedural steps.

The extensive, specific references to remedies in the Rules of the Tribunal as opposed to a general provision leads to the conclusion that, as a rule, further rights for recourse would *prima facie* not be in accordance with the Rules from a systematic point of view. Nevertheless, it is difficult to see significant loopholes in the remedies against decisions of the Registrar. Recourse in one or the other form is provided in every Rule where a decision-making power of the Registrar is established.

Being an organ responsible for judicial administration, it is not unusual for the Registrar to have her decisions subjected to scrutiny by another organ. As far as the right to fair trial of accused is concerned by decisions of the Registrar, according to the current Rules, i.e. the Directive on Assignment of Defence Counsel, recourse against decisions must be had to a Chamber,[32] and before a case is allocated to a Chamber, to the President. As the Registrar is not empowered to take decisions in other areas, no general right to appeal is necessary or provided by the Rules.

As far as the detention regime is concerned, the Registrar's decisions are subject to appeal by the President. As the supervisor of the judicial administration, the President is in the proper position to ensure observance of the rights of detainees. The specific references to recourse rights lead to the conclusion that, systematically and based on a teleological interpretation of the Rules, no further recourse is available for detainees.

5.4 Scope of appeals

An important question is how far the competence of a Chamber or the President to review a decision of the Registrar reaches. Is the competence of the Registrar entirely replaced by the superior organ or is this organ only competent to check the frame of the exercise of the Registrar's functions? By frame, I refer to the limits of an "outer marker" of the Registrar's decision making-power, namely her obligation to act on the basis of a given competence, review all facts before deciding, evaluate facts reasonably, apply the law properly to the facts, select the proper legal consequence, etc.[33]

---

[32] I.e. in legal aid questions.

[33] Galligan, Due Process and Fair Procedures (1996) at p. 395.

Contrary to this, the superior organ could also have the authority to exercise full judgement on the subject matter, thereby substituting the Registrar's competence, including a full evaluation of the facts, the application of the law and particularly the choice of the appropriate legal consequence of the application of the norm. Nevertheless, the Rules of the Tribunal are in most instances explicit on the scope of the review competence. In detention matters, the review competence is described sufficiently – in all cases the President may either confirm the Registrar's decision or quash it.

The Rules on recourse in legal aid matters lack this clarity. The question was however addressed by a Trial Chamber decision in the case *Naletilić and Martinović*.[34] Defining the shape of the administrative powers of the Registrar, the Chamber held that "by refusing the Request of the accused the Registrar *has not committed an obvious error* in her assessment such as to justify, as matters currently stand, that the decision be overturned." (emphasis added).

Thereby the Chamber took the view that even though it is competent to review the Registrar's decision, it will only be checked whether the Registrar has committed any mistake, but a margin of appreciation will be left to her. In accordance with the administrative competence and expertise of the Registrar this appears consequent.[35]

5.5 Appeals against appeals from Registrar decisions

Parties whose appeal against a decision of the Registrar has been unsuccessful may question whether it would not be possible to appeal an appellate decision in such a matter. In cases where the President of the Tribunal has decided upon an appeal this appears not to be the case, as *firstly* no other appeal is foreseen in the Rules and *secondly*, no judicial authority is above the President for matters for which he or she is responsible.

Things may be different for appeals in legal aid matters which are decided upon by a Trial Chamber. Rule 73(B) of the Rules allows for leave to appeal against Trial Chamber decisions if granted by a bench of three judges of an Appeals Chamber, in case the impugned decision would cause prejudice to the final judgement which could not be cured, or the issue is of general importance to proceedings before the Tribunal or in international law generally. It appears that the refusal of assignment of legal counsel could fall under the former ground of appeal. The lack of legal representation before the Tribunal as a criminal court would normally seriously prejudice an

[34] *Prosecutor v. Naletilić and Martinović, Decision on the appeal of the accused Martinović against the Registry's refusal of his request for assignment of counsel*, Case No. IT-98-34-PT, 30 Nov. 1999.

[35] Galligan, Due Process and Fair Procedures (1996) at p. 395, understands this as the regular form of judicial review; from a constitutional law viewpoint, De Smith and Brazier, Constitutional and Administrative Law (1996) at p. 562.

accused.[36] However, one could argue that such an appeal is not possible as the Rules do not explicitly provide for it and it also would constitute a second level of appeal which is not foreseen and no right to it is obligatory under any legal standard.[37]

5.6 The rule of reformatio in peius

Theoretically, the question may arise whether the organ competent for an appeal may reverse a decision of the Registrar in such a way as to disadvantage an applicant even more than the Registrar's original decision did.[38] This may be particularly relevant for a more generally formulated recourse, i.e. the assignment of full or partial legal aid or for recourse of counsel against decisions on his or her fee and expense claims. The Rules are obviously silent on this question. However, the rule of *reformatio in peius* must not necessarily be applied under the rule of law; it is in the will of the legislator to grant this privilege. A legitimate expectation by the applicant cannot be the foundation of the right. As the Rules of the Tribunal are silent, it would be difficult to hold that the principle applies.

6. Conclusion

Thomas Franck, in his book on fairness writes:

> People ... expect that decisions will be made by those duly authorized, in accordance with procedures which protect against ... arbitrary, or idiosyncratic decision-making or decision executing. The fairness of international law ... will be judged ... by the extent to which the rules are made and applied in accordance with what the participants perceive as right process.[39]

The Rules of the International Tribunal providing the Registrar with competencies to take decisions with effect for third parties, also provide for appropriate possibilities of remedies. The remedies are formulated clearly, and cover the rights of suspects and accused particularly well, thereby ensuring procedural fairness in an adequate manner.

---

[36]See also Rule 62(i) RPE which stresses that the judge at the initial appearance has to satisfy himself that the right to counsel is respected.

[37]Birkinshaw, Grievances, Remedies and the State (1985) at p. 89.

[38]Roxin, Strafverfahrensrecht (1998) at p. 343 *et seq*.; Kleinknecht and Meyer-Gossner, Strafprozessordnung (1999), para. 331 No. 1 *et seq*.

[39]Franck, Fairness in international law and institutions (1995) at p. 7.

PART XII

Review and Enforcement of Sentences

NIKOLAUS TOUFAR*

38. State Request for Review

The co-operation of States, especially that of the States of the former Yugoslavia, is one of the most delicate areas in the work of the Tribunal. The history of the Tribunal shows a number of conflicting interests in the judicial and political contexts in which this institution operates. This is evidenced by cases involving a State request for review of decisions, where the issues at stake were closely connected to the role and functioning of the Tribunal as well as the positions of sovereign States. This article examines the history, context and development of the relevant Rule, Rule 108*bis*. In addition, it analyses the relevant jurisprudence of the Tribunal, followed by a discussion of past developments and future perspectives.

1. Introduction

In addition to the right of parties to appeal a judgement, as set out in Rule 108, the Tribunal recognises the specific position of States in the performance of the Tribunal's functions and, through Rule 108*bis*, provides them with a legal framework to assert their position.

Upon its adoption, Rule 108*bis* read as follows:

> (A) A State directly affected by an interlocutory decision of a Trial Chamber may, within fifteen days from the date of the decision, seek a review of the decision by the Appeals Chamber if that decision concerns issues of general importance relating to the powers of the Tribunal.

*Associate Legal Officer, Registry Legal Advisory Section, United Nations International Criminal Tribunal for the former Yugoslavia; *Magister der Rechtswissenschaften, Universität Wien*. The views expressed herein are those of the author alone and do not necessarily reflect the views of the International Tribunal or the United Nations in general.

R. May et al., Essays on ICTY Procedure and Evidence in Honour of Gabrielle Kirk McDonald, 525–532.

(B) The Prosecutor and the defence shall be entitled to be heard by the Appeals Chamber.

(C) The Appeals Chamber, if it considers the request for review admissible may, if it deems it appropriate, suspend the execution of the impugned decision.

(D) Rule 116*bis* shall apply *mutatis mutandis*.

A review of the text of Rule 108*bis* (A) shows that two elements were established for the application of the right of a State to request review:

(1) The State needed to be "directly affected by an interlocutory decision of a Trial Chamber"; and

(2) The impugned decision had to concern "issues of general importance relating to the powers of the Tribunal".

These two elements were clarified in the subsequent cases of the Tribunal and will, therefore, be examined within that context.

2. History of the Rule

2.1 Adoption

Rule 108*bis* was adopted on 24 July 1997 at the ICTY's thirteenth plenary session. On 18 July 1997, six days before the adoption of the new Rule 108*bis*, Trial Chamber II had rendered its decision on the objection of the Republic of Croatia to the issuance of *subpoena duces tecum* in the *Blaškić* case,[1] a decision which was criticised by Croatia. On 25 July 1997, Croatia submitted a request for review, based on Rule 108, which was subsequently considered as falling within the scope of the new Rule.

2.2 Further amendments of the Rule

Sub-Rule 108*bis* (D) was amended at the fourteenth plenary session on 12 November 1997 to refer to Rule 116 (B), i.e., to the power of the Presiding Judge to determine delays and other procedural requirements. This amendment was supplemented at the eighteenth plenary session on 9–10 July 1998, by reference to Rule 116*bis* in its entirety. The jurisprudence of the Tribunal, which is discussed below, relates to the Rule in its initial form as outlined above.

---

[1]*Prosecutor v. Blaškić, Decision on the Objection of the Republic of Croatia to the Issuance of Subpoena Duces Tecum*, Case No. IT-95-14-PT, 18 July 1997 ("*Blaškić* Subpoena Decision").

The most recent amendments concerned sub-Rules 108*bis* (A) and (B) and were effected during the twenty-first plenary session on 15–17 November 1999. The text was amended to read as follows:

> (A) A State directly affected by an interlocutory decision of a Trial Chamber may, within fifteen days from the date of the decision, file a request for review of the decision by the Appeals Chamber if that decision concerns issues of general importance relating to the powers of the Tribunal.
>
> (B) The party upon whose motion the Trial Chamber issued the impugned decision shall be heard by the Appeals Chamber. The other party may be heard if the Appeals Chamber considers that the interests of justice so require.

As can be noted with regard to sub-Rule (A), the phrase "seek a review" was replaced by the wording "file a request for review". This change purported to underline the formalised character of the review proceedings. Sub-Rule (B) was rephrased completely. The entitlement of both the Prosecutor and the defence to be heard by the Appeals Chamber was removed. Instead, only the party upon whose motion the impugned decision was issued is entitled to be heard. The other party may be heard if the Appeals Chamber considers that the interests of justice so require. This amendment took into account the fact that so far the main "antagonist" of the State in review proceedings had been the Prosecutor, while the defence did not always play an active role. It might have also been due to the consideration to ensure an expeditious procedure.

3 Jurisprudence regarding the Admissibility of a State Request for Review

3.1 Blaškić *case*

Rule 108*bis* was for the first time discussed in the Appeals Chamber's decision regarding the admissibility of Croatia's request for review in the *Blaškić* case.[2] Croatia submitted its request for review on 25 July 1997, one day after Rule 108*bis* was adopted at the Tribunal's plenary session.[3] Croatia based its request on Rule 108,[4] a ground which was consequently denied by the Appeals Chamber, since Croatia lacked standing as a party under that

[2]*Prosecutor v. Blaškić, Decision on the Admissibility of the Request for Review by the Republic of Croatia on an Interlocutory Decision of a Trial Chamber (issuance of subpoena duces tecum) and Scheduling Order*, Case No. IT-95-14-AR108*bis*, A. Ch., 29 July 1997 ("*Blaškić* Subpoena Appeal Decision").

[3]*Prosecutor v. Blaškić, Notice of Appeal of the Republic of Croatia and Request for Stay of Trial Chamber's Order of 18 July 1997*, Case No. IT-95-14-AR108*bis*, 25 July 1997.

[4]Id., p. 1.

Rule.[5] However, the Appeals Chamber subsequently examined the new Rule 108*bis* as a basis of Croatia's request and found that the Rule "was adopted to fill a perceived *lacuna* in the Statute and Rules, namely that a State whose interests were intimately affected by a decision of a Trial Chamber could not request that decision to be submitted to appellate review".[6] The Appeals Chamber, therefore, found it appropriate to consider Croatia's request under the new Rule. Prior to examining the criteria set out in the new Rule, the Appeals Chamber examined a possible "retroactive or otherwise aspect" of the amendment, since the impugned decision was rendered on 18 July 1997, i.e., before the new Rule was adopted. In this regard, the Appeals Chamber found that the rights of the accused would not be prejudiced provided that the appeal was heard expeditiously and that it did not unduly delay the trial proceedings.[7]

Having established the applicability of Rule 108*bis*, the Appeals Chamber then proceeded to the admissibility test of whether Croatia was "directly affected" by the decision and whether it concerned "issues of general importance relating to the powers of the Tribunal". It found that the decision met both requirements. Regarding the first element, the Appeals Chamber held that Croatia was "clearly directly affected" by a decision stating that both Croatia and high officials of Croatia may be ordered to produce documents, in particular military records, before the Tribunal. Regarding the second element, the question of the Tribunal's power to subpoena States and high officials of States was considered to fall within that category since it related to the Tribunal's competence.[8]

Although the Appeals Chamber did not elaborate further in this regard, an examination of Croatia's arguments demonstrates that the decision was reasonable. Croatia raised nine counts[9] in order to object to the issuance of *subpoena duces tecum*. It objected to any competence of the Tribunal or possible inherent or express powers to issue compulsory orders. It then disputed the form of *subpoena duces tecum* and the Tribunal's power to enforce or sanction orders. In its last three counts, Croatia maintained a strong view on the immunity of state officials under international law, disputed the Tribunal's power to determine national security interests of States and dismissed possibilities to hold State officials acting in their official capacity in contempt or to sanction them. In view of the fundamental nature of Croatia's arguments, the elements of "being directly affected" and "issues of general importance" are arguably well established.

---

[5] *Blaškić* Subpoena Appeal Decision at para. 6.

[6] Id., paras. 8 and 9.

[7] Id., paras. 10 and 11.

[8] Id., paras. 13 and 14.

[9] *Prosecutor v. Blaškić, Notice of Appeal of the Republic of Croatia and Request for Stay of Trial Chamber's Order of 18 July 1997*, Case No. IT-95-14-AR108*bis*, 25 July 1997 at para. 3, subparas. (A) to (I).

3.2 Kordić and Čerkez *case*

The admissibility of a State request for review was again examined in the *Kordić and Čerkez* case, in which Croatia requested the Appeals Chamber to quash an order for the production of documents. The Appeals Chamber in its order on admissibility[10] confirmed that both requisite elements were met in this regard. It stated that Croatia was clearly directly affected by an order for the production of documents.[11] The Appeals Chamber also confirmed that questions regarding the meaning and intent of Article 29 of the Statute were issues of general importance relating to the powers of the Tribunal.[12] In this regard, the Appeals Chamber noted that the Prosecution, "in view of the experience concerning the issuance and enforcement of binding orders by the International Tribunal over the past eighteen months", had favoured the appellate review.[13]

4. Analysis

4.1 Principles emerging from the cases

4.1.1 Blaškić case

The Appeals Chamber in its Judgement on Croatia's request for review[14] delineated a general framework of the law on State co-operation with the Tribunal. The following principles could be discerned:

The power of the Tribunal to issue binding orders to States was generally upheld, while the form of *subpoena* was considered to be not applicable in relation to States, since the Appeals Chamber favoured a narrow interpretation of the term, referring only to binding orders *under the threat of penalty*.[15] Furthermore, the established principle of sovereign equality of States precluded the issuance of binding orders to state officials acting in their official capacity. The Tribunal, therefore, had to turn to the State itself.[16] The Appeals Chamber, in this regard, again preferred a cautious approach as to the extent of the powers of the Tribunal.

Regarding the content of a binding order for the production of documents issued under Article 29 (2) of the Statute, the Appeals Chamber established

[10]*Prosecutor v. Kordić and Čerkez, Order on Admissibility of State Request for Review of Order to the Republic of Croatia for the Production of Documents Issued by Trial Chamber III on 4 February 1999 and Request for Suspension of Execution of Order*, Case No. IT-95-14/2-AR108*bis*, A. Ch., 26 March 1999.

[11]Id., p. 3.

[12]Id.

[13]Id., p. 2.

[14]*Prosecutor v. Blaškić, Judgement on the Request of the Republic of Croatia for Review of the Decision of Trial Chamber II of 18 July 1997*, Case No. IT-95-14-AR108*bis*, A. Ch., 29 Oct. 1997 ("*Blaškić* Subpoena Judgement").

[15]Id., para. 21 (emphasis added).

[16]Id., para. 43.

certain criteria. It held that the order must identify specific documents rather than broad categories, set out the reasons why the documents are deemed relevant or at least general grounds therefore, not be unduly onerous, and give the requested State sufficient time for compliance.[17]

The Appeals Chamber asserted a general principle that States may not withhold documents because of alleged national security concerns alone and that the ultimate decision must rest with a Judge of the Tribunal. The Tribunal should, however take such concerns into account, and, if necessary, provide practical procedures[18] such as the scrutiny by one Judge,[19] the provision of a certified translation by the State concerned, *in camera ex parte* proceedings, no deposition or filing, and finally partial redaction of documents by the State. In addition, the State's previous record regarding co-operation should be taken into account.[20]

The provision of national security information was also discussed in relation to the establishment of the permanent International Criminal Court (ICC). A proposal presented by the United Kingdom reflected the intentions of the Subpoena Judgement to put the Court into a position to decide over the issue of security information.[21] The discussions resulted in stronger protection for the security interests of States. The State, while generally being obliged to co-operate with the Court, was provided with a right to intervene. The procedure for the disclosure itself was made dependent on who was in control of the information. The Court could order disclosure if the information was within its control or when it could be obtained by methods other than by request for co-operation under Part 9 of the Statute. In case the State had control, the Court could refer the matter to the Assembly of States Parties.[22]

4.1.2 Kordić and Čerkez case

In its decision on another request for review of a binding order by Croatia,[23] the Appeals Chamber dealt with Croatia's request to quash the binding order on two grounds; firstly, that the order was issued without Croatia

[17] Id., para. 32.

[18] Id., para. 68.

[19] Judge Karibi-Whyte dissented on that issue and held that the full Trial Chamber should decide. See: *Blaškić* Subpoena Judgement, *Separate Opinion of Judge Adolphus G. Karibi-Whyte*, Case No. IT-95-14-AR108*bis*, 29 Oct. 1997 at para. 14. This issue was also raised by G. Sluiter who criticised the Appeals Chamber as being "over-zealous" in proposing this practical solution; see G. Sluiter in A. Klip and G. Sluiter (Eds.), Annotated Leading Cases of International Criminal Tribunals I, pp. 245–285, at 285.

[20] *Blaškić* Subpoena Judgement at para. 68.

[21] For a comprehensive analysis see: R. Dixon and H. Duffy, "Article 72", in O. Triffterer (Ed.), Commentary on the Rome Statute (1999), margin no. 2; see also R. Wedgewood, "International Criminal Tribunals and State Sources of Proof: The case of Tihomir Blaškić", 11 *Leiden Journal of International Law* (1998), pp. 635–654.

[22] R. Dixon and H. Duffy, see supra footnote 21, margins no. 3, 4.

[23] *Prosecutor v. Kordić and Čerkez, Decision on the Request of the Republic of Croatia for Review of a Binding Order*, Case No. IT-95-14/2-AR108*bis*, A. Ch., 9 Sept. 1999.

having been given notice and an opportunity to be heard and secondly, that the order did not comply with the criteria regarding the content of a binding order established in the Subpoena Judgement.

Croatia alleged that a binding order for document production could not be issued without affording the requested State notice and an opportunity to be heard. The Appeals Chamber held that both elements were sufficiently provided through Rule 108*bis* and that Croatia had no right to be notified or heard before the issuance of a binding order.[24]

Regarding the alleged inconsistency of the Binding Order with the criteria established in the *Blaškić* Subpoena Judgement, the Appeals Chamber held that the Trial Chamber in its Binding Order characterised the Judgement's criteria to be "mandatory and cumulative" and, therefore considered itself bound by them.[25] The Appeals Chamber then examined the four requirements set out in the Judgement.[26] Regarding specificity, it held that the Judgement prohibited broad categories, but not the use of categories as such. It further argued that the issue of relevance fell within the discretion of the Trial Chamber and States from which documents were requested lacked *locus standi* to challenge that issue. As regards the amount of documents requested, the Appeals Chamber held that there were no absolute terms in numbers, which would render the request unduly onerous. However, proportionality between the difficulty to produce evidence and the exigencies of the trial should be kept in mind. Lastly, the requirement of sufficient time limits did not create an obligation for the Trial Chamber to consult the State before the issuance of a Binding Order, since that matter could sufficiently be dealt with within the procedure of Rule 108*bis*.

4.2 Discussion

The establishment of a request for review undoubtedly led to important decisions regarding the area of State co-operation and helped clarify parts of the powers of the Tribunal and the corresponding obligations of States. As noted above, the Subpoena Judgement made detailed observations regarding the powers of the Tribunal, their use and mechanisms to be used in delicate situations involving national interests.

However, a preliminary question, i.e., why it was felt necessary to provide States with a separate legal instrument to challenge decisions, does not seem to be clearly answered. The argumentation used in the Subpoena Appeals Decision on the admissibility of a State request for review does not appear to contain detailed reasoning. The statement that Rule 108*bis* was adopted "to fill a perceived *lacuna* that States whose interests were intimately affected by a decision of the Trial Chamber should be given the right to seek review" does not add much clarity. By nature, the creation and mandate of

[24] Id., paras. 16–20.
[25] Id., para. 33.
[26] Id., paras. 33–44.

the Tribunal "intimately affects the interests of States", especially when orders under Article 29 of the Statute are issued.

Did the introduction of the Rule stem from the recognition of the increased importance of the role of States in the functioning of the trial procedure, so that there had to be a legal instrument similar to that of a party to the proceedings? The context of the case at hand, i.e., the role of General Blaškić as one of the higher-ranking leaders, might have underlined the importance of such co-operation and might have played a part in the considerations of the Appeals Chamber.

If one of the reasons for the introduction of the Rule was indeed to ensure State co-operation, especially in high-level cases, the question remains if that goal has been achieved. The recent history of the Tribunal seems to indicate that the level of co-operation is, to a large degree, dependent on the political situation in States. The introduction of a review mechanism of decisions did not seem to significantly change the attitude of States on co-operation with the Tribunal. Until now, only one State, Croatia, resorted to that mechanism. It is, therefore, difficult to assess its significance in a broader context.

Furthermore, it is interesting to note that the right for States to request review is unique to the Rules of the ICTY, although the work of both Tribunals is dependent on State co-operation. In connection with the ICTR, concerns and interests of Rwanda and other, mainly African States, came to the surface in the recent *Barayagwiza* case where Rwanda claimed to be "intimately affected" by decisions of the Tribunal, without having the possibility to formally request review. It remains to be seen if, in that light, the ICTR might consider the establishment of a State request for review.

Another aspect concerns possible developments of the Rule. The latest changes in the Rule seem to indicate that it is deemed appropriate to expedite the review procedure by making the participation of the other party dependent on the decision of the Appeals Chamber. Since there has been no new case law as yet, it cannot be certain at this stage if this will be achieved.

5. Conclusion

From the relevant case law of the Tribunal it follows that the jurisprudence has not yet sufficiently crystallised in order to answer the question if the Rule had contributed to close a *lacuna* regarding the role of States or if the Rule was merely a reaction to a "factual situation on the ground" that needed to be resolved at that time. Future cases of States invoking that Rule might shed more light on this question.

DAVID TOLBERT[1] and ÅSA RYDBERG[2]

39. Enforcement of Sentences

1. Introduction

As an international criminal court, it is axiomatic that the ICTY faces the issue of how to enforce its sentences. The Tribunal's Statute has placed the onus of housing convicted individuals on co-operating States, but it has made this a voluntary undertaking.[3] Thus, while States have specific legal obligations to co-operate on a range of issues with the Tribunal, including making arrests and turning over evidence,[4] they have no specific legal duty to house convicted persons. The ICTY has thus had to rely on the goodwill of co-operating States to assist it in enforcing its sentences.

During the early days of the Tribunal, its requests to States for assistance regarding enforcement of sentences, by entering agreements to enforce the Tribunal's sentences, generally and understandably fell on deaf ears, as the ICTY had few detainees and was just beginning to commence its first trials. This situation has now been transformed, with almost 40 persons in detention and a number of convictions as of the time of writing. Thus, issues relating to the enforcement of the Tribunal's sentences are now coming to the fore. However, it must also be noted that the Tribunal has been active in seeking agreements from States to enforce its sentences. President Gabrielle Kirk McDonald, working with the Registrar, took a particularly active role in attempting to persuade States to enter into agreements and during her term

[1]Senior Legal Adviser, Registry and Chef de Cabinet to President McDonald, ICTY. B.A. *magna cum laude*, Furman University; J.D., University of North Carolina; LL.M *with distinction*, University of Nottingham. Formerly: Chief, General Legal Division, UNRWA; Lecturer, University of Hull School of Law; Partner, Gerdes, Mason, Wilson, Tolbert & Simpson.

[2]Associate Legal Officer, Registry, ICTY; Master of Laws, Uppsala University, Sweden.

The views expressed herein are the view of the authors alone and do not necessarily represent the views of the ICTY or the UN.

[3]ICTY Statute, Art. 27.

[4]Cf. ICTY Statute, Art. 29.

R. May et al., Essays on ICTY Procedure and Evidence in Honour of Gabrielle Kirk McDonald, 533–543.

a number of agreements were concluded and negotiations commenced with other States.[5] Thus, shortly after the end of President McDonald's term, seven (7) States had signed agreements with the ICTY.

There are a number of practical and theoretical issues that arise in relation to enforcement of the Tribunal's sentences which explain the fact that only a relatively small number of States have been willing thus far to enter into agreements with the UN. These primarily relate to difficulties arising for States in enforcing the judgement of an international court and then remaining subject to the supervision of that court regarding the enforcement of the sentence. While States are familiar with treaties for enforcement of judgements of foreign courts, in which the enforcing State essentially takes over the enforcement of the sentence of the foreign court,[6] their laws generally need some adaptation to enforce the sentence of Tribunal. In particular, issues relating to pardon, commutation and early release raise difficulties, as well as to a lesser extent the inspection regime that the Tribunal requires to ensure that human rights standards are observed by the enforcing State. This chapter will examine these and other issues relating to the enforcement of sentences in the context of the Tribunal's Statute, Rules and practices.[7]

2. Legal Framework

The legal framework for the enforcement of the Tribunal's sentences is established in Articles 27 and 28 of the Statute. Article 27 provides that the convicted person will be imprisoned in a State that has indicated that it is willing to do so, "in accordance with the applicable law of the State concerned, subject to the supervision of the International Tribunal".[8] Article 28 addresses issues of pardon and commutation of sentence, providing that if the convicted person is eligible for pardon or commutation of sentence under the law of the enforcing State, it shall so notify the Tribunal, and the President, "in consultation with the judges, shall decide the matter on the basis of the

[5]See Report of the Expert Group to Conduct a Review of the Effective Operation and Functioning of the International Criminal Tribunal for the Former Yugoslavia and the International Criminal Tribunal for Rwanda, A/54/634, 22 Nov. 1999 ("Experts Report"), at para. 110.

[6]See 1983 Council of Europe Model Convention on the Transfer of Sentenced Persons, 112 ETS (1983), Art. 9(3). David Tolbert, "The International Criminal Tribunal for the former Yugoslavia", 11 *Leiden Journal of International Law* (1998), pp. 655–669, at pp. 660–1 ("Tolbert").

[7]The authors note that this chapter overlaps conceptually with a previous article written by one of them, see supra note 6. Therefore, the authors have endeavoured to cover developments since the publication of that article while providing background necessary to understand the general practice of the Tribunal regarding enforcement of sentences. Readers are referred to the previous article for a fuller discussion of the theoretical and conceptual issues relating to the enforcement of sentences, which cannot be addressed in the present chapter due to reasons of space.

[8]For a discussion of the meaning of "supervision", see supra note 6, at pp. 659–60.

interests of justice and the general principles of law". Rules 103 and 104 essentially repeat the provisions of Article 27, adding that until the arrangements for transfer are finalised, "the convicted person shall remain in the custody of the Tribunal". Moreover, Rules 123–125 address matters relating to pardon and commutation of sentence and provide for general standards applicable to granting such pardon or commutation of sentence.[9]

It is clear that the Statute and the Rules only provide a general framework for the enforcement of sentences in co-operating States and do not address the modalities of enforcement or other important issues, such as issues relating to early release of the convicted person. The United Nations and the ICTY have drafted a Model Agreement, which establishes a framework for enforcement and addresses issues relating thereto.[10] The Model Agreement starts from the premise that the State is "bound by the duration of the sentence" pronounced by the Tribunal.[11] Building on this concept and the Tribunal's overall supervision of the enforcement, the Model Agreement provides that issues relating to early release will be treated in the same matter as pardon and commutation of sentence under Article 28, i.e., the President decides if early release is appropriate. Moreover, the Model Agreement establishes mechanisms for communications between the parties and for decisions on enforcement requests, which are made by the Tribunal and accepted by the State on a case by case basis.

3. Pardon, Commutation of Sentence and Early Release

As previously noted, the Tribunal retains the power to grant pardon and commutation of sentence. A pardon is usually granted when the executive determines that the crime should be forgiven or that there had been a miscarriage of justice and that sentence should not have been imposed in the first place.[12] A commutation of sentence has similar implications, as the original sentence is substituted by a lesser penalty, which may imply recognition that the original sentence was overly harsh or otherwise defective.[13] Given

[9]ICTY Rule 125 provides: "In determining whether pardon or commutation is appropriate, the President shall take into account, inter alia, the gravity of the crime or crimes for which the prisoner was convicted, the treatment of similarly-situated prisoners, the prisoner's demonstration of rehabilitation, as well as any substantial cooperation of the prisoner with the Prosecutor."

[10]The ICTY's agreement with Norway is, *mutatis mutandis*, identical to the Model Agreement. Agreement Between the Government of Norway and the United Nations on the Enforcement of Sentences of the International Criminal Tribunal for the former Yugoslavia, 24 Apr. 1998, UNTS Registration No. 34525 ("Norwegian Agreement").

[11]References to the Model Agreement can be found in the Norwegian Agreement.

[12]See *generally* 1 International Encyclopaedia of Laws, Criminal Law, Sections 626–628 (Jan. 1993).

[13]Id.

this and the fact that the Tribunal has jurisdiction over very serious crimes, the granting of pardon and commutation must be treated with the utmost seriousness.[14]

With regard to early release, the term is a broad one, thus implying that it covers parole, non-custodial measures or any other similar programs and was thus deliberately chosen for use in the Model Agreement. The Statute and the Rules are, however, silent with regard to the granting of early release.[15] This is surprising, given that most convicted persons can be expected to become eligible for some form of early release under the applicable domestic law of the State in which the sentence is being served.

While the legal basis for treating, in the Model Agreement, early release similar to pardon and commutation of sentence has been described above, there are also a number of policy reasons for doing so. These include the fact that early release, like pardon or commutation, also ends the incarceration or, in the alternative, fundamentally changes the conditions of the enforcement of the sentence.[16] Thus, the Model Agreement was drafted to provide that if, pursuant to the national law of the enforcing State, the convicted person becomes eligible for early release, the final decision rests with the President, in consultation with the Judges of the Tribunal, as to whether any early release is appropriate. If not, the enforcing State shall continue to enforce the sentence.[17]

One issue that arises in connection with early release is that by tying the early release to State law, convicted persons serving similar sentences may be subject to different early release regimes. Thus, there is a theoretical possibility of unequal treatment of similarly situated convicted persons. In practice, this difficulty is ameliorated in two ways. First, the early release regimes are, at least in European countries (where most of the sentences probably will be served), broadly similar, with eligibility for early release generally after two-thirds of the sentence has been served.[18] Moreover, the President is in the position to review all applications for early release and thus can ensure that unequal treatment does not occur. The President will need to take these concerns into account when considering requests for early release. The President should also take into account the early release regimes of the different States when he or she designates the State in which the sentence will be served.

---

[14]Tolbert, supra note 6, at pp. 661–662.

[15]The Secretary-General's Report is also silent on this matter.

[16]The fact that any early release is subject to the approval of the President of the Tribunal must also be seen as part of the Tribunal's broad supervision of the enforcement of the sentence, as expressed in Art. 3(2) of the Model Agreement. See Tolbert, supra note 6, at pp. 664–667.

[17]Norwegian Agreement, supra note 10, Art. 3, paras. 3–4.

[18]See *generally* International Encyclopaedia of Laws, supra note 12.

The President of the Tribunal has issued a Practice Direction[19] on the Procedure for the Determination of Applications for Pardon, Commutation of Sentence and Early Release of Persons Convicted by the International Tribunal, which establishes the internal procedure to be used in connection with applications for pardon, commutation of sentence and early release.[20] Concerning pardon and commutation of sentence, the Practice Direction simply provides a procedure for the principles provided in Article 28 and Rule 125. With regard to early release, the Practice Direction follows the Model Agreement, and the agreements that have been actually negotiated with States, and provides that early release should be dealt with in the same manner as pardon and commutation of sentence.

Under the Practice Direction, when a convicted person becomes eligible for pardon, commutation of sentence or early release under the law of the State in which the sentence is being served, the State shall, in accordance with the enforcement agreement, notify the Tribunal accordingly.[21] Upon receiving such notification, the Registry of the Tribunal shall inform the convicted person, request reports and observations from the relevant authorities in the enforcing State as to the behaviour of the convicted person and the general conditions under which he or she was imprisoned, and request any psychiatric or psychological evaluations prepared on the mental condition of the convicted person. Moreover, the Registry shall also request from the Prosecutor a detailed report of any co-operation that the convicted person has provided to his or her office and the significance of such co-operation.[22] Copies of the above mentioned information shall be forwarded to the President of the Tribunal as well as to the convicted person. Following this, the President of the Tribunal shall hear the convicted person either through written submissions, or alternatively, by video- or telephone-link.[23] The President will determine whether pardon, commutation of sentence or early release is to be granted, having regard to the above noted criteria specified in Rule 125, and taking into account the views of the members of the Bureau and the sentencing Chamber.[24] The decision of the President is final and can

---

[19]Pursuant to ICTY Rule 19(b), the President of the ICTY may, in consultation with the Bureau, the Registrar and the Prosecutor, issue Practice Directions, consistent with the ICTY Statute and the ICTY Rules, addressing detailed aspects of the conduct of proceedings before the Tribunal.

[20]Practice Direction on the Procedure for the Determination of Applications for Pardon, Commutation of Sentence and Early Release of Persons Convicted by the International Tribunal, IT/146, 7 Apr. 1999 ("Practice Direction on Pardon, Commutation of Sentence and Early Release").

[21]Id., para. 1.

[22]Id., para. 2; para. 6 provides that all information received by the President pursuant to paragraphs 2 through 5 shall be considered confidential.

[23]Id., paras. 3–4.

[24]Id., para. 7. However, it should be pointed out that it is possible that the members of the sentencing Chamber are no longer serving as Judges at the Tribunal at the time of the application for pardon, commutation of sentence or early release.

thus not be appealed.[25] However, with regard to applications for early release, in the event that the President decides that early release is inappropriate, the decision shall specify the date on which the convicted person will next become eligible for consideration for early release, unless it is specified by the domestic law of the enforcing State.[26]

The decision shall be made public, unless the President decides otherwise.[27] The President can also direct the Registry to inform witnesses about the release of the convicted person, the destination of the convicted person upon his or her release and about any other relevant matters, where appropriate.[28] Such information may be of particular importance for witnesses who are victims of crimes committed by the convicted person and who testified about these crimes during the trial.

While the Tribunal has no practice regarding these matters to report, there are several issues raised by the Appeals Chamber in its Sentencing Judgement in the *Tadić* case. The Appeals Chamber sentenced the accused to 20 years imprisonment, but makes the recommendation that "unless exceptional circumstances apply, Duško Tadić should serve a term of imprisonment ending no earlier than 14 July 2007",[29] which is approximately two-thirds of the 20 year sentence. Such a recommendation is best interpreted as a recommendation to the President of the Tribunal rather than to the enforcing State; the judgement could hardly be seen as overriding Article 28. Thus, the applicable national law on early release should still work as the trigger for eligibility and the ensuing application for early release, regardless of what the Sentencing Judgement recommends. However, if the recommendation were interpreted as pre-empting the President's power to decide on whether an application for early release should be granted, this could be seen as eroding the power implicitly granted to the President by Article 28. Moreover, the Sentencing Appeals Chamber would be involving itself in administrative matters outside its area of competence.

In another case, the Trial Chamber sentenced Goran Jelisić to 40 years imprisonment and recommended that he receive psychological and psychiatric follow-up treatment and requested "the Registry to take all the appropriate measures in this respect together with the State in which he will serve his sentence".[30] In a footnote, the Trial Chamber points out that the concluded Agreements all provide that when the Registrar presents her request to the enforcing State, she will attach any appropriate recommendation relating to continued treatment in the State where the convicted person serves the sentence.[31] Thus, given the fact that Article 27 provides

[25] Id., para. 9.
[26] Id., para. 8.
[27] Id., para. 7.
[28] Id., para. 11.
[29] *Prosecutor v. Tadić, Judgement in Sentencing Appeals*, Case No. IT-94-1-A and IT-94-1-*bis*, A. Ch., 26 Jan. 2000 at para. 76.
[30] *Prosecutor v. Jelisić, Judgement*, Case No. IT-95-10-T, 14 Dec. 1999 at para. 140.
[31] Id., footnote 185.

that the imprisonment shall be in accordance with the applicable law of the State where the sentences is being served, the Trial Chamber's request must be seen as a mere recommendation to the enforcing State to provide psychological and psychiatric follow-up treatment to Jelisić.

It should be noted that the Model Agreement's requirement that States adapt to the Tribunal's primacy, by allowing the Tribunal to make the final determination on pardon, commutation of sentence and early release matters, may cause difficulties for some States, as they will have to adopt a procedure which is not in conformity with the procedures provided for by their domestic laws.[32] The power to grant a pardon is generally reserved for the executive, such as the President or Queen and is so often vested by the Constitution of the State. Given this, a number of States have, in fact, had difficulty with the provisions of the Model Agreement relating to pardon, commutation of sentence and early release; these difficulties are discussed below.[33]

4. Supervision of Prison Conditions

Another matter addressed in the Statute and the Model Agreement is the conditions of imprisonment of the convicted person and the inspections of these conditions. The Model Agreement, building on Article 27, provides that the conditions of imprisonment shall be compatible with certain standards applicable to the treatment of prisoners. In order to ensure appropriate implementation of those standards, the Model Agreement stipulates that the International Committee of the Red Cross ("ICRC") shall conduct inspections of the conditions of detention and treatment of prisoner(s) on a periodic basis.[34] The ICRC reports its findings to the State and to the Tribunal, which then consult on the appropriate steps to be taken on the basis of the reports. This use of a respected independent body, specialising in prison conditions, ensures that the applicable human rights standards are being enforced. However, as is discussed below, some States have had difficulties with the inspection regime.

---

[32]Tolbert, supra note 6, at p. 665.

[33]See Contribution of the Chambers of the International Criminal Tribunal for the former Yugoslavia (ICTY), submitted at the 13–31 March 2000 Preparatory Commission for the International Criminal Court, on the provisional Rules of Procedure and Evidence for the Court, V(D), at pp. 17–18.

[34]See the Norwegian Agreement, supra note 10, art. 3(5). The standards include the Standard Minimum Rules for the Treatment of Prisoners, ECOSOC Resolution 663 C(XXIV) of 31 July 1957; the Body of Principles for the Protection of all Persons Under any Form of Detention or Imprisonment, UN Doc. A/RES/43/173 of 9 Dec. 1988; and Basic Principles for the Treatment of Prisoners, UN Doc. A/RES/45/111 of 14 Dec. 1990. The inspections by the ICRC are provided for in Art. 6 of the Norwegian Agreement.

5. ICTY Practice in Relation to Enforcement of Sentences

5.1 Agreements concluded

Thus far, the United Nations has concluded seven agreements with individual States on the enforcement of sentences of the Tribunal. Italy, Finland, Norway, Austria, Sweden, France and Spain have each signed such agreements.[35] These agreements are all based on the Model Agreement, with some differences, as discussed below.

Some of the agreements contain provisions that limit the scope of application. However, while discussing these restrictions or conditions it should be kept in mind that all the agreements are framework agreements which treat all the requests to a State to enforce a particular sentence on a case-by-case basis. Thus, while some States have chosen to include their restrictions or conditions in the agreement, other States may have chosen to limit the scope of application of the agreement by simply intending to reject requests to enforce certain sentences, e.g., sentences of high profile figures or sentences longer than the maximum sentence under domestic law in the State.

The Agreement with Spain provides that it will only consider enforcing sentences pronounced by the Tribunal that do not exceed the highest maximum sentence for any crime under Spanish law.[36] The Swedish Agreement requires that the convicted person have "strong ties" with Sweden.[37] Obviously, such requirements limit the scope of application of the Agreement considerably, particularly in the case of Sweden. Moreover, the Italian, Swedish, French and Spanish Agreements all differ from the Model

[35] Agreement Between the Government of the Italian Republic and the United Nations on the Enforcement of Sentences of the International Criminal Tribunal for the former Yugoslavia, 6 Feb. 1997, UNTS Registration No. 36198 ("Italian Agreement"); Agreement Between the International Criminal Tribunal for the former Yugoslavia and the Government of Finland on the Enforcement of Sentences of the International Tribunal, 7 May 1997, UNTS Registration No. 34918 ("Finnish Agreement"), Norwegian Agreement, supra note 10; Agreement Between the United Nations and the Government of Sweden on the Enforcement of Sentences of the International Criminal Tribunal for the former Yugoslavia, 23 Feb. 1999, UNTS Registration 35517 ("Swedish Agreement"); Agreement between the United Nations and the Federal Government of Austria on the Enforcement of Sentences of the International Criminal Tribunal for the former Yugoslavia, 23 July 1999, UNTS Registration 35959 ("Austrian Agreement"); Accord entre l'organisation des Nations Unies et le Gouvernement de la République française concernant l'exécution des peines prononcées par le Tribunal pénal international pour l'ex-Yougoslavie, 25 Feb. 2000, UNTS Registration pending ("French Agreement"); and Agreement between the United Nations and the Kingdom of Spain on the Enforcement of Sentences of the International Criminal Tribunal for the former Yugoslavia, 28 Mar. 2000, UNTS Registration pending ("Spanish Agreement"). The Agreements with Italy, Finland, Norway, Sweden and Austria are in effect; the Tribunal has not yet received notification that France and Spain have ratified their respective Agreements.

[36] Spanish Agreement, id., Art. 3(2). Currently, the maximum sentence for a crime under Spanish law is 30 years.

[37] Swedish Agreement, supra note 35, Art. 2(2)(d).

Agreement with regard to certain provisions relating to pardon, commutation of sentence and early release.[38] The Spanish Agreement also deviates from the Model Agreement on inspections of the conditions of imprisonment.

5.2 Issues in negotiation

As noted above, in the case of pardon, commutation of sentence and early release, the "trigger mechanism" lies with domestic law but the Tribunal retains the power to actually grant these measures. This approach led to problems for Italy, as its law did not allow for such decisions to be made by an outside power. The Italian Agreement thus provides that in the event a convicted person becomes eligible for pardon, commutation of sentence or early release under Italian law and the President of the Tribunal does not find this to be appropriate, the convicted person will be immediately re-transferred to the Tribunal.[39] The Swedish, French and Spanish Agreements provide for similar solutions.[40] Needless to say, in the event that such a transfer takes place, the convicted person will thereafter be transferred to another State for continued enforcement. While these problems are perhaps more theoretical than real, it points to one of the substantive difficulties that impede certain States from entering in enforcement of sentences agreements with the Tribunal.

Other States have had difficulty with the inspection regime and have not been willing to accept the provisions of the Model Agreement in this regard. Alternative inspection procedures have therefore been adopted in these cases. The Austrian Agreement states that "the conditions of imprisonment shall be equivalent to those applicable to prisoners serving sentences under Austrian law and shall be in accordance with relevant human rights standards".[41] It also provides that the inspections shall be performed by the "International Tribunal, or a body designated by it".[42] The Spanish Agreement provides for yet another approach. It stipulates for monitoring of the conditions of detention and treatment of the convicted persons by a Parity Commission, composed of two representatives of the Tribunal and two representatives of Spain. The Parity Commission will perform inspections upon the request, and at a time to be stipulated by, any two members of the Commission.[43] This ensures that the Tribunal representatives may insist on

---

[38]Italian Agreement, supra note 35, Arts. 3(4) and 8(2), Swedish Agreement, supra note 35, Art. 8(2)–(3), French Agreement supra note 35, Arts. 3(4) and 8(2), Spanish Agreement, supra note 35, Arts. 3(5) and 8(2). The reasons for this are explained below.

[39]Italian Agreement, supra note 35, Arts. 3, 8 and 10.

[40]Swedish Agreement, supra note 35, Arts. 3, 8 and 9; French Agreement, supra note 35, Arts. 3, 8 and 10; and Spanish Agreement, supra note 35, Arts. 3, 8 and 10.

[41]Austrian Agreement, supra note 35, Art. 3(3).

[42]Austrian Agreement, id., Art. 6. In this connection it should be noted that ICTY Rule 104 provides that "[a]ll sentences of imprisonment shall be supervised by the Tribunal or a body designated by it."

[43]Spanish Agreement, supra note 35, Art. 4.

inspections. Like the ICRC, the Parity Commission will prepare reports on the conditions of detention and treatment of the convicted person and make recommendations to the President of the Tribunal and to the competent authorities of the State in question.[44] As the two Tribunal representatives can request inspections at any time as well as submit independent reports, the important principle that inspections can be initiated and performed without the control of the enforcing State is retained, albeit in a somewhat different way.

5.3 Designation of State

In domestic systems the prison authorities, normally falling under the ministry of justice or a correctional department, decide where a convicted person shall serve his or her sentence.[45] Since the Tribunal has no justice ministry or other prison or correctional authority, the Rules now provide that the President shall make the decision as to the selection of a State for enforcement.[46] The President of the Tribunal has adopted a Practice Direction for the designation of a State in which a convicted person shall serve his or her sentence.[47] The Practice Direction establishes the modalities of how that decision is made, giving the President the discretion to undertake consultations in determining the appropriate State for enforcement. Such a procedure appears to be appropriate, as the President, being the highest-ranking officer of the Tribunal, is in the best position to make the decision, which is primarily an administrative decision but with certain political and quasi-judicial elements as well.[48]

The procedure established provides that once the sentence of the convicted person becomes final, the Registrar of the Tribunal shall make a preliminary inquiry of the States that, pursuant to Article 27, have declared their willingness to accept convicted persons and which have signed an enforcement agreement to that effect.[49] Following their replies, the Registrar prepares a confidential memorandum for the President of the Tribunal enumerating which States have indicated that they are willing to enforce the sentence. The memorandum shall contain information concerning the convicted person's marital status, dependants, usual place of residence,

---

[44]Spanish Agreement, supra note 35, Art. 4(2)–(3). Cf. Norway Agreement, supra note 32, Art. 6.

[45]See, e.g., 2 International Encyclopaedia of Laws, Criminal Law, Supplement 10, sections 520–522, (Jan. 1993).

[46]ICTY Rule 103(A). Tolbert, supra note 6, at p. 668.

[47]Practice Direction on the Procedure for the International Tribunal's Designation of the State in which a Convicted Person is to Serve His/Her Sentence of Imprisonment, IT/137, 9 July 1998, para. 2 ("Practice Direction on Designation of State").

[48]Tolbert, supra note 6, at pp. 668–669. For a different view, see André Klip, "Enforcement of Sanctions Imposed by the International Criminal Tribunals for Rwanda and the Former Yugoslavia", *European Journal of Crime, Criminal Law and Criminal Justice*, Vol. 5/2, (1997), 144–164, at pp. 156–157.

[49]Practice Direction on Designation of State, supra note 47.

linguistic skills and, where appropriate, any medical or psychological reports on the convicted person. Moreover, the confidential memorandum shall state if the convicted person is expected to serve as a witness in further proceedings of the Tribunal and whether he or she is expected to be relocated as a witness.[50] Finally, if possible, the memorandum shall also note the general conditions of imprisonment and the rules governing security and liberty in the States that have indicated their willingness to enforce the sentence of the convicted person.[51] The President will, on the basis of the submitted information and on any other inquiries that he or she chooses to make, determine the State in which imprisonment is to be served.[52] This decision is final and can thus not be appealed. Before deciding the matter, the President may consult with the Sentencing Chamber or its Presiding Judge as well as request the opinion of the Prosecutor.[53] It is interesting to note that it is optional for the President to request the opinion of the convicted person.[54] The President may decide that the designation of the State shall not be made public.[55] This provision can thus be applied when there are serious security concerns in connection with the transfer of the convicted person to the designated State or during the enforcement in the designated State.

6. Conclusion

The enforcement of the Tribunal's sentences remains an important aspect of the Tribunal's work. Without an adequate number of States willing to enforce the Tribunal's sentences, the Tribunal's work is endangered. Fortunately, under the leadership of President McDonald progress has been made, but much more needs to be done. The experience to date demonstrates the difficulty of reaching agreements with supportive States. However, while issues relating to enforcement, notably pardon, commutation and early release, and matters relating to inspections, have caused difficulties, the Tribunal's practice shows that these difficulties are not insurmountable.

---

[50]Concerning witness relocation, see further e.g. Åsa Rydberg, "The Protection of the Interests of Witnesses: The ICTY in Comparison to the Future ICC", 12 *Leiden Journal of International Law* (1999), pp. 455–478, at pp. 463–465, and Contribution of the Chambers of the International Criminal Tribunal for the former Yugoslavia (ICTY), Submitted at the 13–31 March 2000 Preparatory Commission for the International Criminal Court, on the provisional Rules of Procedure and Evidence for the Court, III(D), at p. 10.

[51]Practice Direction on Designation of State, supra note 47, at para. 3.

[52]Id., at para. 4. When determining in which State the imprisonment is to be served, particular shall be given to the proximity to the convicted person's relations.

[53]Id.

[54]Id. Cf. Art. 103(3)(c) of the Statute of the International Criminal Court, UN Doc. A/CONF.183/9 (1998).

[55]Practice Direction on Designation of State, supra note 47, at para. 5.

PART XIII

The ICTY and its Relationship with the Former Yugoslavia and the ICC

LAL C. VOHRAH[1] and JON CINA[2]

40. The Outreach Programme

> It is likely that, except for a very small proportion of the populations of the former Yugoslavia and elsewhere, there is large-scale, if not total, lack of knowledge regarding the ... ICTY and ICTR.[3]

It is a great pleasure to be able to contribute this paper in honour of Judge Gabrielle Kirk McDonald. She devoted six full years to the Tribunal, first as Judge of a Trial Chamber of the ICTY and subsequently as Presiding Judge of the Appeals Chamber of the ICTY (and ICTR). As one of the founding Judges of the ICTY, she played an important part in making the ICTY the viable institution that it has become today. During her tenure as President of the ICTY one of her pet projects was the Outreach Programme and this paper is a tribute to her unsparing efforts in launching it. The paper is confined to the Outreach Programme pursued in the ICTY.

1. Introduction

The ICTY's Outreach Programme was established in late 1999 as both a response to widespread ignorance concerning the Tribunal's activities and objectives and to facilitate the realisation of some of those objectives. In

---

[1]Judge, Appeals Chamber ICTY/ICTR. *Formerly,* Justice, High Court of Malaya (1978–1993).

[2]PhD Candidate, University of Melbourne. Formerly Special Assistant to President McDonald and Legal Assistant, Registry; LLB Hons., University of Strathclyde.

The authors gratefully acknowledge the assistance of David Tolbert, Senior Legal Officer, ICTY. The views expressed herein are those of the authors and do not necessarily represent those of the United Nations, ICTY or ICTR.

[3]See Report of the Expert Group to Conduct a Review of the Effective Operation and Functioning of the International Criminal Tribunal for the Former Yugoslavia and the International Criminal Tribunal for Rwanda, A/54/634, 22 Nov. 1999 (*Experts' Report*), at para. 97.

R. May et al., Essays on ICTY Procedure and Evidence in Honour of Gabrielle Kirk McDonald, 547–557

thus focusing on its responsibilities towards the populations of the former Yugoslavia, the Tribunal signalled that it had truly moved from creation to implementation. For the court to fulfil its broader mandate of contributing to peace and reconciliation, it must be able to build a positive, direct relationship with those affected by the crimes it was created to prosecute. It is this, rather than the *per se* convictions of and issuance of judgements against those responsible for violations of international humanitarian law in the former Yugoslavia that will have a decisive impact on the Tribunal's success.

The Programme was thus designed to operate at the Tribunal's seat in The Hague and in field offices to be created throughout the conflict region. Together, these units would provide a direct link between the area and the court, allowing the Tribunal to interact directly with and disseminate information to the communities concerned and provide a channel of communication for the communities and their representatives.

2. Rationale

The Tribunal, like its Nuremberg and Tokyo predecessors, occupies a distinctive place in the pantheon of legal institutions. In creating it, the Security Council intended that there be an express link between the court's activities and the politico-sociological situation in the former Yugoslavia. In both Resolutions 808 and 827 it stated its conviction that the establishment of an international tribunal would put an end to the crimes being committed there and constitute an "effective measure to bring to justice the persons responsible for them," thereby contributing to the restoration and maintenance of peace.[4]

Clearly, the court did not "put an end" to the crimes: the conflict in Bosnia and Herzegovina continued and the savagery of the crimes increased. Massacres in Srebrenica and the outbreak of renewed conflict in Kosovo underlined the Tribunal's frailty, both as a nascent organisation wholly dependant on external support to function and as a judicial body supposed to have a real time impact on the conduct of a very real war.[5] It is

[4]See Security Council Resolution 808, S/RES/808 (1993); Security Council Resolution 827, S/RES/827 (1993); Report of the Secretary General pursuant to paragraph 2 of Security Council Resolution 808 (1993) at paras. 25–6.

[5]Equally clearly, the continuation of conflict and massive criminality *prima facie* within the Tribunal's jurisdiction does not represent a failure on its part. Lack of resources and the means to secure custody of indicted persons, many of whom were located in the conflict zone, was the cause of its impotence while the conflict in Bosnia and Herzegovina continued. However, one year after the signing of the General Framework Agreement for Peace in Bosnia and Herzegovina (*GFAP*), when sixty thousand NATO troops patrolled that State, the *de facto* deprioritisation of the Tribunal left over 80% of publicly indicted persons at liberty. The Tribunal was viewed as an impediment, rather than a prerequisite, to comprehensive peace.

only recently that the court's belief that it was "a fundamental piece of the highly complicated jigsaw"[6] – the task of fostering peace and security in the Balkans region – has been endorsed in deed by the international community. The detention of indicted persons, the provision of physical and financial support and the relatively significant progress made lately in securing crucial intelligence material held by various States has finally endowed the court with the means to begin the effective discharge of its mandate to prosecute those responsible for serious violations of international humanitarian law committed in the former Yugoslavia.[7]

Having begun to overcome external obstacles, the contradiction intrinsic to the Tribunal's existence assumes greater significance: it is connected to the former Yugoslavia only tenuously, by the wording of Security Council resolutions. It is thus handicapped unlike any other contemporary analogous legal body.[8] Courts function as a mechanism for delineating standards in the society over which they have jurisdiction. Typically, they have a tangible bond with such societies: the judicial system is either located within the community, or in the case of supra-national courts, individuals have a right of direct petition. Moreover, the existence of a comprehensive criminal justice system,[9] media and legislature, which are established institutions in most States, provides a means of interpreting and disseminating the results of criminal proceedings within those communities. It is thus rarely, if ever, that a court speaks beyond its judicial pronouncements.

In contrast, the Tribunal functions on behalf of all States, rather than within any one. It operates without certain common institutions – enforcement agency, legislative forum, media – in the international community. Crucially, it is located far from the territory and people over which it has jurisdiction, and is mandated to work in only English and French.[10] This institutional vacuum is completely at odds with its purposes. In trying and convicting perpetrators, it aims to provide their victims with a sense of justice. At an individual level, it must acknowledge suffering and punish those who inflicted it. At the community level, it should establish a historical record of the conflict and its causes, insuring against revisionism and the assignation of responsibility to communities, rather than to specific members. Globally, its proceedings are intended to deter others and to prove the efficacy of what is nebulously referred to as international justice.

---

[6]See Antonio Cassese, Address to the General Assembly, 4 Nov. 1997

[7]While arguably one may discern different motives behind the various actions by NATO SFOR to detain indictees within Bosnia and Herzegovina, the moral, legal and practical imperatives of removing and holding to account those responsible for violations of international humanitarian law have been accepted at a policy level, by, *inter alia*, both senior NATO officials and governments such as that of the United Kingdom.

[8]The ICTR faces similar problems.

[9]This includes police, prisons, a parole system and extra-territorial judicial co-operation agreements.

[10]Proceedings and relevant documents are translated into local languages.

The Tribunal's ultimate objective is thus to apply the legal process in helping create conditions for reconciliation leading to peace. Accordingly, it is critical to the success of the court that the victims and perpetrators of the crimes, and the general populations of the states in which they occurred, are made aware of it and its activities and have the opportunity to apply its work to their own communities. If it is to succeed, the ICTY must be relevant to those whose rights it seeks to vindicate.

Disappointingly, the opposite has generally been true: the ICTY's relationship with the people of the former Yugoslavia has been characterised by the latter's lack of knowledge of the former and by the court's inability hitherto to address this.

Of necessity, the first five years of the Tribunal's life were taken up in building its judicial infrastructure. Although a public relations capacity has existed since very early in its creation, the court's primary constituency – the population of the former Yugoslavia – was typically not its principal focus. Instead, efforts focused on States, academics, human rights organisations, and international law activists worked to ensure that the Tribunal's potential effect on the development of those fields was maximised. Although the first two Prosecutors, Goldstone and Arbour, visited the former Yugoslavia relatively frequently, their purpose was predominantly to address operational issues, while the two Presidential visits so far undertaken – in 1996 and 1998 – were similarly focused.[11]

The court was thus perceived at times more as an intellectual exercise than as a body charged with prosecuting the most serious crimes committed in Europe for fifty years. To take one example, no facility existed for transmitting decisions and judgements to the very communities which they concerned nor for reducing the often highly complex and lengthy legal discussions they contained to a format more amenable to mass consumption. Whilst interested individuals in other parts of Europe and in America could obtain copies of ICTY documents, those in the former Yugoslavia were left wondering "what The Hague is doing."

It is easy to criticise this approach. However, as noted, in addition to the difficulties that might reasonably be expected from the creation of a new criminal judicial institution, unprecedented in jurisdiction or legal authority, the international community's apathy towards it undermined the Tribunal to such an extent that its ability to function even as an effective criminal court was questioned.[12] It could only be understood and embraced by its constituents if it was first able to carry out its purely judicial functions.

---

[11]However, in May 2000 President Jorda will attend a conference in Croatia the primary aim of which is to encourage discussion and increase awareness of the court. See Section D infra.

[12]See, for example, Theodor Meron: "Answering for War Crimes", *Foreign Affairs*, Jan. 1997, p. 2.

The predictable consequence of this approach, combined with a number of other factors, was within the former Yugoslavia a proliferation of misperceptions affecting the credibility and the impact of the Tribunal, and consequently its ability to discharge its mandate. The ruling nationalist parties, the media within their control and other interest groups systematically exploited this lack of understanding of the institution. As the Tribunal's judgements have established, many of these groups are themselves responsible for creating the atmosphere conducive to the ethnic conflicts which occurred. Its work to identify individuals in these groupings and hold them accountable for their roles was subject to misrepresentation, politicisation and adverse propaganda. Politically motivated allegations were and continue to be perpetuated against the court, asserting *inter alia*, a bias in its activities, to the benefit or detriment of one or other ethnic group, and mistreatment of persons detained under its authority:

> The impact of the media distortions [within Bosnia and Herzegovina] concerning the Tribunal should not be underestimated: given what their media have to say on the subject of the ICTY, it would be difficult to find Bosnians who do not have misconceptions concerning the Tribunal and its work. This conclusion is supported by the number of government officials directly involved in these issues, including Ministry of Justice officials and public prosecutors, who have revealed [...] basic gaps in their understanding of the Tribunal's role during discussions with [institutions involved in the peace process].[13]

In addition to militating against reconciliation, the impact of such views impedes the work of the Prosecutor and is readily exploited by authorities who do not recognise or do not co-operate with the Tribunal, as for example in the arrest or surrender of indicted persons or the adoption of legislative procedures to govern such co-operation.[14]

The existence of such a state of affairs stood in striking contrast to the Tribunal's relative institutional stability; throughout 1999 the situation became a policy priority within the court.

---

[13] 1998 letter from an institution established under the General Framework Agreement for Peace in Bosnia and Herzegovina to oversee its implementation, to President McDonald. At the time, similar situations existed in the Republic of Croatia and the Federal Republic of Yugoslavia, with the Tribunal in general portrayed as persecuting the Croatian or Serbian people.

[14] As will be discussed below, the political situation in various parts of the former Yugoslavia has since evolved.

3. The Origins of the Outreach Programme

The creation of the Programme marked a significant formal shift in the way in which the Tribunal perceived itself, signalling both the replacement of typically responsive public relations with proactive efforts and its refocusing towards the former Yugoslavia. It was, however, preceded by a variety of *ad hoc* and uncoordinated activities, usually undertaken by external actors.

One of the first was in 1996: the US-based Court TV Network used audio-visual transmissions from the ICTY to broadcast the *Tadić* trial in parts of the former Yugoslavia. Although this was discontinued due to funding shortages, the initially high viewing figures dropped sharply anyway as the intricacies of court proceedings, particularly the one in which the Tribunal "learned to fly",[15] reduced the perceived impact and symbolism of the first trial. Such an enterprise may have been more successful had a daily television digest of the proceedings complemented it but this was not possible at the time.

A significant force for disseminating the work of the Tribunal has been the Coalition for International Justice (CIJ). It was formed under the American Bar Association's Central and East European Law Initiative (ABA-CEELI) after the court's establishment, to co-ordinate several NGOs supporting both the ICTY and the ICTR.[16] The CIJ's internet site was for a time a key source of ICTY information,[17] containing documents and publicity materials both on its work and general issues of international justice. More importantly, through the regular work of the ABA-CEELI's legal training field offices throughout the States and entities of the former Yugoslavia, it was able to channel information between the Tribunal and the region: *inter alia*, engaging the interest of prospective defence counsel; making unofficial translations of simple documents; and speaking to victims' associations, other human rights groups and legal associations about the work of the Tribunal.

In late 1997, Judge McDonald was elected President of the Tribunal, and, in that capacity, declared it a priority to attempt to increase awareness of the court. Although not able to travel to the region herself,[18] she actively supported efforts to enhance perceptions of the Tribunal as being a relevant actor in the peace process, rather than an abstract and distant international

[15]President McDonald, presiding judge in the trial, frequently compared the *Tadić* trial to an aeroplane's test flight.

[16]Through its liaison officer at the Tribunal, the CIJ provided legal research resources and various other forms of assistance to the Judges, the Registry and the Office of the Prosecutor as the court struggled to function.

[17]The website was not endorsed by the ICTY. After protracted discussions with United Nations Headquarters in New York, where the homepage was based for financial reasons, the court launched its own homepage in April 1997.

[18]A variety of reasons precluded her doing so.

institution.[19] In addition to giving a considerable number of interviews with media from the former Yugoslavia and using her international public speaking opportunities to promote the concept, she proposed extending the ICTY's Hague-based press office by establishing a dedicated press unit in Bosnia. Regrettably, budgetary considerations effectively terminated the idea.

President McDonald, the court's Registrar[20] and the CIJ then organised, with external funding,[21] an "Outreach Symposium" at the Tribunal's seat in The Hague, in October 1998.[22] The two-day intensive introduction to the ICTY brought "leading figures from the judicial and legal communities of the former Yugoslavia[23] [together with representatives of international institutions working in Bosnia and Herzegovina] and gave them the opportunity to listen to and question senior members of all sections of the Tribunal."[24] Notwithstanding the limitations of the exercise, the participants agreed that the conference was "highly constructive",[25] a number *proprio motu* submitting proposals to help increase communication and understanding.

Efforts to build on this momentum through a visit by President McDonald to the region were handicapped when the trip was cancelled for security reasons. She thus sent in November 1998 the court's press spokesman and one of her staff to meet with local and international governmental and non-governmental representatives, lawyers, judges, activists, and international institutions, to listen to their views of what the Tribunal could or should be doing to improve its image. What they found was instructive.[26]

During their discussions, many of the individuals emphasised that the time was ripe for thc Tribunal to undertake such a study. Other sentiments indicated that attitudes towards it among both lay and professional populations of the region have improved considerably since 1993 and that the court had been accepted as a reality. While there was unanimous support for the institution and acknowledgement of its special status, set

---

[19]See, for example, "Gabrielle Kirk McDonald: From Civil Rights To War Crimes, A Pioneer Promotes The Rule Of Law", Los Angeles Times Interview, Los Angeles Times, Feb. 7, 1999, by Kitty Felde.

[20]Dorothee de Sampayo Garrido-Nijgh.

[21]From the United States Institute for Peace.

[22]Although it was a priority, the vigour of efforts devoted to increasing awareness was necessarily constrained by other Presidential commitments. See Cina and Tolbert "The Office of the President: A Third Voice" in this collection of essays.

[23]Including Belgrade, Banja Luka, Mostar, Podgorica, Sarajevo, and Tuzla.

[24]See "Outreach Symposium Marks The First Successful Step In Campaign For Better Understanding Of The ICTY In The Former Yugoslavia", ICTY Press Release CC/PIU/355-E, 20 Oct. 1998.

[25]Id.

[26]They conducted in excess of 100 interviews with individuals from different locations and professions in Croatia and both entities of Bosnia and Herzegovina (the Federation of Bosnia and Herzegovina and Republika Srpska).

apart from other international actors in the area, there was a strong perception that the Tribunal was shrouded in mystery, depersonalised, distant and unresponsive; too narrow in its focus; and too legalistic in its outlook. Many considered that local legal systems were subservient to it, which some professed to understand and some to resent, and that it influenced their lives without any input from them. Nevertheless, an equally strong desire existed for greater access to the Tribunal, through both its jurisprudence and, in particular, through direct interaction with court representatives stationed in the region.[27] Equally pertinent, the international organisations consulted perceived an absence of an overall strategy for the execution of the court's mandate, namely how criminal trials will have positive effects on the ground: the need to clarify "the gap between international mechanisms of justice and the rebuilding of societies [...]".[28] Not surprisingly, there was unanimity that the immediate establishment of a local ICTY presence was the only way to combat misperceptions, misinformation and propaganda; also it would free up the resources used by those agencies in their efforts to do so.[29]

These views, coupled with the Tribunal's relative stability and the increasing activism of President McDonald and the support given by the Registrar, provided the momentum for the proposal to establish the Outreach Programme. While the ICTY's budget submission for 1999 had already been finalised, the depth of feeling, both expectant and dismissive, and President McDonald's commitment to address the situation, led the court to seek external funding. By mid-1999, finance had been secured from the Austrian, Dutch, Finnish and US Governments and the US-based Macarthur Foundation to hire a co-ordinator in The Hague and establish at least two staffed and equipped offices in the region.

4. Outreach in Practice

The longest journey begins, as has been said, with the first step, however small. Since the Programme's functional commencement in October 1999

---

[27]The Humanitarian Law Centre organised a Conference on War Crimes Trials in Belgrade in November 1998. Focusing on the ICTY and its relevance to the region, international and indigenous participants met for two days. As expected, several attempted to politicise the agenda but in general, it was regarded as an extremely useful exercise, indicating the extent to which local actors could work with the ICTY to promote justice. President McDonald and Prosecutor Arbour were invited; both declined to enter the Federal Republic of Yugoslavia after its Government refused Arbour a visa to travel on to Kosovo to commence on-site investigations there.

[28]Justice, Accountability and Reconstruction in the former Yugoslavia, Human Rights Centre, University of California, Berkeley, Oct. 1998, at p14. This project, *inter alia*, a study of attitudes in areas of the former Yugoslavia to justice and the ICTY, should be of considerable benefit to the Outreach Programme.

[29]The Office of the High Representative, for example, often acted to counter media and political propaganda directed at the Tribunal.

with the recruitment of a co-ordinator, offices have been established in Zagreb and, in early 2000, in Banja Luka/Sarajevo. Since opening in December, the Croatian office has developed comprehensive local media and NGO contacts and is making real time information available through media and academic outlets. Staff have established distribution systems to place paper and electronic versions of Serbo-Croatian translations of ICTY documents in libraries, governmental and judicial institutions around the country and has organised talks at various fora, as well as provided a fixed contact point for enquiries from a diverse range of sources. The office has also been active in organising a conference scheduled for mid-2000, at which members of the Croatian legal community and government (including the Prime Minister) are expected to meet the President and other ICTY representatives. Given the former Croatian administration's attitude towards the court,[30] this portends a considerably improved relationship between the two.

While specific sensitivities pertain to each State, Province and Entity, it can be expected that this operational model will be followed as new field presences are established. It is hoped that the next one will be in Pristina, Kosovo. Notwithstanding the complexities inherent in such action, a proactive public relations presence there offers the potential for avoiding the steady erosion of ICTY credibility evident elsewhere in the region. Moreover, following the extremely positive reception and feedback received by three of the Tribunal's judges who made an orientation visit to Sarajevo in 1999, it is expected that visits between the court's seat and the conflict region will soon become a regular feature.

In The Hague, the Programme has, *inter alia*, facilitated a co-operative venture sponsored by private donors to provide trilingual live internet broadcasting of proceedings from the Tribunal's three courtrooms;[31] a Serbo-Croat digest of news, interviews and information about the Tribunal, the latter being distributed on-line[32] and to television networks in South Eastern Europe for re-broadcast; and a weekly radio programme summarising court proceedings.[33] It is also co-ordinating a series of six ICTY-focused symposiums to take place in the former Yugoslavia during 2000 and has supplied collections of ICTY documents to the Belgrade Media Centre, Serbia and to a number of libraries in Bosnia and Herzegovina. The co-ordinator has apparently made visits to the region to discuss further Programme initiatives.

---

[30]See "Primacy of the Tribunal and State Non-compliance", ICTY Annual Report 1999, for examples.

[31]Domavina Net:http://www.domavina.xs4all.nl.

[32]SENSE, South East News Service Europe: http://www.sense-agency.com/.

[33]From April Radio Free Europe/Radio Liberty has broadcast "Hague Chronicle" (Haagska Hronika), a 30-minute weekly programme in Serbo-Croat that uses audio material from Domavina Net's live coverage.

The Programme's designers intended that it should be complemented by an enhanced role for the Tribunal's existing press and publicity unit.[34] In this area, the court appears to have made significant progress, making information available for outreach purposes as part of a general improvement in the quality and quantity of its public relations activities. Regular press briefings are held in The Hague and in Brussels; additional staff enables the monitoring of judicial proceedings and the publication of summaries of both these and all major decisions; the internet site and many of the documents it contains are available in Serbo-Croatian; and a mass distribution ICTY information video, funded by the UK Government, is under development.[35]

It should be noted that the ICTR has launched an analogous outreach initiative, *inter alia*, providing facilities for a radio service to broadcast from the Tribunal's seat in Arusha. Given the high quality of the programming and the prevalence of radios within households in Rwanda, this portends a greatly increased connection between community and court.

5. Idealism and Realism

"The value of these programs is incalculable".[36] It would be illusory, however, to link their success or failure to the future peace of the former Yugoslavia (or Rwanda). Reconciliation cannot be imposed and, experience suggests, is impossible in the short term. Rather, their significance is in the potential of their activities. In the regions themselves, the pre-requisites for peace are chiefly structural, legal, political and economic change. Events during the six years that have passed since the active conflicts were halted have demonstrated both the lack of "solutions" and the need for an approach that emphasises variety and flexibility in attempting to remove the causes of conflict. Both Tribunals' Programmes aim to inform, educate and involve; if they can do so effectively, informed popular participation and debate may help catalyse the process of change.[37] Thus, for example, in the Republika Srpska, Radovan Karadžić's official removal from power four years ago[38]

[34]The Public Information Unit of the court's Registry.

[35]Further, the appointment of a Prosecution spokesperson has allowed clearer and more consistent institutional dissemination of information as the interests and priorities of the Prosecutor frequently differ from, or conflict with, those of the Chambers or Registry.

[36]Experts' Report, supra note 3.

[37]Or it may continue to be based on economic rationale.

[38]Karadžić retreated from public life in the summer of 1996. He was indicted one year earlier, in July (and again in November 1995) for genocide, crimes against humanity, grave breaches of the 1949 Geneva Conventions, and violations of the laws or customs of war. Nine months earlier, Slobodan Milošević signed the GFAP on behalf of the Republika Srpska, expressly committing the government of RS to co-operate fully with the Tribunal (General Framework Agreement, Article IX) and prohibiting indicted individuals from holding public office within Bosnia and Herzegovina (Annex IV, Article IX (1)).

and the international community's subsequent convoluted relationship with the Entity's successor personalities – Plavsić, Dodik and Poplasen – have supported the emergence of a moderate, albeit minority, civil society; here is both a channel for outreach activities, and a platform through which the RS's nascent human rights, legal and judicial communities can seek to influence the Tribunal, in a benign manner, such as through the submission of proposals for the court's Rules of Procedure and Evidence. Public suggestions in early 2000 by incumbent Prosecutor Del Ponte that she would welcome ICTY trials taking place in the region are an encouraging indication of how the Tribunal may in future move closer to overcoming the problems inherent in its location and status. Ultimately of course, only legitimate trials by the courts of the region will fully address this problem but the Tribunal's legal and moral relationship with the domestic criminal justice systems is central to the attainment of this goal.[39]

The longer-term implications of the Outreach Programmes are likely to be felt outside the former Yugoslavia and Rwanda: they should eventually contribute to an "understanding of how the judicial mechanism contributes to processes within communities that lead to reconstruction and reconciliation".[40] Indeed, they are illustrative of "a growing and elevated awareness of the roles of the Tribunals in protecting and enhancing humanitarian values"[41] and, in conjunction with various publishing[42] and other initiatives,[43] provide a critical practical example of the recent phenomenal growth in interest in the practice of international criminal law.

Further discussion of the Programme's potential and benefits, beyond this necessarily short survey, would currently be precipitate. The proactive nature of its activities to date is extremely encouraging; however, it faces shortfalls in financing and personnel. The ICTY must therefore continue to support it vigorously, in particular by ensuring a regular source of financing.[44] Simply put, of all the innovations that the Tribunal has stimulated, this offers the most far-reaching opportunity to demonstrate the utility of international criminal prosecution[45] to every level and segment of society in the former Yugoslavia.

---

[39]The Rules of the Road programme creates a direct practical link: the ICTY Prosecutor reviews all proposed Bosnian prosecutions of crimes within the Tribunal's jurisdiction.

[40]Supra note 25.

[41]Experts' Report, supra note 3.

[42]These include the Crimes of War Project, launched on the 50th anniversary of the signing of the 1949 Geneva Conventions to further awareness and understanding of this aspect of modern conflicts: see www.crimesofwar.org.

[43]See for example supra note 25.

[44]Ideally through the Programme's inclusion in the court's annual budget submissions. Although a sizeable donation is expected from the European Union in the course of 2000, the Programme continues to rely on *ad hoc* donations in place of regular budgetary funding.

[45]Already, the important educational role of the International Criminal Court has been recognised, the US delegation indicating during the negotiations that this would be a primary function of the court.

KEN ROBERTS*

41. Aspects of the ICTY Contribution to the Criminal Procedure of the ICC

The Rome Statute of the International Criminal Court ("Rome Statute" and "ICC") was adopted in Rome on 17 July 1998 with 120 states voting to adopt the Statute, 7 states voting against and 21 states abstaining.[1] The establishment of this permanent institution may be seen as a logical progression from the existing *ad hoc* international criminal tribunals (the ICTY and the ICTR), another step on the path towards an effective international criminal justice system. As such, the ICC has been described as a turning point in the world community for what it may possibly contribute to international criminal justice.[2]

The adoption of the Rome Statute followed five weeks of intense negotiations between national delegations in Rome, which in turn followed years of preparatory work. During both the preparatory and negotiation phases of this process, those involved had the benefit of an increasing body of experience from the functioning *ad hoc* international criminal tribunals, in which criminal procedures were being tried and tested with varying degrees of success. This paper will focus upon the extensive contribution made by the ICTY to the criminal procedure of the ICC as set out in the

---

*Ken Roberts, Legal Officer, ICTY. BA (Toronto), LLB (Western Ontario), LLM (London School of Economics). Barrister & Solicitor (Law Society of Upper Canada). The author would like to thank Fabricia Guariglia and Helen Duffy for their comments on an earlier draft of this paper. The views expressed herein are those of the author and do not necessarily reflect the views of the United Nations.

[1]See ICC web-site *http://www.un.org/icc*. While there was widespread support from all continents, two permanent members of the Security Council, the United States and China, did not join in the vote for the establishment of the ICC.

[2]See Antonio Cassese, "The Statute of the International Criminal Court: Some Preliminary Reflections", *European Journal of International Law* 10 (1999), p. 145. While to date most analysis of the Rome Statute has focused on the substantive law to be applied, Judge Cassese argues that the major contribution of the Rome Statute lies in the field of international criminal procedure, at p. 146.

R. May et al., Essays on ICTY Procedure and Evidence in Honour of Gabrielle Kirk McDonald, 559–572.

Rome Statute.[3] The ICTY has served as a valuable resource in many ways, as noted by the ICC Liaison Committee of the Chambers of the ICTY:

> The creators of the ICC have acknowledged the importance of taking advantage of the experience of judges of the Tribunal, through such means as importing ICTY Rules or jurisprudence into the ICC Statute, through reference to ICTY caselaw or Rules in ICC Preparatory Committee and commission documents, through inviting Tribunal staff to participate as observers to each of the PrepCom sessions, and through sending experts to the Tribunal to seek advice from the judges and other organs of the Tribunal.[4]

A definitive analysis of the ICTY contribution and a detailed account of individual procedural mechanisms are beyond the scope of such a brief paper; the examples that follow must of necessity be illustrative of the larger contribution. These examples focus in particular on judicial aspects of the ICTY contribution, leaving aside other areas which have also been heavily influenced by the ICTY, such as administration, other Registry matters and prosecutorial issues.

On a final preliminary note, it is hoped that these brief illustrations may serve a secondary purpose. Just as the ICTY has contributed to the ICC, there would appear to be an emerging symbiotic relationship between the two institutions in which the permanent court is also likely to exert influence upon the ICTY. Some of the examples below touch upon this symbiotic relationship.

---

[3]At time of writing, the rules of procedure and evidence of the ICC were still in preparation by the Preparatory Commission, with the final version to be completed for 30 June 2000. However, a great deal regarding procedure before the ICC can already be gleaned from the Rome Statute itself. Indeed, as noted by the ICC Liaison Committee of the Chambers of the ICTY, "many of the ICTY Rules are reproduced in the Rome Statute" (Contributions of the Chambers of the International Criminal Tribunal for the former Yugoslavia, 13 August 1999, PCNICC/1999/WGRPE/DP.38, Annex, para. 9.). While this paper focuses solely on the ICTY, it is noted that the ICTR has made an equally significant and often similar contribution.

[4]Supra note 3, para. 3. ICTY President Gabrielle Kirk McDonald showed a particular interest in the development of the ICC during her Presidency. See e.g., Remarks made by Judge Gabrielle Kirk McDonald, President of the International Criminal Tribunal for the former Yugoslavia, to the Preparatory Commission for the International Criminal Court, *Press Release JL/P.I.S./425-E*, ICTY, The Hague, 30 July 1999; and Remarks by Her Excellency Judge Gabrielle Kirk McDonald, President, International Criminal Tribunal for the former Yugoslavia, 16 June 1998, unpublished document. The ICTY continues to serve as a valuable resource in the Preparatory Commission negotiations concerning the ICC Rules of Evidence and Procedure and Evidence, as may be seen in *inter alia* the recent "Contributions of the Chambers of the International Criminal Tribunal for the former Yugoslavia (ICTY)", submitted at the 3–31 March 2000 Preparatory Commission for the International Criminal Court, on the provisional Rules of Procedure and Evidence for the Court.

1. The Nature of the ICTY Contribution

The ICTY has made its contribution to the criminal procedure of the ICC in different ways. In its most obvious form, the drafters of the Rome Statute followed the ICTY experience by directly incorporating procedures used before that Tribunal, as set out in the ICTY Statute, Rules or case law. For various reasons, such procedures have often been incorporated only in part or in modified form. However, the contribution of the Tribunal goes further than this. The ICC has also benefited from the Tribunal's experience to identify shortcomings or lacunae in that institution's procedures; particular provisions of the Rome Statute attempt to remedy these perceived inadequacies.

1.1 The Rome Statute: incorporating ICTY procedures

The most obvious and far-reaching example of the ICC adopting a procedure in place before the ICTY is the common-law derived adversarial nature of ICC proceedings with an independent Prosecutor. However, there are also examples with respect to other procedures of more limited scope, some of which are detailed below.

(a) Disclosure of national security information

In general, state co-operation with the ICC follows a different model than that in place before the ICTY. However, with regard to the protection of national security information, the ICTY experience was imported into the Rome Statute in part. The procedure adopted by the ICC with regard to the disclosure of information affecting national security represents a compromise between States favouring absolute state control over the invocation of the national security exception under Article 93(4) of the Rome Statute[5] and those favouring the court as the ultimate arbiter of such disputes.[6] Significantly, Article 72 of the Rome Statute ensures that the final decision on whether the disclosure of information would prejudice its national

---

[5]Art. 93(4) provides that "a State Party may deny a request for assistance, in whole or in part, only if the request concerns the production of any documents or disclosure of evidence which relates to its national security".

[6]Rodney Dixon and Helen Duffy, "Article 72: Protection of national security information", in Otto Triffterer (Ed.), Commentary on the Rome Statute of the International Criminal Court (1999), pp. 937–946, at p. 939. See also Bert Swart and Göran Sluiter, "The International Criminal Court and International Criminal Co-operation", in Herman A.M. von Hebel, Johan G. Lammers and Jolien Schukking (Eds.), Reflections on the International Criminal Court (1999), pp. 91–127, at p. 99.

security is in most cases left to the state itself.[7] This was considered by the United States in particular to be a victory in the negotiations. According to David Scheffer, US Ambassador-at-Large for War Crimes Issues and Head of the US delegation to the Rome Conference, the US "applied years of experience with the ICTY on this issue to the challenge of similar co-operation with a permanent court".[8]

However, the ICTY experience did have some influence on the Rome Statute in this area. Article 29 of the ICTY Statute reads in part

> 2. States shall comply without undue delay with any request for assistance or an order by a Trial Chamber, including but not limited to: ...
> (b) the taking of testimony and *the production of evidence*. (emphasis added).

This provision was interpreted by the ICTY Appeals Chamber in the *Blaškić subpoena decision* to make "clear that [the provision] does not envisage any exception to the obligation of States to comply with requests and orders of a Trial Chamber",[9] thus leaving the Tribunal as the ultimate arbiter in cases of dispute. The *Blaškić* approach is incorporated into Article 72 of the Rome Statute, in the sense that the provision is designed to induce a state invoking national security concerns to disclose as much as possible the information it wishes to withhold. In addition, in those situations in which the Court has the relevant information within its control or can obtain it other than through a request for co-operation from the state in question, it may order disclosure if it determines that this is appropriate in light of any representations made by the state.[10]

---

[7]In the case of a government's refusal, the Court may seek a remedy from the Assembly of States Parties or the Security Council pursuant to Article 87(7). Despite this recourse, it appears that the state has wide latitude in deciding the disclosure of evidence in any form. See David J. Scheffer, "The United States and the International Criminal Court", 93 *American Journal of International Law* 1 (January 1999), pp. 12–22 at p. 15. This procedure was heavily debated and has since been described as a "retrogade step"; Swart and Sluiter, supra note 6, at p. 120.

[8]Scheffer, supra note 7, at p. 15.

[9]*Prosecutor v. Blaškić, Judgement on the Request of the Republic of Croatia for Review of the Decision of Trial Chamber II of 18 July 1997*, Case No. IT-95-14-AR108*bis*, A. Ch., 29 Oct. 1997 at para. 63.

[10]Dixon and Duffy, supra note 6, at p. 940. Since the adoption of the Rome Statute, there has been some development with regard to the ICTY procedure concerning orders directed to States for the production of documents. At the twenty-first plenary session (15–17 November 1999), Rule 54*bis* of the ICTY Rules was adopted. This rule appears to reflect aspects of Art. 72 of the Rome Statute, particularly with respect to the necessity to negotiate with the state, the documents of which are being sought. However, the Tribunal remains the final arbiter in the event that a state objects to the disclosure of documents on the basis that this would prejudice national security interests.

(b) Preconditions to the exercise of jurisdiction

The permanent Court also imports in part a procedure in use before the ICTY concerning preconditions to the exercise of jurisdiction. In general, the mechanism established under Article 12 of the Rome Statute differs from that before the ICTY in that it relies on state acceptance of the court's jurisdiction. Concern was expressed during negotiations that this formulation could create problems in the event that a state does not accept the court's jurisdiction, effectively providing a loophole to escape prosecution (at least at the international level). An attempt to address such concerns was made under Article 13(b), drawing in part on the ICTY experience. Under this provision, the Security Council may decide to refer a situation to the Prosecutor, in which case state acceptance of the Court's jurisdiction is not required. This has been described as the "Sledgehammer" of the ICC:

> In effect, the mechanism by which the Security Council established the ICTY and ICTR is imported into the ICC. This mechanism may prove to be the most effective to seize the Court whenever situations similar to those in the former Yugoslavia and Rwanda occur.[11]

(c) Proceedings on an admission of guilt

The contribution of the ICTY with respect to ICC proceedings on an admission of guilt is of particular interest and merits development in some depth. The Tribunal would appear to have both influenced the drafters of the Rome Statute and, at the same time, have been influenced by early negotiations on the subject leading up to the Rome Conference.

Article 65 of the Rome Statute was the subject of an early consensus at the Rome Conference,[12] in part as a result of the ICTY experience. Preliminary discussions with respect to guilty pleas under the Rome Statute had begun on the basis of Article 38(1)(d) of the ILC Draft Statute.[13] The ILC provision had adopted a classic common law guilty plea formula, allowing the accused to "enter a plea of guilty or not guilty". However, the Commentary to the ILC Draft Statute made it clear that this provision did not necessarily imply a summary end to the trial or an automatic conviction. Indeed, such a classic common law approach was openly rejected by many delegations during negotiations on the Rome Statute, for reasons including

---

[11]Cassese, supra note 2, at p. 161.

[12]Fabricio Guariglia, "Article 65: Proceedings on an Admission of Guilt", in Otto Triffterer (Ed.), Commentary on the Rome Statute of the International Criminal Court (1999), pp. 823-831, at p. 823, para. 1.

[13]Draft Statute for an International Criminal Court ("ILC Draft Statute"), in Cherif Bassiouni, The Statute of the International Criminal Court: A Documentary History, at pp. 657–673. The ILC Draft Statute was prepared by the International Law Commission and attached to its Report on the Work of its 46th Session (1994). This served as the basis for discussion in early negotiations leading to the adoption of the Rome Statute.

the fear that this would automatically allow for the practice of plea bargaining in the context of the ICC.[14]

Concerns with respect to the approach taken in the ILC draft provision were reflected in the Preparatory Commission's discussions in August 1996. Intending to bridge the gap between different legal systems, it was suggested that

> if the accused admitted the facts contained in the indictment, the trial chamber could decide to conduct an abbreviated proceeding to hear a summary of the evidence presented by the prosecution or to continue with the trial if the accused failed to reaffirm the admission or to accept the proceeding...the trial chamber should determine whether the accused fully understood the nature and consequences of admission of guilt, whether the admission was made voluntarily without coercion or undue influence and whether the admission was supported by the facts contained in the indictment and a summary of the evidence presented by the prosecution before deciding whether to request additional evidence, to conduct an expedited proceeding or to proceed with the trial.[15]

Issues similar to those raised in discussion before the Preparatory Commission were also surfacing before the ICTY. The drafters of the ICTY Statute did not provide for the eventuality of guilty pleas being entered without a subsequent full trial.[16] This was eventually envisaged with the adoption of ICTY Rule 62 (concerning the "Initial appearance of the accused"), which provided in part that

---

[14]Supra note 12, at p. 824, para. 2. Art. 65(5) was adopted to ease the concerns of some delegations which wanted to ensure that the procedures under Art. 65 would not open the way to the introduction of plea-bargaining in the context of the Statute. The paragraph was intended to underline the independence of the Trial Chamber with respect to any agreement reached by the parties. However, it has been noted that, although the ICTY Statute makes no room for plea bargaining, the first valid guilty plea in the history of the ICTY (*Prosecutor v. Erdemović*) was the result of a plea bargain agreement between the accused and the Proecutor. By providing that a guilty plea may dispense with the need for trial, the Tribunal paved the way for both plea agreements and plea-bargaining. See Vladimir Tochilovsky, "Rules of procedure for the International Criminal Court: Problems to address in light of the experience of the *ad hoc* Tribunals", *Netherlands International Law Review* XLVI (1999), pp. 343–360 at p. 347. For an analysis of plea-bargaining and the ICTY, see also the contribution by Michael Bohlander in this collection of essays.

[15]Report of the Preparatory Committee on the Establishment of an International Criminal Court, UN GAOR, 51st Sess., Supp. No. 22, UN Doc. A/51/22 (1996), Vol. I, in Cherif Bassiouni, The Statute of the International Criminal Court: A Documentary History, at p. 424, para. 263.

[16]Art. 20 of the ICTY Statute provides that "the Trial Chamber shall read the indictment ...and instruct the accused to enter a plea. The Trial Chamber shall then set a date for trial".

> Upon his transfer to the seat of the Tribunal, the accused shall be brought before a Trial Chamber without delay, and shall be formally charged. The Trial Chamber shall:
>
> ...
>
> (iii) call upon the accused to enter a plea of guilty or not guilty on each count; should the accused fail to do so, enter a plea of not guilty on his behalf;
> (iv) in case of a plea of not guilty, instruct the Registrar to set a date for trial;
> (v) *in case of a plea of guilty, instruct the Registrar to set a date for the pre-sentencing hearing.* (emphasis added).

This provision closely reflected the draft provision put before the Preparatory Commission by the ILC, in that there was no qualification of the mandatory nature of the requirement to accept a plea of guilt without a full trial.

In 1997, the procedure under ICTY Rule 62 was scrutinised by the Appeals Chamber in the *Erdemović Appeals Judgement*.[17] The Chamber raised preliminary issues *proprio motu* pursuant to its inherent powers as an appellate body seized of an appeal pursuant to Article 25 of the ICTY Statute.[18] The issue of the validity of the plea of guilty entered by the appellant was considered in detail in the *Joint Separate Opinion of Judge McDonald and Judge Vohrah*[19] appended to the judgement.

In the *Joint Separate Opinion*, the judges found that the institution of the guilty plea must not in any way prejudice the appellant's rights as provided for in Article 20(1) of the ICTY Statute.[20] They found that, as a result, certain minimum pre-conditions must be satisfied before a plea of guilty can be entered:

> (a) The guilty plea must be voluntary. It must be made by an accused who is mentally fit to understand the consequences of pleading guilty and who is not affected by any threats, inducements or promises;
> (b) The guilty plea must be informed, that is, the accused must understand the nature of the charges against him and the consequences of pleading guilty to them. The accused must know to what he is pleading guilty;
> (c) The guilty plea must not be equivocal. It must not be accompanied by words amounting to a defence contradicting an admission of criminal responsibility.[21]

With respect to the particular circumstances in that case, Judge McDonald and Judge Vohrah found that for the guilty plea to be informed, the accused must understand the nature and distinction between the alternative charges and the consequences of pleading guilty to one rather than the other.[22] They

---

[17] *Prosecutor v. Erdemović, Judgement,* Case No. IT-96-22-A, A. Ch., 7 Oct. 1997 ("*Erdemović Appeals Judgement*").
[18] Id., para. 16.
[19] *Prosecutor v. Erdemović, Joint Separate Opinion of Judge McDonald and Judge Vohrah*, Case No. IT-96-22-A, A. Ch., 7 Oct. 1997 ("*Joint Separate Opinion*").
[20] Id., para. 7.
[21] Id., para. 8.
[22] Id., para. 14.

found that the plea was not informed because "[i]t was not clearly intimated to the Appellant that by pleading guilty, he would lose his right to a trial, to be considered innocent until proven guilty and to assert his innocence and his lack of criminal responsibility for the offences in any way".[23] Defence counsel consistently advanced arguments contradicting the admission of guilt and criminal responsibility implicit in a guilty plea.[24]

In addition, the *Joint Separate Opinion* found that the difference between a crime against humanity and a war crime was not adequately explained to the appellant by the Trial Chamber, and that defence counsel statements indicated a lack of understanding of the offence of a war crime. This led the appellant to plead guilty to the more serious of the two charges, that alleging the crime against humanity.[25] It was thus concluded that the appellant did not understand the true nature of the charges he was facing nor the charge to which he pleaded guilty.[26] The Appeals Chamber, following the reasoning set out in the *Joint Separate Opinion*, held by four votes to one[27] that the plea was not informed and remitted the case to another Trial Chamber for the Appellant to re-plead in full knowledge of the consequences of pleading guilty *per se* and of the inherent difference between the alternative charges.[28]

Following the *Erdemović Appeals Judgement*, the need for clear procedures with respect to admissions of guilt was evident. At the 14th plenary session of the ICTY,[29] new Rule 62*bis* was adopted, establishing a specific procedure for proceedings following a guilty plea. Therefore, at the time of the Rome Conference,[30] ICTY Rule 62*bis* provided as follows:

> If an accused pleads guilty in accordance with Rule 62(v), or requests to change his or her plea to guilty and the Trial Chamber is satisfied that:
> (i) the guilty plea has been made voluntarily;
> (ii) the guilty plea is not equivocal; and

[23]Id., para. 15.

[24]Id., para. 16.

[25]Id., para. 19. It is beyond the scope of this paper to address the issue of whether crimes against humanity are inherently more serious offences than war crimes, but it is noted that there is a move away from this view in the Tribunal's most recent jurisprudence. See *Prosecutor v. Tadić, Judgement in Sentencing Appeals*, Case No. IT-94-1-A and IT-94-1-A*bis*, A. Ch., 26 Jan. 2000 at para. 69 and in the *Separate Opinion of Judge Shahabuddeen* at pp. 35–49. See also the discussion in Bing Bing Jia, "The Differing Concepts of War Crimes and Crimes against Humanity in International Criminal Law", in Guy Goodwin-Gill and Stefan Talmon (Eds.), The Reality of International Law: Essays in Honour of Ian Brownlie (1999), pp. 243–271.

[26]Supra note 19, at para. 18.

[27]Supra note 17, at Disposition, para. 3 (Judge Li dissenting).

[28]Supra note 19, at para. 91.

[29]20 October and 12 November 1997.

[30]A minor amendment to ICTY Rule 62*bis* was made at the 17th plenary session (11–13 March and 20 March 1998), allowing the Trial Chamber to instruct the Registrar to set a date for the sentencing hearing, rather than for the *pre*-sentencing hearing. However, this amendment only entered into force in Revision fourteen of the Rules, on 17 December 1998.

> (iii) there is sufficient factual basis for the crime and the accused's participation in it, either on the basis of independent indicia or of lack of any material disagreement between the parties about the facts of the case,
>
> the Trial Chamber may enter a finding of guilt and instruct the Registrar to set a date for the sentencing hearing.

As well as reflecting the general concerns raised about the validity of guilty pleas, this revision introduced discretion on the part of the Trial Chamber as to whether or not the plea would be accepted and the need for a trial averted.

The problems raised and addressed by the ICTY in the *Erdemović Appeals Judgement* and in the subsequent rule changes were a concrete example of the concerns that led to the adoption of the corresponding provision at the Rome Conference.[31] In its form adopted at the Rome Conference, Article 65 of the Rome Statute provides in part:

> 1. Where the accused makes an admission of guilt pursuant to article 64, paragraph 8(a), the Trial Chamber shall determine whether:
>
> (a) The accused understands the nature and consequences of the admission of guilt;
>
> (b) The admission is voluntarily made by the accused after sufficient consultation with defence counsel; and
>
> (c) The admission of guilt is supported by the facts of the case that are contained in:
>
> (i) The charges brought by the prosecutor and admitted by the accused;
>
> (ii) Any materials presented by the Prosecutor which supplement the charges and which the accused accepts; and
>
> (iii) Any other evidence, such as the testimony of witnesses, presented by the prosecutor or the accused.

In addition, paragraph 2 of Article 65 provides discretion for the Trial Chamber to decide that, although the guilty plea is valid, normal trial procedures will be followed regardless. Conversely, paragraph 3 emphasises that, following a rejected admission of guilt, trial procedures must be continued as if the plea had not been made.

Article 65 of the Rome Statute follows what has been described as a "third avenue" between the classic common and civil law approaches.[32] Its structure and wording clearly reflects the development of the procedure upon admissions of guilt before the ICTY. It is interesting to note that it was not until after the adoption of the Rome Statute that ICTY Rule 62*bis* was amended[33] to include the requirement that the Trial Chamber be satisfied

---

[31] Guariglia, supra note 12, at p. 826, para. 5.

[32] Id., p. 825, para. 5.

[33] After the 19th plenary session (3–4 December 1998).

that the guilty plea is informed, corresponding to ICC Article 65(1)(a).[34] Clearly the drafters of the Rome Statute drew support not only from the status of ICTY Rule 62*bis* at the time of the Rome Conference, but also the principles enunciated in the *Joint Separate Opinion*, which largely reflected concerns voiced in earlier Preparatory Commission discussions.

Article 65(4)(a) of the Rome Statute would seem to further substantiate this point of view. This provision allows the Trial Chamber to request the Prosecutor to present additional evidence, including the testimony of witnesses, in cases in which a more complete presentation of the facts of the case is required in the interests of justice, and in particular the interests of victims. The Appeals Chamber followed a similar procedure in the *Erdemović* case, issuing a Scheduling Order to the parties asking for further information regarding guilty pleas.[35]

The *Erdemović Judgement* called for clear procedures on an admission of guilt, which were subsequently introduced by means of amendments to the ICTY Rules. Article 65 of the Rome Statute has endorsed and reinforced these procedures. The Rome Statute unequivocally provides the Trial Chamber with the discretion to accept an admission of guilt and to dispense with the need for trial, or to reject such an admission and continue with trial proceedings.[36]

1.2 A different path: rejecting ICTY procedures or filling in lacunae

In some instances, the drafters of the Rome Statute chose to adopt different procedures from those in use before the ICTY, either because the experience of the Tribunal was not seen to be a positive one, or because ICTY procedure was seen to be insufficient to address all relevant concerns. In these cases the ICTY contribution has been indirect in nature.

(a) Adopting and amending rules

One area in which the drafters of the Rome Statute chose to depart from procedure before the ICTY is in the mechanism established for the adoption and amendment of rules. The ICTY model permits judges to establish the rules pursuant to which the Tribunal functions. In contrast, the ICC Rules must be adopted by a two-thirds majority of the members of the Assembly of States Parties (pursuant to Article 51(1) of the Rome Statute). Only in urgent cases where the ICC Rules do not provide for a specific situation may the judges, by a two-thirds majority, draw up provisional rules.

[34]It was pursuant to this amended version of ICTY Rule 62*bis* that Trial Chamber I accepted an admission of guilt from the accused in *Prosecutor v. Jelisić, Judgement*, Case No. IT-95-10-T, 14 Dec. 1999, paras. 24–58. It is noted that, although outside the scope of this paper, valid guilty pleas have also been made before the ICTR in the cases *Prosecutor v. Kambanda* and *Prosecutor v. Serushago*.

[35]Supra note 17, at para. 16.

[36]Tochilovsky, supra note 13, at p. 348.

Even these, however, must be adopted, amended or rejected at the next ordinary or special session of the Assembly of States Parties.[37]

There is no doubt that this departure from the ICTY mechanism for adopting or amending rules was the result of a conscious decision. The antipathy to judge-made rules was in part the result of a perceived difference in circumstances between the permanent Court and the *ad hoc* Tribunal. Substantial flexibility was required by the ICTY in order to provide for numerous unforeseen circumstances. The ICC, having had the benefit of the ICTY experience, is arguably less likely to require the same volume of amendments, thus permitting greater political control of the amendment mechanism. However, it seems clear that Article 51 also reflects a desire by the drafters to establish certainty in procedure before the Court to the benefit of the parties to proceedings, an aspect which is felt to be missing before the Tribunal where the Rules have been revised frequently.

Nevertheless, the judges of the ICTY have argued that judicial input could still be of use, suggesting that "nothing seems to prevent the Assembly of State Parties from electing judges prior to adopting the Rules"[38] and that "[t]he judges wish to encourage the Preparatory Commission to include a provision that would allow judicial participation with the Assembly of States Parties in the adoption of the Rules. Even though the ICC judges will not have drafted the rules themselves, as did the ICTY and ICTR judges, their input before adoption is critical and cannot be overemphasised".[39]

(b) Rights and role of the victim

With respect to the procedural rights and role of the victim, the drafters of the Rome Statute specifically addressed a perceived lacuna in the ICTY Statute and Rules, which deal with victims principally in their role as witnesses, focusing on their protection.[40] While victims are thus largely given an auxiliary role before the Tribunal, the ICC provides for victims not only in the role of witness but also in their own right.[41] Article 68 of the Rome Statute follows the tradition of many civil-law jurisdictions, providing for the views of victims to be presented at some point during the proceedings, either

---

[37]Rome Statute Art. 51(3).

[38]Supra note 3, at para. 6.

[39]Id., para. 7, footnote omitted.

[40]See e.g. ICTY Statute, Arts. 15, 20(1) and 22.

[41]See e.g. Rome Statute Arts. 15(3), 19(3), 68, 75 and 79; Theo Van Boven, "The Position of the Victim in the Statute of the International Criminal Court", in Herman A.M. von Hebel, Johan G. Lammers and Jolien Schukking (Eds.), Reflections on the International Criminal Court (1999), pp. 77–89 at pp. 85–87. The difference in procedure between the ICC and the ICTY is recognised in the "Contributions of the Chambers of the International Criminal Tribunal for the former Yugoslavia (ICTY)", supra note 4. However, this submission stresses that "while these provisions are clearly important steps in addressing the fundamentally important position of victims in international justice, it must be remembered that the principal way in which individual victims will come into contact with the Court will be as witnesses" (at p. 7).

by the victims themselves or by their legal representatives.[42] Article 75 establishes reparations for victims of crimes. These provisions were adopted in order to account for perceived lacunae in Tribunal procedure, and represent a substantial advance with respect to the status of victims.

(c) Pre-Trial Chamber

Drafters of the Rome Statute also addressed problems related to the expeditiousness of trials before the ICTY by providing for specific powers to be exercised by a Pre-Trial Chamber. Such pre-trial procedures were not envisaged by the Draft Statute prepared by the ILC in 1994, nor did they exist before the ICTY prior to the Rome Conference, although provision was contemporaneously made for a Pre-Trial Judge pursuant to ICTY Rule 65*ter*.[43] During the ICC negotiations leading up to the adoption of the Statute, support increased steadily for the establishment of a Pre-Trial Chamber to carry out those judicial functions foreseen under the Statute which are to be exercised prior to the commencement of trial.[44] Informal consultations on the specific modalities of the Pre-Trial Chamber took place in the spring of 1998 at the final Preparatory Committee prior to the Rome Conference. At the conference itself, negotiations took place in earnest and led to the adoption of Article 57 as it now reads, which includes most of the Pre-Trial Chamber's powers.

The emphasis placed on the important role of the Pre-Trial Chamber in the ICC is evident from the organisation of Chambers to include three distinct divisions: Appeals, Trials and Pre-Trials. Pursuant to Article 39(1), the Rome Statute stipulates that judges with the appropriate criminal trial experience shall be responsible for conducting pre-trial matters:

---

[42]See Tochilovsky, supra note 13, at 348–349. It would appear that the ICTY has followed the ICC lead in adopting Rule 84*bis* at its 20th plenary session (30 June–2 July 1999). This Rule permits the accused to make a statement, if the Trial Chamber agrees, after the opening statements of the parties (or after the opening statement of the Prosecutor, if the Defence chooses to delay its opening statement until after the conclusion of the Prosecutor's presentation of evidence). The accused is not required to make a solemn declaration, nor can he be examined about the content of the statement.

[43]Art. 65*ter* of the ICTY Statute concerning the use of a Pre-Trial Judge was added at the eighteenth plenary session (9–10 July 1998) and extensively amended at the twenty-first plenary session (15–17 November 1999). It was adopted because of concern with delays in trials and a desire to conduct proceedings in the most efficient and expeditious manner possible (*ICTY Bulletin*, No. 21, 27 July 1998 at p. 1 and p. 20). This provision was first applied in *Prosecutor v. Delalić and Others, Order Appointing a Pre-Appeal Judge*, Case No. IT-96-21-A, A. Ch., 12 Oct. 1999. The Appeals Chamber considered that it was in the interests of justice and of a more expeditious and effectively managed appeal to appoint a pre-appeal judge responsible for matters arising prior to the commencement of the hearing of the appeal.

[44]Fabricio Guariglia and Kenneth Harris, "Article 57: Functions and powers of the Pre-Trial Chamber", in Otto Triffterer (Ed.), Commentary on the Rome Statute of the International Criminal Court (1999), pp. 743–752 at p. 744.

> the assignment of judges to divisions shall be based on the nature of the functions to be performed by each division and the qualifications and experience of the judges elected to the Court, in such a way that each division shall contain an appropriate combination of expertise in criminal law and procedure and in international law. The Trial and *Pre-Trial Divisions shall be composed predominantly of judges with criminal trial experience*. (emphasis added).

This provision is aimed at improving the efficiency of pre-trial procedures, addressing some of the problems encountered by the ICTY and taking into account the diverse background from which the judges will likely be drawn.[45] It is intended to "strike a proper balance between criminal law and procedure and international law".[46]

While certain functions in Article 57 of the Rome Statute were considered significant enough that they should be exercised by the whole Chamber,[47] other more routine powers may be exercised by a single judge of the Pre-Trial Chamber in the interests of expediency and efficiency.[48] In certain cases, the particular complexity of the case will determine whether powers are exercised by the Chamber or by a single judge.[49] The Pre-Trial Chamber's powers to facilitate expeditious trials include the power to issue orders and warrants as required for the purposes of an investigation[50] and to provide for the protection and privacy of victims and witnesses, preservation of evidence, protection of national security information, and the protection of persons who have been arrested.[51]

Other powers of the Pre-Trial Chamber are provided outside of Article 57. While the Pre-Trial Chamber must hold hearings to confirm charges in the presence of the person charged, in exceptional circumstances this may be done in the absence of the person charged.[52] At the request of the Prosecutor, the Pre-Trial Chamber may take measures necessary to avail itself of a unique opportunity to collect evidence that may not be available subsequently for the purposes of a trial.[53] In addition, a decision of the Prosecutor not to investigate or not to prosecute may be reviewed by the

---

[45]Rome Statute Arts. 36(3)(b)(ii) and 36(5) provide that candidates for the position of judge shall be registered on one of two lists: List A for specific competence in criminal law and procedure, List B for specific competence in international humanitarian law and human rights.

[46]Jules Deschênes, "Article 39: Chambers", in Otto Triffterer (Ed.), Commentary on the Rome Statute of the International Criminal Court (1999), pp. 615–617 at p. 616.

[47]For example, orders or rulings issued under Rome Statute Arts. 15, 18, 19, 54(2), 61(7) and 72.

[48]Pursuant to Rome Statute Art. 57(2)(b).

[49]Guariglia and Harris, supra note 44, at p. 745.

[50]Rome Statute Art. 57(3)(a).

[51]Rome Statute Art. 57(3)(b).

[52]Rome Statute Art. 61.

[53]Rome Statute Art. 56.

Pre-Trial Chamber on its own initiative, in which case the Prosecutor's decision must be confirmed by the Chamber.[54]

The establishment of a Pre-Trial Chamber and the powers delegated to it are proof that the drafters of the Rome Statute learned from problems experienced by the ICTY in trial management and that the ICC has already taken significant steps in order to "give Judges the tools [they need] to expedite proceedings".[55]

2. Conclusion

There is no doubt that the influence of the ICTY was dictated to a certain degree by the circumstances in which the Rome Statute was drafted. The *ad hoc* Tribunal, deriving its powers directly from Chapter VII of the UN Charter and concerned with a defined conflict in a single region, was created in a situation that allowed for easier consensus and, in some aspects, the allocation of greater powers. The drafters of the Rome Statute were more constrained by the need to compromise, stemming from political concerns emanating from a large number of states representing a broader background of legal systems. This need for compromise inevitably played a major role in shaping the final text and defining the limits of the ICTY contribution.[56]

Regardless of such considerations, it is apparent that the ICTY contribution to the criminal procedure of the ICC has been substantial. The Rome Statute has in some cases directly incorporated procedures used by the ICTY, and in other cases has profited from the Tribunal's experiences in order to choose a new procedural path. The view advocated by some that, in certain instances, the correct procedural lessons were not learned from the ICTY, does not in any way diminish the enormous contribution that this *ad hoc* Tribunal has made.

---

[54] Rome Statute Art. 53(3)(b).

[55] Remarks of Judge Richard May, Judge of the International Criminal Tribunal for the former Yugoslavia, to the Fourth Session of the Preparatory Commission for the International Criminal Court, *Press Release JL/P.I.S./479-E*, ICTY Trial Chambers, The Hague, 20 March 2000.

[56] Swart and Sluiter, supra note 6, at p. 127.

Index

International Humanitarian Law Series

1. Michael J. Kelly: *Restoring and Maintaining Order in Complex Peace Operations.* The Search for a Legal Framework. 1999 90-411-1179-4
2. Helen Durham and Timothy L.H. McCormack (eds.): *The Changing Face of Conflict and the Efficacy of International Humanitarian Law.* 1999 90-411-1180-8
3. Richard May, David Tolbert, John Hocking, Ken Roberts, Bing Bing Jia, Daryl Mundis and Gabriël Oosthuizen (eds.): *Essays on ICTY Procedure and Evidence in Honour of Gabrielle Kirk McDonald.* 2000 90-411-1482-3

KLUWER LAW INTERNATIONAL – THE HAGUE / LONDON / BOSTON